THE POLITICS OF
THE COMMON LAW
Perspective, Rights, Processes, Institutions

The Politics of the Common Law is an introduction to the English legal system that places the law in its contemporary context. It is not like other conventional accounts that simply seek to describe institutions and summarise details. The book is a coherent argument, organised around a number of central claims. Can today's common law be characterised as a series of emergent practices that articulate the principles of human rights and due process? The common law is presented as historical experience; the authors present the perspective that we are in the opening of a new chapter.

The argument examines the impact of the European Convention on the structures and ideologies of the common law, and suggests that there is now a general jurisprudence of human rights stemming from the Human Rights Act. The Human Rights Act has also led to more pronounced judicial intervention into politics, and is precipitating a debate on the forms that the rule of law should assume in contemporary British democracy. Equally important is the function of European Union law, and the extent to which it is also committed to due process and the rule of law. These themes are read into civil and criminal procedure, and broader concerns about the tensions between the requirements of economics and the demands of justice. Can a revitalised common law address a plural, post-colonial future?

Dr. Adam Gearey is a reader in law, Birkbeck College, University of London. He has been a visiting professor in the Faculty of Law at Makerere University, Uganda; and the University of Pretoria, South Africa.

Professor Wayne Morrison is director of the University of London External Undergraduate Laws Programme and professor of law, Queen Mary, University of London.

Robert Jago is a lecturer in law at the University of Surrey and is the postgraduate director of studies within the School of Law. He was involved in Surrey University's Joint Infrastructure Fund Project on Defining Excellence in Teaching and is a regular visitor to SPACE, University of Hong Kong where he teaches Public Law and Civil and Criminal Procedure.

THE POLITICS OF THE COMMON LAW

Perspectives, Rights, Processes, Institutions

Adam Gearey, Wayne Morrison and Robert Jago

Routledge·Cavendish
Taylor & Francis Group
LONDON AND NEW YORK

Published 2009 by Routledge-Cavendish
2 Park Square, Milton Park, Abingdon, Oxon, OX14 4RN

Simultaneously published in the USA and Canada
by Routledge-Cavendish
711 Third Ave, New York, NY 10017

Routledge-Cavendish is an imprint of the Taylor & Francis Group,
an Informa business

© 2009 Adam Gearey, Wayne Morrison and Robert Jago

Typeset in Sabon by Keyword Group Ltd
Printed and bound in Great Britain by
CPI Antony Rowe, Chippenham, Wiltshire

All rights reserved. No part of this book may be reprinted or
reproduced or utilised in any form or by any electronic,
mechanical, or other means, now known or hereafter invented,
including photocopying and recording, or in any information
storage or retrieval system, without permission in writing from the
publishers.

British Library Cataloguing in Publication Data
A catalogue record for this book is available from the British Library

Library of Congress Cataloging-in-Publication Data
A catalog record has been requested

ISBN 13: 978-0-415-48153-3 (pbk)
ISBN 10: 0-415-48153-8 (pbk)

'Difficult to know what one means
– to be serious and to know what one means –'

George Oppen, 'Ballad'

CONTENTS

Authors' acknowledgements		viii
Publisher's acknowledgements		ix
	Introduction	1
1	'As a system … the common law is a thing merely imaginary'	19
2	Recording law's experience: features of the 'case'	47
3	Institutionalising judicial decision making: the judicial practice of precedent	71
4	The judicial practice of statutory interpretation	101
5	The politics of the judiciary revisited: rights, democracy, law	123
6	Racism and law: 'no dogs, no blacks, no Irish'	156
7	Rights, politics and the law of the European Union	185
8	Constituting human rights	210
9	Human rights and the integrity of the law	229
10	The general jurisprudence of human rights	248
11	The jurisprudence of Article 6: due process and the common law	271
12	Imagining civil justice	289
13	The principles of civil procedure	311
14	Imagining criminal justice	333
15	The principles of criminal procedure	354
16	The politics of representation: legal aid, human rights and access to justice	379
	Conclusion	398
	Bibliography	400
	Index	408

AUTHORS' ACKNOWLEDGEMENTS

Mary Gearey – shaping spirit, forger of bodies of prose – my love and thanks. My thanks also to Sally Cartledge, Robert Cartledge, Valerie Kelley, Costas Douzinas, Michelle Everson, Bill Bowring, Peter Goodrich, Peter Finnemore and Paul Virr. For instruction in obligations and rights: thanks to Niamh Gearey and Arthur Gearey.

    The Gay Hussar, Soho and the National Liberal Club proved convivial places to discuss this book, argue about its contents and toast its coming into the world.

A.G.

With love and thanks to my parents, my three 'sisters' and the Three Musketeers. You know who you are.

R.J.

With thanks and love to Michele for all her support and to Tzu His for keeping me sane. And respect to all the external students who do their best to drive me insane.

W.J.M

PUBLISHER'S ACKNOWLEDGEMENTS

Routledge-Cavendish and the authors wish to thank the institutions and individuals that have kindly provided photographic material for use in this book. Full caption and source information is listed below. We apologise in advance for any unintentional omissions or errors, and will be pleased to insert the appropriate acknowledgements to any companies or individuals in any subsequent edition of this book.

Chapter 1

1.2, 1.3, 1.4, 1.6, 1.8 – Mary Evans Picture Library

1.5 – Title page, *Leviathan*, Hobbes, 1651, London. © Bettmann/Corbis

1.7 – *The Polling*, engraved by George Presbury, from *The Works of William Hogarth*, 1833 (litho) by Hogarth, William (1697–1764) (after) Private Collection/ Ken Welsh/ The Bridgeman Art Library

Chapter 2

2.1 – Victoria and Albert Museum, London

2.2 – Mary Evans Picture Library

2.3, 2.4 – Joseph Mallord William Turner, English, 1775–1851, *Slave Ship* (Slavers Throwing Overboard the Dead and Dying, Typhoon Coming On), 1840 Oil on canvas 90.8 × 122.6 cm (35 3/4 × 48 1/4 in.) Museum of Fine Arts, Boston Henry Lillie Pierce Fund 99.22. © 2008 Museum of Fine Arts, Boston. All rights reserved.

Chapter 3

3.1 – Mary Evans Picture Library

Chapter 5

5.1 – Mary Evans Picture Library

Chapter 6

6.1 – *Hey Bros*, Ian Waldron, 1998. Acrylic on canvas. 122 × 176 cm © Ian Waldron

6.2 – Unknown artist, *Illustrated London News*, 1870. Collection Wayne Morrison

6.3 – Mary Evans Picture Library

Chapter 12

12.1 – University of Glasgow Library, Department of Special Collections, Hepburn

Chapter 14

14.1 – © *The Independent*, 6 December 2007

THE COMMON LAW: RIGHTS, POLITICS AND PROCEDURES

INTRODUCTION

For us, the contemporary common law is defined by the Human Rights Act 1998, the presence of European Convention rights in English law and the reality of European Union law. Equally important is the political situation of the United Kingdom in a post-colonial world characterised by the globalised flows of capital, commodities and people.

In this introduction, we will argue that the study of the common law can be organised around four main themes: (1) an engagement with the cultures of the post-colonial common law, (2) the notion of judicial practices, (3) an engagement with the notion of procedure or process and (4) human rights. There is also an underpinning concern with the legitimacy of the law that runs through all four areas. This approach allows us to impose a certain form on our understanding of the common law.

Our first theme will take us towards a general understanding of the different versions of the common law that articulate conflictual understandings of its role and purpose. The second theme is an engagement with the common law practices of precedent and statutory interpretation. The third theme allows us to discuss the principles that animate common law civil and criminal procedure. Our fourth theme is focused primarily on Article 6 of the European Convention on Human Rights. Article 6 defines fair trial rights.

Our concern with Article 6 connects together the concern with human rights and procedural law. Our framing of this concern as one of human rights needs to be carefully understood. If one looks at the history of the common law the principles that regulated criminal and civil trials were not framed in the language of human rights. Human rights represents a fairly recent understanding of legal processes. While remaining cognisant of the immanent principles of the common law, we will argue that looking at common law procedures through human rights allows us a focused analysis of the principles of procedural law. Reference to Article 6 also means that we can examine the extent to which the common law measures up to international standards of due process. This is a salutary reminder that the common law cannot be studied in a vacuum.

Our concern with the values or principles of law is not restricted to our analysis of due process. It can be observed at a number of levels throughout the book, from the opening concerns with the narratives of law, through to the politics of the judiciary, the structure of the European Convention and the law of the European Union. Our discussion raises some general questions about the legitimacy of law. This theme is pervasive. It is underpinned by a number of arguments. Law is legitimate to the extent that its authority rests on a concept and practice of due process. This stresses that law's authority rests on reasoned and neutral adjudication of disputes. Parties to a dispute must have had access to an open court, broadly equal resources and the decision that resolves the dispute must have been made by an impartial judge within a reasonable time.

This definition of due process is, to some extent, consistent with a narrow notion of the rule of law, which would hold that even legal decisions which would otherwise be in breach of human rights can be justified provided there was some degree of due process in their resolution. Our notion of law's legitimacy avoids this 'thin' version of due process. This is because Article 6 exists within a context of substantive human rights. A national government committed to the due process guarantees of the Convention, must also be committed to upholding the other rights contained in the document. Thus, due process as an element of the law of human rights is inseparable from a much broader network of rights that go far beyond the internal structure of the law.

We are limited in the extent to which we can develop this theme. In a book of this length, we cannot conduct any real engagement with the broad question of human rights in English law. This takes us to our argument about the 'internal' structure of the law. The Convention and its protocols articulate human rights law through a series of what we call integrity rights that can be seen as attempts to provide a structural form of law that is coherent with a human rights regime. Integrity rights are thus rights that protect and define the legitimate form of law. Does the common law measure up to these international standards?

Our concern with law's legitimacy also runs through our engagement with the politics of the judiciary. We will argue that we need to look at the way that judges are engaged in a 'dialogue' with Parliament. We need to appreciate that present constitutional arrangements in the United Kingdom show a degree of strain. While fundamental constitutional structures remain largely unchanged, the conventional concept of the deference of an unelected judiciary to a sovereign Parliament is being slowly redefined by the impact of the Human Rights Act 1998. Understanding the politics of the judiciary requires a subtle appreciation of the political structures on which the contemporary common law rests, and the part that law plays in a broader culture of democracy and human rights. The relationship between the common law, democracy and human rights is not straightforward. It is not simply a question of tracing 'direct' lines between legal and political concepts. Indeed, we need to see how the common law, the law of the convention, European Union Law and other sources of international law are involved in ongoing struggles to define the nature of the links between these terms.

THE POST-COLONIAL COMMON LAW

The opening chapters of this book are concerned with the post-colonial common law.[1] From the perspective of British history, the common law was central to the production of a 'nation' and an 'English speaking people'. The common law was fundamental to the centralisation of power, and the subtle networks that brought together forms of direct and indirect rule over colonised territories. There are complex and sophisticated links between processes of nation building, the creation of a colonial empire and its formal dismantling in more recent times. This history of law would find law's proper place in the perpetuation of a certain cultural, social and economic hegemony.

Whereas the story of nation building and empire has been the dominant account, and it would be wrong to downplay the legacies of colonialism in which we are all implicated, we need to link these issues to a new set of questions. In our time, can the common law help build plural communities that are committed to democracy and the rule of law?

This question requires another historical perspective on the common law. This is why one of our early chapters examines two 'slave' cases from the seventeen and eighteen hundreds. In these cases we can see a battle taking place over the proper role of the law; and indeed, we are also concerned with the proper language in which to talk about the law. Is the proper task of the common law the protection of property rights, even if this extends to the right of a master to own his slaves? Or must the common law realise the exemplification of the spirit of liberty, equality and dignity, and affirm that a human being is not a chattel? There are a number of compromises between these positions – and it could no doubt be seen as traditional English duplicity to affirm that there can be no slavery in mainland Britain, while enjoying the economic products of systems of slave-holding safely located on the colonial periphery. The slave cases show how different narratives about the law circulate, and how different political claims about the values of law oppose one another. Law's 'open texture' has allowed (at least to some extent) legal challenges to be mounted on even the most seemingly settled of cultural institutions, even if the courts prefer not to develop the law in a progressive manner.

What else do these cases suggest? As Granville Sharp appreciated (see Chapter 2), to engage with the law necessitates a legal training. This means that the tyro must submit to a course of study and 'become' a lawyer – a process that testifies to law's (relative) autonomy as a discipline. It is this autonomy, and its contemporary forms, that interests us in this book. In order to make this theme manageable, our starting point is an engagement with the practices of legal education, precedent and statutory interpretation, the two areas of study that have traditionally served as something of a portal into an understanding of law's peculiar form.

These early chapters also make use of the un-scholarly 'I'. As these chapters concern the interlinking of personal histories and biographies with broader structures of legal ideology, we wanted to make use of the 'I' as a foregrounding device. If political

---

1 'Post-colonial' is a difficult term to define. We mean it in its least problematic sense: the period after 1945 when European Empires were either dismantled or fell apart. See Douzinas and Gearey (2005).

sentiments begin with the questioning of one's teachers and traditions, then the 'I' is a (limited) way of examining the values of law, and opening up important political questions.

JUDICIAL PRACTICES, LEGITIMACY AND DEMOCRACY

The doctrines of precedent and statutory interpretation have to be understood as judicial practices.[2] To describe precedent and statutory interpretation as practices draws attention to the way in which judges interpret the law and act on the basis of those interpretations. Practices take shape within a culture that determines how they are composed.[3] Chapters 3 and 4 will present an account of judicial legal interpretation within these terms. This approach will allow us to discuss judicial law making and to understand its contemporary dynamic. Our discussion of precedent and statutory interpretation thus raises the question of institutional legitimacy. The doctrine of the separation of powers (to the extent that it applies to the constitution of the UK) would stress that judicial law making should be kept within careful boundaries, lest the judges usurp Parliament's law-making powers. The judiciary, the executive and the legislature are to be kept to their correct constitutional provinces. This theme needs to be connected with fundamental questions about British democracy.[4]

Without trespassing too far into the province of public law, we can observe that the British constitution rests on the doctrine of the sovereignty of Parliament. That Parliament should be able to make or unmake any law that it so chooses is justified by the claim that it is elected by 'the people'. It is thus entirely proper (so the argument goes) that in a democracy, the legislature should be sovereign – and the executive's domination of the legislature is justified by the fact that the majority of people have voted for it and its legislative programme. The sovereignty of Parliament thus rests on a majoritarian thesis about its 'popular' legitimacy.

However, one of the central themes of constitution in recent years has been the extent to which a political party with a large majority can exploit the sovereignty of Parliament to push through its policies unhindered by checks or balances on its power. The political accountability of the executive to Parliament appears too remote to make much of a difference to the activities in which government engages.

To understand our arguments it is necessary briefly to outline the way in which judicial review operates in English law. Judicial review allows the High Court to examine

---

2   The philosophical orientating points for a proper understanding of the practice of precedent would have to draw on Wittgenstein – perhaps even as mediated by de Certeau (2006).
3   Any sensible development of these themes would have to take into account Peter Goodrich's work, especially *Reading the Law* (1986) and *Languages of Law*. These are essential texts for understanding the dynamics of the common law traditions.
4   See Lord Steyn (2005). Lord Steyn posits two 'strands' to the 'democratic ideal'. The first relates to the notion that Parliament is an elected body, accountable to the people. The second is that 'the basic values of liberty and justice for all and respect for human rights and fundamental freedoms must be guaranteed'. Where there is conflict between these values, an 'impartial and independent judiciary' must find the balance 'in accordance with principles of institutional integrity'.

the way in which public bodies exercise their powers. The doctrine of Parliamentary sovereignty defines the fundamental parameters of judicial review. The court cannot declare an empowering Act void. It is entirely concerned with whether or not a public body has acted within the powers given either by common law or statute.

Judicial review thus raises the issue of the rule of law. It concerns the extent to which the courts can control executive agencies of the state. If the political checks and balances of the constitution have been thrown out, to what extent can they be 're-set' by judicial review? We don't want to be misunderstood on this point. At no point do we argue that there is any real support for a doctrine of judicial review that would allow the courts to strike down Acts of Parliament. However, in the wake of the Human Rights Act, there is a sense in which the constitutional balance is shifting. Empowered by the Act, certain judges are willing to question their traditional deference to Parliament, and to be more critical of the executive. To what extent is this judicial 'activism' legitimate if it protects human rights against executive encroachment?

Our assessment of the judiciary will be made in this constitutional context. Arguments about the legitimacy of judicial law-making must also take into account the claim that human rights are not justified on majoritarian grounds. Rather, they raise certain values above 'political' processes. These concerns will also take us towards an assessment of the procedures for the appointment of judges. We will argue that given the constitutional shifts underway, the present reforms of the system leave a lot to be desired and that further reforms are required to produce a judiciary that is democratically accountable, transparent and 'representative' of contemporary British society.

In Chapter 5, we will urge caution lest this theme be misunderstood. We are not asserting that the judges should always decide cases where human rights are in issue against the executive. Such a position would clearly be stupid to assert as the overriding judicial function is one of neutral adjudication. However, to the extent that post-war public law shows a predominant (but by no means exclusive) sympathy towards the executive, the relevant question is the extent to which the judiciary can, while remaining neutral, legitimately decide cases against the government.

How can we engage with these general concerns? In Allen's words:

> We may imagine a dialogue between the judge and the representative legislator ... [t]he opposition between parliamentary sovereignty and the rule of law has been conceived too starkly. On close examination these principles are more interdependent than independent, enabling legislative will and common law reason to be combined in accordance with the demands of justice and the common good.[5]

While we do not accept the concept of dialogue between the judges and Parliament in unqualified terms, we do think that it is a useful way of describing the post-Human Rights Act constitutional settlement.[6] The dialogue is no longer one where the courts assume deference to Parliament. They attempt to define the correct roles of each branch of the State in a constitution that upholds human rights values. Those commentators who have objected to the idea of dialogue from various republican premises have

---

5   Allen (2003).
6   Cohn (2007). The judge is as an 'actor in a continuous multi-participant process or network of decision-making'.

indeed articulated a valid criticism of the term.[7] It is still necessary to be critical of the constitutional propriety of unelected, unaccountable and unrepresentative judges. However, any scepticism directed towards the judges has to be tempered by criticism of executive dictatorship. With radical democratic reform off the political agenda, it would appear that a rather skewed dialogue between the courts and Parliament is the best for which one might hope. It still remains to be seen whether the British constitution can move from its tendencies towards centralisation of power to meaningful democratic accountability.

This connects with our engagements with race, plurality and the law. Chapter 6 shows how race and racism have been central to the cultural expression of the common law. There are fundamental continuities between the experiences of Empire and the history of 'race relations' in the post-war period. Can the common law put its house in order? Can it articulate meaningful forms of protection to those oppressed by racial discrimination? This is a question of law and politics. It is inseparably connected with what we call the realisation of plural communities. While not seeking to present this as the only issue in British politics, it strikes us that this is one of the most pressing concerns. We will deal with it through a study of the Begum case and the issues it raises about multiculturalism and the role of human rights in defining the way in which people can live together in mutual respect.

THE EUROPEAN CONTEXT

The common law cannot be studied in a vacuum. The European context takes us to law of the European Union (EU) and the European Convention on Human Rights (ECHR). Our chapters on the EU and the ECHR elaborate the themes that we have discussed in the introduction. To take the EU first, understanding our approach requires a little history.

The European Union was founded in 1992 with the Treaty on European Union. It was formerly known as the European Community. Defining the Union is a difficult task; and indeed, the political implications of various definitions of the Union are currently being fought out in European politics. A basic working definition is, however, possible. The European Union is essentially a common market. Linked to the common market, and open to varying degrees of acceptance by the member states of the Union is an ongoing experiment in social democracy. This means that the common market is subject to regulation, and, that there is a commitment to various social, economic and welfare rights. From a legal perspective the most important aspect of the Union is the fact that it is a supranational institution. Lawyers have tended to link law to the nation state. There is thus something of a challenge in conceiving a legal order that is international but creates rights that can be used in national courts.

Our focus on the EU is provided by the question of its legitimacy. To what extent do the institutions of the EU bring together due process, human rights and democratic politics to legitimise an international legal order? We will argue that the EU

---

7 See Tomkins (2005).

is characterised by ongoing reforms that are endeavouring to give form to the values of accountability, transparency and the rule of law.

Our engagement with the Convention is also concerned with the functions of an international legal order dedicated to the provision of basic human rights. The European Convention on Human Rights (ECHR) was signed in Rome in 1950 and entered into force in 1953. The Convention guarantees certain rights including the right to life, freedom from torture, freedom from arbitrary arrest, the right to a fair trial, the right to privacy, freedom of religion, freedom of expression, and freedom of assembly and association. Institutionally, the Convention provided for an international court, the European Court of Human Rights (ECtHR) and a Commission to consider complaints and decide whether or not to remit them to the court.

We will argue that the Convention creates a human rights 'regime' – a coherent statement of the relationship between due process and substantive human rights. This regime provides the terms in which we can think about the legitimacy of sovereign states. These themes are developed below under the heading of 'integrity rights'.

In turning to the impact of Convention rights on the common law, we will consider what we have called the 'general jurisprudence' of the Human Rights Act. Matters that fall into the general jurisprudence can be described as follows: we will be concerned, first of all, with the general structure of the Act and the mechanisms that it sets up. We will then turn our attention to the linked concerns of the vertical and horizontal effect of the Human Rights Act and the vexed question of the definition of public authority. After examining the equally troubled question of the Act's retrospective effect, we will look at the relationship of common law and European human rights law, and the question of whether or not the judges have seized upon the HRA as a catalyst to develop an indigenous human rights law that draws on the traditions of common law as much as the European legal inheritance.

INTEGRITY RIGHTS

If human rights provide the foundational standards of law, a number of crucial concerns must be addressed. What is the precise form of the international standard provided by human rights? We will argue that, as far as the institutional nature of European Human Rights law is concerned, this takes us to the structure of the Convention, and the precise ways in which breaches of human rights can be remedied. This can be linked to the justification of a series of rights which preserve the coherence of intentional human rights law and hence the integrity of law. We will call these 'integrity rights' or rights that protect rights and thus define law's legitimacy. One could perhaps see integrity rights as 'second-order' rights that enshrine due process. In Chapter 9, we show that Articles 7, 13, 15, 17, 18 and 57 and Protocol 7 can be understood in precisely this sense.

Our argument about integrity rights should not be confused with Fuller's notions of an integral ordering of law, and we are entirely agnostic in relation to Dworkin's claims about the structure of law. Integrity rights reflect an entirely contingent legal reality: to the extent that a nation commits itself to the Convention, it is compelled to adhere to a certain set of legal values. This does not mean that law in general must have any particular form or that the inherent indeterminacy of rights are limited. We will return to this latter point below.

As well as mandating a fundamental procedural structure for law, integrity rights prevent rights being used 'against themselves'. There are two elements to this issue. Rights give the executive the power to limit or suspend their operation in certain limited circumstances. Unless this power is circumscribed, the guarantees provided by human rights are meaningless. This is inseparable from the problematic concern of how European democracies respond to 'terrorism', or a violence that opposes itself to the lawfully sanctioned violence of the state. The second problem that integrity rights thus confront is the possibility that certain groups might use rights arguments to limit rights. An example of this would be a placard observed in 2007 during a demonstration by Islamic fundamentalists in London in 2007 which read 'Death to freedom of speech'. We can thus appreciate the scope of Article 17. It gives expression to the 'spirit' of human rights as it prevents rights being used in such a way as to destroy Convention rights. It is worth remembering that Article 17 is invoked in situations which fall short of those dealt with under Article 15, which allows the state to suspend rights in a time of emergency or war.

The pressing issue, therefore, is the extent to which we can distinguish between legitimate and illegitimate limitations of human rights. As with our discussion of Article 13, we will be concerned with finding precisely where this line might lie. Indeed, integrity rights are not themselves immune from certain criticisms about the precise form of the legal order they create. They rest on a problematic distinction between the rights of European nationals or citizens, and those others to the European order that present themselves as migrant workers, refugees or asylum seekers or 'sans papiers'. Although this category of persons is not entirely deprived of rights, they are accorded rights of a lesser status.[8] Integrity rights make necessary distinctions between an 'inside' and an 'outside' of a legal order, and a limnic zone through which people move between nations either with or without the blessing of the law.

PROCEDURE, FAIRNESS AND POWER

Integrity rights inform us about the general structure of the law. In turning to issues of due process and Article 6 we are focusing on the structure of the law at the more specific levels of civil and criminal procedure. While Article 6 and procedural law can be seen as forms of integrity rights, we will use this term primarily with reference to the Articles discussed in the section above. Furthermore, in our discussion of procedure we will not just be concerned with Article 6. Due process is inseparable from wider concerns that take us beyond human rights law and require an engagement with democratic culture. How do we approach these themes? We need to begin with a reference to important scholarship on common law procedure and its values.

---

8   This position has a striking resemblance to the way in which colonial law operated. See the work of Mamdani (1996).

Jeremy Bentham provided an early approach to common law procedure.[9] His work is underpinned by the wider principle that asserts the utility of settled laws for social cohesion. Thus, the trial as a procedure is meant to achieve an accurate outcome through the application of clear legal principle to the facts.[10] While this interpretation of procedure was certainly influential, contemporary writers have criticised the fundamental reduction of procedure to the single notion of accuracy.

For instance, if one examines the common law, it is hard to see how adversarial procedures are explicable solely by reference to a notion of accuracy. Furthermore, institutions such as the jury, and the standard of 'popular morality' that it brings to the criminal trial, cannot be explained entirely by a single concept. Bentham's hostility to safeguards in the criminal trial also detracts from the contemporary relevance of his work. Thus, those scholars drawing on Bentham's work have argued that his fundamental insight should be updated, to allow us to see that 'legal standards' are 'supplemented by other normative standards and values'.[11]

This takes us to an appreciation of the importance of participation as a procedural value.[12] Accounts of participation in political and legal fields share certain important similarities as elements of a democratic culture. At a general level, participation can be linked to a diverse set of themes which develop related concerns: a person should be able to influence processes in which their interests are at stake.[13] But it is not just these ethics of citizenship that underpin participation. The importance of participation also lies behind procedural principles that enable a person to give evidence and respond to questions aimed at elucidating the issues of the case and the possibilities of their resolution. By making information available in this way, it enables the adjudicator to make a full and 'balanced' decision. Participation of the accused in the criminal trial requires that the defendant has a chance to reply to the charge and to take part in the search for 'truth' that requires the accused to question their own behaviour. As a form of 'moral criticism', the trial attempts to confront the accused with the consequences of his or her act, and this would lack legitimacy if the findings of the court were simply thrust upon them.[14]

The key point about the normative relevance of participation is thus the instrumental role it plays in the delivery of accurate outcomes. Participation brings together social and legal elements in allowing confidence in the accuracy of procedures that have

---

9   Although his thoughts on the criminal and civil trial developed throughout his work, certain generalisations can be hazarded.
10 Opposed to the law of evidence of his day, Bentham argued that this last objective would be provided by a system of 'natural proof' that offered a common sense approach to forensic proof, rather than the arcane rituals that he saw taking place in the courtroom.
11 Galligan (1996).
12 Participation is difficult to define, as it covers a range of different concerns. Participation in forensic processes relates to the rights of the parties to 'present their cases and respond to the cases against them' (ibid., 130). Parties can also call witnesses and choose whether to give evidence themselves. This full adversarial model is perhaps the most realised form of participation, which can also include far more minimal forms of involvement, such as 'the barest opportunity to present a statement of facts and perhaps an expression of opinion'. At an administrative level, participation tends to be 'consultative' in nature, which again takes different forms from the full public inquiry to the mere chance to 'submit a written statement'. Participation in politics is generally expressed through voting either in local or general elections, but it can also mean party activism.
13 Supra n. 11.
14 Ibid., 138.

made use of the 'best' sources of information.[15] In this way, participation makes for the legitimacy of legal procedures.

The importance of participation can also be linked to arguments about the availability of public resources that allow individuals to gain access to the courts. When we look at the economics of legal aid in Chapter 16, we will see that the access to justice agenda can be understood as a realisation of the importance of participation. A citizen should be able to access the courts to protect his or her rights; and cost or inefficiency should not impact unduly so as to restrict the use of the courts. However, while these arguments are compelling, we will see that it is not simply the case that the access to justice agenda is driven by values such as participation. The government is also motivated by the need to keep down the costs of legal aid.

We can elaborate this point. While participation is clearly important, it is not the only value that informs procedure. It is indeed possible to conceive of a fair trial that had not had a significant element of participation by the accused. A decision could be justified without the participation of the accused if other safeguards were in place and the procedure appeared fair overall. The view that participation is 'necessary' in justifying moral blame of the accused can also be criticised.[16] The trial can equally be seen as a way of securing a decision. Certainly in historical terms, the idea of the trial as characterised by safeguards for the defence is a relatively recent idea; at least, there is little warrant for seeing it 'primarily as a moral dialogue with the accused'.[17]

These criticisms of procedure lead us to suggest that we also need to appreciate the relationship between procedure, the right to a fair trial and power. Rights are 'procedural restraints' on 'state power'. For instance, in criminal proceedings fairness militates against claims that the 'public interest' is best served by 'fact finding' or what Packer would call 'crime control values'.[18] Fairness is achieved (in part) through the rational nature of procedures that are defined by legal norms. By providing norms that regulate the terms of the trial, the concept of fairness imposes limits on both executive power, and the way in which the power of the courts can be used. What do we mean?

There are undoubtedly different 'forms' of power which are normally bracketed together under the concept of state power. We want to distinguish between executive/administrative and judicial power. A proper consideration of democracy would have to consider legislative power – the power of 'the people' to elect governments – but this would take us too deeply into public law and political theory. Suffice to say that liberal political philosophy seeks to balance out the relationships between these forms of power.

The sovereign or executive power of the state covers the ability of ministers and other decision makers in central government to command resources, make or refrain from making decisions, and, ultimately, to deploy armed force. This form of power could also be invoked to suspend the order of law and rights in the event of war or emergency. Executive power thus ultimately manifests itself in the state's monopoly on violence. We will return to this point presently. At least from the perspective of our work in this book, we could also specify that there are forms of administrative power.

---

15 Ibid.
16 Ibid.
17 Ibid.
18 Packer (1968).

These can be distinguished from both executive and judicial power as administrative power rests in the hands of civil servants and bureaucrats who run the agencies of government at both local and central levels. At its most developed it undoubtedly overlaps with executive power, but it is perhaps best used to describe the myriad mundane decisions that operationalise government. It can be distinguished both from the power that rests in the hands of ministers, and from judicial power. Judicial power is the power to resolve disputes and to deploy the coercive resources of the state through punishment licensed by the courts. However, it is also the power to control executive and administrative power. How can we think about these relationships?

When we talk of state power, we tend to aggregate executive, administrative and judicial power. Undoubtedly, the executive can use the courts for its own ends. Recalling our comments above on the politics of the judiciary, we argued that one of the fundamental constitutional problems was the inability or reluctance of the courts in England to question robustly executive acts. Executive power is only used legitimately to the extent that it remains within the law. This lies behind the democratic idea that the courts, or judicial power, must keep executive power in check. Judicial power can come into tension with executive power in different ways, from judges declaring cases against the executive, to the provocation of constitutional crises which raise the whole issue of where legitimate power rests.

Due process protects the integrity of legal proceedings against an executive that may want to abuse the law for its own political ends. At the same time, due process articulates the values and structures that legitimise the authority and power of the courts. It might be crude to suggest that these terms exist in opposition. The politics of constitutionalism are to a large extent about the compatibility of legal and executive power, and the extent to which they can be balanced in a democratic polity. The difficulty of achieving this balance rests on the fact that the executive must accept that there are limits on its actions provided by the courts.

Due process also concerns itself with the mundane functioning of the courts, without reference to high constitutional drama. In these instances the power of the law is necessarily exercised against private citizens. This is particularly true in the criminal trial, but it is also true of civil trials, to the extent that they award the compulsory payment of damages and can impose fines and other financial penalties. At this level, due process seeks to place limits that justify and legitimise this exercise of coercive state power. The contemporary law of due process also requires us to engage with many of the specialist courts and tribunals that, standing outside the structure of regular courts, deal with matters such as mental health, the custody of children, welfare benefits and military discipline. These specialist tribunals are central to the regulation of many areas of social life, including those that concern some of the most vulnerable and troubled individuals. Due process also seeks to bring these expressions of administrative power under its control, although, as we will see in Chapter 11, there are problematic questions about precisely where the boundaries should be drawn.

There is one final issue that we have to consider. State power may be the primary concern of due process, but there are other more diffuse expressions of power that are relevant to our discussion. Civil and criminal courts do not just deal with private individuals. There are commercial, industrial and business interests that both make use of the civil courts and find themselves subject to criminal penalties. The power of these bodies to mobilise resources can, in some instances, be equal or greater than that of national governments, and certainly goes far beyond those of individuals or groups of individuals. Due process does, to some extent, take this disparity of resources into account, as indeed it must do if it is linked to the concept that the courts must be open to all. It would arguably be a breach of due process if an individual were deprived of public resources that would enable him or her to sue a powerful company, or indeed to protect him or herself from aggressive assertions of economic power. We will see in Chapters 12 and 13 that one of the longest running pieces of civil litigation in English legal history concerned this very issue. Due process must take into account these issues of access.

If due process protects the integrity of the courts, then it must also be concerned with the ways in which procedures can be abused. While the issue of bribery of judges does not suggest itself as a matter of concern, we will see that some due process cases concern the potential abuse of forensic processes by organised criminals and terrorists who oppose their own violence to that of the state. We do not have the space in this book to thoroughly investigate this issue, which tends to emerge in relation to intimidation of witnesses and other evidential issues. It would also be necessary to observe the differences between criminal and politically motivated violence. Indeed, it might even be possible to argue that elements of Article 6 case law were driven by the post-war crises in Germany and Italy provoked by left-wing armed groups challenging the legitimacy of the State. Cases in which the UK has been forced to defend itself at Strasbourg have also come out of the military and paramilitary policing of the situation in Northern Ireland. Special concerns are raised when the court is faced by those violent or organised enough to oppose their own power to that of the state.

THE PROVENANCE OF DUE PROCESS

We have argued in the section above that the State is legitimate because rights provide checks on its executive powers. This, in turn begs the question of the legitimisation of rights. We do not have the space to examine this issue in detail, but our brief history of due process begins with this point. Thus, regional expressions of human rights, such as the European Convention, and national expressions of rights and liberties, such as those in the English common law, have to be seen within the context of international legal and political norms. Article 6 of the Convention is legitimate because it reflects Article 10 of the Universal Declaration. To what extent is the common law understanding of fair trial guarantees coherent with these international traditions? To what extent is it a problem that until recently the common law contained no statement of human rights? We will now turn to consider these issues.

Article 10 of the Universal Declaration of Human Rights is at the centre of a cluster of rights that protect due process. Article 9 prohibits arbitrary arrest and detention, and Article 11 elaborate fair trial rights with specific reference to the criminal trial. We will focus on the text of Article 10:

> Everyone is entitled in full equality to a fair and public hearing by an independent and impartial tribunal, in the determination of his rights and obligations and of any criminal charges against him.

The due process rights of the Universal Declaration are an attempt to provide an international standard that reflects the values and histories of different national legal traditions. A proper elaboration of this theme would require a close study of the ways in which different traditions give shape to due process values. We can briefly elaborate this theme by looking at the American and English common law traditions. Whereas the former expresses due process as a right, the latter articulated it as the rules of natural justice. This does not mean that English common law is somehow illegitimate as judged by international norms. English and American common law represent different ways of achieving similar ends.

The legal articulation of due process in the American tradition is provided by the Fifth Amendment in the Bill of Rights of the American Constitution. The Fifth Amendment states:

No person shall ... be deprived of life, liberty, or property, without due process of law.

Also relevant is the Sixth Amendment. The core of the Sixth Amendment reads.

In all criminal prosecutions the accused shall enjoy the right to a speedy and public trial, by an impartial jury ...

The presence of due process in the Bill of Rights allows the constitutionalisation of procedure in American law. We can thus clearly see the link between fair trial rights and the guarantee of fundamental human rights. While this is not yet the case in the UK, it may be that one of the impacts of Article 6 will be the constitutionalisation of procedure. However, this is to run ahead with the argument. At this stage, it is necessary to show that, despite certain claims to the contrary, there has always been an understanding of due process in English common law.

Prior to the Human Rights Act, English law provided no explicit general statement of rights in relation to the conduct of the legal process. However, due process does appear as part of a general legal inheritance. Commentators have traced it to clause 39 of the Magna Carta in 1215 which refers to 'lawful judgement ... and the law of the land' and the term 'due process' does occur in a statute of 1354. Somewhat later in the seventeenth century Edward Coke referred to the 'due process of the common law' and the right of access to the courts was affirmed by Blackstone in his *Commentaries* in 1765-9. There are also undoubtedly due process ideas in the Bill of Rights of 1689. For instance, the Act specifies that jurors should be duly empanelled and returned (Article 10). The independence of the judiciary is specifically affirmed in the Act of Settlement of 1701. These historic reference points form the backdrop to Dicey's definition of the rule of law.[19] This can be read as an articulation of due process values:

When we say that the supremacy or the rule of law is characteristic of the English Constitution, we generally include under one expression at least three distinct though kindred conceptions.

---

19 *Thomas* v. *Baptiste* [1999] 3 WLR 249.

We mean in the first place, that no man is punishable or can be made to suffer in body or goods except for a distinct breach of law established in the ordinary courts of the land. In this sense the rule of law is contrasted with every system of Government based on the exercise by persons in authority of wide, arbitrary, or discretionary powers of constraint.

We mean in the second place ... not only that with us no man is above the law, but that every man, whatever his rank or condition, is subject to the jurisdiction of the ordinary tribunal.

There remains yet a third and different sense in which the rule of law ... may be described as a special attribute of English institutions. We may say that the constitution is pervaded by the rule of law on the ground that the general principles of the constitution (e.g. the right to personal liberty, or the right to public meetings) are with us the result of judicial decisions before the courts; whereas under many foreign constitutions the security given to the rights of individuals results, or appears to result, from the general principles of the constitution.

The rule of law is understood in terms of the 'supremacy of regular law as opposed to arbitrary power and equality before the law'.[20] We could suggest that common law provides the parties to both criminal and civil proceedings with a number of protections and safeguards which, taken together, form the framework of the common law 'right to fair trial'. There are two 'minimum' fair trial principles: 'nemo judex in causa sua' and 'audi alteram partem'. The first maxim states that nobody must be the judge in their own case. It can thus be linked to the requirement of the objectivity and neutrality of the judge. The second maxim is difficult to translate. It is normally rendered as 'let the other side be heard'. It can perhaps be seen as the 'right' to address the court. These principles indicate that the common law never turned its back on an understanding of the integral values of the law.

If common law never developed an overarching human right to due process, why should it be necessary to talk in these terms? This is certainly a compelling criticism. In Chapters 13 and 15 we will see that certain features of procedure are indeed hard to describe in human rights terms. For instance, it is difficult to see how the 'institutional value' of a public hearing can be described as a 'right' in criminal procedural law. As commentators have pointed out, it may even be the case that some defendants would prefer not to face the publicity of a trial. That an accused person cannot opt out of a public trial also makes it hard to account for it in the terms of traditional rights theory. Thus not every aspect of due process can be described in the terms of rights. It is also necessary to appreciate the 'institutional context' of common law.[21] However, we will use the language of human rights because, for reasons explained in our discussion of the Human Rights Act, the common law tradition now has an intrinsic link to international traditions. So, our argument will make use of the language of rights, but will also be aware of the inherent limits of rights analysis.

---

20 Clayton and Tomlinson (2001: 7).
21 Summers (2007: 170).

We need to be clear about the precise terms of Article 6 before we can develop this argument. Article 6 of the European Convention on Human Rights states:

> In the determination of his civil rights and obligations or of any criminal charge against him, everyone is entitled to a fair and public hearing within a reasonable time by an independent and impartial tribunal established by law. Judgment shall be pronounced publicly but the press and public may be excluded from all or part of the trial in the interest of morals, public order or national security in a democratic society, where the interests of juveniles or the protection of the private life of the parties so require, or to the extent strictly necessary in the opinion of the court in special circumstances where publicity would prejudice the interests of justice.
>
> 1 Everyone charged with a criminal offence shall be presumed innocent until proved guilty according to law.
> 2 Everyone charged with a criminal offence has the following minimum rights:
>   (a) to be informed promptly, in a language which he understands and in detail, of the nature and cause of the accusation against him;
>   (b) to have adequate time and the facilities for the preparation of his defence;
>   (c) to defend himself in person or through legal assistance of his own choosing or, if he has not sufficient means to pay for legal assistance, to be given it free when the interests of justice so require;
>   (d) to examine or have examined witnesses against him and to obtain the attendance and examination of witnesses on his behalf under the same conditions as witnesses against him;
>   (e) to have the free assistance of an interpreter if he cannot understand or speak the language used in court.

We can see that Article 6 expressly confers fair hearing rights in broad and unqualified terms.[22] In our consideration of the Article, we will see that the court has also recognised the 'implied rights' of access to the courts and a series of other fair trial rights. This will take us to a consideration of the doctrine of equality of arms. The concept is not mentioned in the Article, and is thus distinct from requirements that the trial should be held in public before an independent tribunal.[23] The court's cognisance of the relationship between adversarial procedure and equality of arms shows the Strasbourg court attempting to bring within the range of the Article an important feature of the common law trial.[24] In Chapters 10 and 11 we will develop these themes, and examine the extent to which the common law is compatible with Article 6.

IMAGINING CIVIL AND CRIMINAL JUSTICE

To imagine a system of justice is to imagine a process which is fair both procedurally and substantively. Laws mean nothing if their application goes unconsidered. Our chapters

---

22 Supra n. 21.
23 Ibid., at 103.
24 Ibid. As Summers points out, adversarial procedure is not an exclusively common law concept.

on imagining civil and criminal justice ask some critical questions about how these areas of procedure operate.

In our consideration of civil justice, we use the work of John Rawls to demonstrate why civil justice is important. This also allows us to move away from traditional accounts of civil procedure which tend merely to summarise the detailed bodies of rules. We prefer to encourage our readers to think about how the civil justice system 'actually' works. To this end we will critically describe the problematic way in which civil justice has attempted to deal with three concerns: (1) the allocation of medical resources; (2) claims made to land by a minority group; and (3) the operation of legal aid.

There is a second difference between our work on procedure and that of traditional textbook accounts. The latter tend to present the law and its processes in a 'whiggish' fashion where the history of an institution is a story of its gradual improvement. Thus, the injustice of civil law in the 1800s is demonstrated by reference to Charles Dickens' novel *Bleak House*. Contemporary civil justice can then be triumphantly presented as the realisation of a rational form of civil procedure and the achievement of a better future. In our consideration of Lord Woolf's reforms, we want to show how many problems remain.

While the criminal justice process is also characterised by intractable problems, it is also worth pointing out that the issues raised in this area are quite different from the problems we describe in civil justice. For a start, state punishment impacts more seriously upon an individual's liberty than the remedies available in a civil trial. Furthermore, the competing aims and values at play in the criminal justice system tend to undermine the consistent functioning of the system. We want to raise some questions about the legitimacy and integrity of criminal justice processes.

We begin with a study of police powers to stop and search. While this practice can be justified as necessary to effective policing, the operation of stop and search powers impacts upon minorities in a disproportionate way. We then turn our attention to the way in which criminal process increasingly relies on scientific evidence. This form of evidence is meant to allow the court to find out the truth in any given case. In the words of Jerome Frank, science serves as something of 'a procedural opiate'. We will show that scientific evidence is far more problematic than most would want to believe.

The final section of the chapter looks at the role of judges in the sentencing process and the problem of prison overcrowding. Once again we come across profound tensions within the system. Although the battle between the judiciary and the executive over sentencing powers is not new, in the last decade it has assumed particularly 'sharp' form. This is driven, in part, by the executive's commitment to an expansionist prison policy which appears to have popular support. To pick up on themes developed earlier on in the book, we feel that this is another area in which the judges, rather than Parliament, have stood up for the principles of individual liberty.

The excessive use of the prison comes at a time when the population of incarcerated people is at its highest in this country. Prisons are packed to such a degree that overcrowding has a severe detrimental impact upon the conditions prisoners must endure when serving their sentences. The public, fuelled by the press, may imagine a room with a view, a satellite dish and a few cuddly toys. This is far from the reality of Britain's prisons.

We are often told that problems and abuses within civil and criminal justice are inevitable. This is a lazy excuse to forget those who suffer at the hands of the system. It is a failure of imagination!

THE PRINCIPLES OF CRIMINAL AND CIVIL PROCEDURE

Can we suggest that there are certain key principles that underlie procedural law? Jacob traces them to the concepts of open justice. His thesis is congruent with the work of Jaconelli. Open justice has a specific content that reflects Article 6. It includes 'provision of adequate facilities' for the public and the press, and an 'associated right to report' that requires that trial documents are published and available for public scrutiny. In the criminal trial, the accused must be present, and must be given the opportunity and resources to challenge prosecution evidence. Jacob argues that the effect of the doctrine of natural justice is a clear influence on this concept of procedure. Justice must be seen to be done.

We will see that the concept of open justice is certainly useful. However, when we examine specific areas of civil procedure, we need to appreciate that the animus in this area of law is the requirement that competing values are, as far as possible, placed in a balance. For example, one of the fundamental areas of procedural law is structured on the need to allow the full disclosure of evidence, while accepting that there are certain areas where evidence can be withheld for compelling reasons. Similar points can be made about the development of the law relating to self-incrimination.

Turning our attention to concerns with finality in litigation, we can see that the court has attempted to articulate the acceptable boundaries on the instances where a case can be reopened through appeal. The law has to balance the need for a clear decision with the countervailing requirement that the interests of justice demand, in certain circumstances, that an appeal should take place. In the area of due notice, there are tensions between the need for a person to be present when his or her rights are being determined, and the award of certain injunctions that would not be effective if the respondent was on notice. In civil law as a whole, there is also a need to understand that the duty to give reasons for a decision is not absolute. The duty to give reasons reflects law's fundamentally rational nature. A judgment has authority to the extent that it is reasoned argument, rather than simply an assertion of power. However, the case law also suggests that in certain circumstances it may be legitimate not to do so. In all these areas we can thus see tensions between the values of open justice, and the competing values of the civil justice system that privilege expediency, finality and the balance between the plaintiff and the defendant.

At a general level, we could say that criminal procedure shows a tension between Packer's concepts of due process and crime control. While this model of criminal justice has a relevance to our consideration of arrest, for example, we will see that the notion of crime control is simply too remote from criminal procedure to be a generally useful term. This suggests that we are far more concerned with arguments about the form of due process itself, and the tensions that characterise the forensic process. To what extent can the court articulate a balance between defence and prosecution; between values and principles that operate in favour of defendants, and those that suit the prosecution? We will refer to these as defence- and prosecution-orientated values. How can we develop our analysis of these issues?

Although there is a rhetorical commitment to the due process values, commentators have often suggested English criminal process operates in favour of the prosecution. While this is perhaps generally true, we will see that there is an ongoing commitment to defence-orientated values in the common law, and, in recent years, an interesting relationship between the common law and European human rights has developed. Human rights law carries within it the same tensions that we have described above. However, human rights cases do suggest new ways of thinking about the clash of values in the criminal procedural law, and the broader operation of the courts in a democratic society committed to the rule of law. Thus, our analysis of criminal procedural law will begin with a consideration of the pre-trial stage of arrest, before examining the presumption of innocence and the privilege against self-incrimination. The last section of the chapter will look at the issue of bias and the jury.

CONCLUSION

We are aware that studying the common law through an idea of human rights has its problems. Traditions of thinking on the common law were certainly not sympathetic to the 'rights of man'. Whether or not these prejudices are still alive in the opposition to thinking of the common law in terms of human rights is an open question. While it would be wrong to try and reduce all common law institutions, or indeed all aspects of common law procedure to issues of human rights, we will use the term (to some extent) as both a focus and a provocation. The language of rights allows us to think about those elements of the common law that are coherent with international traditions, and those that reflect different values. While human rights does not even come close to solving the problems that we will discover (and certainly does not define politics) it does allow us to speak in terms of value tensions in the law. This allows us to see that the common law is returning to a sense of an inherent politics of rights. Law is not politically neutral. It has to reflect the values of a democratic culture.

1

'AS A SYSTEM...THE COMMON LAW IS A THING MERELY IMAGINARY'[1]

English legal development appears as a historical continuum. There is no obvious rupture, no wholesale wiping out of the legal wisdom of centuries and no division of the law into a pre- and a post-revolutionary era. In English law the present is never completely shut off from the past and its historical roots are easily perceived.[2]

Out of hard and bitter experience, Englishmen had come to learn that the remorseless, incalculable power of the past over the present was not to be dispelled by the strivings of a single generation. From 1660 onwards, England was never again entirely to forget that the secret of a nation's strength is to have the power of the historic past behind it, not against it.[3]

INTRODUCTION: ORIENTATION AND THE USE OF HISTORY

What is the role of history in the common law world?

Where did Australian law begin? According to traditional legal historiography the origins of Australian law are found in England, around the time of the Norman Conquest in 1066. The English law that developed in the succeeding centuries was ultimately imported to Australia by the British colonists, laying the foundations for an Australian law which grew to have a separate existence from its English parent. This account assumes that the history of law in Australia, like all other Australian histories, began only with the 'discovery' of Australia by Captain Cook in 1770.[4]

As with this account of Australian law so my [WJM] legal education. I attended law school at the University of Canterbury (New Zealand) in the mid to late 1970s. The first

---
1   This title is an edited version of a quote from Jeremy Bentham (1928: 125); the full quote reads 'as a system of rules'.
2   Van Caenegem (1986: 8).
3   S. Chrimes, discussing the events of the civil war, overthrow of Charles I and virtual replacement by the army under Oliver Cromwell and the attempt to create a new system of government (along with a written constitution), the failure of that enterprise and the recall to the throne of the heir of Charles Stuart, in the small work on English Constitutional History I [WJM] used as a supplementary text, S. Chrimes, 1st ed. (1948). We used the 3rd ed. (1965: 158).
4   Mathew, Hunter and Charlesworth (1995: 3).

year of the four-year law degree contained only one law subject – *Legal System*. This was a 'filter subject', which one had to pass along with the non-law subjects at a good grade to allow one to enter law school proper. It was not even called *New Zealand Legal System*. Perhaps that was as well, for it was a trawl through a set of historical events and institutions, images in words, of England. Beginning with an idea of rough and ready customs before the Norman Conquest of England in 1066, we sat in the same packed lecture hall (and the lectures were repeated twice as demand for places so great) week in and week out to construct a set of notes concerning such items as Shire Courts and the Curia Regis, the Magna Carta, the role of juries (which protected us subjects of England's great providential history from the terrors of continental torture), Chief Justice Coke's confrontation with the Crown in which he reminded the king that the king was not above the law but partly constituted by the law, the development of the 'spirit of judicial independence', the glories of equity (and Lord Mansfield's attempts to fuse equity and the common law), the development of the 'modern' courts (and there was a certain repugnance attached to the word 'modern'). Students and lecturer were in New Zealand, yet we were not working with New Zealand material and it seemed as if the lecturer did not particularly like being in New Zealand (the bearing that he presented was very much of a colonial administrator having worked as a public prosecutor in Kenya prosecuting, solid rumour had it, members of the Mau Mau uprising/insurgency against British rule), but he was sure that the common law – along with parliamentary democracy and cricket – were gifts that New Zealanders ought to appreciate. Later in the year we did legal method using a mixture of English and New Zealand cases, but legal method was prefaced by legal history; it was through legal history that we were told the identity of that strange phenomenon that we were to study – the common law legal system.

I was bemused by that lecturer and his style. He began sometimes with, 'Now last time I saw you I ended with [dramatic pause] ... a comma, after the comma comes the word ...', and on it would drone at a pace just sufficient for us to sit there writing down his words as a comprehensive set of 'lecture notes', but the impact of those classes lingers on and the implicit pedagogical answer to the issue of modern law's identity – history – needs evaluation. It is important to distinguish my distaste for the experience from the act of questioning what 'legal history' is a history of. And why was that presentation of *Legal System* a collection of 'images' from the past? And what now, in 2008, located in London, can I make of it all?

Pedagogy, content and ideology

I now label this early experience 'instructionist teaching' that did not involve students in doing any real activities. We faced activities later in the second part of the course which focused on legal method and they were very much concerned with reading case reports, identifying key common law features (many defined in Latin such as *ratio decendidi* and *obiter dicta*), and getting to know how to find and use the 'sources' of law such as the techniques of finding case reports, digests and legislation in the library and then using these sources to construct arguments. I went faithfully to my *Legal System* lectures; I did not to *Introduction to Sociology*. The *Legal System* module was assessed by examinations (25 per cent mid-sessional and 75 per cent final year); two of my other subjects were largely coursework-based with the examinations only taking up 30 per cent of the assessment. In *Introduction to Politics* I completed projects on Japan (on the Liberal Democratic Party and the Japanese Constitution [written unlike New Zealand and the UK]), while in *Sociology* I was faced virtually from day one with the necessity of reading scholarly journals (with their rather peculiar language) to construct a series of assessed essays (on 'father figures' such as Weber and 'concepts' such as power and social development). I hardly attended the lectures in *Sociology* and my memory presents me with a rather different and revealing counter position to *Legal System*. As I remember it, I was put off by the presentation of a young lecturer (dressed in jeans and shirt) from the north of England who claimed that Marxism was the most relevant theoretical stance to explain then contemporary New Zealand (including its legal distribution of 'rights' and 'property') and if we would not see that then we were in the grip of 'ideological mystification'. Through his performance I sat, hardly taking notes, thinking, 'Who is this "outsider", this "whinging POM?" ' (as we termed anyone from England who complained about our country). Coming from a small town and partly raised on a farm, I gave more attention to the statements in *Introduction to Economics* on the role of pork bellies in the construction of the Chicago Futures Market (the 'MERC') and decided to invest what spare cash I had in the Stock Exchange (later taken out and the practice not continued at ongoing considerable loss to my potential economic benefit).

The small figure lecturing in full academic gown in *Legal System* carried more 'authority'; after all as a public prosecutor in Kenya he had defended the state (and possibly 'civilisation') from the Mau Mau 'emergency'. If he thought that legal history was our route into law, then who were we to question?

This, in both crude and sophisticated forms, has been until recently a standard view. Consider the following two quotations:

> Speculation about law and politics is an attractive pursuit. More especially is it attractive to the young. A small knowledge of the rules of law, a sympathy with hardships which have been observed, and a little ingenuity, are sufficient to make a very pretty theory ... It is a harder task to become a master of Anglo-American law, by using the history of that law to discovery the principles which underlie its rules, and to elucidate the manner in which these principles have been developed and adapted to meet the infinite complexities of life in different ages. But those who have chosen to endure this harder task have chosen the better part ... for, as Hale said, 'It is most certain that time and long experience is much more ingenious, subtle and judicious, than all the wisest and acutest wits in the world coexisting can be.'[5]

> The English legal system, which includes for this purpose that of the United States of America and most of the British Commonwealth of Nations, is peculiar among modern systems in this unbroken link with the past. It is the heritage of a profession which made its own law and whose debt to foreign systems is small.[6]

---

5   Holdsworth (1928: 104–105).
6   Potter (1943: 2).

Both date from the first half of the twentieth century. The first writer is William Holdsworth, a greatly respected legal historian; the second is a more mundane but respected law professor. While very much a history in which we have 'an eye on the end of the story' (perhaps a version of the progress wins in history meta-narrative), Holdsworth's legal history was self-consciously educative; 'effective legal history' rather than 'mere antiquarianism' enabled us to learn lessons about what was successful, about those things that underpinned the contemporary. By contrast I have little recollection of any normative thread to the 'history' I was recounted, perhaps there was but I took the message to be more celebratory, rejoice (New Zealanders) in what you are a product of. While Holdsworth was a comparativist, asserting that both the legal systems of England and of Rome had solved the 'difficult problem of combining stability with elasticity',[7] a Potter style history (as displayed in the second quotation above) disavowed that there was any worth in presenting a multiplicity of perspectives. The narrative we were implicitly presented with may be then of one story, one past and one future. Perhaps again I am simplifying my recollection of the pedagogy I experienced, or perhaps the lecturer had already dumbed-down the message or, more prosaically, had simply inherited the course and someone else's notes; alternatively this may have been just the first stage of the intellectual apprenticeship of joining the legal profession and we needed a course on its tradition as a precursor before we got down to the more practical task of learning the 'rules' and policy disputes of contemporary practice. After all, until relatively recently one did not learn the common law by going to university; one learnt it by observing others in practice, by apprenticeship, and there is justification for that. If we assume that law has its own realm, and it has developed in accordance with a set of processes and practices that have given it its own specificity then it follows that we learn what law is by entering into that realm and learning to accept and play the game by the 'rules' of its internal dynamics, customs, methods of arguing and persuading and ways of action, and that this is the true method of understanding, not seeking knowledge from some 'external' vision such as that of a sociologist. Take the words of the legal historian and writer on 'legal transplants', Alan Watson, who presents the growth and evolution of the law as largely determined by an autonomous legal tradition that exists and operates independently of the demands of societal factors.

> There is a lawyer's way to approach a problem. This mode of thinking inoculates them from too much concern with the demands of society.[8]
>
> Law ... is above all and primarily the culture of the lawyers and especially of the law-makers, that is, of those lawyers who, whether as legislators, jurists, or judges, have control of the accepted mechanisms of legal change. Legal development is determined by their culture; and social, economic, and political factors impinge on legal development only through their consciousness ... Law is largely autonomous and not shaped by societal needs; though legal institutions will not exist without corresponding social institutions, law evolves from the legal tradition.[9]

---

7 Ibid., 9.
8 Watson (1985: 42).
9 Ibid., 119.

For Watson the success of what he termed legal transplants provided a conclusive demonstration for his arguments:

> To a large extent law possesses a life and vitality of its own; that is, no extremely close, natural or inevitable relationship exists between law, legal structures, institutions and rules on the one hand and the needs and desires and political economy of the ruling elite or of the members of the particular society on the other hand. If there was such a close relationship, legal rules, institutions and structures would transplant only with great difficulty, and their power of survival would be severely limited.[10]

So then for us in New Zealand, and elsewhere in the lands affected by British imperialism (the common law world), the common law had been 'transplanted' and our law, New Zealand law, gained its identity not by politics or struggle in particular socio-economic domains but through the internal dynamics and culture of the common law 'tradition'. The small amount of New Zealand history that we did note consisted in the acts whereby we, seemingly without much more than instances of a little 'local trouble', adopted English common law as our law.[11]

But I knew from undertaking my *Introduction to Politics* course that the Japanese constitution (and legal system) adopted after the Meiji Restoration in 1889 was very much a political act in response to acts of an external power (the difficulty of maintaining Japan's isolation after the display of power by Commodore Perry of the US Navy). But that was a university course where we learnt about 'them'; it was a course in understanding another system and culture, undertaken on borrowed time (before I did proper legal studies); we did no such 'external' accounts to our own.

The difference may in part be explained as a matter of assigning identities to the different players: the sociologist is given the status of an observer, a spectator who seeks to attain a distancing from practices, the regularities, the human actors, to cast aside any familiarity he has from that what he is observing so that he can gain the grasp of an independent 'science' and return with greater insight and deeper familiarity. The lawyer, in counter-position, gains the status of an actor, who takes his or her meanings from the viewpoint of the internal participant, one who is engaged, who participates in practices that are value laden.

So what then of the images I had been presented with? What was my role as audience? Why do I have no recollection of any narrative binding them together? Should some intellectual order have been imposed so strongly upon them that I can still recollect a message as to what the 'system' added up to? But whose system was it? There was a certain existential imbalance. Why were we students given a history, but not of 'our' system? Did New Zealand have a legal system or a simple 'import'? What was,

---

10   Watson (1978: 314–315).
11   So, in a small book we used as a back up in constitutional law: Chrimes (1965) 3rd ed. (my copy had been bought and sold in the law students' second-hand book sales eight times before my purchase, an indication of its centrality) we read: 'The English Constitution is remarkable for many reasons. Alone among existing Constitutions it is the product of a history never entirely broken over a period of some fourteen centuries. Notwithstanding its long history, it is in the highest degree adaptable to the needs of changing circumstances and conditions ... It is remarkable also in having been exported whole-scale, often more or less *en bloc*, to distant lands...' (pp. 2–3).

if any, the link between the history of the first term and the analytical training – the techniques of legal method in the second?

Nearly 30 years later as a legal academic I accept there are at least two different ways of approaching the study of a 'legal system'; one is analytical, defining the constituent elements and tracing their functional or logical interconnections; another is historical. Contemporary legal system texts and courses largely ignore history; accounts of purposes, functions and social policy have replaced it.[12] I do not seek to analyse the reasons for this, merely to note it. I take this to be what Bentham – a great believer in the enlightenment drive for rationality, system and order – meant in his late eighteenth century criticism that the common law as presented by people such as Blackstone (who portrayed it as historical creation) was not really a system of law at all. Perhaps what I experienced was the repetition of an act of recounting that once was vital but had become a tired old trope. If so then that recounting of the history of the common law was an exercise that once had given it legitimacy and identity, but was now simply a genuflection to ritual where the real action was becoming learning sets of rules and proceedings with discussions of policy, or functions, or effectiveness, disentangled from history.[13] What can I re-imagine? Perhaps not a system of law, but elements of a tradition....

ORIGINS

The Norman Conquest is a catastrophe which determined the whole future of English Law.[14]

Britain had not been conquered ... she felt no need to exorcise the past.[15]

Time has a particular relationship with common law. On one level the acceptance of custom – historically the first major source of common law – was that it ran from time out of mind, from time immemorial, later accepted as from 1189 (the first year of the reign of Richard I). Another is of the common law as a unique combination of continuity and change. Sir Mathew Hale presented an analogy with the ship of the Argonauts: thus although continually changing, the common law kept its essential nature.[16] The two quotes immediately above reflect a dilemma at the heart

---

12   See Partington (2003), beginning with 'Knowledge, themes and structure', then 'Law and Society: the purposes and functions of law'. Cownie and Bradney (1996) in *English Legal System in Context* begin by asking 'What is "the English Legal System"?'
13   Allison (2007) in a text entitled *The Historical Constitution: Continuity, Change and European Effects* presents the two sides of Dicey.
14   Pollock and Maitland (1898: 79).
15   Jean Monnet (one of the intellectual figures behind the EU), in his memoirs (Monnet, 1978) reflecting upon the different attitude Britain took to the European community than France and Germany.
16   'But tho' those particular Variations and Accessions have happened in the Laws, yet they being only partial and successive, we may with just Reason say, They are the same English Laws now, that they were 600 Years since in the general. As the Argonauts Ship was the same when it returned home, as it was when it went out, tho' in that long Voyage it had successive Amendments, and scarce came back with any of its former Materials; and as Titius is the same Man he was 40 Years since, tho' Physicians tells us, That in a Tract of seven Years, the Body has scarce

of understanding the interconnections of common law tradition, British identity and constitutionalism. The history of gradualism and piecemeal change inherent implicit in Monnet's succinct statement contrasts to most countries; the United Kingdom has few overriding constitutional movements or events of great change such as revolutions. One context for the argument for and practical creation of the European Community, now the European Union, was the catastrophic wars continental Europe experienced over the centuries and in particular in World War I and World War II. Whereas China, for example, had in the twentieth century three radically contrasting systems of government and three entirely rewritten constitutions; the twentieth century saw great changes in the UK but its land was never invaded and its constitutional developments, such as its reform Acts or devolution of power on Scotland and Wales, and the significance of the joining the evolving EEC/EU were gradual rather than revolutionary, evolutionary rather than imposed by events and people from outside.

Under the narratives of gradualist legal evolution the common law of England is traced back in its development as the oldest state law in Europe in the sense that England existed as a state (though not in the sense of a nation-state that was to become the popular motif of state formation in modern society) as old as the Anglo-Saxons with a relatively centralised currency, law (albeit customary based) and an administration of justice that gave a role for central officials. It developed as the oldest body of law that was common to a whole kingdom and administered by a central court with a nationwide competence in first instance. In the rest of Europe at that time, the law was either European or local, not particular to a state. Some European countries adopted the cosmopolitan *jus commune* (Roman or canon law, shared by learned lawyers over Europe) to provide a national legal system that their divergent customs could not produce. In England, a common law was produced out of the mixture of Norman land law and the courts dealing with English customs and via an administrative class linked to the crown. Ironically that class was not English at all but kings and justices of continental extraction: the disputed point of origin was the invasion of the Anglo-Saxon kingdom by the Normans under William Duke of Normandy. I will begin by contrasting two images concerning the Norman Conquest: one of violence and the other of administration and centralisation.

First a central image to British historical consciousness is the famous Battle of Hastings, often called the cataclysm of 1066, when the Norman Duke William defeated the English King Harold and claimed the throne of England.

The victory of William Duke of Normandy poses a problem for any ideology of continuity and unbroken evolution for it led to the succession of a new dynasty, the dispossession of a native aristocracy and the creation of a split society. The *Franci* became the dominant minority, introducing values, rules and a language different from those of the native masses (the *Anglici*). This is dramatic change: how then is the image of the laws of England being the expression of national identity preserved?

The traditional explanation, which preserves the identity of the common law from being seen as actually foreign, is a paradox: William was a political victor (he who

---
any of the same Material Substance it had before.' From Hale (1971: 39) *The History of the Common Law*, written in the seventeenth century.

26 ~ The Politics of the Common Law

Figure 1.1 Death of King Harold at the Battle of Hastings.
Source: Cassell's *Illustrated History of England* (1900) p. 81, which states 'the great battle of Hastings, which lasted from sunrise to sunset, and which, for the valour displayed by both armies and their leaders, was worthy to decide a contest for a crown'. The term 'Conqueror' here bears the original meaning of 'the Gainer'. William claimed not the right of a usurper but those of a lawful heir to the English throne.

'gained' the Throne) who left the law alone. But this is partly, at least, mythological. Of course, it was an important tool of ruling that one could present it as preserving an existing system, but there were many changes and introductions. The Anglo-Saxon system of administration had many features that we can see as more efficient than those in use on the continent – such as the use of a centralised system of money exchange with taxation – and so preservation of the main features of the system was efficient as well as good rhetoric. Yet the fact remains that the resulting system was a blend. Take the situation of Henry II (1154–1189), who is often referred to as the father of the common law. Here the system was not just English: Henry was titled King of the English, Duke of the Normans and Aquitanians and Count of Angevins. Under his administration locally chosen sheriffs were changed into royally appointed agents charged with effectively enforcing the law and collecting taxes in the counties. Henry made use of juries (then used as instruments for the presentation of facts of the locality) and reintroduced the sending of justices (judges) on regular tours of the country to hear cases for the crown. His legal reforms led him to be called the father of the common law; he died in France in 1189 at war with his son Richard (later Richard I, the Lionheart).

My second image reflects the opportunity that the pre-existing system gave to this new energised and competent élite.

Figure 1.2 The Domesday Book.
Source: MEPL.

Twenty years after the Battle of Hastings, William I faced pressures from the Danes and the King of Norway in particular which necessitated a significant expenditure. William ordered a great survey be made and that a book be compiled containing information on who owned what throughout the country. This book would strengthen the tax revenue as it would provide the record against which nobody could dispute or argue against a tax demand. (One story [mythical] of the title is that it brought doom and gloom to the people of England – hence 'Domesday Book'.) Each record includes, for each settlement in England, its monetary value and any customary dues owed to the Crown at the time of the survey, values recorded before Domesday, and values from before 1066. The Domesday survey is far more than just a physical record though. It is a detailed statement of lands held by the king and by his tenants and of the resources that went with those lands. It records which manors rightfully belonged to which estates, thus ending years of confusion resulting from the gradual and sometimes violent dispossession of the Anglo-Saxons by their Norman conquerors. It was moreover a 'feudal' statement, giving the identities of the tenants-in-chief (landholders) who held their lands directly from the Crown, and of their tenants and under tenants. The fact that the scheme was executed and brought to complete fruition in two years is a tribute of the political power and formidable will of William the Conqueror. It was compiled by (1) collecting existing information about manors, people and assets, including documents dating from the Anglo-Saxon period and post-1066 which listed lands and taxes in existence, and each tenant-in-chief, whether bishop, abbot or baron, and each sheriff and other local official, was required to send in a list of manors and men; (2) verifying or correcting this information – commissioners were assigned sections of England called circuits and travelled around the country; in every town, village and hamlet, the commissioners asked the same questions to everyone with interest in land from the barons to the villagers; (3) recording all of this in three stages: as it was in the time of King Edward, as it was when King William gave it and as it is now.

I use this image as symbolising the formation of central government. Baker relates that the earliest form of justice was not seen as coming from a ruler or the state employed learned judges but communal justice or the custom of the people.[17] As feudalism developed, the style of authority that came with being a lord gave rise to a set of courts

---
17 Baker (2002).

relating from a developing personalisation of authority. The most important long-term effect of this, once England became a single kingdom in the tenth century, was the constitutional ascendancy of the king. William and the new élite worked with and developed further the existing institutions. The growth of the common law was owed in great part to the ability of a central court to fashion and administer a set of remedies and in the process of deciding disputes articulate principles and rules. Without a developing strong central government it would not have been possible to unify the norms and customs of the country into a centralised form administered by a common set of courts and each area of the country would have been able to develop its own traditions and customs in conflicting and competing ways. The growth of the common law was in one sense a victory of centralised authority over a host of competing local forms.

Land law was central and here the rise of royal actions, in particular the royal order of *reseisin*. Here, as elsewhere, the crucial process was procedural. Fees had to be paid for this justice but 'the main attractions for the private litigant were no doubt the effective process and enforcement which royal writs procured, and the availability from the late twelfth century of a central written record which would end the dispute for all time'.[18] The common law developed because of the strength of the king's (institutional) power behind the writ (royal commands addressed to officials to 'do' something), and the development of a professional body of persons and settled behaviour in the processing of claims and the enforcement of judgment. Predictability of process was a key factor. Judgments were not *ad hoc* but followed from similar forms through real actions and the processes whereby cases were structured, presented and resolved in court.[19] Delegation of authority to decide led to the rise of a legal profession with judges at the peak. Another factor leading to the pre-eminence of English judges was the fact that the law was not placed in the first place in any one learned 'Holy Writ'; that is, codification, hence it did not fall into the hands of a guild of scholarly jurists who had sole access to its bookish sources. Although there were statutes, the central lawgiver remained largely inactive. By contrast there was the strength and continuity of the central courts competent in first instance for a wide variety of cases over the

---

18   Ibid., 14–15.
19   Judicial reasoning is not a mechanical process; it is better seen as an **art form** developed over time and through many political and social battles. For centuries, until the Judicature Acts of the 1870s, the common law of England consisted of a system of actions or legal remedies, each commanding its own procedure. It was crucial to get the procedure correct, to specify the right pleading (the oral presentation of the issues and facts); early books on English law tended to be compilations of correct procedures or collections of moves that had worked in the past. Breaking out of those procedure-based actions, legal doctrine developed but it was essential to use established concepts, principles and arguments that had been approved in earlier cases. In this way we say that English law prefers **precedent** as a basis for legal judgments, and moves empirically from case to case, from one reality (actual case) to another. Continental law (from the civil or Roman law tradition) tends to move theoretically by deductive reasoning, basing judgments on abstract principles. It is more conceptual, more scholastic and works with definitions and distinctions. The common law is for the most part not a codified law. Rules and principles are made clear by the examination of decided cases. We do this by drawing generalisations from the cases, but there is argument as to the exact status of decided cases: are they 'the law' or are they (as per Blackstone) 'evidence of the law'? In the declaratory theory, the common law is always something more than what is contained in the judgments. The legal reasoning and rules expounded in the cases can be good or bad, and we say that the law works itself out through the cases. This implies that the law is always something other than the cases, and being faithful to the law means being faithful to something beyond what we can see written down; it means being faithful to a tradition and to historically entrenched ideals.

whole kingdom. They acted with royal power behind them and were staffed by professionals. These royal judges shaped the common law in cooperation with barristers and serjeants (the small group of leading barristers of the time; in modern time that order has been replaced by King's/Queen's Counsel) and were at the same time its guardians.

The continental development of civil law is considerably different. Several countries in the European continent in the late middle ages came to adopt the law as contained in the *Corpus Juris*; the Code Civil became the lawyer's bible. These texts were treated by many as *Ratio scripta*, 'reason put into writing', so legal science was based on great authoritative texts and consisted in large part of glosses and commentaries. This was different from the Roman production of these texts and seems strange, almost religious, to the practically focused English frame of mind.

Thus the continent accepted a great law book of a society that had been gone for centuries as its ultimate authority, and entirely reshaped its own law through scholastic gloss, disputations and commentaries based on the Roman model.

The English way came to be to create relatively settled modes of presenting arguments, developing existing rules, modernising the courts and their procedures and gradually building up case law. Perhaps it would occasionally appeal to the lawgiver, but otherwise it let the professionals get on with the task of pleading and adjudicating. The conquest of Normandy by the French monarchy and the gradual introduction of Roman-inspired French law into the duchy turned Anglo-Norman law into purely English law. What became the common law tradition started as Anglo-Norman law, shared by a kingdom (England) and a duchy (the French duchy of Normandy) that were not separated but united by the Channel; what came to be the hallmark of England's difference from Europe was initially not insular at all.

I now look at another image which deals with a famous, if rather misunderstood legal document, the Magna Carta, which has for a long, long time held a place in popular consciousness, at least, as the nearest thing to a written foundational document. John's reign has been termed 'a career in tyranny'[20] and the document was not understood at the time as it became to be. A grasp of the rhetorical appeal of the Magna Carta may be gauged from Cassell's glowing tones in the 'century edition' of 1902:

> To the Englishman of modern times, the event of that day bears a deep and solemn interest, far surpassing that of battles or of conquests. He is surrounded now by many of the blessings that freedom gives to all who live beneath her sway. Under her warm smile civilisation grows and flourishes, knowledge sheds around her calm, undying light; wrong is redressed by free opinion; and man, with brow erect, throws off the tyranny of man. In the green meadow of the Thames was sown the seed which bears such fruits as these. Centuries more of toil and struggle may be needed to bring it to maturity. The progress of the human race is slow, and beset with difficulties: amidst the present material prosperity, with all the advantages of civil and religious liberty, we are still far from the goal which lies before us ... Now at least, the way is open to us, and cannot be mistaken; the light of Heaven shines full upon it, the obstacles grow fewer and weaker

---

20   Cassell (1902: vol. I, 266).

Figure 1.3 King John Granting Magna Charta (on the Thames island of Runnymede, near Windsor) by Ernest Normand (1859–1923), a notable painter in Victorian England for works on historical and orientalist scenes. This is a painting in canvas the same as the *King John Granting the Magna Carta* fresco at the Royal Exchange in London (painted 1900, restored 2001).
Source: Cassell's Frontispiece to Vol. I.

Figure 1.3 Continued

This image of course obscures (it does not present) the fact that on 15 June 1215, the action by King John, pressured by the barons and threatened by insurrection, was one of extreme reluctance. John assumed that the pope would give him permission to retract his agreement immediately once he could get himself into a better political position on the grounds that he signed under duress.

The charter, however, also established a council of barons who were to ensure that the sovereign observed the charter, with the right to wage war on him if he did not. The Magna Carta was the first formal document insisting that the sovereign was as much under the rule of law as his people, and that the rights of individuals (at least those of a certain status) were to be upheld even against the wishes of the sovereign. As a source of fundamental constitutional principles, the Magna Carta came to be seen as an important definition of aspects of English law, and in later centuries was popularly perceived as the basis of the liberties of the English people. It has of course long been superseded but in the absence of a written constitution it retained almost mythological status.

The Magna Carta lives on as a central trope to be deployed in narratives of democratic progress and struggle. For example in 2007 the British Cabinet Minister Jack Straw, as leader of the House of Commons, claimed that the 'fight now against unbridled terror' should be part of a story, 'alongside the Magna Carta, the fight for votes and emancipation of Catholics, women, ethnic minorities and World War II' which makes it 'clearer about what it means to be British' and its roots in democracy to challenge those opposed to Britain's core values. Some rights and responsibilities were a non-negotiable part of being a British citizen and it would help reduce segregation in an increasingly mixed society. While conceding that the British had often looked or acted like oppressors 'to the Irish and to many of the peoples of the British Empire', the freedom preached by Britain helped ensure that the empire had collapsed 'with less bloodshed than many other decolonisation struggles'. A stronger 'British story' would challenge those with a 'single, all-consuming identity' at odds with democratic values, such as minority fringe Muslim groups. Thus society should stress how democracy could serve 'as the means to allow different groups with often competing interests to live together in relative harmony'. But while there was room for 'multiple and different identities', they could not take precedence over the British 'core democratic values of freedom, fairness, tolerance and plurality'. 'To be a British citizen, fully playing your part in British society, you must subscribe to that. It is the bargain and it is non-negotiable.' (Cyril Foster Lecture at Oxford University, reported by the *Guardian*, 25 January 2007.)

In February 2008, when now Lord Chancellor (the reformed post) and Secretary of State for Justice, Jack Straw gave a lecture at George Washington University in the US, he began 'where so much of our legal, governmental and social systems begins – with the Magna Carta'. The Magna Carta, the Declaration of Independence, and the Bill of Rights and the Constitution constituted the 'political scriptures'. In Straw's narrative:

'In the late eighteenth century, the Founding Fathers searched for an historical precedent for asserting their rightful liberties from King George III and the English Parliament. They found it in a parley which took place more than 500 years before that, between a collection of barons, and the then impoverished and despotic King John, at Runnymede in 1215. On that unremarkable field they did a remarkable thing. They demanded of the king that their traditional rights be recognised, written down, confirmed with the royal seal and sent to every county to be read aloud to all freemen.

Let us, however, prick the illusion, that the Magna Carta was precipitated by the equivalent of thirteenth century civil rights campaigners. The Magna Carta was a feudal document – designed to protect the interests, rights and properties of powerful landowners with the temerity to stand up to the monarch. Given its provenance, it is a paradox that a document which was founded on the basis of class and self-interest has over centuries become one of the basic documents for our two constitutions, and one of the icons of the universal protection of liberty.

This is a measure of how constitutions evolve, grow and develop with changing circumstances; in this sense they can be very much like scripture. This is the process by which a document just shy of its eight-hundredth birthday still has a resonance and relevance today. In more than 100 decisions, the United States Supreme Court has traced dependence on the Magna Carta for understanding of due process of law, trial by one's peers, the importance of a fair trial, and protection against excessive fines and cruel and unusual punishment. These are principles which similarly have long formed the bedrock of our system of common law in the United Kingdom – as admired as it is emulated in democracies around the world.

I dwell on this historical point to demonstrate that in spite of the very different systems of governance in the UK and the US, there is an enduring bond between our two democracies, a shared legal culture, a common thread that can be followed back to the Magna Carta. At the heart of each, of both, is a powerful and everlasting idea of liberty and of rights.'

(Mr Jack Straw, Modernising the Magna Carta – Ministry of Justice, website, delivered 13 February 2008 at George Washington University, Washington, DC.)

by the day, the efforts to oppose them grow stringer, and the final triumph is secure. The value and importance of Magna Charta is not to be estimated by its immediate application to ourselves. Those positive laws and institutions of later times, all have their root in this charter.[21]

John ruled an England officially Catholic. He may have been an able administrator interested in law and government but he neither trusted others nor was trusted by them. His despotic tendencies, refusal to honour agreements, heavy taxation, disputes with the Church (John was excommunicated by the Pope in 1209) and unsuccessful attempts to recover his French possessions made him unpopular. Many of his barons rebelled and in June 1215 they forced the king to sign a peace treaty accepting their reforms. The barons took their stand on feudal law and followed its formalities. For, if the king was their divinely ordained ruler he was also their feudal lord and as such had obligations towards them. King and barons entered into a contract and the contractual nature of medieval feudalism coloured the constitutional outlook at this time.

As a peace treaty, the Magna Carta was a failure and the rebels invited Louis of France to become their king. When John died in 1216, England was in the grip of civil war. The treaty was later seen as a key constitutional document and the name Magna Carta has great rhetorical power; it limited royal powers, defined feudal obligations between the king and the barons, and guaranteed a number of rights. The most influential clauses concerned the freedom of the Church; the redress of grievances of owners and tenants of land; the need to consult the Great Council of the Realm so as to prevent unjust taxation; mercantile and trading relationships; regulation of the machinery of justice so that justice should be denied to no one; and the requirement to control the behaviour of royal officials. The most important clauses established the basis of the writ of habeas corpus ('you have the body, bring it to me'); that is, that no one shall be imprisoned except by due process of law, and that 'to no one will we sell, to no one will we refuse or delay right or justice'.

METHODS OF PROOF AND THE RISE OF THE JURY

While to the participant, who we assume believed deeply in God, the practices held respect, to modern senses early modes of procedure and proof 'in contentious matters was calculated to avoid reasoned decision-making'.[22] If the parties, either in a dispute we would now call criminal matters or civil, could not be persuaded to settle, then resort would be had to proof by oath, backed up by a physical test. The complainer would have to demonstrate that his case was believable and worthy of taking action by bringing a group of supporters who would back up his story, the defender may be allowed to respond by 'proof by oath', that is to swear on the holy book to the truth of the case and he was expected to bring neighbours as 'oath helpers' to back up his word. But if this form of proof was not allowed, either because of the gravity of the accusation

---

21 Ibid., 268–70.
22 Baker (2002: 4).

Figure 1.4 Trial by ordeal by water (unattributed woodcut, probably of a supposed witch, sixteenth century). Credit: MEPL

or the unreliability of the party's word, the oath might have to be proved by test of an ordeal. There were two main ordeals, by fire or by water (and occasionally the oath was to be proved by making the oath taker swallow a large piece of hardened dry bread!). In the ordeal of fire a piece of iron was put into a fire and then into the party's hand, the hand was bound and inspected a few days later: if the burn had festered, God was taken to have decided against the party. The ordeal of water required the party to be tied and lowered into a pond; if she/he sank the water was deemed to have received her/him with God's blessing, and she/he was quickly fished out.

Ordeals were a unilateral appeal to the judgement of God. These relied upon the help of the Church for a priest was required to perform the rites necessary to call upon divine aid. The priest must heat the iron or *adjure* the pool of water to receive the innocent who, if they sank, were declared to have come clean from the ordeal (the ordeal of cold water). A priest bound up the hand that carried the hot iron and unbound it to see whether the burn had healed thereby showing a stainless conscience (ordeal of hot iron). The priest adjured the morsel of bread (*cosned*) to choke the swearer of a false oath. In 1215 the Lateran Council resolved to withdraw the sanction of the (Roman Catholic) Church from the ordeal. In consequence the ordeal soon became virtually obsolete (with the exception of 'witches').

Its disappearance enabled the jury trial to take its place. It is important to understand how this enabled law and facts to be separated and how the difference enabled 'law' to develop over time. The ordeal was inscrutable.

> There was a prolonged intellectual debate about the legitimacy of the ordeal. It was not clear how man could expect God to answer human questions: might He not, for instance, choose to absolve men who had broken the law but repented? And what if He decided not to intervene at all, but to leave the matter to be settled by His ordinary laws of nature? Could one be sure in a given case whether He has intervened? There is some evidence that those who administered ordeals, perhaps because of such doubts, began to feel a responsibility to facilitate the result they considered right: for instance, by letting the iron cool in cases where suspicion was weak, or by interpreting a burned hand liberally. In the last days of the ordeal, the acquittal rate was surprisingly high. Above all, it was not clear that humans had any right to invoke God's miraculous intervention in mundane affairs: indeed, the Church taught that is was wrong to tempt the Almighty. In 1215, the Lateran Council, after discussing these problems, took the decisive step of forbidding clergy to participate any more in ordeals.[23]

Under the old system 'judgement preceded proof: once it was adjudged that one of the parties should swear or perform a test there was no further decision to make, except whether he has passed it'.[24] However separating law and facts enabled judgments to be produced by the application of legal rules to accepted facts (it was the role of the jury to rule on competing versions of facts) and judges to develop the rules and issue directions to the jury on how, given what version of the facts they accepted, a valid verdict was to be reached.

SOVEREIGNTY AND THE RISE OF POSITIVISM

My next image I will call an 'anti-common law' image. It was presented by the English political theorist Thomas Hobbes in 1651 as the frontispiece of *Leviathan*, regarded as a foundational text for English political liberalism. Writing against the backdrop of a bloody civil war in England and widespread war and unrest in Europe, Hobbes sought to present an image of authority and reason to avoid the dangerous and bloody quarrels over the respective claims of political and religious leaders by defining the law of practical human association (the Commonwealth) as the command of the sovereign. '[I]t is not wisdom but authority that makes a Law.'[25] If we did not agree on a stable institutional authority for (human) law we would be lost in different claims about law and reason, and everyone would have grounds for questioning laws validity. Positive law was an instrument of power; where there is no sovereign, such as in the case of so-called international law, there is no real law.

---

23   Ibid., 5.
24   Ibid., 5.
25   Hobbes, *Dialogue*, 55.

This simplifies Hobbes, but in *Leviathan* and his related *Dialogue* law fits the paradigm of the legislator; that is, the political power centre as the king of the law, and all further legal officials operating as deputies of that sovereign power.[26] Hobbes may be called an 'anti-common law' writer as he seems to present a theory of 'positive law' (or law posited by a human power centre) before its time. His essential themes were picked up in the late eighteenth and nineteenth centuries by the English legal philosophers Jeremy Bentham and John Austin to found a perspective entitled legal positivism, which for much of the 'modern' era has been the dominant approach to understanding law in Anglo-American jurisprudence.

Positivist sovereignty is hierarchy ('sovereign and subject' in John Austin's terms), law – whatever rational or theoretical justification for it – is an emanation of sovereignty. By contrast the idea of the rule of law presents another articulation of the relationship of sovereignty and law in which law is not the emanation of sovereignty but sovereignty operates subject to law. *Leviathan* presents hierarchy as the solution of the impasse of a harsh meta-narrative of the human condition, one which gives the natural condition of mankind as a state of 'warre' of all on all, where reason has little chance against the violent passions of man, and the life of man is solitary, poor, nasty, brutish and short. Humanity is rescued from this condition by fear and our use of reason to overcome the essential weakness of our natural condition. Fear of death drives man to act rationally and combine together, forming a strong, even totalitarian government, through accepting that power – might – lies at the heart of all social organisation and that whoever possesses power has both the ability and the right to dominate. The commands of the government – the sovereign – are the law and ultimately it is power that makes law effective. We are simplifying but Hobbes places the achievement of security – the pacification of violence – before all else and demands performability (the power to enforce or to make a predictable, repeatable occurrence) as his criteria for success.[27] In a Hobbesian world the sovereign must be effective; it was not feudal obligation but rational calculation that founded the social bond.

Leviathan, whether or not the author understood it as such, is a prototypical modernist text. Although the author tries to work with the allusions and language of the past (except that he wrote it in English and not Latin as was expected) he gives a new beginning to stories of our social life. He is termed the father of 'political liberalism' since he says we must start our notions of human interaction with the basic premises that we are first all relatively equal and that we are also to be treated as autonomous individuals, and he is a modernist when he gives us the task of creating, of moulding the conditions of social life anew and doing that through the use of scientific knowledge, not the historical narratives or epics of the traditions. The political power centre is to use law as our instrument of command, of enforcing political will, of getting social projects done.

---

26 Blackstone grasped this clearly; sovereign or supreme power articulated itself, made law, through legislation: 'For legislature ... is the greatest act of superiority that can be exercised by one being over another.' (*Commentaries*, I, 46*).

27 In today's conditions – post-11 September 2001, and observing the instability of Iraq and many other countries around the globe – Hobbes' message rings true to many.

Figure 1.5 In the frontispiece of *Leviathan* (1651), we are presented with an image of sovereignty – it concerns both protected (civilised) space and embodiment. The body of the sovereign towers over the protected space; the sovereign is the highest, it is the summit towering over what it dominates and protects. Note that the body of the sovereign is composed of the bodies of the subjects and the reality of the body limits, of the vulnerability of all humans to pain and death, provides a key element in Hobbes' narrative of the human condition that he used to legitimate sovereign power. The frontispiece concerns the creation of civilised space, a realm of civil society where a civilised humanity can flourish beneath the watching gaze of the sovereign. We know that Hobbes placed the control of social violence, the widespread nature of which in the early seventeenth century could hardly even be described as the waging of 'war', as key.

Figure 1.5 Continued

On the page, an interlocking set of images gives a visual presentation of the benefits of security and stability; in effect an existential world picture. For us of course this is a classical text: we cannot recreate the experience of encountering it during the time of its writing. We acknowledge that it was written at the time of the passing in Europe of the superordinate authority of the Christian church; it was a time when religious authority, instead of being a binding force, had itself become a major source of conflict. What should replace the claims to loyalty of religious brotherhood or localised relations? The Thirty Years War – the most bitter European campaign then seen – had laid waste to much of central Europe and drastically reduced the German-speaking population. Few people thought globally as we mean it; but, using our current language, the major blocs of that time appear as a divided European Christendom, with the strongest world powers being the Chinese Empire, localised in its concerns, and the Islamic Ottoman Empire, somewhat at odds with Islamic Persia. For centuries Islam, not Christian Europe, had been the place of learning; but a grand European project was to change that world. Spain destroyed the last Muslim (Moorish) enclave in Western Europe – the Emirate of Granada – in 1492, in the aftermath of which Columbus was allowed to sail in search of a new route to India. From that time, the ships and military power of Europeans entered into the wider realms of the globe, overwhelming cultures and peoples that could not withstand the onslaught, and creating new social and territorial relations in a European image.

Driving this world shift in power was an existential perspective on life itself. Hobbes postulated the basis of the social bond – in place of dynasties, religious tradition or feudal ties – as rational self-interest exercised by calculating individuals. As bearers of subjective rationality, individuals were depicted as forming the social order and giving their allegiance to a government, a sovereign, because it was in their rational self-interest to do so and the metaphor for the social bond was contractual, not traditional. The sovereign was now to have a particular territory, which many have rather loosely termed the 'nation state', wherein he was the representative of a people and was ultimately composed of the people who occupied that territory. To ensure security and maintain peace, Hobbes knew the sovereign must be well armed. The armaments he gave him were dual: the public sword and the weapons of the military, but there are also the weapons of metaphysical awe, the emblems of the Church, of solace as well as respect. The sovereign would use the weapons of power and awe; his word would make law. But what of justice? The common law views of the time stressed that judges did not make law as a representative of the power centre – deputies of the sovereign – but either declared what the custom of the locality had been (and in this, as later writers such as Blackstone stated as if a legitimating factor, would be law by the acceptance of the people).

THE CENTRALITY OF JUDGES

To accompany the next image consider an extract from the English twentieth century poet W.H. Auden's poem *Law like love*.[28]

> Law, says the judge as he looks down his nose,
> Speaking clearly and most severely,
> Law is as I've told you before,
> Law is as you know I suppose,
> Law is but let me explain it once more,
> Law is The Law

I interpret this extract as representing a peculiarly English way of expressing an attitude and understanding of law that has become common sense. Is there any philosophical point being expressed there, and why should Auden have a 'judge' as the speaker?

In my own reading the quotation expresses the anti-theoretical leaning of much of English writing about law; law was simply the law, get on with it: work within the

---

28   Auden (1976).

Figure 1.6 Earl Mansfield, wearing the Robes of a Peer, engraved by H.T. Ryall after a painting by Sir Joshua Reynolds (MEPL). Mansfield is known as the father of English commercial law for his influence while Lord Chief Justice, but like the educationalist, William Blackstone, he became a judge through politics (and was better at law than politics). He was born 1705 in Scotland, the fourth son of the fifth Viscount Stormont. He was a King's Scholar at Westminster School (a leading private school), and Christ Church College, Oxford, and was called to the Bar at Lincoln's Inn in 1730. He became an MP and made his in name in 1737 with his speech to the House of Commons in support of a merchants' petition to stop Spanish assaults on their ships. In 1742 he became Solicitor General. In 1754 he was appointed Attorney General and was leader of the House of Commons under the Duke of Newcastle. In 1756 he was appointed Chief Justice of the King's Bench, being raised to the peerage, a post he held until 1788. The role of the judge as the central actor in the legal system is displayed by the fact that he rationalised many of the rules of procedure, reduced expense and delay, and tried to fuse the principles of law and equity. Though not fully successful in renovating the medieval law of property, he developed a theory of contract that laid the foundation for modern commercial law. His role in the development of commercial law owed a lot to listening to commercial practitioners and coming up with a decision that fitted with their notions of practice (what we may call commercial custom). He attempted to apply continental analogies in order to bring English law closer to international practice. Mansfield was unpopular for his opinions on seditious libel and for his judgments in the case of the radical politician John Wilkes, and his house was burned (1780) in the anti-Catholic Gordon riots. In preparing *Commentaries on the Laws of England*, Blackstone was clearly influenced by Mansfield and incorporated many of his opinions into his exposition of the law.

tradition (and the tradition, of course, gave you ways of thinking that you took for granted). Law did not need defining, it did not need some overriding theoretical framework, it was better understood through practice, through the experience of it rather than some logical scheme and the prince of law was the judge. The judge, not the politician, not the academic commentator and certainly not the administrator, was the key figure, the controller of meaning, the arbitrator of application. Thus the imagery of English law abounds with portraits of judges, some famous (or infamous) at the time and now forgotten by history, others immortalised as famous figures of the common law. The image I present is of Lord Mansfield, perhaps the most famous of the classic common law judges. In the common law tradition the judges are central. Since the so-called constitutional settlement which gave the English throne to William and Mary in the late seventeenth century, judges have security of tenure; in other words the government cannot dismiss them at will. The Act of Settlement provided that judges' commissions should be during good behaviour and they should be removable only upon the address of both Houses of Parliament (a very unlikely event). Much of the actual law of England and Wales has been developed out of judges' decisions – this is often said to be the narrow meaning of the phrase 'common law'; that is, case law, as opposed to statute law which has been made by the legislature. In Chapters 3 and 4 we expand on the basic arguments that exist on how much law-making judges do when deciding cases and interpreting earlier decisions to draw out the principles earlier used therein, and apply them in fresh conditions; whatever position one holds on the extent of judicial law-making, all agree that in common law jurisdictions judges control the process of declaring what the law is in practical application of resolving disputes. You should note that even in the case of statutes – where it seems that that control is given to the legislature – the judges retain ultimate control, for they declare what the statute 'means'. They declare, in reality, how the statute is to be applied. Many scholars, however, hold that in declaring what the law is, the judges extend law; put starkly, they make law. How can this difference be reconciled? In practice the complexity of the issues – both factual and legal – presented in a particular case and the wealth of competing analogies available with the circumstances of previous cases ('precedents' or 'authorities') frequently allow a judge to make his own constructive choice without appearing to breach the doctrine of binding precedent (the key doctrine of the modern common law system, which is literally to stand by what has previously been decided).

INTERNAL AND EXTERNAL PERSPECTIVES IN LEGAL EDUCATION, INSIDERS AND OUTSIDERS

University education in common law is relatively recent and it was only in the 1960s and 1970s that the legal profession in England began to be a profession of law graduates. Law has been a subject of exposition and study in universities from the thirteenth century formation of 'university life' in Bologna, Italy, but it was study of Roman Law, the classical codes and glosses on them derived from the system of governance of the Roman Empire. As late as 1881 Dicey gave his inaugural lecture with the title 'Is English Law a fit topic for study at University?' The common law was learnt by apprenticeship and seemed unsuitable for university study; it was law without clear foundations, bastard law (law without a 'father' or sovereign, everywhere a mass of cases, or so it seemed). My assertion, simply put, is that these two sets of images – that of the sovereign power presented by Hobbes as above and directing society on the one side, with that of the judge epitomised by Earl Mansfield (or Blackstone himself) on the other – represent radically different ways of understanding law and its relation to social order. On the one side we have law as the expression of power, law as *imperium*, law as an instrument of the power élite moulding and changing society; on the other, law as community and tied in with the mysterious science of the common law, known primarily by the judges, where law reflects the organic social order that is built up from below and the judges when they decide actual disputes are conduits for this process and bring out its inherent rationality. This distinction has an inbuilt inside–outside distinction. On the one side the commentator stands outside the legal tradition and adopts an external perspective, ideally trying to understand the entirety of law and its role in society; on the other side one works within the tradition, within its narratives and its sets of meaning, adopting an internal attitude, one of striving to be faithful to your (interpretative) understanding of the enterprise you are part of.

While Hobbes was in many respects an outsider – performing a supportive role to members of the establishment (*Leviathan* was written to be presented to the members of the exiled English Court who at that time were living just outside Paris while conflict raged in England) – Blackstone, the author of the first comprehensive scholarly work presenting the common law as a whole (written at Oxford and published first in 1765–1769), was an insider, a person who desired to become a central member of the establishment élite. For Blackstone considered that the pinnacle for his life's achievements would be to become a judge, and he first studied law at Lincoln's Inn, was a junior barrister, became a scholar and lecturer at All Souls College, Oxford, a member of its governing body, then a Member of the National Parliament (when the Tory Party effectively bought the local MPship for him for two periods), before succeeding in becoming a judge. But it is as the author of the famed *Commentaries on the Laws of England* that Blackstone's place in the intellectual history of England and the common law is assured (we may note that the text also made him a wealthy man!).

I will not go into great detail on the *Commentaries on the Laws of England*, save to say that it stands as the great educational testament to the classic common law. The *Commentaries* is not a dry cataloguing of legal rules and maxims. It had been written by Blackstone principally in order to establish English law as a fit subject for university education, but it was also an extended essay which celebrated the genius and liberty of the English people. He also claimed it demonstrated how English common law exemplified 'the general spirit of laws and principles of universal jurisprudence' (*Commentaries*, Preface). The common law was held out as a product of English exceptionalism – that is to say that it could only have been created out of the heritage of England and its institutions. And yet (and here Blackstone seemed to imply it was as a result of God's divine providence) the result was of universal applicability and enshrined positions and concepts of value elsewhere. Blackstone presented the common law as both a particular product of a specific historical development and also an entity that could be taken elsewhere, perhaps partly explaining why he has been termed its saviour, preserving it from codification, founding its modern academic study, and popularising its study through teaching the lawyer not only to speak the language of a scholar and a gentleman, but also to present the common law as forming a system. The *Commentaries* were the legal publishing sensation of the eighteenth century and new editions appeared well into the nineteenth; in addition they spawned a diverse series of works which were at first based on the *Commentaries* but went on to have lives of their own. The text continued in smaller student editions in England well into the twentieth century. In America many copies of the editions printed in England circulated. Additionally a first American edition, Bell's, appeared almost immediately in 1771–1772. Tucker's 1803 five volume edition proved a benchmark in that Blackstone's *Commentaries* were taken as the authoritative statement of the common law by reference to which American writers could display the well-founded continuity of American law or choose to differentiate new, specifically American, paths. Future American editors felt able to preserve the original text of the ninth edition and add on their own commentaries in well-used editions until the late nineteenth century.

The imagery of Blackstone's *Commentaries* – of the common law as a traditional and customary system that contains in its present forms the features of the past and that would hand on that historical identity to the future – appears at odds with the rationalising impulse of modernity. Yet it is precisely this aspect that gave it its enduring appeal.

It is hard for outsiders to appreciate the interlocking nature of the common law heritage and the constitution of the United Kingdom. Both are in a sense unwritten – the constitution and indeed the common law cannot be found in one authoritative text (hence we say it is unwritten) – and yet there are so many written texts or judgments to consult. We look to the past, yet the past is always open to interpretation. So it was with the success of Blackstone's *Commentaries*; they are full of history, yet the aim was to expound and explain English law as history had organically produced it. He asserted the existence of the common law from time immemorial and followed the earlier judge and writer Sir Mathew Hale (who objected strongly to Hobbes' image of law) in denying that William the Conqueror had altered or could 'alter the laws of this kingdom, or impose laws upon the people *per modum conquestus* or *jure belli*'. A narrative of national identity of epic proportions runs throughout the text, one in which the common law, and the judges, preserve the liberty of the Englishman and develop a country whose air is even too pure to allow slavery.

I have called Blackstone an insider, by which I mean someone who lives, breathes and desires those things that the tradition bequeaths. Consider the places where Blackstone produced the *Commentaries*, his life as a member of one of the Inns of Courts in London and his academic base in All Souls College, Oxford. First consider Oxford University, with its traditions, solid feeling and robust buildings. The four volumes of the *Commentaries* were partly an essay heralding the past congratulating England upon its social constitution and offering images imbued with complacency. The past was to be a reservoir feeding confidence into future actions. A sense of general improvement had been established by the greater political stability and domestic peace after the turmoil of the sixteenth-century Wars of Religion and the Thirty Years War (1618–1648). The scientific revolution of the seventeenth century and the advent of capitalist industrialisation gave hope for progress through science and commerce. The test of legal identity for the common law offered in the *Commentaries* lay not in analytical consistency to any body of political or legal principles, but historical evolution. The legal scholar was to be asked to treat the common law as an intricate legacy, one to be carefully studied with no part easily vanquished.

CELEBRATING THE MYTHOLOGIES OF POPULAR HISTORY

There is more than one story of legal history. Consider the separation of powers and the rule of law. When Dicey came to formulate the analytical structure of the British constitution in the late nineteenth century it seemed that he could celebrate the first of its historical creation but now present the features of the constitution as if they could be henceforth divorced from history. Yet features of the constitution understood historically show the contingency and malleability of social institutions.

Another image comes from what we may term the 'subversive media'. In the early months of 1754, the painter and satirical engraver William Hogarth was working on what eventually became a set of four paintings and prints dealing with electoral corruption. This subject dominated London's newspapers and journals because of the general election of that year and in particular because of the notoriously corrupt election campaign in Oxfordshire. The first of these, *An Election Entertainment* was put on display just days before the election itself. In this quartet of pictures, Hogarth shows the various stages of an election campaign in the fictional country town of Guzzledown. The first scene depicts an electoral feast organised by the Whig Party to garner support. *Canvassing for Votes*, the second scene, is set outside the Royal Oak inn, and focuses on a farmer who is being offered bribes by representatives of both the Tories and the Whigs. The sense of a nation being failed by their political leaders is made even more explicit in the third scene, *The Polling*, where a broken-down coach, representing Britain itself, has ground to a halt. Meanwhile every available male is being dragged to a polling booth to vote. In the final scene the Tory victory parade is violently interrupted and upset by a riotous cluster of people and animals.

Dicey could by the late nineteenth century assert as an analytical principle of modern constitutional law that the Crown in Parliament is sovereign. Yet the composition and relationship between the analytical or constituent parts of government is no logical concept, Parliament evolved and for much of history was in a series of complex power struggles with the Crown, viewed than as separate. Crown (here directly referring to 'royal') patronage made the constitutional balance later called the separation of powers work by royal 'influence'.

Chrimes[29] summarises the revolution of 1688–1689 as bequeathing the eighteenth century as its form of government a partnership of king, lords, common and common law: 'The link between the executive and the Parliament which was most effective in keeping the wheels of government turning in the eighteenth century and the early nineteenth century was what we would call bribery and corruption, but which was usually regarded as merely the obvious exercise of influence.' The settlement had led to recognition of the independence of the judiciary which enabled the courts to

---
29   Chrimes (1965: 170–1).

Figure 1.7 The Polling (third engraving in *Four Prints Of an Election* by William Hogarth [1697–1764]) illuminates how a Member of Parliament is elected. Ballots were not secret but held under the watching eyes of clerks who may or may not be in the influence of one or either of the competing groups. First in line at the polling station is a soldier who has lost three of his limbs. A clerk tries to subdue his laughter as the veteran places his hook on the Bible. Lawyers from opposing parties flank him and argue the validity of his 'handless' oath. Next an imbecile locked in his chair is taking the oath. He is being prompted by an individual standing behind him whose leg is also manacled to the chair. Third in line is a dying man who is dragged up the stairs by his nurses. One is lacking his nose, a symptom of advanced venereal disease. A blind man – guided by his stick and a boy – walks up the stairs; behind him is a cripple. The two candidates appear in highchairs with a sleeping beadle between them. Other men around them share a ballad or drink merrily together. In the background, 'Britannia's' coach (the State) has broken down and is about to overturn. Involved in their game of cards, the coachmen ignore the dangerous situation. The ship of state is not in safe hands. The … *of an Election* set was published by William Hogarth from February 1755 to February 1758. It represents Hogarth's last great set of engravings and is loosely based upon the riotous Oxfordshire election of 1754, where the Whig candidate, the Duke of Marlborough, challenged the incumbent Tories. Hogarth's satirical works strove to provide images to mock and critique existing political and aristocratic methods to bribe, coerce and generally exploit the populace and manage the constitutional process. Hogarth partly engraved the pieces assisted by other engravers working in London to complete the series. (*The Polling* was designed by William Hogarth, engraved by Le Cave and published by William Heath in 1822.) William Hogarth is the unquestioned father of England's rich tradition of satire and remains one of the most original and lively minds in the entire history of British art. The *Election* series that he produced over 1754–1755 signalled a new kind of artistic venture on Hogarth's part, in which he offered a beautifully painted but severe indictment of modern electoral corruption. This turn to political subject matter became more pronounced with the publication of his print *The Times* in 1762, which saw Hogarth becoming actively involved in a bitter and personalised war of political images and texts. Largely thanks to this intervention into the field of political satire, Hogarth had become both the most celebrated and most vilified artist in Britain by the time of his death in 1764.

arbitrate within the law between the executive and the people subject to the overriding supremacy of Acts of Parliament, the royal prerogative of refusing assent to bills passed by both Houses of Parliament was not used after 1701, the Commons gained the rights to discuss any matter freely, to criticise executive power, and be supreme in matters of financial supply. But if a system of checks and balances was created, how was deadlock prevented? Normally the Crown, if it could not rely upon the loyal support of majorities in the House, 'could and did attach to its interest the needful balance of votes in either House by exercising its "influence" '. Without clear party organisation, Members of Parliament supported the Crown either because they saw it in the national interest to do so or as a result of personal advantage. 'The Crown's powers of patronage were ample; the favours, the honours, the pensions, the sinecures it could bestow were great – greater than those within the gift of any of the powerful and wealthy leaders of whichever group happened at any time to be resisting the "influence" of the Crown.' Factors which led to the contemporary balance include the rise of political parties, the changing electorate and the overriding principle of democracy.

RULE OF LAW AS INSTITUTIONAL FREEDOM FOR THE LEGAL PROCESS

To understand this, consider another image, that of the Queen's Bench, an important central court.

The rule of law means in social reality a *set of social conventions and practices* that enscribe concepts such as professional duty, respect for conventions, the power of restraining influences. Consider the image of the Court of Queen's Bench of 1870. The image presents a social space dominated by legal professionals, texts and counsel making oral presentation (argument) in front of judges. The Common Law Procedure Act of 1854 gave the possibility of trying facts by judges alone in civil cases and this led in time to the virtual disappearance of the jury from civil trials. This changed the nature of the judgment delivered with the resultant statement a combination of the trial judges' notes on evidence, the previous 'direction on law' (which would have been given to the jury), verdict and the courts decision (and often comment on the counsel's argument). Barker comments: 'Now that law and fact are no longer decided separately, it is never certain to what extent judgments turn on the facts and to what extent the judge's comment on particular facts are intended to create legal distinctions. In theory every case now establishes some new point, however minute.'[30]

The image opposite also represents adversarial proceedings. Litigation at common law was a system in which the parties themselves set the agenda and the pace of proceedings. At its apex was the image of the trial at which all the business was conducted orally, even documents and legal authorities being read out in public court (in the above image clerks appear to be consulting reports, checking that counsel's statements are accurate). 'Co-operation was not expected, and the parties did their utmost to hinder or ambush their opponents. Costs were unpredictable and often disproportionate

---

30 Baker (2002: 93).

Figure 1.8 The Court of Queen's Bench in session (1870) unattributed artist in *The Graphic*.
After the reorganisation of the courts in the Judicature Act 1873 the court system returned to its foundational structure of a single Curia Regis and the distinction between courts of equity and common law was abolished.

to the matter in dispute.'[31] From the time of the Victorian criticism (see Chapter 12 for Charles Dickens's critique of the Court of Chancery in *Bleak House*) reforms seemed unable to fundamentally change these elements. All socio-legal studies in the twentieth century, however, and the legal realism movement, stressed that the pre-trial stage had gained in importance, that the majority of 'cases' never culminated in final court trials, that retention of documents which would show the real 'facts' was substantially unfair, that 'ambush' infringed in spirit if not in the letter of the law the principles of due process, that 'expert witnesses' had increased in use, that many cases pitted parties against each other that were radically unbalanced in terms of resources and knowledge (for example, major corporations and insurance companies against sole litigants) and that the growing complexity of commercial transactions meant the old reliance on orality was counter-productive. How could the system gain access to the array of complex documents buried deep in filing systems or in computer memories, easily shredded or wiped, multinational corporations could simply transfer information out of the jurisdiction. Early action was needed, such as discovery, pre-trial injunctions, freezing orders and orders to preserve evidence. Both sides could commission experts to provide technical evidence. But if these measures were designed to address one set of problems, they could be weapons to harass opponents and add unnecessarily to delay and cost.

---

31   Ibid.

In the 1980s and 1990s the solution increasingly was seen in changing the role of the judge: instead of the traditional role of umpire, the role of 'case manager' was envisaged. After a comprehensive review Sir Harry Woolf (later Lord Woolf) proposed radical changes aimed at simplifying litigation, encouraging alternative dispute resolution and reducing cost. His recommendations were mostly adopted and formed the basis of the Civil Procedure Rules adopted in 1999. Cases were to be differentiated on grounds of complexity and amount. Not only was English finally to replace some of the terms inherited from the French–Latin mixture of the formation of the common law but an overriding objective – to deal with cases 'justly' – was established with the court required to further this objective by 'actively managing cases'. The new procedures are designed to reduce the role of orality with a great deal of the work finding, reading and analysing the documentation taking place long before the trial, if one results at all. If this was a new landscape, its proponents also stressed it was a work in progress.

> The message for all those involved in the civil justice system, judges, practitioners and court staff alike, is that the changes being introduced in April (1999) are as much changes of culture as they are changes in the Rules themselves. We have to be ready to be proactive, not reactive. And we must see this as the beginning, not the end, of the process of change.[32]

CONCLUSION

This chapter began with reflection and questions, I now think I have an answer. Today I am one person who speaks (along with many others) a particular language of law. Semantically it can be called a language frame that certain fellow lawyers – those who study and practise in the common law world (within the common law legal family) – recognise, understand and communicate within. This language, this set of tropes, rhetorical appeals, processes and shared invocations has an internal aspect in which we users think of it as some natural form of being, of its users as sharing if not a uniform concept of law then a set of concepts within a relatively friendly 'family' with a basic identity. From an external view, and that is a view adopted by both those who are not speaking the language of the common law (and it may also be said those who refute the whole idea of 'law' as some form of uniform entity) this language use may give a greater confidence in identity and coherence than is warranted. But it is an evolving language and it has given us today basic legal concepts and rules, like the concept of rights, duties and remedies, due process, the concept of a sanction and a competence. This language is deeply penetrated by historical legal experiences, some of which have been imaged in this chapter and some we can put under broader headings, such as the struggle for democratic procedures of legitimate legislation. Many people who refer to law, who raise a legal claim assume, consciously or otherwise, these basic experiences. This idea of the common law and its politics is more than a theoretical hypothesis; it is living history.

---

32 Lord Irvine of Lairg, 'Foreword' to the Civil Procedure Rules. (S.I. 1998 No. 3132 L. 17).

2

RECORDING LAW'S EXPERIENCE: FEATURES OF THE 'CASE'

Last Friday morning early, two poor negroes came to inform me that one of their friends was [word illegible] by his Master on shipboard at Gravesend to be sent as a slave to Barbados. All the judges being out of town on the circuit I could not obtain either warrant or writ of *habeas corpus* after the most unwearied endeavours till late on Saturday night and in the meantime I had notice that the ship was sailed from Gravesend. However I sent [the writ] off by an attorney and the young man's friend in a post-chaise that same night to Deal in hopes that the ship might not yet have quitted the Channel and they happily arrived in the Downs just in time to save the poor despairing man: a delay even of a single minute more would have been fatal! However they brought the young man safe to me yesterday at noon and after proper consultation I sent him this morning with officers to catch his master but he had prudently decamped and fled to Scotland. The young man confessed that he had intended to jump into the sea as soon as it was dark in order to avoid slavery by death![1]

Figure 2.1 Granville Sharp (1735–1813), the abolitionist, rescuing a slave [Jonathan Strong] from the hands of his master, by James Hayllar (1829–1920). Oil painting, England, 1864.

1 Letter from Granville Sharp to the Archbishop of Canterbury about helping a slave, 1 August 1786 [Gloucestershire Archives, Ref D3549 13/1/C3].

CONSTRUCTING LAW'S EXPERIENCE

The American jurist and Supreme Court Judge Oliver Wendell Holmes Jr. (1841–1935) famously said that the life of the law was not logic but experience.[2] But how does the common law record and present its experience? For generations of lawyers and law students the answer is simple: through the institutional processing, deciding and recording of *cases*. Cases are not dry 'law', decided under the sway of some mechanical jurisprudence; they are more. They are collections of stories, narratives where human characters make appeals to the law (often in practice stopped by their lawyers who turn what they want to say into language that is regarded as legally relevant), ask for rights, assert that others owe them duties and seek remedies for supposed breaches of those duties. Within the context of the case, interpretation of legal sources takes place and arguments are engaged in. Some cases may be termed easy; there the facts are regarded in such a way that the interpretation of the legal sources seems to indicate that legal argument is one sided, that the strength of the arguments as to what the law is and how it applies to the factual situation are so unbalanced that only one outcome seems justified in good faith. But others, and – by dint of the institutional framework of the court structure of legal systems – most appeal cases, are harder; there the sources are open to an array of interpretations, both as to their importance and as to their 'meaning in application'. Whether hard or easy, whether reflected upon or not, within the confines of the case, propositions of law are advanced, contested, and in the adversarial setting of the common law institutions, success will flow to the party that has demonstrated their superiority in the argumentative practice.

A great deal of legal writing tends to obscure the reality that this is a very human process. Common law jurists, such as Ronald Dworkin,[3] may define the common law as the depository of a society's legal and political commitment to principle but others champion the joy of encountering the vagaries of human existence and story telling:

> The Common Law possesses a great deal of historical and contemporary colour: it is lively, realistic and, incidentally, eminently teachable. The student of common law rubs shoulders with Indian princes, fishwives, conjurors, shopkeepers and sea-captains of the East India Company. Translated into statutory language, only the pale shadows of this colourful assembly would remain, they would become plaintiffs, traffic accident witnesses, promisors of rewards, hire-purchasers and applicants for public office.

---

2 Justice Oliver Wendell Holmes, Jr., began his book *The Common Law* in 1881: 'The life of the law has not been logic: it has been experience. The felt necessities of the time, the prevalent moral and political theories, intuitions of public policy, avowed or unconscious, even the prejudices which judges share with their fellow-men, have had a good deal more to do than the syllogism in determining the rules by which men should be governed. The law embodies the story of a nation's development through many centuries, and it cannot be dealt with as if it contained only the axioms and corollaries of a book of mathematics. In order to know what it is, we must know what it has been, and what it tends to become. We must alternately consult history and existing theories of legislation. But the most difficult labor will be to understand the combination of the two into new products at every stage. The substance of the law at any given time pretty nearly corresponds, so far as it goes, with what is then understood to be convenient; but its form and machinery, and the degree to which it is able to work out desired results, depend very much upon its past.'
3 Dworkin (1986).

> The common law is a storehouse for worm tubs, ornamental broughams, snails in ginger beer bottles and fancy waistcoats, all of which would long since have turned to rust and rubbish had the cases which brought them into prominence been governed by some statute.[4]

Law's collective experience is recounted through narrative and the power of the state to apply coercion in giving effect to legal judgment is in turn judged, in part at least, by the aptness of that application in light of the events recounted in narrative. The appeal to justice, the application of logic, the reference to past 'cases' (legal precedents), the structuring of arguments so that they are legally relevant, so that they fit the matter at hand, so that they carry substantive weight, is located amidst and between many factors. We may mention for example, the court hierarchy, the adversarial profession, the variability of audiences, and one may start with the imbalance of resources, both material and intellectual of the parties (the State against an individual defendant, a well-resourced insurance company against an individual on state pension). A great deal of this richness is lost in any legal education that deals with textbooks, where, in the name of a positivist science of law, cases are reduced to one-line catchphrases, where we are told that such and such a case stands for a particular rule or interpretation of principle. The desire to present the full 'syllabus' leads to teaching the width of contract law, or insurance law, or of the law of Torts, a teaching that runs against the desire to show depth, to uncover how, where and when, a principle came out of the 'swamp' of law's existence in social life.[5] By contrast, problem-based modes of learning start from a factual scenario and cast the student(s) in the semi-professional role of legal advisors, asked to research and reconstruct the social situation into arguments, propositions in legal discourse that strive to command attention as valid assertions to conclude the argument. The successful conclusion is one that best fits with the collective memory of law's enterprise, but this memory may be of tactics, of procedure, of the actual and not the ideal which may manifest itself in the conclusion that the outcome fits with what the law is, but is not 'just'. Law's stories are always partial, incomplete and never fully innocent. Law's storytelling is purposeful, undertaken within constraints of time, finance and the vagrancies of the adversarial profession. There is no one story, although only one story may be told (and how that story, and only that story surfaced, was allowed is again another story). The choices may reveal an ongoing and constant contest between shifting narratives about the role of and claims of law, government, political and social interests and identities. The resultant decision, the decided case, is also not a simple plain fact; its holding is interpreted and in the hands of future lawyers may be confined, extended, distinguished or even overturned. A particular legal case may be formally located in terms of historical categories, such as forms of 'trust' recognised in law, but these themselves are presented in argumentative propositions structured in narrative (lawyers may say that such and such judge got it wrong, and they got it wrong because they listened to that argument, gave weight to this or that specific consideration, but if they had read the story of the development of the principles in this

---
4   Luke (1982).
5   Maughan and Webb (2005).

area better, then they would have ...). Understood thus the appeal of law's experience is neither logical (analytical power) nor empirical (grasp of facts or secure reference) but historical.

> The life of the law is not a vision of the future but a vision of the past; its passions are unleashed, to use Benjamin's words, 'by the image of enslaved ancestors rather than that of liberated grandchildren'.[6]

Let us illustrate. This chapter began with a quotation from the 1 August 1786 entry in the diary of the eighteenth century social activist Glanville Sharp and another image, a painting of Sharp rescuing Jonathan Strong – formerly a slave but abandoned and later recaptured by his 'master' – from being sent back as a slave to Jamaica in 1767 by successfully pleading Strong's case before the Lord Mayor of London. Between that date and that of the diary quotation where the writ of *habeas corpus* was granted as a matter of normal legal course lies Sharp's historic legal victory in the *Somerset* case of 1772.[7] There, in a judgment barely 200 words long, Lord Mansfield responded to five days of arguments by England's finest barristers (spread over several months as he tried to arrange for the case to be settled out of court), including the legal and emotive appeals to him to recognise that the air of England was too pure for a slave to breathe and that the category of slavery must not be recognised by English courts. His judgment, often misunderstood as freeing all slaves in England, awarded the writ to free the black slave Somerset who had been bound in chains awaiting shipment to Jamaica. The impact on Somerset was a freedom, albeit socially restricted for Somerset would not have been on the same status as an Englishman, and we do not know the subsequent events in the personal narrative that was Somerset's life story.[8] The decision, more broadly, became a classic referent, a trope in the narrative of English law's protection of rights and adherence to due process, confirming that whoever was resident in England was able to use the law to protect their rights (other than those that had been expressly taken away by positive law).[9]

---

6   Luban (1994: 211).
7   The importance of this writ in the history (and mythology) of the common law may be gauged from the words of Chrimes (1965: 61): 'The writ of Habeas Corpus is the great and effective remedy to protect the individual from unlawful imprisonment and detention. Any imprisoned or detained person, or any person acting on his behalf, may apply for the writ to any judge of the High Court, who is bound, under heavy penalties, to issue the writ on prima facie cause being shown. The procedure is simple and expeditious. On cause being shown, the judge, as a matter of course, issues a peremptory order to the detainer to appear and show cause why a writ of Habeas Corpus should not be issued against him. If on appearance and argument, the judge is satisfied that the application is sound, the writ is forthwith issued, requiring the production of the prisoner in court on an appointed day, whereupon he is released if no sufficient cause for detention is proved. If sufficient cause is proved, then a speedy trial is ensured, thus making it impossible for the executive to detain a person for an indefinite period. The writ is issuable to anyone, whether a Secretary of State, a Minister, military authority, or any person whatsoever. It is a highly effective remedy for unlawful detention, but it does not of itself provide damages or penalties for unlawful detention or assault, to obtain which separate proceedings are required and available.'
8   Jonathan Strong never fully recovered from his beating and died in April 1773. Nothing is known of James Somerset after 1772. Extract from Granville Sharp's diary, 19 April 1773 [D3549 13/4/2 book G]: 'Poor Jonathan Strong, the first negro whose freedom I had procured in 1767, died this morning.'
9   Somerset had been taken from Africa as a slave to the Americas in 1749 where he was sold in Virginia to Charles Steuart, a Scottish merchant and slave trader in Norfolk who served after 1765 as a high-ranking

In this image Granville Sharp is portrayed by the Victorian popular artist Hayllar as the protector of the black and the invoker of law's spirit. It fits with the symbolic invocation of the names of Somerset's case and Granville Sharp as a narrative demonstration of law's experience that whatever your social status you are the subject of the law, and are not subject to the arbitrary capriceness of man without legal protection and that the common law has due process values inscribed in it. It is an imaginary representation to the public of what Holdsworth later asked law schools to achieve, namely:

> To put and keep before the minds of their students that sense of the sanctity of the law, and of its great civilizing mission, which is and always has been present to the minds of the great administrators of the law.[10]

We may be more sceptical. Read from a 'subaltern' position the image is also the message that the civilisation that carries the spirit of the law, law's civilising mission, is white and male. The space of action in the painting is largely that inside the door of the courtroom where a substantial group (of white males), including lawyers and on the bench the Lord Mayor as judge, watch Sharp prevent a sea captain from taking Strong away from the court. This portrays the courtroom as the gateway to rights, to performance, the place where a claim is registered, heard and action ordered. This is in many ways a particular Western conception of law as an ensemble of rights and legal process as the establishment and authoritative pronouncement of those rights and court orders as their enforcement.

Hayllar's painting was a popular celebration:[11] yet the image is an illusion of law's justice and the ease of claiming rights. Images partly create illusions and illusions often create images. The artist had, of course, no first-hand knowledge of the events he portrayed; this was an image of historical recall, one of the victory of the spirit of English law in the protection of the rights of the oppressed.

There *is* in this story a narrative of distress and the appeal to the courts as the guardians of rights, and also of the reading of English history as such that it *must* grant rights.[12] But it is by no means a linear or autonomous story of law's progress. One question concerned standing, basic identity: who was the bearer of rights? Was the answer Free Englishmen, and only those of the correct Church (i.e. members of the Anglican Church), or any human that was in England?

At the time of the case Strong had been baptised and had English godparents. This ritual, this joining the Christian brotherhood, was undertaken to grant him a

---

British customs official. In 1769, Steuart took Somerset with him to England. After two years in England, Somerset escaped from Steuart, but was recaptured. Steuart decided to sell Somerset back into slavery in Jamaica, and, in late November 1771, Somerset was bound in chains on a ship on the Thames, the *Ann and Mary*, awaiting shipment.
10   Holdsworth (1928b: 183).
11   James Hayllar had come from a family of artists and came to London in 1848, studied with F. S. Cary and at the R.A. Schools. Having spent a fashionable two years in Italy he made money painting humorous genre pictures involving children and later adopted a style of painting historical paintings with a popular appeal.
12   The following story is in essence well known: my particular sources are Guildhall Library Manuscripts Section – Strong, Somerset and Sharp – liberating black slaves in England (Guildhall Library Manuscripts Section, online resources), Gloucestershire Council library resources.

substance, a presence and a voice. In eighteenth century Britain and the colonies, it was popularly believed that baptism made African slaves free; common references to slaves as 'heathens' served to buttress the slave trade, and passages from the Bible were used to suggest that becoming a Christian conferred freedom. As a result, many plantation owners refused to allow their slaves baptism and several American colonies passed laws which explicitly outlawed freedom by baptism. However there was no British legal opinion until 1729, when the Attorney General and the Solicitor General ruled that 'baptism doth not bestow freedom' (the Yorke–Talbot ruling).

Nonetheless a popular belief persisted that coming to Britain and being baptised released you from slavery though not service – so that you could not be bought and sold, nor beaten. Many slaves brought to Britain by their masters did seek baptism, finding a sympathetic clergyman and English godparents.

Granville Sharp met the young runaway slave Jonathan Strong by chance in 1765. Strong had been brought as a slave from Barbados to London before being savagely beaten with a pistol by his master David Lisle and abandoned by Lisle in the street.

However, Strong found his way to the surgeon William Sharp's house, where Sharp treated the poor of the City of London for free. Sharp's brother Granville was taken by Strong's condition and enquired about his serious injuries.[13] He then arranged for Strong to be admitted to St Bartholomew's Hospital where Strong received treatment for four months. On his discharge, the Sharp brothers found him employment as errand boy with a surgeon, with whom he lived for two years. Lisle saw Strong by accident one day and having followed him home, entered into an agreement to sell the slave he had left for dead and obtained £30 for him, to be paid when Strong was aboard a West Indian ship ready to sail. Lisle therefore paid two slave-hunters to kidnap Strong and deliver him to the Poultry Compter (a jail in the City of London) until a West India ship was ready to sail.

Strong's employer was only interested in financial compensation for his loss. Strong realised his only chance of avoiding going back to Jamaica as a slave, was to contact Sharp who appealed to the Magistrates and used his influence to call a hearing in front of the Lord Mayor. The action was heard at Mansion House on 18 September 1767 where the Lord Mayor discharged Strong because 'the lad had not stolen anything, and was not guilty of any offence, and was therefore at liberty to go away'. As the painting presents it, in the courtroom, in front of the Lord Mayor, the captain of the ship attempted to seize Strong but Sharp prevented him being taken away. Another conflict then ensues: 'David Lisle, Esq. (a man of the law) called upon me … to demand gentlemanlike satisfaction … I told him, that, "as he had studied the law for so many years, he should want no satisfaction that the law should give him".' Lisle responded to Sharp's refusal to fight a duel by joining with the Jamaican planter who had bought Strong to sue the Sharp brothers for trespass in depriving them of their property. Sharp's success

---

13   The occasion is recorded in Sharp's own words (1820: 33): 'Nothing can be more shocking to Human Nature than the case of a Man or Woman who is delivered into the absolute Power of Strangers to be treated according to the New Masters Will & pleasure; for they have nothing but misery to expect; and poor Jonathan Strong, who was well acquainted with West India Treatment seemed to be deeply impressed with that extreme horror which the poor victims of the inhuman Traffic generally experience.'

in gaining Strong his liberty had betrayed their property rights, guaranteed by law. The Sharp brothers engaged lawyers to defend them, but those lawyers quoted the Yorke–Talbot ruling of 1729 that a slave did not become free on coming to England, he did not become free by baptism and that any master might compel his slave to return to the West Indies.

Sharp was shocked: he 'could not believe that the Laws of England were really so injurious to natural Rights' and began studying the law to conduct his own defence. He was a clerk in the Ordnance Office at Tower Hill and had 'never opened a lawbook (except the Bible) in my life'.

For over two years Sharp committed himself to legal research seeking to trace the original sources of the laws of England and interpret the history of villeinage, the British form of feudal serfdom. His was a well-known and socially connected family, he spoke with many of the leading legal officials and remained convinced that English law did not sanction slavery. He learnt the language in which to construct and frame his counter argument, his assertion as to what the law really was. The lawyers he commissioned presented Sharp's arguments to the opposing set with 'the desired effect, for it intimidated the Plaintiffs' lawyers from proceeding in their action' and in 1769 Sharp published his answer to Yorke–Talbot, *A Representation of the Injustice and Dangerous Tendency of Tolerating Slavery; or of Admitting the Least Claim of Private Property in the Persons of Men, in England*. The central proposition was that any person who came to England and lived there became a subject of the king and therefore subject to *habeas corpus* which prevented forcible removal to another country. And he cast the legal proposition against which he argued into a social language of humanitarian appeal: 'a toleration of slavery is, in effect, a toleration of inhumanity'.

Sharp, who had now left his job and was financially supported by his brothers, became the conduit for social activism in the cause of fighting slavery, assisting other runaway slaves to find safety and bringing a number of cases before the courts, seeking in vain a definitive judgment on the legality of slavery in four separate cases. The climax came with James Somerset. Somerset was an African slave sold in Virginia to Charles Steuart, a colonial customs official, later based in Boston. He arrived, with Steuart, in London in 1769 and was baptised as James Somerset on 20 February 1771 at St Andrew Holborn. He left Steuart's service on 1 October 1771. Steuart hunted him, and he was seized and confined in irons aboard a ship bound for Jamaica on 26 November 1771. His godparents, Thomas Walklin, Elizabeth Cade and John Marlow, applied for a writ of *habeas corpus* to prevent his removal and sale in Jamaica and paid for Somerset's bail. Somerset visited Granville Sharp and persuaded Sharp to become involved.

Sharp organised counsel to argue for Somerset and published an appendix to *The Injustice of Tolerating Slavery* which drew on the cases he had brought previously and implicitly criticised Lord Mansfield for impeding law's development. Indeed, he arranged for James Somerset to deliver a copy directly to Mansfield. West Indian planters rallied round Steuart, determined too that this should be a test case, and framed their response to the *habeas corpus* very carefully. Their position was simple: 'negro slaves' were chattel goods, and as Somerset was a slave according to the laws of Virginia and Africa, his master had rightfully detained him to send him to Jamaica for sale.

The hearing began in February 1772; Hochschild terms it 'high theatre, prolonged over several months by recesses when Mansfield vainly kept pushing for an out-of-court.[14] A central focus was whether slavery was legal in England and whether if not was it then possible for an English court to uphold colonial laws which did not have an English parallel. Steuart's lawyers stressed the harmful economics of letting slaves go; they did not appeal to a proposition that it was God's will that Blacks be inferior, or that it was even in line with natural justice that slavery exist, but that it was simply so: slavery was in their eyes a legal fact and the court must recognise that. It was the legal and social order and the court should not act so as to disturb that order. Mansfield wished to avoid a decision and tried to persuade Elizabeth Cade, Somerset's godmother, to buy him and Charles Steuart, his former owner, to set him free. Both refused because they wanted the case settled and the law made clear. Feeling the significance of the case Mansfield is said to have finally exclaimed: '*Fiat justicia, ruat coelum*' (Let justice be done, though the heavens fall) and delivered a carefully worded judgment on 22 June 1772.

> We feel the force of the inconveniences and consequences that will follow the decision of this question. Yet all of us are so clearly of one opinion upon the only question before us, that we think we ought to give judgment, without adjourning the matter to be argued before all the Judges, as usual in the Habeas Corpus, and as we at first intimated an intention of doing in this case. The only question then is, Is the cause returned sufficient for the remanding him? If not, he must be discharged. The cause returned is, the slave absented himself, and departed from his master's service, and refused to return and serve him during his stay in England; whereupon, by his master's orders, he was put on board the ship by force, and there detained in secure custody, to be carried out of the kingdom and sold. So high an act of dominion must derive its authority, if any such it has, from the law of the kingdom where executed. A foreigner cannot be imprisoned here on the authority of any law existing in his own country: the power of a master over his servant is different in all countries, more or less limited or extensive; the exercise of it therefore must always be regulated by the laws of the place where exercised. The state of slavery is of such a nature, that it is incapable of now being introduced by Courts of Justice upon mere reasoning or inferences from any principles, natural or political; it must take its rise from positive law; the origin of it can in no country or age be traced back to any other source: immemorial usage preserves the memory of positive law long after all traces of the occasion; reason, authority, and time of its introduction are lost; and in a case so odious as the condition of slaves must be taken strictly, the power claimed by this return was never in use here; no master ever was allowed here to take a slave by force to be sold abroad because he had deserted from his service, or for any other reason whatever; we cannot say the cause set forth by this return is allowed or approved of by the laws of this kingdom, therefore the man must be discharged.

A legal judgment is addressed to at least three audiences: the legal profession, the parties and the public. The narrow focus should be appreciated along with the wider impact.

---

14   Hochschild (2005: 50).

Focused on the legality of forcible deportation the decision looked extremely narrow: Steuart was not entitled to seize and deport Somerset under the laws of England and the writ was available to stop him and bring 'the man', the slave, before the courts so that they, and they alone, could determine his legal status.

The wider holding concerned the status of the applicable law: the laws of Virginia supported slavery but there was no law in England which did and in 'a case so odious as the condition of slaves' the master was not given the power claimed under common law and only a positive law could grant such power. 'No master ever was allowed here to take a slave by force to be sold abroad because he deserted from his service ... and therefore the man must be discharged.'

A set of common distinctions characterise the many projects of understanding law in general: one is between law as power and law as reason; another is between law as the upholder of justice and law as the upholder of social order. In the later contrast, law as the upholder of justice requires a decision to be made that may result in social unrest, one seeks justice, not what the demands of utilitarian calculation advises; with law as the upholder of social order, one preserves and defends the institutional state of affairs, which may be achieved only at the expense of justice.

We know of Mansfield's attempts to have the case settled out of court (he is said to have muttered that he wished all blacks thought they were free and all masters thought they were slaves). At first sight his decision to 'let justice be done' is narrowly focused, a compromise image of law as the upholder of due process, a formal definition of justice as following the correct procedures, of sidestepping the arguments of Somerset's lawyers concerning the big picture of the inhumanity and injustice of slavery. Another reading is to see it as an example of law's characteristic role of mediating between the ideal and the real. The 'pure' legality of the decision seems to reduce the appeal of justice to a procedural calculation of due process: 'Is the cause returned sufficient for remanding him? If not, he must be discharged.' That is, a simple question, namely did the response to the writ reveal a reason recognised in law for holding the person. But the distinction drawn between the narrow procedural outcome and the wider holding becomes legally radical when one realises that the comments on the state of slavery, namely that it was not covered by common law, means that Mansfield is stating that the legal status and effectiveness of slavery must only flow from positive legislative enactment or long-standing custom: 'The state of slavery is of such a nature, that it is incapable of now being introduced by Courts of Justice upon mere reasoning or inferences from any principles, natural or political'; or for that matter, the courts cannot declare what was legal to be now illegal by resort to reasoning or inferences from principles, natural or political.

But if slavery was a creation of 'positive law'; that is, law consciously made by man as an act of legislative will, or simply a longstanding custom of that region, then we have a separation that is at the same time both conservative and radical. It is conservative in that we face a claim of the purity of legal process and reasoning that in this operation law can have a socially neutral realm; radical in that if the status of slave was a creation of positive law, then why not gender, class or race more generally?

Somerset confirms Sharp's legal analysis: English law protects certain fundamental 'rights of man' even for African slaves in England, including the right of access to the courts to protect against unlawful imprisonment or abuse, and freedom from chattel slavery. *Somerset* thus becomes a trope in the narrative of English laws protection of freedom: core legal freedoms such as access to the courts and protection from arbitrary, unlimited physical abuse, were available to all subjects as 'rights of man', not dependent upon birth, race, religion, or free status, and could only be denied by statute or express, longstanding custom. The decision separates a claim to the naturalness of the common law from the arbitrariness of positive law.

For Van Cleve, Lord Mansfield's decision that positive law, not common law, must authorise slavery both in England *and* in its colonies, as opposed to deciding *Somerset* under English common law and limiting its holding to slavery in England only, was a 'transformative decision'.

Mansfield's positive law holding, Van Cleve reads, was legally novel, unnecessary to Mansfield's substantive holding in Somerset, seemingly supportive of the status quo, and yet deliberately subversive of both metropolitan and colonial slavery. Mansfield's holding had both domestic and imperial political motives, but reflected Mansfield's beliefs as well. As to English domestic politics, Mansfield's holding was an effort to eliminate slavery litigation in the English courts and to commit the slavery issue to Parliament. As to imperial politics, Mansfield's positive law holding avoided a difficult imperial governance problem, but did so by exacting a substantial price from colonial slaveholders. Positive law holding also knowingly devalued slave property by making slave status wholly dependent on the law of individual jurisdictions, which he (and slave owners) knew meant that slave flight would increase because fugitive slaves could become free or protected against excessive force and compelled return, not just in England but in the colonies.[15]

The holding on slavery's status was 'profoundly destructive of the moral and legal legitimacy of slavery, since it made slave property an artificial creature of statute and deprived slavery of the sanction of the common law'.

As for the effect on the public, many thought that Mansfield's decision freed the slaves of England. The *St James' Chronicle and General Evening Post* and the *Middlesex Journal* (both of 23 June 1772) and Felix Farley's *Bristol Journal* thought so, reporting 'that every slave brought into this country ought to be free, and no master had a right to sell them here'. Other papers more accurately reported that the Somerset case had decided only that black slaves in England could not be forcibly removed from England. The trial had been attended by a large number of black people who celebrated the verdict with delight. A ball for black people only was arranged at a pub in Westminster where Lord Mansfield's health was drunk. James Somerset wrote to a friend that the judgment meant all slaves were now free. But there were still many slaves in England long after 1772 – adverts for finding and returning runaway slaves continued to appear in English newspapers, especially in Bristol. West India planters ignored Mansfield's judgment, or got round it by apprenticing their slaves. They lobbied, unsuccessfully, for an Act of Parliament to reinstate the Yorke–Talbot ruling.

Public opinion was changing. Somerset's case was influential, widely reported in newspapers that portrayed it as a drama with human interest as well as great legal importance. Many English people found that they could not tolerate a man or woman being owned as a chattel, especially in London, where a free (albeit poor) black

---

15   Van Cleve (2006: 109–113).

community developed in the late eighteenth century. The slave trading ports of Bristol and Liverpool were more aware of the foundations of their prosperity.

LOST PRECEDENTS? FROM DUDLEY AND STEPHENS BACK TO THE *ZONG*

R. v. Dudley and Stephens

On 9 December 1884 Lord Coleridge, C.J., read out the verdict of a five-judge court which on 4 December in Westminster, London had heard arguments around a rather unusual situation both legally and factually. At the Devon and Cornwall Winter Assizes, 7 November 1884, the jury, at the suggestion of the trial judge, had found the facts of the case in a special verdict in which they asked for a set of judges to take the responsibility of actually determining whether a conviction of murder should be given.[16] The special

JUSTICE COLERIDGE, WEARING THE BLACK CAP.

Figure 2.2 Lord Coleridge, Chief Justice, puts on the black cap which signifies that he is about to pass the death sentence.
Source: Engraving by an unnamed artist in the *Illustrated London News*, 1845.

---

16 The jury in Dudley and Stephens' murder trial issued a 'special verdict', which included several findings of fact as reproduced in our text. It failed to reach a 'general verdict' regarding the men's guilt or innocence: 'But whether upon the whole matter by the jurors found the killing of Richard Parker by Dudley and Stephens be felony and murder the jurors are ignorant, and pray the advice of the Court thereupon.' This was highly unusual at the time. The judge, Baron Huddleston, persuaded the jury at the trial of Dudley and Stephens to enter a special verdict in lieu of a general verdict as he apparently wanted to ensure that the judges of the Queen's Bench, rather than a lay jury, would have the chance to resolve whether the killing constituted murder. See Simpson (1984: 208–223).

verdict revealed the facts of a case of human cannibalism on the high seas and the plea of necessity as a defence to the charge of murder. It stated:

> That on July 5, 1884, the prisoners, Thomas Dudley and Edward Stephens, with one Brooks, all able-bodied English seamen, and the deceased also an English boy, between seventeen and eighteen years of age, the crew of an English yacht, a registered English vessel, were cast away in a storm on the high seas 1600 miles from the Cape of Good Hope, and were compelled to put into an open boat belonging to the said yacht. That in this boat they had no supply of water and no supply of food, except two 1lb. tins of turnips, and for three days they had nothing else to subsist upon. That on the fourth day they caught a small turtle, upon which they subsisted for a few days, and this was the only food they had up to the twentieth day when the act now in question was committed. That on the twelfth day the remains of the turtle were entirely consumed, and for the next eight days they had nothing to eat. That they had no fresh water, except such rain as they from time to time caught in their oilskin capes. That the boat was drifting on the ocean, and was probably more than 1000 miles away from land. That on the eighteenth day, when they had been seven days without food and five without water, the prisoners spoke to Brooks as to what should be done if no succour came, and suggested that some one should be sacrificed to save the rest, but Brooks dissented, and the boy, to whom they were understood to refer, was not consulted. That on the 24th of July, the day before the act now in question, the prisoner Dudley proposed to Stephens and Brooks that lots should be cast who should be put to death to save the rest, but Brooks refused to consent, and it was not put to the boy, and in point of fact there was no drawing of lots. That on that day the prisoners spoke of their having families, and suggested it would be better to kill the boy that their lives should be saved, and Dudley proposed that if there was no vessel in sight by the morrow morning the boy should be killed. That next day, the 25th of July, no vessel appearing, Dudley told Brooks that he had better go and have a sleep, and made signs to Stephens and Brooks that the boy had better be killed. The prisoner Stephens agreed to the act, but Brooks dissented from it. That the boy was then lying at the bottom of the boat quite helpless, and extremely weakened by famine and by drinking sea water, and unable to make any resistance, nor did he ever assent to his being killed. The prisoner Dudley offered a prayer asking forgiveness for them all if either of them should be tempted to commit a rash act, and that their souls might be saved. That Dudley, with the assent of Stephens, went to the boy, and telling him that his time was come, put a knife into his throat and killed him then and there; that the three men fed upon the body and blood of the boy for four days; that on the fourth day after the act had been committed the boat was picked up by a passing vessel, and the prisoners were rescued, still alive, but in the lowest state of prostration. That they were carried to the port of Falmouth, and committed for trial at Exeter. That if the men had not fed upon the body of the boy they would probably not have survived to be so picked up and rescued, but would within the four days have died of famine. That the boy, being in a much weaker condition, was likely to have died before them. That at the time of the act in question there was no sail in sight, nor any reasonable prospect of relief. That under these circumstances there appeared to the prisoners every probability that unless they then fed or very soon fed upon the boy or one of themselves they would die of starvation. That there was no appreciable chance of saving life except by killing

some one for the others to eat. That assuming any necessity to kill anybody, there was no greater necessity for killing the boy than any of the other three men. But whether upon the whole matter by the jurors found the killing of Richard Parker by Dudley and Stephens be felony and murder the jurors are ignorant, and pray the advice of the Court thereupon, and if upon the whole matter the Court shall be of opinion that the killing of Richard Parker be felony and murder, then the jurors say that Dudley and Stephens were each guilty of felony and murder as alleged in the indictment.

We have an opportunity to decide denied to the jury, whom we suppose may have found a verdict of 'not guilty' on humane grounds. If a verdict of 'guilty' was to be found the penalty was death. Coleridge's judgment relates a story wherein he is conscious of the human appeal: 'The prisoners were subject to terrible temptation, to sufferings which might break down the bodily power of the strongest man, and try the conscience of the best. Other details yet more harrowing, facts still more loathsome and appalling, were presented to the jury.' Yet he finds the facts clear: 'The prisoners put to death a weak and unoffending boy upon the chance of preserving their own lives by feeding upon his flesh and blood after he was killed, and with the certainty of depriving him of any possible chance of survival.'

The first major argument put to the court was that it had no jurisdiction to try the matter. This was quickly disposed of, for it had been 'declared by Parliament to have been always the law' that:

> All offences against property or person committed in or at any place either ashore or afloat, out of her Majesty's dominions by any master seaman or apprentice who at the time when the offence is committed is or within three months previously has been employed in any British ship, shall be deemed to be offences of the same nature respectively, and be inquired of, heard, tried, determined, and adjudged in the same manner and by the same courts and in the same places as if such offences had been committed within the jurisdiction of the Admiralty of England.

The only real question in the case was whether 'killing under the circumstances set forth in the verdict be or be not murder'. Coleridge then relates how the argument that it could be anything other seemed absurd:

> The contention that it could be anything else was, to the minds of us all, both new and strange, and we stopped the Attorney General in his negative argument in order that we might hear what could be said in support of a proposition which appeared to us to be at once dangerous, immoral, and opposed to all legal principle and analogy.

He then sums up the arguments to the ploy that the only possible excuse in law could be that the killing was justified by what has been called 'necessity'.

> But the temptation to the act which existed here was not what the law has ever called 'necessity'. Nor is this to be regretted. Though law and morality are not the same, and many things may be immoral which are not necessarily illegal, yet the absolute divorce of law from morality would be of fatal consequence; and such divorce would follow if the temptation to murder in this case were to be held by law an absolute defence of it.

It is not so. To preserve one's life is generally speaking a duty, but it may be the plainest and the highest duty to sacrifice it. War is full of instances in which it is a man's duty not to live, but to die. The duty, in case of shipwreck, of a captain to his crew, of the crew to the passengers, of soldiers to women and children, as in the noble case of the Birkenhead; these duties impose on men the moral necessity, not of the preservation, but of the sacrifice of their lives for others, from which in no country, least of all, it is to be hoped, in England, will men ever shrink, as indeed, they have not shrunk.

The narrow point is positioned within a story of law's relationship to morality and to the past and Coleridge was certain: Englishmen had never shrunk from those duties, the law never knew of a defence of necessity. On a positivist reading that was true; the law, the collective experience of previous cases, did not know, but this is not innocent, it did not know because it had not been allowed to.

The voyage of the *Zong*: a precedent that never was

The basic facts are clear. The *Zong* was a slave ship owned by James Gregson and a number of others who were directors of a large Liverpool slaving company. In 1781 it travelled the triangle from Liverpool to West Africa and onwards with a cargo of slaves to the Caribbean, thence to return with a cargo of sugar for the English tea-houses. The *Zong* left West Africa on 6 September with a cargo of 470 slaves bound for Jamaica; when it approached its destination some 12 weeks later more than 60 Africans and 7 of the 17-man crew had died.[17] The captain, Luke Collingwood, was more used to being a ship's surgeon (a position it should be noted that meant he was responsible for picking out the slaves most likely to survive the journey) and had packed even more slaves on board than usual. Shyllon[18] states that 'chained two by two, right leg and left leg, each slave had less room than a man in a coffin'. The result was a high mortality level, for both black and white, but commentators consider it far less than the catastrophic losses suffered by some other slave ships. The British ship the *Hero*, for example, once lost 360 slaves (over half of its cargo), while the *Briton* lost over half of its 375 slaves on one voyage. The main cause of death in the middle passage was generally virulent dysentery that the sailors called the 'flux', though some slaves could be lost by being beaten to death or, in the case of women, killed when resisting sexual abuse. Slaves also tried to starve themselves to death as an act of resistance and had to be force-fed using mechanical devices that prised open their jaws.

On 29 November Collingwood called his officers together and proposed that the sick slaves should be jettisoned – thrown overboard – in order to secure the rapidly dwindling supplies of water and to allow the shipping company to claim their loss on insurance. In Walvin's words: 'It was, even in the age of the slave trade, a grotesque suggestion.'[19]

---

17   A voyage with favourable trade winds from Senegambia to Barbados might take as little as three weeks, but a ship travelling from Guinea or Angola might be becalmed by lack of wind or be driven back by storms and take as long as three months.
18   Shyllon (1974).
19   Walvin (1992).

Given the conditions, there were plenty of slaves who appeared sick. Collingwood explained to his officers that 'if the slaves died a natural death, it would be the loss of the owners of the ship; but if they were thrown alive into the sea, it would be the loss of the underwriters'. As a 'humane', though obviously specious, justification, he suggested that 'it would not be so cruel to throw the poor sick wretches into the sea, as to suffer them to linger out a few days, under the disorders with which they were afflicted'. Of course, no such proposal was made to put an end to the suffering of sick crewmen. Charles MacInnes explains that such actions were not uncommon:

> If the ship proved unseaworthy or if the food and water began to run short in consequence of an unduly prolonged voyage resulting from calms, adverse winds, or any other difficulties, a simple remedy lay at hand. A sufficient number of slaves would be thrown overboard.[20]

What was Collingwood's understanding of the law? He would have been familiar with the terms and conditions of the voyage which would have been covered by a 'standard' marine insurance policy. In that same year, a digest of insurance laws and practice was published in London on behalf of the Clarendon Press of Oxford. It stated:

> The insurer takes upon him the risk of the loss, capture, and death of slaves, or any other unavoidable accident to them: but natural death is always understood to be excepted:– by natural death is meant, not only when it happens by disease or sickness, but also when the captive destroys himself through despair, which often happens: but when slaves are killed or thrown into the sea in order to quell an insurrection on their part, then the insurers must answer.[21]

So the 'law' was clear! But was sickness alone a sufficient reason for drowning the slaves? Collingwood's excuse was that the ship was running short of water, due in part to his own navigational error that had mistaken Hispaniola for their destination, Jamaica. His argument was that to kill the sick slaves would mean that the healthy could be sustained on the dwindling supplies. Not to kill the slaves would be to jeopardise the safety and health of everyone on board. This was later to be the crucial factual issue at the court and seemed to others to be an unconvincing line of self-justification not least because water was not rationed until after the killing of the slaves had begun and, second, because no attempt was made to put ashore to replenish supplies. Moreover, according to the sailors' accounts, before all the sick slaves had been killed, 'there fell a plentiful rain' that was admitted to have 'continued a day or two'. They collected six casks of water, which was 'full allowance for 11 days, or for 23 days at half allowance'. When the *Zong* landed in Jamaica on 22 December, it had 420 gallons of water on board. It had left in its wake 132 drowned Africans.

The chief mate James Kelsal at first opposed the proposal to drown the slaves but Collingwood insisted, and the killings began. The crew selected those who 'were

---

20 Charles MacInnes (1934).
21 Weskett (1781: 525).

sick, and thought not likely to live'. On 29 November, the first batch of 54 was pushed overboard and a day later 42 more were drowned, while on the third day the slaves were fighting back with the result that 26 were thrown overboard with their arms still shackled. The remaining ten 'sprang disdainfully from the grasp of their tyrants, defied their power, and, leaping into the sea, felt a momentary triumph in the embrace of death'. One of the jettisoned slaves managed to catch on to a rope and climbed back safely on board. In Walvin's words: 'A total of 131 slaves were coolly murdered from the deck of a Liverpool vessel, for no good reason save the economic calculations of Captain Luke Collingwood and the physical compliance of his crewmen'.

Walvin has no trouble calling this 'murder', but we are concerned with the process whereby it avoided ever becoming recorded or labelled murder in the legal literature. On 19 March 1783 Sharp was visited by Olaudah Equiano (sometimes called Gustavus Vassa), an African and former slave who was emerging as the most prominent spokesman for the black community living in London: 'Gustavus Vassa, Negro, called on me with an account of 130 [sic] Negroes being thrown alive into the sea, from on Board an English Slave Ship'. The *Zong* affair was already before the courts some two weeks earlier, when the case of *Gregson* v. *Gilbert* had been heard in the Guildhall in London. Gregson, on behalf of himself and the other ship owners, were claiming for the loss of their slaves (£30 each) from their underwriters (Gilbert). The latter refused to pay, and the case was presented as a simple matter of maritime insurance.

The jury in that trial sided with the ship owners, ordering the insurance company to pay compensation for the dead slaves. In a letter to the *Morning Chronicle*, an eye-witness at the trial wrote: 'The narrative seemed to make every one present shudder; and I waited with some impatience, expecting that the jury, by their foreman, would have applied to the Court for information how to bring the perpetrators of such a horrid deed to justice.' Perhaps one way out was the suggestion that Captain Luke Collingwood – by now safely dead – 'was in a delirium, or a fit of lunacy when he gave the orders'. This was not to happen: the case was to retain its basic inhuman simplicity: a claim for insurance. Yet the correspondent went on to identify the *Zong* as involving questions beyond the particularities of an argument about insurance:

> That there should be bad men to do bad things in all large communities, must be expected: but a community makes the crime general, and provokes divine wrath, when it suffers any member to commit flagrant acts of villainy with impunity ... it is hardly possible for a state to thrive, where the perpetration of such complicated guilt, as the present, is not only suffered to go unpunished, but is allowed to glory in the infamy, and carries off the reward for it.

Walvin's language is clear and is worth reading for his invocation of the close ties between the law and the economic system:

> The crime had been committed on board a British ship, and was so startling in the crudity and extent of its violence that it clearly shook observers. But where would the pursuit of criminality end if, let us say, the crew were arraigned for their crimes?

Although the murder of African slaves was unusual, it was common enough in pursuit of slaves, in securing the safety of a slave ship, in defeating ship-board resistance – to say nothing of the endemic violence which helped keep slavery in place throughout the American slave colonies. Slavery begat the slave trade, and the slave trade was, in origin, in conduct and in its very being, the crudest of violations, which encompassed, when necessary, the death of its victims. For the system to survive in its economic viability, some slaves had to pay the ultimate sacrifice. It took no great leap of the imagination to appreciate that the logic of pursuing the murderers of the slaves on the *Zong* would be the first tug which would unravel the entire garment of the slave system. And in some respects this is precisely what happened, for it was around the small band of men of sensibility, outraged by events on the *Zong*, that there developed the first powerful body of abolitionist feeling and action. The line of dissent from the *Zong* to the successful campaign for abolition was direct and unbroken, however protracted and uneven.

Granville Sharp tried to get together a body of like-minded men to pursue the prosecution of the *Zong* sailors. He was not to succeed. The *Zong* affair came to trial again on a matter of insurance for the underwriters refused to pay the compensation ordered, and the matter came before Lord Justice Mansfield sitting with two other judges in May 1783. The slave owners, claiming the insurance on the slaves, were represented by John Lee, the Solicitor-General. What was Lee's professional and ethical interest in the case? He certainly seemed aware of the potential implications of the case. At the trial he turned towards Granville Sharp in the public gallery and argued that there was a person in court who intended to bring on a criminal prosecution for murder against the parties concerned: 'But it would be madness: the Blacks were property'. Walvin describes the line he adopted as 'casually dismissive':

> What is all this vast declaration of human beings thrown overboard? The question after all is, was it voluntary, or an act of necessity? This is a case of chattels, of goods, it is really so: it is the case of throwing over goods – for to this purpose, and the purpose of the Insurance, they are goods and property: whether right or wrong, we have nothing to do with it. This property – the human creatures if you will – have been thrown overboard: whether or not for the preservation of the rest – that is the real question.

The slave system hinged on the concept of the slave as a thing: a chattel, a piece of property. Both law and economic practice had, from the early days of the Atlantic slave trade, accepted the chattel status of the slave, thus what objection could there be to the killing of chattel? Mansfield himself accepted the point: 'They had no doubt (though it shocks one very much) that the case of the slaves was the same as if horses had been thrown overboard'.

Mansfield conceded the importance of the case but contended that the owners had not definitively established that the ship's water supply was so low that there was an absolute 'necessity' to throw the slaves overboard to be drowned and so ordered a new trial (no one has found any evidence of a further trial being held or even identified the next legal step in the *Zong* affair). The owners of the *Zong* were not the last slave-ship owners to claim insurance for dead slaves. Granville Sharp continued his campaign and tried to persuade government officers to bring murder charges against those involved, telling Admiralty officials that he had 'been earnestly solicited and called upon by a poor Negro for my assistance, to avenge the blood of his murdered countrymen'. Marshalling all the supporting evidence he could find, Sharp hoped to present an unanswerable case for a prosecution.[22] But as Walvin concludes:

> Again, he confronted that official silence and inactivity born of the realisation that any such action would corrode the system. Once an English court began to discuss murder and cruelty in the conduct of the slaving system, there was no knowing where the questions – and the consequent material damage – would end.

How was the case contained?

The image with which this chapter began depicted the courtroom as an ethical space wherein the rights of man were defended. The modern rule of law finds its institutional space in the proceedings of a case, in the barrier of the courtroom and the inside–outside distinction. Inside the courtroom law provides the discourse for resolution. But legal discourse has its own distinction between what is relevant and what is irrelevant. Movement occurs between the formal and the specific, between abstract and the concrete.

As Baucom[23] relates, Sharp's appeal to use criminal discourse and test necessity is at odds with the meaning it held in Mansfield's courtroom. The use of necessity in the criminal law case of R. v. *Dudley and Stephens* and another could not be called upon since necessity was understood as a particular stipulation within the *Zong*'s insurance contract and to the general insurance principle underlying that stipulation. Inside the courtroom, whatever the appeal from the public gallery, whatever the concern of those who sat with Sharp observing to 'see' justice done, the question of necessity was circumscribed by the terms of an insurance contract. Necessity thus meant for Mansfield not an ethical or moral question, not an issue of man's treatment of man, not whether or not it had been necessary for Collingwood to sacrifice some lives to save others; necessity meant whether his actions met the standard of necessity (for the throwing overboard of 'goods') of his contract's jettison clause and whether, accordingly, the owners were or were not entitled to compensation for those lost 'goods' in accord with the rules laid down by the bedrock insurance principle of the 'general average'. In their appeal for a new trial following the Guildhall jury's initial ruling in favour of the owners (and initial determination that Collingwood's actions had indeed met his contract's standard of necessity), the underwriters were clear: 'The [owners] have since pretended

---

22   Although there was no further legal action Parliament was petitioned. It refused to intervene, accepting that only 'cargo' was involved. The Quakers organised a general petition for the abolition of the slave trade but encountered the strong resistance of commercial interests. Four years later Granville Sharp joined with many others to form the Anti-Slave Trade Society. Today, this society continues to fight against modern forms of slavery and child trafficking that occur in many places around the world.
23   Baucom (2005: 139ff).

that the Sd. 133 slaves which were thrown alive out of the Sd. Ship Zong into the sea and perished ... were at the rate of 30 per head and according to the Stipulation and Agreement in the Afsd. Policies of Insurance of the value of 3990 & that the loss of the Sd. Slaves was a general Average Loss which ought to be born & paid for by the Underwriters.' The question before the court was whether or not the loss to the overall value of the *Zong*'s cargo was or was not a general average loss 'according to the Stipulation and Agreement' of its insurance policy. There were two main ways in which the underwriters' attorney could have pursued that question: either by suggesting that that policy did not include slaves among the list of 'goods' that could be treated as a general average loss or by suggesting that the policy did include slaves among that full list of 'commodities that had become the subject of insurance', but that, in this case, it had not been necessary for Collingwood to destroy these 'goods' and thus no compensation was owed. The first option would have entailed a fundamental engagement with the legality of slavery and the extant theory of property. The second, which is the option that the attorney chose to pursue, depended more simply on a matter of fact.

The 'standard' marine insurance policy of the period stipulated that:

> Whatever the master of a ship in distress, with the advice of his officers and sailors, deliberately resolves to do, for the preservation of the whole, in cutting away masts or cables, or in throwing goods overboard to lighten his vessel, which is what is meant by jettison or jetson, is, in all places, permitted to be brought into a general, or gross average: in which all concerned in ship, freight, and cargo, are to bear an equal or proportionate part of what was so sacrificed for the common good, and it must be made good by the insurers in such proportions as they have underwrote: however, to make this action legal, the three following points are essentially necessary; viz – 1st. That what was so condemned to destruction, was in consequence of a deliberate and voluntary consultation, held between the master and men: - 2dly. That the ship was in distress, and the sacrificing the things they did was a necessary procedure to save the rest: – and 3dly. That the saving of the ship and the cargo was actually owing to the means used with that sole view.

The *Zong* then is a referent both for the ship, the decision of its captain and crew towards their 'cargo' (not passengers), and it is also referent for the legal event and for absence. The *Zing*'s identity is as an exemplar of the contemporary, of the success of legal relevancy and the failure of the ethical appeal.

How can this be represented?

I pose another image, that by J.M.W. Turner and one which was the chief Academy picture of the Exhibition of 1840; when it was said later, 'Nothing could exceed the critical violence with which it was attacked.'[24]

---

24   The view is today different: Simon Schama: 'Though almost all of his critics believed that the painting represented an all time low in Turner's reckless disregard for the rules of art, it was in fact his greatest triumph in the sculptural carving of space.' See http://www.bbc.co.uk/arts/powerofart/turner.shtml.

Figure 2.3 Slave ship (slavers throwing overboard the dead and dying, typhoon coming on), Joseph Mallord William Turner, English (1775–1851), oil on canvas, 1840, Museum of Fine Arts, Boston. (The original is of course in vibrant colour). The painting was accompanied by a poem that described a slave ship caught in a typhoon, and based on the *Zong*. The critic John Ruskin, wrote, 'If I were reduced to rest Turner's immortality upon any single work, I should choose this.' When Turner exhibited the work at the Royal Academy in 1840 he paired it with the following extract from his unfinished and unpublished poem *Fallacies of Hope* (1812): 'Aloft all hands, strike the top-masts and belay;/Yon angry setting sun and fierce-edged clouds/Declare the Typhon's coming/ Before it sweeps your decks, throw overboard/ The dead and dying – ne'er heed their chains/Hope, Hope, fallacious Hope!/ Where is thy market now?' (For the full text of Turner's verse see Finberg (1961). Ruskin: 'I think, the noblest sea that Turner has ever painted, and if so, the noblest, certainly, ever painted by man, is that of the Slave-ship. It is a sunset on the Adriatic [*sic*, he means Atlantic], after prolonged storm; but the storm is partially lulled, and the torn and streaming rain clouds are moving in scarlet lines to lose themselves in the hollow of the night. The whole surface of sea included in the picture is divided into two ridges of enormous swell, not high, nor local, but a low, broad heaving of the whole ocean, like the lifting of its bosom by deep-drawn breath after the torture of the storm. Between these two ridges, the fire of the sunset falls along the trough of the sea, dyeing it with an awful but glorious light, the intense and lurid splendour of which burns like gold, and bathes like blood. Along this fiery path and valley, the tossing waves by which the swell of the sea is restlessly divided, lift themselves in dark, indefinite, fantastic forms, each casting a faint and ghastly shadow behind it along the illumined foam. They do not rise everywhere, but three or four together in wild groups, fitfully and furiously, as the under strength of the swell compels or permits them; leaving between them treacherous spaces of level and whirling water, now lighted with green and lamp-like fire, now flashing back the gold of the declining sun, now fearfully dyed from above with the indistinguishable images of the burning clouds, which fall upon them in flakes of crimson and scarlet, and give to the reckless waves the added motion of their own fiery flying. Purple and blue, the lurid shadows of the hollow breakers are cast upon the mist of the night, which gathers cold and low, advancing like the shadow of death upon the guilty ship as it labours amidst the lightning of the sea, its thin masts written upon the sky in lines of blood, girded with condemnation in that fearful hue which signs the sky with horror, and mixes its foaming flood with the sunlight, – and, cast far along the desolate heave of the sepulchral waves, incarnadines the multitudinous sea.'

The Victorian art critic and one time owner of the picture Ruskin understood that Turner presented nature about to punish guilty human beings. In his eyes it was a masterpiece in its combination of inspiration and technique:

> Its daring conception – ideal in the highest sense of the word – is based on the purest truth, and wrought out with the concentrated knowledge of a life; its colour is absolutely perfect, not one false or morbid hue in any part or line, and so modulated that every square inch of canvass is a perfect composition; its drawing as accurate as fearless; the ship buoyant, bending, and full of motion; its tones as true as they are wonderful; and the whole picture dedicated to the most sublime of subjects and impressions.

The work counter-poses detail and distance: in the left distance the guilty vessel is about to meet its deserved end, while in the right and central foreground we see the cast off slaves being devoured by the sea and its creatures.

Turner presents us with fanciful ocean predators to play on the gothic fear of imagined consequences and while John McCoubrey states Turner painted this image specifically for an anti-slavery campaign, the image is ambiguous when we understand the full context. The year 1840 was to be a celebration of Britain's stance on slavery and the abolitionist movement were to hold an international convention of the great and good to express righteous indignation against slavery in the United States. Turner had been introduced to the cause many years before by his patron, Walter Fawkes, and wanted to make a contribution, but his work punctures any feeling of superiority. By going back to the *Zong*, Turner points to the failure of human justice; turned by the courts into the discourse of insurance and the claim of necessity, it is nature, the same nature that has terrible fates for the cast off slaves, that will punish those on the ship that threw them overboard. Turner's words in his poem 'Hope, Hope, fanacious Hope!/Where is thy market now?' is an attack not just on the slave trade but the way in which the humans of the *Zong* had not even gained a recognition as passengers but

Figure 2.4 Detail of the *Slave Ship* by Turner.

only as items of cargo that bore an insurance value. Turner's work opposes vantage points to communicate both sympathy and judgment leading the viewer to sympathise with the victims of those about to receive deserved retribution. Since this opposition of near and far in this way demonstrates for the viewer the essential justice of the ship's destruction, the very closeness of the dying slaves to the spectator creates a second effect, which is the recognition that the nature which will justly punish the ship is the same nature that is already unjustly devouring the ship's innocent victims. The law has denied justice: only nature will deliver it, but can we trust this nature? Turner may be with the classical Greek poet Hesiod: 'The immortals are ever present among men, and they see those who with crooked verdicts spurn divine retribution and grind down one another's lives ... [They] keep a watchful eye over verdicts and cruel acts as they move over the whole earth, clothed in mist ... so that people pay for the reckless deeds and evil plans of kings whose slanted words twist her straight path.'[25] We, however, may not share this confidence.

CONCLUSION: LAWS OPENNESS AND CLOSURE

Murphy reminds us that the common 'law is a matter of judgment in a particular place from which things can be seen in their proper arrangement'.[26] In this chapter we have been concerned with rights, due process, discourse, decision and vision: the ability to see and decide, whether 'justly' or not. Turner reminds us that the visibility of the courtroom is consequent to the structuring of the case. The court's ability to see, to have the facts and issues brought before a judge or panel of judges, is at the end of processes of inclusion and exclusion, both in terms of legal discourse (conceptualisation) and justicability (of allowing issues and facts to be in issue at the court). We will not in this text do more than note the widespread concerns over access to justice deserving of greater attention (the name of Bhopal and the denial of justice to the victims of that chemical disaster in the 1980s is but illustrative). Our concern is primarily the politics of the common law system in England and Wales and we shall look at some access to justices issues when we come to consider the values associated with legal aid, but viewed globally the rise of rights discourse also demonstrates how so few of the victims of abuses of rights can access any form of 'international justice'.[27] And while transatlantic slavery no longer exists, people trafficking is still extensive and monthly some choices are made in boats and containers over which illegal immigrant is to be taken on or sometimes pushed off into the sea – bodies of the not so lucky regularly wash up in the Mediterranean.

Law's domain is ambiguous: expansive and yet particular. Law appears to be able to answer any question that is turned into its particular forms of discourse, discourse that fits the constraints of the 'case'. Understood contextually, we need to be aware of the social, political and economic forces that structure the case and in scholarly terms

---

25   Hesiod (1983: vol. II, 73).
26   Murphy (1997: 116).
27   On the rise of rights discourse see Sellars (2002); among the growing list of works defining the twentieth century as one of mass crimes and little prosecution see Ball (1999); Rubenstein (2000); Morrison (2005).

there is much to be gained in knowledge from sociological, anthropological, historical, political and economic analysis to position the case, to position law's operation and its ability (or forgetfulness) to record laws experience. In this sense whatever the outcome of the (to law students often arbitrary) disputes as to whether multidisciplinary study should take 'law and society' or 'law in society' as its target law in the sense of the case *is* law in society. This might give rise to optimism: structure our understanding of the case so that we are aware of these constraints and law is free to be law and not politics, the case contains the interests, the law is impartial. However, the boundaries are not clear and are increasingly complex. We witness an expansion of the range of issues, parties and inherent conflict (if not outright contradiction) between them. The rise of the global economy presents environmental, economic and political interdependency as never before. Complex multinational organisations make identifying responsibility, cause and effect, extremely difficult. New technologies push out the boundaries of the possible, and create, for example, forms of bio-power that allow for the state to regulate 'life' – the rise of biotechnologies present ethical and political dilemmas that the courts struggle to cope with. The factors to be taken into account in the construction of a case expand, the outcomes of particular 'cases' may increasingly reflect compromises, criticised by observers as not settling the issues, but can such issues be settled?

For example, the seemingly relative simplicity of *R* v. *Dudley and Stephens* – and the patronising language of Coleridge's judgment – came back to play in the case of *Re: A (Children)* [2000]. Jodie and Mary were conjoined twins, joined at the pelvis, born to devout Roman Catholic parents. Mary was the weaker of the two twins and would not have survived if she had been born alone. She was being kept alive by virtue of Jodie's own circulatory system. Jodie was considered to be capable of surviving a separation procedure; Mary was not. The courts accepted that if no separation took place, both would die within a matter of months, due to the added strain on Jodie's circulatory system. The medical team looking after the twins wished to separate them, in the knowledge that Mary would die as a direct result of the operation. The twin's parents, however, would not sanction the operation. In their eyes, both twins were God's creatures, each having a right to life. They could not sanction the shortening of Mary's life in order to extend that of Jodie. If it was God's will that they die, then so be it. The medical team sought a ruling from the High Court that an operation to separate the twins, knowing that such a procedure would result in the death of Mary, would not be unlawful; that is, murder.

At the first instance trial, Johnson J tried to avoid calling this murder by ruling that such an operation would not be unlawful because in his view the proposed operation was not a positive act but represented a 'withdrawal of blood', a situation analogous to the withdrawal of feeding and hydration in *Airedale NHS Trust* v. *Bland* [1993]. The parents appealed on the grounds that Johnson J was wrong in finding that the proposed operation was in either Mary's or Jodie's best interests, and that the operation should not be held legal. Ward LJ, Brook LJ and Walker LJ of the Court of Appeal therefore considered submissions from all interested parties, and came to the same outcome – that the separation would not be unlawful. But they rightly saw the operation in terms of the doctors doing an intentional action and each judge used different routes to find the operation lawful. Each decided to concentrate on dealing with different spheres of principles of medical law, family law, criminal law and human rights principles and legislation. Each concluded that the operation would result in the death of Mary, an act that was intentional and was therefore murder. In order to be considered 'lawful', the operation would therefore have to be carried out under the auspices of an exception or defence to murder, or be 'excused' in some way. They considered the defence of 'necessity' to be applicable to this situation, Brook LJ giving the most detailed assessment of the relevant law (Brook LJ in *Re: A (Children)* part 4 sections 16–24). The defence was accepted with the compromise to restrict the applicability of this defence, for the purposes of public policy, to the very 'unique circumstances' of this case. But how did this fit in the narrative structure of law's predictability? Did the case give a result that ensured predictability? In other words could other doctors know whether the principles of 'necessity' will be applied in other aspects of medical practice, where decisions are made as to the relative worth of an individual's life, in comparison with that of another? It seemed not.

There were two sets of criticisms: one that the judgment did not enter into a deep enough discussion of the ethical and moral responsibilities. The other that the issues were not reconciled in law. The following was representative:

> Future criminal cases will find little material with which to generalise in Re A. Robert Walker LJ's judgment can largely be disregarded, and the analyses of Ward and Brooke LJJ tread different paths. Indeed, their Lordships' mutual declarations of agreement are undermined by the reasoning in their judgments. No ratio decidendae emerges with clarity from the decision. Nonetheless, authoritative dicta may be drawn upon to support arguments about the scope of self-defence (in Ward LJ's judgment) and especially necessity (in Brooke LJ's judgment). And one may be confident in future that a defence to murder will be available to D in situations where a blameless victim is, by her conduct, posing an unjustified threat to the lives of others, at least provided the victim's death is not directly sought and is only a virtually certain side-effect of the life-preserving actions taken by D.[28]

We will not go into further detail, we may or may not agree that 'the extension of what it is possible to do, from more efficient ways of killing people to the cloning of humans, have fast outstripped the ability of society to come to a consensus on what is permissible or right'. But one message is that more and more factors, parties and issues may be packed into a case; we have to accept that law's ability to see, in the confines of the case, seems destined to become simultaneously more opaque and more complex. If the common law's traditional practicality can provide answers, they will be increasingly temporary and open to analysis from many perspectives. But as this chapter has alluded to, the connection between law and truth may always have been the product of the confines of the 'case'.

---

28   Case Note, *Criminal Law*, Simester and Sullivan, Hart Publishing, updated 14 October 2002 (http://www.hartpublishingusa.com/updates/crimlaw/crimlaw_med.htm)

3

INSTITUTIONALISING JUDICIAL DECISION MAKING: THE JUDICIAL PRACTICE OF PRECEDENT

The law of England would be a strange science if indeed it were decided by precedents only. Precedents serve to illustrate principles and to give them a fixed certainty. But the law of England, which is exclusive of positive law, enacted by statute [i.e. Mansfield specifies he is referring to case law developed by the courts], depends upon principles, and these principles run through all the cases according as the particular circumstances of each have been found to fall within the one or the other of them.[1]

If a group of cases involves the same point, the parties expect the same decision. It would be a gross injustice to decide alternate cases on opposite principles. If a case was decided against me yesterday when I was a defendant, I shall look for the same judgment today if I am plaintiff. To decide differently would raise a feeling of resentment and wrong in my breast; it would be an infringement, material and moral, of my rights. Adherence to precedent must then be the rule rather than the exception if litigants are to have faith in the even-handed administration of justice in the courts.[2]

The paradigm case of injustice is that in which there are two similar individuals in similar circumstances and one of them is treated better or worse than the other. In this case, the cry of injustice rightly goes up against the responsible agent or group; and unless that agent or group can establish that there is some relevant dissimilarity after all between the individuals concerned and their circumstances, he or they will be guilty as charged.[3]

If lawyers hold to their precedents too closely, forgetful of the fundamental principles of truth and justice which they should serve, they may find the whole edifice comes tumbling down about them. Just as the scientist seeks for truth, so the lawyer should seek for justice. Just as the scientist takes his instances and from them builds up his general propositions, so the lawyer should take his precedents and from them build up his general principles. Just as the propositions of the scientist have to be modified when shown not to fit all instances, or even discarded when shown in error, so the principles of the lawyer should be modified when found to be unsuited to the times or discarded when found to work injustice.[4]

1 Lord Mansfield, *Jones* v. *Randall* [1774] 1 Cowp. 37.
2 Cardozo (1921: 33–4).
3 Frankena (1973: 49).
4 Lord Denning, former Master of the Rolls (1979: 292).

INTRODUCTION: DETERMINING THE AUTHORITY OF WORDS IN CASES

Case law is the product of judicial determination; it is sometimes referred to as judge-made law. Yet common law systems claim they operate the rule of law, not of men (and traditionally, and in large part continuing today, appellant courts are staffed by male judges). The human element to law's operation appears inescapable; how is case law justified, legitimized and rescued from claims of arbitrariness and subjectivity? At one time – following on from the eighteenth century enlightenment desires for system, clarity and systematic rationality – a progressive view was that codification was the solution to the problem of a perceived chaos of competing cases and seemingly ad hoc, if not retrospective judicial 'law making'.[5] With limited (if sometimes, as in India, notable) exceptions this did not occur and most large-scale schemes of converting case law into statutes consisted mainly of consolidating legislation where the aim was to preserve and consolidate the existing structure of principles and rules developed over time by common law judges.

In addition, common law systems with their variety of formal sources of law (historically custom, case law, national statutes, transnational agreements and institutional links, academic commentary) specify that predictability and recognisability of law are features of their systems. Identifying precision in the relevant 'law' – a crucial element in legal research – is not always easy. The central paradox of case law is that it is both written and yet never completely or finally written, the statements of the judge(s) are, in Blackstone's classic words of 1765 (at the peak of the 'declaratory' theory of the common law), 'evidence of what is the common law'; they are not themselves the final word. While the declaratory theory may have lost its grip, it still continues that the words of a judgment are judicial pronouncements, articulations, which will be interpreted and reinterpreted. At times some of the words will be taken as pointing to principles of wider application, at times some will be rejected while others, or competing words (for example of the dissenting judgment and not the leading judgment), preferred as accurate statements of the 'law'; the crucial distinction is that *judicial fidelity is owed not to the articulations of previous judges, but to the law*.

Another central doctrine is that of judicial independence, and, since the Act of Settlement 1701, processes are in place to ensure that judges are not politically or financially controlled. How are the ideas of the rule of law and judicial independence reconciled? Our answer here is through the location of judicial decision making in sets of judicial 'practice', a central element of which is the practice of precedent.

The modern practice of precedent is a practical solution to changing circumstances, such as changes in theories of the nature of law generally held (such as declaratory theory versus legal positivism), the nature of the legal community (such as the rapid expansion

---

5   The reference to case law and 'judge-made' law began with Bentham, who so defined it in the hope of destroying its legitimacy.

of numbers of legal professionals in the twentieth century), issues in structuring the expansion of the court system, and the nature of law reporting which has developed from an ad hoc private enterprise of opportunistic barristers to, in part at least, large-scale enterprises of multinational media conglomerates.

The evolving historical constitution, not some analytical set of logical related and clearly specified concepts and ideas, provides the guiding force for the common law. Judges, human figures, pronounce on 'the law', make judgments, find in one party's favour, and claim legitimacy for their decisions. At least three audiences are listening and watching the judicial display: the parties to the dispute, the public, and other legal professionals. The latter include fellow judges and in particular the judges who are likely to hear the case again if the legal issues go to appeal, as well as legal academics eager to write case notes or articles and books in which particular cases are described as correct, others 'wrong', certain judgments as incisive, others as not particularly well reasoned and so forth. This process of interpretation and pronouncement on the law is not mechanical; if it were then the issue should not have reached court. Legal audiences applaud judicial style and recognise judicial creativity, but this must be within constraints as both the public and legal audiences consider that there is an answer to legal problems, that there was law to be found, and that judges should strive to do justice according to the 'law' and not their bias. Is there a logical set of binding rules that settle all these issues? No.

A characteristic and vital concern in the common law world is the determination of the authority of propositions found in the law reports to be considered to be accurate statements of the law; that is, strategies of reading and giving weight and according substance to the recorded statements by the judges in making judgment in deciding cases. Put simply, what is the status of the words therein contained? As generations of introductory books state, the most important method of ranking and weighing judgments is adherence to the 'doctrine' or 'rule' of precedent (in modern form a tightening of the older principle guiding judicial determination called *stare decisis*). The doctrine may be relatively easily stated in crude terms but it soon becomes more complex when we perceive the multifaceted calls a lawyer makes when working on a difficult case. Reading case reports to find relevant propositions of 'law', negotiating between 'leading' and 'dissenting' judgments, weighing up whether statements are 'ratio' or 'obiter' is no mechanical process, but more aptly described as an art, as a learned craft. Statements are given differing weight depending on how they contribute to developing an answer to a legal question and as material to evaluate the arguments of the opponent or formulate legal arguments that best fit with his or her sense of the case 'for' his or her client.

A term that is often used is 'authority': What is the authority *for*, or *against*, the argument? This is not an abstract consideration but deeply practical. Put another way, one part of legal research is about the technical problems of how to find or look up 'the law'; but faced with one set of concrete results of those searches – that is, a range of decisions and judgments – how should the lawyer rank and differentiate the material that he or she finds? One answer is by following the doctrine of precedent.

It is relatively easy to paraphrase scholarly descriptions of precedent; it is usually explained by reference to the English translation of the Latin phrase *stare decisis*, which literally translates as 'to stand by decided matters'. The phrase *stare decisis* is itself a shortened version of the Latin phrase *stare decisis et non quieta movere*, or 'to stand by decisions and not to disturb settled matters'. In student books it is common to run together *stare decisis* and the modern doctrine of precedent as if they were the same, but technically, *stare decisis* is the older term referring to the practice before the modern doctrine of 'binding precedent'. Historically, it appears to have given judges flexibility; one stood by previous decisions but weighed up their effects and their meaning in the overall understanding of the common laws' conception of the just state of affairs for the community. Precedent, in its modern form (i.e. binding precedent), developed from the looser *stare decisis* in the course of the nineteenth century and took on more of the character of a binding set of rules, whereby the decision of a higher court within the same national or provincial, state or district jurisdiction acts as *binding* authority on a lower court within that same jurisdiction. The decision of a court of another jurisdiction only acts as *persuasive* authority. The degree of persuasiveness is dependent upon various factors, including, first, the nature of the other jurisdiction and second, the level of court which decided the precedent case in the other jurisdiction. Other factors include the date of the precedent case, on the assumption that the more recent the case, the more reliable it will be as authority for a given proposition, although this is not necessarily so. And on some occasions, the judge's reputation may affect the degree of persuasiveness of the authority.

If things seem simple at this level of generality they get complex when we realise that all cases are an intermixing of procedure, facts and 'law', and that it is only particular parts of a decision that are called upon as authority, but often it is not easy to differentiate between the different parts. Glanville Williams described it for generations of law students thus:

> What the doctrine of precedent declares is that cases must be decided the same way when their material facts are the same. Obviously it does not require that all the facts should be the same. We know that in the flux of life all the facts of a case will never recur, but the legally material facts may recur and it is with these that the doctrine is concerned. The *ratio decidendi* [reason of deciding] of a case can be defined as the material facts of the case plus the decision thereon. The same learned author who advanced this definition went on to suggest a helpful formula. Suppose that in a certain case facts A, B and C exist, and suppose that the court finds that facts B and C are material and fact A immaterial, and then reaches conclusion X (e.g. judgment for the plaintiff, or judgment for the defendant). Then the doctrine of precedent enables us to say that in any future case in which facts B and C exist, or in which facts A and B and C exist the conclusion must be X. If in a future case A, B, C, and D exist, and the fact D is held to be material, the first case will not be a direct authority, though it may be of value as an analogy.

It follows from Williams's analysis, however, that the addition of fact D to a future case means that conclusion X may or may not follow. In other words, the presence of a new fact D may have the effect of distinguishing the future case from the precedent or conversely the precedent may be extended to apply to the future case.[6]

There has been considerable writing on whether the doctrine of binding precedent is good or bad but the doctrine is usually justified by arguments which focus on the desirability of stability and certainty in the law and also by notions of justice and fairness. Examples are:

- Reliance upon precedent promotes the expectation that the law is just. Specifically if we accept that the idea that like cases should be treated alike is anchored in the assumption that one person is the legal equal of any other. Thus, persons in similar situations should not be treated differently except for legally relevant and clearly justifiable reasons. Precedent promotes judicial restraint and limits a judge's ability to determine the outcome of a case in a way that he or she might choose if there were no precedent. This function of precedent gives it its normative force.
- Precedent enhances efficiency. Reliance on the accumulation of legal rules helps guide judges in their resolution of legal disputes. If judges had to begin the law anew in each case, they would add more time to the adjudicative process and would duplicate their efforts.

The use of precedent is related to and dependent upon the publication of law reports that contain case decisions and the articulated rationale of judges. The paucity of law reports until their reorganisation under the Council of Law Reporters and the adoption of 'official' series meant that uncertainty existed as to the actual words that justified early decisions (many early reports were more reporting the procedure or the argument used; often the decision was not included!).

Location: that is the position of a judge (and their court) within the structure of the court hierarchy is crucial. How do we understand the complex of factors cohering? We contend that the doctrine of precedent is best seen as a practice through which many competing pressures are, if not reconciled, at least kept in a workable equilibrium.

PRECEDENT AS JUDICIAL PRACTICE

To restate our analytical stance: precedent is not to be understood as a rule or doctrine but as judicial practice.[7] That practice is shaped by, among other things, the rules on court hierarchy, ideas as to the nature of case law and the 'law-making' nature of judicial determination of disputes. Such ideas reflect general jurisprudential beliefs, even if not

---
6   References to Williams are to his *Learning the Law*, 9th ed. (1973) [my student copy, WJM]. In this account, legal rules, embodied in precedents, are generalisations that accentuate the importance of certain facts and discount or ignore others. The application of precedent relies on reasoning by analogy. Analogies can be neither correct nor incorrect but only more or less persuasive. Reasonable persons may come to different yet defensible conclusions about what rule should prevail.
7   A thorough study of the judicial practice of precedent would analyse the interpretative techniques that determine the statements of ratio and *obita dicta*. It would also have to concern itself with the techniques of overruling, distinguishing and following previous decisions. The most thorough account of judicial practice would then have to go on to study the education and training of judges, and their embedding within a particular culture or cultures of legal behaviour.

so clearly articulated by the judge. In particular the historical link between acceptance of 'custom', natural law and the declaratory theory, contrasted to the 'modern' view of positivism that law must be traced to some determinable origin and is the creation of human agency, that is it is posited. The rise of legal positivism has highlighted judicial creativity as an active process of making law, not declaring what already existed or finding.

To describe precedent as a practice is to draw attention to the location of the activity of judges interpreting law and acting on the basis of those interpretations.[8] While interpretation is central to all judicial reasoning – whether in statutory interpretation or in the reading of previous judgments and indeed, the presentation of facts in legal claims – interpretation is not freestanding but exists in sets of activities, the various activities that make up legal systems, and involve a host of legal actors (such as the police, court reporters, lawyers, judges and those who provide in wider writings the jurisprudential ideas of the age). Practices are shaped by the legal culture and the practices in turn affect legal culture (an important contribution to culture is the activity of procedure and pleading in an adversarial system). This chapter is mostly concerned with aspects of the institutional context of judicial interpretation, in particular understanding the hierarchy of courts as a factor that has influenced and determined the forms of the judicial practice.[9] However, practices are never unitary. They are animated by tensions that reflect disagreements over the precise way in which the practice should be performed. A consensus shared between practitioners over the techniques and performances that constitute a practice reflects the stability of the practice as a whole. We will see that judicial interpretation is a relatively stable practice. However, there have been important disputes over its precise operation and in some important areas, notably human rights, debates are ongoing.

What are the consequences of this argument? If practices are essentially ways of acting in given circumstances, any general theory may be too distant from the practice to capture how judges actually interpret cases. Judicial interpretation is always a matter of a specific case and a singular set of facts. To understand why a judge in a particular case comes to the conclusion that s/he does necessitates a study of a precise legal context. In other words, a general account of precedent perhaps tells us more about the practice of academic writing than it does about the work of judges. It may be that the best way to

---

8   Appellate courts create precedents in common law system. The most famous common law court, the Supreme Court in the US, settles conflicts over the status of law within a particular constitutional framework laid down at independence. A key factor in the choosing of new Supreme Court judges is their attitude to precedent. Court decisions either reaffirm or create precedents. It is clear that despite its reliance on precedent, the Court will depart from its prior decisions when either historical conditions change or the philosophy of the Court undergoes a major shift. The most famous reversal of precedent is *Brown* v. *Board of Education* [1954] 347 U.S. 483, 74 S. Ct. 686, 98 L. Ed. 873, in which the Supreme Court repudiated the 'separate but equal' doctrine of *Plessy* v. *Ferguson* [1896] 163 U.S. 537, 16 S. Ct. 1138, 41 L. Ed. 256. This doctrine had legitimated racial segregation for almost 60 years but finally gave way in *Brown*, when a unanimous court ruled that separate but equal was a denial of equal protection of the laws.
9   'Underlying precedent is an emphasis on stability, permanence and the wisdom of the past – the common law being conceived as an accumulation of such wisdom – combined with reverence for the higher courts as the "elders and betters" of the lower courts. Precedent reflected the vision of law as an undertaking based on learning, acquired skills and experience. At the same time, since precedents exist in order to be applied, the system essentially empowered the higher courts to legislate. Presented as a restraint, precedent camouflaged law-making while in reality constituting law-making.' Nicol (2006).

understand the practice of judicial interpretation is to background any general account, and see how it proceeds in different doctrinal areas of law. This would indicate that the best way to understand the practice of precedent is to study cases within their specific contexts.[10]

Specific contexts are, however, historically positioned. The transition from *stare decisis* to binding precedent may be reflective of changing ideas on the degree to which judicial practice is creative. Under the positivist account, popularised by Bentham and then put into mainstream jurisprudential form by Austin, judges make law.[11] Those who wished to defend traditional common law ideas of community, accumulated wisdom and balancing concerns felt it necessary to deny this fact in order to stress stability, certainty and continuity amidst change. This was inexorably linked to the hierarchy of courts and the need to institutionalise and strengthen that hierarchy after the reforms of the late 1800s. Stability and regularity in decision making required each court to respect its place in the hierarchy that stretched from trial courts, through to the ultimate appellant tribunal, the Appellant Committee of the House of Lords. Deviations could not be tolerated. There was also a constitutional argument. Judges could not trespass on the province of parliamentary legislation, as constitutional doctrines stressed the legal and political sovereignty of Parliament.

It became untenable to deny judicial law making, in part because it went against the older doctrine of judicial competence over the common law. It also proved a difficult line to hold because the need to do justice could not so easily be removed from judicial practice in the name of unqualified procedural regularity. The demands of justice disturbed both the settled hierarchy and the sense of constitutional boundaries. Cases presented compelling arguments for departure from the hierarchy of courts, and even for urgent changes in the law to be made by the courts themselves. A central tension emerged between hierarchy and flexibility in judicial practice. This can be understood as an issue of institutional legitimacy.

Judicial creativity raises the question of institutional legitimacy because it puts at stake the legitimacy of judicial law making. This, of course, raises the question of the relationship of parliamentary and judicial 'legislation'. Our UK constitution affirms the priority of the former over the latter. However, given that judges do make law, the real question is the extent to which this is legitimate, 'just' or acceptable within current understandings of constitutional propriety. Judicial practice has responded to issues of institutional legitimacy by providing guidelines that define and regularise the practice,

---

10 English legal education does not contain a formal training in precedent. The study of precedent is restricted (for the most part) to an element of a first-year introductory course of the LLB (and was absent from the CPE and now the GDL). To understand the law is to read cases and to engage in practical arguments about them. Likewise, professional training does not consist of training courses on the interpretation of cases. On the whole this reflects the empirical and practical culture of the common law, and the fact that until relatively recently legal training was more akin to an apprenticeship than a course of university study. The law in general and precedent in particular are thus essentially ways of 'doing' law that have never seen the usefulness of general or abstract accounts of their operation.

11 'The theoretical position has been that judges do not make or change the law: they discover and declare the law which is thought the same. According to this theory, when an earlier decision is overruled the law is not changed; its true nature is disclosed, having existed in that form all along ... In truth judges make and change the law. The whole of the common law is judge made and only by judicial changes in the law is the common law kept relevant in a changing world.' Lord Browne-Wilkinson *Kleinwort Benson* v. *Lincoln City Council* [1998] 4 All ER 513.

although a definitive articulation of the relationship of the courts and Parliament has been avoided. We will see that this debate now proceeds increasingly in human rights terms. It cannot be understood in the terms of the conventional practice of precedent. Indeed, disagreements reflect the transitional nature of the practice itself, although it would be too soon to say whether or not we are witnessing a fundamental shift in judicial practice.

Our study of precedent will begin with an overview of the tension between hierarchy and flexibility that underlies the broad issues of institutional legitimacy. We will then look specifically at the relationship between the House of Lords and the Court of Appeal, and the possible development of an alternative practice of judicial interpretation. The final sections will engage specifically with the judicial law making and human rights. The chapter will conclude with some final reflections on substantive justice and procedural legitimacy.

Figure 3.1 Members of the Four Inns of Court, the Middle Temple (barristers, judges and benchers) dinning in common, Great Hall, Middle Temple, 1840s.

Why put so much emphasis upon the idea of practice? Legal education in the common law until the advent of university education in law in the later nineteenth century and developing through the twentieth century was a matter of apprenticeship, of learning in practice and for those who wished to participate in the dealings of the courts of joining one of the four Inns of Courts, attending lectures and most importantly living the common life (dining and drinking). One way of understanding the need for modern rules of precedent is proposed by A.W.B. Simpson, namely that historically 'the common law is best understood as a system of customary law, that is, a body of traditional ideas received within a caste of experts'. Practice determines the reality of a rules operation and acceptance, since 'as a system of legal thought the common law ... is inherently vague' (Simpson, 1973: 90). It is not that everything is always in the melting pot, 'but that you never quite know what will go in next'. Simpson identifies the common law system as 'a body of practices observed and ideas received by a caste of lawyers, those ideas being used by them as providing guidance in what is conceived to be the rational determination of disputes litigated before them, or by them on behalf of clients and other contexts. These ideas and practices exist only in the sense that they are accepted and acted upon within the legal profession, just as customary practices can be said to exist within a group in

Figure 3.1 Continued

the sense that they are observed, accepted as appropriate forms of behaviour and transmitted both by example and precept as membership of the group changes' (Simpson, 1973: 94). The modern (positivist) rules of binding precedent and determination of the 'authority' of the statements to be found in the mushrooming sources of law (the vast expansion of law reports) is a response to the breakdown of the previous largely unstated techniques of acceptance on the corpus of ideas and processes, and requires new mechanisms for the transmission of the traditional ideas and the encouragement of orthodoxy, new forms of learning the processes of deference, and learning when to innovate and when to follow almost mechanically. In a time when the legal profession was small 'the law was the peculiar possession of a small, tightly organised group comprising those who were concerned in the operation of the Royal courts', and within this group the judges and senior barristers were crucial. 'Orthodox ideas were transmitted largely orally, and even the available literary sources were written in a private language as late as the seventeenth century. A wide variety of institutional arrangements tended to produce cohesion of thought.' These have changed and diversity now is sought, the common law is no longer able to be confined as a system of customary law and arrangements, but the basic point remains that 'to argue that this or that is the correct view, as academics, judges, and counsel do, is to *participate* in the system, not simply to study it scientifically' (Simpson, 1973: 97).

This is also the rise of the textbook. As Birks puts it: 'It ought to be possible to take any legal subject and to cut away its detail so as to reveal the skeleton of principle which holds it together,' and then keep that elementary structure under constant review. This skeleton of principle is a particular organisation, 'a version chosen from a number of possibilities'. The choice is made, not in the cases themselves but found outside the adversary institutions in the production of the 'textbook'. Since the late nineteenth century, 'textbooks have borne the responsibility for restraining the centrifugal tendencies of case-law. If subjects such as contract or tort now are accepted as having a settled structure it is not because of some pure structure that the subject rationally follows, but 'because generations of textbooks, from different hands and going through successive editions, have selected and evolved a structure which for the moment seems best fitted to the matter' (Birks, 1985: 1–2).

HIERARCHY AND FLEXIBILITY

The practice of precedent works within the context of the court structure; the hierarchy of the courts provides the fundamental institutional structure.[12] The doctrine asserts that decisions of the Appellant Committee of the House of Lords bind all the courts below it in the hierarchy.[13] *London Tramways* v. *London City Council* (1898) was central to the foundation of what was to become the conventional form of the doctrine. In *London Tramways*, the House of Lords decided that it was bound by its own previous decisions:

> Of course, I do not deny that cases of individual hardship may arise, and there may be a current of opinion in the profession that such and such a judgment was erroneous; but what is that occasional interference with what is perhaps abstract justice, as compared with the inconvenience ... of having each question subject to being rearguarded and the dealings of mankind rendered doubtful by reason of different decisions, so that in truth there is no final court of appeal. My Lords, '*interest rei publicae*' is that there should be '*finis litium*' sometime and there can be no *finis litium* if it were possible to suggest in

---

12 This can be seen as having three distinct elements: 'These are the respect paid to a single decision of a superior court, the fact that a decision of such a court is a persuasive precedent even as far as the courts above that from which it emanates are concerned, and the fact that a single decision is always a binding precedent as regards courts below that from which it emanated'. (R. Cross and J.W. Harris, 1991, p. 3). The hierarchy of the courts is based on the 'respect' given to the decisions of superior courts. The 'binding' nature of precedent applies to the inferior courts. However, as the persuasive nature of an inferior court on a superior court has not been a particularly contentious issue, we will not consider it in this chapter. However, note that these distinctive features of precedent are introduced as being an accurate description '[a]t present' (ibid., p. 5). This is somewhat peculiar. It suggests that the doctrine itself is developing and changing over time. Any global definition has to be sensitive to this particular problem; a problem that corresponds with the idea that precedent is a practice, and that practices themselves develop.

13 This could be linked to the dominance of the declaratory theory of common law interpretation.

each case that it might be rearguarded because it is 'not an ordinary case' whatever that may meant'.[14]

Lord Halsbury acknowledges that cases of individual hardship may result from the House of Lords being bound by its own decisions. However, the need for clear general principles overrides the hardship caused in individual instances. Does the need for general principles also override the requirement that the court make just judgments? Lord Halsbury rules that justice is of little consequence in comparison with the need for finality in litigation. His argument denies that there could be such a thing as an extraordinary case where justice may demand a departure from general principles.

London Tramways lays down the parameters of modern practice demonstrating a preference for a clear, unambiguous statement of the binding nature of precedent. Very little allowance is made for a departure from the hierarchical ordering of the courts.[15] Sixty-eight years later the Practice Statement of 1966 stressed the need for the flexible development of the law:

> Their Lordships regard the use of precedent as an indispensable foundation upon which to decide what is the law and its application to individual cases. It provides at least some certainty upon which individuals can rely in the conduct of their affairs, as well as a basis for the development of legal rules.[16]

What does this tell us about the reshaping of the practice? Precedent is now described as fulfilling a dual function: it has a doctrinal aspect – the development of legal rules – and a social function as well. We find a different argument from that of Lord Halsbury:

> Their Lordships nevertheless recognize that too rigid adherence to precedent may lead to injustice in a particular case and also unduly restrict the proper development of the law.[17]

The Practice Statement reclaims the concern for the individual case; it asserts that there is no point having general rules, if these lead to injustice in individual instances. What is to be done? Their Lordships resolve to 'modify' the way they approach precedent: they will consider that they are normally bound by their previous decisions, but, in certain cases they will depart from previous decisions when 'it is right to do so'.[18] How are we to know when the time is right? Their Lordships will consider:

> The danger of disturbing the basis on which contracts, settlements of property and fiscal arrangements have been entered into and also the especial need for certainty as to the criminal law.[19]

---

14   *London Tramways v. London City Council* [1898] AC 375.
15   *Rookes v. Barnard* [1964] AC 1129.
16   Practice Statement (Judicial Precedent) [1966] 1 WLR 1234, at 1234.
17   Ibid., 1234.
18   Later in this chapter, we will see that this claim coordinates with one about the need to do justice in individual cases.
19   Practice Statement, at 1234.

This gives some general guidelines as to how the judges will understand the institutional legitimacy of their practice. The law would be illegitimate if it simply asserted the need for general rules, and ignored the fact that justice required general rules to be changed. However, the law would also become illegitimate if it simply treated each case as exceptional and failed to develop general rules. Law fulfils a social function: there is a social interest in settled general principles of law. If there is an implicit acknowledgement of judicial law making in the Practice Statement, there is also an understanding that the power should be used sparingly, and that stability would ultimately be preferred to creativity.

In the years after 1966, it indeed became clear that departing from precedent decisions would only take place in very rare circumstances.[20] We can develop this point by examining some important decisions. In *Miliangos v. George Frank*[21] the House of Lords departed from a previous decision, arguing that changing the law would enable the courts to 'keep step with commercial needs' and, furthermore, would not lead to 'practical and procedural difficulties'. The following passage from Lord Wilberforce's judgment is worth considering in detail:

> The law on this topic is judge-made: it has been built up over the years from case to case. It is entirely within this House's duty, in the course of administering justice, to give the law a new direction in a particular case where, on principle and in reason, it appears right to do so. I cannot accept the suggestion that because a rule is long established only legislation can change it – that may be so when the rule is so deeply entrenched that it has infected the whole legal system, or the choice of a new rule involves more far-reaching research than courts can carry out ... Indeed, from some experience in the matter, I am led to doubt whether legislative reform, at least prompt and comprehensive reform, in this field of foreign currency obligation, is practicable. Questions as to the recovery of debts or of damages depend so much upon individual mixtures of facts and merits as to make them more suitable for progressive solutions in the courts. I think that we have an opportunity to reach such a solution here. I would accordingly depart from the Havana Railways case and dismiss this appeal.[22]

Lord Wilberforce argues that because the law in this area is judge made, it is legitimate to alter it provided that 'on principle and in reason, it appears right to do so'. The sterling principle for the award of damages had become anachronistic. The law of damages has to keep pace with modern developments. There is thus a strong argument

---

20 Some indications are given in *Jones v. Secretary of State for Social Services* [1972] 1 AC 944. It is insufficient that the case was wrongly decided. Lord Reid refused to give precise criteria, arguing only that experience would prove to be a guide for discretion. He indicated that it would involve 'broad issues' – of both justice and legal principle – and that in the instant case neither of these criteria were present. Lord Wilberforce argued on slightly different grounds that if an interpretation of a statute had been given, then, unless Parliament was to change that statute, the interpretation was to stand. Lord Pearson's argument stressed the idea of 'finality of decision' supported by arguments with which we are already familiar. Of all the judgments, Lord Simon's is perhaps the most interesting, because he provides a list of reasons for not departing from the earlier case. Alongside reasons with which we are already familiar, he added a consideration of the nature of the parties and the litigation in issue – it was a revenue case with frequent litigants.
21 *Miliangos v. George Frank* [1975] 3 WLR 758.
22 Ibid., at 470.

for change. However, it is also important to note that the rule can be changed without upsetting other deep-seated principles. Miliangos thus refers to a set of rules that may be of ancient providence, but, because they are in an area of judge made law, it would not be necessary to defer to Parliament. The particular mixture of 'facts and merits' makes this pre-eminently an area for judicial law making.[23]

Miliangos suggests factors that legitimize judicial law making in civil law. Are there similar considerations in criminal law? Given limitations of space, we will look in detail at two important cases: *Shivpuri* and *Howe*. In *R. v. Shivpuri*[24] the House of Lords overruled itself. The case concerned the construction of s.1 of the Criminal Attempts Act 1981.[25] In an earlier case, *Anderton v. Ryan*,[26] the House of Lords had argued that the section could be approached on the basis of a distinction between acts that were 'objectively innocent', and those that were not so considered. However, in *Shivpuri* they were of the opinion that *Anderton* had been wrongly decided.

Lord Bridge's judgment in *Shivpuri* is worth looking at in detail; in particular his criticisms of the notion of objective innocence. He argues that the concept is 'incapable of sensible application' in criminal law. This is very emphatic language. The concept of objective innocence makes little sense because it avoids the central concept of the actor's intention. This is the essential ingredient in the law of attempt. Thus, if a person attempts to buy drugs, but is sold a harmless substitute, the criminal law must approach the attempted offence from the viewpoint of the actor's criminal intention. It would be wrong to argue that 'objectively' the act is innocent because the drugs did not exist. Acts cannot be considered 'independently' of the state of mind of the actor.[27] Lord Bridge also stressed his own 'conviction' as a 'party to the decision' that *Anderton* was 'wrong'.[28]

If *Anderton* was so clearly flawed, what course of action was open to the House of Lords? It was not possible to distinguish *Anderton* from *Shivpuri*. If their Lordships were bound by the unworkable test, the law of attempt would be based on flawed concepts. The only alternative would be to invoke the Practice Statement. Was this a justifiable course of action? Departing from a precedent case would lead to uncertainty

---

23   A close reading of the relevant cases might suggest the presence, or variation, of some of Lord Wilberforce's concerns in *Jones*. Arguments about social change lie behind *Herrington v. British Railways Board* [1972] AC 877. It is no longer acceptable that a property owner should have limited responsibilities to trespassers, and the law must be amended accordingly. However, in *Knuller v. D.P.P.* [1973] AC 435 the House of Lords refused to overrule *Shaw v. D.P.P.* [1962] AC 220. Does this suggest that there are slightly different considerations in criminal law? In *Shaw*, the court made the claim that it had a jurisdiction to try offences against good morals, even though Parliament had not legislated to cover such behaviour, or the existing law was either ambiguous or silent. In *Knuller*, the court refused to overrule the earlier case even though it was wrong. Does this suggest that their Lordships are willing to go much further in the area of social control than they are in commercial law or tort?
24   *R. v. Shivpuri* [1986] 2 WLR 988.
25   The section provided that a person is guilty of an offence if s/he does an act which is 'more than merely preparatory'. Section 1(2) goes on to state that even if 'the facts are such that the commission of the offence is impossible', a person may still be found guilty of an attempt to commit an offence.
26   *Anderton v. Ryan* [1985] AC 560.
27   Ibid., at 22. An alternative ground to justify the decision in *Anderton* was to analyse attempts in terms of the actor's 'dominant intention'. However, this test also runs into difficulties, because it is very difficult to distinguish between dominant intention and incidental beliefs; there are also problems in devising any way of articulating a meaningful test that would be helpful to a jury.
28   Ibid., 22.

in the law. However, in *Shivpuri* this was justifiable. As *Anderton* was a recent decision, settled law had not yet developed. However, this is not the determining factor. The most pressing factor is the need to correct a 'serious error', 'a distor(tion)' in the law.[29]

It might appear, then, that any understanding of the interpretation of *Shivpuri* is rooted in the context of the criminal law, and the serious error in which the House of Lords had fallen into in *Anderton*. Can we observe a similar pattern if we turn our attention to R. v. *Howe*?[30]

In *Lynch*[31] the House of Lords had held that the defence of duress was available to someone who had been charged with aiding or abetting murder.[32] In R. v. *Howe*[33] the House of Lords overruled this decision. As with *Shivpuri*, we encounter very strong language. Lord Bridge asserted, 'I can find nothing whatever to be said for leaving the law as it presently stands'.[34] He went on to argue that an 'odd quirk of the system' had allowed the decision in *Lynch* to stand, despite the fact that four out of the seven presiding law lords (in the appellate courts in Northern Ireland and England) had rejected the reasoning in the case.[35]

Lord Hailsham argued that R. v. *Howe* afforded an ideal opportunity to re-consider the issue from the standpoint of 'authority'.[36] A review of the law of homicide stretching back to *Hale* and *Blackstone* showed that duress had never been available for murder. It was possible to invoke the Practice Statement because *Lynch* could not 'be justified on authority'.[37] Furthermore, 'judicial legislation [had] proved to be an excessive and perhaps improvident use of the undoubted power of the courts to create new law by creating precedents in individual cases'.[38] The improvident use of judicial legislation in *Lynch* was also indicated by Parliament's refusal to legislate on the issue. Lord Bridge pointed out that Parliament had not acted on the Report of the Law Commission's recommendation to allow a defence of duress.[39] Parliament's refusal to legislate suggests that the judges should not have taken upon themselves the reform of the law.

Lynch was fundamentally wrong in principle: Lord Hailsham justified this criticism by referring to the overriding objects of the criminal law to set standards of conduct that are clear in specifying how people are to 'avoid criminal responsibility'.[40] This means that the duress defence must not blur the offence of murder. The law must be based on the principle that it is never justifiable to commit murder, even to save one's own life. Does this mean, though, that as other offences allow a duress defence, the criminal law is inconsistent? This criticism is met with an argument from principle: 'consistency and

---

29   Ibid., 12.
30   R. v. *Howe* [1987] 2 WLR 568.
31   *DPP for Northern Ireland* v. *Lynch* [1975] 2 WLR 641.
32   Per Lord Bridge: in the law established by *Lynch* and *Abbott*, duress is a complete defence to a murderer otherwise guilty as a principal in the second degree; it is no defence to a murderer guilty as a principal in the first degree.
33   R. v. *Howe* [1987] 2 WLR 417.
34   Ibid., at 437.
35   Ibid., at 436.
36   Ibid., at 427.
37   Ibid., at 429.
38   Ibid., at 430.
39   Ibid., at 437.
40   Ibid.

logic ... are not always prime characteristics of a penal code based like the common law on custom and precedent'.[41] Indeed, if law is an art, rather than 'an exact science',[42] a pragmatic response to problems is more important than a consistent development of abstract principles.[43]

What, then, can *Howe* and *Shivpuri* tell us about the practice of precedent within criminal law? The law lords in both cases approach the law from the perspective that there has to be very compelling arguments for change. The House of Lords will overrule itself when it has fallen into serious error, and when the circumstances of the case are such that it is practical to overrule an earlier decision. These narrow guidelines preserve the legitimacy of judicial law making. The House of Lords is ensuring the consistent development of principles. Criminal law is legitimised as the courts dispel the errors into which they have fallen. It is not necessary to depart from the hierarchical organisation of the courts to achieve this end. However, in turning to the question of the Court of Appeal's jurisdiction, we now have to grapple with this very problem. How does this raise the problem of institutional legitimacy in a slightly different context?

THE HOUSE OF LORDS AND THE COURT OF APPEAL: PRECEDENT AND JUSTICE

Perhaps one of the most fraught questions in the area of precedent relates to the right of the Court of Appeal to depart from a judgment of the House of Lords. This is linked to the question of whether the Court of Appeal was bound to follow its own decisions.

Tensions between the Court of Appeal and the House of Lords had developed in *Schorsch Meier*. The Court of Appeal had argued that circumstances had changed so much since the House of Lords ruling in *Havana Railways*[44] that 'the sterling judgment rule' principle should no longer apply. Denning MR stated that the underlying reason for damages being given in sterling was essentially 'practical'.[45] He went on to invoke the principle *cessante ratione legis cessat ipsa lex*[46] or – as he pithily put it – 'Seeing that the reasons no longer exist, we are at liberty to discard the rule itself'.[47] Lord Denning justified this principle by arguing that it would be wrong to abrogate substantive rights by reference to procedural concerns.[48] Furthermore, he pointed out (and Lawton LJ agreed) that Article 106 of the Treaty of Rome required

---

41   Ibid., at 423.
42   Ibid.
43   Ibid., 434.
44   In *Re United Railways of Havana* [1961] AC 1007.
45   *Schorsch Meier v. Henin* [1975] QB 416., at 425. It was outside the competence of the court to determine the value of a currency other than sterling; besides, it was 'appropriate to trading conditions' in a time before instantaneous communications (ibid.).
46   Ibid., at 428.
47   Ibid., 425.
48   However, it would appear that there are at least two factors that justify the use of the principle. In a prior case, *Jugoslavenska Oceanska Plovidba v. Castle Investment Co. Inc.* [1974] QB 292, the court had allowed arbitrators

that judgment should be given in the currency of the member state in which the creditor resided.[49]

This suggests the development of an alternative practice of interpretation that departs from the conventional understanding of the doctrine of the hierarchy of the courts.[50] The response of the House of Lords to the Court of Appeal in *Schorsch Meier* came in *Miliangos*. Lord Simon, with the explicit agreement of Lord Wilberforce, rejected Lord Denning's use of the *cessante ratione cesset ipsa lex* principle. The wide meaning of the principle would mean that any court could 'disclaim any authority of any higher court on the ground that the reason which had led to such higher court's formulation of the rule of law was no longer relevant'. Application of the principle would mean that the court could even overrule Acts of Parliament, if it judged that the reasons for the rule no longer applied; as such the rule has 'no place in our own modern constitution'.[51]

This reassertion of the conventional understanding of the practice did not prevent another deviation arising on a later occasion. However, the matter now concerned the question of whether the Court of Appeal could depart from its own previous decisions. The conventional position, as stated in *Young v. Bristol Aeroplane Co.* asserted that even if the Court of Appeal regretted a previous decision, it was obliged to follow it and recommend an appeal to the House of Lords.[52] As the Court of Appeal was created by statute, it had to adhere to its statutory powers, and could not exceed its limited role.[53]

Lord Denning attempted to avoid this rule in *Davis v. Johnson*.[54] In *Davis v. Johnson*, the Court of Appeal considered the case of a victim of domestic violence. Ms Davis had unsuccessfully asked the court for an order to compel her abusive partner to leave the flat that they had been sharing. To allow her appeal, the Court of Appeal would need to depart from previous decisions where injunctions had not been awarded in similar situations.[55] Lord Denning made a strong argument from principle. He began

---

to make awards in foreign currency. Denning MR also made reference to this principle in the Court of Appeal's hearing of Miliangos.
49   *Schorsch*, at 431.
50   See also *Broome v. Cassell* [1972] AC 1027. The Court of Appeal had attempted to show that the House of Lords had acted *per incuriam*, or incorrectly, in the case *Rookes v. Barnard* [1964] AC 1129. The case concerned the issue of damages. Lord Hailsham articulated the conventional position clearly: 'In the hierarchical system of courts which exist in this country, it is necessary for each lower tier, including the Court of Appeal, to accept loyally the decisions of the higher tiers'. Lord Hailsham's words return to the notion that 'far worse than individual injustice is the compromise of general principles'.
51   *Miliangos*, at 476.
52   *Young v. Bristol Aeroplane Co.* [1944] KB 718, at 725. This would also apply whether the Court of Appeal was sitting as a 'full court' or as a division with only three members present.
53   Lord Greene concludes: 'On a careful examination of the whole matter we have come to the clear conclusion that this court is bound to follow previous decisions of its own as well as those of courts of co-ordinate jurisdiction. The only exceptions to this rule (two of them apparent only) are those already mentioned which for convenience we here summarize: (1.) The court is entitled and bound to decide which of two conflicting decisions of its own it will follow. (2.) The court is bound to refuse to follow a decision of its own which, though not expressly overruled, cannot, in its opinion, stand with a decision of the House of Lords. (3.) The court is not bound to follow a decision of its own if it is satisfied that the decision was given per incuriam'.
54   *Davis v. Johnson* [1974] AC 264.
55   In *B v. B* [1978] 1 All ER 821 and *Cantliff v. Jenkins* [1978] 2 WLR, it was held that the county court did not in fact have the power that it claimed under the Act. The task of the court in *Davis v. Johnson* is to 'review' the

by admitting that, in normal cases, the Court of Appeal was bound by its own previous decisions. He went on to criticise the consequences of this argument. It may be that an appeal is never made to the House of Lords, or that there is a long delay before the House of Lords has an opportunity to overturn an incorrect decision.[56] It may also be that an individual lacks the financial means to bring the appeal to the House of Lords. This problem is compounded by the fact that wealthy litigants can 'pay off' appellants, and so perpetuate a decision erroneous in law. Moreover, in the present case, the delay that an appeal would cause would add to Ms Davis' hardship. She was resident in a battered women's refuge in 'appallingly' overcrowded conditions:

> In order to avoid all the delay – and the injustice consequent upon it – it seems to me that this court, being convinced that the two previous decisions were wrong, should have the power to correct them and give these women the protection which Parliament intended they should have.[57]

There is a compelling case for the avoidance of delay. However, what are the consequences of allowing the Court of Appeal to overrule itself? Would the lower courts be left in confusion? For instance, a judge in a county court would not know which Court of Appeal case stated the correct law. Lord Denning argues that the lower court would simply follow the later decision, based on the principle that as long as the later case contains a 'full consideration' of the earlier cases, it was the preferable authority.[58]

This is a good illustration of the conflict between general procedural principles and individual injustice. But, how, as a question of law, would it be possible to get around *Bristol Aeroplane Co.*? Lord Denning showed that *Bristol Aeroplane Co.* was not an accurate statement of the law. This argument returns to roots of the jurisdiction of the Court of Appeal. When the Court was set up in 1873, it was the final appellate court, as the jurisdiction of the House of Lords was not established until 1875. The Court 'inherited' the jurisdiction of the Exchequer Chamber and the Court of Appeal in Chancery. As these courts were always considered to have the power to review their own decisions, it would be fair to assume that the new court had inherited this jurisdiction.[59] The argument also returns to *Hutton* v. *Bright*[60] which held that 'every court of justice possesses an inherent power to correct an error in which it had fallen'. What conclusion can be drawn from this argument? As Lord Denning succinctly puts it, *Young* v. *Bristol Aeroplane Co.* 'overruled the practice of a century'.[61] The Court of Appeal is not, as a matter of law, bound to follow its previous decisions. It does so

---

decisions, and if they are wrong, to articulate correct principles. Clearly, against this position is the conventional argument that the Court of Appeal is bound to follow its own previous cases in the area, and if the law is incorrect, it must be altered by an appeal to the House of Lords.
56   The example is the 60-year period before the wrong decision in *Carlisle and Cumberland Banking Co. Ltd. v. Bragg* [1911] 1 KB 489 was corrected in *Gallie v. Lee* [1971] AC 1004.
57   *Davis*, at 280.
58   *Minister of Pensions* v. *Higham* [1948] 2 KB 153, 155.
59   *Davis*, at 195.
60   *Hutton* v. *Bright* (1852) 3 HL Cas. 341.
61   *Davis*, at 196.

as a 'matter of judicial comity'.[62] Arguing that the 1966 Practice Statement effectively overturns the London Tramways case, Lord Denning concludes:

> A rule as to precedent (which any court lays down for itself) is not a rule of law at all. It is simply a practice or usage laid down by the court itself for its own guidance: and, as such, the successors of that court can alter that practice or amend it or set up other guide lines, just as the House of Lords did in 1966.[63]

We are compelled to the conclusion that the Court of Appeal can follow the 1966 Practice Statement and depart from its own decisions if it considers them wrongly decided.

These arguments were not ultimately successful. The conventional form of the doctrine was reasserted by the House of Lords.[64] The court considered the alternative approach to the problem articulated by Sir George Barker P and Shaw LJ in the Court of Appeal.[65] The latter had argued that '*stare decisis* should be relaxed' only when applying a precedent would mean that 'actual and potential victims of violence' would be deprived of the protection afforded them by an Act of Parliament. It was stressed that this situation would be very rare. However, Lord Diplock preferred that the House of Lords should 're-affirm expressly, unequivocally and unanimously' the rule in *Bristol Aeroplane Co*.[66]

Viscount Dilhorne elaborated this argument. It had to be the case that the 1966 Practice Statement applied only to the House of Lords. If it did not, any court could argue that it was not bound by its previous decisions. Lord Denning's argument ignored 'the unique character of the House of Lords sitting judicially'.[67] As the Practice Statement was based on this feature of the House of Lords, it could not be extended to another court. Lord Salmon and Lord Diplock elaborated this point by citing the concluding words of the 1966 Statement: 'This announcement is not intended to affect the use of precedent elsewhere than in this House'.[68] Furthermore, the fact that there are up to 17 Lord Justices in the Court of Appeal meant that, if Lord Denning's arguments were followed to their conclusion, there was the risk that there would be a 'plethora of conflicting decisions' which would lead to great confusion in the law. Lord Salmon's argument goes some way to countering some of Lord Denning's points about the denial of justice, by proposing that the Court of Appeal could be granted a power to grant, when circumstance dictated, the payment of costs out of public funds.

Davis v. *Johnson* is a unique case. Although Lord Denning's arguments make a compelling case for the Court of Appeal to respond to the demand for justice, the House of Lords effectively asserted that there are no exceptions to the priority of general

---

62   Ibid.
63   Ibid., at 197.
64   The House of Lords rejected the argument that the CA could depart from its own decisions if it considered itself to be in error, and affirmed the doctrine with which we are familiar. The CA is bound by its own decisions, except in the exceptions laid down in *Bristol Aeroplane*.
65   *Davis*.
66   Ibid., at 328.
67   Ibid., at 336.
68   Ibid., at 344.

procedural rules. The case shows judicial law making at its most dramatic. Perhaps this is precisely the problem. Lord Denning has an eccentric appreciation of the boundaries of institutional legitimacy. He raises the protection of substantive rights over the general understanding of the limits of judicial creativity. For the purposes of our argument, we need to locate a more modest understanding of the legitimate parameters of judicial legislation. However, as we will see towards the end of the chapter, substantive issues of justice cannot be entirely expelled from judicial practice.

JUDICIAL LAW MAKING

Determining the boundaries of judicial law making is partly a doctrinal and partly a constitutional question. If we require some broad guidelines, a useful place to start is Lord Scarman's speech in *McLoughlin Appellant* v. *O'Brian*.[69] The appeal in this case raised the very question of the relationship between the legislature and the judiciary. Lord Scarman argued that the judge had a jurisdiction over a common law that 'knows no gaps' and no '*casus omissus*'. If this is the case, the task of the common law judge is to adapt the principles of the law to allow a decision to be made on the facts in hand. This may involve the creation of new law. Whatever the case, judicial reasoning begins from 'a baseline of existing principle'. The judge works towards a solution that can be seen as an extension of principle by process of analogy. For Lord Scarman, this is the 'distinguishing feature of the common law': the judicial creation of new law, as the justice of the case demands. This process may involve policy considerations, but the judge can legitimately involve him/herself in this activity, provided that the primary outcome is the formation of new legal principles. In those cases where the formation of principle involves too great an intrusion into the field of policy, the judge must defer to Parliament:

> Here lies the true role of the two law-making institutions in our constitution. By concentrating on principle the judges can keep the common law alive, flexible and consistent, and can keep the legal system clear of policy problems which neither they, nor the forensic process which it is their duty to operate, are equipped to resolve. If principle leads to results which are thought to be socially unacceptable, Parliament can legislate to draw a line or map out a new path.[70]

This argument demarcates quite clearly the role of judge and Parliament. Judicial interpretation keeps the common law 'flexible' and responsive to change, and defers to Parliament on those issues with which the courts are not well equipped to deal. Parliament also acts as a final adjudicator. If the courts make mistakes, they can be corrected by legislation. Whilst this argument is compelling, it is hard to see precisely where the dividing line lies between principle and policy. We will examine this issue below, but it is perhaps worth bearing in mind that where this line falls is a rather

---

69 *McLoughlin* v. *O'Brian* [1983] 1 AC 410.
70 Ibid., at 430.

complex issue that cannot be precisely determined by some general theory. Before we examine this issue, however, it is worth looking at another aspect of Lord Scarman's argument:

> The real risk to the common law is not its movement to cover new situations and new knowledge but lest it should stand still, halted by a conservative judicial approach. If that should happen, and since the 1966 practice direction of the House it has become less likely, there would be a danger of the law becoming irrelevant to the consideration, and inept in its treatment, of modern social problems. Justice would be defeated. The common law has, however, avoided this catastrophe by the flexibility given it by generations of judges.[71]

This is the second reference to justice in this passage, and it might suggest that Lord Scarman's account of judicial creativity is indeed underpinned by such a concept. It is a description of the common law judge as the guardian of the conscience of the common law. The judge is charged with the development of the law in such a way that its principles remain coherent as it develops and adapts itself to changing social conditions. Thus the flexibility of the common law is an element of what makes it just.

However, things are somewhat more complicated. Flexibility is inseparable from the 'risk' of 'uncertainty in the law'. This risk varies with the context of the legal problem under consideration. In other words, problems of uncertainty take a different form in areas of 'commercial transaction' and 'tortious liability for personal injuries'. Returning to the issue of justice, Lord Scarman argues that justice can demand a degree of loss of certainty in the law ('the search for certainty can obstruct the law's pursuit of justice, and can become the enemy of the good'). In the area of damages for nervous shock, certainty could have been achieved by leaving the law as it stood as stated by authorities in the early 1900s.[72] However, the law has had to respond to advances in 'medical science' and technology, and adapt the relevant test for foreseeability. The extent of these developments means that the problem has now become one for Parliament. Arguments of principle have become over-determined by arguments of policy. We could say, then, that one important element of this theory of interpretative justice is that the judge should know when it is necessary for Parliament to intervene.

What do we make of Lord Scarman's presentation of the role of the judge? It would be too bold to argue that all judicial accounts of their task make use of a theory of interpretative justice. However, in looking at some other important cases in which the role of judicial law making has been considered, we can pick up and develop the concern with judicial development of the common law. We will examine a sample of cases from different areas of law.

Regina v. *R.*[73] is perhaps one of the best examples of judicial creativity. The House of Lords determined that a husband could be held guilty of raping his wife. This involved a particularly bold interpretation of the Sexual Offences (Amendment)

---

71   Ibid.
72   *Victorian Railways Commissioners* v. *Coultas*, 13 AC 222; *Dulieu* v. *White & Sons* [1901] 2 KB 669; or in 1970, *Hinz* v. *Berry* [1970] 2 QB 40.
73   *Regina* v. *R.* [1991] 3 WLR 767.

Act 1976, which would otherwise seem to perpetuate the husband's exemption to a charge of rape. Indeed, Lord Lane asserted that this was precisely the conclusion to which a literal interpretation of the Act would come. He proposed a 'radical' solution.[74] It was necessary to:

> disregard the statutory provisions of the Act of 1976 and [thus] ... it is said that it goes beyond the legitimate bounds of judge-made law and trespasses on the province of Parliament. In other words the abolition of a rule of such long standing, despite its emasculation by later decisions, is a task for the legislature and not the courts. There are social considerations to be taken into account, the privacy of marriage to be preserved and questions of potential reconciliation to be weighed which make it an inappropriate area for judicial intervention.[75]

Lord Lane's interpretation of the Act is creative enough to amount to judicial legislation. However, against these 'formidable objections' is the authority of the judge to update the common law to 'changing social attitudes'. Furthermore, the powerful authority *S. v. H.M. Advocate*[76] would appear to be on Lord Lane's side. In the wake of this case, the exception is revealed as 'a fiction'; and 'fiction is a poor basis for the criminal law'. The conclusion of the argument is compelling:

> It seems to us that where the common law rule no longer even remotely represents what is the true position of a wife in present day society, the duty of the court is to take steps to alter the rule if it can legitimately do so in the light of any relevant Parliamentary enactment.[77]

The legitimacy of the court's action is further justified by the fact that it is not creating a new criminal offence, but removing from the 'common law?' an anachronism that is 'offensive' to contemporary social attitudes and standards of behaviour.

R. v. Clegg[78] suggests the kind of situation in which a judge will not legislate. The House of Lords held that on a charge of murder, there was no distinction between the use of excessive force in self-defence, and the use of force in crime prevention. Most importantly for our purposes though, the House of Lords refused to change the law in relation to the reduction of murder to manslaughter, stating that it was a matter for parliamentary legislation.

Why, in this instance, did their lordships refuse to alter the law? Lord Lloyd's speech is instructive. Interestingly, he refers back to Lynch as encouraging judicial legislation. In particular he refers to Lord Wilberforce's argument[79] that asserts that in 'the domain of the common law' judges have the power and authority to interpret legal principles in the light of the facts that are presented to them. There are of course problems with

---

74   Ibid., at 609.
75   Ibid.
76   *S. v. H.M. Advocate* [1989] SLT 469.
77   *Regina* v. *R.* at 610.
78   *R. v. Clegg* [1995] 2 All ER 43.
79   Ibid., 684–5.

this position. As we know, *Lynch* was overruled in *Howe*. There are also important distinctions between the contexts of *Lynch* and *Clegg*. Although the defences of duress, self-defence and the use of force in the prevention of crime were created by judges, the essential difference is that in the latter case Parliament had passed the 1967 Act which did not create a defence that related to the excessive use of force. This would make the present case very different from *Lynch*, precisely because one of the most compelling reasons for overruling this case was the fact that Parliament had not legislated. Lord Simon's speech from *Lynch* thus becomes relevant. Although Lord Simon acknowledges that judges do make law, they have to refrain from so doing when policy matters are involved. Picking up on Lord Simon's principle, Lord Lloyd argues that in distinction to *Reg. v. R.*[80] where the House of Lords did change the common law without waiting for Parliament to legislate, the present issue is indeed one for the legislature.

A variation on this theme can be found in *C. v. DPP*.[81] The case concerned the concept of *doli incapax*, or the presumption that a child between 10 and 14 was incapable of committing a crime. The House of Lords refused to abolish the rule, arguing that although it was not consistently applied, it was necessary for Parliament to legislate. A number of Acts showed a definite legislative position on the presumption of *doli incapax*. Legislation stressed that it was still necessary for the prosecution to show that the child knew that what s/he was doing was 'seriously wrong'.[82] Although this policy had met with objections and criticism, this was not enough to justify judicial legislation. Again, though, this begs the question of where the line between judicial intervention and the correct province of Parliament lies. Lord Lowry is careful to point out that this is indeed a difficult line to draw. He draws support for the refusal to overturn the presumption from *R. v. Kearley*[83] where the House of Lords refused to alter the hearsay rule. This allows certain guidelines to be posited:

(1) If the solution is doubtful, the judges should beware of imposing their own remedy. (2) Caution should prevail if Parliament has rejected opportunities of clearing up a known difficulty or has legislated, while leaving the difficulty untouched. (3) Disputed matters of social policy are less suitable areas for judicial intervention than purely legal problems. (4) Fundamental legal doctrines should not be lightly set aside. (5) Judges should not make a change unless they can achieve finality and certainty.[84]

It is hard to know what the status of these guidelines is. Although *C. v. DPP* has been an influential decision in the area of criminal responsibility, Lord Lowry's thoughts on judicial activism do not appear to have been cited. However, these principles go some way to articulating the areas where judges can safely legislate. The grounding idea appears to be deference to Parliament when the 'solution is doubtful', or Parliament has already considered the issue and refused to legislate. There is also a presumption against changing the law; and change should only come when it brings with it 'finality

---

80   *R. v. R.* [1992] 1 AC 599.
81   *C. v. DPP* [1995] 2 WLR 383.
82   White Paper entitled 'Crime, Justice and Protecting the Public' (1990) (cited by Lord Lowry), p. 26.
83   *R. v. Kearley* [1992] 2 AC 228.
84   Ibid., at 228.

and certainty'. Lord Lowry's guidelines are congruent with those of Lord Lloyd in *Clegg*.

In case it seems like all the examples that we have chosen come from criminal law, consider *Airedale NHS v. Bland*[85] – a case that raised difficult moral, ethical and legal issues about the role to be played by medicine in keeping alive someone in a persistent vegetative state (PVS). On the facts of this case, the court had to determine whether or not the patient's treatment could be continued. Medical opinion was unanimous that there was no hope of recovery. The court found that there could be no further benefit to the patient of continuing medical treatment; and held the medical staff no longer under a duty to continue treatment sustaining the patient's life.

Lord Browne-Wilkinson took the opportunity to consider the correct role of the courts in such a fraught area. Precisely because there was no consensus in society about the correct values that should inform this area of medical ethics, it was not fitting for the judges to 'develop new, all embracing, principles of law' that only reflect 'individual judges' moral stance'. A judge thus must work with the 'existing law'. Although this is in itself 'unsatisfactory', a judge was unsuited to consider the wider issues that were attendant on the decision in this given case. Given these circumstances, Lord Browne-Wilkinson considered that it was 'imperative that the moral, social and legal issues raised by this case should be considered by Parliament'. It was up to Parliament, and the 'democratic process' to give voice to principles that reflected a consensus.

Clearly the legitimate boundaries of judicial law making are difficult to draw precisely. Lord Lowry's guidelines suggest some of the factors that a judge would take into account, however, how these factors are weighed, or, the extent to which other factors may be influential, is impossible to determine in abstraction. That common law interpretation proceeds for the most part without such guidelines being absolutely explicit, suggests they may be embedded within judicial culture in such ways that many elements remain obscure to observers and commentators. A general statement about institutional legitimacy may allow us to glimpse the contours of the practice, but it will never allow us to get 'inside' its operation. We are able, however, to further explore the way in which the practice is transforming itself, and the parameters of institutional legitimacy are being renegotiated.

THE HUMAN RIGHTS ACT AND JUDICIAL LAW MAKING

Has the Human Rights Act impacted on the judges' perception of the boundaries of their law-making powers? This is a difficult question to answer; indeed, to get a good grasp of this issue, it is necessary to engage with the other chapters in this book. Whether or not we are looking at a moment as definitional as *London Tramways* is hard to say. We will see that, while judges are still working within the broad terms of the doctrine of precedent, but in certain areas, the courts have seized the chance to create new law and to make bold decisions.

---

85   *Airedale NHS v. Bland* [1993] 1 All ER 821.

These issues can be further explored if we turn to the series of cases that considered mandatory life sentences. These cases show how the appellate courts are defining their relationship to Parliament after the Human Rights Act.[86] Unless one remembers the political context of these cases, this issue can seem rather abstract. The Crime (Sentences Act) 1997 was passed by Michael Howard, the Conservative Home Secretary. s.2 of the Act required judges to pass mandatory life sentences when a person convicted of a serious offence had a previous conviction for a similar offence. The judges considered this to be an unjustifiable intervention into an area of judicial competence by the executive. One might expect, therefore, that the Human Rights Act would be seized upon as a way of redressing the balance. In *R. v. Offen and others*[87] the Court of Appeal could have issued a declaration of incompatibility; however, it chose to employ a less confrontational approach. It used its discretion to limit the reach of the provisions of s.2 of the 1997 Act. Lord Woolf argued that s.2 would be Convention compliant if the courts interpreted it in such a way that people convicted of a second serious offence would not receive an automatic life sentence if they did not present 'a significant risk to the public'. Assessing whether or not there was a significant risk fell to the courts and had to be considered on the facts of each case.[88]

We will see in the next chapter that in *R. v. A.*, the courts took a very bold approach to s.41 of the Youth Justice and Criminal Evidence Act 1999. As this case is perhaps most usefully read as an exercise in statutory interpretation, we will look at it in detail in the next chapter. To the extent that it shows the court making a particularly creative interpretation of the Act, it could also be seen as an example of judicial law making. Similarly to *R. v. Offen*, the courts did not issue a declaration of incompatibility, and, along with *Offen* perhaps, shows that the courts, under certain circumstances, assert their will against Parliament in the area of criminal evidence and forensic procedure. However, it would be wrong to suggest that this is a general principle, and, like *Offen*, *R. v. A.* needs to be seen as a case limited to its context.

Other cases show the courts using the HRA to develop the common law.[89] *Venables and Thompson*, *Douglas* and *Campbell* are important test cases for judicial creativity, because they are essentially concerned with whether or not the judges will give 'horizontal' effect to the HRA, and bring its effects into areas of private law. The extent to which they are willing to so act is a useful indicator of the degree to which the Act is creating new practices, but once again we should be wary of finding new patterns which do not exist. *Venables and Thompson v. Newsgroup Newspapers*[90] supports this argument. The case concerned two children who were convicted of the murder of another child. Venables and Thompson won the continuation of injunctions preventing newspapers publishing information about them. We need to consider the ratio of the case and identify the precise conditions that the court argued allowed them to employ the HRA in a dispute between private parties.

---

86 See in particular *Re S* [2002] 2 WLR 720.
87 *R. v. Offen and others* [2001] 1 WLR 253.
88 Ibid., 277.
89 Wadham, J. and Mountfield, H. 2003. Wadham has argued that the courts have a duty to develop the common law in line with Convention rights by virtue of 6(3).
90 *Venables and Thompson v. Newsgroup Newspapers* [2001] 2 WLR 1038.

In granting the injunctions, the court argued that it could protect confidential information in 'exceptional cases where it was strictly necessary'. Given the notoriety of Venables and Thompson, it was very likely that they would be seriously injured if the press did reveal their identities or whereabouts on their release from custody. Most interestingly, the court argued that:

> The ECHR applied in this case via the obligation on the courts in the Human Rights Act, even though the defendant newspapers were not a public authority and the dispute was one between private parties. The claimants' rights under Articles 2, 3 and 8 of the ECHR were at risk, and had to be balanced against Article 10.

What can we summarise from this argument? It would appear that the court will utilise the HRA in disputes between private parties only in exceptional circumstances, and where there were significant human rights issues at stake. This probably means that the courts will refrain from employing the HRA in all but the most extreme cases.

This authority can be placed against *Douglas* v. *Hello*.[91] On very different facts, the court showed that it was willing to protect the privacy of celebrities against journalists using particularly intrusive methods of photography. Consider Sedley LJ's argument that the courts should recognise a right of privacy. Sedley LJ begins by pointing out that the common law and equity have developed slowly and 'by uneven degrees'; moreover, they have tended to be 'reactive'. Arguably, the time has come for the articulation of 'discrete principles of law' that relate to the protection of privacy. Why is this?

> The reasons are twofold. First, equity and the common law are today in a position to respond to an increasingly invasive social environment by affirming that everybody has a right to some private space. Secondly, and in any event, the Human Rights Act 1998 requires the courts of this country to give appropriate effect to the right to respect for private and family life set out in Article 8 of the European Convention on Human Rights and Fundamental Freedoms.[92]

So, in *Douglas*, the court felt that it was now necessary to develop a 'positive institutional obligation to respect privacy'. Clearly, this is a bold decision, and the courts had been struggling with the issue of privacy for a long time prior to this case. What *Douglas* does not suggest is that, in all areas of law, the courts will take upon themselves the obligation to extend both the common law and the range of the HRA to cover private parties. Nevertheless, *Douglas* does suggest that the courts will take seriously the need, in certain situations, to make sure that a limited definition of public authority does not lead to rights abuses.

In *Campbell* v. *MGM*[93] the House of Lords expanded the law of confidentiality so as to cover pictures taken of Naomi Campbell[94] and details of the therapy that she was undergoing for drug addiction. As Baroness Hale pointed out, the case concerned the

---

91 *Douglas* v. *Hello* [2001] QB 967.
92 Ibid., 997.
93 *Campbell* v. *MGM* [2004] 2 AC 457.
94 Baroness Hale pointed out that 'even the judges know who Naomi Campbell is', p. 493.

balancing of human rights 'between two private persons'.[95] In holding that Campbell's rights under Article 8 took precedence over MGM's[96] freedom of expression under Article 10, the House clearly saw the Act as creating remedies available against a private company.[97] The argument made by the court was not that the Act created new causes of action 'between private persons', but only to the extent that there is 'a relevant cause of action'. If there was a relevant cause of action, then the court was bound to act 'compatibly with Convention rights'. Although the case was difficult because it required the courts to balance two competing rights, we can try and draw some general conclusions.

Despite a three-to-two split in the House, there appeared to be some consensus on the question of the Act's capacity to bind private parties. Baroness Hale appeared to accept Lord Woolf's claim in *A. v. B.*[98] that the HRA created 'new parameters'[99] for breach of confidence, a position which Lord Hope appeared to agree, referring to the 'new breadth and strength' that Articles 8 and 10 provide. The minority judgments seemed to concur on the point that Articles 8 and 10 are as applicable to 'disputes between individuals ... as they are in disputes between individuals and a public authority'.[100] Lord Hoffmann cited Sedley LJ's judgment in *Douglas v. Hello*, as 'perceptive[ly]' identifying that the approach under the HRA takes a 'different view' of the 'underlying value which the law protects'.[101] The duty to protect a confidence is now based on 'the protection of human autonomy and dignity'.[102] This begged the question of why this right should be applicable against the state, but not against a private party.[103] For Lord Hoffmann, however, the instant case fell under the old law, and did not require a resolution of these broader points.

Commentators have been critical of the reasoning in *Campbell*, and suggest that it contains no clear statement of the extent to which the judges will elaborate horizontal effect of the Act in the area of breach of confidence. Later cases such as *Re S*.[104] and *Douglas III*[105] do not provide any greater clarification.[106] However, while not articulating a position on the horizontal effect of the Act, the judges have 'left themselves the ability to bring Convention principles into private law'.[107] Their reluctance to offer clear principles perhaps allows the maximum space for manoeuvre. The 'flexibility' of 'judicial reasoning' is retained.[108] Within the terms of the generally accepted position,

---

95 Ibid., 493.
96 MGM Ltd was the company that owned the Mirror Newspaper that had published the pictures and the story.
97 The House of Lords held that the photographs and the details of the treatment were 'were akin to the private and confidential information contained in medical records and their publication required specific justification'. Ibid., 458.
98 *A v. B plc* [2003] QB 195., cited p. 494.
99 Ibid.
100 Per Lord Nicholls, ibid., 465.
101 Ibid., 472.
102 Ibid.
103 Ibid.
104 *Re S* [2005] 1 AC 593.
105 *Douglas III* [2006] QB 967.
106 Phillipson (2007: 167–72).
107 Ibid., 172.
108 Ibid.

that the Act does not create new cause of action for private parties that replace common law actions, there are a range of possible positions. These allow an individual judge to make the Convention applicable at the level of procedure, remedy, or even to invoke the underlying applicability of the 'values'[109] of Convention rights. How does this relate to judicial law making? Although we cannot indicate any clear definition of the extent to which the Act will be applied to private parties, the very fact that such a debate surrounds the issue testifies to the power of the judges to develop the common law. The debate about horizontal effect only makes sense if we acknowledge that this power exists. It would be hard to make any sense of the judgments considered in this section unless one agreed that the development of the law was driven by the judges and not Parliament.

THE HUMAN RIGHTS ACT AND PERTURBATIONS IN JUDICIAL PRACTICE

That the HRA introduced a disturbance or a perturbation into the judicial practice of precedent is evidenced by the cases *R. v. Lambert*[110] and *R. v. Kansal*.[111] We will discuss them in detail in a later chapter. At this point, we need to understand how *Lambert* and *Kansal* raise questions about the operation of the doctrine of precedent. In *Lambert* the House of Lords held that the HRA should not have retrospective effect. The same question was raised in *Kansal*, and their lordships felt that, although *Lambert* was a doubtful authority, it should be followed. Thus *Kansal* shows the judges feeling their way into a new jurisprudence of the Human Rights Act; their different approaches all suggest the various orientating points that a new interpretative practice might take.

The tentative nature of the arguments in *Kansal* is indicated by the slightly different approaches to the issue taken by the majority. Lord Slynn argued that *Lambert* should be followed as the case was close enough in fact and law to be bound by the earlier decision. The fact that the House, almost identical in its composition to that which decided *Lambert*, was dealing with 'a transitional provision' also made it wrong to depart from *Lambert*. Lord Lloyd argued that *Lambert* had to be followed unless the 1966 Practice Statement applied. Lord Hutton argued that although the decision in *Lambert* was probably wrong, it was still an 'eminently possible one'[112] and the case should be followed. His argument focused on the 1966 Practice Statement and *Fitzleet Estates v. Cherry*[113] where Lord Wilberforce contended that the Practice Statement did not allow an appellant to argue that the minority should be preferred over the majority. Lord Wilberforce went on to say that: 'Nothing could be more undesirable, in fact, than to permit litigants, after a decision has been given by this House with all appearance of finality, to return to this House in the hope that a differently

---

109   Ibid.
110   *R. v. Lambert* [2001] HRLR 55.
111   *R. v. Kansal* [2001] UKHL 62.
112   Para 111.
113   *Fitzleet Estates v. Cherry* [1977] 1 WLR 1345, 1349.

constituted committee might be persuaded to take the view which its predecessors rejected'.[114]

Lord Steyn was perhaps more forceful in his opinion about *Lambert*. He argued that it was wrongly decided, but should still be followed. He referred to Lord Reid's argument in *R. v. Knuller*.[115] In *Shaw*, the House of Lords had decided that the crime of conspiracy to corrupt public morals did exist in English law, and Lord Reid had dissented. However, in arguing that *Shaw* should be followed, Lord Reid pointed out that the 1966 Practice Statement did not mean that 'whenever we think that a previous decision was wrong we should reverse it'. The requirement for certainty in law was paramount. Precisely because it was only transitional provisions of the Act that were at stake, *Lambert* should be the binding authority.

Lord Hope dissented. His argument was that in 'a developing field of jurisprudence' it was legitimate to depart from *Lambert* in order that mistakes be swiftly corrected; besides *Lambert* was out of line with *ex parte Kebilene*, which was a majority decision of the Lords. The only way to resolve the deadlock was for the 'the present appeal to be reargued before a panel of seven Law Lords'.[116] This is because a panel of five judges should not 'depart from *Lambert*' and the effect of their decision on other cases 'in the pipeline' should be taken into account. The nature of Lord Hope's arguments, was that they should be seriously considered by a panel of seven law lords. Lord Lloyd refers to *Lewis v. Attorney General of Jamaica*[117] and the analogous argument that the Privy Council used the power to overrule its own previous decisions.

Despite the differences of opinion shown in the reasoning in *Kansal*, perhaps the most interesting factor is the assertion of the importance of a coherent practice of precedent in a time of doubt. It is perhaps not so much motivated by a political conservatism, as an inbuilt appreciation that a practice takes its primary orientating points from what has been; from the way in which people have behaved in the past. These issues returned in two later cases. In *Leeds City Council v. Price/Kay v. London Borough of Lambeth*[118] Lord Bingham outlined the key issue:

> Whether a court which would ordinarily be bound to follow the decisions of another court higher in the domestic curial hierarchy is, or should be, no longer bound to follow that decision if it appears to be inconsistent with a later ruling of the court in Strasbourg.[119]

To understand this question, we have to reconstruct the context, and this takes us to a line of cases that considered Article 8 in the light of fundamental principles of the

---

114 Para 110.
115 *R. v. Knuller (Publishing, Printing and Promotions Ltd)* [1973] AC 435.
116 Para 19.
117 *Lewis v. Attorney General of Jamaica* [2001] 2 AC 50. Lord Hoffman asserted that: 'no judicial system could do society's work if it eyed each issue afresh in every case that raised it ... Indeed, the very concept of the rule of law underlying our own Constitution requires such continuity over time that a respect for precedent is, by definition, indispensable'.
118 *Leeds City Council v. Price/Kay v. London Borough of Lambeth* [2006] UKHL 10.
119 Ibid., para 40.

law of property. In *Harrow LBC* v. *Qazi* the plaintiff had attempted to use an argument based on Article 8 to defeat possession proceedings brought against him by the local authority. Despite the dissent of Lords Bingham and Steyn, the House asserted that property law rights could not be limited by Article 8. In *Connor* v. *UK*[120] the ECtHR found that there had been a breach of Article 8 on similar facts relating to the eviction of travellers from local authority land. Strasbourg held that the council had to establish that there was a compelling reason for the interference with Article 8 rights. In *Leeds City Council* v. *Price/Kay* v. *London Borough of Lambeth* a specially convened House of seven law lords had to reconcile *Qazi* and *Connors*. They did so by arguing that someone who claimed that his or her Article 8 rights had been breached must be given an opportunity to show that Article 8 did apply. However, there was no obligation on the party seeking to assert their property law rights to show that their argument was justified.

Having reconstructed the context, we can turn to the issue of precedent. The Court of Appeal had considered themselves bound by *Qazi*, but this case was out of line with *Connors*. What was the correct course of action? The civil liberties groups who had intervened in the case urged that a lower court should be entitled to follow ECtHR rulings clearly inconsistent with earlier domestic authorities. This course of action would be open to a court when a Strasbourg case laid down a clear principle that comprehended both Convention law and domestic law and was not inconsistent with any relevant statute. The House of Lords did not agree. Lord Bingham's leading judgment began by stressing the centrality of the doctrine of precedent to the development of English law. He quoted the 1966 Practice Statement, and returned to the words with which we are now familiar: precedent is 'an indispensable foundation' to the common law.[121] An integral part of the jurisprudence of the 1966 Practice Statement is that it only applies to the House of Lords. Lord Hailsham's argument in *Broome* v. *Cassell & Co Ltd*[122] is not cited because it is 'too well known to call for repetition'.[123] If Lord Denning was unable to disturb this principle, it is unlikely that human rights will upset the fundamental terms of judicial practice.

The House had been presented with arguments that called for a modification of the rules of precedent. They rested on assertions that a lower court could follow a Strasbourg ruling in preference to one of the House of Lords where there is clear inconsistency between the ECtHR and the English authority. However, as Lord Bingham argued, the present appeal shows that inconsistency is itself difficult to determine. The appellants and the Court of Appeal in *Leeds* v. *Price* had argued that there was a clear inconsistency between *Qazi* and *Connors*; the respondents and the Court of Appeal had taken the opposite position. Echoing the criticisms made of Lord Denning's attempts to apply the Practice Statement to the Court of Appeal, Lord Bingham invoked the spectre of confusion that would haunt the common law if the settled arrangements for the creation of authorities were disturbed. The appellant's argument suggested that 'different county court and High Court judges, and even different divisions of the Court of Appeal'

---

120   *Connor* v. *UK* [2004] 40 EHRR 9.
121   Supra n.110, at para 42.
122   *Broome* v. *Cassell & Co Ltd* [1972] AC 1027 at 1053–5.
123   Supra n. 110, at para 42.

might take 'differing views of the same issue'.[124] In face of the challenge of human rights law, then, we fall back on our trusted institutions. The certainty of the common law is achieved by 'adhering, even in the Convention context, to our rules of precedent'.[125] If an authority is inconsistent with a Strasbourg ruling, then it is best dealt with as an appeal – and the House of Lords given the opportunity to produce a definitive statement of the law.

Lord Bingham supports his position with a second argument. The Convention requires a constructive dialogue between national courts and the ECtHR. The ECtHR has the authority to pronounce on the Convention and the correct interpretation of its principles. However, in its 'decisions on particular cases'[126] the ECtHR allows a significant 'margin of appreciation'[127] to national courts, and in particular to their understanding of the facts of the case. This means that the national court must decide precisely how the Convention applies and 'how the principles expounded in Strasbourg should be applied in the special context of national legislation'.[128] If the national courts have to apply Convention jurisprudence, then they must do so in the prevalent terms of a national legal system: thus, as far as the UK is concerned 'the ordinary rules of precedent should apply'.[129]

There is one 'partial exception' to this principle. In *D. v. East Berkshire Community NHS Trust*[130] the Court of Appeal had argued that the House of Lords in *X (Minors) v. Bedfordshire CC*[131] should not be followed. The decision in *X v. Bedfordshire* was prior to the Human Rights Act and, based on reasoning, that and 'policy considerations' those were inconsistent with the Act.[132] The House of Lords in *D* had agreed with the Court of Appeal.[133] Note, however, the special considerations that applied in this case. The 1995 ruling of the House of Lords had contained no reference to the Convention. Furthermore, the applicants in *D* had successfully argued a breach of Article 3 in Strasbourg, and obtained significant damages. Lord Bingham notes: 'Such a course is not permissible save where the facts are of that extreme character'.[134]

What do we make of this? Could the case be seen as a failed opportunity to re-invent both the doctrine and judicial practice? Harris has suggested, albeit in a different context, that the principle of overruling needs to be reconsidered.[135] He argues that the present practice of allowing wrong precedents to stand stresses the value of certainty at the cost of the 'quality of justice'. He argues that the better approach would be for the final appellate court to 'depart from precedent after systematically weighing up all the competing considerations'.[136] In some cases there may be compelling reasons for the

---

124 Ibid., para 43.
125 Ibid.
126 Ibid., para 44.
127 Ibid.
128 Ibid.
129 Ibid.
130 *D. v. East Berkshire Community NHS Trust* [2004] QB 558.
131 *X (Minors) v. Bedfordshire CC* [1995] 2 AC 633.
132 Supra n. 110, at para 45.
133 *X (Minors) v. Bedfordshire CC* [2005] UKHL 23.
134 Supra n. 110, at para 45.
135 Harris (2002).
136 Ibid., 427.

decision to stand, in others the weight of the argument may be to overrule and restate the correct principles. The doubts expressed by the Lords suggest that the issues raised in *Leeds City Council* v. *Price/Kay* v. *London Borough of Lambeth* were not crisp enough to make this case a clear authority for the need to redefine precedent in such a dramatic way. In a later chapter, we will see that *Leeds City Council* v. *Price/Kay* v. *London Borough of Lambeth* is inconsistent with the so called mirror principle that the Lords have established should guide the relationship between domestic courts and Strasbourg. This might indicate the reassertion of traditional practices in the face of a developing human rights jurisprudence, but we have to be a little careful with this argument as it does raise problematic issues about the relationship of common law and European human rights law. Perhaps we can indicate at this point no more than the case suggests the perturbations the practice of precedent is experiencing in the wake of the HRA.

CONCLUSION

Historical practices of their nature evolve. Precedent is fundamental to the institutional structures of the common law and it would be hard to think about the impact of human rights on judicial practice in the terms of the hierarchy of courts, and the debates centring on *Schorsh Mier* and *Davis* v. *Johnson*. While *Kay* shows that the courts are not suddenly going to depart from the hierarchic structure of the common law, human rights law has, in certain areas, been the spur to the creation of new law. It would be presumptuous to see this as a constitutional revolution. After the Human Rights Act, judges are doing precisely what they did before the Act came into force: making law. It may be that the mechanisms of the Human Rights Act lead to a reworking of judicial practice, subtly shifting the sense of where the legitimate boundaries of judicial legislation lie. Ultimately, this is what makes it difficult to offer any final conclusion. Practices take time to develop, and time to shift the terms in which they are performed. It will be interesting to see the precise form that the judicial practice of precedent will assume – and the tensions between flexibility and hierarchy balance out.

4

THE JUDICIAL PRACTICE OF STATUTORY INTERPRETATION

An act of parliament is the exercise of the highest authority that this kingdom acknowledges upon earth. It hath power to bind every subject in the land, and the dominions thereunto belonging; nay, even the King himself, if particularly named therein. And it can not be altered, amended, dispensed with, suspended or repealed, but in the same forms and by the same authority of parliament.[1]

Parliament generally changes law for the worse, and ... the business of the judges is to keep the mischief of its interference within the narrowest bounds.[2]

I shall ... state, as precisely as I can, what I understand from the decided cases to be the principles on which the Courts of Law act in construing instruments in writing; and a statute is an instrument in writing. In all cases the object is to see what is the intention expressed by the words used. But, from the imperfection of language, it is impossible to know what that intention is without inquiring farther, and seeing what the circumstances were with reference to which the words were used, and what was the object, appearing from those circumstances, which the person using them had in view; for the meaning of words varies according to the circumstances with respect to which they were used.[3]

I remember only too well my first intervention as a new Minister at the Treasury on the Finance Bill in the very early hours of the morning on a subject about which I knew absolutely nothing but on which I had a marvellously thick book of briefing from the Inland Revenue. I appropriately read out the response to some detailed points that had been made by one of the Opposition spokesmen who stood up afterwards to say how well I had dealt with the point he had raised and welcomed my first intervention in Finance Bill Committees. However, I discovered from my private office afterwards that I had read out the wrong reply to the amendment. Clearly, it made not the slightest bit of difference.[4]

---

1   Blackstone, *Commentaries*, Vol. I, p. 185*.
2   Pollock (1882: 85).
3   Lord Blackburn in *River Wear Commissioners* v. *Adamson* [1877] 2 AC 743 at 763.
4   Lord Hayhoe, as reported in *Hansard*, 27 March 1996 reflecting upon the circumstances in which 'explanations' on proposed legislation are given in parliament. In the Westminster Parliament, exchanges sometimes take place late at night in nearly empty chambers while members have dinner, drink and discuss in places often away from the actual building but are called back to vote. Often a bill reflects a party political debate with party 'whips' ensuring that party members vote on one side or the other. The questions are often difficult but political warfare sometimes leaves little time for reflection. These are not ideal conditions for the making of authoritative statements about the meaning of a clause in a bill.

INTRODUCTION

We begin with a mixture of views on constitutionalism, political reality and separation of powers therein expressed. Statutory interpretation as performed by the judiciary is a subset of constitutional practice. The first, from Blackstone, can be seen as a representative statement of the doctrine of parliamentary supremacy. The second, from Pollock, may be seen as a more or less accurate description of the judicial mindset in Victorian times. While the common law could be presumed to be the repository of the community's collective wisdom as expressed through its judiciary, legislation was the imposition of a political will for reform. This could, and was perhaps best presumed to be, partisan and unreflective of the nuances of social life. This approach led to restrictive interpretation by literalist methods which sometimes blocked social progress. It remained the approach of English judges until some time after the Second World War, yet Lord Blackburn's comments show that it is not correct to hold that one approach dominated.

The first part of this chapter outlines the concept of the contemporary practice of statutory interpretation. Understanding statutory interpretation has not been helped by references – in decades of student orientated texts at least – of a model of 'rules' of interpretation, which, if they ever did convey any feel of what went on, were a relatively constrained account of options in practice. Instead we need to see it as a dynamic engagement with legal texts. We will not in this chapter present a guide to interpretation; instead, after setting the scene, we will concentrate upon certain recent developments, namely the impact of *Pepper* v. *Hart*, European methods of interpretation and the interpretative provisions of the Human Rights Act 1998. Our stance is to focus on the parameters or limits of judicial interpretation. Although the vast bulk of everyday practices of interpretation seem to pose few constitutional issues, we argue that the general practice operates within constraints of institutional legitimacy; any act of statutory interpretation involves matters of constitutional propriety. Indeed, writing in 1999 about the Human Rights Act, Lord Irvine (1999) spoke of the judiciary as 'an integral component in a constitutional machinery that seeks to secure accountable government'. Similarly, Lord Steyn has argued: 'The language used by Parliament does not interpret itself. Somebody must interpret and apply it. A democracy may, and almost invariably does, entrust the task of interpretation to the neutral decision-making of the judiciary'.[5] What are the current limits of this interpretive role? We will suggest that contemporary practice can be seen as evolving. informed by a democratic vision where the courts and Parliament operate in dialogue about the relationship of legislation and human rights.

STATUTORY INTERPRETATION AND INSTITUTIONAL LEGITIMACY

Statutory interpretation has very little to do with so-called 'rules' of interpretation. Whether or not these rules accurately reflect the approach of the courts in the past,

---

5 Lord Steyn (2004: 248).

they are largely irrelevant to the contemporary practice. At best, the priority of the literal approach stressed a general problematic: interpretation needs to be kept within certain constitutional constraints.[6] The main question in this chapter is thus a variation on one of the key points of the previous chapter: what picture can be drawn of the constitutional arrangements in which interpretation takes place? To what extent can interpretation be seen as law making, and, if so, what are the acceptable constraints of judicial legislation? This is, of course, a question of institutional legitimacy. Again we may have settled on a practice wherein interpretation takes place on a daily basis in such a fashion that the majority of cases do not appear to raise this problem of where the boundaries of interpretation lie. If the language of a statute is clear then interpretation is presumably entirely secondary to the application of the statute to the facts. While all interpretation occurs within an interpretative community and there are interesting issues in explaining interpretation in an increasingly pluralist social body, we are more concerned in this text with the constitutional propriety of interpretation in those instances where statutory language is ambiguous or capable of carrying different meanings, or where the law places on judges a particular set of interpretative demands stemming either from European law or the interpretative provisions of the Human Rights Act. The choice of one meaning rather than another may amount to law making. As the courts cannot be seen to overstep the boundaries in their legislative role, and intrude upon the province of Parliament, the real issue in terms of the constitution of the practice is where this boundary lies.

In elaborating this issue, we need to remind ourselves of some important arguments from the previous chapter. One should be careful when discussing rules of statutory interpretation not to impose too great a degree of rigidity or a level of generality that fails to reflect what the judges are actually doing when they interpret statute. There are a couple of points to bear in mind. Any discussion of these 'techniques' as 'rules' is problematic, not least because we will be concerned with a practice as a rule in a non-legal sense: a rule as a guide to action. Future references of the rules of statutory interpretation will be understood as referring to the techniques that compose judicial practice. There is a second problem. Statements of practice in one case may or may not be understandable as general theories of interpretation. Judges tend not to give methodological statements that reflect in a general sense on what they are doing. This begs another question: if judges practice statutory interpretation without a textbook, then why do textbooks have chapters on statutory interpretation?

This chapter offers an engagement with a number of key cases in order to try and determine how different judges in different areas of law deploy the techniques of interpretation. It is only at this level that anything useful or relevant can be said about statutory interpretation.

---

6 In *Duport Steels Ltd* v. *Sirs* [1980] 1 WLR 142, Lord Scarman stressed: 'In the field of statute law the judge must be obedient to the will of Parliament as expressed in the enactments. In this field Parliament makes and unmakes the law, the judge's duty is to interpret and to apply the law, not to change it to meet the judge's idea of what justice requires. Interpretation does, of course, imply in the interpreter a power of choice where differing constructions are possible. But our law requires the judge to choose the construction which in his judgment best meets the legislative purpose of the enactment' (p. 169).

It is worth considering another point that will run through this chapter. If we were trying to describe contemporary judicial practice, then we would have to take into account European 'purposive' methods of interpretation. The rules of interpretation have the virtue of reminding us that – at least in a historical perspective – purposive interpretation was always part of the common law.[7] Indeed, Twining has argued that purposive interpretation by British judges is justified not by references to European law, but to common sense.[8] Twining argues that interpretation of statutes can be analysed as falling into two stages. The first stage is to acquire a general sense of both the legal and factual context and the intention of the legislature; the next stage is to read the particular words in their primary and natural meaning if they are ordinary words, or according to their technical meaning. If this leads to an absurd interpretation, the interpreter may put forward an interpretation that avoids the absurdity. With reference to this second stage, there are limits to the kind of materials of which the interpreter can make use. Another misleading aspect of statutory interpretation is that it suggests that there may be more of a clear distinction between literal and purposive interpretation than there in fact is in practice. It suggests a rather artificial approach that imagines a judge asking first about whether the words are unambiguous and if not, then how can they be read so as to give effect to the intention of Parliament.[9]

Twining *is* describing modern judicial practice. It is largely determined by pragmatism, and an engagement with the language of the Act in question in its legal context. This goes a long way to suggesting how judges approach statutory interpretation in those cases where no European or human rights issues might impinge; or, indeed, where no reference to *Pepper* v. *Hart* is necessary. We need, therefore, to move towards an engagement with these problematic and developing areas. However, for the moment we can ask some further questions about the suppositions that inform modern practice, and examine the role of the presuppositions of statutory interpretation.[10] The presumptions reflect the cast of the common law and the orientation of practice towards

---

7   The literal approach reflects the relatively recent dominance of Parliament over the courts.
8   Twining (1992: 368). We also need to be careful with the argument that community or civilian manners of interpretation should be adopted, or are being adopted by English judges. The problem is in part definitional. It is not entirely clear what is meant by continental ways of interpretations, other than stating that they are purposive. As the mischief rule is purposive, English judges have always had recourse to purposive interpretation; *Re Marr* would also suggest that the judges themselves do not necessarily see purposive interpretation as European. It is a question more of preserving the idea that the court defers to Parliament. In European law purposive interpretation may be legitimate, but there is the risk that if followed too far, it would involve the courts in making rather than interpreting the law. Besides, as Twining writes: 'the pragmatism of English judges makes discussion of the proposition that they ought in general to adopt a purposive approach a little unrealistic'.
9   Glanville Williams has suggested that a more accurate description of the judge's practice would read as follows: 'What was the statute trying to do? Will the proposed interpretation [be] ruled out by the language of the statute?' What does this mean? He explains: 'literal and purposive interpretation may be seen to represent varying emphases on how these questions are to be answered; in particular, on how far a judge is prepared to go in deciding whether a proposed interpretation is or is not sustained by the language of the statute. In short, context, language and purpose are all relevant, but there is still no settled priority rules for weighting these factors'. Cited in Twining (1992: 369).
10 The presumptions are: against the alteration of the common law; that *mens rea* should be an element in criminal offences; against the retrospective application of statute; against the deprivation of individual's liberty, property or rights; a presumption that legislation does not apply to the Crown; a presumption against breach of international law and a presumption that words take their meaning from their context.

pragmatic questions of context and sense. A review of the presumptions may develop this argument.

The first presumption, against the alteration of the common law, suggests that interpretation is inherently conservative: the law appears as a repository of meanings that are authorised by its history. Thus, rather than presuming a change in the law, a judge will presume that the law is coherent and without gaps. There are also presumptions that have a particular slant towards rights or liberties.[11] That the Human Rights Act contains an interpretative provision suggests that these presumptions may not have been as effective as they might have been in protecting rights and liberties. Nevertheless, we could say that common law interpretation appears to have always had a commitment to preserving these values. The presumptions against breach of international law can be seen as informing a notion that common law is coherent with international law, unless Parliament has stated otherwise. It suggests some interesting points about the relationship of national and international legal norms, but we cannot engage with this material in this chapter. The presumption that legislation does not apply to the Crown is historic and suggests the privileges accorded to the Crown. The seventh presumption reflects on the aids to construction that can be utilised. Within this catalogue, there is a basic distinction between intrinsic and extrinsic evidence, and a grouping of rules that relate to presumptions about how certain verbal formulations are to be understood. We could say that this represents the legal employment of certain grammatical rules. These rules reflect more on the micro-economic level of interpretation, and stress that statutory interpretation is inherently a form of textual close reading. It is as much about resolving grammatical and syntactical problems as it is about the operation of specifically legal principles of interpretation. The presumptions remind us that statutory interpretation is about rules that are necessarily involved in acts of reading that operate within a specifically legal context.

PEPPER V. HART[12]

To return to our principle of analysis: we will examine statutory interpretation through a close reading of some central cases. One of the most important cases defining contemporary practice is *Pepper* v. *Hart*. Here the Judicial Committee of the House of Lords sat nine strong (over half of the total membership of the Judicial Committee) to hear an appeal in which the plaintiff, irrespective of the clear words of the Act, claimed that the movers of the bill had a quite different intention for the Act than the one put forward by the Inland Revenue. The minister had actually said on the floor of the House of Commons that teachers in private schools who had their children take up spare places at discounted fees would not be taxed on the difference as if this was a financial benefit in kind, whereas the Inland Revenue wanted to tax the teachers as if the teachers had received the benefit of the discounted school fees (as the clear words of the Act seemed to indicate). The Lords took the opportunity to consider whether when

---

11 The requirement that criminal offences have *mens rea*; that statute does not apply retrospectively; that people are not to be deprived of rights and liberties.
12 *Pepper* v. *Hart* [1993] 1 All ER, 42.

applying a statute the judges should consider only the words of the Act or whether they could look at *Hansard* to see evidence of the clear intention of the progenitors. They decided in favour of the teachers.

To what extent did *Pepper* v. *Hart* revolutionise methods of interpretation by allowing judges access to parliamentary materials to which they would not otherwise have access? The case shows that defining the parameters of judicial interpretative practice involves questions of constitutional propriety and the very function of the forensic process. Indeed, the subsequent case law attempts to define a line between the political and the judicial that may be very difficult to hold.

Prior to *Pepper* v. *Hart*, the courts had not been able to look at the *Hansard* debates[13] as an aid to interpreting statute. Although the case changed this rule, it went on to narrowly define the occasions when a court could make reference to *Hansard*. To enable a reference to *Hansard*, legislation must be ambiguous. To resolve the ambiguities, the court can make use of ministerial statements. This clearly means that the courts cannot make use of statements made by MPs in debate or argument, and the statements themselves have to be clear.

How can this approach be justified? Why should the rule that had always structured judicial practice be relaxed? Lord Browne-Wilkinson began the leading speech in *Pepper* v. *Hart* by reviewing the arguments as to why references to *Hansard* should still be prohibited. The primary reason was constitutional. The courts must look only to the words used in the Act, as otherwise there is a risk of judicial legislation. Lord Browne-Wilkinson then touched upon a related issue. *Hansard* material may not be forensically suitable, as it may have been said in the heat of debate, or from a politically partisan position. Difficulties in providing access to definitive text of debates and cost implications had also militated against the use of *Hansard* in the court.[14]

If these are the arguments for preserving the existing practice, what are the issues that compel change? It would appear that practice itself has already moved beyond the constraints of the old approach:

> the courts have departed from the old literal approach of statutory construction and now adopt a purposive approach, seeking to discover the Parliamentary intention lying behind the words used and construing the legislation so as to give effect to, rather than thwart, the intentions of Parliament. Where the words used by Parliament are obscure or ambiguous, the Parliamentary material may throw considerable light not only on the mischief which the Act was designed to remedy but also on the purpose of the legislation and its anticipated effect.[15]

This speech stresses that there is a historical shift in judicial interpretation. This is, in part, due to the impact of purposive styles of European interpretation; it is no wonder that *Pepper* builds on *Pickstone* v. *Freemans*.[16] Note that a difference has

---

13   The official record of debates in Parliament.
14   Against this position, the Law Commissions reporting in 1969 and the Renton Committee had recommended that the rule outlawing the use of *Hansard* be reconsidered.
15   *Pepper*, at 633.
16   *Pickstone* v. *Freemans* [1988] 3 WLR 265.

to be observed in the interpretation of domestic and European legislation. It is with the latter that the court can be 'more flexible'.[17] However, there is another factor in the argument that suggests that purposive interpretation cannot be so neatly limited to European law. Lord Griffith's speech elaborates this point. He argued that the increasing volume of legislation carries with it the risk that 'ambiguities in statutory language' are not apparent at the time the bill is drafted. It would seem that the form of judicial practice had not kept up with practical developments. How should the new approach be defined? It is necessary to return to fundamental principles. The task of the court is to interpret the intention of Parliament. If the court cannot use *Hansard* to interpret ambiguous language then it may become frustrated in this task.[18]

What does this mean? How is the purposive approach to be defined? It is a question of carefully plotting the parameters that are discoverable in the cases where *Pepper v. Hart* has been applied.[19] In *R. (on the application of Spath Holme Ltd) v. Secretary of State for the Environment, Transport and the Regions*,[20] the House of Lords considered an argument that it was necessary to make a reference to *Hansard*. The reference would show that the powers of a minister granted by the Landlord and Tenants Act 1985 to restrict rent increases were narrow and applied only to the restriction of inflation in the economy. Rejecting this approach, the court stressed the importance of the first limb of the ratio of *Pepper v. Hart*. Unless this first condition was satisfied, there was a danger that any case that raised an issue of statutory construction would necessitate disproportionate costs as lawyers researched the relevance of parliamentary statements. However, there is also a constitutional element to the House of Lord's argument that returns us to one of the structuring concerns of statutory interpretation. Whereas it may be acceptable to rely on the statements of the minister sponsoring the bill, the court cannot consider parliamentary exchanges in debate. Such matters are unsuited for the forensic process. Furthermore, such scrutiny comes close to breaching

---

17   The precise parameters of this flexibility will have to be defined by subsequent case law.
18   *Pepper*, at 617. In summary: Lord Browne-Wilkinson's guidelines show that a reference to *Hansard* is only acceptable when three conditions applied. First, the legislation in question was 'ambiguous or obscure, or led to an absurdity'. Second, that the material to which reference would be made were 'statements by a minister or other promoter of the Bill' with material that might support these statements which, third, had to themselves amount to a clear statement.
19   *Melluish (Inspector of Taxes) Appellant v. B.M.I. No. 3* [1996] AC 454 affirmed that the rule in *Pepper* was narrow; the case should not be seen as an opportunity to begin to 'widen' the kinds of materials that could be considered to interpret legislation. This rule was clarified still further in *Three Rivers DC v. Bank of England No. 2* [1996] 2 All ER 363. The court asserted that speeches made in Parliament could be used by a court to ascertain both the true meaning of statutory language and the intention of Parliament in passing a particular Act. More recently, the issue of the correct use of *Hansard* has arisen with respect to construing the Human Fertilization and Embryology Act 1990 s. 28(3). The question facing the court in *U v. W (Attorney General Intervening)* No. 1 [1997] Eu. LR 342 was whether a licence was required for certain forms of fertility treatment. The court held that *Hansard* could be used to resolve the issue of whether or not the restriction on licences was justifiable. This was because relevant issues arose in the discussion of the bill in the House of Lords. The second and third parts of the *Pepper v. Hart* conditions also applied. However, in an interesting adaptation of the test, it was held that *Hansard* could be referred to even though the first part of the *Pepper v. Hart* conditions did not apply.
20   *R (on the application of Spath Holme Ltd) v. Secretary of State for the Environment, Transport and the Regions* [2001] 1 All ER 195.

Article 9 of the Bill of Rights. This prohibits the court from questioning proceedings in Parliament.

The case concluded with the court asserting that as the meaning of the relevant section was not ambiguous, there was no need to make use of *Hansard*.[21] *Spath Holme Ltd* thus goes some way to determining the form of the post-*Pepper* v. *Hart* practice. We can see that, while *Pepper* v. *Hart* acknowledges that a new practice is necessary, this practice has to be informed by a conventional understanding of the role of the courts. The techniques of purposive interpretation are thus 'revolutionary' only to a degree. They work within the existing constitutional settlement. It is worth clarifying this point still further. Just because a new practice is under development, this does not mean that the institutional or doctrinal structure of law is also being transformed. A significant development in a practice is thus entirely consistent with the continuity of other institutions. Furthermore, the fundamental 'shape' of the practice remains continuous with its general orientation, despite its own transformation. Purposive interpretation might thus realign, but it does not fundamentally alter the relationship between Parliament and the courts.

EUROPEAN INTERPRETATION

To what extent has the court's interpretation of European law influenced the forms that judicial practice is taking? Lord Denning provides a starting point:

> No longer must they [the judges] examine the words in meticulous detail. No longer must they argue about the precise grammatical sense. They must look to purpose or intent. To quote the words of the European Court in the Da Coasta case they must deduce from the wording and the spirit of the Treaty the meaning of the Community rules ... They must divine the spirit of the Treaty and gain inspiration from it. If they fill a gap, they must fill it as best they can. They must do what the framers of the instrument would have done if they had thought about it. So we must do the same.[22]

The impact of European methods of interpretation is undoubtedly having an important impact on the practice of statutory interpretation. But think about what Lord Denning is saying. The claims about 'no longer' are somewhat misleading. We have seen above that common law judges always made use of a form of purposive interpretation. The need to interpret European law lifts this into a new context; it may even be that this means that the courts have to follow European law rather than English law if there is a conflict. We will deal with this matter presently. For the moment, let us focus on one of our key concerns: how do European methods of interpretation shape

---

21   Also relevant to the argument in this case was the status of the 1985 Act as a consolidating statute. The normal rule for the interpretation of this kind of statute is that it is not permitted to look at the law that it replaced as an aid to its interpretation. It was only possible to make use of the old law when the Act itself was ambiguous.
22   *Bulmer* v. *Bollinger* [1974] Ch 401, at 426.

or reshape the constitutional parameters of interpretative practice. We need to return to the principle of the supremacy of European law. Lord Denning outlined this doctrine in *Macarthys v. Smith*:

> It is important now to declare – and it must be made plain – that the provisions of Article 119 of the Treaty of Rome take priority over anything in our English statute on equal pay which is inconsistent with Article 119. That priority is given by our own law. It is given by the European Communities Act 1972 itself. Community law is now part of our law: and, whenever there is any inconsistency, Community law has priority. It is not supplanting English law. It is part of our law which overrides any other part which is inconsistent with it.[23]

European law takes priority over English statutes because Parliament has so provided. How does the doctrine of sovereignty relate to judicial interpretation? Our concern could be phrased as follows: in understanding the judicial interpretation of community law and the extent to which it allows a distortion of the literal meaning of statute, to what extent is judicial creativity limited by their perception of constitutional boundaries?

Once again, answering this question means looking at the development of the judicial practice. In *Garland v. British Rail Engineering Ltd*[24] the House of Lords held that s.6(4) of the Sexual Discrimination Act should be interpreted in such a way as to make it consistent with Article 119 of the EEC Treaty. The problem was that the words of the relevant section were capable of two different and opposed interpretations: one that suited the applicants and one that suited the respondents. Lord Diplock argued, and the rest of the House concurred, that the meaning of the section which was consistent with Article 119 had to be preferred. Lord Diplock also made use of a principle of interpretation 'too well established to call for citation of authority' that a statute passed after an international treaty had to be interpreted as consistent with the obligations that the country had undertaken. Interestingly, he avoided the question of whether or not a provision expressly intended by Parliament to contravene European obligations would be so interpreted by the court.

The parameters of this mode of interpretation can be seen in the later case *Duke v. GEC Reliance*.[25] In this case the House of Lords interpreted sections 2(4) and 2(6) of the Sexual Discrimination Act. It was asserted that the 1975 Act was not meant to give effect to the Directive on Equal Treatment issued in 1976. As s.2(4) of the EC Act did not allow a court to 'distort' the meaning of the statute, European employment rights should not be available in English law. This is surprising. One would expect that the court would have to the construe the British statute in such a way as to make it harmonise with Community law. However, the court followed an earlier precedent. *Marshall*[26] promoted a much narrower approach to the interpretation of statute; stressing that if

---

23 *Macarthys v. Smith* [1979] 3 All ER 32, at 218.
24 *Garland v. British Rail Engineering Ltd* [1982] 2 WLR 918.
25 *Duke v. GEC Reliance* [1988] 2 WLR 359.
26 Case 152/84, *Marshall v. Southampton and South West Hampshire Area Health Authority* [1986] ECR 723; [1986] 1 CMLR 688; [1986] QB 401.

the domestic statute had not been 'intended'[27] to give effect to European obligations, then the court was limited by the words of the Act. On the facts of the present case, as the provisions of the 1976 Act could not carry the interpretation urged by the appellants, the court had to give effect to the literal meaning of the Act. The 1986 Sex Discrimination Act was passed to bring retirement ages into line with European law, but, as this Act was not retrospective, it did not help the appellant's case.

What conclusions can we draw from these two cases? Although the issues raised are similar, and the same sections of the 1975 Act are interpreted in both cases, it would seem that the central difference relates to the court's understanding of the 1976 directive and its effect in English law. As the 1986 Act did not have retrospective effect, it was not possible to apply a strained interpretation to the 1975 Act to make it consistent with the directive. Some commentators have argued that Duke was wrongly decided.[28] *Marshall* had held that a directive could not create obligations between individuals. In *Marleasing*, the ECJ had relied on an earlier authority, *Van Colson*, to assert that a court had to interpret national law as consistent with European obligations whether or not the national law pre- or post-dated a directive.[29] From this perspective, it would appear that the courts have a much bolder role to play in the interpretation of national legislation, and that judicial practice could make use of the *Van Colson* doctrine to assert, against *Duke*, that there was an overriding objective to ensure judicial protection of European rights.[30]

Pickstone v. *Freemans*[31] shows the court approaching the interpretation of national legislation far more robustly than they had in *Duke*. In this case, the House of Lords had to interpret s.1(2) of the Equal Pay Act 1970. The Act had been amended to make it coherent with obligations arising under Article 119 of the Treaty of Rome. The key question was whether the amendment of the Act actually did give effect to the obligations under the treaty. In approaching the interpretation of the Act, their lordships began from a purposive position. Lord Nicholls, for instance, determined that purpose of the Article was twofold: to ensure consistency in the legal systems of member states across the community, and to improve working conditions. These objectives are furthered by a directive, and by ECJ cases that clarify the precise terms of community law. A problem arose because on at least one interpretation of the relevant sections of the UK Act, it did not accord with European law. Furthermore, the 'broad' interpretation of the section that would have made the law coherent was difficult to square with the wording of the Act.

What, then, should be the correct approach? Lord Diplock's argument in *Garland* provided a point of reference. Only express wording in an Act passed prior to the date that the UK had joined the Community would allow a court to conclude that it was not

---

27 *Marshall* v. *Southampton and South West Hampshire Health Authority* [1986] 2 All ER 584, cited in *Duke* at 639.
28 Mead (1991).
29 The ECJ argued that the obligation to enforce directives was a duty under Article 5 and Article 189 of the Treaty of Rome.
30 See *Marleasing SA* v. *La Commercial Internacional de Alimentacion SA* [1992] 1 CMLR 305. The issue in these cases is also the extent to which European law is enforceable against private parties as well as the state. Marleasing went beyond Marshall, and extended European law rights to private parties.
31 *Pickstone* v. *Freemans* [1988] 3 WLR 265.

intended to be consistent with European law. The court was thus justified in particularly 'wide' departures from the wording of the Act 'in order to achieve consistency'. Argument focused on whether 'exclusionary' words in the Act had the effect of limiting the section in such a way as to not give full effect to Convention Rights.[32]

What are the consequences of this argument? The literal interpretation would compel the conclusion that the Act was in breach of European law; furthermore, it would not be consistent with the principle articulated by Lord Diplock. In Lord Oliver's opinion, the Act was reasonably capable of bearing the interpretation that would make it consistent with European law. Ultimately, it was held that a purposive interpretation allowed the appellant's case to succeed. Their argument was helped by the fact that the court took into account the Equal Pay Regulations of 1983 that had brought the statute in line with Community law. Although these draft regulations had not been subjected to the same parliamentary process as a bill, they had been passed to give effect to a decision of the ECJ. It was thus legitimate to take into account Parliament's purpose in interpreting the draft regulations.

In *Litster and Others Appellants* v. *Forth Dry Dock & Engineering Co. Ltd*[33] the House of Lords went even further than *Pickstone*. The court gave a purposive interpretation to a statutory instrument that concerned rules relating to the transfer of employees' rights in the event of the sale of a business. The court 'implied' words into the terms of the regulation so as to make it compatible with obligations under European law. Lord Oliver provided a useful summary of the court's approach in *Litster*. The court must first of all determine the precise nature of the obligations concerned by construing the wording of both the relevant directive, and the interpretation given to that directive by the ECJ. If it can be 'reasonably construed' in such a manner, UK legislation must then be purposively interpreted so as to give effect to European law. This approach can allow the courts to depart from the literal meaning of the words used.

Pickstone v. *Freemans* and *Litster* certainly seem to show the development of a new judicial practice that moves beyond the restraints on statutory interpretation prior to 1972. However, it would be wrong to assume from these cases that practice has so moved on that literal interpretation is 'dead'. The starting point remains a literal reading of the statute. Thus, in *Carole Louise Webb* v. *EMO Air Cargo (UK) Limited No. 2*[34] the 1975 Sex Discrimination Act was again subject to interpretation. As the House of Lords could interpret the relevant sections of the Act in such a way, there was no need to distort the language of the statute or to otherwise alter the literal sense. It is also worth remembering that the law of the EU itself limits the purposive approach.

---

32   This impacts on interpretative techniques. Lord Keith argued that it was 'plain' that Parliament could not have 'intended' to depart from its European law obligations. Under the circumstances of the case, he felt it was entirely legitimate that the court should consider the draft regulations. Lord Oliver was concerned that the case did indeed raise issues that made for a 'departure' from the normal rules of statutory interpretation. It would not normally be open to a court to depart from a literal interpretation of an Act simply because the Act was passed to give effect to an international treaty. Furthermore, parliamentary materials cannot normally be relied upon as aids to construction. However, European law was different. Parliament had in s.2(1) of the EC Act, incorporated European law into domestic law.
33   *Litster and Others Appellants* v. *Forth Dry Dock & Engineering Co. Ltd* [1989] 2 WLR 634.
34   *Carole Louise Webb* v. *EMO Air Cargo (UK) Limited No. 2* [1995] 1 WLR 1454.

This can be seen in *Grant* v. *South Western Trains*.[35] The ECJ refused to prohibit discrimination based on sexual orientation. In theory, they might have been able to broaden the terms of Article 119 and the relevant directives. However, the court felt that as community law did not recognise homosexual marriages, this issue could only be dealt with at a national level. *Grant* indicates one extreme constitutional line that Community law will not cross. It is interesting that this raises a question of sexual morality. The consequence of this means that while issues of sexual discrimination have frequently formed the context for tensions between UK and Community law that have occasioned debates on the acceptable boundaries of judicial discretion, the resistance to equal rights for gays and lesbians means that it is unlikely to give rise to acts of bold interpretation.

THE POLITICS OF INTERPRETATION UNDER THE HUMAN RIGHTS ACT

The interpretative provisions of the Human Rights Act have had a major impact in judicial interpretative practices. Our consideration of the new practices has to begin by looking at section 3 of the Act. Note first of all that the range of this provision – it applies to primary and secondary legislation 'whenever enacted' – before or after the Act. The effect of s.3(2)b, however, is that the incompatibility of a piece of primary legislation with the HRA does not mean that this legislation is held to be void.[36] In other words, parliamentary sovereignty is left in place. We are thus concerned with the realignment of a judicial practice rather than its complete redefinition. The pressing question is: how will the courts interpret legislation in the light of s.3? The government White Paper, *Rights Brought Home* stated that s.3 would go 'far beyond' the rules prior to the HRA which had allowed the court to take into account the ECHR in interpreting legislation and clarifying ambiguity: 'The courts will be required to interpret legislation so as to uphold convention rights unless the legislation itself is so clearly incompatible with the Convention that it is impossible to do so'.[37] While this clearly articulates a rule of interpretation, it leaves a great deal of discretion in the hands of the interpreter to determine whether or not it is impossible to interpret legislation as compatible with the Convention. We are concerned once again with the constitutional boundaries of the judicial practice.

One of the first key authorities is *Wilson* v. *First County Trust*.[38] Let us consider Lord Nicholls' argument. He addressed the idea that the courts are themselves public

---
35   *Grant* v. *South Western Trains* (Case 249/96) (1998) *The Times*, 23 February.
36   Moreover, it does not allow a court to hold subordinate or secondary legislation to be invalid if the primary legislation does not allow the incompatibility with the HRA to be remedied
37   *Rights Brought Home: The Human Rights Bill*, Command Paper No. Cm 3782, para 2.7
38   *Wilson* v. *First County Trust* [2003] HRLR 33. Mrs Wilson had argued that a loan that she had taken from a pawnbroker and not repaid was unenforceable, because the agreement did not contain all the prescribed terms, contrary to the Consumer Credit Act of 1974. In particular Mrs Wilson was objecting to a fee for preparation of documents that she had been charged and which was not mentioned in the loan agreement. Her argument was that the 1974 Act made the agreement unenforceable. The County Court held that the agreement was enforceable, and Mrs Wilson had appealed to the Court of Appeal, which reversed the County Court's judgment. The Court

authorities, and therefore bound by the HRA. Would this mean that as the courts are bound by the Act, they would be compelled to discount an Act of Parliament that was inconsistent with the Act? This would clearly be a very broad interpretation of the Human Rights Act. Indeed, it would effectively make the Human Rights Act itself sovereign, and bring to an end the sovereignty of Parliament. As this was never the intended effect of the Act, it could not be a valid interpretation. In interpreting a statute in the light of the HRA, it was necessary to abide by constitutional principles and give effect to the will of Parliament; however, the court could consider the 'proportionality of legislation'. In approaching the issue of proportionality, the court was fulfilling a reviewing role. Parliament retained the primary responsibility for deciding the appropriate form of legislation. The court would reach a different conclusion from the legislature only when it was apparent that the legislature had attached insufficient importance to a person's Convention right. The readiness of the court to depart from the views of the legislature depended on the circumstances, one of which was the subject matter of the legislation. The more the legislation concerned matters of broad social policy, the less ready a court would be to intervene.

These are nuanced arguments. Insofar as it is possible to draw a conclusion, the House of Lords might be suggesting that legislation would be interpreted to protect Convention rights if the court considered it necessary when considering the 'proportionality of legislation'. In so doing, the Court would defer to Parliament, but would reserve for itself the power to 'reach a different conclusion from the legislature' if 'the legislature had attached insufficient importance to a person's Convention right'.[39] We will see that the precise terms of the proportionality test became one of the sites over which the applicability of the Human Rights Act to statutory interpretation was fought out. This is one of the key concerns in *R. v. A* where disputes between the judges represent rival ways in which a doctrine of human rights interpretation could be forged.

In *R. v. A*,[40] the House of Lords considered whether s.41 of the Youth Justice and Criminal Evidence Act 1999 amounted to a breach of the defendant's right to a fair trial.[41] How could the House of Lords interpret this section? Would they have to issue a certificate of incompatibility? Or would the court assert that the Act had to be followed? Lord Steyn argued that the starting point for the interpretation of the Act was the 'mischief' that Parliament had 'decided' to address. However, at the same

---

of Appeal also made a declaration under s.4 of the HRA. The Court of Appeal argued that the 1974 Act was incompatible with the rights guaranteed to the creditor by Article 6(1) of the European Convention on Human Rights ('the Convention'). The Secretary of State, who had been added to the proceedings, appealed, and the House of Lords allowed the appeal.

39   Ibid., H17.
40   R. v. A. [2001] 2 WLR 1546.
41   Section 41 prohibits the questioning of a complainant of rape about previous sexual behaviour, except in certain narrowly defined circumstances. This section of the Act serves a clear purpose. It both prevents irrelevant evidence being given in court and the perpetuation of harmful stereotypes. However, at the same time, the courts were aware that s.41 might lead to a breach of Article 6 if an accused was never able to put evidence before the court about consensual sexual relations. Although this evidence could never be used to suggest that because a woman had consented to sex in the past, she was likely to be consenting at the time in question, it may have some relevance to the case in hand. Depriving the accused of this right could conceivably be a breach of a right to a fair trial, as it could jeopardise 'the overall fairness of the proceedings' by excluding relevant evidence.

time, the House of Lords had to decide whether the Act made 'an excessive inroad into the right to a fair trial'.[42] How, then, was the court to assess where this particular provision fell? Reference was made to an important piece of extrajudicial writing by Lord Lester. This suggested a two-tier approach to the assessment of legislation in the light of the HRA. The first question that the court had to ask was whether or not the provision in question 'interfered'[43] with a Convention right. Answering this question does not require an essential reference to parliamentary intent, because it will hardly ever be the case that Parliament deliberately intended to breach a Convention right. It is at the second level of the test where the government attempts to justify the particular provision, that parliamentary intention becomes more relevant. This raises the question of whether or not the provision falls into one of the 'exception clauses' under the HRA. The court must then move to consider the issue of proportionality.[44]

What sense does proportionality make in the present context? We need to start from the assertion that Article 6 lays down a fundamental set of guarantees to enable a fair trial to take place. The only way in which this right can be restricted is by reference to Article 6 itself. Lord Steyn summarised this as determining a balance between 'the interests of the accused, the victim and society'. Applying this set of considerations to the test of proportionality requires reference to Lord Clyde's guidelines in the key authority *de Freitas* v. *Permanent Secretary of Ministry of Agriculture, Fisheries, Lands and Housing*.[45] These guidelines allow a court to decide whether a restriction on a right is acceptable, or 'arbitrary or excessive'. The guidelines ask the court to determine, first of all, whether the objective of the legislation is 'sufficiently important'; then the court must decide if the actual limitations in the legislation achieve this end. Applied to the issues of *R.* v. *A*, the court must thus be sure that the restrictions of the accused's right to give evidence of consent to the court in the Act are 'proportionate' to the goal of limiting fair trial rights: preventing irrelevant evidence and perpetuating stereotypes of women's sexual behaviour.

This is essentially an act of interpretation. Section 41 may be subject to certain exceptions, but it is effectively a 'blanket ban'.[46] Note how Lord Steyn then makes explicit reference to techniques of interpretation:

> Ordinary methods of purposive and contextual interpretation may yield ways of minimizing the prima facie exorbitant breadth of the section. Secondly, the interpretative obligation in section 3(1) of the 1998 Act may come into play. It provides that 'So far as it is *possible* to do so, primary legislation ... *must* be read and given effect in a way which is compatible with the Convention rights'. It is a key feature of the 1998 Act.[47]

In the context of this chapter, it is important to remember here that this is simply a reference to 'purposive and contextual' methods; it is not any explicit evocation of

---

42 Ibid., 65.
43 Ibid.
44 See also Wilson (1988: 371–2) and Feldman (1999: 122–3).
45 *de Freitas* v. *Permanent Secretary of Ministry of Agriculture, Fisheries, Lands and Housing* [1999] 1 AC 69.
46 R. v. A., ibid., 66.
47 Ibid.

the mischief rule or the golden rule. Note also how it is offered as one way in which judicial discretion can limit the range of s.41, and thus grant some power to a judge to determine whether or not evidence can be admitted. This requires an understanding of the statute in its common law context. Alongside this is a literal reading of the section; or, rather, what is termed the 'interpretative obligation' that is required of the judges by the HRA. We do not have the space to go into the detailed interpretation of the relevant case law. We can, however, consider the conclusion to which Lord Steyn comes:

> In my view ordinary methods of purposive construction of section 41(3)(c) cannot cure the problem of the excessive breadth of the section 41, read as a whole, so far as it relates to previous sexual experience between a complainant and the accused. Whilst the statute pursued desirable goals, the methods adopted amounted to legislative overkill.[48]

We can see how this relates back to the previous paragraph. The purposive interpretation cannot 'cure' the breadth of the section. The judge must therefore make use of the 'interpretative obligation'. Section 3 applies even where 'there is no ambiguity' in the Act; it does not just mean, therefore, that the Court must take the Convention into account in interpreting ambiguous statutory language. The 'duty' placed on the court by s.3 requires the court to 'strive' to make the statute coherent with the Convention. This takes us beyond normal methods of statutory interpretation. Normally a court can 'depart from the language of the statute to avoid absurd consequences', but s.3 is a far more 'radical ... general principle'[49]: interpretation must make Act and Convention 'compatible'. Following *Pepper* v. *Hart*,[50] this could amount to an interpretation 'against the executive'. Thus:

> In accordance with the will of Parliament as reflected in section 3 it will sometimes be necessary to adopt an interpretation which linguistically may appear strained. The techniques to be used will not only involve the reading down of express language in a statute but also the implication of provisions. A declaration of incompatibility is a measure of last resort. It must be avoided unless it is plainly impossible to do so.[51]

It may be that Parliament expresses a *'clear* limitation on Convention rights'.[52] However, this is not one of those cases. In Lord Steyn's opinion, this requires an interpretation of the statute informed by 'common sense', and by a supposition that Parliament itself would not have intended that the Act would prevent an accused making

---

48   Ibid., 67.
49   Ibid., 68.
50   Citing '*Pepper* v. *Hart*; A re-examination' (2001) 21 *Oxford Journal of Legal Studies* 59; see also Baker (1993).
51   R. v. A., at 69.
52   See R. v. *Secretary of State for the Home Department, Ex p Simms* [2000] 2 AC 115.

a full defence, so long as it made use of 'truly probative material'. Words can thus be read into the statute: an 'implied provision' that evidence which is probative and is necessary to a fair trial cannot be excluded. It is up to the trial judge to determine when evidence is probative, and when it is merely irrelevant or insulting to the victim of rape. Following this line of argument, it is not necessary to issue a declaration of incompatibility.

Lord Hope did not agree with Lord Steyn, asserting that s.41 was proportionate to the end it sought to achieve, particularly because the overenthusiastic use of judicial discretion had resulted in a loss of public confidence in the fairness of rape trials. Moreover, he argued that the section of the Act itself preserved the defendant's right to ask questions.[53] This case, then, does not present itself as an opportunity to consider whether or not issues of general unfairness are raised. Only in this instance would there be grounds to hold an incompatibility with Article 6.[54] Furthermore, on this argument, the case does not raise the need to apply s.3 of the HRA; it is not necessary to 'modify, alter or supplement the words used by Parliament'.[55] Lord Hope would not, then, see this case as calling for the 'radical' approach:[56]

> [S]ection 3 does not entitle the court to legislate; its task is still one of interpretation. Compatibility is to be achieved only so far as this is possible. Plainly this will not be possible if the legislation contains provisions which expressly contradict the meaning which the enactment would have to be given to make it compatible. It seems to me that the same result must follow if they do so by necessary implication, as this too is a means of identifying the plain intention of Parliament.[57]

This interpretation of the acceptable use of s.3 also begins with the idea that it is based on the intention of Parliament. However, in a partial agreement with Lord Steyn, Lord Hope concludes that if the trial judge found it necessary to use s.3, he should do so by following the test articulated by Lord Steyn.

Lord Clyde was also perhaps not as forthright as Lord Steyn. He admitted that it might be possible to resolve the case without 'straining' the language of the provision. Failing this approach, though, s.3 of the HRA could be applied; and the issue of compatibility with the Convention did not arise.[58] Lord Hutton agreed with Lord Steyn.[59]

---

53 R. v. A., at 85.
54 Ibid., 86.
55 Ibid.
56 He cites Lord Woolf in *Poplar Housing and Regeneration Community Association Ltd v. Donoghue* [2001] QB 48
57 R. v. A., at 86.
58 Ibid., at 97.
59 Ibid., 106. 'Therefore pursuant to the obligation imposed by section 3(1) that section 41 must be read and given effect in a way which is compatible with article 6, I consider that section 41(3)(c) should be read as including evidence of such previous behaviour by the complainant because the defendant claims that her sexual behaviour on previous occasions was similar, and the similarity was not a coincidence because there was a causal connection which was her affection for, and feelings of attraction towards, the defendant. It follows that I am in full agreement with the test of admissibility stated by my noble and learned friend Lord Steyn in paragraph 46 of his speech.'

The disagreements among the law lords as to the precise way in which the Human Rights Act is to be applied leads to the possibility of two approaches. The relevant section of the 1999 Act could be interpreted by reference to s.3 and along the lines suggested by Lord Steyn, and broadly consented to by Lords Clyde and Hutton, or in the way suggested by Lord Hope. In Lord Steyn's understanding, the proportionality test suggests 'legislative overkill', and this requires words to be read into the Act so as to make it consistent with Article 6. Lord Hope did not feel the case raised a s.3 point, and it was not necessary to apply the proportionality test. Note that this is not a disagreement over the proportionality test as such, rather, whether it is a dispute over whether it applies on the facts. It is interesting though, to point out that when this case was applied in *Goode* v. *Martin*,[60] it was held that *R.* v. *A.* authorised the 'reading in' of certain rules into the Civil Procedure Rules. This might suggest that the terms of the test proposed by Lord Lester and adopted by Lord Steyn are feeding into judicial practice.

The Human Rights Act may allow judges to consider the proportionality of legislation, but what are the boundaries of the test? This perennial concern lies behind the concerns of the subsequent case law. In *Re S*[61] the House of Lords considered the compatibility of care orders with Articles 6(1) and 8 of the ECHR. The Court of Appeal had used s.3 of the ECHR and interpreted the Children Act 1989 in order to make it Convention compliant. The House of Lords held that this use of s.3 overstepped the power given to judges by the HRA. Lord Nicholls pointed out that:

> In applying section 3 courts must be ever mindful of this outer limit. The Human Rights Act reserves the amendment of primary legislation to Parliament. By this means the Act seeks to preserve parliamentary sovereignty. The Act maintains the constitutional boundary. Interpretation of statutes is a matter for the courts; the enactment of statutes, and the amendment of statutes, are matters for Parliament.[62]

This restates a fundamental constitutional principle. It is clear that the HRA is meant to preserve the distinction between interpretation and enactment of statutes. To some extent this rather bald distinction does not engage with the difficulty of drawing the line between the interpretation and the creation of the law. However, Lord Nicholls did acknowledge the inherent difficulties in the next part of his argument. He pointed out that the more 'liberal' modes of interpretation make it harder to locate the boundary between the 'robust' and the 'impermissibly creative'. He proposes a rule of thumb test:

> For present purposes it is sufficient to say that a meaning which departs substantially from a fundamental feature of an Act of Parliament is likely to have crossed the boundary between interpretation and amendment.[63]

---

60   *Goode* v. *Martin* [2002] 1 All ER 620
61   *Re S* [2002] UKHL 10.
62   Ibid., para 39.
63   Ibid.

Elaborating this test returns us to themes with which we are familiar from earlier in this chapter. Particularly creative acts of interpretation depart from fundamental principles of an Act, and also bring matters to court that are ill-suited to the forensic process. The reinterpretation of the Children's Act by the Court of Appeal did just this. In a sensitive area, where Parliament had entrusted powers to local authorities, the courts should not intervene so as to interfere with this statutory regime.

A good example of a case where a broad interpretation of an Act leads to an acceptable piece of judicial law making is *Ghaidan* v. *Godin-Mendoza*.[64] The case saw the House of Lords dealing with a question of property law that related to succession to a tenancy under paragraph 2 of schedule 1 to the Rent Act 1977. The defendant was contending that the Rent Act discriminated against him as a homosexual in depriving him of rights over the flat of his deceased partner. What precisely was the issue in *Ghaidan*? Paragraph 2(2) makes a distinction between a heterosexual and a homosexual couple who are living together. For the former, the survivor can take over the tenancy if the property was in the name of the deceased, whereas for the latter, the survivor cannot. The survivor in a gay relationship is not deprived of all rights over the property. He/she is entitled to an assured tenancy. However, in terms of both rent protection and rights against eviction, the survivor of the homosexual relationship is clearly not in as beneficial a situation as the survivor of the heterosexual relationship.

The Court of Appeal had held that the Act amounted to an infringement of the defendant's rights under Articles 8 and 14 of the Convention. The Court of Appeal had used s.3 of the HRA to read the Act in a broad way, thus allowing the defendant to take over the tenancy of the flat. The House of Lords dismissed the appeal against this ruling, and confirmed the approach of the Court of Appeal. It was thus not necessary to issue a declaration of incompatibility, as the Act could be read in such a way as to make it Convention compliant. The House of Lords did note, however, that the new meaning of the Act must be 'consistent with the fundamental features of the legislative scheme'.[65] We need to investigate this argument in a little more detail.

Lord Nicholls pointed out that there are a number of ways of reading s.3 as there is a certain degree of ambiguity in the word 'possible'. A narrow reading would hold that s.3 only allowed courts to resolve ambiguities in statutory language in favour of Convention-compliant interpretations. A much broader interpretation of the section has been preferred, which allows the courts to give a different meaning to the language of the statute in order to make its meaning consistent with the Convention. This could involve reading in words, as in *R.* v. *A.* There is no need for the language of the Act to be ambiguous for the Court to take this course of action.[66] This means that the court can 'depart from the unambiguous meaning the legislation would otherwise bear'. Normally, the court would have to determine the intention of Parliament by using the language in the Act. However, s.3 means that the court may have to 'depart from the intention of the enacting Parliament'.

---

64 *Ghaidan* v. *Godin-Mendoza* [2004] UKHL 30.
65 Ibid., 558.
66 Ibid., 570–1.

We can begin to appreciate how the Human Rights Act makes for a potentially radical departure from conventional methods of interpretation. However, this does not extend to the idea that the court is now an equal partner with Parliament when it comes to legislation. The fundamental requirement is that the courts should follow Parliamentary intention in interpreting an Act. The question becomes: how would a court know that it is legitimate to depart from Parliamentary intention? The answer to this question depends on the degree to which Parliament intended that the 'actual' words of a statute, as opposed to the concept that those words express, is to be 'determinative' of the Act's meaning. What does this mean? Lord Nicholls argues that the determinative factor cannot be the word of the Act, since the HRA allows them to be interpreted against their obvious sense. It would be possible, therefore, for a court to read words into an Act. This would be consistent with the fact that s.3 'requires' that courts read in words to make an Act compliant with the Convention.[67] There is a limit to this process. Although the court can read in words, Parliament could never have intended that 'the courts should adopt a meaning inconsistent with a fundamental feature of legislation' (ibid.). This would cross the line, and show the courts interfering with the sovereign rights of Parliament.[68]

DEFINING THE PARAMETERS OF THE NEW PRACTICE

The sample of cases that we have been examining suggests that we are at the cutting edge of a new kind of judicial practice. Perhaps we can think of the practice of statutory interpretation as the judges as entering into some form of dialogue with Parliament. This would certainly have the authority of Jack Straw, who, in a Parliamentary debate, argued that:

> Parliament and the judiciary must engage in a serious dialogue about the operation and development of the rights in the Bill ... this dialogue is the only way in which we can ensure the legislation is a living development that assists our citizens.[69]

If we accept that the idea of dialogue is useful then it is necessary to determine the precise terms in which it operates. If this is a democratic dialogue, then it cannot simply be a judicial usurpation of legislative power in the name of human rights. As Lord Irvine's words quoted in the introduction suggest, the dialogue must take place within a constitutional settlement that stresses separation of powers. However, it is necessary to accept that the dialogue does open up a new judicial vocabulary. Does this take us back to the proportionality test? The proportionality test is a powerful mechanism that can allow either the broad interpretation of statutory language or the reading in of words in order to make legislation Convention compliant. However, the

---

67 Ibid., 572.
68 Ibid.
69 Jack Straw, 314 HC 1141, June 24. Cited in Klug (2003: 131).

test, as shown by *Ghaidan* v. *Godin-Mendoza*, must itself be subject to some constraints, otherwise the courts would be moving far beyond the powers given to them by the Human Rights Act, as the intention of the Act was to preserve parliamentary sovereignty. The approach in *Ghaidan* was legitimate because the interpretation proposed by the House of Lords was consistent with the fundamental policy objectives of the legislation, which were to provide security of tenure. Clearly, where a judicial interpretation moved beyond the policy of legislation, the courts could not effectively legislate in Parliament's place. It could thus hesitatingly be suggested that after the Human Rights Act judicial practice is changing to such an extent that judges now have an acknowledged legislative power. This allows them to make legislation Convention compliant. Compared to the legislative power of Parliament it is limited, but the interpretative provisions of the 1998 Act effectively makes judges the legislators of human rights.

This is perhaps coherent in some way with Klug's interpretation of the Act.[70] She argues that sections 3 and 4 bring an end to 'judicial deference to the legislature'; in particular, judges need to appreciate that s.4 allows them to enter into a dialogue with Parliament. It would be a mistake to see s.4 as mandating a change of law, rather the Act 'was specifically structured to allow the courts to uphold rights while also retaining parliamentary authority'. Klug suggests that the HRA was intended to 'inject principles of parliamentary accountability and transparency into judicial proceedings without removing whole policy areas to judicial determination'. Changes in judicial practice would have to be seen as driven by the 'new dynamic' that the Act attempts to create.[71]

This would suggest that the precise terms of the practice or dialogue of statutory interpretation in the wake of the HRA are focused on sections 3 and 4. Kavanagh has made similar points. We can consider her response to the criticisms of *R. v. A*.[72] The critical issue is of the nature of the obligation under s.3(1), and whether it allows or requires the court to depart from the intention of Parliament expressed in the words of the statute. Placing *R. v. A.* in the context of *Lambert*, Kavanagh asks why this authority has been singled out for criticism, when in *Lambert* the court went against the clear intention of Parliament. This begs the question about how parliamentary intention is understood. Recent authorities[73] on s.3(1) suggest that there are two legislative intentions at play, namely that which is underlying the statute in question, and that which is 'expressed' in s.3(1). Section 3(1) only becomes relevant when there is a 'conflict' between these two intentions. How should this conflict be resolved? If one applies the doctrine of implied repeal, the later Act would repeal the earlier, but as the

---

70 F. Klug (2003).
71 Ibid., 130.
72 Commentators have been critical of Lord Steyn in *R. v. A*. Ekins (2003) argues that approaches such as that of Lord Steyn subvert the fact that the judges are trying to determine Parliament's intention: 'Thus, statutory interpretation in a rights-conscious era remains a search for legislative intent and judgment and s.3 should therefore be understood simply as a rule that stipulates defeasible presumptions of legislative intent and which acts as a tiebreaker in the event of genuine interpretative uncertainty ... Given the indeterminacy of rights adjudication and the democratic unaccountability of the judiciary, we would do well to be grateful for that fact' (p. 650).
73 Kavanagh relies on Lord Nicholls' and Lord Steyn's speeches in *Ghaidan* [2004] UKHL 30; [2004] 2 AC 557 at [30] (Lord Nicholls), [40] (Lord Steyn).

HRA applies to legislation 'whenever enacted', then it would apply to legislation after 1998. The 'effect' of s.3(1) is thus quite specific:

> Ordinarily, Parliament intends its legislation to be understood in accordance with its ordinary meaning. By empowering judges to go beyond the ordinary meaning, s.3(1) instructs judges to go against that legislative intention.

This is supported by the AG reference 4 of 2002[74] which describes s. 3(1) as 'very strong and far reaching' and can require a departure from the 'intention of Parliament'. This would justify the approach of Lord Steyn in *R. v. A.*, but also in his wider reflections on the justification for a more expanded role for the judiciary. Elaborating these arguments is best left for Chapter 5 on the Politics of the Judiciary, but we need to move away from static understandings of the court somehow mechanically trying to discover the intention of Parliament, through a literal reading of an Act, and understand the practice of statutory interpretation as a dialogue. In this democratic dialogue the courts do not usurp the legislative power of Parliament, but on a mandate given to them by Parliament itself, engage in articulating legislation that is compliant with human rights.

CONCLUSION

Statutory interpretation is a pragmatic practice within constitutional limits. In attempting to define the parameters of the contemporary practice of statutory interpretation we have avoided any approach that stressed the centrality of the rules of interpretation and have attempted instead to see how, in important cases, judges actually interpret the statutory language with which they have been presented. We have hazarded a general thesis. Alongside the presumptions of interpretations, which describe the concern with the general structure of the law as meaningful language, there is a structuring concern with the parameters of the practice. This can only be described in constitutional terms. Where does the boundary lie between interpreting a statute and creating new law? This raises the issue of institutional legitimacy. For us the development of the practice is itself bound up with three important recent developments: the ruling in *Pepper* v. *Hart*, the impact of European interpretative methods, and the powers of interpretation created by the Human Rights Act. As a general point, describing judicial practice requires an engagement with specific legal issues, the tensions in approach that show an interaction between different judicial understandings of practice, and the spaces in the law that allow these arguments to be made.

Building on the previous chapter, we could say that practices always allow for a degree of dispute over their central terms and suppositions. Over time, these disputes may become resolved, or at least less 'hot', and the practice assumes a conventional form. Given the impact of so many recent legal developments in statutory interpretation, it would not be surprising to find some degree of dispute over the precise

---

[74] Att-Gen's Reference (No. 4 of 2002) [2004] UKHL 43 [2004].

constitution of legitimate techniques. However, this can exist alongside a more or less settled understanding of the fundamental orientation of the practice. What we find in recent statutory interpretation is just this mixture of coherence and dispute. Thus a central strand in the emerging practice of statutory interpretation can be seen as an ongoing dialogue with Parliament over the relationship between domestic legislation and human rights.

5

THE POLITICS OF THE JUDICIARY REVISITED: RIGHTS, DEMOCRACY, LAW

The seat of judgment is like the throne of God. Let the unwise and unlearned not presume to ascend it, lest he should confound darkness with light and light with darkness, lest with a sword in the hand, as it were, of a madman he should slay the innocent and set free the guilty, and lest he should tumble down from on high, as from the throne of God, in attempting to fly before he has acquired wings ... Even when a man is obliged to decide cases and to be a judge, still let him beware of the dangers to himself, lest by judging perversely and against the laws, through entreaties or for a price, he should purchase for himself the measureless sorrows of eternal damnation for the momentary enjoyment of a paltry gain. Let him take thought lest in the day of the wrath of the Lord he should incur the vengeance of Him Who has said, *Revenge is Mine: I will repay*. On that day, the kings and princes of the earth shall behold the Son of Man, and shall weep and wail in fear of His punishments, and gold and silver will not avail to set them at liberty.[1]

All the judges, without exception, are members of the Athenaeum [a private club], and I presume that you will wish to be a member.[2]

The English judiciary includes few women, even fewer blacks and nobody under the age of 40. English judges tend to be elderly gentlemen most of who have had a public school education. It is disturbing that our judges come from such a narrow range of the community. To adjudicate cases is to exercise discretion in fact finding, sentencing, applying the law and awarding costs. Such powers should be exercised by judges of different backgrounds, ages, races and sexes. This is for two main reasons. First, it is inequitable in a democratic society that one set of values should predominate on the Bench. Secondly, there is a danger that minority groups and women faced by a Bench on which they see few, if any, of their number will lose respect for the law. A more diverse judiciary is unlikely to be attained while appointment is confined to practising barristers. There are few blacks, women and Labour Party supporters among the ranks of senior barristers.[3]

---

1 Bracton (c. 1235).
2 The Master of the Rolls, Cozens-Hardy, writing to Lord Buckmaster when Lord Buckmaster was appointed to the Lord Chancellorship in the early twentieth century, quoted in Pannick (1989: 50).
3 Pannick (1989) making the argument for a more representative judiciary.

INTRODUCTION

Writing in the thirteenth century, Bracton – one of the 'fathers' of the common law – used the image of a severe divine judge to warn human judges against corruption, prejudice, rashness and ignorance. In Bracton's world view the eschatological teachings of Christianity provided final accountability. He wrote before notions of human sovereignty, or the rise of the legal positivist philosophy which defined law as something totally and wholly posited by man; instead he held broad and encompassing notions of humanity's place in the cosmos and considered virtue and prudence to be guides to decision making:

> The King himself, however, ought not to be under man but under God, and under the law, for the law makes the king. Therefore, let the king render back to the Law what the Law gives to him, namely dominion and power; for there is no king where will, and not Law, wields dominion.

We are dealing with a holistic conception of location and responsibility. Although one mythic conception of the common law presents it as arising out of custom and the role of the judge as simply the finder and declarer of the rationale of local customs, common law evolved from the interaction of a small group of court related officials, the Curia Regis and the forms of argument and procedures for bringing disputes before judges who owed their position to central authority (the Crown). The primary procedure that gave power to the common law was 'the use of documents in good and due form that ordered subjects of the crown to appear before a judge under penalty for contempt of writ'.[4] Kriegel finds a major factor in understanding the different constitutional history of France from England in the early and enduring role of the judge: arguing that in England centralisation was achieved through law, and thereby that developments of political society and of law were not separate processes he finds that 'a judge was a man of the state; by the same token he is a judge'.

> The judge played a major role in English society, perhaps because he was from the beginning a buttress of the state [royal authority], and the law has remained an indisputable authority, perhaps because an offence against the law was an offence against a society composed of members who were all subject to the law but who also held the power to judge whoever disobeyed or transgressed the law.[5]

Against the idea of sovereignty as the source of law and therefore of law beneath sovereignty we have sovereignty AND the rule of law. The rule of law, therefore, is a mode of participation, a form of association. What today should the judge be faithful to? And does it matter who the human beings that make up the judiciary are?

Our discussion takes a path founded on returning to Griffith's seminal text: *The Politics of the Judiciary*.[6] It is necessary to both continue and update the critical thinking

---

4   Kriegel (1995: 73).
5   Ibid., 73–4.
6   First edition 1977, the text soon provided a point of writing from which to analyse notions of bias, competence and impartiality. For an interesting debate between Sir Stephen Sedley and J.A.G. Griffith, see Sedley (2001).

initiated thereby. However, we now turn to a more explicitly political context to examine the proper task of the judge within a democratic state as exampled by the UK. As indicated in this chapter's beginning we accept that any attempt to try and answer questions on judicial competence and impartiality requires some holistic model of law; it would also be inaccurate to borrow too heavily from Griffith's understanding of the inherently conservative nature of the judiciary. It is necessary to assess the impact of human rights, the legislative response to terrorism and the constitutional reforms of 2005; matters that were simply not on Griffith's agenda. We will see that judges are capable of making decisions that bring them into conflict with executive government, and of furthering a human rights agenda in ways that the Labour administration from 1998 onwards appeared reluctant to countenance. We will argue that the politics of the judiciary must now be understood as a form of dialogue between the judges and the executive that is characterised by tensions over the correct balance between judicial and governmental power. It is not simply a case of judges versus the executive, but a complex rearticulation of positions around matters of national importance. Democracy and human rights require that the traditional subservience of the courts to Parliament, seemingly inherent in the notion of parliamentary supremacy, be reassessed. This argument requires that we acknowledge that the 'politics' of the judiciary are not simplistic or 'party political', but a complex conjunction of arguments over values that are fundamentally legal, or relate to legal concepts and their development. Depending on the case in issue, such arguments have a more or less direct link with broader political concerns. We will track these issues through some of the most important Human Rights Act cases.

THE POLITICS OF THE JUDICIARY

The contents page of Griffith's text shows the study split into a number of engagements with judicial activity. The book concerns itself with industrial relations, personal rights, property rights, government secrecy, and students and trade unions. It reflects areas of importance at the time of writing in 1977. In brief, Griffith discussed the political problems of his day: concerns over the power of trade unions and the parlous state of industrial relations, student demonstrations, the early years of race relations, the tensions that resulted from economic recession and the impact of the equality agenda. We are in a time prior to the Thatcherite reforms of the 1980s that changed the face of British politics. What conclusions are drawn about the role of the judges in this period?

> My thesis is that the judges in the UK cannot be politically neutral because they are placed in positions where they are required to make political choices which are sometimes presented to them, and often presented by them, as determinations of where the public interest lies; that their interpretation of what is in the public interest and therefore politically desirable is determined by the kind of people they are and the position they hold in society; that his position is part of established authority and so is necessarily conservative and illiberal. From all this flows that view of the public interest which is shown in judicial attitudes such as tenderness towards private property and dislike of trade unions, strong adherence to the maintenance of order, distaste for minority opinions, demonstrations and protests, the avoidance of conflict with Government policy even

where it is manifestly oppressive of the most vulnerable, support of government secrecy, concern for the preservation of the moral and social behaviour to which it is accustomed, and the rest.[7]

Griffith stressed that, contrary to conventional opinion, judges are political, and that their politics are essentially those of an illiberal clique dedicated to frustrating progressive government policies. This was, of course, a bold and shocking statement for the time. Judges are meant to be neutral and impartial. Griffith demonstrated that, in the areas of decision making he examined, this was far from the truth. Whilst this suggests that in other areas of decision making, judges retained their impartiality, it did suggest that, in those areas of contentious policy, a right-wing bias was manifest. What do we make of this?

The evidence suggests that Griffith was correct, and an examination of recent history shows that judges conceived their role in conservative political terms. Progressive administrations explicitly took into account this reality in pushing through the creation of the welfare state and its institutions. However, in more recent years there has been something of a shift in the politics of the judiciary. Indeed, while Griffith's (and Pannick's) point about the composition of the appellate courts remains accurate, it would appear that important senior members of the judiciary have begun to champion and support human rights in such a way that brings them into conflict with the executive. This has also produced tensions within the judiciary itself. Understanding these developments requires us to carry forward Griffith's essential thesis, that judges are inherently political, but to appreciate that these politics are now articulated over the meaning of human rights within a democratic polity.

If one considers the judiciary from the perspective of a time frame broader than that of Griffith, one realises that their 'politicisation' began well before the 1970s. Stevens seeks to analyse the politics of the judiciary in the context of modern British history. Although the identification and division of historical periods is always rather arbitrary, this approach does allow us to identify certain overarching themes. The period 1900–1960 covers two world wars, and significant social, economic and political changes. To what extent do these broader concerns affect the composition of the judiciary and their awareness of their role? At the end of the 1800s, the Conservative Prime Minister, Lord Salisbury, appointed Lord Halsbury as Lord Chancellor. Lord Halsbury immediately began to staff the junior and senior ranks of the judiciary with his political allies. While these appointments did not always meet with the approval of the legal profession, they reflected what Salisbury saw as an unwritten rule of the constitution: the ruling party could explicitly influence the composition of the bar on ideological lines. Indeed, in the 1870s, with the establishment of the House of Lords as the final court of appeal, Salisbury had observed that it merely made judicial law making more explicit.

However, although momentarily in the ascendant, Conservative political philosophy did not go unopposed. If Tory ideology stood for the beliefs of an old order of privilege and settled practices, there were strong currents of reform in British politics. The extension of the franchise in 1832 had changed the political landscape significantly.

---

7   Griffith (1977).

Government was now to be increasingly accountable to a Parliament elected on a broad franchise. Influential ideas of law reform stressed the need for clear principles, downplaying the role of judicial creativity and privileging the authority of Parliament.[8]

Nevertheless, Lord Halsbury presided over a number of important decisions that reflected his biases, although these cannot perhaps always be explained in party political terms. In *London Tramways* v. *London City Council*[9] a case that we have already seen was central to the development of the modern doctrine of precedent; Lord Halsbury's ruling was a way of preserving the political influence of the Conservative House of Lords. However, he was also capable of affirming that the balance of power between legislature and executive lay firmly with the latter in the *Earldom of Norfolk Peerage Case*.[10] There were also a number of cases that sought to limit the power and influence of the trade unions. After suffering a reverse in *Allen* v. *Flood*,[11] despite attempting to make use of political allies on the bench, Halsbury managed to carry the day in *Quinn* v. *Leatham*.[12] This anti-union decision depended as much on Halsbury's political manoeuvring as the legal reasoning of the court; a strategy repeated in the celebrated *Taff Vale* decision.[13]

The political repercussions of this case helped lead to the Tory defeat in the elections of 1906. The Lord Chancellor in the new Liberal government, Lord Loreburn, made a number of new appointments. Although those to the High Court appeared not to be party political, the more senior appointments continued the 'tacit assumptions' that the new government shared with the Tories. At the same time, Lord Loreburn understood that judges had to be kept away from trade union cases, and also prevented from sabotaging the government's project: the construction of the welfare state. It was necessary to stress the neutral nature of judicial decision making, and where the Liberal government was rebuffed by the courts, to legislate. The 1913 Trade Union Act thus reversed the decision of the Lords in *Amalgamated Society of Railway Servants* v. *Osborne*.[14] Thus it would be possible to observe a change in judicial appointments that went alongside the pushing through of the political reforms of the Liberal and, later on, Labour governments. The legal regulation of the welfare state was to be achieved by a system of tribunals and administrative law that bypassed the formal court system, where the Conservative Law Lords had entrenched their position. Stevens points out that the move to appointment by merit rather than patronage in this period reflects this broader project.

We cannot dwell upon the appointments made by the Liberal Prime Minister, Lloyd George and Loreburn's replacement, Lord Haldane, other than to note that appointments to the Law Lords, and in particular to the office of Lord Chief Justice, were made on political grounds, and also reflected the alliances and falls from favour of ministers and their allies within the party. By the 1930s, the system of legal

---

8 Stevens (2002) who sees this as the legacy of utilitarian thought, which drew on Bentham's hostility to the obfuscations of the judges and Blackstone's defence of the common law.
9 *London Tramways* v. *London City Council* [1898] AC 375.
10 *Earldom of Norfolk Peerage Case* [1898] AC 375.
11 *Allen* v. *Flood* [1898] AC 1.
12 *Quinn* v. *Leatham* [1907] AC 10.
13 *Taff Vale Railway Company* v. *Amalgamated Society of Railway Servants* [1901] AC 426.
14 *Amalgamated Society of Railway Servants* v. *Osborne* [1910] AC 87.

regulation of the institutions of the welfare state was such that the role of the courts was increasingly sidelined through statutory clauses that protected legislation from challenge in the courts. Courts also refrained from examining executive acts done under prerogative powers and the decisions of administrative bodies. Following the report of the Committee on Ministers Powers in 1928, an 'official' understanding of the relationship between the courts and administrative tribunals stressed the distinct and separate spheres in which the institutions operated. While the former dealt with disputes by ruling on the facts with reference to objective rules, the latter dealt with administrative matters through the use of discretion, which was not the proper province of the judge. As Stevens points out, this presupposed the 'objectivity of legal rules and the feasibility of interpreting statutes "impartially"'.[15] Underpinning this position was the declaratory theory of law, which further sought to stress the formalism of common law decision making and reject any emphasis on creativity.

It was in this environment that the perception of the class bias of the Law Lords became increasingly apparent. It was as if the Law Lords revenged themselves on the executive, by using what powers they had to limit or undo progressive legislation. Thus, in *Roberts* v. *Hopwood*[16] minimum wage policy was effectively 'struck down'. The judges also busied themselves dismantling (as far as they could) the tax statutes and the taxation regime that they made for. This showed their class bias, to the extent that they privileged the protection of propertied interests over the funding of the welfare state. Stevens argues that the courts, and in particular, the House of Lords and the Court of Appeal, made themselves increasingly irrelevant in the period from 1939 to 1960. This can be shown by the number of cases these courts heard. In 1953 half as many cases were heard as in 1939.[17]

The 1945 election returned a Labour government committed to the economic and social reconstruction of the country. This added to the sense in which the defence of privilege by the courts was out of step with the will of the country. However, the reluctance or refusal of the courts to engage in any meaningful collaboration with the executive arguably resulted in a public law characterised by the failure to develop notions of both substantive and procedural due process. Furthermore, the commitment of the 1945 Labour government to radical reform might have led to reforms of the judiciary and the legal profession itself. Proposals were made at a Cabinet level for a new system of courts, and a movement towards continental styles of litigation and procedure. The Labour Lord Chancellor, William Jowitt was not of a radical cast of mind. He managed to limit proposals for reform, and preserve the structure and institutions of the profession.[18] The civil courts continued working on private disputes, in the 'most formalistic manner'[19] and eschewed the development of public law.

It would be simplistic, however, to think of the immediate post-war period as entirely characterised by the irrelevance of the courts to constitutional development broadly conceived. Voices within the Labour government spoke of the need to involve

---

15   Stevens (2002: 23).
16   *Roberts* v. *Hopwood* [1925] AC 578.
17   Stevens (2002: 26–7).
18   Ibid., 31, suggests that the 'conservative provenance' of the Evershed Committee, who had been tasked to report on the courts, cast its shadow on developments 'for the remainder of the century'.
19   Ibid.

the law in the management of the state, and more independently minded judges began to make their influence felt. The career of Lord Denning prompted a reappraisal of formalistic methods of interpretation, and suggested that the common law might be open to creative development by judges. Alongside Lord Denning, other important figures such as Lord Gardiner also opened up new possibilities. Although Lord Gardiner was more of a formalist than Lord Denning, he played an important role in arguing that the House of Lords could overrule itself, asserting that it would lead to a more coherent development of the law. When the House of Lords began to feel the influence of Lord Reid, public law was also reinvigorated, with a series of important judicial review decisions that developed notions of due process. Labour relations remained troubled, and led to tensions between the courts and Parliament. As a response to House of Lords rulings in *Rookes* v. *Barnard*[20] and *Stratford* v. *Lindley*[21] the Labour government proposed that labour relations be regulated by an administrative board. Failure to resolve these issues prompted the Conservative government to introduce the Judges Industrial Relations Court in 1971. With the change from a Conservative to a Labour government in 1974, the court was disbanded, but not before its president, Sir John Donaldson, had nearly been impeached for his political prejudice. This might show nothing more than the repetition of old patterns; a suspicion confirmed by Lord Diplock's statement that the task of the judge was to stick to the interpretation of the law made by Parliament – especially in politically contentious issues.

Although judges appeared to be playing a more prominent role in politics, their work in the courts was characterised by formalistic interpretations of the law that confirmed some opinions that the Law Lords were establishment figures incapable of criticising government. The succession of senior judges who presided over reports on the situation in Northern Ireland also 'threw doubt on the impartiality and independence of the British judiciary'.[22]

While these concerns suggest the right-wing prejudice of the Law Lords, developments throughout the 1980s and the 1990s indicated that an activist judiciary were inventing themselves around a new set of challenges. Other factors that led to a reinvention of the judiciary and their increasing involvement in politics were the accession of the UK to the EEC in 1972, and the shift in the political landscape with the election victory of Margaret Thatcher's Conservative Party in 1979. The judges were propelled into the centre of British politics, a space that was created by a populist 'right' government, intent on pushing through a package of reforms, and a Labour Party that turned sharply to the left. While the Conservative government remained somewhat sceptical towards Europe, and insisted on the 'sacrosanct' nature of parliamentary sovereignty, the House of Lords enthusiastically applied European Community law, most notably suspending the operation of a UK statute in *ex parte Factortame*.[23] The House of Lords also showed itself willing to take a stand against the executive in *M.* v. *The Home Office*[24] and *Woolwich* v. *IRC*.[25] While the

---

20 *Rooks* v. *Barnard* [1964] AC 1129.
21 *Stratford* v. *Lindley* [1965] AC 269.
22 Stevens (2002: 43).
23 *R.* v. *Secretary of State for Transport, ex parte Factortame* [1989] 2 CMLR 353.
24 *M.* v. *Secretary of State for the Home Office* [2006] EWCA Civ. 515.
25 *Woolwich* v. *IRC* [1993] AC 70.

European Convention was not part of UK law, influential judicial voices argued for its incorporation. The old stereotypes of a politically quiescent or pro status quo judiciary appeared to be breaking down. Indeed, in the 1990s, there were frequent clashes between the courts and the Conservative administration over immigration, sentencing policy, criminal justice and international development.[26] The invigorated approach to the development of the common law was strikingly evidenced when Lord Bingham and Lord Hoffman argued that the right to privacy should be created by judges if Parliament refused to legislate.[27] Furthermore, with the ruling in *Pepper* v. *Hart* 'judicial power was dramatically extended'.[28]

Can we hazard any general conclusions? Reflecting on the recent history of public law, Sir Stephen Sedley, writing extra-judicially, argued:

> The subsequent reassertion of judicial oversight of government which has been the achievement of the 1970s and 1980s in this country has been replicated all over the common law world as judiciaries have moved to fill lacunae of legitimacy in the functioning of democratic polities.[29]

The reassertion of the judicial scrutiny of the executive represents an important reinvention of democratic politics. Lord Woolf has articulated a sense of the courts as central to maintaining 'the delicate balance of a democratic society'.[30] This did not mean loyally accepting the will of Parliament, but asserting such values as due process and human rights. In one public address, he referred to the 'limits on the supremacy of Parliament' that were linked to the operation of judicial review. Stevens suggests that certain judges began to see themselves, albeit in an undeveloped way, as a 'separate branch of government', along the lines of the American judiciary.[31] The sense in which judges are working towards a more enhanced understanding of their role can also be seen in the extra-judicial writings of Sir John Laws. His understanding that the 'doctrine of Parliamentary sovereignty' was itself dependent on, and limited by, a 'higher order law'[32] can be seen as paralleling the jurisprudence of Ronald Dworkin, and suggesting a sympathy for a notion of fundamental human rights. The Human Rights Act 1998 encouraged these tendencies within the judiciary.[33]

---

26 For instance, In R. v. *Secretary of State Ex parte World Development Movement*, a successful challenge was launched to the Foreign Secretary's decision to go ahead with a decision to support a hydroelectric scheme in Malaysia despite the findings of the Overseas Development Administration that it was uneconomical. The Foreign Secretary had argued that the World Development Movement did not have *locus standi* to challenge his decision. The courts held otherwise. They held that having regard to the merits of the challenge and the importance of vindicating the rule of law, the applicants could make the application. Moreover, they held that the Foreign Secretary's decision was not within the terms of the statute which empowered him, the Overseas Development and Co-operation Act, as he should be promoting economically sound development.
27 Stevens (2002: 54).
28 Ibid.
29 Sedley (1995: 386–400).
30 Stevens (2002).
31 Ibid.
32 Ibid., 60.
33 To understand the origins of the Human Rights Act, we need to turn to the White Paper 'Rights Brought Home'. It is necessary to appreciate the political context: John Major's Conservative government had just been removed from office by an overwhelming Labour majority in 1997. Conservative governments had always been

In order to study the way in which some important and influential judges now understand their role, it is worth looking in some detail at a recent lecture by Lord Steyn.[34] Although some of the points that he considered are perhaps original to him, we may be able to appreciate that it resonates with the approach suggested by the statements of the other senior figures we briefly reviewed. Lord Steyn locates the judiciary within the 'two strands' of democracy in the UK. The 'principle of majority rule' translates itself into the supreme law-making power of Parliament, and the function of the executive, which is to carry on 'the business of the country'. Lord Steyn is primarily concerned with the Cabinet. The Cabinet is composed of ministers drawn from the ruling party. To the extent that it is in charge of policy execution, and to the extent that it is executing the political programme of a democratically elected party, the Cabinet represents the way in which the 'will of the people' expresses itself in party political terms.

In distinction to the executive, the judiciary is not elected, and has no popular mandate; it 'adjudicates disputes between the state and individuals, and between individuals and corporations'.[35] From what source, then, does the judiciary draw its legitimacy? We could say that it is rooted in a broad set of values. First, those of 'liberty and justice for all'.[36] This is precisely linked to 'fundamental freedoms'[37] as stated in the Human Rights Act 1998. Second, the legitimacy of the judiciary is founded on the extent to which they are 'independent, neutral, and impartial'.[38] None of these values are necessarily based on the idea of a political majority. Indeed, some human rights, the rights of immigrants for example, are particularly unpopular. Lord Steyn defines liberty, the spirit of the common law, in traditional terms. An individual can do anything that the law does not explicitly prohibit. Note, however, that this definition is much narrower when applied to the state and its agencies, who 'may only do what the law permits'.[39] This is because 'what is done in the name of the people requires constant

---

reluctant to incorporate the Convention into domestic law, and had not appreciated the need for legislation on human rights.
34   Baron Steyn PC, is such an example of a senior judge being a human rights activist. Born in 1932 in South Africa he was educated in South Africa and Oxford, being called to the Bar in South Africa in 1958 but leaving because of his opposition to apartheid, coming to the UK and joining the English Bar in 1973, and was made a Lord Justice in 1992, a Lord of Appeal in Ordinary in 1995 and created a life peer as Baron Steyn. While a Law Lord he gained recognition for his liberal views and espousal of human rights, including fierce criticism of Augusto Pinochet's claim to stand immune from prosecution. He openly criticised Camp X-ray at Guantanamo Bay and came under pressure from the UK government to make himself unavailable for the hearing on the indefinite detention of suspects under the Anti-terrorism, Crime and Security Act 2001 that began on October 4, 2004. The decision in that case caused the government to review its policy of indefinite detention of terror suspects and led to the equally controversial Terrorism Bill 2005. At the forefront of embedding the Human Rights Act into the contemporary common law he was also a moderniser and supported calls for the abolition of the role of Lord Chancellor. While a Law Lord he did not speak in the House of Lords, instead developing his views on democracy and human rights through judgements and lectures. Upon his retirement as a Lord of Appeal in Ordinary in 2005 he became the Chairman of the human rights organisation JUSTICE and has been vocal in his criticism of the Labour government and its approach to human rights. He has opposed proposed powers to allow detention without trial and expressed concern about the use of existing anti-terror powers.
35   Ibid. 246.
36   Ibid.
37   Ibid.
38   Ibid.
39   Ibid.

examination and justification'.[40] It would thus seem that the courts also obtain their legitimacy from their ability to scrutinise the executive, and demand that they justify their actions. How does this argument develop?

Lord Steyn's examples are interesting. The Hunting Act 2004 shows that 'even ancient liberties are not immune from abolition by a government set on doing so for party political reasons'. While it is only perhaps a vocal minority who engage in hunting, or would even be particularly concerned about the 'ancient liberty' to kill animals, the point is somewhat broader. It recalls (and Lord Steyn is later specific on this point) Lord Hailsham's warning that the British political system does not offer sufficient restraints on an executive with a large majority.[41] Parliamentary government is effectively 'an elected dictatorship'.[42] However, this legitimacy gap is to be filled by a newly empowered judiciary who can rise to the challenge of protecting minority rights and articulate the democratic culture of a 'multicultural society'. Lord Steyn goes on to argue:

> The public is now increasingly looking not to Parliament, but to the judges to protect their rights. In this new world, judges nowadays accept more readily than before that it is their democratic and constitutional duty to stand up where necessary for individuals against the government. The greater the arrogation of power by a seemingly all-powerful executive which dominates the House of Commons, the greater the incentive and need for judges to protect the rule of law.[43]

It is now the judges, not Parliament, who can give authentic voice to a human rights culture. This is evidenced by a number of recent decisions. *Director of Public Prosecutions of Jamaica* v. *Mollison*[44] show that the independence of the judiciary is a 'constitutional fundamental' and cannot be trespassed upon by other branches of government. In *Anufrijeva*,[45] the House of Lords held that the executive could not make unilateral determinations of people's rights which bypassed the scrutiny of the courts. This right of 'access to justice' could also be considered a 'fundamental' constitutional principle. In the Belmarsh case,[46] the House of Lords stated that indefinite detention of foreign terrorism suspects was in breach of the ECHR. In so doing, the House of Lords was giving effect to section 6 of the HRA. It would thus be hard to say that this decision lacked any kind of democratic legitimacy.

Lord Steyn's notion of the legitimacy of the court is thus twofold. There does appear to be something of a democratic justification, to the extent that the court acts 'in the name of the people' and has enabled Britain to become a 'constitutional state'. Support for this vision of the politics of the judiciary can be found in Lord Hope's speech in Jackson. Lord Hope points out that the rule of parliamentary sovereignty might rest on a 'political reality', but this in turn requires that the 'legislature [maintain] the trust of the electorate'. Bringing together Lord Hope's and Lord Steyn's views, we could

---

40 Ibid.
41 Lord Hailsham (1978: 126).
42 Steyn (2006).
43 Ibid., 247.
44 *Director of Public Prosecutions of Jamaica* v. *Mollison* [2003] 2 AC 411.
45 *R. (Anufrijeva)* v. *Secretary of State for the Home Department* [2003] UKHL 36.
46 *A.* v. *Secretary of the State for the Home Department* [2004] UKHL 56.

suggest that the court is precisely the body that inculcates and preserves this trust by ensuring that government remains within the law. If we assert, as Lord Hope does, that the sovereignty of parliament was 'created by the common law', and Parliament 'represents the people whom it exists to serve',[47] then we can appreciate that these arguments envisage a far more central role for the court in preserving the constitutional legitimacy of the state. Lord Hope also said:

> The rule of law enforced by the courts is the ultimate controlling factor on which our constitution is based ... Parliamentary sovereignty is an empty principle if legislation is passed which is so absurd or so unacceptable that the populace at large refused to recognise it as law.[48]

Regina (Jackson and others) v. Attorney General[49] is a key case for understanding the judge's perception of their role. Lord Bingham pointed out that the constitutional balance has been thrown out, and the 'Commons, dominated by the executive, [has become] the ultimately unconstrained power in the state'.[50] However, his speech is also noteworthy for stressing an important constitutional convention. It is 'inappropriate for the House in its judicial capacity'[51] to elaborate political criticisms of the Executive. The point made, though, corresponds with the arguments made by Lord Steyn extra-judicially. As far as his speech in *Jackson* is concerned, and acknowledging that there is a certain circumspection to what can be said in the House of Lords, the comment that the HRA 'created a new legal order' and the 'pure and absolute doctrine' of parliamentary sovereignty is 'out of place', must be considered radical statements.[52]

Central, then, to the new politics of the judiciary is the development of a body of human rights law. This uses the inspiration and resources of the HRA and the Strasbourg court, to adapt European rights jurisprudence to a common law context.[53] This represents the courts developing the powers given to them by Parliament under the HRA. It should not be seen as a judicial attempt to usurp the will of Parliament. The main thrust of the different judicial statements and writings suggest that the intention of the judges is to use the powers that Parliament has given them to remake the checks and balances of the constitution. What this might mean in terms of concrete adjudication can be glimpsed in *R. (on the application of ProLife Alliance) v. BBC*.[54]

The case was argued in relation to freedom of expression under Article 10. The ProLife Alliance, an anti-abortion group, had fielded enough candidates in the 2002 General Election to entitle them to a short public broadcast to be shown in Wales. The BBC refused to show the film that they produced, on the grounds that it would be offensive to public feeling under s.6(1)(a) of the Broadcasting Act 1990. The ProLife Alliance sought judicial review of this decision. Although they were successful in the

---

47 *Regina (Jackson and others) v. Attorney General* [2005] UKHL 56, at para 126.
48 Ibid.
49 Ibid.
50 Ibid., at para 41.
51 Ibid.
52 Ibid., at para 102.
53 We return to this theme in the chapter on the general jurisprudence of the HRA. It is a little more complex than this sentence allows.
54 *R. (on the application of ProLife Alliance) v. BBC* [2003] UKHL 23.

Court of Appeal, the House of Lords affirmed the decision of the court of first instance that the refusal to transmit the film was not a breach of their freedom of expression.

We are not so much concerned with the technical arguments about judicial review or Article 10, as with the broader constitutional issues that this case raised. How could the decision of the court be justified? It would be possible to argue that this was an interference in the democratic process; that the imposition of standards of taste on party political broadcasting was inappropriate in a mature democracy. A variation on this argument would assert that the courts were not taking their human rights obligations seriously enough, and should have affirmed that the right to freedom of expression against any limitations in the 1990 Act. Counter arguments would stress that even after the HRA, the courts are bound to follow statutes, and not to substitute their own decisions in place of laws passed by a democratically elected Parliament. But, does such an argument suggest that the HRA changes nothing? That human rights are entirely subordinate to the will of Parliament?

The starting point of our discussion is the bold statement of Laws LJ. He argues that the authority of the court 'rests in its constitutional duty to protect and enhance the democratic process, irrespective of the wisdom or the rightness of any or all the diverse political opinions which in the course of that process are paraded before the people'.[55] The court has to hold the line between various opinions, and in so doing contribute to the development of a democratic culture by allowing a public domain in which all shades of opinion can be articulated. In such a culture there should only be minimum restrictions on freedom of speech – a position which Article 10 itself acknowledges. The pressing question is how the court's obligation to give effect to Article 10 affects their relationship with Parliament. Should the House of Lords have been bold in this case, and argued that the ban on transmission went beyond a minimal restriction on freedom of speech? How can the judges understand the correct role of human rights in the democratic process?

Lord Hoffman considered the argument that the courts should show 'deference' to Parliament and asserted that, if the word carried the meaning of subservience, then it was not an accurate description. The question of the precise powers of the different branches of government, and their relationship to each other, was a matter for the 'rule of law and the separation of powers': in every instance, it had to be determined where supreme decision-making power lay, and the limits on that power. As a question of law, this was a matter for the courts.[56] This of course means that the 'courts themselves often have to decide the limits of their own decision-making power', but it does not follow that these limits are out of deference. Respective powers rest on a differentiation of the tasks of the courts and Parliament: 'Independence makes the courts more suited to deciding some kinds of questions and being elected makes the legislature or executive more suited to deciding others'.[57] Underlying this distinction are principles:

> The principle that the independence of the courts is necessary for a proper decision of disputed legal rights or claims of violation of human rights is a legal principle. It is

---

55 Ibid., para 5.
56 Ibid., para 75.
57 Ibid., para 76.

reflected in article 6 of the Convention. On the other hand, the principle that majority approval is necessary for a proper decision on policy or allocation of resources is also a legal principle. Likewise, when a court decides that a decision is within the proper competence of the legislature or executive, it is not showing deference. It is deciding the law.[58]

This is a powerful statement of the rule of law, and its relationship to human rights. Underlying the constitution are legal principles that assign the executive, the legislature and the judiciary to their respective sphere of competence. This is 'reflected' in Article 6. In other words, European human rights are entirely coherent with the common law on this particular principle. The relationship of the courts to Parliament is thus based on the law of human rights to the extent that it is not based on deference, but is a matter of principle. On the facts of the present case, the decency requirements for political broadcasts reflects the view of Parliament, and is based on the finding of the Annan Committee who stated that public opinion cannot be totally disregarded in the pursuit of liberty.[59] To the extent that this is an argument of principle, it was said to involve no arbitrary or unreasonable restriction on the right of free speech.

Lord Hoffmann's arguments address broad matters of principle. Lord Walker considered a more technical issue. How do constitutional principles translate into the way in which the courts should review legislation and executive decisions in the light of the Human Rights Act? Prior to the HRA, the test was based on the principle of Wednesbury irrationality.[60] After the HRA, the courts felt that a more exacting standard was required, and looked increasingly towards the concept of proportionality. In other words, in considering human rights, the court had to ask itself not was the executive decision irrational, but was it proportionate to the end to be achieved, taking into account the human rights obligation of the 1998 Act? In applying this test, the courts determined that they would have to show a certain degree of deference to Parliament. Lord Steyn's guidelines in *R. (Daly)* v. *Secretary of State for the Home Department*[61] are seen to be an accurate description of the path the court had to tread: to determine whether a limitation imposed by either a statutory rule or an executive decision is 'arbitrary or excessive', the court had to ask three questions. First, whether or not the objective of the Act is important enough to justify a limit on human rights; second, whether or not the precise measures in the Act are 'rationally connected' to the restriction on a right(s); and third, whether the 'means' put in place to 'impair' the right are 'more than is necessary to accomplish the objective'.[62]

This new test does not mean that the courts are reviewing the merits of a decision, but nor does it mean that the old Wednesbury test is still in place. This is because the 'intensity' of the proportionality review is much greater. Thus, the court would have to ask itself not whether the decision made was within 'the range of rational or reasonable decision', but to 'assess' the 'balance' between the limit of the right and

---

58 Ibid.
59 Report of the Annan Committee, Cmnd 6753, 1977.
60 After the decision *Associated Provincial Picture Houses Ltd* v. *Wednesbury Corporation* [1948] 1 KB 223.
61 *R. (Daly)* v. *Secretary of State for the Home Department* [2001] 2 AC 532.
62 Cited in ProLife Alliance, at para 133.

the need to preserve the fundamental right that the decision maker had made. This can involve the court in question of whether or not the 'limitation of the right was necessary in a democratic society, in the sense of meeting a pressing social need'.[63]

To return to a broader constitutional argument, this does not mean that there has been a blurring of judicial and executive functions, but it does mean that the HRA requires the courts to carefully scrutinise both legislation and executive decisions stemming from statutory powers.[64] Lord Justice Laws guidelines in *International Transport Roth Gmbh* v. *Secretary of State for the Home Department*[65] are definitional of this new understanding. Laws LJ argues: 'Greater deference is to be paid to an Act of Parliament than to a decision of the executive or subordinate measure'. There will be a greater scope for deference when the Convention requires it. The courts must also afford greater deference to democratic powers acting within the sphere of their constitutional competence, and the courts must observe that, within the constitutional settlement, they are entitled to pay less deference to a matter that falls within their area of 'expertise'. Lord Walker singled out the first of the guidelines as of particular relevance not only to the case in hand, but, also as an interpretation of the underlying foundation of the Convention: to strike a 'fair balance between individual rights and the general interest of the community'.

Figure 5.1 Being 'called' to the bar, Middle Temple, 1840s.

This image captures the traditional process of joining the professional élite, along with its rituals and ideologies that many believe protect members of the bar and the judiciary from undue influence. The argument of this chapter holds that judges are political and that it is better to have openness about the politics of their role than hold to some version of an apolitical rule of law. This will appear strange to some people who will prefer an ideal of judicial neutrality and may argue that recognising the politics of the judicial runs against their professional ethics and professional institutional belonging which should insulate them from the political. Traditionally judges in the UK were appointed from the ranks of senior barristers. The background of their role and politics was the culture of the bar and the

---

63 Ibid., para 135.
64 See *R. (Mahmood)* v. *Secretary of State for the Home Department* [2001] 1 WLR 840.
65 *International Transport Roth Gmbh* v. *Secretary of State for the Home Department* [2003] QB 728, 765–7.

Figure 5.1 Continued

oath of office. Barristers are officers of the court, and in most countries judges on appointment take an oath to uphold the constitution and/or support the rule of law.

There are numerous instances, however, when judges have supported legal or quasi-legal orders to produce clearly (to an outsider) unjust processes and decisions. In the cases, for example, of the American judges who applied the Fugitive Slave Laws, German judges who implemented Nazi law, or South African judges who imparted legal legitimacy to apartheid, professionals charged with administering justice provided institutional support passively and sometimes directly for state-sponsored (and often arbitrary) degradation, repression and brutality. Should judges bear a particular moral expectation? Clearly, in rule of law societies judges are central professionals, and, as Camenish in his classical work on ethics and professionals in society put it, are 'bearers of a public trust, bestowed upon them in the form of a professional degree and title, and endowing them with a monopoly in the provision of a service which is crucial to society'. Their role provides them with a power that can be used either 'for great societal benefit or to considerable societal harm', and thus 'they can rightly be accused of failure not only when they use their power, influence and expertise for the wrong purposes, purposes which are positively harmful, but also when they fail to use them for the proper purposes, or even fail to do so with sufficient energy and perseverance'.[66] Judges are subject to particular scrutiny because they are trained and take oaths to administer justice, or at least to uphold the constitution and the laws, which contain principles of justice.

In one interesting study Hilbink[67] analyses the submissive role that the judges in Chile played under the military dictatorship of General Pinochet even though they had been trained and appointed under a democratic regime and had taken an oath to uphold the constitution of that regime, which provided a host of liberal and democratic protections. Their support for the illiberal, antidemocratic, and anti-legal agenda of the military government (for example, of the more than 5400 habeas corpus petitions filed by human rights lawyers between 1973 and 1983, the courts rejected all but ten) is explained institutionally. In common with some who have sought to explain the behaviour of the judges who supported the Nazi regimes he first finds the ideology of legal positivism, as (mis)understood as making morality irrelevant to law and thus as consigning judges to be 'slaves of the law'. This view developed into a legal essentialist or 'antipolitics' conception of the judicial role among judges. Judges understood 'law' and 'politics' as two entirely distinct and unrelated pursuits, and considered the goals of judges and legislators to be completely separate and divergent; the less 'political' judges were, the more 'legal' they would be. This understanding was strengthened and reproduced by the institutional structure that was established in the 1920s, when reformers sought to end executive manipulation of the courts and professionalise the judicial career. A formal judicial hierarchy was established and the Supreme Court was given control over discipline and promotion within the career, even controlling nominations to its own ranks. Although this structure successfully increased judicial independence from executive control, it henceforth provided incentives for judges to look primarily to their superiors – rather than to any other audience or reference group – for cues on how to decide cases. Judges thus learned that to succeed professionally, the best strategy was to eschew independent or innovative interpretation in favour of conservative rulings that would please the high-court justices. In this way, conservatism and conformity were continually reproduced within the inward-looking judicial ranks.

Thus after the 1973 military coup even judges personally at odds with the laws and practices of the military regime were professionally unwilling or unable to defend liberal democratic principles and practices. Publicly challenging the validity of the regime's laws and policies in the name of liberal–democratic values and principles was viewed as unprofessional 'political' behaviour, which threatened the integrity of the judiciary and the rule of law. Under the watchful eye of the Supreme Court, any judge who aspired to rise in the ranks of the judiciary learned not to take such stands. Instead, judges conformed to the conservative line set and policed by the Supreme Court. Hilbink does not imply that the judiciary functioned in a social and cultural vacuum, the institutional structure and ideology of the Chilean judiciary embodied and reproduced the interests and ideas of its nineteenth- and early twentieth-century designers and so his study is historically bounded. However, he proposes a mix of personal policy preferences, legal philosophy, class-based interests, and regime-related variables such as fear and manipulation by the executive all factors in explaining the judicial behaviour. She offers several lessons. First, formal judicial independence, even when achieved and respected, is not sufficient to produce a judicial defence of rights and the rule of law. Indeed, institutional variables appear to impact significantly whether or not judges will be willing and able to assert themselves in defence of rights and the rule of law. Second, it is important to understand not only the way institutions constrain the expression of judges' pre-existing attitudes but also to how they constitute judges' professional identities and goals. Judicial role conceptions matter, and we need to understand better how they are formed, maintained or altered. Third, 'apoliticism' appears to be the wrong ideal around which to construct a judiciary in service of liberal democracy. Although judicial independence and professionalism are desirable for any polity committed to the rule of law, it is neither possible nor desirable to construct a judiciary beyond politics. For when judges are prohibited by institutional structure and/or ideology from engaging with the wider polity, they are unlikely to cultivate the professional attributes necessary for them to defend and promote liberal–democratic constitutionalism. She concludes that an 'apolitical' judiciary is thus far better suited to authoritarianism than to democracy.

....

66   Camenish (1983: 15, 17).
67   Hilbink (2007); remaining text summarises her argument.

THE JUDGES, THE EXECUTIVE AND THE RESPONSE TO TERRORISM

Tensions over the application of human rights continue into one of the most important and pressing areas where conflict has developed between the executive and the judiciary: the legislative response to terrorism. What has been the judicial response to these Acts? While some judges have shown themselves willing to follow the executive, and not to challenge legislation in the courts; others have attempted to stress the importance of human rights values, and court's scrutiny of executive actions.[68] Nicol argues that the issue of 'who has ultimate authority to determine the dividing line between the state's judicial and elective officers ... is contested and will remain so'.[69]

The response of the government to the terrorist attacks of September 2001 had two main aspects: the enactment of Part 4 of the Anti-terrorism, Crime and Security Act 2001, and the passing of a statutory instrument, the (Designated Derogation) Order 2001[70] derogating from certain Articles of the ECHR. Section 23 of the 2001 Act allowed the Home Secretary to detain foreign nationals under suspicion of involvement in terrorism if they are believed to be a risk to national security. The detention of foreign nationals must be under such circumstances that they cannot be deported from the UK if this would expose them to the possibility of torture. This would put the UK in breach of both Article 3 of the Convention Against Torture and other Cruel Inhuman or Degrading Treatment or Punishment (CAT) and Article 3 of the ECHR. However, it was still necessary to derogate from Article 5 of the ECHR to constitute these detention powers. This is because immigration detention powers are limited to the period that is required to deport the person in question. If there is no possibility that the individual will be removed from the UK in a reasonable time, then that individual cannot be lawfully detained. Thus, to make sure that the UK was not in breach of the European Convention on Human Rights (ECHR), the government used the power allowed by Article 15 to derogate from Article 5 (and also Article 9 of the International Covenant on Civil and Political Rights [ICCPR]).

The legislation thus shows a desire to remain human rights compliant with Articles 3 of the CAT and the ECHR, while using derogations to strengthen the Home Secretary's power to detain terrorist suspects. It would therefore be wrong to see the struggle

---

68   Answering these questions demands that we look at the general legal context. The UK ratified the Convention Against Torture in 1988, and it entered into force in January 1989. The European Convention, which also came into force in January 1989, also supplements the protection offered by the Convention for the Prevention of Torture. However, opposition to torture in English law existed prior to the undertaking of these international commitments. The common law has had its face set against torture since the seventeenth century. The Treason Act 1709 definitively stated that no one accused of crime could be tortured, and, alongside this Act, both the common law and the Offences Against the Person Act 1861 criminalised the act of torture. The law against torture was updated at the time the UK acceded to the Convention with s.134 of the Criminal Justice Act 1988. This made it an offence for a public official, or someone acting in a public capacity, to commit torture or engage in cruel, inhuman or degrading treatment or punishment. Criminal liability attaches to the act of torture under this section irrespective of the nationality of the alleged torturer, or where in the world the offence was committed (CAT Report, November 2004, p. 3). The commitment outlawing torture in domestic law and honouring international obligations must be seen in the light of recent legal reforms as part of the ongoing response to international terrorism.
69   Nicol (2006: 741).
70   SI 2001/3644.

between the judges and the courts over the response to terrorism as simply that of an anti-rights executive and a pro-rights judiciary. The legislation itself shows an intent to abide by human rights standards. The issues that we must examine lie within this general context.

We will be concerned with the House of Lord's ruling in the *A* case.[71] It focuses attention on the nature of the Home Secretary's power to make political decisions that are outside the province of the courts. The House of Lords held, first of all, that although there was not a specific terrorist threat, this did not invalidate the judgement that there was a real risk of a terrorist attack at some point in the future. This assessment of risk was a political judgement. Great weight must be accorded to the decision by the court. Despite Lord Hoffman's dissent, the court believed that the Home Secretary had made an accurate assessment that the nation was facing a public emergency. However, the House of Lords also held that the deference that the court owed to Parliament did not prevent the court from considering the proportionality of measures made by the executive to restrict rights. On this ground, s.23 was a disproportionate response to the terrorist threat.[72]

On these grounds the measure was illogical, disproportionate to the threat faced and the limitation on the right to liberty was therefore not justifiable. The House of Lords was also concerned that there had been no derogation from Article 14 and the effect of the section was discriminatory. Finally the House held that the measures were not coherent with international human rights obligations, citing the Refugee Convention and the Convention on the Elimination of All Forms of Discrimination, to protect the rights of those in a national territory and secure equality before the law.

How are we to understand this decision? The courts affirm that they respect the political nature of the Home Secretary's decision and accord 'great weight' to his conclusions. However, this deference to the Home Secretary does not prevent judicial assessment of the proportionality of the legislation that Parliament has passed. From this perspective, it would appear that the courts are political actors, assuming the power to assess executive decisions, and not to defer to them. How acceptable is it for judges to proceed in this way? This is a difficult question to answer. How one approaches it depends on where one feels ultimate authority lies in the constitution. Does it rest with the protection of human rights, or the executive's 'right' to protect national security, even if this means restricting human rights protection? The real answer to this question probably rests in a dialogue around the values of national security and human rights where both the courts and Parliament contribute to a meaningful articulation of democratic values. Whether or not the *A* case and the cases that we will now examine establish this dialogue, remains open to question.[73]

---

71   *A. and others* v. *Secretary of State for the Home Department* [2005] 2 WLR 87.
72   This was because, inter alia, the section applied to non-nationals, but not to nationals; moreover it permitted non-nationals to leave the UK, and did not assess the threat from British nationals. Finally, the court argued that s.23 could also apply to those who did not present a threat.
73   The government responded to the House of Lords' ruling in *A* with the Prevention of Terrorism Act 2005 (PTA). Amnesty International has argued that this 'broke the spirit, if not the letter, of the Law Lords' ruling'. This is because the 2005 Act gives a government minister 'unprecedented powers' to issue control orders to those suspected of terrorism. These orders can be made on the basis of 'secret evidence'. Further legislation has been passed in the wake of the bombings in London in July 2005 and another Terrorism Bill is presently before Parliament.

The issue of torture is certainly one where differences of opinion between judges and between the courts and Parliament, has emerged. The key case is *A. v. Secretary of State* (No. 2).[74] The case also concerns emergency powers enacted in Part 4 of the 2001 Act. One of the points of the appeal addressed rule 44(3) of the Special Immigration Appeals Commission (Procedure) Rules 2003. This rule allowed the Commission to receive evidence that would not be admissible in a court of law. This could include evidence obtained by torture by officials acting for foreign governments. The Court of Appeal stated that provided that the Home Secretary had neither procured or connived in torture, and provided that he was acting in good faith. The Home Secretary could use evidence 'which had or might have been obtained through torture by agencies of other states over which he had no power'.

The Court of Appeal thus shows less willingness than the House of Lords in the previous *A.* case to question the executive's actions in defence of national security. How is this justified? No doubt it would be correct to say that the courts must follow the legislature, but is one then compelled to agree that if the legislature makes a law that condones or authorises torture, the courts must follow it? From the viewpoint of the CAT, such laws would be in immediate violation of the Convention, and hence a nation's international human rights commitments.

In 2005, the House of Lords[75] reversed the Court of Appeal. The House of Lords held that evidence obtained by torture was unreliable and 'incompatible' with a principled administration of justice. As such, evidence obtained by torture, no matter whether or not this was by a third party outside of the UK, was inadmissible in court. The House of Lords also went on to consider the use of such information in the detention or arrest of a person ordered by the Home Secretary. Although the Home Secretary did not act 'unlawfully' in making use of 'tainted' information in these decisions, the Commission reviewing the reasonableness of the Home Secretary's suspicion could not admit evidence obtained by torture. However, the Commission was entitled to admit 'a wide range of material' that would not be inadmissible in 'judicial proceedings'. Furthermore, as those detained pursuant to the Home Secretary's decision had 'only limited access' to the evidence that was being used against them, it was necessary to use a specific approach to the issue of whether or not a statement had been obtained by torture. The correct approach was to be found in Article 15 of the Torture Convention. If, on the balance of probabilities, evidence has been obtained by torture, it should not be admitted. However, if the Commission was in doubt as to whether evidence had been so obtained, the evidence should be admitted. If a detainee was able to show a 'plausible reason' that evidence was obtained by torture, then the Commission had to 'initiate relevant inquiries'.

What sense do we make of this decision? Does it show the House of Lords championing human rights against a pusillanimous Court of Appeal? It would perhaps be more accurate to read this ruling as indicative, albeit in a rather limited form, of the dialogue that we have been describing in the section above. Although the House of Lords does overrule the Court of Appeal with a bold statement of principle, and

---

74   *A. v. Secretary of State* (No. 2) [2005] UKHL 71.
75   Ibid.

asserts that such evidence cannot be used in court, they assert that it is the Commission reviewing the Home Secretary's decision that cannot make use of torture evidence, and that the Home Secretary himself would not be acting unlawfully in making use of such evidence. The Commission might also be able to make use of torture evidence given the nature of the test under Article 15 of the CAT. If there is a dialogue taking place between the executive and the judiciary in this case, it suggests that the courts will police the due process and integrity of forensic processes, to the extent that torture evidence cannot be used. However, at the same time, they appear to acknowledge that such evidence may be used by the Home Secretary, and that given the terms of the relevant test, torture evidence might be used in court. This suggests a subtle and shifting alliance between the court and the executive. Although the Court of Appeal was in error in *A.* in suggesting a broad discretion to use torture evidence, the House of Lords do not go as far as asserting a general ban.

THE POLITICS OF APPOINTMENT

If, as we have argued above, judges are fundamentally political creatures, then to what extent are they subject to democratic scrutiny and accountability? Gearty argues that one of the most potent sources of current tension 'lies in the fact that judges are not democratically accountable'.[76] Precisely because the HRA has empowered judges, it may be necessary to reassess the checks and balances that exist over the judiciary. This is not to suggest that it is necessary to move towards a system where judges are elected. However, with the creation of a supreme court, these matters are brought to a head. As the issue of the democratic accountability of judges is quite broad, we will examine one particular aspect of this problem: the reforms in the area of judicial appointment. To what extent do they open judicial appointments to democratic scrutiny? Why should this be important?

Baroness Hale has argued, and most would agree, that it is a matter of principle:

'In a democratic society, in which we are all equal citizens, it is wrong in principle for that authority to be wielded by such a very unrepresentative section of the population.'[77]

That the composition of the judiciary should reflect that of society is a claim about the composition, rather than the function of the body. The argument for a representative judiciary is founded on the assertion that institutions should reflect the nature of the society in which they operate. This can be justified by principles of democratic pluralism, or equality of opportunity. Arguments for a representative judiciary are not the same as arguments for a representative legislature. Parliament is elected on a broad democratic franchise. Its function is to represent the interests of the electorate as a whole. While judges should be more representative of the society from which they are drawn, their predominant function is that of neutral adjudication. Indeed, the first report of the Select

---

76 Gearty (2004: 209).
77 Hale (2001: 502).

Committee on Constitutional Affairs stressed that reforms in judicial appointments should be driven by a notion of 'democratic accountability' that sought to achieve a balance between the need to secure the transparency of the appointments procedure, and the requirement of judicial independence within both the domestic and European contexts of the British state.[78] It was becoming increasingly clear that the old system was lacking in democratic credibility.

Prior to the 2005 Act, the Lord Chancellor's 'power' to appoint judges[79] meant that the process was secretive and headed by a person who held political office. The pool of possible appointments was small and almost entirely composed of senior barristers, or, in the case of most appointments to the office of High Court judge, those who were currently practising as recorders. It became increasingly difficult to justify this unaccountable and untransparent system of 'secret soundings'.[80] Furthermore, the blurring of judicial and executive functions in the office of Lord Chancellor appeared to be in breach of democratic principles. The Human Rights Act 1998 signalled the reform of the system. Proposals focused on the need for a judicial appointments body that would bring to an end obscure methods of appointment and limit the power of the Lord Chancellor.

The different forms that the body might take reflect different understandings of where the balance of power should lie between ministers, lay members, the legal profession and judges themselves.[81] An appointing committee, at least in the form presented in the government's consultation paper, would take over the appointment powers of the Lord Chancellor and the Prime Minister. Power to appoint judges would effectively be removed from the hands of ministers. This would have the virtue of independence from the political process, but it would also be necessary to make sure that the Commission was not biased with views from the profession or other sources. Although there are regulatory bodies that have no ministerial presence, and this model removes whatever political influence a minister might bring to bear on judicial appointments, it raises a serious constitutional issue. The removal of ministerial input also compromises the element of parliamentary scrutiny, because a minister is responsible to Parliament.

---

78   The government was also keen to promote a diversity agenda, but within the context of cost and efficiency. There were some arguments that the creation of a Judicial Appointments Committee would simply be too expensive; or would take up too large a part of a budget that had to be shared between the Court Service and the provision of legal aid. Indeed, there were misgivings about the time scale in which reforms could be worked out and then implemented. The reason for haste was seen as 'primarily political', although it is hard to understand this point. Is this a criticism of the party political agenda that lay behind the reforms, or an acknowledgement that reforms are necessary to make British institutions human rights compliant? See http://www.parliament.the-stationery-office.co.uk/pa/cm200304/cmselect/cmconst/48/4803.htm#a2.
79   Appointments to higher judicial positions, to the Court of Appeal, the Appellate Committee of the House of Lords and to offices of Lord Chief Justice and President of the Family Division were made by the Queen, on the advice of the prime minister after consultation with the Lord Chancellor, who had himself consulted with senior members of the judiciary. High court judges, circuit judges, recorders and stipendiary and lay magistrates were appointed by the Queen on the advice of the Lord Chancellor.
80   Although solicitors were allowed for some posts in the early 1990s, in the mid-1990s it was still the case that information on potential judges was kept in the Lord Chancellor's department in closed files (containing for barristers pink cards and for solicitors yellow cards) consisting of a range of appreciative and not so favourable comments, some related to much earlier stages in a person's career. A person's reputation could be made or unmade by comments, phrases and allegations that were never fully scrutinised.
81   See http://www.dca.gov.uk/consult/jacommission/index.htm#ch2.

A recommending commission reflects a different understanding of the balance of power. This model retains the involvement of ministers, and hence the element of responsibility to Parliament. The Commission itself makes the recommendation, and the minister rejects or accepts the recommendation. The model requires a precise demarcation of responsibilities between Commission and minister to be worked out, as otherwise a minister might find him or herself in the position of responsibility for appointments in which he or she had little or no input. A hybrid commission represents a variation on this theme: the power to make junior appointments would rest with an appointing commission, but appointing to senior positions would require ministerial input. A hybrid commission would allow ministerial responsibility to Parliament, while also creating an independent body. Once again, however, the precise demarcation between junior and senior judicial roles would have to be carefully addressed so as not to balance the powers of the body and the responsibilities of the minister.

The government's preference for a recommending body was ultimately successful, and suggests that the major ways in which transparency will be maintained is through the traditional constitutional mechanism of accountability to Parliament. Whilst this stresses the element of political accountability in appointments, it does beg the question of the terms of this constitutional convention. There is an argument that should a sufficiently strong government choose to support a minister's decision, then he or she would be unlikely to resign. Such criticisms of Parliament's weakness in the face of the resolve of governmental power suggest wider concerns about the 'democratic deficit' in British politics. While we cannot consider them in detail in this chapter, we could suggest that the weaknesses of the present reforms to achieve a transparent and democratic system of appointments are inseparable from wider concerns about the unrestrained power of the executive and the ongoing need for general constitutional reform.

How does the Constitutional Reform Act structure the operation of a recommending commission? The Act begins by reaffirming the independence of the judiciary. This is the first time in British history that a statement of this value has taken a statutory form. Give the absence of a fundamental document that describes the relationship between the executive, the legislature and the judiciary, this particular statement of judicial independence reflects the need to define a constitutional settlement without committing to a written constitution. It thus needs to be read in the context of 'constitutional' statutes such as the Human Rights Act 1998 and the European Communities Act 1972 that are seen as structural to the legal form of the British state. The other point that needs to be borne in mind is the sense in which the Constitutional Reform Act is driven by the political need to ensure that British institutions are compliant with the European Convention on Human Rights.

The Constitutional Reform Act makes a number of changes to the office of the Lord Chancellor, but most importantly for our purposes, we need to realise that the Lord Chancellor retains an important set of powers to affect and influence the appointment of judges. Although these powers are offset by those of the appointments committee, it would be wrong to see the new system as bringing to an abrupt end the influence of the executive in the appointment of judges.

Section 3(1) of the 2005 Act thus places a duty on the Lord Chancellor and other ministers with responsibility for the 'administration of justice' to 'uphold' the 'independence of the judiciary'. This section of the Act also contains provisions in relation to the independence of the judiciary in Scotland and Northern Ireland, but we do not have the space to consider these in detail. This is not too problematic, as they follow the general schema of the Act outlined below.

The general duty at s.3(1) is elaborated in a number of more specific responsibilities. Section 3(5) prohibits the Lord Chancellor and other ministers from influencing judicial decisions 'through any special access to the judiciary'. It is hard to know precisely what this notion of 'special access' covers. The notes for guidance put it in the following way: ' "special access" is intended to refer to any access over and above that which might be exercised by a member of the general public'.[82] It is hard to believe that ministers will be prevented by the Act from influencing decisions through subtle forms of political pressure. It is also difficult to see how a member of the general public may be able to question any particular decisions. Despite these criticisms, s.3 (1) has the virtue of a clear statement of the broader constitutional principle of the division of power. Ministers must leave the judiciary to their own sphere of competence. Likewise, judges must not trespass on executive or legislative functions. Given the cult of secrecy in much of central government, and our general ignorance of how judges make decisions, it is hard to know whether or not the branches of the state keep to their respective fields of competence. The Lord Chancellor is given specific duties to ensure the defence of judicial independence and the reflection of the 'public interest' in matters relating to judges and the administration of justice.

The main structural provisions are provided for by s.61 of the Act, which sets up the Judicial Appointments Commission. The Act goes on to specify that appointments must be solely on merit[83] and the Commission must be certain that the appointee is of 'good character'.[84] There is also a statutory duty to ensure that appointments are made in such a way as to achieve diversity in the composition of the judiciary, although such a duty is subject to the requirements of the sections described above. The Lord Chancellor retains an advisory role with respect to both procedure and the selection of candidates, and the Commission is under a duty to take into account the advice that may be given. However, given the importance of this guidance for the operation of the Commission, the Act does specify that the Lord Chancellor must consult with the Lord Chief Justice and bring the advice to the attention of the Commons for its approval. We could see this mechanism as the way in which the system of 'secret soundings' is opened to the democratic process.

The appointment powers of the Commission are also defined by the Act. The Act effectively divides judicial appointments in terms of the hierarchy of seniority. As far as appointments to senior positions[85] are concerned, the Lord Chancellor must first request the Commission to select a person if a vacancy arises in one of these offices.

---

82 See http://www.opsi.gov.uk/acts/en2005/2005en04.htm.
83 Constitutional Reform Act 2005, 63(2).
84 Ibid., 63(3).
85 This group includes: the Lord Chief Justice, who, among other offices and duties is the head of the judiciary and president of the Criminal Division of the Court of Appeal; The Master of the Rolls, who presides over the Civil Division of the Court of Appeal, and the three division heads of the High Court: The president of the Queen's Bench Division, The president of the Family Division, and the chancellor of the High Court.

Once the selection has been made, the Commission must submit a report to the Lord Chancellor. When he is in receipt of the report, the Lord Chancellor may accept or reject the selection; he also has the power to require the Commission to reconsider its choice of person. The procedure the Act determines is rather complicated, but the Lord Chancellor can refuse a selection on the basis that the person is not suitable or that the person is not the best candidate on merit. The Act requires the Lord Chancellor to put his decision in writing.[86]

The Judicial Appointments Commission [JAC] consists of a chairman and 14 other members who are appointed by the Queen on the recommendation of the Lord Chancellor. The composition of the Commission is crucial as it must achieve a balance between those who represent the legal profession, and those who are drawn from a non-legal background. As the select committee report argued, there was a fear that if judicial members of the Commission predominated, they would recruit 'in their own image'. Indeed, it was pointed out that the Appointments Commission in Scotland was considered successful despite the fact that judges and lawyers were in the minority. The structure of the Act reflects a partial triumph of this position. The chairman has to be a 'lay member' rather than a judge. Of the other commissioners, five must be judicial. The five judicial members must reflect a cross-section of judicial ranks, from Lord Justice of Appeal to district judge. Two members must be professional, representing the bar and the solicitor's branch of the profession. The five lay members are defined as those who are not practicing lawyers, and have not held judicial office.[87]

Criticisms have been made of the composition of the JAC. The Law Society has argued that the government still has too much control, as it appoints the Commission's staff, 82 per cent of which are seconded from the Ministry of Justice. They have also argued that the members of the Commission are 'selected primarily by the Lord Chancellor and the Lord Chief Justice'; the latter retaining a great deal of control over final appointments. Within the Commission, there are fears that the view of the judiciary predominate: five of the 15 JAC members must be judges, while at present three others happen to be current or former judges. Judicial influence is also cemented by the practice of obtaining references before interview, as this operates as a kind of filter. The JAC is also slowed down by cumbersome bureaucracy – a vice that the old system did not suffer from (at least in the opinions of some judges).[88]

---

86   The next group of judicial offices, as defined by s.85 of the Act includes puisne judges or the High Court judges, circuit judges, who sit in the regional Crown and County Courts, and recorders, who also sit in the Crown or County Court and hear less complex matters than circuit judges and district judges, who preside over County Courts and Justices of the Peace. The rules in relation to consultation and selection are similar to the group of senior judges.
87   The Act also sets up a Judicial Appointments and Conduct Ombudsman s.62(1). It also creates a set of disciplinary procedures. Based on s.108, these allow the Lord Chancellor to remove holders of judicial office and sit alongside the powers of the Lord Chief Justice that are also subject to statutory procedures. The Lord Chief Justice, with the agreement of the Lord Chancellor, may formally reprimand or suspend from office a judicial office holder who is, among other concerns, subject to criminal proceedings or convicted in criminal proceedings. The objective of this disciplinary code is to preserve public confidence in the judiciary. These disciplinary powers themselves sit within a system of checks and balances. Section 110 empowers the ombudsman to review disciplinary cases in certain circumstances, but, it is worth remembering that this is a review of procedure, rather than the substance of the claim made against the judicial office holder. Under s.111, the ombudsman has the power to set aside a decision, and to order that the matter be reconsidered.
88   See http://business.timesonline.co.uk/tol/business/law/columnists/article3283286.ece.

Will the JAC create a more diverse judiciary? In January 2008, with the appointment of the first ten high court judges, many people began to think otherwise. Of a group of 21 candidates who have been approved, the first ten to obtain appointments 'are white male former barristers and six of the nine educated in Britain went to leading independent schools'. The group of approved candidates consists of three women, none of whom are ethnic minority appointments.[89] The Commons Inquiry into Judicial Appointments found that although some progress had been made at lower judicial levels, there was a 'glass ceiling' at recorder level. As the position of recorder was the 'bridge' to more senior appointments, it would appear that while the lower courts and tribunals are becoming more diverse, the higher courts remain the preserve of white males.

To some extent it is unfair to criticise the JAC for this problem as the last two rounds of appointments to Recorder were made by the Ministry of Justice. Complaints were also made over the advertisements for specialist circuit judges that appeared to exclude applications from district judges. While there is a degree of diversity amongst district judges, there is very little among circuit judges. This would also suggest that there is another failure to push through a coherent agenda. Commentators have also pointed out that it will take some time for new appointments to be made. However, there are also problems with this gradualist approach:

> Once enough women, members of ethnic and religious minorities, gays, and other non-standard issue have been at Bar for long enough, they are bound to come through to the higher positions. Most serious outside observers know that it is not so simple ... There are also systemic obstacles to making sufficient progress to be regarded as a serious candidate.[90]

It is not simply a question of taking a 'wait and see' approach, and believing that the most able candidates will come to the top. The 'systemic obstacles' in the system of appointments mean that the system itself, despite the reforms and protestations to the contrary, still is in the control of social groups who recruit in their own image. This has been commented on by Mrs Justice Dobbs, one of the ten female High Court judges, and the only one from an ethnic minority. She cites Lady Justice Arden on the 'notable lack of progress for women at a time when there is considerable pressure for diversity in the profession and on the bench'.[91] It would seem that, at least for now, the old order remains in control of appointments to the judiciary.

THE JUDGES, PLURALITY AND RELIGION

The Politics of the Judiciary can be seen as an attempt to deal with one of the most pressing questions facing British democracy in the contemporary period: how to create

---

89   Reported in *The Guardian*, January 28, 2008. See http://www.guardian.co.uk/uk_news/story/0„2247993,00.html.
90   Hale (2001: 492).
91   See http://business.timesonline.co.uk/tol/business/law/article1984466.ece.

enduring plural and inclusive communities. Griffith did not make use of a concept of pluralism. Can this term help us to analyse the role of the judges in articulating modes of social life that are accessible to all citizens?

What is a plural society? A plural society is perhaps best understood as one where different communities can exist along side each other, and achieve a degree of mutual tolerance, respect and solidarity. Is it necessary to have a dominant culture within which minority cultures find some form of accommodation, or is a 'non-hierarchical' community possible, where different cultures accommodate themselves to each other without any privileged set of values? In present years, these issues have tended to play themselves out in terms of race and religion; and in particular around Article 9 of the Convention. These are difficult and pressing matters. We cannot deal with them in the detail that they deserve. However, we can focus on one case. *R (On the Application of Begum (By Her Litigation Friend, Rahman)) v. Headteacher, Governors of Denbigh High School*[92] raises precisely these concerns with the extent to which a minority faith position can be accommodated with the values of the majority.

What role do the judiciary play in this complex situation? If we accept the argument made in this chapter that the judges are playing an increasingly central role in the debate over the way in which British democracy operates, then we need to examine the impact of ideas of plurality in cases where community relations are at stake. Of course, it could be said that any consensus about the values that should define British society is a matter for public debate and the democratic process. It is not the job of the judiciary to determine the way in which a plural society should define itself. The matters at stake go beyond the law, and may not be capable of legal definition. Whilst there is a certain degree of truth in this claim, the courts have the obvious task of resolving those disputes where different values have come into conflict.

Shabina Begum was a pupil at a state-maintained school that required pupils to abide by its uniform policy. This policy had been developed in consultation with a number of local faith groups. It allowed female pupils to wear a variety of forms of dress including the shalwar kameeze. The shalwar kameeze is a form of dress, Pakistani in origin, which includes a headscarf. The majority of pupils at the Denbigh High school were Muslim, and the issue of school uniform had not arisen before the litigation occasioned in this case. Indeed, it was noted that Ms Begum had herself been happy to comply with the uniform rules when she first attended school. However, Ms Begum had come to the conviction that the shalwar kameeze was not an acceptable form of dress for a mature Muslim woman. She began to attend school wearing the jilbab. The jilbab provides covering for the wearer's arms and legs. Shabina Begum was suspended from school because she refused to stop wearing the jilbab.

Ms Begum applied for judicial review of the decision to exclude her from school, arguing that the uniform policy was in breach of Article 9[93] of the Convention. Her case

---

[92] *R. (On the Application of Begum (By Her Litigation Friend, Rahman)) v. Headteacher, Governors of Denbigh High School* [2006] UKHL 15.
[93] Ms Begum also alleged a breach of Protocol 1 of the Convention.

was dismissed, and she appealed to the Court of Appeal. The Court held that her rights under Article 9 had been breached. The Court of Appeal stated that:

> Although her belief that the shalwar kameeze was not a religiously acceptable form of dress was shared by only a minority of Muslims in her community, it was sincerely held. It was not for school authorities to pick and choose between religious beliefs; every shade of religious belief, if genuinely held, was entitled to due consideration under Article 9.[94]

The court is concerned with the boundaries that can be legitimately placed by the state on the symbols that are used by believers to manifest their faith. The Court of Appeal's makes a pluralist argument. Even if only a minority of Muslim opinion hold that the jilbab is the form of acceptable dress for a mature Muslim woman, the state – or its institutions – do not have the 'right' to determine whether or not this is acceptable. However, this argument has to be placed in the context of the Court's interpretation of the human rights position. The Court of Appeal suggested that the school's uniform policy could be justified under Article 9. The 'correct starting point' was to accept that the claimant had a valid right to 'manifest her belief'. The onus was then on the school to show that there was a legitimate aim that justified restricting the claimant's religious freedom. The restrictions are those that are justifiable by law in a democratic society. Evidence given to the court suggested that if some students wore the jilbab, others would view them as extremists. This would be 'divisive' and have a negative effect on school discipline. Concerns were also expressed on health and safety grounds. The High Court had accepted the school's evidence on this point, and held that limitations on the claimant's rights were necessary to allow the protection of the rights and opinions of others.

The House of Lords overturned the Court of Appeal.[95] Lord Bingham argued that ECtHR had accepted that limitations on Article 9 are permissible. Because of the limitations on Article 9, the respondent's decision to wear the jilbab could not be considered a breach of the Article. The test for interference is strict, and on the facts there was no interference with the Article. Brooke LJ's judgment in the Court of Appeal was criticised for being too proceduralist in approach. Lord Bingham asserted that the court must approach the substantive claim as to whether Convention rights had been breached, rather than focusing on the issue of correct procedure. The correct approach is provided by a proportionality test. In applying the test, the court must defer (to some extent) to the original decision maker's own understanding of the facts. Baroness Hale's judgment shows a very interesting approach to the facts of the case. She refers to the dissenting judgment in *Sahin* v. *Turkey*:[96]

> If a woman freely chooses to adopt a way of life for herself, it is not for others, including other women who have chosen differently, to criticise or prevent her. Judge Tulkens, in *Sahin* v. *Turkey* draws the analogy with freedom of speech. The European Court of Human Rights has never accepted that interference with the right of freedom of

---

94   R. *(On the Application of Begum...)* para 93.
95   Ibid.
96   *Leyla Sahin* v. *Turkey*, Judgment of 10 November 2005.

expression is justified by the fact that the ideas expressed may offend someone. Likewise, the sight of a woman in full purdah may offend some people, and especially those western feminists who believe that it is a symbol of her oppression, but that could not be a good reason for prohibiting her from wearing it.[97]

Rather than justify the limitations on Article 9 rights, Baroness Hale is arguing that they should be interpreted as broadly as possible. The act of wearing the jilbab has to be seen as freely chosen, and must be protected as such. Just because some may object to seeing veiled women in public life, does not mean that Article 9 should be limited. What is at stake is the means by which a particular form of Muslim culture allows women to enter the public world. A public ban on the jilbab would thus unduly affect a particularly discriminated minority. However, this argument has to be read in the following context. The primary concern is with education. Baroness Hale points out that schools must 'educate the young from all the many and diverse families and communities in this country in accordance with the national curriculum'.[98] An essential part of this task is to encourage mutual respect between those of 'diverse races, religions and cultures'.[99] On this point, Baroness Hale stresses that she was impressed by a particular piece of evidence: 'Girls have subsequently expressed their concern that if the jilbab were to be allowed they would face pressure to adopt it even though they do not wish to do so.[100] Preventing this kind of social pressure to conformity is achieved by a 'uniform dress code', but there is a much broader issue:

> Like it or not, this is a society committed, in principle and in law, to equal freedom for men and women to choose how they will lead their lives within the law. Young girls from ethnic, cultural or religious minorities growing up here face particularly difficult choices: how far to adopt or to distance themselves from the dominant culture. A good school will enable and support them.[101]

This argument undoubtedly proceeds from pluralist principles. It accepts that the individual has a choice as to what extent they will share the values of 'the dominant culture', while stressing that (at least in Baroness Hale's understanding) that culture is dedicated to equality. Equality is obviously compatible with plurality. This is because it attempts to prohibit forms of discrimination that prevent certain people from accessing cultural goods. In order to further equality, it is necessary that certain boundaries are placed that on the whole achieve the goals of equality. Privileging this goal means that the autonomous choices of individuals can be restricted if they are judged on balance to be discriminatory. Does this strike the right balance?

Clearly if one is a devout Muslim, then the decision in the Begum case shows that the 'state' will impose restrictions on what can be worn in public places. However,

---
97 R. (On the Application of Begum...) para 96.
98 Ibid, para 97.
99 Ibid.
100 Ibid.
101 Ibid.

to what extent did the school's uniform policy reflect the majority wishes of the community? If there was not a consensus that the jilbab was the required form of dress for Muslim women, then it is hard to justify its use, especially given the evidence that Baroness Hale cited. From this perspective, the court is indeed attempting to define a boundary that most people within the community in question would probably accept. The Law Lords themselves appreciated that the case should not be generalised. Lord Bingham stressed, 'This case concerns a particular pupil and a particular school in a particular place at a particular time'.[102] It could thus be tentatively suggested that the ruling in *Begum* is entirely consistent with a form of pluralism where the state must act to ensure that compromises are imposed on different groups with conflicting ideas. These compromises must be consistent with the underlying concepts that justify pluralism.

SHARIA IN THE UK

In February 2008, the Archbishop of Canterbury, Dr Rowan Williams, gave the foundation lecture at the Royal Courts of Justice.[103] In his address, Dr Williams engaged with the status of Islamic sharia law in the UK. He was careful to stress, however, that the issues raised by his lecture were not peculiar to sharia. They concern broader relationships of faith and law. How should a democratic society respond to the tensions between secular values and those based on religious codes?

---

102 Ibid. at para 2. Lord Bingham went on to say that: 'The House is not, and could not be, invited to rule whether Islamic dress, or any feature of Islamic dress, should or should not be permitted in the schools of this country'.
103 Thursday 7 February, 2008, full text at www.archbishopofcanterbury.org/1575. The Archbishop's lecture ranged over jurisprudential and institutional issues. He recognised that in contemporary society 'our social identities are not constituted by one exclusive set of relations or modes of belonging', thus he rejected the view 'that to be a citizen is essentially and simply to be under the rule of the uniform law of a sovereign state, in such a way that any other relations, commitments or protocols of behaviour belong exclusively to the realm of the private and of individual choice'. This, he called a positivist account of law that reduced the complexity in the legal category of modern citizenship and social interdependency. The Archbishop asked for a 'higher level of public legal regard' to be paid to 'communal identity' and argued for greater thought to be given to what it means to live under more than one jurisdiction. There was controversy and a degree of hostile reaction to the speech. On Thursday July 3, 2008 the Lord Chief Justice Phillips (the most senior Judge in the UK, who had Chaired the Archbishop's lecture) gave a less wide-ranging speech to the London Muslim Council in which he said Islamic law could benefit society and that he was willing to see sharia law operate in the country, so long as it did not conflict with the laws of England and Wales, or lead to the imposition of severe physical punishments. Phillips reiterated there was 'widespread misunderstanding' of the nature of sharia law, and argued: 'There is no reason why sharia principles, or any other religious code, should not be the basis for mediation or other forms of alternative dispute resolution [with the understanding] ... that any sanctions for a failure to comply with the agreed terms of mediation would be drawn from the Laws of England and Wales.' He also suggested sharia principles should be applied to marriage arrangements. The Lord Chief Justice stressed that he was not countenancing any notion of sharia courts operating as a separate, competing jurisdiction in the UK. 'So far as the law is concerned, those who live in this country are governed by English and Welsh law and subject to the jurisdiction of the English and Welsh courts.' However, he was clear that 'It was not very radical to advocate embracing sharia law in the context of family disputes, for example, and our system already goes a long way towards accommodating the archbishop's suggestion ... It is possible in this country for those who are entering into a contractual agreement to agree that the agreement shall be governed by a law other than English law. Those who, in this country, are in dispute as to their respective rights are free to subject that dispute to the mediation of a chosen person, or to agree that the dispute shall be resolved by a chosen arbitrator or arbitrators.'

The Archbishop pointed out that sharia law has been subject to a certain degree of misrepresentation at the hands of certain self-appointed spokesmen for western 'liberal' values. Their proselytising has led to a simplistic idea of a 'clash of civilisations' where the enlightened values of human rights are opposed to a supposedly pre-modern and socially conservative religious world view. While the use made of sharia law by extremist movements may be seen as exemplary of some 'primitivist' understanding of Islam, traditions of Islamic jurisprudence are far too complex and sophisticated to be reduced to such caricatures. Thus, the first key element of Dr Williams' argument is that any sensible arguments about sharia have to understand the richness and diversity of its traditions.

Sharia can be understood as a practice of interpretation. Rather than a 'monolithic' set of enactments or a 'single code', it is a way in which the Koran and other sacred texts have been read so as to 'actualise' the principles of Islam in 'human history'. Indeed, the major traditions of Islam are identified with different ways in which sharia can be interpreted. These traditions are now established, and have such historical authority that there can be no further attempts to open new ways of interpreting the sacred texts. However, there are also a 'good many voices' arguing that new interpretations can be forged by 'reasoning from first principles' rather than entirely remaining within the historical traditions. It is from this position that it might be possible to outline a 'just and constructive relationship between Islamic law and the statutory law of the United Kingdom'. The search is thus for those points at which two legal traditions can 'talk' to each other and find points at which they overlap.

The Archbishop's argument is profoundly pluralist and rests on an understanding of the part that law plays in social communication. We will elaborate these two themes in turn. The law of the secular state serves to licence the acceptable forms of social communication, and is the dominant way in which public discourse is constituted. Where disputes concerning religious issues are being adjudicated, the court substitutes its own legal understanding of the nature of the dispute for the meaning(s) that it might have for the parties concerned. This takes us towards the pluralist elements of the argument. Once it is accepted that religious opinions have to be taken seriously, it raises the question of plural jurisdictions.

Where does this argument lead? Dr Williams refers to the need to think about whether or not there could be 'something like a delegation of certain legal functions to the religious courts of a community' – a question not just of sharia, but of other bodies of 'religious' law. To some extent this is already taking place. There is an Islamic Sharia Council that gives rulings on matters such as marriage and divorce. Dr Williams argues that 'access' requires that this body be given proper resources and a 'sophisticated' role in the adjudication of disputes. It is perhaps a little unclear what this might mean at the level of institutional reform, but the general direction of the argument is clear. Reforms are necessary to give such a body a significant role in adjudication, so that it can claim a 'high degree of community recognition'. Only then will there be a more or less acceptable way of distinguishing between real and vexatious issues.

There are, of course, objections. A sincere attempt to achieve the kind of rights that create a truly plural society might in fact serve to entrench patterns of subordination and disadvantage. Moreover, how would conflicts between human rights and religious values be resolved? The fundamental response to these concerns is simple: 'If any kind of plural jurisdiction is recognised, it would presumably have to be under the rubric that no supplementary jurisdiction could have the power to deny access to the rights granted to other citizens or to punish its members for claiming those rights'. This suggests that there are limits to pluralism, but that these limits are justifiable. Moreover, it allows minority groups to live in both communities: that of faith and that of the secular state with its commitment to equality.

CONCLUSION

In this chapter we have been describing a transformation of the politics of the judiciary. We have been suggesting that there is an understanding that the judges must play a more pronounced role in the constitution. However, while the HRA has been a 'catalyst' for change, it must also operate the necessary restraint and work within the doctrine of the 'separation of powers'.[104] This suggests a renewed importance for the judiciary, perhaps even a dialogue between the courts and Parliament. It also indicates the lines around which judicial practice will work itself in the wake of the HRA. These themes come together interestingly in the following paragraph:

> And if in our own society the rule of law is to mean much, it must at least mean that it is the obligation of the courts to articulate and uphold the ground rules of ethical social existence which we dignify as fundamental human rights.[105]

This kind of statement would have been unimaginable in the 1950s or, one might imagine, a Law Lord fulminating about the threat posed to good order by invoking radical ideas like 'ethical social existence'. Sedley's statement represents his views – it does not necessarily mean that he is representative of the senior judiciary. Indeed, we have seen that the politics of the judiciary is characterised by tensions (although these should not be seen in party political terms). We should also not be too hasty in thinking that judges are all strong advocates of human rights, or that the reawakened sense of judicial activism is not uncontroversial.[106] However, what is clear is that, at least since 1998, there has been a significant shift in the judge's own understanding of the role that the judiciary plays in a democratic state, and a new sense in which we can speak of the politics of the judiciary.

This begs a number of serious questions. While doctrines of human rights are employed as ways of justifying the political role of judges, human rights does not allow us to address the range of institutional and constitutional issues that arise. Human rights are themselves indeterminate. For instance, Begum's case shows that Article 9 could be used to either protect Ms Begum's right to manifest her faith, or to limit that right. It is entirely a question of the values that the court chooses to privilege. This may suggest to some that there should be far more public scrutiny of the judiciary, and the

---

104 Lord Irvine (1999: 371).
105 Sedley (1995).
106 See Tomkins (2005), who puts forward a 'republican' reading of the British constitution and argues against seeing the common law and the courts, rather than parliament, as the central players holding government to account.

hence the values that they bring to their decision making. Whether or not the JAC can be reformed in such a way as to open judicial appointments to the necessary degree of scrutiny is perhaps one of the most pressing political questions, and necessarily linked to the creation of a democracy worthy of its name.

POSTCRIPT: THE POLITICS OF THE NEW LEGAL OFFICIALS IN A GLOBALISED LEGAL ORDER

Our chapter on the politics of the judiciary has been focused entirely on a national context. Perhaps this approach is too narrow. Moreover, we appear to assume that the decisions of judges, rather than other officials, are central to law and regulation. This brief postscript intends to meet these criticisms.

Within the modern common law nation-state (as represented by England and Wales, the USA, Canada and, increasingly, countries such as New Zealand, Australia and Singapore), judges are not in charge of the actual operation of law. While judges may still be the Kings of doctrinal development the court is being displaced from the centre of process or institutional reality. Irrespective of the claims as to a variety of forms of 'law' made by legal pluralists, it is undeniable that in large part, legal specialists are moving from the litigation model to a dispute-management model, organised so as to settle disputes far from the courts. The courts system, in which the judge reigns, appears somewhat side-lined. The dispute resolution function has shifted elsewhere. 'If lawyers once followed judges and clustered around courts, now increasingly lawyers follow the client.'[107] These lawyers or service providers are located in a vast diversity of firms and modes of organisation, but the power and prestige of lawyers is at its most concentrated in international law firms.

The international law firms operate in a globalised legal order that seems resistant to democratic accountability. Globalisation renders problematic the paradigm of the nation-state. It has made important sources of social, political and (especially) economic-related lawmaking autonomous of the nation state, and hence difficult to trace, let alone control. Key examples would include commercial rules, like the *lex mercatoria*, which come from outside national legal systems. How can national legal systems exert any control over these international bodies of commercial law? Whose ethics, rights and claims hold sway? These new rules and forms of understanding are based on and determined by market-based economic interests and concerns, which often purport to be devoid of value underpinnings or implications, yet implicitly carry value presuppositions and have value consequences. To what legal order, to what system of scrutiny do the legal officials belong? Other examples are the legal, political and economic reforms routinely forced upon countries seeking economic aid from international lenders and relief agencies. More examples exist, varying in the degrees of their 'voluntary' nature, including the legal reforms necessary for membership in the General Agreement on Tariffs and Trade (GATT) of the European Union, and the adoption of child and sweatshop labour regulations to satisfy consumer groups from abroad.

---

107   Murphy (1997: 192).

In these situations local conditions, customs and values have a minimal influence on the creation of law, although they will experience the consequences of its implementation, and the norms and ethics of those responsible for implementation may or may not be resonant with those of local officials.

Whatever, the impact on democratic accountability globalisation is however already affecting the culture and ethics of judges in national context. As Slaughter put it:

> Judges are building a global community of law. They share values and interests based upon their belief in law as distinct but not divorced from politics and their view of themselves as professionals who must be insulated from direct political influence. National and international judges are networking, becoming increasingly aware of one another and of their stake in a common enterprise. The most informal level of transnational judicial contact is knowledge of foreign and international judicial decisions and a corresponding willingness to cite them.[108]

The movement of students from one jurisdiction to another, for postgraduate legal studies (such as the Masters in Law) in particular, offers one piece of the picture of an emerging legal culture for the globalization of law, towards the development and solidification of a transnational legal culture. Ideas, texts, bites of knowledge, will float and be transmitted and used in settlings far from the locality of the utter. The idea of the rule of law will need to be rethought and if different bodies of official law are at play, the question as to who and what holds these legal actors accountable is not just one of process but of belief system. If accountability to democratic process and positive rights provides one answer to that question for the nation-state the outcome for an emerging transnational, global practice is far from certain.

What ideal, or set of understandings, could guide for this new reality? Perhaps we can see an emerging global code of legality (undoubtedly with human rights central to it), but who is to judge the judges; where will accountability lie? The chapter began with Bracton's appeal to the judges to remember that they would be held accountable in a day of final judgment. Tim Murphy explains that the common law has a particular claim to be 'the oldest social science' dating from its early days when judges were a feature of the (Royal) court and the court practiced 'adjudicative government'.[109] In adjudicative government decisions were made in accordance with a particular way of looking at things, specifically the manner in which things looked if you sat behind a bench – or a table – and listened to an argument before giving judgment. Murphy reminds us that in Occidental culture 'such a tableau unfolded, of course, at the every end of time itself, in the Last Judgment'. This was not a version of natural law where one was meant to follow God's will and the task was to create rules to be strictly applied based on what God had given but of choice and responsibility. 'A greater weight is carried by the image of God as judge than by that of God as Lawgiver. The Laws, as given, are given.' The image of God as judge is not mechanical jurisprudence, it is not

---

108   Slaughter (1997: 186).
109   Murphy (1997).

a matter of applying what is laid down in some simple allocation of facts to easy law: once we put emphasis on the seat of judgement the central question concerns how as king of heaven or his regent on earth, should one judge. This in the end means 'how to weigh in the balance good and evil, or how to determine what is good and what is evil. This is the character of the question of truth, which is not really imaginable outside the setting of power and judgement.' Yet if we are to conceive of a politics of judging transnationally – given we are in an era where it is clear that forces prevent knowledge of global interconnectedness, and 'realistic' notions seem akin to announcing that one is too exhausted to care for more than a sympathetic moment – it will need great powers of judgement to link law, democracy and truth.

6

RACISM AND LAW: 'NO DOGS, NO BLACKS, NO IRISH'[1]

The best remedy for whatever is amiss in America would be if every Irishman should kill a negro and be hanged for it.[2]

A car drove by with a loudspeaker saying that all Hutus had to defend themselves, that there was a single enemy: the Tutsis. I heard that. I jumped out of bed, grabbed a club, I went out, and I began killing. There was an old woman nearby, with two young children who had not reached school age yet. We took them outside and made them stand by a pit ... I killed the children and [....] killed the old woman. Then we climbed back out [of the pit] and found an old man hiding behind the house. I knocked him out with a club ...; I did not know the people I killed very well. All we were told was to hunt down the Tutsis, and we began to slaughter them ... While I was killing, I thought there was no problem, no consequences, since the authorities said the Tutsis were enemies.[3]

It was the British idea of the rule of law that ... guaranteed free disposition of one's own body, a shift that constitutes the origin of both liberty and property. Liberty is not exhausted by the right to make contracts; it begins with the protection of life secured by law. Consequently subjective rights are directly linked to the conception of power that rejects slavery and domination. They are inseparable from the new political arrangements and a new conception of rights as law.[4]

It is a great and dangerous error to suppose that all people are equally entitled to liberty. It is a reward to be earned, not a blessing to be gratuitously lavished on all alike – a reward reserved for the intelligent, the patriotic, the virtuous, the deserving – and not a boon to be bestowed on a people too ignorant, degraded, and vicious, to be capable either of appreciating or enjoying it.[5]

---

1   The later part of the title being from a sign on accommodation in London in the early 1970s.
2   The comment of an Oxford academic cited in Jamieson (1992: 79).
3   The account of a man held in central prison in Kigali, Rwanda, for his part in the genocide that took the lives of 800,000 in 1994, 'We Were Calling to Death', *Harpers Magazine*, February 2003, pp. 14–15.
4   Kriegel (1995: 37).
5   John C. Calhoun (1782–1850), a leading US southern political and social philosopher [7th Vice President of the US] and an outspoken proponent of slavery, which he defended as a positive good. Quoted in Becker (1942: 252).

INTRODUCTION: THE LONG VIEW, WHOSE PERSPECTIVE?

This text began in New Zealand in the 1970s with one of the authors listening to first year Legal System lectures on (English) legal history from a figure wearing black academic gown who had been a public prosecutor in Kenya and whom, it was rumoured, laid claim to have hung a considerable number of the Mau Mau. The 'I' voice of that first chapter is white (as are the other two co-authors), a *Pakeha*, as the Maori would call the white settlers – predominantly from Europe – who came (with superior technology; i.e. guns) to the lands they occupied.

The contemporary common law world – as with the civil law world – was built through the global spread of colonialism and capitalism.[6] The interaction of race and law is not innocent; European expansion carried a story of delivering law as its gift, bringing order to chaos, light to darkness. But imperialism relied on violence and the violence of imperialism was 'legitimate'. For Fitzpatrick, 'racism' solved the contradiction between enlightenment ideal of universal freedom and equality and the undeniable fact of European colonialism (and the inherent violence to the other inherent in that).[7] For Patricia Tuitt, the colonial state was 'monstrous' in its racial denial of what should be the 'most fundamental of securities, the persistent recognition of the human state to all, irrespective of race'. Race allows types of pairings or conjunctions with the now disputed human subject: the human subject's universality is demarcated and partitioned. Learning law is in part learning a language, a vision and an inheritance.[8] For many, and with considerable justification, the story of the development of modern law is a story of overcoming slavery, of developing ideas of subjective rights and then institutionalising those ideas in law and in international conventions.[9] For the French writer Kriegel the law provides the only route out of slavery: 'The chains of oppression can be broken and a community of men [sic] freed from bondage only by passing through a narrow gate', that of law.[10] But for Kriegel and for the authors of this text, law is no simple fact, no positive thing, but a complex that needs human action and ethical responsibility for it to live up to this narrative, else it may falsify and entrap. For others, such as Tuitt, modern law cannot be divorced from the violence and violent counter-violence of colonialism.[11] What is the responsibility in legal education of considerations of time, place and race?

---

6   Admitting there is no one form of colonialisation, and generalisations are always subject to qualification, the spread of Europe into the globe owed much to its technological, military and naval supremacy and its competitively minded nation states. It also owed greatly to its private entrepreneurs who had or organised capital to export, and its crowded populations that gave human resources for ships, military and people to settle other lands.

7   Fitzpatrick (1991: cf. 63–72).

8   'The knowledge of the law is like a deepe well out of which each man draweth according to the strength of his understanding. He that reacheth deepest, he seeth aimiable and admirable secrets of the law, wherein, I assure you, the sages of the law in former times ... have had the deepest reach'. (Coke Upon Littleton, 71a).

9   Slavery is unfortunately still practiced today in far too many places – see Bales (1999) and the regular postings of Anti-Slavery International. It is of course officially condemned by virtually every government, even those that tolerate it.

10 Kriegel (1995: 148).

11 Tuitt (2004).

If one narrative of common law's development *within* its homeland of England (allowing for the constant and, one suspects, deeply ontological engagement with continental Europe) is of the levelling of hierarchy, of the claiming (and acceptance) of legitimacy through democracy and 'the rule of law', what of the places 'other'? For many, particularly non-white Europeans (and we include as quasi-Europeans the white inhabitants of the Americas, Australia and sectors of Asia and Africa), the foundations of modern law are cast in the violence of colonisation – the other side of the European Enlightenment. We cannot here offer a major essay or series of reflections, only a small engagement with perspectives, walls and the fractured division of the human world. Law categorises; that is part of its utility. It seems to reflect division; it can demarcate and differentiate with precision. Oppositions seem also existentially inbuilt to conceiving of law; much thinking and speaking (and although not often articulated, of experiencing) about law is done in terms of internal and external, of inside and outside; perhaps better understood as by the insider and the outsider.

So with the university-education beginning of the first chapter: I [WJM] sat in a class of white faces, listening to a legal history and various courses on law delivered by white males (almost entirely) that had little role for the Maori (the brown skinned Polynesian inhabitants of the islands to be called New Zealand at the time of European arrival). Was the silence of these lectures towards the Maori and the Aboriginal, the absence of the 'other' to our real Australasian history, a form of racism? I have ambivalence. I had no consciousness of any absence, but I am white and now conscious of the words of Patricia Williams that it is one of the privileges of whiteness to appear 'unraced'.[12] I was not so conscious of being and not-being then. In the concluding section of *Peau Noire, Masques Blancs* (translated as Black Skins, White Masks), the Caribbean social theorist Frantz Fanon existentially denies any plain fact view of the world, stating words to the effect that the black man is not; nor is the white.[13] The English translation of his work subdues his existential sense (such as the title of Chapter 5 being presented as 'The Fact of Blackness', rather than a more subtle 'The Lived Experience of the Black Man'). Fanon is no positivist, the blackness of race is not a 'fact', not a reflection of natural state (and the same goes for whiteness); both are a form of lived experience (*expérience vécue*). The ontology of social reality is lived experience. Existentially we have an abyss of meaning: the black man and the white man are not, and yet they are. The reality of their being is co-joined. Practical concern and much scholarly work on racism has emphasised the 'victim': key concepts such as racism, discrimination and prejudice seem to carry a certain direction that leads legal discourse and practical legal measures being orientated to helping, to avoiding harm to (an)other cast as the 'victim'. There is in this a certain one-sidedness. The 'coloured', the 'black' fight as terms to reclaim a human dignity for those who they were once addressed to in disdain, in placement beneath; by contrast whiteness does not seem to exist. To the revisionist post-colonialists, by contrast, being white 'means that God put you on the planet to rule, to dominate, and occupy the centre of the national and international universe – because you're white'.[14] For Toni Morrison whiteness is not static but defined in relationship to 'otherness'.[15]

---

12   Williams (1997).
13   Fanon (1952) English translation 1986.
14   Jordan (1995: 21).
15   Morrison (1992).

At times those who were 'white' were seen as dangerous and not-really-white. The identity of the white-non-white (and potential contagion) varies. In the US the 'Irish were niggers turned inside out'; and only by a combination of fortunate political and religious alliances were they recast as part of the mainstream. Has consciousness of inter-connectedness in New Zealand increased?

Again I am ambivalent. The monolithic history has fractured, and there are many ceremonies which declare the heritage of the space constituting New Zealand/Aotearoa as one of diverse life experiences that have made and make the life that exists. But is this superficial or a real recognition of what has structured this space and life, impacting on how and what is currently lived? Certainly, first year law students in New Zealand in the 2000s face a different educational perspective on the common law and a different heritage. Both interweave. New Zealand now has a distinctive constitutional development with a relatively recently established Supreme Court and Bill of Rights. Common law methodology, adherence to precedent, the language of Appeal Court decisions, has been 'enriched' and a 'moral imperative' appears clear from judgements of the highest courts.[16] The treaty of Waitangi (signed in 1840 by representatives of the British government and over 500 Maori chiefs) is now seen as the foundational legal document of the 'partnership' at the basis of New Zealand constitutional arrangement.[17] At the time I attended first-year lectures the Maori had engaged in sustained land marches that claimed 150 years of broken promises and absent legal presence. If for the Maori the treaty was a solemn legal compact in which they had surrendered certain things for recognition of *tino rangatiratanga* of the chiefs, tribes and people, and promises of equal protection, including protection of Maori property rights, then much of the 'real' history of New Zealand was of broken promises and denial of legal recognition. In Maori subject position the lesson of the rule of law appeared largely one-sided, of a violence being done to them (either through the taking of land or military action when they resisted). The words of Judge F.R. Chapman, sentencing a Maori activist to prison in 1917 for resisting arrest are illustrative:

> You have learnt that the law has a long arm, and that it can reach you, however far back into the recesses of the forest you may travel, and that in every corner of the great

---

16 The leading Constitutional Law text, Joseph 2007, discusses the impact of the New Zealand Bill of Rights at pp. 871–3, 880–1, 1140 and 1175–82. His essential thesis: 'The Bill of Rights has enriched common law method. It requires courts to consult openly the range of public law values that underpin rights adjudication, making it a more evaluative jurisprudence. The instrument extricated the courts from the crude, self-sustaining "balancing of interests" approach that beset earlier rights adjudication, when the State's interests readily subsumed individual rights of protest, association and free speech. The instrument also "internationalised" New Zealand's human rights law ... The instrument has engaged New Zealand in an international conversation about human rights that has broadened and enriched its legal culture. A more evaluative and principled approach to rights adjudication has replaced the "public versus private interests" approach of pure common law method. The courts apply the European doctrine of proportionality when delineating reasonable limits on guaranteed rights and appeal directly to international comparisons when assigning content to rights.' (Joseph, 2007: 1140). For Richard Scragg (personal conversation, Canterbury University, April 2008) after the Bill of Rights New Zealand judgments 'have a more democratic ring', they 'read differently', with a 'greater sense of the bench grappling with deep issues of social policy and social values'.

17 Although there are debates over what exactly the Treaty 'meant' to both parties, and the difficulties in translation between the English and the Maori copies. As Seuffert (2006) points out, the process of settling Treaty claims undertaken from the mid-1980s and continuing is government sponsored and one can identify one aim as the re-creation of the story of national identity, now with the Maori being incorporated as economic entrepreneurs.

Empire to which we belong the King's law can reach anyone who offends against him. This is the lesson your people should learn from this trial.[18]

However, Maori activism had won from the Labour government the Treaty of Waitangi Act 1975; it was to be largely a dead letter for some years until another Labour government in 1985 extended the Waitangi Land tribunal to reopen old transactions, to look into historical breaches of the treaty and give financial compensation. The tribunal became flooded with claims, and Pakaha-orientated history was turned into an unsettled history of claim, counter-claim and anxious race relations.[19]

Anderson reminds us that nations are imagined political communities.[20] If we were to attempt to include the colonial experience, what does the rule of law *look* like? What does one see? We will consider two images: one of the Aboriginal perspectives of the settlement of Australia and the other of the Mau Mau 'emergency'.

Figure 6.1 Hey Bros, Ian Waldron, 1998, acrylic on canvas.

At first sight this looks like a straight copy from a very famous English painting (*The Hay Wain* by John Constable painted in 1821) and then one notices a small Aboriginal figure with the Aboriginal flag and the caption 'Hey Bros...' what is going on? The English painter Constable desired to be a landscape painter though this was not popular and he had to produce portraits to ensure a good living. However, he made many sketches in pencil and oil paint in the open air as he observed the natural world and the effects of the weather and changing seasons on the countryside, with the

---

18 Quoted in King (2003: 222).
19 To note the title of one book, *An Unsettled History: Treaty Claims in New Zealand Today*, Ward (1999).
20 Anderson (1991).

Figure 6.1 Continued

final paintings composed back in his studio using the sketches as component parts. The resulting landscapes have a spontaneous appeal, despite the fact that they have been so carefully arranged. The dog, the fisherman and boat in The Hay Wain exist as separate sketches, often reappearing in other works by Constable, and the artist made several changes to the composition of this painting before deciding on this version. There is a full-sized oil sketch in the Victoria and Albert Museum in London but this final painting is held in the National Gallery. In The Hay Wain we see on the left-hand side a mill-house, rented by a farmer called Willy Lott from Constable's father, who owned both the house and surrounding land. The house is often referred to as 'Will Lott's cottage' to reinforce the quaintness and rusticity of the scene, but it was in fact a much more sizeable property. To the extreme right, beside the fisherman's boat on the far side of the river, we can see the beginning of a red brick wall belonging to a water-mill, just out of sight in this view. Constable drew much of his initial inspiration for scenes such as this one from memories of the childhood he had spent in the area. The wisps of smoke curling from the chimney of the house, and the woman beside it drawing water from the river, give the scene a harmonious, domesticated atmosphere. In the background, in the yellow and green fields, dappled with sunlight, we can see workers, one sharpening his scythe, others pitchforking hay onto an already laden wagon, and one man stacking the load from the top. The time of year must be between June and early August – haymaking season. The cloudy, windswept sky would seem to indicate the possibility of rain and certainly evokes English summertime weather. Constable actually made many of the cloud studies for this painting on Hampstead Heath in London. The hay wain itself ('wain' is an old word for 'wagon') is crossing the river at a ford to continue into the fields. The driver has stopped for a moment, perhaps to let the horses drink. The usually steep wooden sides of this type of vehicle have been cropped and we can see the two workers riding on the wagon. Constable's innovative technique, with looser brushwork and the use of white paint to suggest reflections of light upon the water, was not very popular with contemporary English critics, who preferred a more traditional style of painting and more 'serious' subject matter. He did, however, achieve considerable success in France, winning a Gold Medal at the Paris Salon of 1824 with this painting. The French Impressionists were to be very much influenced by Constable's ideas about sketching outdoors and observing the effects of nature.

The painting by the Australian Aboriginal artist is actually a play on the politics of colonialisation in Australia. The common law incorporated settled international (i.e. European) rules for the 'acquisition' of territory and added its own rules regarding the application of English law within the colonies established in the acquired areas. Blackstone explains in the Commentaries:[21]

> Plantations or colonies in distant countries are either such where the lands are claimed by rights of occupancy only, by finding them desert and uncultivated, and peopling them from the mother country; or where, when already cultivated, they have been either gained by conquest, or ceded to us by treaties. And both these rights are founded upon the law of nature, or at least upon that of nations. But there is a difference between these two species of colonies, with respect to the laws by which they are bound. For it has been held, that if an uninhabited country be discovered and planted by English subjects, all the English laws then in being, which are the birthright of every subject, are immediately then in force. But this must be understood with very many and very great restrictions. Such colonists carry with them only so much of the English law, as it is applicable to their own situation and the condition of an infant colony ... But in conquered or ceded countries, that have already laws of their own, the King may indeed alter and change those laws; but, till he does actually change them, the ancient laws of the country remain, unless such as are against the law of God, as in the case of an infidel country.

In a 'desert and uncultivated' land one could occupy and 'people from the mother country'; that is, settle, then the law in force would be all the English laws then in being as applicable to their situation. A 'settled colony' drew upon the notion of terra nullius (a Latin expression deriving from Roman law signifying 'land belonging to no one'; i.e. 'empty land'). In the sixteenth and seventeenth century expansion this blended into meaning in practice land that was unclaimed by a sovereign state recognised by European powers. The Swiss philosopher and international law theorist Emerich de Vattel, building on the philosophy of John Locke and others, proposed that terra nullius applied to uncultivated land. As the indigenous people were not (in this view) using the land, those who could cultivate the land had a right to claim it. English political and legal authorities accepted that the Australian colonies were 'settled', as opposed to conquered, colonies. On his later voyage after his 'discovery' of the lands in the south, Cook could not nor was he instructed to specifically conclude any treaty with any of the Aboriginal peoples, but he had been given vague instructions to take possession of land 'with the consent of the natives'. Cook recorded that he took possession through symbolic acts of planting a flag and firing a gun, ignoring some Aboriginal people, 'who follow'd us shouting'. Both Cook and Sir Joseph Banks concluded that there were few inhabitants, living only in the coastal area, and they could not be in possession of the land as they did not cultivate it.

The historian Henry Reynolds[22] argues that, regardless of the first impressions of Cook and Banks, it became clear to the British settlers who followed that the Australian colonies were not terra nullius. On the basis of a detailed examination of historical evidence he argues that the imperial government was prepared to accept that, while English law applied in the Australian colonies, that law should and could recognise Aboriginal title to land. Reynolds contends that the colonists failed to observe imperial instructions by continuing to ignore the Aborigines, and the common law followed suit. The Aboriginal artist is asking what would happen if an Aboriginal came to England and claimed the territory on the grounds that the English had misused the land. Would it be a question of force?

---

21   Blackstone, *Commentaries* (I, pp. 107–8*):
22   Reynolds (1987: 31).

REPLYING TO HEY BROS

It is now widely acknowledged that European incursion into the Americas, Australia and New Zealand led to the displacement and genocide of the indigenous populations of these areas, not by accident but in order to create the optimum conditions for white domination.

In the Caribbean, Newfoundland, and Tasmania all but a remnant of the resident Aboriginal peoples had been murdered. In practice, the choice between killing and 'a temperate line of conduct' was often beyond the control of colonial administrators. As settlement expanded, Aboriginal peoples were deprived of their lands and conflict was inevitable. However, once a sufficient number of Aboriginal peoples had been killed (i.e. enough to ensure British dominance), a set of policies based on a 'temperate line of conduct' frequently became possible. These policies relied upon a dominant military or civil police force for their ultimate enforcement and were aimed at managing Aboriginal peoples by controlling their land use, settlements, government and daily life. They also called for the introducing of Aboriginal peoples to missionaries.[23]

Against Armitage, the author of the extract above, it is *not* now widely acknowledged that genocide universally occurred throughout the lands mentioned; the earlier conquest and settlement of the Americas is now labelled genocide by some of those who claim descent from the original inhabitants, and the claim for genocide in Australia is hotly contested.[24] It is undeniable, however, that genocide has occurred when settler interests were threatened and where the means and authorisation (at least implicit) was available; the culmination of European colonialisation was the Nazi pursuit of life space in Eastern Europe and the calculated denial of life to the 'sub-human Jews and lesser-human Poles'.[25]

Access to and recognition in space – land in time – is central and here the prime place of law reveals itself: 'law as an ultimate and authoritarian assertion of position'.[26] The imperial (European) law, brought from outside, enabled the colonist's claim to objectivity in relations. Consider the personal history and the most remembered judgment of Prendergast, first Chief Justice of New Zealand to be appointed from among the persons actually practicing in New Zealand.

Born in London in 1826, the youngest son of a QC, James Prendergast graduated from Queens' College, Cambridge and enrolled in the Middle Temple in London in 1849. However, he joined the gold rush in 1852 to Victoria, Australia. While not unsuccessful in the diggings he contracted dysentery and moved back to town where he became a magistrate's clerk and in 1856 met another Londoner, the young Julius Vogel, later to be a famous Prime Minister of New Zealand. Prendergast crossed

---

23 Armitage (1995: 5).
24 For the lively claims of a part American Indian, see Churchill (1977) for a damning indictment of the whole settlement of the Americas. See also Stannard (1992) who gives his text the controversial title of *American Holocaust*. For the Australian situation see Reynolds' early work (1971) *An Indelible Stain? The Question of Genocide in Australia's History*.
25 See Zimmerer (2004); Morrison (2006).
26 Fitzpatrick (2001: 180).

over to New Zealand in 1862 and was admitted to the bar in Otago that year. His arrival in Dunedin coincided with the great goldrush and dramatic expansion of legal business in Otago. Thirty-three lawyers were enrolled in Dunedin in 1862, and 20 more over the next three years (Prendergast's first client was Julius Vogel, then editor of the *Otago Daily Times* in Dunedin). Prendergast prospered in practice and in 1863 he was appointed acting solicitor for Otago Province, in 1865 becoming Crown Solicitor. In 1865 Prendergast was appointed as a Member of Parliament to the Legislative Council, the then upper house of parliament. In 1865 he also became a non-political Attorney General of New Zealand. As Attorney General Prendergast's task was to consolidate the criminal law and in the process he drafted 94 Acts. He also helped to create order in the legal profession – in 1870 the New Zealand Law Society was formed with Prendergast as its first president. Prendergast was appointed Chief Justice of New Zealand on 1 April 1875 on the advice of Vogel. His most (in)famous decision came in *Wi Parata* v. *Bishop of Wellington* in 1871, where he sidestepped two New Zealand precedents and asserted that the British government had never recognised Maori law and custom because such an entity had never existed.

The case involved land that was given by local Maori to the Anglican Church for the purpose of building a school. The school was never built and Parata asked the land given to the Church be returned to the Ngati Toa iwi. In his judgment, Prendergast took the view that 'native' or 'Aboriginal' customary title, not pursuant to a Crown grant, could not be recognised or enforced by the courts; the Treaty of Waitangi was a 'simple nullity' as 'no body politic existed capable of making cession of sovereignty, nor could the thing itself exist'. The Maori tribe had no juridical status, but neither did individual Maori have the rights of Englishmen; British subjecthood and the rights that went with that apparently conferred by Article 3 of the Treaty, were denied. This was standard practice as it was legally recognised until – in practice – into the 1980s that for it to take effect the Treaty would have had to be incorporated into New Zealand law by specific statutory adoption. Instead relations between Crown and Maori were 'to be regarded as acts of State, and therefore are not examined by any Court'. Maori were labelled 'primitive barbarians', 'incapable of performing the duties, and therefore of assuming the rights, of a civilised community'. Consequently, 'in the case of primitive barbarians, the supreme executive Government … of necessity must be the sole arbiter of its own justice'.

> At common law, then, Maori lacked any original or subsisting juridical status. Their relations with the crown, including any 'rights' they might hold, were judicially recognised as being at the absolute discretion of the crown.[27]

In Nan Seuffert's words:

> His decision literally re-members the nation by erasing or cutting off not only any recognition of Maori laws and practices in colonial law, but any existence at all of those

---

27   McHugh (2001 194).

laws and practices. He recreates the nation as one in which Maori laws and customs never existed.[28]

The decision was extremely convenient for the Crown: native title matters involving the Crown now fell entirely within the jurisdiction of the Crown's prerogative powers, and so were outside the jurisdiction of the municipal courts. This meant that native title claims were not enforceable against the Crown within these courts, nor could these courts refer such matters to the Native Land Court against the wishes of the Crown. Rather, the Crown was to be the 'sole arbiter of its own justice' on native title matters. The subsequent case law largely follows this case – even in the face of an open breach with the Privy Council in 1903 over this issue – and much of Prendergast's reasoning was not clearly rejected until 1938 when *Te Heuheu Tukino* v. *Aotea District Maori Land Board* was decided, where the Court ruled that the Treaty was seen as valid in terms of the transfer of sovereignty, but as it was not part of New Zealand statute law it was not binding on the Crown.

Prendergast's judgment contains various conflicting positions and almost certain contradictions. John Tate explains it in terms of a 'colonial consciousness' which shaped the way in which issues of land settlement were understood within settler societies largely.[29] While seeming to accept a view of the land before the British settlement as *terra nullis*, the decision, and consequent decisions, were more a logical game of being a servant to Crown interests and prerogative: Prendergast accepts that the common law could recognise native title, but if it would have existed as a matter of fact – if native title could be shown to have existed as a form of (customary) legal right – then the common law as understood in New Zealand courts and legislature would already have recognised it. In other words he assumes that the New Zealand government would have taken that into account in framing its statutes. The fact that they had not served to demonstrate that no such legal rights existed! But there were phrases in Crown statutes that implied customary ownership insofar as they made reference to 'the rightful and necessary occupation and use' of land by the 'Aboriginal inhabitants', such as in the Land Claims Ordinance of 1841. Prendergast blankly denied that they implied Crown recognition of native title. As he stated: 'These measures were avowedly framed upon the assumption that there existed amongst the natives no regular system of territorial rights nor any definite ideas of property in land'. He insisted that the absence of stated legal recognition of such 'territorial rights' or 'definite ideas of property in land' among Maori was due not to any oversight on the part of the Crown, rather it was due to their non-existence in fact. He stated: 'Had any body of law or custom, capable of being understood and administered by the Courts of a civilised country, been known to exist, the British Government would surely have provided for its recognition, since nothing could exceed the anxiety displayed to infringe no just right of the Aborigines'. Given this assumption of the Crown's desire to do everything in favour of the natives the fact that they had not recognised native title was proof of the absence of a 'body of law or custom' relating to property within Maori society which, Prendergast believed,

---

28   Seuffert (2006: 36).
29   Tate (2003).

rendered English law incapable of recognising any native title rights to which Maori tribes might be able to lay claim![30]

What was the threat to settler society? The Native Land Court posed a threat to Crown title in that if the Act recognised native title then matters would be referred to the Court and Maori understandings as to possession rights may determine the issue. If, however, Prendergast could claim that all native title matters involving the Crown were subject to the Crown's prerogative, this would exclude the jurisdiction of the municipal courts, and so undermine their capacity to refer native title matters to the Native Land Court under the Native Rights Act 1865. Further, if he could claim that this Act itself was not intended to intrude on the Crown's prerogative, the jurisdiction of the Native Land Court would be limited as well.

Tate defines a 'colonial consciousness' as an outlook informed by the material interests of a settler society. Foremost among these interests is a necessary concern for the process of land settlement, since it is this process which, more than anything else, defines a 'settler' society. These material concerns were exacerbated in New Zealand society because of the open military conflict that had erupted between Maori tribes and the Crown over precisely this issue in the middle decades of the nineteenth century. For Tate the members of the New Zealand Bench were affected by these interests and concerns and these intruded on their legal outlook and judgment in native title cases. 'In particular, this "colonial consciousness" explains the Court of Appeal's tenacious commitment to the precedent of Wi Parata, its willingness to misread previous native title cases as consistent with this precedent, and its willingness to defend Wi Parata even to the point of an open breach with the Privy Council.' This colonial consciousness then manifested itself in some very traditional legal language, namely the defence of the stability and security of the young nation. It also surfaced in the implicit defence of the New Zealand bench that they were – more than the Privy Council in London – being faithful to the law; the inherited 'common law'. Defined as the bearers of one universal law, the lack of a jurisprudence of legal pluralism, meant that to deny competing legal foundations meant that everything was to be decided in accordance with 'principle of law', 'settled principles of our law', and 'the common law of England'. So the Bench reacted furiously to the Privy Council accusing the Law Lords of not being as familiar with the operation of the common law in settings outside of the UK as they were and not following the precedent of Wi Parata.

The end of empire frees up the writing of history. Post-colonial histories and institutional arrangements are heavily debated, though it is also a melancholy observation that the debate may be tangential to the power flows establishing the institutional re-recognition and redefining of forms of association of the indigenous peoples as constituting 'indigenous law' and giving historical redress to the lack of recognition of that law. This is a politics of recognition, identity and imaging the nation. Recognising that the indigenous peoples had law complicates the historical picture of settlement and raises the issue of its relationship to the law of the new state in a 'post-colonial' era (post-colonial here meaning not just 'independence' but a reworking of historical narratives of foundation and identity). In New Zealand an alternative story of foundations – the

---

30   Discussion pp. 77–78 Wi Parata...

Figure 6.2 New Zealand war dance of the past, unknown artist, *Illustrated London News*, 1870.
Source: collection WJM.

King argues that one feature that saved the Maori from the genocidal practices elsewhere under colonial settlement was their ability to be imaged as proud, independent fighters. Note that this image, presented in the popular *Illustrated London News* is titled 'New Zealand war dance *of the past*'. Many assumed that the Maori, as with other native groups, would die out; that the future would not contain them. In this way it was assumed nature was genocidal. In Wi Parata, the colonial law rejects Maori as any form of partner in the colonial nation's development. Nan Seuffert analyses another, less known case: *Rira Peti* v. *Ngaraihi To Paku* [1888] where Prendergast effectively denies Maori custom in marriage effective legal recognition in colonial marriage law (Seuffert, 2006: 37). This was at odds with social reality – most marriages between Maori up until c. 1936 were customary rather than conducted according to settler ritual and legal form. Earlier New Zealand legislation and court decisions *could* have been interpreted so as to recognise Maori customary practices and 'law'. This would, however, meant that there were two narratives of original sources for New Zealand law. This, as the extract from Blackstone (see our discussion in Hey Bros, Figure 6.1) specifies, was able to be recognised by the common law: the argument then must be that it was Colonial consciousness or settler interests that shaped the courts reasoning. The post-colonial court structure in New Zealand gave a different story in *Ngat Apa* v. *Attorney-General* relegating Wi Parata 'to an appendix of colonial injustices' (Ibid., p. 133). But while this decision overturns much of the past, Seuffert argues that 'the founding violence of the nation … as a result of the repression of the Maori version of the Treaty remains unrepaired. Common law native title is a colonial legal invention, a view of indigenous law, customs and relationship with the land through the lenses of colonial courts … It is not power sharing or self-determination' (ibid., p. 135). We may note that the New Zealand war dance, the Haka, is now ritualised as the central feature of the New Zealand rugby team, the All Blacks, a title itself a misspelling of an English reporter's text to London on watching the first New Zealand team to tour England (he actually sent 'all backs').

recognition of the Waitangi Treaty – could be constructed and is under critique and reconstruction. But what of Australia?

In recent times the question of settlement came up in *Mabo* (1992),[31] a claim to recognise native title. Before the arrival of the Europeans, the lands in question (three islands constituting the Murray Islands, Mer, Dauar and Waier) were already occupied by the Meriam people. In 1879, they were annexed to the colony of Queensland, although a few years later, the islands were reserved by proclamation

---

31   *Mabo* v. *Queensland* (No. 2) (1992) 175 CLR IF 92/014.

for the 'native inhabitants'. Some years later still, in 1912, the islands were permanently reserved, being placed in trust in 1939. In this case, the Meriam people were arguing that they had good title to lands, that they had never been 'Crown lands'. In 1992, after a decade of litigation, the High Court ruled that the land title of the indigenous peoples, the Aborigines and Torres Strait Islanders, was recognised at common law. This indigenous peoples' land title, or native title, stemmed from the continuation within common law of their rights over land which pre-date European colonisation of Australia. In the absence of an effective extinguishment by the crown, this title presents through inheritance the original occupants' right to possession of their traditional lands in accordance with their customs and lores. The judgment rejected the *terra nullius* concept, bringing Australia almost in line with other common law countries; that is, the US, Canada and New Zealand.

Reynolds provides some evidence that Aboriginal ownership of land has always been recognised by Britain, providing extracts from early dispatches to Australia from the British Colonial Office, proclamations in the House of Commons and private correspondence between officials.[32]

One of the central themes in *Mabo* was a question of the authority of the court. The court had to affirm its own authority to develop the law of Australia, to deal with the problem of native title from the perspective of a nation that considers itself to be a modern democracy. At the same time, the court is a product of its history. It cannot simply be a question of departing from the common law if jurisprudence is out of step with a contemporary political reality. The view then is that Australian law is both more than English common law, but enabled by the English common law tradition. Thus, it can develop 'independently' from the authorities of the English courts, and it is 'free' of the control of the 'imperial' centre. However, to retain its common law tradition legal principles can be updated, but not to the extent that they completely break or throw over the basic 'skeleton of principles'.

We are dealing with a politics of memory. Clearly, the settlement in accordance with *terra nullis* rested on the notion that those living in the territory were without law. *Mabo* now rereads the position of indigenous peoples and gives them legal being, as far as the common law was concerned. However, in *Mabo*, the people who are to be one under the law are included into a common law history, are given an 'origin' synonymous with the arrival of the common law.[33] Effectively, while the common law is recognised as a particular relationship to time – existing from time immemorial – the Australian Aboriginal existence is recognised only as at the time of settlement.

---

32 Reynolds (1987). The 1837 House of Commons Select Committee's report on Australian colonies, for example, stated that 'the native inhabitants of any land have an incontrovertible right to their own soil however, which seems not to have been understood'.

33 One of the issues in the case was justiciability. Whether or not territory had been acquired was not justiciable; however, the court accepted it had the jurisdiction to determine the consequences of acquisition under municipal law. The court's conclusions were somewhat double handed. Native title was affirmed, even though it did not fit within the categories of possession at common law. Indeed, the precise terms on which native land was to be held could only be resolved by reference to the laws and customs of indigenous peoples. However, the final conclusion, that the Meriam people could claim good title to the land, was qualified. Such native title was subject to the power of the Parliament of Queensland. Moreover, the courts did not have the jurisdiction to challenge the issue of the Crown's acquisition of territory.

Under this assumption native 'law' is drawn unproblematically into the fold of a common law that can adapt to history, and a foreign clime. After all, this grounds the claim that the common law is able to resolve the issue of native title by drawing into itself those social relations that it can order, determine and articulate in the best possible way. Behind this claim is a far more difficult and subtle operation. *Mabo* effectively denies the reality of the indigenous claim, at the same time as acknowledging it. The *Mabo* judgment in no way challenges the legality of non-Aboriginal land tenure; settler interests are undisturbed. The Court went to considerable lengths to establish that the impact of its judgment will be minimal on non-Aboriginal Australians. Only land such as vacant Crown land, national parks and possibly some leased land, where the lease is subject to Aboriginal rights of access to the land, can be subject to Aboriginal claims. Further, no native title is automatically recognised in law. The Aboriginal claimants either have to go to court, or possibly tribunals, and prove that they continually maintained their traditional association with the land they are claiming. Anyone can appeal against the claims and the *Mabo* judgment ensures that whenever there is conflict between titles granted by the Crown and the native title, the native title loses. It is only in the case of titles newly established since 1975 that Aborigines can even claim compensation for extinguishment of title.

Thus, any claim to Aboriginal title or law has to be made through the medium of the common law of the colonist. It appears unlikely, especially in the wake of the *Mabo* decision and the law's retreat from a notion of native title that the ongoing violence of the original imposition of settler's law can move towards reconciliation.

THE MAU MAU 'EMERGENCY'

What of our lecturer? As students we knew little of what the reference to the Mau Mau emergency was; all we understood was that it had been important and that our lecturer was to be respected for his role as an official operating the rule of law. Perhaps even if we had known that Kenya had declared a 'state of emergency', and that this provided a space of exception to the normal rule of law, we would not have understood what lessons can be learnt about the normal from the exceptional. In the last few years two books have appeared that have shattered any illusions about the heroic defence of the civilising mission in Kenya. I now read:

> State execution is a mighty weapon, and in the colonial context it has generally been used sparingly. Not so in the Mau Mau emergency. Kenya's hanging judges were kept busy. Between April 1953 and December 1956 the Special Emergency Assize Courts tried a total of 2609 Kikuyu on capital charges relating to Mau Mau offences in 1211 trials. Around 40% of those accused were acquitted, but 1574 were convicted and sentenced to hang over this period. Others still had been convicted in the Supreme Court before the Special Emergency Assize Courts were created in April 1953, and there would be a smattering of further Mau Mau trials throughout 1957 and even into 1958. In total, approximately 3000 Kikuyu stood trial between 1952 and 1958 on capital charges relating to the Mau Mau movement. In all, over the course of the emergency, 1090 Kikuyu would go to the gallows for Mau Mau crimes. In no other place, and at no other

time in the history of British imperialism, was state execution used on such a scale as this. This was more than double the number of executions carried out against convicted terrorists in Algeria, and many more than in all the other British colonial emergencies of the post-war period – in Palestine, Malaya, Cyprus and Aden.[34]

Of the accounts in the Western media of the Mau Mau a telling account concerns a small event in 1955, reported in *Time* magazine, March 21 1955, under the heading 'Mau Mau in the Cathedral'.

> In the blue–black darkness of an African night last week, a gang of Mau Mau warriors crept out of the squalid shantytown where the huge Negro majority of Nairobi's population lives, and moved, unseen, into the heart of the white city. It was Sunday evening, and the sexton had locked the doors of the Anglican cathedral after the evening service, but the Mau Mau broke in and gathered in a group in the chancel. They splashed water from the font for more than an hour in a weird pagan ceremony performed at an altar that faces Mt. Kenya (17,040 ft.). The mountain is the Mau Mau's sacred symbol, and British officers who investigated concluded that the terrorists had been ordaining a new Mau Mau general for the Nairobi area.

Consider again the foundational image Hobbes gave as the frontispiece of the *Leviathan*. There, in the protected space of the sovereign's gaze and reach, lies civilised space, at the centre of which is the Cathedral. Hobbes had set up the natural necessity of the sovereign because of the natural condition of humanity as (relative) equality and (relative) autonomy. Since no one was naturally superior to the other, any could be killed by the other; since each was similar yet not the same, all were in competition. Many have misunderstood Hobbes. He has become a name called into action (intellectually) to defend authoritarian states and the radicalism of Hobbes was denied. His message has been (mis)presented as an issue of autonomy and identity, of essential blocs of sameness in competition – that is, as stating that the difference of humanity (grades of humans) was a basic feature of existence rather than recognising that above relative difference was an essential equality. The spatial protection offered by the sovereign was in principal open to everyone, and global in space; in practice it pertained only to civilised space.[35] David Sibley provides a helpful discussion of spatial purification. Purification reflects deep-seated paranoias concerned with defilement and pollution, the language of leaking and contamination refers both to individual bodies and national borders.[36] Perhaps both are inherent in the images which appeared in the Western media after the attack upon a white settler's farm which killed the farming couple and their young son.

What was presented in the Western media in 1952/1953 as a sudden explosion of violence and rejection of the civilising mission had deep roots. Kenya displayed settlement colony tactics but in a land clearly not empty. Railway construction towards Uganda had opened up land and it appeared sensible to the colonialists to reserve the

---

34 Anderson (2005: 6–7).
35 Developed further in Morrison (2006).
36 Sibley (1995: 77).

Figure 6.3 'Kitty Heselburger and Dorothy Raines-Simpson successfully defend themselves against the Mau Mau terrorists'. Source: Walter Molinoin in 'La Domenica del Corriere', 18 January 1953.

Kenya looks beautiful this week. The Nandi flame trees are ablaze with crimson against the clear blue sky, and in the sky glisten the snowy crests of Mount Kenya and Kilimanjaro. The giraffes gracefully nod their tall necks on the plains. Even the Aberdares, if you do not know what they shelter, could be called beautifully peaceful.

But it is really a land of murder and muddle. And there is little likelihood that either murder or muddle will halt soon. The sullen masses of evicted blacks in the overrun reserves; the white farmers and their wives besieged in their farmhouses with revolvers next to the dinner plates; the bearded commandos stumbling through forests after the elusive Mau Mau; the brittle Mayfair-in-suburbia life of spuriously gay Nairobi; the purple-faced ex-colonels in the very, very particular Rift Valley Club – none of them seeming to know what to do. Not even the Mau Mau themselves seem to know what they really want – except to kill and disembowel as many whites, chiefs, head men, and non-Mau Mau Kikuyu as possible.

Nobody can guess how long it may drag on, how far Mau Mauism may spread, how infectious its example might prove to be. What thoughts pass through the minds of Samburu, Turkana, Wakamba or Masai tribesmen as they watch the white man harried by the hitherto despised and pacific Kikuyu?

Figure 6.3 Continued

What thoughts down in Central Africa, where the British plan a political federation opposed by the natives, or in Uganda or the Belgian Congo? In South Africa, the Negro-hating Boers use the Mau Mau's terror to win support for even more brutal suppression of the nonwhites. Kenya, the Land of the Shining Mountain, has become a smoldering ember in Africa. And the surrounding brush vast, white-run, black-populated, miles of it, is tinder-dry.
'A Report from Kenya', *Time* magazine, March 30, 1953

This report by *Time* was representative of the first wave of reporting in Western media on the events in Kenya. Labelled terrorists, the Mau Mau were depicted as a primitive return to barbarism and rejection of Western civilisation. By 1960 the *Time* magazine reports moved on to summing up what was seen as central to this movement: the oath (note: the figures quoted are subject to official revision and the numbers of Europeans and Africans killed by the Mau Mau drastically lowered).

Of all the colonial revolts that have convulsed Asia and Africa since World War II, none have matched Kenya's Mau Mau movement for sheer grisliness. In seven years of terror beginning in the autumn of 1952, 95 Europeans, 29 Asians and 12,423 Africans were slain by methods ranging from merciful garroting to having their heads bashed in and their brains removed, dried and ritually eaten. Last week the British finally got around to releasing the first complete and authoritative account of the Mau Mau disaster – an almost clinically detached, 322-page report by Career Colonial Administrator Frank D. Corfield, 58, onetime Governor of Khartoum.

Corpses and orgies

Like African leaders everywhere, the men who organised the Mau Mau faced one basic difficulty in forging a nationalist spirit: for the ordinary African, a man's overriding loyalties are to his family and his tribe. By compelling Mau Mau members to violate not only Christian ethics but every tribal taboo as well, says Corfield, Mau Mau leaders deliberately reduced their victims to a state where a man who took the Mau Mau oath was cut off 'from all hope, outside Mau Mau, in this world or the next'. To achieve this, the Mau Mau leadership forced its recruits, voluntary or involuntary, to seal their oaths by digging up corpses and eating their putrefied flesh, copulating with sheep, dogs or adolescent girls, and by drinking the famed 'Kaberichia cocktail' – a mixture of semen and menstrual blood. And when he was assigned to kill an enemy of the movement, a sworn Mau Mau pledged himself to remove the eyeballs of his victim and drink the liquid from them. Once the blood lust had been aroused to this pitch, the oath taker was easily led to kill his own father or mother, wife, child or master at Mau Mau command. And any local Mau Mau leader devising a fouler ritual was under obligation to pass along his recipe immediately to his less inventive colleagues. Since there were seven basic oaths, which could be taken over and over again, Mau Mau ceremonies thus became perpetual orgies. The result was that, when a Mau Mau convert did repent and vomit out his story to authorities, he sometimes ended by humbly asking to be taken out and shot. His sense of absolute degradation and 'absolute sin', says the Corfield report, left him no choice.

The Expert

Personally responsible for the 'general pattern' of this horror, charges the Corfield report, was Jomo ('Burning Spear') Kenyatta, sixtyish, longtime Kikuyu nationalist leader still under house arrest in a remote Kenya mountain village. A mission-educated nationalist fanatic who spent 17 years in England and Europe, where he made himself an expert in primitive anthropology and published a scholarly work on Kikuyu customs, Kenyatta diabolically parodied the traditional religion of his people in Mau Mau ritual – much as occultists did in the legendary Black Mass. In fact, reports Corfield, Kenyatta's work showed 'at least a passing acquaintance' with European witchcraft'.
'The Oath Takers', *Time* magazine, Monday, June 13, 1960[37]

---

37 Kenyatta was released from prison and in 1963 became Kenya's first prime minister.

supposedly 'empty' and climatically suitable highlands for the Europeans. Consequently the African tribes were forced into reservations and excluded from the thinly settled highlands in order to create the prerequisites for gentleman farming. Little analysis appears on the conditions of the natives.

In 1999 a new imaginary of the Mau Mau was shown in Britain: *How Britain crushed the 'Mau Mau rebellion'* was a controversial episode in Channel 4's Secret History series (screened 15 September 1999). This presented an opposing story to the previous orthodoxy. The Mau Mau 'rebellion' (from 1952 to 1959) and the response to it by the colonial government and European settlers was presented through documentary footage, narration and interviews with participants from both sides, plus background material on the Channel 4 website. The programme began by reversing the terrorist label describing a 'gang of freedom fighters' called Mau Mau, who had vowed 'to free Kenya from colonialism at any cost'. It was the British response that was now to be seen as 'brutal and shocking'. Film footage of Kenya before the uprising showed smug Europeans living a life of idle luxury based on African land and labour, a life that was increasingly resented after World War II. Having fought with the British the Kenyans now wanted some return, while the settlers were presented as living in an ideological mist of superiority. The Kikuyu tribe had 50 years earlier been evicted from their traditional areas to make way for European farmers. By the end of the World War I, 3,000 European settlers owned 43,000 square kilometres of the most fertile land, only 6 per cent of which they cultivated, while the African population of 5.25 million occupied – without ownership rights – less than 135,000 square kilometres of the poorest land. Pushed into 'native reserves' on which much of the land was unsuitable for agriculture, the rural Africans were not able to operate their traditional methods of extensive agriculture, but nor did they have access to the new technology that would make intensive agriculture viable. Presenting a picture where the population was having severe problems feeding itself a dramatic dislocation existed between the rural black African population and a white (and small black élite), the programme pointed to a rumour-led situation where a secret society had been formed among the Kikuyu, Kenya's largest tribe, one-fifth of the population, called the Land Freedom Army (LFA). The society forced the Kikuyu to swear an oath to take back the land the white man had stolen. The term that was applied to this group, the 'Mau Mau', was never used by the Kikuyu and does not exist in their language and could have been coined by the British as part of an attempt to demonise the Kikuyu people. The core of the LFA was the Kikuyu Central Association (KCA), which was formed in 1924. Its original programme was a combination of radical demands such as the return of expropriated lands and the elimination of the passbook scheme (similar to the internal passport system in South Africa), with a striving to return to the traditional pre-colonial past. In the late 1930s the KCA led a wave of mass peasant struggles against the forced sale of their livestock to the government. In the 1950s the KCA began conscripting support from the Kikuyu masses, believing it was possible to consolidate their support through the administration of 'the oath'. When a staunch British loyalist, Chief Waruhu, was killed on 7 October 1952, the government saw the LFA as the first serious threat to colonial rule in post-war Africa. Two weeks later, on 20 October, a state of emergency was declared. Thousands of British troops and equipment were flown in to 'clear the colony of the menace of Mau Mau'. Over 100 leading members of the Kenya

African Union, a political party demanding greater African self-rule, were arrested. Along with others, Jomo Kenyatta was put on trial for subversion.

What of due process? Kenyatta had publicly denounced Mau Mau and advocated peaceful change; however, the British and the white settlers were convinced that he was the driving force behind the movement. There was no evidence. Nevertheless, Kenyatta was found guilty of incitement and imprisoned in a remote part of Kenya for seven years' hard labour. In the first ten days of emergency rule, almost 4,000 Africans had been arrested, but the attacks from the LFA continued. A wave of hysteria swept through the European settlers. In January 1953, a European farmer and his family were killed and angry settlers stormed Government House demanding stronger action. In fact, more white settlers died in road accidents on the streets of Nairobi during the emergency than at the hands of the LFA. On 25 March a loyalist village was destroyed and most of the inhabitants were killed, including Chief Luka and his family. This clearly seemed to be the slaughter of innocent Kikuyu but a short time before almost 100,000 Kikuyu farm workers and their families had been evicted from their homes in the Rift Valley – where they had been living as squatters on settler farms – and driven back to the reserve. Some of them had already been evicted 20 years earlier to make way for European settlers. Chief Luka, who had been personally rewarded with good land, had negotiated this government's 'land exchange scheme'. The farm workers vented their anger against the chief, whom they considered to be responsible for their plight. In a revenge attack the following day, 10 times more Kikuyu were killed by government forces and more houses were destroyed. The LFA faced the full force of British colonial power. The forests of Mount Kenya, where the LFA had their base camps, were designated a 'prohibited area' and heavily bombed. Peasants living on the fringes of the forest were evicted from the land, their animals confiscated and crops and huts burned to clear the way for the 'free fire zone'. Thousands were herded into overcrowded, heavily militarised 'protected villages' and a policy of 'terror' and 'containment' employed by the British. The programme reports various atrocities culminating in the death from beating of 11 men and serious injury of 60 at Hola camp.[38] The reports of the beatings

---

38   Among the claims: 1. In the 'free fire zones' Africans could be shot on sight with rewards offered to the units that produced the largest number of 'Mau Mau' corpses, the hands of which were chopped off to make fingerprinting easier; 2. Settlements suspected of harbouring 'Mau Mau' were burned, and 'Mau Mau' suspects were tortured for information; 3. Officers who paid their men five shillings a head for every 'Mau Mau' they killed. 4. In late 1953 the British opened a new campaign, code named Operation Anvil, to cut off the supply network to the LFA. The first target was Nairobi, which was believed to be the centre of their organisation. On 24 April 1954, the police rounded up all the African inhabitants in the city – around 100,000 people. The 70,000 Kikuyu were separated and screened. Of them, up to 30,000 men were taken to holding camps. The families of the arrested men were pushed into the already overcrowded native reserves. In rural areas Kikuyu were forced into fortified villages, where they lived under 23-hour curfew. This policy, known as 'villagisation', was claimed to be 'purely protective and beneficial for the Africans'. It gave the colonial authorities total control over the Kikuyu. 5. Taking the Mau Mau oath was made a capital offence. Between 1953 and 1956 more than 1,000 Africans were hanged for alleged Mau Mau crimes. Public hangings, which had been outlawed in Britain for over a century, were carried out in Kenya during the emergency. A mobile gallows was transported around the country dispensing 'justice' to 'Mau Mau' suspects. Dead 'Mau Mau', especially commanders, were displayed at crossroads, at market places and at administrative centres. 6. By 1954 one-third of all Kikuyu men were said to be in prison. These detainees had not been convicted of any crime and were held without trial. The British government insisted that every prisoner had to denounce 'the oath' and submit to a 'cleansing ceremony'. By 1956 the LFA had been militarily defeated, but the camps still held 20,000 detainees who refused to confess to taking the oath, so the emergency remained in force. The huge cost involved forced London

and deaths caused political uproar in Britain as it was now the British authorities that were exposed as brutal thugs. Within weeks the camps were closed and the detainees released. The Mau Mau oaths became irrelevant. In 1960 the state of emergency was lifted. The LFA death toll during the emergency was 11,500, of whom around 1,000 were hanged. Eighty-thousand Kikuyu were imprisoned in concentration camps and it is now claimed that 150,000 Africans, mostly Kikuyu, lost their lives, with many dying of disease and starvation in the 'protected villages'. On the other side, the KFA killed around 2,000 people, including 32 European civilians and 63 members of the security forces. In 1961 Jomo Kenyatta was freed from jail and in 1963, four years after the Hola massacre, Kenya was granted independence. The Mau Mau fighters were mostly excluded in independent Kenya from public life and preferment, the spoils of independence going to the wealthy and educated Africans who had a vested interest in marginalising them; a black-African élite simply replaced the white one.[39]

Writers in critical legal studies, feminist and race theory fields have stressed the complexity of the violence of colonial regimes. Patricia Tuitt sees the formation of the colonial state in terms of 'causal' and '(a)causal'. Drawing on Fanon and others, Tuitt locates a world of 'causal' relations and flows of events and an (a)causal world in which normal, expected relations are inverted, in which there is a perversity of moral connections. A causal world experiences 'the constant sequence or conjunction of events, relations, state and moral precepts', which in an (a)causal world are suspended (an example of this chapter 'the state of emergency', which allowed the repression of the other as part of the state apparatus). The latter is inherently racist in the sense that it displaces 'the most fundamental of securities, the persistent recognition of human state to all, irrespective of race'.[40] This state form signifies sustained systemic violence by the dominant, going beyond the immediate realities of the racially dominated. It persists as well as a diffuse contemporary form in which 'the project of the history of racial harm, domination, and violence' stands subjected to other histories of past wrongs, in all their unending, even infinite, assertions of 'innocent causes' and to 'the unreliability of memory and testimony'.[41]

Tuitt argues, for example, that the 'counter-violence' of colonial subjects as needing to be understood by the 'full gaze of history', but this is no easy or certain task.[42] In our

---

to demand that a faster way be found to 'cleanse' detainees of their oaths; and 7. The method found was physical beating to confess an oath. 8 The Hola event. Detainees were to be made to obey work orders and beaten if not. On 3 March 1959, 85 prisoners were marched out to a site and ordered to work and then systematically beaten for several hours resulting in 11 dead and 60 seriously injured. The prison officials attempted a cover-up by claiming that the men had died from drinking contaminated water but the survivors told a different account, which found its way back to London and the truth could not be suppressed.

39 Kenya was not alone in achieving political independence. In 1960 Prime Minister Harold Macmillan, in his 'wind of change' speech, recognised the necessity for Britain to find a new form of rule in its colonial possessions in Africa. In Kenya political control was passed into Kenyatta's 'safe pair of hands' and the European settler farmers found that they were more prosperous after independence than they were before.
40 Tuitt (2004: 32).
41 Ibid., p. 33.
42 Ibid., p. 96. For an idea of some of the contemporary discussion on the history of the 'emergency', see Anderson (2005: 2–3). This article highlights the division of the Kenyan nation over the efforts of the former members of Mau Mau, a nationalist and former insurgent organisation in Kenya, to mount a prosecution of Great Britain for war crimes. Anderson *et al.* (2006: 20–22) is an article that asserts that the Freedom of Information Act is being used to protect the perpetrators of a war crime that took place in Kenya in June 1953. It tells the story of an atrocity

contemporary times, we are awash with narratives and counter narratives and the idea of modernity as a coherent, transparent whole, in which truth and reason would be the guides to policy and law is undone. A lot of so-called post-modern (or post-structural or post-Marxist, or hyper-liberal) writings stress the difficulty of viewing, asking whose gaze is it that determines understanding, policy and connections between law and justice? We may take the Kenya case as an example of the intellectual, political and ethical problems associated with understanding resistance and insurgency. How may reading divergent stories found in post-colonial law and literature enable us to resituate the law of violence and violence of law discourse?

RETURN TO EUROPE: READING THE INTERNAL AS A FEATURE OF THE COLONIAL

It takes under three hours to travel by Eurostar from London to Brussels, the home of the European Parliament and the administrative capital of the EU. The Channel Tunnel is a late modern testament to decreasing fears of European contamination and hopes for European integration. It can also appear as a conduit of crime:

> A man from the Congo, living in Brussels, travelled regularly to London on Eurostar to collect housing benefit, an Old Bailey jury heard today. Ngolompati Moka, 33, who is a Belgian national, used fake tenancy agreements to persuade the boroughs of Hounslow and Haringey to pay him a total of £4,653.36, said the prosecution. The court was told that Moka, who was born in the Congo, used a series of identities to claim the cash. After he was arrested in a Hounslow Job Centre last August, police found a number of documents that incriminated him. These included bogus tenancy agreements, a Belgian ID card and receipts from Eurostar trains. 'These show he was making trips from Brussels to claim benefit in this country', said counsel. (*Evening Standard*, 28 January 1999)

For the media this was an everyday crime, one that was, moreover, evidence of the need to strengthen immigration control and border policing. Doing justice meant punishing an individual. It did not invite analysis as to the complex intertwining of the Congo and Brussels, nor of past exploitation justice and reparations. In this exercise of justice – concerning 'a man from the Congo, living in Brussels' – we are dealing with politics of the visible and the invisible.

Awareness of the colonial upsets the comfortable narrative where law represents the totality of shared habits, conventions and traditions; law and its institutions are seen as embodying the spirit of the nation or at least as representing a nation's historical

---

committed by British military forces in colonial Kenya. The story of the shooting of 20 Kenyan civilians at Chuka in June 1953 has been hidden behind a veil of official secrecy. The British Ministry of Defence has still retained some of the papers on the case relating to the role of the two junior British officers in the massacre. Two books about Kenya: *Histories of the Hanged: The Dirty War in Kenya and the End of Empire* by David Anderson; and *Imperial Reckoning: The Untold Story of Britain's Gulag in Kenya* by Caroline Elkins have created controversy. Elkins's work, while winning the 2006 Pulitzer Prize for non-Fiction has been criticised for uncritical use of high estimates of civilian deaths.

and cultural achievements.[43] Colonialism shaped both geographical centres and margins (the cities in Europe are in many ways the product of the colonial).[44] Post-war immigration provides a particular challenge to this construction of the present and the past.[45] As Gilroy writes, the contemporary perception of the problem was not so much the volume of black settlement but rather its character and effects, specifically the threat to legal institutions.[46] Immigration was perceived as a threat to English constitutional values, and in its most paranoid form, saw the destiny of the West at stake.[47] This perception of immigration as threat, rather than an opportunity to create a different history or a different institutional response, represents the failure of English law when faced with race.

This is part of a broader cultural and political failure that reveals blindness to the wider problem. The industrialisation of the First World at the expense of the Third has produced a developed core, and an underdeveloped and exploited periphery.[48] The political will to deal with the redistribution of resources that would help repair this situation does not exist; but the dislocations wrought by the process continue to cause social and economic effects. It is from this perspective that British immigration and race-relations law must be considered.

THE STRUCTURE OF IMMIGRATION LAW

An overriding concern in immigration law is the distinction between 'colonial periphery' and 'imperial centre'.[49] In the post-war period, despite differences in political ideology, a broad consensus emerged among the political élites about the need to stem and control immigration. A useful starting point is the 1962 Commonwealth Immigrants Act,

---

43 See Fitzpatrick (1987). One development of Marxism would understand racism as alien to capitalism's ideology of universal rights; another approach would see a symbiotic relationship where migrant workers provide cheap labour. Fitzpatrick's point is not that Marxism must be rejected, but that questioning race can also lead to a different understanding of Marxism. This appears coherent with the work of cultural theorists such as Paul Gilroy. More importantly, Fitzpatrick is concerned with a dynamic of liberalism that both links race to law, and then denies that racism is a central problem. Understanding the reach of this problem demands a work of historical and philosophical acumen that can trace the inter-relations between liberalism, enlightenment reason and a colonial project. Fitzpatrick is clear: 'liberal capitalism [both] opposes and is maintained by racism' (p. 121), a particularly pithy summary of a central tension that runs in different ways through British and American law.
44 For reflections on Brussels and its connection with the imperial project of King Leopold II see Morrison (2006). Chapters 5 and 6.
45 See Fitzpatrick (1992). The nation is defined in terms of race; the colonised people are everything that the English are not. While sustaining this division, the constitution of Englishness is largely left unexamined. In the wider colonial world view, although there are differences between, say, the English and the French, they are still united by a 'something' that allows them to be posited as the colonisers and the natives as the colonised. Race is therefore in some senses empty. It can be filled with the contents of Englishness and Frenchness yet still be opposed to the otherness of the savage. Moreover, it raises a standard against which the 'new' nations can be judged, but which they must always fall short. The native can only be civilised to a certain extent; they can never quite be 'one of us'.
46 Gilroy (1987b).
47 For instance, following Enoch Powell's 'Rivers of Blood' speech in 1968, race was presented in the terms of the disastrous encounter of two different civilisations.
48 In the sense developed by Etienne Balibar: 'the (shifting) distinction between the core and the periphery of the world economy corresponds also to the geographical and politico-cultural distribution of strategies of exploitation' (1991: 177).
49 Paul (1997: 184).

passed in the context of reducing immigration through issuing employment vouchers.[50] The organising concept of the Act was that of 'belonging', defined as having a link with Britain either through birth or the possession of a British passport. At a symbolic level, the Act signified the withdrawal from Empire and the Commonwealth and created the 'blueprint' for a regime of racial control.[51] While the government was concerned about the social problems that resulted from coloured immigrants settling in Britain, they were less concerned about white immigrants from the 'old dominions'.[52] This distinction was made through acts of overt discrimination between coloured and white immigrants:

> Operating the 1962 Act [in this way] reinforced the differentiation of communities of Britishness: the imperial, familial community consisting of white-skinned Britons was privileged and protected from the letter of immigration law, while the political community of Britishness consisting of black skinned Britons was subjected to increasingly tight regulation.[53]

The defeat of the Conservative government in 1964 did not produce any change in the law by the incumbent Labour administration. The second Commonwealth Immigration Act 1968 attempted to create an even tighter legal definition of British nationality. At one point, the Home Secretary proposed to increase the powers of immigration officers and effectively redefine immigrant British subjects as aliens[54] (although these proposals did not move beyond the White Paper). Debates in the press and in Parliament contributed to the impression that both settled coloured peoples and immigrants were suspect communities whose presence was problematic and troublesome for the majority. Given this background, it is no wonder that the later Race Relations Act in 1965 was also severely compromised. It would not be going too far to suggest that the 1965 Act perpetuated the idea of hierarchised 'communities' of Britishness.[55] This weighting towards separate and not particularly equal spheres undercut any official commitment to ideas and practices of neutrality or integration. In its most

---

50 Juss (1993) argues that the 1962 Act ended what had been an 'open door policy' to Commonwealth citizens. It was a knee-jerk response rather than a reasoned consideration of factors such as housing, education and health which could have given some indication of the country's capacity to accommodate immigration: 'The result was the enactment of an exclusion policy rather than an immigration policy so called' (1993: 4). Although this ad hoc feature of the Act is important to note, it is worth stressing the racist attitudes that also fed into the legislation; attitudes that were the legacy of empire. Holmes writes that 'pre-existing hostility towards Blacks and those from the Indian subcontinent ... can hardly be ignored' (1992: 262).
51 As Solomos (1993: 57), points out, this reflects a set of concerns developing slightly earlier, as the Labour and Conservative governments of 1945–51 attempted to develop policy for stemming the flow of black migrant workers coming to Britain: 'It was during this time that the terms of the political debate about "coloured" immigration were established, leading to a close association between race and immigration in both policy debates and in popular political and media discourses'.
52 Paul (1997: 173).
53 Ibid., 173. Solomos (1993: 61) quotes William Deedes, minister without portfolio, who wrote: 'The Bill's real purpose was to restrict the influx of coloured immigrants, We were reluctant to say as much openly. So the restrictions were applied to coloured and white citizens in all Commonwealth countries – though everybody recognised that immigration from Canada, Australia and New Zealand was no part of the problem'.
54 Paul (1997: 175). For a broader perspective on this process, see Miles (1989) who points out that the notions of alien and foreigner are predicated on the entire history of the nation state.
55 Ibid., 176. For a more radical account of the thinking behind the Act, which sees the state as acting on behalf of capitalists' interests, see Sivandan (1982).

extreme form the discourse of the National Front can be seen as the logical extension, rather than any great departure from the official government discourse on the need to police race.

The colonial background of the legislation is also starkly apparent in the background to the 1968 Commonwealth Immigrants Act. Prior to the Act, Commonwealth citizens who had a parent or grandparent 'born, adopted, registered, naturalised or naturalised' in the UK had an automatic right of entrance. A large group of Kenyan citizens of Asian descent were facing discrimination in Kenya and sought to enter the UK. The law was changed to restrict their right of entrance. Later, in 1972, similar treatment was meted upon the 'Ugandan Asians', albeit under a different legislative regime. The European Commission of Human Rights found that this amounted to 'inhuman and degrading treatment'.[56] The reason for allowing this group to enter the UK was thus not associated with any enlightened immigration policy, but with the impact of the Commission's ruling.[57]

A racist logic works itself through into the 1971 Immigration Act. Largely informed by the 'separate spheres' concept of nationality, it gave legislative form to overtly discriminatory practices that had long been in operation by dividing British subjects into 'patrials' and 'non patrials', non patrials being so deprived of rights of settlement and work as to be 'virtually aliens'.[58] The practical upshot of this definition also meant that patrials were almost completely white. Despite the language of the 1976 Act, and the developing case law, the immigration law remained racist in the crudest of senses. Reflecting continuing public concerns with the 'swamping' of the nation, the 1981 British Nationality Act provides a further attempt to classify and control. Nationality was divided into British Citizenship, British Dependent Territories Citizenship and British Overseas Citizenship. These classifications and the hierarchy of rights they reflected were predicated on notions of descent, themselves dependent on a notion of Britishness that excluded any broader notion of belonging to the Commonwealth.[59]

THE RACE RELATIONS ACTS

The 1965 Race Relations Act was expanded by the 1968 Act, redefined by the 1976 Act and redefined again in 2000. The Acts themselves are largely compromised, and leave racism largely intact.

The 1965 Race Relations Act was passed by a Labour government with a small majority and was profoundly affected by political compromises that were necessary to

---

56   Paul (1997: 182).
57   Ibid., 182. Juss (1993) also describes this later Act as marking another watershed. After 1968, government controls increasingly targeted secondary immigration. For example, the 1962 Act had retained the right of a child to join their his/her parent in the UK. The 1968 Act limited this provision by stating that both parents had to be resident in the UK before the right could be exercised.
58   Juss (1993: 181). Fryer (1984), states that this Act, when it came into effect in 1973, virtually ended all primary immigration. As well as increasing the power of immigration officers and the police to detain immigrants, it came into force in a context of increasing violence against black communities.
59   There is a problem with research into recent history. The 30-year rule over the release of official papers means that the following discussion is not up to date.

achieve the necessary parliamentary support on the eve of a general election.[60] It was a limited measure, creating a criminal offence of incitement to racial hatred and an overseeing body, the Race Relations Board, which lacked basic powers to call for witnesses and documents. The emphasis was on conciliation; only if conciliation failed could the Board refer the case to the Attorney General who had discretion to determine whether litigation was necessary or not.[61]

Political exigencies combined with wider ideological failures to severely limit the Act's effectiveness. The 1965 Act was explicitly linked to the problem of a coloured immigrant population that had to be controlled both at the point of entry and in their ongoing settlement and 'integration'.[62] The claims made by apologists for the Act can be unpicked by looking at the following extract written by Anthony Lester, one of the major champions of the bill:

> Our law has two faces. One face confronts the stranger at the gate, grudgingly and suspiciously; the other is turned benevolently towards the newcomer and his descendants within the gate, guaranteeing the treatment of members of ethnic minorities as individuals on their merits, rather than discriminatory treatment on the basis of racial stereotypes, prejudices and assumptions. With one face, the law embodies and reinforces racial inequality; with the other it expresses and urges racial equality. The positive impact of race equality law continues to be diminished by the negative impact of unfair and discriminatory immigration and asylum laws.[63]

Our law has two faces, without being two-faced. This passage accepts the necessary linkage between immigration and anti-discrimination law, but, projects the tension into an image of balance, and potential resolution. To resolve the problem, we need only identify the 'negative' elements and work to expunge them. However, we have seen that the legal response was so thoroughly bound up with political priorities as to be inextricable from them. The racism of immigration law feeds into and sustains the failures of anti-discrimination law. It would be harder, from this perspective, to blame the Act's failure on external elements, those 'Maoists' and 'other militant tendencies, brought together under the tattered banner of "Black Power"'.[64] Instead of the tired rhetoric of law's balance, what is needed is an understanding of law's wider implication in sustaining a post-colonial order. One might have to search much deeper than a limited criticism of the common law that 'had at best been neutral, at worst [given] preference to property and contract rights over the right to equality of treatment'.[65] Policymakers had missed the opportunity to link anti-discrimination legislation with poor social conditions, exclusion and policy failures in housing, education and welfare. Thus, the 1965 Act did not apply to areas of education and housing. The Act conceived

---

60 McCrudden *et al.* (1991: 9).
61 Ibid., 9.
62 Miles and Phizacklea (1987: 57).
63 Lester (2000: 29).
64 Ibid., 27.
65 Ibid., 29.

of the problem as one of 'biologically discrete populations'[66] whose interactions with the white majority had to be protected by the law.

An overview of more recent legislation displays an ongoing inability to understand the nature of racism. The 1968 Act extended the provisions of the 1965 Act. It made discrimination in housing and employment subject to civil remedies. Discrimination was defined as less favourable treatment on the grounds of colour, race or ethnic or national origins. The Race Relation Board's conciliatory role remained, but the Board was now empowered to litigate cases in the county court. Alongside the Board a new body was created. The Community Relations Commission was to sponsor 'harmonious community relations'. But the 1968 Act was as flawed as its predecessor, since most of it was orientated towards individual forms of behaviour it failed to generate resources needed to implement effective programmes.

The 1976 Act widened the scope of anti-discrimination law still further.[67] The statutory definition of discrimination specified that a higher proportion of the group experiencing discrimination must be unable to comply with the condition than the population at large. As there was no guide to this proportion, the court has to use its discretion; a discretion that also applied to the question of whether the condition was justified. Given that 'tribunals and courts tend to be norm reflecting' and not likely to encourage interpretations that disturb or challenge norms, these terms were always going to be limited by the courts inherent conservatism.[68] An Act that presented, at least potentially, a challenge to ingrained practices was profoundly compromised by its reliance on mechanisms that would, either directly or indirectly, allow old modes of thinking to perpetuate themselves.

This problem can be traced into the Act's definition of indirect discrimination. Indirect discrimination went some way to acknowledging the social reality of racism's operation. Acts of discrimination are often not obvious and direct, but have a more sophisticated and covert nature. The kind of indirect discrimination covered by the Act is the imposition of a condition that on the face of it is colour blind but, in application occasions, discrimination. Take for instance, the situation that led to litigation in *Mandla* v. *Lee*. A Sikh boy was unable to conform with a school rule that forbade non-regulation clothing at school. Clearly no direct discrimination had taken place: the boy had not been refused entrance to the school because he was a Sikh. However, a condition

---

66 Fryer (1984: 58).
67 Problems with the Act do not end with the definition of discrimination. There are other critical approaches to both the failures of the Act itself, and the case law that develops around it. As Lustgarten (1980) argues, no matter how the Race Relations Act is assessed, one is compelled to acknowledge that it has been largely ineffective. Thus, a consideration of incidents of successful prosecution after the Act became law shows that in 1982, 30 out of 200 cases heard in ITs were successful. This is lower than the 25 per cent success rate in unfair dismissal cases. (Information from the CRE consultative document The Race Relations Act [1983].) If one looks at evidence for changes in employers' attitudes, one finds patterns of 'ignorance and inaction'; see Young and Connelly (1981). Solomos (1993) argues that '[a]lmost all the academic research that has been done on the effectiveness of the 1976 Act has pointed to three ways in which policies have proved to be ineffective. First, the machinery set up to implement the Act has not functioned effectively. Second, the policies have not produced the intended results. Third, the policies have failed to meet the expectations of the black communities. The other glaring omission was the exclusion of the police from the provisions of the Act.
68 Lustgarten states: 'in every case in which there was a split tribunal decision against the complainant, the non specialist wingman joined the chairman to make the majority'.

had been applied which would have made it impossible for Sikhs to comply because wearing a turban is an expression of ethnic identity. Thus, the statutory test concerns the imposition of a condition that significantly fewer people in the discriminated group could comply.

As commentators have suggested, this concept of indirect discrimination falls far short of any meaningful idea of institutional discrimination.[69] As we shall see, the Lawrence inquiry stressed the institutional nature of racism as the

> Collective failure of an organisation to provide an appropriate and professional service to people because of their colour, culture or ethnic origin. It can be seen or detected in processes, attitude and behaviour which amount to discrimination through unwitting prejudice, ignorance, thoughtlessness and racist stereotyping which disadvantage minority ethnic people.[70]

This is a more useful definition than that provided by the 1976 Act. It draws attention to the informal networks, the unofficial but influential social interactions where a culture's racism coheres. The concept of discrimination in the 1976 Act was limited as the condition that allegedly discriminated had to be an absolute bar. A 'preferred profile' would not constitute a condition for the purposes of the Act. Thus, the reality of prejudice operating at a shop floor or informal level would not necessarily be prohibited by the Act. Arguably, the Act should have covered any practice that had a 'significant adverse impact' on levels of employment among ethnic minorities. Institutional racism thrives in an environment where unreflective and conservative thinking persists.[71] Weaknesses in the definition of key terms meant that it was difficult to combat this thinking.

The failures of the 1976 Act can be seen in the murder of the black teenager Stephen Lawrence. The subsequent inquiry into the failure to obtain a prosecution revealed the continuing nature of British racism.

THE LAWRENCE INQUIRY

The first report into the murder investigations, the Kent Report, found no evidence that racism had significantly contributed to the failures to make arrests. Admittedly, the Kent Report addressed complaints against individual officers, and did not have a remit to research wider issues, but this in turn reflects the nature of the problem; an inability to conceptualise racism, and an underestimation of its persistence.

Lord Scarman's report into the Brixton Disorder in 1981 had rejected the allegation that British institutions were systematically involved in racial discrimination. The Lawrence Inquiry picked up on this explanation of the problem as one of 'unwitting'

---
69 Bob Hepple's chapter was entitled 'Have twenty five years of race relations Acts in Britain been a failure?', in Hepple and Szyszczak (1992).
70 *The Lawrence Inquiry*, 6: 34.
71 *The Lawrence Inquiry*, Cm 4662-I (London: HMSO, 1999).

racism.[72] Thus, the Metropolitan Police were not racist; apparent prejudice at an operational level was to be explained by 'errors of judgement ... lack of imagination and flexibility'.[73] At the level of everyday policing, 'occasional' racism could be explained as the 'immaturity' of certain officers. In Lord Scarman's report, however, there is an acknowledgement that the problem is wider and more structural. It appears as an explanation as to why individual officers, who are not racist, may become so. Because of racial stereotyping, officers facing a rising tide of 'street crime' may 'lapse into unthinking assumptions'.[74] It is not as if Lord Scarman is dismissive of racism. Where unwitting racism has been proved, it warrants remedy. Racism is the cause of social tension that cannot be allowed to fester and destroy good order. However, the legacy of the Scarman Report is an understanding of racism that distracts attention from its invasive, systematic or institutional nature, and tends to see it as either unconscious or the unwitting acts of individuals.

The limitations of Lord Scarman's definition of racism were apparent to the Lawrence Inquiry.[75] Both the Police Complaints Authority (PCA) and the police had failed to understand the problem of discrimination as it was limited to the acts of a few 'rotten apples', who 'let the side down'.[76] Equally at fault was the practice of following the 'traditional way of doing things'. The over-arching aspect of this ideology is the reluctance to come to terms with the need to police a multiracial society. For a police force that is attached to a notion of unarmed and consensual policing, such a refusal to move with the times is profoundly damaging.

The Lawrence Inquiry also found that the culture of policing does not encourage a critical self-understanding that would make prejudice easier to identify and to challenge. Evidence from officers in the Black Police Association (BPA) drew attention to a powerful 'occupational culture'[77] which was shaping or influencing black officers' own views about race and crime from the perspective of 'white experience, white beliefs and white values'. This was self-perpetuating, as white officers tended only to meet black people in 'confrontational' situations that supported assumptions and stereotypes about black criminality and lawlessness. As the Lawrence Inquiry was told, it 'may be' that these attitudes are prevalent throughout British society. Such a concern was obviously outside the inquiry's terms of reference, although some tentative suggestions were made about wider attitudes. As institutional racism it is expressed not only in the failures of the Lawrence murder investigation, but also in the disparity in the numbers of black people stopped and searched,[78] the underreporting of 'racial incidents'[79] and the inability of the police to take the issue seriously at the level of training.[80]

---

72   Ibid., at 6:7.
73   Ibid., at 6:8.
74   Ibid., at 6:10.
75   For the Stephen Lawrence case see *The Guardian*'s special report – http://www.guardian.co.uk/lawrence/0,,179674,00.html.
76   Ibid., at 6:14.
77   Ibid., at 6:28.
78   Ibid., at 6:45.
79   Ibid., at 6:45.
80   Her Majesty's Inspectorate of Constabulary Report: *Winning the Race* showed that before 1998, not a single officer had received training in racism awareness.

The law might begin to understand racism through a concept of 'institutional' discrimination.[81] The report itself refers back to a text by two black American activists, Stokely Carmichael and Charles V. Hamilton, to develop this definition. Racism must be seen as operating within the most 'respected forces' and as a combination of both 'active' and 'pervasive' racist attitudes; underlying these is a belief in black inferiority. This does need supplementing by assumptions about black lawlessness that have their own particular history. For instance, one account of black history in Britain quotes a Metropolitan Police Commissioner as saying: 'In the Jamaicans, you have people who are constitutionally disorderly ... It's simply in their makeup. They are constitutionally disposed to be anti authority'.[82]

Also important is the perception of mugging as a 'race' crime. Although official Home Office investigations into race relations tended to stress the role of a difficult minority of among a fairly respectable majority, the panic over mugging in the later seventies led to a series of violent confrontations between the police and black youths. Still the subject of complex and fierce debate in criminology and policy circles, it is difficult within the space of this chapter to account for these explosions of violence. One fact is salient. Official accounts tended to play down the political motivations of the rioters. In the wake of the Notting Hill riots of 1976, a new set of stereotypes was created. The image of the black mob entered into the public imagination; violence seemed to make the link between blackness and disorder more complex and profound.[83] This in turn perhaps led to a new escalation in the tensions that had produced rioting in the first place. The police strategy of containment and aggressive use of powers of search and arrest led to further riots in the 1980s.

After the Lawrence Inquiry these attitudes are no longer acceptable. In the words of Sir John Woodcock, the Chief Inspector of Constabulary in 1992, the inquiry reveals a wider 'cultural failure'.[84] Thus in its recommendation for tackling English racism, there is a need for, in the words of the Reverend David Wise, a 'radical transformation' involving not only the police but all levels of society. The inquiry becomes the point at which a previously radical critique enters within official discourse. Again, with reference to the words of Sir John, the police remain a nineteenth century institution, a 'mechanism set up to protect the affluent from what the Victorians described as the dangerous classes'.[85]

CONCLUSION: LAW'S PAUSE IN THE POST-COLONIAL?

Whether or not one accepts that the global was first understood practically through the practices of colonialism, the post-colonial and the global interact. Europe may defend its 'civilised space' through strategies of boundary drawing, creating a common space

---

81 Ibid., at 6:22.
82 Fryer (1993: 37).
83 See Gilroy (1987a); more generally Phillips and Bowling (2002).
84 Lawrence Inquiry, 6:61.
85 Ibid., at, 6:61.

which demarcates itself from the other, but it is constituted by relationship with the other and the colonial violence that has shaped so much of modern law. What of justice? In her review Tuitt seems to hope that our intellectual work of rewriting histories and identities may provide for 'law's pause, and ... hesitation', offering some place 'for justice' precisely where 'the law sees the terror of its own force'.[86] Yet we may suspect that there are many forces preventing the interconnections – and racism of the global order – being in view. To end: the current war on terror, presented in an iconic image by the *Economist* magazine as the globe in the shape of a human skull,[87] may be itself read as a continuation of the strategies of allowing some narratives of case and effect and not others. If 11 September 2001 brought images of terror, fear, mistrust and death, as part of normal reality to the West, to others these images were only a realisation by the powerful of the terror that many in the world already lived with on a daily basis. Then there was the question of interdependency. In 1994, Rwanda experienced genocide. This was perhaps the easiest of the great massacres of the twentieth century to have been stopped. But the West refrained from action, resulting in over 880,000 deaths (see quotation at this chapter's beginning). This was a state-sponsored massacre that was planned and with considerable measures taken to achieve it (such as buying and distributing machetes to approximately one-third of the population). If, in the years immediately afterwards, the stories were confusing and contested, we now know that the power élites of the West (the white nations) knew of the plans and the event and deliberately decided to do nothing. We will end with the words of William Rubinstein, himself an historian who has done much to defend settler interests against the charge of genocide of Australian Aboriginals:

> While overt racism certainly played no part in the attitude of the Western world towards the Rwandan genocide, it is difficult to believe that many people in the West really cared whether 100,000 or 500,000 or 800,000 perceived as illiterate savages who had contributed nothing to the world's stock of achievement and culture lived or died. An interesting experiment in fact suggests itself. If two collectors had been stationed in any shopping mall in the Western world at the time of the genocide, one raising money to stop 100,000 Tutsi children from being murdered by Hutus, the other raising money to stop 100 elephants from being slaughtered by poachers, which would collect more? If you had bet on the elephants, it is safe to say you would have put some change in your pocket.[88]

---

86   Tuitt (2004: 114).
87   The front cover of the *Economist*, 30 Nov–6 Dec 2002, under the heading of *Preparing for Terror*, made the globe as one human skull. The cover of the 19–25 October 2002 issue, under the heading *A World of Terror*, was of a small figure standing before a forest of tall sticks of dynamite with their fuses lit.
88   Rubinstein (2004: 291). We may add the caveat that it may be that 'overt' racism played a significant role. See Melvern (2004) who provides an indictment of the Western powers (and the UN) who knew what was planned and happened and chose not to intervene.

7

RIGHTS, POLITICS AND THE LAW OF THE EUROPEAN UNION

INTRODUCTION

Our argument so far has been that due process legitimises the law. What sense can we make of European Union (EU) law from this perspective? This chapter will argue that EU law is characterised by rival notions of legitimacy. Although the courts of the Union are bound by the foundational treaties, they have also invoked principles that go beyond the letter of the law. Is this legitimate?

This question takes us to a second point. Legitimacy is a legal and political concept. Legal notions such as due process relate to democratic political values. This raises the problematic issue of the fundamental values of the Union. Is the EU a democratic order capable of developing so as to become open and transparent to its citizens? To what extent are its political and administrative processes 'self regulating' or open to legal challenge? The most recent attempt to reorder the Union has been to orientate EU law towards human rights. The question remains whether this approach is capable of providing a coherent foundation for EU law and its political order.

This chapter will begin with a discussion of the Charter of Fundamental Rights. We will then turn to the issue of standing and the judicial protection of rights. We will see that the tensions between different versions of the test for standing relate to competing ways of accounting for the legitimacy of the EU. We will trace this concern through the law on the transparency of the Union's institutions and the jurisprudence on the rights of the defence. Our final section is an examination of the status of the Commission;[1] a matter that raises a fundamental Article 6 concern: the neutrality of a judicial tribunal.

We will argue that the EU is an ongoing experiment in the creation of a legal and political order. Its legitimacy is a work in progress. While the courts have, to some extent, been able to develop a jurisprudence of due process (with the caveats we outlined in the introduction), the question remains as to whether a meaningful link can be forged between law and democracy, rights and politics.

THE CHARTER OF FUNDAMENTAL RIGHTS 2000

We will begin with a backward glance over EU law from the perspective of the Charter. Although the foundational 1957 Treaty of Rome contained certain social and economic

---
1 See Appendix to this chapter for a description of the institutions of the European Union and a basic guide to the key terms of European Union law.

rights, the Charter is the first attempt to use human rights as a way of ordering EU law. What is at stake in this endeavour? After placing the Charter in its political context, we will analyse two of its Articles that are most central to the concerns of this book: Article 41, the right to good administration and Article 47, the right to a fair trial and an effective remedy.

The Charter of Fundamental Rights came out of the recommendation of the European Council in 1999. Annex IV is worth considering in some detail. It draws attention to the rationale for a statement of human rights in the EU:

> Protection of fundamental rights is a founding principle of the Union and an indispensable prerequisite for her legitimacy. The obligation of the Union to respect fundamental rights has been confirmed and defined by the jurisprudence of the European Court of Justice. There appears to be a need, at the present stage of the Union's development, to establish a Charter of fundamental rights in order to make their overriding importance and relevance more visible to the Union's citizens.[2]

This paragraph returns to the foundational values of the Union. It is interesting that the statement links together rights and legitimacy, and presents the 'overriding' importance of rights as central to the ongoing legitimisation of the Union. The law of the Union is a developing body of principles that need to be coordinated with the contemporary appreciation that human rights are central to both legal and political legitimacy.

If this argument is placed in its historical context, the political importance of orientating the Union to human rights becomes clearer. There are at least two distinct concerns. Since the foundation of the Union, there has been a growing sense that its institutions remain opaque and somewhat distant from those whose lives they govern. The incomprehension and distrust of the Union has expressed itself in the politics of different member states. Such a 'legitimacy gap' is clearly worrying. Commitment to human rights provides one possible way of stressing that the Union is transparent, accountable and dedicated to the rule of law. The second concern relates to the expansion of the Union to include nations that had been under communist or state socialist control prior to the collapse of the USSR. The economic and political restructuring necessary for membership in the Union required the EU to stress its own democratic credentials, and to promulgate these doctrines in the management of the affairs of the new member states.

However, commitment to human rights is not the only value to which the Union adheres. If we return to the Treaty of Rome, we can also clearly see that it is an economic bloc, operating through the free movement of goods, resources and personnel within the countries that constitute the Union. While human rights and economic goals are not necessarily incompatible, tensions can clearly develop between the profit-driven requirements of capitalist economics and the social justice imperatives of human rights. As this problem can only be appreciated through an in-depth study of EU law,

---

[2] Cologne European Council, Conclusions of the Presidency, June 1999, at http://www.europarl.europa.eu/summits/kol2_en.htm#an4.

we are forced to deal with it at a rather general and abstract level. However, our first point is that the Charter represents at least one way in which these tensions are managed.

The Charter does not give human rights 'teeth'. It is not a binding document, and it does not create new rights. It is intended to be a coherent statement of the rights that already exist in EU law and to act primarily as an interpretative aid for the community courts.[3] Human rights are thus a factor to be taken into account in the polity of the EU and weighed against other compelling arguments that reflect the competing goals of the Union. However, this is not to suggest that the Charter is somehow secondary and unimportant. We will see below that the Charter is influencing the reasoning of the courts, and allowing them to express principles of Union law in human rights terms. It is perhaps too soon to say how this process will play itself out; it would also be a major project to understand the dynamics of this process across the entirety of EU law. We will thus restrict ourselves to some provisional arguments about how Articles 41 and 47 can be understood, and how they can be traced in the Court of First Instance (CFI) and the European Court of Justice (ECJ).

It is worth bearing another point in mind. We will be looking at cases decided prior to the Charter, and doctrines developed before the orientation to human rights took place. Weighing up the due process elements of EU law will thus require us to think about law that does not express itself in human rights language. As argued in the introduction, this is not necessarily problematic. Due process can take the form of institutional principles that are not expressed as human rights. This leads to the difficult coordination of two forms of legal language, but as we will see, this is only one of a complex of issues that confront us when we examine due process in EU law. At the very least, we should not assume that if a principle does not express itself as a human right it lacks structure, clarity or legitimacy.

We will now review Articles 41 and 47. Article 41 is the statement of right to good administration. As there is no comparative right in the European Convention, Article 41 represents something of an innovation within European human rights law. The first paragraph details a broad, overarching right that creates a duty for the institutions of the Union:

> Every person has the right to have his or her affairs handled impartially, fairly and within a reasonable time by the institutions and bodies of the Union.

The wording of 41(1) echoes Article 6 in its requirement for an impartial consideration of an individual's affairs and the 'reasonable time' requirement. However, it is immediately worth pointing out that Article 41 is much wider than Article 6, which remains fairly narrowly focused on courts and tribunals. In this sense 'administration' can include political as well as legal or quasi-legal forms

---

3   The Charter was part II of the 2004 treaty that established a constitution for Europe. Ratification required consent from all member states. 'No' votes in referenda held in France and the Netherlands meant that the Treaty was not adopted. The issue of a European constitution remains problematic.

of deliberation. Subsequent paragraphs expand the terms of the right within the context of administrative law. Paragraph 41(2) states that 41(1) includes

> the right of every person to be heard, before any individual measure which would affect him or her adversely is taken.

This takes us to the test for standing (or *locus standi*) that we discuss below. Suffice to say that 41(2) is a key requirement for a right to good administration in that it clarifies when an individual is considered to have the necessary standing to challenge an administrative decision. Our discussion below will elaborate why this kind of test is necessary, and how it relates to the test that is current in EU law.

Paragraph 41(3) takes us to the essential concern with transparency and accountability:

> The right of every person to have access to his or her file, while respecting the legitimate interests of confidentiality and of professional and business secrecy.

While the concern with the 'file' represents the civil law context (common lawyers might not talk in these terms) the sense of the paragraph is reasonably clear. The right of access to relevant documents is limited by two grounds: confidentiality and business secrecy. The definition of the right and its limitations makes an engagement with the case law necessary, but as we point out, this in turn requires us to understand that the CFI and the ECJ have developed a jurisprudence on transparency that pre-dates the Charter.

The final paragraph, 41(4), elaborates a right with which we will become quite familiar:

> the obligation of the administration to give reasons for its decisions.

We will elaborate the courts' understanding of this duty below. The key point is that it stresses a fundamental idea of the rule of law in this administrative setting. Arbitrary expressions of power are illegitimate and unlawful. The legitimacy of the law is based on the way in which it requires decision makers to provide reasons to justify the actions that they have taken. This allows the affected person(s) to understand why a decision has been made, and also, if necessary, enables the articulation of grounds of appeal. Paragraph 41(4) thus requires administrative proceedings to be conducted in accordance with the rule of law.

Article 47 is the right to a fair trial and an effective remedy. It is based on Articles 6 and 13 of the Convention (the right to an effective remedy). Unlike Article 6, Article 47 does not limit fair trial rights to determination of civil obligations or criminal charges, although the core values of an 'independent and impartial tribunal' and determination within a reasonable time are the same as Article 6:

1   Everyone whose rights and freedoms guaranteed by the law of the Union are violated has the right to an effective remedy before a tribunal in compliance with the conditions laid down in this Article.

2 Everyone is entitled to a fair and public hearing within a reasonable time by an independent and impartial tribunal previously established by law. Everyone shall have the possibility of being advised, defended and represented.
3 Legal aid shall be made available to those who lack sufficient resources in so far as such aid is necessary to ensure effective access to justice.

Article 47 rests on the fundamental assertion that rights correlate with remedies. What follows from this basic position is the requirement that the integrity of legal proceedings are themselves protected. This returns us to one of the main claims of this book. Law has to be understood as structured on certain principles and values. This fundamental structure of law is reflected in the overlap between Articles 41 and 47. Good administration and fair trials make necessary impartial judges/decision makers who make a decision within a reasonable time. Obviously Article 47 goes further in also specifying a right to representation. This important right is dealt with in Chapter 16.

What do we make of Articles 41 and 47? We have described their location within European human rights law and the coherence of the fundamental principles that they articulate. The remainder of this chapter will review some important areas of due process in the law of the Union, and assess it from the perspectives of the fundamental requirements of due process and of human rights. We will see that while human rights are not irrelevant, the key arguments take place in relation to the principles of EU law. This point will be further elaborated in the conclusion to the chapter.

STANDING AND EFFECTIVE JUDICIAL PROTECTION

Our consideration of due process in EU law requires a brief consideration of the way that standing operates in administrative law. So far in the book, we have not engaged expansively with this issue. We have argued that its proper consideration belongs in the province of public law. However, to the extent that we are concerned with the values of law, and the conflicts over their meaning and range, we must touch upon this doctrine. As far as our discussion of EU law is concerned, this argument links with those that will be developed in Chapter 16 on access to justice. The issue that we want to explore can be outlined as follows. If the Union is to be responsive to its citizens and democratically accountable, then there must be mechanisms to allow citizens and pressure groups to challenge the decisions of Union institutions. These mechanisms must operate (as far as possible) to enable, rather than frustrate, the ways in which citizens and their representatives can claim rights to review. To understand the issues in this area, we need to make another preliminary point. Standing is a peculiar product of judicial review. As we are not concerned with private rights derived (for example) from a contract or a tortuous act, but with public rights, the law needs to define their nature and their scope. This technical concern with the nature of a public law right thus conceals the pressing question of how a legal system can empower its citizens and the extent to which a court is open to a broad range of interests, not just commercial operators protecting their private (or indeed public) rights.

Thus the law has to create a balanced test that allows those affected by a general decision to obtain review, while filtering out those who are too remotely interested to plead an interference with their public law interest. How does this general concern relate to the specific legal order created by the EU?

The ECJ has provided a useful overview of the fundamental concerns of EU law:

> By Article 173 and Article 184 (now Article 241 EC), on the one hand, and by Article 177, on the other, the Treaty has established a complete system of legal remedies and procedures designed to ensure judicial review of the legality of acts of the institutions, and has entrusted such review to the Community Courts (see, to that effect, *Les Verts* v. *Parliament*, paragraph 23). Under that system, where natural or legal persons cannot, by reason of the conditions for admissibility laid down in the fourth paragraph of Article 173 of the Treaty, directly challenge Community measures of general application, they are able, depending on the case, either indirectly to plead the invalidity of such acts before the Community Courts under Article 184 of the Treaty or to do so before the national courts and ask them, since they have no jurisdiction themselves to declare those measures invalid (see Case 314/85 *Foto-Frost* [1987] ECR 4199, paragraph 20), to make a reference to the Court of Justice for a preliminary ruling on validity.[4]

The foundational law on judicial review is contained in the EC Treaty, as amended. The reviewing body are the Community Courts. They have the jurisdiction to hear challenges of community measures from individuals, business organisations and associations. The second mechanism allows individuals to challenge community measures in the courts of the member states. This is an indirect way of obtaining judicial review, as it compels the courts of member states to make reference to the ECJ. The key issue, then, is to see EU law as an interface with the law of member states, but, as we argued above, EU law is an overarching supranational legal order that must be supreme. This leads to some specific concerns about review in the EU system. Let us deal with a general point before outlining these themes. What is the nature of the test for standing in EU law on judicial review?

The general position is that the EU law on standing has not developed in favour of the citizen, nor indeed, commercial interests. *Plaumann* v. *Commission*[5] laid down the fundamental test. The case refers back to Article 173 of the EEC Treaty, which states: 'Any natural or legal person may ... institute proceedings against a decision ... which although in the form of a decision addressed to another person, is of direct and individual concern to the former.'[6] There are two matters of definition: the nature of a 'decision' and the precise way in which a person can claim to have an individual concern. By reference to Articles 189 and 191 of the EEC Treaty, decisions are defined by the fact that they concern specific persons. It is equally important to know in what circumstances a person can issue proceedings when his/her issues are affected by a decision that addresses another person. The test for 'individual concern' would be met if

---

4   UPA, para 40.
5   Case 25/62, *Plaumann and Co.* v. *Commission* [1963] ECR 95.
6   Ibid.

'by reason of certain attributes which are peculiar to them or by reason of circumstances in which they are differentiated from all other persons', they are 'differentiated' to such an extent that they are individually affected in the same way as the person directly addressed.[7]

While the wording of the test is somewhat complicated, it is clear that the test could be given either a broad or a narrow meaning. One would imagine that the court would be willing to take the latter option. However, in *Plaumann*, the test was given a very restricted interpretation. The applicant was an importer of fruit into the EC. The court held that because this form of business could be carried on by any other commercial concern, the applicant was not individually concerned. The applicant was thus not able to question a decision of the Commission to suspend custom duties on the import of fresh fruit into the EU. An equally narrow test for regulations was laid down in *Calpak*,[8] which was also difficult to apply because of the technical way in which it was framed.[9]

The Plaumann test was considered in *Unión de Pequeños Agricultores [UPA]* v. *Council of the European Union*.[10] UPA was a trade association of Spanish farmers. It was challenging a Regulation that made for certain reforms in the European olive oil market, in particular the termination of aid for small producers. UPA's argument, in part, alleged that this measure was in breach of both a fundamental principle of Community law (equal treatment of producers and consumers) and the objectives of European agricultural policy.

The CFI argued that the opportunities for a challenge were defined by the Plaumann test. Standing could be shown on one of three possible grounds. UPA would have to prove either that the Regulation provided the right to challenge the measure, or that the members of the association had interests affected by the measure, or that the association itself was 'distinguished individually' by the measure. UPA would be able to make out this last ground if, for example, its negotiating position had been affected by the Regulation.[11] The CFI held that none of these conditions applied. Would this mean, though, that the Court had denied an effective remedy for a matter of public interest?[12] The CFI argued that Article 230 EC prevented a substantive ground (i.e. a matter of public interest) being used as a reason for standing. UPA had one final argument. It asserted that it could make an 'indirect' challenge to measures that affected it. As there are no remedies under national law, it could ask the ECJ for a preliminary ruling that would review the 'legality of the legislation' under Article 243 EC. The CFI stated that this was not a correct application of 243 EC to the facts of the case.

In order to understand these arguments and the broader issues they raise, it is useful to look at the opinion of the Advocate General. He had a degree of sympathy

---

7   Ibid.
8   Cases 789 and 790/79, *Calpak SpA* v. *Commission* [1980] ECR 1949.
9   In the wake of Plaumann, there were arguments that an 'indirect' challenge to Community measures was possible under Article 243. This approach would effectively allow an applicant to begin proceedings in a national court as a way of accessing the ECJ. It is discussed below in Advocate General's opinion in the UPA case. The court rejected this approach in *Asocarne*. See case C-10/95 P. *Asocarne* v. *Council*.
10 Case C-50/00 *Unión de Pequeños Agricultores* v. *Council of the European Union*.
11 Ibid., para 13.
12 Ibid., para 15.

for UPA's position: the rules on standing were 'problematic'.[13] The restrictions on the right to challenge a Regulation were 'unacceptable'. Article 230 should be interpreted in such a way as to make it consistent with the principle of effective judicial protection. However, the CFI were correct to reject the doctrine of indirect challenge. As national courts could not declare Community law invalid, they were not the appropriate forum for review cases. Indeed, an indirect challenge would appear to be a breach of the principle of effective judicial protection, as the applicants require 'access to a court which is competent to grant remedies capable of protecting them against the effects of unlawful measures'.[14] There was a second fundamental problem with this argument. It would make *locus standi* dependent on national law. As this differs between member states, it would result in a loss of certainty and lead to the unacceptable situation where, for example, a measure could be challenged in a Spanish court, but not in a court in the UK. Such an anomaly would 'infringe the principle of equal treatment'.[15]

What, then, was the solution? The Advocate General proposed a test of 'individual concern' based on paragraph 4 of Article 230 EC. He argued that it was not necessary to read into the Article the requirement that an individual challenger of a measure needs to be 'differentiated' from others that might be affected by it. The peculiar consequence of this test was that the greater the number of people affected by a measure, the 'less likely' it was that judicial review would be available. This seems against the logic of the position: 'The fact that a measure adversely affects a large number of individuals, causing widespread rather than limited harm, provides … a positive reason for accepting a direct challenge by one or more of those individuals.'[16] The test in its most expanded form becomes: 'a person is to be regarded as individually concerned by a Community measure where, by reason of his particular circumstances, the measure has, or is liable to have, a substantial adverse effect on his interests.'[17] Such a test would meet UPA's arguments about the weakness of the judicial protection principle when applied to standing; it would also provide a more 'generous' test and 'improve judicial protection', values consistent with the fundamental principles of community law.[18] Finally, it would resolve the problems that had come out of the incorrect use of Article 243 for indirect challenges to community measures.

What do we make of this opinion? The Advocate General's proposed test would liberalise the law on standing. It would make it easier for those affected by Community measures to make use of the courts to protect their rights and hence play more of a role in the development and ultimately the legitimisation of Community policy. A restrictive test gives the courts a much less pronounced role, and might open the Community to the charge that its institutions were difficult to subject to judicial control. If we accept the reasoning of the Advocate General, though, how can we (in turn) justify his interpretation of the law? Surely this runs the risk of going beyond the letter of

---

13 Ibid., para 37.
14 Ibid., para 42.
15 Ibid., para 53.
16 Ibid., para 59.
17 Ibid., para 60.
18 Ibid., para 63.

the treaties. The Court could be accused of acting illegitimately in granting itself a broad interpretative power that the Treaty did not bestow.

Could we justify this opinion as a 'use of background rights as a mechanism for a re-assessment of existing doctrine'?[19] This reading would allow us to legitimise the argument by presenting it as coherent with the fundamental principles of the Union. While this approach is compelling, it is worth noting that the 'background rights' are those derived from the Treaty of Rome and EU law in general. Article 47 is only mentioned in passing. However, the relative unimportance of the Charter is not our key point. If the Advocate General's opinion can be seen as legitimate, then it suggests that the ECJ can re-orientate doctrine to principle. What are the boundaries of this practice? The Advocate General himself states that there is a legitimate concern in protecting Community law from 'undue judicial intervention'. A balance has to be struck. The Advocate General argues that this lies in the development of 'substantive standards of judicial review' rather than 'by the application of strict rules on admissibility' which have the effect 'of blindly excluding applicants without consideration of the merits of the arguments they put forward'.[20] This argument is legitimate because it attempts to balance competing interests. It suggests a pragmatic policy dimension to the Advocate General's reasoning. Legitimacy is thus not entirely a matter of law. A legitimate position is both legally consistent and politically acceptable.

The response of the ECJ to the Advocate General is an indication that his reasoning was not persuasive. The ECJ had a different understanding of how the 'rule of law'[21] applied to the facts of the present case. The Court returned to the Plaumann test and argued that any test of standing had to return to the Treaty.[22] The test proposed by the Advocate General was too broad, and amounted to the ECJ exceeding its role as an interpreter of the Treaty. The correct way forward would be for the member states themselves to reform the test, in accordance with Article 48 EU.[23] The opinion of the Advocate General was not followed. This led to certain problems in *Jégo-Quéré*.

Jégo-Quéré v. *Commission*[24] concerned an appeal from a French company active in the fishing industry. The Commission had promulgated a Regulation that reduced net sizes in order to conserve fish stocks. The applicants argued before the CFI that, should its action be dismissed, they would be denied the possibility of legal remedy, because the Regulation did not provide a right to bring an action before a court of a member state. Framing its argument with reference to Articles 6 and 13 of the Convention and Article 47 of the Charter of Fundamental Freedoms, the CFI held that Articles 243 and 235 EC (and Article 288) had to be interpreted along the lines proposed by the Advocate General in *UPA*. This would mean applying the test of 'individual concern', and allowing the applicants to make a 'direct action' in the CFI. The Commission then appealed to the ECJ, and the case was considered directly after the ruling in *UPA*. The reasoning of the Advocate General that had been so influential in the CFI could not

---

19   Craig (2007: 337).
20   Supra n. 10 at 66.
21   Ibid., para 38.
22   Ibid., para 44.
23   Ibid., para 45.
24   Case 263/02, *Jégo-Quéré* v. *Commission*.

stand against the authority of *UPA*. The 'narrow' test for standing was once again reaffirmed.

Where does this leave us? The flip-flopping between the argument of the Advocate General and the ECJ certainly suggests that there is a profound tension in the law. It would be too simplistic to assert that the Lord Advocate's version of the standing test was the most coherent working out of the principles of the rule of law to the Union. This is because the position of the ECJ is clearly consistent with a version of the rule of law that would stress the need to keep to the terms of the foundational treaty, and to keep the power of the Court in check. Our problem in weighing up this case law is the absence of a constitutional document that would clarify the relative powers of Union institutions. A new form of the test was indeed made part of the proposed Treaty Establishing a Constitution for Europe in 2004, but the Treaty failed to become law. What might this tell us about the relationship between law and politics? We will postpone our provisional conclusion until we have considered one further related concern. To what extent is there a right to be heard in legislative, rather than administrative or legal procedures? This question returns us to the issue of the role that individuals and business entities can play in the development of EU law.

In *Atlanta AG* v. *Commission*[25] the appellants argued before the ECJ that the right to be heard in administrative proceedings could be 'transposed'[26] to legislative procedures that were geared towards the creation of law. Atlanta based their argument on Article 173 (230 EC, after amendment) of the EC Treaty. They asserted that the 'procedural right' to a defence in judicial proceedings could be read broadly. This would entitle them to damages as an EC Regulation that affected their business was in breach of international trade rules.[27] The ECJ rejected this argument. The Court held that Article 173(4) merely specified that individuals could issue annulment proceedings against an Act that directly affected them. It was not possible to 'logically conclude'[28] that this right could be used in the 'context' of 'legislative Acts' such as EC Regulations.[29] However, there is a narrow line between the unsuccessful argument of the appellants and those instances where affected parties can bring annulment proceedings in the CFI. The crucial question is the 'manner in which' the claimants interests are 'affected by the contested Acts'.[30] An applicant would have to show that his or her 'individual situation' is 'directly at issue'.[31] Where, as in this case, a legislative Act 'affects' all businesses alike, the 'infringement' of individual rights is general, and the 'rights of the defence' cannot be invoked.[32]

---

25   Case C 104/97 P, *Atlanta AG* v. *Commission* [1999] ECR I-6983.
26   Ibid., para 58.
27   Atlanta were alleging that EC Regulation 404/93 of 13 February 1993 was in breach of World Trade Organisation (WTO) rules on the regulation of the banana market.
28   Ibid., para 63.
29   Ibid.
30   Ibid., para 65.
31   Ibid.
32   Ibid., 66.

The principles articulated in Atlanta have been consistently developed in the subsequent case law. For instance, the difference between legislative and judicial proceedings was stressed in *Pfizer* v. *Council*[33] so as to deny an affected individual of the right to be heard even though they had been directly affected by a Regulation. The principle was broadened still further in *UEAPME* v. *Council*.[34] The applicants were challenging a policy on parental rights which would affect their members' rights. UEAPME had been in contact with the Commission and had sought unsuccessfully to be included in the negotiation process. The CFI held that this could not be construed so as to give them an interest that could be protected by the Court. Even participation in negotiating processes does not necessarily give an affected party a judicial right to question a legislative measure in court. The cases *Greenpeace*[35] and *Merck*[36] show that unless a relevant piece of legislation gives a person or a group a right to bring an action, the Court is not going to construe involvement in a policy-making process, or communications with a Community institution as amounting to a legally enforceable right.

Can the approach of the Court be justified? Commentators have suggested that while the distinction between judicial and legislative proceedings can be drawn at a general level, it is largely a matter of degree. There is no hard and fast distinction between measures that only directly affect an individual and those that affect a general category of persons. The fundamental problem in the jurisprudence of the Court is the 'narrow definition of individual concern'.[37] This seems inconsistent with the recent orientation of the Union towards transparency and accountability. The present stance of the Court would also militate against the encouragement of participation in the law-making process. If participation does not give rise to rights, it would seem that any attempt to make 'dialogue' an essential element of the creation of law has not been achieved. At the same time, there is a need to ensure that political processes do not become excessively 'legalised' to the extent that legal wrangling impeded the delivery of policy. It would appear that, at least for the moment, the line has been too firmly drawn on the side of protecting policy from the courts.

Our provisional conclusion is that the problems in the case law indicate a need to resolve the relative importance of conflicting principles at a political level. Whether or not the balance will be reassessed has to be linked to the broader debate about the democratic processes in the Union. Thus, the failure to agree a European constitution does draw attention to an important concern. Unless there is some congruence between legal and political orders, the courts cannot be relied upon to generate the principles that legitimise a polity. This would suggest that catalogues of human rights are, in themselves, incapable of providing a principled overarching order. Human rights can be part of a general orientation of principles towards important values. However, doctrines of human rights leave the Court without political guidance. Its decisions thus lack grounding in a broader reality.

---

33   Case T-13/99, *Pfizer Animal Health* v. *Council* [2002] ECR II-3305.
34   Case T-135/96, *UEAPME* v. *Council* [1998] ECR II-2335.
35   Case T-583/93, *Stichting Greenpeace Council* v. *Commission* [1995] ECR II-2205.
36   Case T-60/96 *Merck and Co. Inc., and others* v. *Commission* [1997] ECR II-849.
37   Craig (2007: 19).

TRANSPARENCY AND THE RIGHTS OF THE DEFENCE

The issue of access to documents raises a fundamental due process issue, and a concern with the extent to which the institutions of the Union are accessible to the 'citizens' of Europe. We will examine the law on transparency both before and after the significant Treaty on European Union 1992 (the Maastricht Treaty), before weighing up the impact of transparency reforms and the Fundamental Charter.

As Craig has pointed out, transparency has become a pressing issue since the 'near failure' to have the Treaty on European Union ratified in Denmark and France.[38] The institutions of the Union appear distant and secretive. Prior to Maastricht, however, there was a realisation that this problem needed to be addressed. In 1992, the European Council issued the 'Birmingham Declaration: A Community Close to its Citizens'.[39] As the title suggests, the document set out to explore 'ways of opening up the work of the Community's institutions' and tasked the Commission with improving 'public access' to information held by Community bodies.[40] This led to an incorporation of Declaration No. 17 in the 1992 Treaty on European Union:

> The Conference considers that transparency of the decision-making process strengthens the democratic nature of the institutions and the public's confidence in the administration.[41]

The Declaration went on to recommend that the Commission should submit a report to the Council on ways in which public access to information relating to Community institutions could be improved. In 1993, a joint Code of Conduct was issued by the Commission and the Council.[42] This led to the 1993 Decision 93/731/EC on public access to Council documents. Article 1 gave the public 'access to Council Documents' subject to certain restrictions.[43] These were provided by Article 4. Non-disclosure is justified on the grounds of 'the protection of public interest', or (4(2)) to protect the 'confidentiality of the proceedings of the Council'.[44]

These provisions were the subject of test cases in *Carvel and Guardian Newspapers* v. *Council*[45] and *Netherlands* v. *Council*. In the former, the applicant

---

38 Supra n. 19, at 351.
39 Available at http://aei.pitt.edu/1455/01/Birmingham_oct_1992.pdf.
40 Ibid., para 1.8.
41 Ibid.
42 Code of Conduct Concerning Access to Council and Commission Documents, OJ 1993 L340/41. De Burca (1996) suggested that this was a positive achievement in the development of consistent practices and concepts of transparency.
43 See also Commission Decision 94/90/ECSC.
44 Article 4(1) of Decision 93/731 states: 'Access to a Council document shall not be granted where its disclosure could undermine: the protection of the public interest (public security, international relations, monetary stability, court proceedings, inspections and investigations), the protection of the individual and of privacy, the protection of commercial and industrial secrecy, the protection of the Community's financial interests, the protection of confidentiality as requested by the natural or legal person who supplied any of the information contained in the document or as required by the legislation of the Member State which supplied any of that information.'
45 Case T105/95 *Carvel and Guardian Newspapers* v. *Council* [1995] ECR II- 2765.

sought to gain access to a number of documents that related to international policing. An application to the relevant Swedish authorities had led to the successful disclosure of a significant number of the requested documents. However, the Council was not as forthcoming, revealing only a small proportion of the relevant documents and justifying non-disclosure on the grounds of public interest.

The applicant's arguments covered a number of points. They alleged that the failure of disclosure by the Commission breached 4(1), 4(2) of Decision 93/731and one of the 'fundamental principles of Community law'[46] that required the fullest possible access to documents. They also alleged breach of Article 190 of the EC Treaty. The CFI found for the applicants on the basis of a breach of Article 190, and argued that it was not necessary to consider the other arguments that had been put forward.[47]

In *Netherlands* v. *Council*[48] the status of the 1993 Code of Conduct was questioned. The CFI held that the Code was a 'voluntary agreement' between the Commission and the Council and did not have legal effects. Furthermore, the Council could develop principles relating to disclosure as a matter of its own internal procedure. Before the ECJ, the government of the Netherlands argued that this was not the correct way for such an important matter to be resolved. Precisely because 'openness is a fundamental characteristic of a democratic system'[49] access to information should be regulated more formally and include the 'necessary safeguards'.[50] This argument was rejected. The ECJ held that as the Union as a whole had not adopted 'general rules' on public access, it was up to individual institutions to deal with the issue as a matter of internal procedure.

It would thus seem to be the case that whilst the Council is bound to give access to documents, there is no general position on a right to information in EU law. This would appear to be the ruling of the ECJ in *Hautala* where the CFI was held to be wrong to find that there was a general 'principle of the right to information'.[51]

The Union's ongoing endeavours to ensure its transparency led to the promulgation of Regulation No. 1049/2001.[52] This measure was designed to give 'the fullest possible effect to the right of public access to documents'.[53]

To what extent have the CFI and the ECJ been able to develop a meaningful jurisprudence of transparency and disclosure? In *IFAW*[54] an environmental group sought disclosure of documents held by the Commission relating to the decision to allow the extension of a factory into an area protected by the Habitats Directive. Relying on 4(5) of Regulation 1049/2001, the Commission stated that it would need to obtain the permission of the member state concerned before the documents could be released. When the relevant permission was not forthcoming, the environmental group brought an

---

46 Ibid., para 88.
47 Ibid., para 127.
48 Case C-58/94 *Netherlands* v. *Council* [1996] ECR-1-2169.
49 Ibid., para 31.
50 Ibid.
51 Case C 353/ 99 *Hautala* v. *Council* [2001] ECR I-9565, para 31.
52 Regulation (EC) No. 1049/2001 of the European Parliament and of the Council of 30 May 2001 regarding public access to European Parliament, Council and Commission documents (OJ 2001 L 145, p. 43).
53 Ibid., Recital 4.
54 *IFAW Internationaler Tierschutz-Fonds GmbH* v *Commission*, judgment of 30 November 2004.

unsuccessful action before the CFI. On appeal, the ECJ held that the overriding concern in the interpretation of the Regulation was to give effect to a number of inter-locking principles. The preamble to the Regulation stressed that it was necessary to 'improve the transparency of the Community decision-making process, since such openness inter alia guarantees that the administration enjoys greater legitimacy and is more effective and more accountable to the citizen in a democratic system'.[55] The effective 'veto' that a member state would have under 4(5) was inconsistent with the wording of the Article. The ECJ determined that IFAW could have access to the relevant documents.

What do we make of this case law? Lenaerts refers to transparency as one of the 'trust enhancing mechanisms' in EU law. He comments that it was one of the great 'non issues' in the jurisprudence of the Community before general distrust of government, and the activity of non-governmental organisations (NGOs) pushed it onto the agenda.[56] The Treaty on European Union can thus be seen as response to this need to open up the Union to scrutiny. The importance of this reorientation of the Union can be seen in the general assertion that decisions should be taken 'as openly as possible and as closely as possible to the citizen'.[57] This represents something of a restatement of Article 255(1) of the EC Treaty itself which specifies that '[a]ny citizen of the Union shall have a right of access to European Parliament, Council and Commission documents'.[58]

Do the reforms go far enough? In *Hautala*, Advocate General Leger called for the recognition of the fundamental right of access to information held by all Community institutions, a proposal which the ECJ did not comment upon. The cautious approach of the Court was reaffirmed in *Interporc v. Commission*.[59]

However, we also need to place the development of the law in the context of the Charter. It has been pointed out[60] that the CFI has begun to make reference to Articles 41 and 47 in its reasoning[61] as an aid to the interpretation of the law. For instance, in *max.mobil Telekommunikation Service GmbH v. Commission*,[62] Article 41(1) was explicitly linked to the Commission's obligation under Articles 85 and 86[63] of the EC Treaty to make 'diligent and impartial examination' of all matters brought to its attention by 'complainants'.[64] In *Technische Glaswerke Ilmenau GmbH v. Commission*,[65] Article 41(1) was linked to the duty on the Commission to 'to treat impartially all the parties concerned in a formal investigation procedure'.[66] Although these two cases cannot be seen as evidence of a clear pattern, they do suggest that the Charter is having some influence on the reasoning of the Court.

---

55   Supra n. 50, at para 54.
56   Lenaerts (2004).
57   Treaty of Amsterdam, Article 1(4).
58   This right is limited by 255(2) 'General principles' and 'public or private interest'. Of course 255(2) provides some sense of the limits of what is possible in the disclosure of documents.
59   Case C- 41/00 *Interporc* v. *Commission*.
60   John Morijn, Judicial Reference to the EU Fundamental Human Rights Charter, see http://www.fd.uc.pt/hrc/working_papers/john_morijn.pdf.
61   Jégo-Quéré and Cie SA.
62   Case T 54/99 *max.mobil Telekommunikation Service GmbH* v. *Commission*.
63   Now Articles 81 EC and 82 EC.
64   Supra n. 62, at para 49.
65   Case T198/01 *Technische Glaswerke Ilmenau GmbH* v. *Commission*.
66   Ibid., para 55.

Considered as a whole then, this area shows a cautious movement forward in the realisation of the centrality of a right to disclosure of documents. However, as Dyrberg points out, although transparency is a 'necessary' condition for legitimacy, it is 'in itself insufficient'.[67] Whether or not it is possible to bring together transparency with other values to produce a more democratically accountable Union is clearly part of ongoing political and legal debates. Although this does make any final assessment impossible, the courts of the Union do seem to be making progress in other areas that we could associate with due process. We will link the concerns raised in the transparency jurisprudence to a series of cases that raise broad issues about the rights of the defence and attempt to define the status of the principles of natural law, and the privilege against self-incrimination in EU law.

In *Transocean Marine Paint Association* v. *EC Commission*[68] the ECJ considered the right to be heard. This specifies that an individual affected by a decision of a public authority must be given the chance to state his/her case, particularly where 'obligations' with 'far reaching effects' are imposed. Applying this rule to the facts of the case, the ECJ annulled part of the Commission's decision on the ground that the applicants had received no advance notice of it. The ECJ went on to consider the status of the principle of *audi alteram partem* in European law. To what extent was this common law doctrine of natural justice part of a general European legal inheritance, and hence part of EU law? There was evidence that a similar principle existed in French law, albeit going under a far more 'sober' title: *les principes généraux du droit*. The Court was made aware of a degree of argument over whether *audi alteram partem* coordinated with the French concept of *les principes généraux du droit*. The consensus was that the relevant decisions of the Conseil d'Etat do show that French law is developing an *audi alteram partem* principle.[69]

The 'hesitancy' in the development of the French doctrine is not evidenced in Belgium and Luxemburg. The situation in these countries contrasts with that in Italy and the Netherlands, where there appears to be no 'general principle of law' that compel public authorities to take into account the interests of those affected by their decisions. What of other jurisdictions? In Germany, Article 103 of the Basic Law provides for the right to be heard in ordinary civil courts. Although there appears to be no requirement for it in administrative law, there were commentators who argued that the right to be heard, *das rechtliche Gehör*, applied as a general principle of law.[70] There was thus a compelling argument to assert that the principle of *audi alteram partem* was part of European law.

The existence of an *audi alteram partem* principle in EU law was further evidenced in *Fiskano* v. *EC Commission*.[71] The ECJ stated that 'the right to be heard'[72] is a

---

67 Dyrberg (2002: 96).
68 Case 17/74 *Transocean Marine Paint Association* v. *EC Commission* [1974] 2 CMLR 459.
69 The ECJ accepted that there are three possible ways in which the principles might apply: first, where a sanction has been applied; second, when a public authority has made a decision based on the behaviour of an individual; and third, in as wide a sense as that of the common law.
70 Usher (1998: 75).
71 Case C-135/92 *Fiskano* v. *EC Commission* [1995] 3 CMLR 795.
72 The principle applies in proceedings which the Commission had begun and which are likely to lead to penalties that will 'adversely affect' the person in question.

'fundamental principle of Community law'. If necessary, this principle can be implied into procedures when the statutes that define them are silent. The right to be heard requires the person who will be affected by the outcome of a case to be 'placed in a position in which he can effectively make known his view of the matters'.[73] This 'general principle' represents a 'minimum standard', and therefore cannot be qualified or restated.[74] In *Al Jubail* v. *Council of the European Communities*,[75] the right to be heard was extended from 'administrative proceedings to investigative procedures'. *Al-Jubail* concerned an investigation pursuant to anti-dumping regulations. The application of the principle was justified because the consequences of the investigation would have had 'adverse consequences' for those affected by them.

Orkem v. *EC Commission*[76] was also important in defining the scope of due process values in EU law. Referring to the laws of member states, the ECJ argued that it would be consistent with the laws of member states not to extend the privilege against self-incrimination in criminal proceedings to the 'economic sphere'. This was linked to an interpretation of Article 6 of the ECHR. A person subject to investigation by an EU authority could rely on the Article, but not to the extent that it provided 'the right not to give evidence against oneself'. However, although EU law did not recognise a right against self-incrimination, it was necessary for the Court to recognise the rights of the defence. The rights of the defence were understood in a broad sense, covering both 'contentious proceedings' and 'preliminary inquiries'.

What conclusions can we draw from this case law? Although these cases predate the Charter, they provide at least some evidence that the values expressed as Articles 41 and 47 in the Charter did already exist in the law of the Union. They show the court developing a jurisprudence that protects the rights of the defence. The specific language of due process may not be a feature of these cases, and it is only in *Orkem* that the Convention is specifically taken into account, but this does not hamper the adoption of the principles of natural justice into Community law. Nor is the limitation on the privilege against self-incrimination inconsistent with due process values. In later chapters, we will see that this is very much a qualified right. Overall, these authorities suggest that, irrespective of the language of human rights, EU law contains principles congruent with international standards of due process.

THE DUTY TO GIVE REASONS FOR DECISIONS

The centrality of this due process value to the law of the EU is stressed by Article 190 EEC, now Article 253 EC. This Article covers a broad range of EU legislation and administrative acts:

> Regulations, directives and decisions adopted jointly by the European Parliament and the Council, and such acts adopted by the Council or the Commission, shall state the

---
73 Supra n. 71. at 798.
74 Ibid., 804.
75 Case C-260/89 *Al-Jubail* v. *Council of the European Communities*.
76 Case 374/87 *Orkem SA* v. *EC Commission* [1989] ECR 3283, [1991] 4 CMLR 502.

reasons on which they are based and shall refer to any proposals or opinions which were required to be obtained pursuant to this Treaty.[77]

As we have argued in the introduction, the duty to give reasons is fundamental to the democratic nature of law. Elaborating this principle, the rationale for the rule given by both the ECJ and the CFI is normally seen to have distinct but interlocking elements. The duty allows interested parties to understand why a measure was made, so as to be able to 'better protect their interests'.[78] Administrators and bureaucrats are compelled by the duty to ensure that their actions are rationally justifiable. The duty also allows the courts to assume their reviewing role over other institutions.[79]

The pressing question is the precise scope of the duty under Article 253. The leading authority is *Sytravel*.[80] The ECJ argued[81] that the Article placed an obligation on the Commission to explain a measure in a manner 'appropriate to the act at issue'. This meant that it was necessary to state in a 'clear and unequivocal fashion' the 'reasoning' behind the adoption of a measure so that those who were affected by the measure could understand it, and the Court could 'exercise its power of review'.[82] The duty had to be interpreted in a context specific way, depending on the 'circumstances of each case' and in particular, taking into account:

> the content of the measure in question, the nature of the reasons given and the interest which the addressees of the measure, or other parties to whom it is of direct and individual concern, may have in obtaining explanations. It is not necessary for the reasoning to go into all the relevant facts and points of law, since the question whether the statement of reasons meets the requirements of Article 190 of the Treaty must be assessed with regard not only to its wording but also to its context and to all the legal rules governing the matter in question.[83]

Commentators suggest that the duty is satisfied if the Commission specifies the Article that gives the authority to act, the relevant facts and the 'purpose' in so acting.[84] This understanding is based on a reading of authorities such as the *Tariff Preferences case*[85] and *Germany* v. *Commission*.[86] In the latter, guidelines were laid down for

---

77 Article 253 EC.
78 Supra, n. 10, at para 116.
79 See Case C-350/88 *Delacre and Others* v. *Commission* [1990] ECR 1-395, paragraph 15 and Case T-85/94 *Branco* v. *Commission* [1995] ECR II-45, point 32).
80 Case C-367/95 P *Commission Chambre syndicale nationale des entreprises de transport de fonds et valeurs (Sytravel)* v. *Commission*.
81 Ibid., para 63.
82 Ibid.
83 See joined cases 296/82 and 318/82 *Netherlands and Leeuwarder Papierwarenfabriek* v. *Commission* [1985] ECR 809, Case C-350/88 *Delacre and Others* v. *Commission* [1990] ECR I-395, paragraphs 15 and 16, and Case C-56/93 *Belgium* v. *Commission* [1996] ECR I-723.
84 Supra n. 26, at 82.
85 *The Tariff Preferences case*. Failure to specify the relevant Articles led to the annulment of a Council measure.
86 Case C 156/98 *Federal Republic of Germany* v. *Commission*. In this case the Commission refused to allow the German government to import a certain quantity of wine into the EU. They alleged that importation would lead to 'disturbance' of the internal market. The lack of specificity in the Commission's justification of their decision led the ECJ to rule that they had not justified their decision.

the way in which matters of law and fact should be treated.[87] As far as refusal to disclose documents is concerned, the Commission must specify why one or more of the legitimate grounds for exclusion from disclosure would apply.[88] If a number of documents are concerned, it is necessary to be precise about the grounds that relate to each document.[89] These cases indicate that the duty to give reasons does act as a way of holding a decision maker to account.

However, limits to the ECJ's willingness to develop a broad application of the doctrine to give reasons have emerged. *Stichting Sigarettenindustrie* v. *Commission of the European Communities*[90] held that Article 253 did not obligate the Commission to 'discuss all the issues of fact and law' that a case raised. Craig suggests that although the CFI may have been more willing to elaborate an expansive set of principles on the duty to give reasons, the ECJ acted as a restraining influence. It would thus be too simplistic to suggest that because Article 253 'embeds' a value in the law of the Union, the courts will develop it so as to broaden the protection it offers.

THE INDEPENDENCE OF THE COMMISSION

This brings us to the thorny issue of Article 6 and its application to the Commission. The Commission has a dual role in the polity of the Union. It is both a law-making body, and a law-enforcement body. It would thus seem to be the case that, as far as Article 6 is concerned, it lacks the necessary neutrality to guarantee a fair trial for those whose rights or obligations are to be determined. The case law does not suggest that this issue has been approached in a principled manner by the Court. In *Heintz van Landewyck SARL* v. *Commission*[91] the applicants argued that the Commission was bound by the procedural guarantees of Article 6 when adjudicating a matter of competition law. They also asserted that it was not an 'independent and impartial tribunal' as it was also an executive agency. The ECJ rejected this argument, holding that precisely because the Commission was an executive body it was not a tribunal under the terms of Article 6.[92] This position was reasserted in *Musique Diffusion Française* v. *Commission*.[93] The ECJ held that although the Commission was bound by 'procedural safeguards' in Community law, this did not mean that it was a tribunal within the terms of Article 6.

It is hard to see from the judgments of the ECJ any reasoned defence of this position. If we remember the arguments made in the previous section about the status of the Convention, it might have been possible for the ECJ to argue that Article 6 was not

---

87 Ibid.
88 Supra n. 7, at 116.
89 Ibid.
90 Cases 240, 241, 242, 261, 262, 268 and 269/82 *Stichting Sigarettenindustrie and others* v. *Commission of the European Communities*.
91 C-209-15/ 78 *Heintz van Landewyck SARL and others* v. *Commission of the European Communities* [1980] ECR 3125.
92 Ibid., paras 80–1.
93 Cases 100 to 103/80 *SA Musique Diffusion Française and others* v. *Commission of the European Communities*.

binding upon them, and that Community law itself contained equivalent due process guarantees. As Craig points out, an alternative would have been to argue that the cases in question did not involve the determination of 'civil rights or obligations'.[94] This would have allowed the ECJ to remain consistent with the Strasbourg jurisprudence. The CFI took this approach in *Enso Espanola*.[95] Drawing on Article 6 case law, they accepted the position of the ECJ in *Heintz van Landewyck* and *Musique Diffusion Française*, arguing that although the Commission was not a tribunal, it was 'independent and impartial' because the CFI had a full power of review over its decisions.[96] The inherent problems and weaknesses of the Court's reasoning perhaps matters a little less after the institutional reforms of 1982, which created the role of Hearing Officer to ensure that due process rights were effectively recognised in the work of the Commission.[97] However, this line of cases does little to assist in the creation of a coherent jurisprudence of due process within the law of the Union.

CONCLUSION

To talk of due process and human rights in the context of EU law is to beg complex questions about the nature of the Union and the ongoing ways in which it attempts to legitimise itself as both a political and legal entity. Commentators have observed that the debates about the legitimacy of the EU are peculiar. This is because the EU is not a nation state, and the term has been primarily deployed in this context. Our analysis has thus encountered two primary obstacles: the question of the correct 'language' in a context where due process has not (until relatively recently) been discussed in the terms of the Convention, and the extent to which a certain set of legal values can be used to justify a supranational legal order.

We have seen that since the Charter a language of fundamental human rights has developed, and that we have used Articles 41 and 47 to assess the due process structures of EU law. Reviewing key areas, we have suggested that there is a marked sense that the EU is moving towards a coherent appreciation of the centrality of certain legal values that define the form and content of the law. However, it would be incorrect to argue that the courts of the Union had produced a jurisprudence that brought together various fair trial rights and rights to good administration. Furthermore, arguing that a commitment to human rights is now the way in which the Union legitimises itself would also misrepresent the complex way in which law and politics are intertwined. The absence of a constitution also makes it difficult to understand the precise structure of the Union.

As Everson[98] has argued, the failure to provide a Constitution for the Union has made for fundamental problems in determining the relationship between law and politics. Hopes that the courts could generate principles that legitimise the Union have

---

94 Supra, n. 26 at 70.
95 Case T-348/94, *Enso Espanola v. Commission* [1988] ECR II-1875.
96 Supra, n. 26 at 70.
97 Ibid.
98 Michelle Everson [with Julia Eisner] (2007).

been frustrated. EU law is characterised by a certain degree of uncertainty and tension. Rather than clarity, the law of the EU can be compared to a dissolving bar of soap left in the bath. How can the law regain its form? One way of recovering clarity would be to link together legal values and a broader political and democratic culture. Whether this can be achieved is one of the key issues that concern the future of the Union. To misquote an old adage, the risk is that the soap is thrown out with the bath water.

APPENDIX

The institutions of the European Union

This appendix is a brief guide to the institutions of the Union: the European Commission; the Council of Ministers, the European Parliament, the Court of First Instance and the European Court. It includes a description of the key terms of EU law. The appendix concludes with a brief summary of the major treaties that underlie the structure of the Union. These texts indicate that the Union is characterised by constant processes of reform, driven by a number of factors such as the enlargement of the Union and the need to streamline decision making, enhance accountability and regulate economic affairs.[99]

It is worth noting that the European Economic Community has experienced a number of 'name changes'. The Treaty on European Union in 1993 changed the name of the European Community to the European Union. This can be somewhat confusing as it is often unclear as to whether one should be referring to the Community or the Union. Within the terms of this Appendix (and the preceding chapter) the term 'Union' will be used when referring to the evolution of those Community institutions that have retained their fundamental identity since their establishment instigation in 1957.

The institutions of the Union achieve two main functions. They create a system of government for the Union as a supranational entity, and allow the interests of member states to be taken into account in the creation of policy and the governance of the Union. Perhaps the most dramatic development is that of the European Parliament. This can be understood as an element of the ongoing endeavour to make the Union accountable and democratically legitimate.

The Union can be traced back to the Treaty establishing the European Coal and Steel Community (ECSC) in 1952. Negotiated between France, Germany, Italy, Belgium, Luxemburg and the Netherlands it gave form to the spirit of post-war economic reconstruction and the coordination of European economies. In 1957 these same six nations agreed the treaty establishing the European Atomic Energy Community (EURATOM). The limited forms of economic cooperation established by the ECSC and EURATOM treaties were expanded by the EEC Treaty of 1957. As will be clear from the discussion below, the EEC Treaty put in place a much more ambitious framework for the creation of a common market and associated social policies.

---

99   Present member states of the EU are: Austria, Belgium, Bulgaria, Cyprus, Czech Republic, Denmark, Estonia, Finland, France, Germany, Greece, Hungary, Ireland, Italy, Latvia, Lithuania, Luxemburg, Malta, Netherlands, Poland, Portugal, Romania, Slovakia, Slovenia, Spain, Sweden and the United Kingdom.

The Union, or the European Economic Community (as it was then known) was established by the Treaty of Rome 1957 (entered into force 1958). This Treaty has been since amended by the Treaty of Amsterdam 1997 (entered into force 1999), and by the Treaty of Nice 2001 (entered into force 2003). We will refer to the consolidated rather than the original Treaty in the discussion below.

In order to understand the institutions of the Union we need to examine the consolidated Treaty of Rome. Article 2 of the Treaty of Rome states:

> The Union shall set itself the following objectives:– to promote economic and social progress and a high level of employment and to achieve balanced and sustainable development, in particular through the creation of an area without internal frontiers, through the strengthening of economic and social cohesion and through the establishment of economic and monetary union, ultimately including a single currency in accordance with the provisions of this Treaty.

Article 6 specifies that the 'Union is founded on the principles of liberty, democracy, respect for human rights and fundamental freedoms, and the rule of law, principles which are common to the Member States'. Paragraph 6(2) specifies that the Union is founded on 'respect [for] fundamental rights, as guaranteed by the European Convention [and] the constitutional traditions common to the Member States'.

Article 3 goes on to specify that the 'Union shall be served by a single institutional framework which shall ensure the consistency and the continuity of the activities'. The central institutions are: the European Commission; the Council of the European Union; the European Parliament; the Court of Justice; and the Court of First Instance.

The European Commission 'upholds the interest of the EU as a whole'[100] and is independent of member states. It is the EU's executive body. It proposes legislation which is then presented to Parliament and the Council. Legislation is informed by the principle of 'subsidiarity'. Action will only be taken at the EU level if a matter cannot be resolved at a 'national, regional or local' level. The Commission is also the EU's executive body responsible for the management and implementation of EU policies. It also enforces EU law. As 'guardian of the treaties' the Commission has the power to ensure that member states are correctly implementing EU law. If necessary the Commission can take a member state to the European Court of Justice. Members of the Commission are nominated by the Union's member states and approved by the European Parliament (EP).

The Council of the European Union represents 'the interests of the member states'.[101] This is reflected in the composition of the body. Its meetings are attended by ministers from the member states, who represent the interests of their states in the matter under discussion. The Council also has a role to play in legislation, but its remit extends to coordinating the economic policies of member states. Through the 'open method of coordination' the Council encourages the coordination of national policies in health, education and welfare. The Council's remit extends over international coordination of legal systems and the policing of the Union.

---

100   http://europa.eu/institutions/inst/comm/index_en.htm#top.
101   http://europa.eu/institutions/inst/council/index_en.htm.

The European Parliament represents the interests of the citizens of Europe. It is directly elected every five years. Parliament plays a central role in the creation of legislation, thus 'guarantee[ing] the legitimacy of European law'.[102] It also has powers of supervision over EU institutions, and the Commission is accountable to Parliament. The European Parliament, alongside the Council, also has 'authority' over the Union's budget and can influence decisions on how money is to be spent.

The European Court of Justice was set up by the ECSC Treaty in 1952. It has the power to interpret EU legislation and ensure its uniform application throughout the Union. The latter function is carried out through the 'preliminary ruling procedure' which enables (and in some instances requires) national courts to apply to the Court for a 'preliminary ruling' on the interpretation of EU law. Its powers extend to ensuring that both member states and institutions act within the law, and it can also adjudicate in disputes between member states. Its composition reflects the fact that it is a Court of a union whose members have different legal traditions:

> The Court is composed of one judge per member state, so that all 27 of the EU's national legal systems are represented. For the sake of efficiency, however, the Court rarely sits as the full court. It usually sits as a 'Grand Chamber' of just 13 judges or in chambers of five or three judges. The Court is assisted by eight 'Advocates General'. Their role is to present reasoned opinions on the cases brought before the Court. They must do so publicly and impartially.[103]

The expansion of the Union, and the increase in the work of the Court, led to the creation in 1989 of the Court of First Instance (CFI) which has a jurisdiction over certain actions brought by private individuals, associations, companies and competition law. It is possible to appeal on a point of law from the CFI to the European Court of Justice.

EU law

> The main goal of the EU is the progressive integration of Member States' economic and political systems and the establishment of a single market based on the free movement of goods, people, money and services. To this end, its Member States cede part of their sovereignty under treaties which empower the EU institutions to adopt laws.[104]

EU law can be divided into two types: primary legislation – the treaties themselves – and secondary legislation. Secondary legislation is defined by Article 249 of the Treaty of Rome:

> In order to carry out their task and in accordance with the provisions of this Treaty, the European Parliament acting jointly with the Council, and the Commission shall

---

102   http://europa.eu/institutions/inst/parliament/index_en.htm.
103   http://europa.eu/institutions/inst/justice/index_en.htm.
104   http://ec.europa.eu/community_law/introduction/treaty_en.htm.

make regulations and issue directives, take decisions, make recommendations or deliver opinions. A regulation shall have general application. It shall be binding in its entirety and directly applicable in all Member States. A directive shall be binding, as to the result to be achieved, upon each Member State to which it is addressed, but shall leave to the national authorities the choice of form and methods. A decision shall be binding in its entirety upon those to whom it is addressed. Recommendations and opinions shall have no binding force.

The early years of the Union generated a great deal of case law over the precise meaning of this Article (which was Article 189). In crudest summary, Regulations are binding on member states. They do not require member states to enact legislation. Provided that they are sufficiently clear and unambiguous, they give rise to rights which can be used in national courts. Directives require member states to give effect to their terms in domestic law. The Court has approached Directives in a creative manner. As explained by the British Court in *Van Duyn* v. *the Home Office*:[105]

> where the Community authorities have, by directive, imposed on member states the obligation to pursue a particular course of conduct, the useful effect of such an act would be weakened if individuals were prevented from relying on it before their national courts and if the latter were prevented from taking it into consideration as an element of community law.[106]

However, as stressed in *Van Duyn*, it is necessary to determine whether 'the nature, general scheme and wording of the provision in question are capable of having direct effect'. The Directive would have to be 'unconditional and sufficiently precise'.

Unlike Regulations and Directives, Decisions are 'addressed to specific parties': a member state, company or individual. Decisions are EU laws relating to specific cases. They emanate from the Council, the Council acting in partnership with the European Parliament or the Commission. They create binding obligations and can be used to prohibit, enable or to 'confer rights'.[107]

The fundamental treaties

The Treaty of Rome has already been described.

The Single European Act entered into force in 1987. It made for institutional changes to encourage European integration. It reformed the decision making procedures of the Union, and enhanced the powers of the European Parliament to address the perceived 'democratic deficit' at the heart of Europe. The Act also laid down the 'foundations' for the CFI.[108] At a policy level, it initiated the creation of a single market.

---

[105] *Van Duyn* v. *the Home Office* [1975] Ch 358.
[106] Ibid.
[107] http://ec.europa.eu/community_law/introduction/what_decision_en.htm.
[108] http://europa.eu/scadplus/treaties/singleact_en.htm.

This is 'an area without internal frontiers in which the free movement of goods, persons, services and capital is ensured in accordance with the provisions of this Treaty'.[109]

The Treaty on European Union (Treaty on Maastricht) entered into force in 1993. The Treaty created the European Union. This consists of the 'the European Communities, common foreign and security policy and police and judicial cooperation in criminal matters'.[110] The Union rests on three 'pillars'. As detailed above, the so-called 'first pillar' of the Union is provided by the European Coal and Steel Community and EURATOM. This is defined as those areas where member states have chosen to 'share their sovereignty'[111] through the Union institutions. These institutions work together to create Community law. The Community method operates in the following manner: a proposal is made by the European Commission which is adopted by the Council and Parliament, while compliance is monitored by the European Court of Justice.[112] The 'second pillar' is a common foreign and security policy. In this area Maastricht amended the Single European Act to enable member states to take joint foreign policy initiatives. The 'third pillar' rests on cooperation in 'the field of justice and home affairs'.[113] Maastricht further enhanced the powers of Parliament and established Union policies in new areas including consumer protection and industry. The single market was also developed through coordination of the economic policies of member states, the imposition of forms of 'financial and budgetary discipline' and the creation of a single currency. A Social Protocol was also agreed which covered employment protection and various welfare provisions. The Treaty on European Union created rights for European citizens and established subsidiarity as a general principle of the Union. The UK is not a member of the single currency and has not signed the Social Protocol.

The Treaty of Amsterdam entered into force in 1999. As new member states joined the Union, further institutional and policy reforms became necessary. The powers of Parliament were again revised, as were methods of voting in the Council. The rights of the Commission to propose legislation were enhanced, and a Protocol agreed that would prevent smaller member states having undue influence in the deliberations of the Commission. The drive for 'greater democratic legitimacy'[114] also led to reforms of the European Court of Justice:

> Article 6 requires the Union to respect fundamental rights, as guaranteed by the European Convention on Human Rights. The amendment is important since it formally gives the Court the power to rule on how the Convention is being applied by the Community institutions. This should spur the Court to greater vigilance.[115]

---

109 Ibid.
110 http://europa.eu/scadplus/treaties/maastricht_en.htm.
111 Ibid.
112 Ibid.
113 Ibid.
114 http://europa.eu/scadplus/leg/en/s50000.htm.
115 Ibid.

The Treaty of Amsterdam also further clarifies the subsidiarity principle and contains some important provisions relating to the enlargement of the Union:

> The increase in the number of Member States will increase diversity within the European Union in terms of each Member State's objectives, sensibilities and priorities. While this diversity is what constitutes the wealth of the European Union, it may also be an obstacle, if the pace of European integration is determined by the slowest.[116]

A major innovation of the Treaty of Amsterdam was the 'concept of variable-speed integration into the EU Treaty.' Articles were added into the EU Treaty (Articles 43 to 45) enabling those states who desired closer cooperation to make use of certain 'institutions, procedures and mechanisms'.[117] Those states unwilling to make use of these procedures are not prevented from so doing at a later stage.

The Treaty of Nice, which entered into force in 2003, continued institutional reforms in the wake of the Union's enlargement. Votes were redistributed in the Council and weighted in favour of the larger nations. The composition of the Commission was modified and changes were made to the CFI and the European Court of Justice. A Declaration on the future of the Union was annexed to the Treaty, and called for a broad debate on the future of the Union. After the Nice Treaty, a draft constitution was prepared for the EU. However, this failed to become law after difficulties in obtaining ratification by all the member states.

The Treaty of Lisbon was signed in December 2007. It contains provisions regarding increased democracy and transparency. The Parliament will be placed on an 'equal legislative footing' with the Council. Voting methods are also to be streamlined in order to improve efficiency and decision making. The Treaty creates the office of President of the European Council and improves policy making in the areas of crime, energy policy and public health. Climate change is also firmly placed on the agenda. The Treaty also stresses the 'democratic values' that underlie the Union.

---

116   Ibid.
117   Ibid.

8

CONSTITUTING HUMAN RIGHTS

AN INTRODUCTION TO THE EUROPEAN CONVENTION

The European Convention (ECHR) 'constitutes' an international human rights regime. What does this mean? 'Constituting' has two different senses, both of which are important to our argument. The first sense relates to the Convention as a document that creates both a catalogue of rights and an institution, the European Court of Human Rights (ECtHR). The Convention puts in place rights that have 'an obligatory judicial character'[1] and the various mechanisms that allow remedies to be sought for their breach. Thus, the Convention is not merely a declaratory statement of those rights that the international community considers desirable. Those states that have ratified the Convention can be held to account in an international court should a breach of their obligations be upheld. Our focus in this chapter will be on the mechanisms that make this radical international legal system possible.

The second sense of 'constitutes' relates to Convention rights as a statement of legal and political values. This begs questions about the principles of human rights, and the order that they put in place. As we explained in the Introduction, this book is not concerned with offering a detailed overview of Convention rights. Its aim is to grasp the fundamental 'regime' that human rights put in place. In this chapter, we will argue that due process and integrity rights only make sense as part of a catalogue of rights that mandate minimal standards for a legitimate political order.

A BRIEF HISTORY OF THE CONVENTION

The origins of the Convention can be linked to the 'growing belief that the protection of human rights against oppressive governments should be embodied in a new world order'[2] that characterised the international mood in the period after the end of the Second World War (1939–1945). Although international institutions such as the League of Nations had been in existence prior to 1939,[3] the cessation of hostilities gave an added impetus to the creation of an institutional structure that would allow a 'just world

---

1 Simpson (2001: 598).
2 Ibid., 219.
3 In 1899 the International Peace Conference adopted the Convention for the Pacific [i.e. 'peaceful'] Settlement of International Disputes and established the Permanent Court of Arbitration, which began work in 1902. After the First World War, in 1919, the Treaty of Versailles created the League of Nations, 'to promote international cooperation and to achieve peace and security'.

order in which governmental misconduct would be brought under the control of the international community'.[4]

The framework for such an organisation was achieved in 1945 when a charter for the creation of the United Nations was drawn up and signed. The first sessions of the UN were dedicated to the promulgation of a Universal Declaration of Human Rights. However, human rights were understood in a very restricted way. This theme is worth developing because it is of relevance to the European Convention. The politicians responsible for creating the UN believed that the post-war order depended on the goodwill and cooperation of sovereign states. Meaningful human rights protection would require an international court with jurisdiction over the domestic affairs of a state. It would be difficult for the UN to encourage states to sign up to international instruments that would limit their sovereign powers. Governments were committed to the doctrines of international law that gave them exclusive control over their internal affairs. Indeed, such was the reluctance to accord a pronounced role to human rights that John P. Humphrey, the first director of the Division of Human Rights at the UN, wrote that human rights would have received a minor place in the Charter, had their importance not been stressed by some of the delegates, and certain private organisations who were involved in the drafting process.

Negotiations over the status of human rights also fell victim to the growing hostilities between the Americans, the European states, the Soviet Union and their respective allies. Indeed, the resulting stalemate meant that the system of UN rights protection did not achieve final form until 1976. One of the consequences of the failure to agree general international human rights protection was a new interest in the possibility of regional systems. The break-out of the Cold War in Europe, the partition of Germany and the building of the Berlin Wall brought protection for human rights in Western Europe to the top of the political agenda. France, Germany and other European states were moving towards closer economic ties with the conclusion of treaties on coal and steel production (1952) and economic energy (1957). This encouraged those lobbying for the agreement of a document that stressed the commitment of nations to democracy and the rule of law.

The politics of this period are complicated, and it should not be imagined that there was universal support either for economic community or for human rights. Although certain German and French politicians were keen to achieve European integration, the British position was peculiar. While Britain's foreign minister, Ernest Bevan, supported regional human rights, he was reluctant to countenance federalism or closer forms of economic integration. The Empire was also an important consideration. Although there was an acknowledgement that the Empire would have to be dismantled and independence granted to colonised territories, the consensus shared by both Labour and Conservative governments was that this process would be gradual. There was a fear in both the Foreign Office and the Colonial Office that human rights were not in Britain's interests, as they might act as a spur to independence movements, and would also bring international scrutiny to bear on what was perceived as a national matter.

---

4 Supra, n. 1, at 12.

In May 1948 delegates from numerous European countries attended the Hague Conference. They resolved (among other matters) to propose the drafting of a Convention on Human Rights. The honorary president, Winston Churchill (then in opposition), was one of the most enthusiastic proponents of a 'statement of Human Rights'.[5] The 'intensely insular legal profession'[6] and certain elements of the British government may not have shared his commitment, but the agenda was seized by supporters of a Rights Convention. In 1949 the Council of Europe was created, and tasked with the creation of the Convention. This body was 'carefully designed to make no significant inroads upon state sovereignty'.[7] Indeed, its composition and status reflects the lack of consensus over the precise form of rights protection in Europe. In some ways the body was deliberately sidelined – it had 'no legal, legislative or executive status'; however, 'its most important asset was the mere fact of its existence'.[8] Although the Council was initially reluctant about the project, it became one of the major champions of the Convention, which began to be seen as an important support for democratic stability in Europe.

The ECHR was signed in Rome in 1950. This text is referred to as the 'Old Convention' as certain significant changes were later made to the structure of the Convention's institutions. These will be considered below. Article 19 of the Old Convention created both the European Commission of Human Rights and the Court. The Commission's primary task was to 'identify those cases which satisf[ied] the admissibility criteria set out in Articles 25–27 of the Convention'.[9] The Commission was more than a filtering body; it was also charged with 'establishing the facts' of the cases under consideration, encouraging conciliation and preparing a legal opinion. If the case was remitted to the Court, the Commission's opinion became a central document in subsequent proceedings. Under Article 53, states undertook to abide by the decisions of the Court in which they were parties. However, states did not have to recognise the jurisdiction of the Court under old Article 46; nor did states have to recognise the right of individual petition under old Article 250.

The original Convention also created a role for the Committee of Ministers.[10] Under the old Convention, the Committee of Ministers examined applications which had been considered by the Commission but not sent on to the Court. The Committee then determined whether or not there had been a breach of the Convention. Although this role of the Committee was brought to an end in 1998, the body still plays an important role in the operation of the Convention system.

This institutional structure operated well in the early years of the Convention's operation. The Convention entered into force in 1953[11] and the caseload for the

---

5   Ibid., 605.
6   Ibid.
7   Ibid., 645.
8   Judt (2005: 155).
9   Harris *et al.* (2005: 573).
10 The Committee of Ministers is the Council of Europe's executive body. It is composed of the foreign ministers of the states that belong to the Council.
11 The first application that was declared admissible by the Commission was brought by Greece against the UK. The Greek government made allegations that British armed forces who were operating in Cyprus had committed acts of brutality against civilians. See 1 Yearbook of the ECHR 1280130 (1955-1956-1957).

remainder of the 1950s was light.[12] The 1960s saw 54 applications to Convention institutions. The Court dealt with 10 cases and the remainder were resolved by the Commission. By the end of the decade, 11 states had recognised the right to individual petition and accepted the jurisdiction of the Court. During the next decade, as more nations signed the Convention and recognised the right of individual petition, the workload of both the Commission and the Court increased.[13] By the end of the 1980s, all the nations who were members of the Council of Europe with the exception of Finland had signed the Convention. The Court had delivered six times as many judgments as it had in the 1970s.[14] The 1990s witnessed the real expansion of the Convention system. The number of signatories doubled as former Eastern Bloc nations sought to reform their legal and political institutions.[15] In 2000 the Convention was ratified by six new nations.[16] The intensity of the Court's work is indicated by the fact that 80 per cent of all its judgments were issued in the first six years of the new decade.[17]

By the end of the 1990s, it was clear that the Court and the Commission were finding it hard to cope with the ever-increasing number of cases remitted to them. Reform of the Convention institutions was overdue. Protocol 11 (ratified in 1998) sought to streamline the system by abolishing the Commission, enhancing the powers of the Court and the means for the enforcement of judgments. The Protocol also made it obligatory for states to recognise both the right of individual petition and the jurisdiction of the ECtHR. Protocol 14 (opened for signature in 2004) made for further reforms. It allowed for single judges to hear cases and refined the rules on admissibility. Although these measures have made important changes to the Convention system, the scale of reforms was indicated in a report submitted to the Committee of Ministers in 2006.[18] It suggested that unless radical measures were taken there would be no 'long lasting solution to ... [the] problems of congestion'.[19] Reform of the Convention institutions will be on the agenda for some time to come.

So far we have been concerned with the institutional structure of the Convention. We will return to elaborate these arguments in a later section of this chapter, as it is important that we understand the relationship of Convention law to English law.

---

12   Janis *et al.* (2007: 21) report that five applications were deemed admissible and the Commission dealt with them all.
13   At the end of the 1970s, there were 20 nations who recognised the Convention, 14 had accepted the right to individual petition and 17 accepted the jurisdiction of the court. 168 applications were declared admissible, and the Court delivered 26 judgments. See Janis *et al.*, supra n. at 22.
14   Ibid. 22, nations were now signatories to the Convention, and had accepted both the right to individual petition and the jurisdiction of the Court. The Court issued 169 judgments during the course of the 1980s.
15   Czechoslovakia (which became the Czech Republic and Slovakia), Hungary and Bulgaria (1992), Poland (1993), Romania and Slovenia (1994), Lithuania (1995), Estonia, Lithuania and Andorra (1996), Macedonia, Ukraine, Latvia, Moldova and Croatia (1997), Russia (1998), Georgia (1999). During the decade nearly 5000 cases were admitted and the Court made 809 judgments.
16   Azerbaijan, Armenia, Bosnia, Herzegovina (2002), Serbia (2004), Monaco (2005), Montenegro (2007). Total signatories to the Convention now number 47. In the first six years of the 2000s over 5000 cases were deemed admissible, and the court made nearly 5000 judgments.
17   Ibid.
18   Ibid., 57 (Cm 2006)88.
19   Ibid.

THE CONVENTION IN ENGLISH LAW

The European Convention on Human Rights is an international treaty. As Hoffman and Rowe argue:

> The Convention was an extremely radical innovation. Never before had there been a system of international law which held states accountable to some superior court in respect of actions against its own citizens: previous international courts and tribunals were constituted solely to settle disputes between states, or, in the case of the Nuremberg Tribunal, to try individuals for their own criminal responsibility.[20]

We can stress a number of points. The ECHR was innovative in that it made sovereign states responsible to an international court. This represents a departure from the previous manner in which international law operated. It was primarily a means for states to resolve disputes with each other. Under the Convention, sovereign states must uphold the human rights of their citizens. The radical nature of the Convention was stressed with the recognition of the right to individual petition.

What, then, is the relationship of the Convention to English common law? Prior to the Human Rights Act, the status of the Convention in English law had to be understood through general principles that determined the relationship of international law to domestic law. Lord Hoffmann explained these principles in *Trendtex Trading* v. *Bank of Nigeria*:[21]

> [I]t is firmly established that international treaties do not form part of English law and that English courts have no jurisdiction to interpret or apply them: J H Rayner (Mincing Lane) Ltd v Department of Trade and Industry [1990] 1 AC 418 (the *International Tin Council* case). Parliament may pass a law which mirrors the terms of the treaty and in that sense incorporates the treaty into English law. But even then, the metaphor of incorporation may be misleading. It is not the treaty but the statute which forms part of English law. And English courts will not (unless the statute expressly so provides) be bound to give effect to interpretations of the treaty by an international court, even though the United Kingdom is bound by international law to do so. Of course there is a strong presumption in favour of interpreting English law (whether common law or statute) in a way which does not place the United Kingdom in breach of an international obligation.

International law only enters into English law if Parliament so legislates. The relevant statute then states the applicable law. This is not incorporation, because international law is only made part of English law if the relevant Act of Parliament so determines. International law binds the UK at an international level. Parliament may have legislated to honour obligations made in international law.

---

20   Hoffman and Rowe (2003).
21   *Trendtex Trading* v. *Bank of Nigeria* [1977] QB 532.

Alternatively, Parliament may have shown in an Act of Parliament that there are derogations or reservations from international obligations. There is, however, an interpretative presumption that the common law is interpreted so as to be coherent with international law. However, if Parliament, or indeed the common law, prevents an interpretation that makes English law coherent with international law, then the courts have to follow English law.

This approach is supported by Lord Goff in *Attorney General* v. *Guardian Newspapers Ltd* No. 2:[22]

> I conceive it to be my duty, when I am free to do so, to interpret the law in accordance with the obligations of the Crown under [the Convention]. But for present purposes the important words are 'when I am free to do so'. The sovereign legislator in the United Kingdom is Parliament. If Parliament has plainly laid down the law, it is the duty of the courts to apply it, whether that would involve the Crown in breach of an international treaty or not.[23]

The key phrase in Lord Goff's argument is 'when I am free to do so'. Lord Goff's argument returns to that of Lord Hoffmann. If a judge is free to interpret English law as coherent with international law he or she will do so.

These principles lie behind the interpretation of the Convention. We cannot deal with the complex issues raised by the constitutional status of the Convention prior to the HRA in this chapter. The general position was that the Convention could be used as an aid to interpreting the common law. It was also possible to take the UK to the ECtHR for breach of its international obligations. A victim of a breach of human rights would have to show that no domestic remedy was available. Some of the difficulties that resulted from this position can be understood if we look at an indicative case, *Malone* v. *Metropolitan Police Commissioner* No. 2.[24]

Malone had been charged with a criminal offence. During his trial the prosecution revealed that his telephone had been monitored on the basis of a warrant issued by the Home Secretary. Malone sought a declaration that this practice was illegal. However, at the time the case was heard, there was no common law rule or statute that supported Malone's position. The court held that since the ECHR had 'the status of a treaty' and 'was not justiciable in England', Malone could not make use of either Article 8 or 13.

Malone's counsel argued that although the Convention was not part of English law, it could 'have some effect'. His position relied on Scarman LJ's argument in *Pan-American World Airways Inc.* v. *Department of Trade*.[25] Lord Justice Scarman asserted that when there were two ways of interpreting the law open to the court, and one interpretation was inconsistent with 'international obligations', the court could take into account a convention or treaty that was not part of English law in order

---

22 *Attorney General* v. *Guardian Newspapers Ltd* No. 2 [1990] 1 AC 109.
23 Ibid., 283.
24 *Malone* v. *Metropolitan Police Commissioner* No. 2 (1979) 69 Cr. App. R. 168.
25 *Pan-American World Airways Inc.* v. *Department of Trade* [1976] 1 Lloyd's Rep. 257, 261.

to understand the law correctly. Could the Convention be used in the same way? Sir Robert Megarry dealt with this point succinctly:

> The Convention is plainly not of itself law in this country, however much it may fall to be considered as indicating what the law of this country should be, or should be construed as being.[26]

Although Sir Robert Megarry was critical of the lack of protection for privacy in English law, he argued that it would not be correct for the courts to develop a right of privacy. It fell to Parliament to legislate if it so chose. Having shown that there were no domestic remedies available, Malone used the Convention to take the UK to the ECtHR. The Court held that there had been a breach of Article 8:

> [T]here must be a measure of legal protection in domestic law against arbitrary interferences by public authorities with the rights safeguarded by paragraph 1. Especially where a power of the executive is exercised in secret, the risks of arbitrariness are evident ... the law must be sufficiently clear in its terms to give citizens an adequate indication as to the circumstances in which and the conditions on which public authorities are empowered to resort to this secret and potentially dangerous interference with the right to respect for private life and correspondence.[27]

The ECtHR argues that at the very least English law lacks clarity and at worst fails to control the power of the executive. If the courts refused to develop a right of privacy, and Parliament was reluctant to legislate, it would appear that the common law was failing to protect human rights at the most basic level. However, defeat in Strasbourg did lead to legislation. In 1985, the Interception of Communications Act was passed. What do we make of this? Even though the UK was ultimately willing to honour its human rights obligations, the Malone litigation suggests that passively awaiting a ruling of the ECtHR was not the most efficient way of ensuring the compliance of English law with international standards. And the Malone case was not exceptional.[28]

As we suggested in the Introduction, this situation could have continued indefinitely. The decision to incorporate the Convention into English law was a political one. Had the Conservative Party remained in office in 1994, then the Human Rights Act would probably never have been passed. The present question of the relationship of the Convention to English law is complex, and is dealt with in Chapter 10. Suffice to say at this stage, that in the absence of a written constitution, the HRA remains a normal statute. Just as the HRA was created, so might it be taken away.

---

26 *Malone* v. *UK* [1985] 7 EHRR 14, 187.
27 Ibid.
28 Between 1966 and the end of 1995, there were 60 cases concerning the UK before the ECtHR. Simpson, supra n. 1 at 7.

THE CONVENTION RIGHTS

This section of the chapter reviews the rights of the Convention. It is not meant to be an exhaustive summary of the Articles, the Protocols and the case law. It is an introduction to our more focused engagement with integrity rights in the next chapter. Integrity rights, as we will show, are primarily concerned with the definition and protection of due process. However, the protection of due process only makes sense within a regime of human rights. A regime of human rights is a consistent statement of the way in which rights act as limits upon the sovereign power of the state. We thus want to deal with two questions. First, what limitations do Convention rights place on a state's executive power? Second, how can the Convention be read as a coherent statement of rights that embeds due process in a complex of interlocking legal and political principles?

In order to answer these questions we will make use of the following categorisations of Convention rights.[29] The categories that we will use are not 'hard edged'. This is not problematic, as we are primarily concerned with making broad points about how the Convention can be conceptualised. Another preliminary point will also avoid confusion. Please note that categorisations do not follow the order of the Convention itself. Our categories 'pull together' different rights to create groups that reflect the 'thematic' structure of the Convention. Our analysis will proceed as follows. After a brief overview of our categorisation of rights, we will go into some detail on each of the groupings that we have defined.

The first group of rights includes Articles 2 and 3. Article 2 protects the right to life, and Article 3 is a prohibition on torture and inhuman or degrading treatment. These rights are aimed at the protection of a citizen's bodily integrity. The rights to bodily integrity thus prohibit certain forms of punishment, torture and also place limitations on the taking of life. However, it is also worth noting that Article 2 creates certain lawful exceptions. We will examine these presently. Article 5, the right to liberty and security, can be placed in this first category, but it also overlaps with the second grouping. This grouping covers due process and integrity rights. This category includes Articles 6, 7, 13, 17 and 18. Turning from due process to rights that protect substantive political

---

[29] To explain the character of rights, we can make use of the traditional typology of 'generations'. First-generation rights can be seen as the 'classical' civil liberties (for example, freedom of speech) which developed in the eighteenth and nineteenth centuries, aimed at providing protection for the individual against the state. Their paradigmatic expression is perhaps the Declaration of the Rights of Man and the Citizen after the French Revolution in 1789. Rights and civil liberties, since this period, have become central to Western democratic political orders. Second-generation rights can be found in the Covenant on Economic, Social and Cultural Rights attached to the Universal Declaration of Human Rights. They are seen as desirable principles rather than legal duties. Third-generation rights can be described as 'solidarity rights', or rights that can only be enjoyed collectively. We are agnostic about the conventional distinction between first-, second- and third-generation rights. Whilst these are perhaps useful as a historical approach, they do not allow us to comprehend the overall dynamic of the Convention. The categories we have chosen reflect the themes of this book. Furthermore, the 'generational' analysis of rights prevents us appreciating the way in which rights have been interpreted. Thus, it may be that the rights of the Convention are primarily those of the first generation. However, as we showed in the chapter on the politics of the judiciary, the litigation concerning Article 9 in the Begum case suggests that Convention rights are being used as solidarity rights in attempts to articulate forms of plural being.

values takes us to the third group. This category describes the 'classical civil liberties' and includes Article 10, the freedom of expression, Article 11, the freedom to assemble and to associate and Article 16.

The fourth group is perhaps the most problematic. In comparison with other international catalogues of rights, such as the International Covenant on Economic, Social and Cultural Rights (ICESCR),[30] the Convention offers rather limited protection of this form of social right. Thus, Article 4, the prohibition on slavery and forced labour can be read as significant not so much for what it does say, as to what it excludes.

The fifth and sixth groups of rights define, respectively, minimal forms of civil society and basic forms of social plurality. In the fifth category we place Article 8, the right to respect for private and family life and Article 12, the right to marry. In the sixth category are Articles 9 and 14. Article 9 guarantees freedom of thought, conscience and religion and Article 14 provides the prohibition on discrimination.

In dividing rights into these categories we intend to show that the Convention provides a coherent statement of basic political and legal principles that are coherent with democracy and the rule of law.[31] Each category guarantees either principles of due process or broader statements of democratic government. The fifth and sixth groups of rights also protect forms of multicultural or plural social being.

However, an important element of the Convention is to define those instances when a state can lawfully limit a human right. These exercises of sovereign power have to be carefully drawn in order to prevent unjustifiable executive acts. As Montesquieu argued, the risk in giving power to an institution is that it will use that power for its own ends, rather than the greater good. The greater good, in this context, is the creation and maintenance of a community protected by the power of the state. A crucial issue for the analysis of Convention rights is thus the extent to which the Court has been careful to enforce consistent understandings of the exceptions to and limits on Convention rights.

---

30   Limitations of space in this chapter prevent us from making a point by point comparison of the Covenant and the Convention.

31   Article 1 specifies that the contracting parties will 'secure to everyone within their jurisdiction the rights and freedoms' that the Convention goes on to define. The Court's understanding of 'jurisdiction' is interesting as it determines the range of the Convention. The definition of territoriality is largely a matter of international law. A narrow approach to jurisdiction would tend to interpret the term as relating to a state's geographical territory. However, in *Assanidze* v. *Georgia* (8 April 2004) the ECtHR acknowledged that territoriality could be defined as relating to territories under de facto control of a state or a state's armed forces. *Al-Skeini and others* v. *Secretary of State for Defence* [2007] UKHL 26 shows what is at stake in this difference of definition. The case concerned the deaths of six Iraqi citizens at the hands of the British armed forces, who were stationed in Basra after the invasion of 2003. The House of Lords held that while the Convention was fundamentally 'territorial' and operated in 'the legal space of the contracting states', there were notable exceptions which included the situation where a contracting state's armed forces had 'effective control' of a territory through 'military occupation' and thus 'exercised all or some of the public powers' which that territory's government would normally exercise. The House relied on *Bankovic* v. *Belgium* [2001] 11 BHRC 435 which ruled that 'acts of the contracting states performed, or producing effects, outside their territories can constitute an exercise of jurisdiction by them within the meaning of Article 1 of the convention'. Applying these principles to the fact of the case, the House held that although the first five claimants did not fall within Article 1, the sixth victim, Baha Mousa, did indeed fall under the scope of the exception.

Rights to bodily integrity

Article 2 defines the right to life. The Article begins by placing a positive duty on a state party to protect 'everyone's right to life'. Exceptions to the principle are then outlined. The first broad exception covers judicial execution pursuant to a sentence pronounced by a court of law. Paragraph 2 then goes on to provide that the right to life will not have been breached if, in cases of 'absolute necessity', force is used: to defend a person from unlawful violence (2a), to make an arrest or prevent an escape of someone who has been lawfully detained (2b). In accordance with 2c, 'deprivation of life' pursuant to lawful actions taken against extreme instances of public disorder such as 'riot or insurrection' are also acceptable. The state or its agents can thus, if absolutely necessary, use lethal force to effect arrests, and to quell violent attempts to overthrow its established order. The fundamental nature of this Article is indicated by the fact that no derogation is possible[32] except for 'deaths resulting from lawful acts of war'.

Article 3 states the prohibition on torture. The Article also covers 'inhuman or degrading treatment or punishment'. Like Article 2, no derogation from this Article is possible.[33] In *Ireland* v. *UK*[34] Judge Fitzmaurice pointed out that Article 3 could not be applied to treatment that fell short of torture. In the same case, the Court defined torture as 'deliberate inhuman treatment causing very serious and cruel suffering'. Certain robust interrogation techniques and even physical assaults on prisoners might thus not fall under the definition. In the Greek case[35] the Commission determined that severe beatings all over the body to extract information did amount to 'the necessary level of suffering'.[36] As torture is such an extreme abuse of due process, it is surprising that the Court has not defined torture more broadly.

Article 5 articulates the right to liberty and security. The Article begins with a positive statement of the right: 'Everyone has the right to liberty and security of person'. Article 5 goes on to prohibit arbitrary detention, except in certain circumstances where it is 'prescribed by law'.[37] In *Engel and others* v. *The Netherlands* No. 1,[38] the Court pointed out that Article 5 concerned 'individual liberty in its classic sense'. Engel suggests that Article 5 requires due process safeguards on forms of arrest and detention. We will analyse it in greater detail in Chapter 15.

---

32 See Article 15(2).
33 Ibid.
34 *Ireland* v. *UK*, 18 January 1978.
35 The Greek Case (12 YB 1 504 Com Rep. 1969).
36 The European Convention for the Prevention of Torture and Inhuman or Degrading Treatment or Punishment, 1998 supplements Article 3. The Convention establishes a European Committee for the Prevention of Torture (CPT). This body has the power to visit detention centres and prisons and monitor the treatment of those detained. The Committee draws up reports after visits. These reports are communicated to the state party concerned.
37 These include: 5(1)(a): lawful detention after sentence has been pronounced by a competent court; 5(1)(b): lawful arrest pursuant to a court order or to 'secure' the fulfilment of lawful obligations; 5(1)(c): detention to enable a person to be brought before a court of law where there is reasonable suspicion of an offence having been committed or to prevent the commission of an offence. 5(1)(d) covers lawful detention of minors for educational purposes or to enable the minor to be brought before competent legal authorities; 5(1)(e) allows lawful detention to prevent the spread of contagious disease or to control certain classes of persons. Finally, 5(1)(e) covers lawful arrest to prevent unauthorised entry into a country or to allow deportation.
38 *Engel and others* v. *The Netherlands* No. 1 [1979–80] 1 EHRR 647.

Due process and integrity rights

Article 6 has been analysed in the Introduction, and is also the subject of Chapter 11. Thus, our main point here is to introduce the concept of integrity rights. These include the following fundamental principles. Article 7 ensures that there should be no punishment without law.[39] It effectively prohibits *ex post facto* laws. In *Kokkinakis v. Greece*[40] the Court pointed out that: 'Article 7(1) ... prohibits the retroactive application of the criminal law and the retroactive imposition of heavier penalties to the detriment of the accused[.]'[41] If Article 7 preserves the integrity of the criminal law, Article 13, the right to an effective remedy, ensures the integrity of the courts as such.

Articles 17 and 18 determine law's place in a broader democratic order. Article 17 prevents both states and individuals or groups from claiming 'any right to engage in any activity or perform any act aimed at the destruction of any of the rights and freedoms set forth herein or at their limitation to a greater extent than is provided for in the Convention'. The Article this safeguards is 'the free functioning of democratic institutions'.[42] Article 18 seeks to prevent restrictions on one set of rights being used as restrictions on other rights. We will explore it in greater detail in the next chapter.

Rights protecting forms of political life

Article 10 articulates the right to freedom of expression. Broadly defined as covering the 'freedom to hold opinions and receive and impart information and ideas', the right is restricted at s.10(2). Freedom of expression may thus be subject to such 'formalities, conditions, restrictions or penalties as are prescribed by law and are necessary in a democratic society'. The list of exceptions covers: 'the interests of national security, territorial integrity or public safety, for the prevention of disorder or crime, for the protection of health or morals, for the protection of the reputation or rights of others, for preventing the disclosure of information received in confidence, or for maintaining the authority and impartiality of the judiciary'. As with the other Convention Articles, the exceptions indicate the legitimate uses of executive power.

Article 11 states two connected freedoms: assembly and association. The latter includes the 'right to form and to join trade unions'. The restrictions on these freedoms are limited to those that are 'prescribed by law and are necessary in a democratic society'. They thus cover restrictions 'in the interests of national security or public safety, for the prevention of disorder or crime, for the protection of health or morals or for the protection of the rights and freedoms of others'. There is an important concluding sentence that stresses that restrictions can be lawfully imposed by 'the armed forces ... the police or ... the administration of the State'.

---

39   Article 15(2) provides that no derogation from this Article is possible.
40   *Kokkinakis v. Greece* [1994] 17 EHRR 397.
41   Ibid.
42   *KPD v. FRG* No. 250/57 1 YB222, at 223 [1957].

Article 16 allows restrictions to be imposed on the political activity of aliens. As we will see in the next chapter, the Convention makes frequent distinctions between aliens, immigrants and citizens. This point will be developed presently.

Social and economic rights

It was suggested above that Article 4 is significant for what it excludes. Article 4(1) begins by explicitly prohibiting 'slavery and servitude' and goes on to prohibit 'forced or compulsory labour'. No derogation is possible from 4(1).[43] Article 4(3) then outlines the exceptions to this general principle. 'Forced or compulsory labour' does not include work carried out in the 'ordinary course of detention', work of 'service or a military character', work carried out in emergency situations or work as part of normal civic obligations.

One of the major criticisms of the Convention is that it is entirely silent on social and economic rights. Rather than compel states to recognise (for instance) the right to work, or the right to social security, it contains this rather limited prohibition on slavery.

It may be, though, that it is precisely the limited form of the Convention article that made it acceptable to nations who were considering whether or not to accept the obligations of the Convention. Control over economic and social policy is often seen as falling entirely within the sovereign power of the state. Thus, the 'price' of the judicial enforcement of rights may be that the social and economic concerns are largely absent from the Convention.

One final point may be made about Article 4. From a Marxist perspective, the Convention can be understood as a set of rights that create and sustain a legal order that enables a certain form of 'democratic' capitalism. To the extent that this theme can appear at all within the Convention itself, Article 4 can be read as enshrining one of the fundamental features of the capitalist social and economic order: it is founded on wage labour. The prohibition on slavery thus places in legal form one of the historical and socio-economic fundamentals of an order that rests on private property, wage labour and the private ownership of capital.

Rights protecting forms of civil society

The right to respect for private and family life is guaranteed by Article 8. Article 8(2) prohibits any 'interference' by public authorities except 'in accordance with the law and is necessary in a democratic society'. The right to marry in Article 12 covers the right to 'found a family' within the context of the domestic laws that govern this area. The Court has held in *Van Oosterwijk* v. *Belgium*[44] that the domestic law of the state parties has not to be arbitrary or effectively prevent the enjoyment of a general right to marry.

---

43   See Article 15(2).
44   *Van Oosterwijk* v. *Belgium* A 40 [1980] Com Rep.

Plurality rights

Article 9 guarantees the freedom of thought, conscience and religion. The second paragraph of the Article, 9(2), places restrictions on the right as articulated in 9(1). The restrictions are ones that are justifiable in a democratic society in the 'interests of public safety, for the protection of public order, health or morals, or for the protection of the rights and freedoms of others'. We have already examined this Article in Chapter 5, and seen the difficult issues that surround it. Perhaps the lack of more sophisticated ways of articulating plurality under the Convention means that this Article is used in an inappropriate manner.

Similar arguments could be made in relation to Article 14. This prohibits discrimination 'on any ground such as sex, race, colour, language, religion, political or other opinion, national or social origin, association with a national minority, property, birth or other status'. The jurisprudence of the Court has made Article 14 'parasitic' on other Convention rights. In other words, although it is widely drawn, it is only possible to argue a breach of Article 14 if another Convention right has also been breached. Article 14 has also proved itself to be difficult to extend to discrimination based on sexual orientation. The failure to provide a free-standing right that prohibits discrimination makes this area of the Convention somewhat weak.[45]

In summary, we have shown that the Convention can be read as a coherent document that provides a minimal standard for a rule of law state. The Convention also seeks to limit those instances where the state can use its executive power. At the heart of the Convention is the protection of due process and the integrity of the law. The integrity of law is fundamental to a democratic state, as without due process the very idea of human rights protected by a court of law becomes meaningless. However, due process itself has to be related to the context of substantive rights.

We also made certain criticisms of the scope of the Convention. To some extent its limitations have been addressed through a number of Protocols. We do not have the space to consider them in detail in this chapter, but we will make one fundamental point. The Protocols have gone some way to updating the rights contained in the Convention. For instance, Protocol 1[46] enshrines the protection of property,[47] the right to education[48] and the right to free elections.[49] The promulgation of further Protocols shows the dynamism of the Convention, and its concern to develop rights protection to cover developing areas of social and economic life.[50]

---

45 But see Protocol 12 (Rome 4. XI.2000). This contains a general prohibition on discrimination.
46 Protocol No. 1 to the Convention for the Protection of Human Rights and Fundamental Freedoms, Paris, 20 III 1952.
47 Article 1.
48 Article 2.
49 Article 3.
50 Protocol No. 4 (16.IX.1963) prohibits imprisonment for debt (Article 1) and guarantees the freedom of movement (Article 2). It goes on to prohibit the expulsion of nationals (Article 3) and the collective expulsion of aliens (Article 4). Protocol No. 6 28.IV.1983 abolishes the death penalty (see also Protocol No 13 Vilnius 3. V. 2002). Protocol No 7 (22.XI.1984) lays down certain rights in relation to procedural safeguards for the expulsion of aliens and conditions relating to criminal law and equality between spouses. It is considered in the next chapter. Protocol 12 was considered above.

The coherence of the Convention does not just relate to the substantive rights that it provides. As we argued in the introduction to this chapter, we are interested in both the right of the Convention, and the way in which the Convention operates as an international legal system. We will now return to this second concern and show that Convention rights have to be understood in the context of the institutions that protect, develop and enforce them.

THE INSTITUTIONS OF THE CONVENTION

In this section we are concerned with the operation of the Convention and the institutional structure of the ECtHR. We will focus on some broad and overarching themes about the nature of the Convention and the enforcement machinery it puts in place. To this end, we can begin by considering the following statement by the ECtHR:

> The Court has repeatedly stated that its 'judgments in fact serve not only to decide those cases brought before the Court but, more generally, to elucidate, safeguard and develop the rules instituted by the Convention, thereby contributing to the observance by the States of the engagements undertaken by them as Contracting Parties'.[51] Although the primary purpose of the Convention system is to provide individual relief, its mission is also to determine issues on public-policy grounds in the common interest, thereby raising the general standards of protection of human rights and extending human rights jurisprudence throughout the community of Convention States.[52]

This paragraph is important because it shows precisely what is at stake in the role of the ECtHR. It is clear that the Court sees itself as providing more than a narrow forum to determine disputes over human rights. The Court conceives of itself as defining a communal and pan-European understanding of human rights at the level of 'public policy'. We will see that something of this spirit has influenced the Court's articulation of its interpretative powers over the Convention, even though this might have led to somewhat contentious decisions in the opinion of certain nation states.

Section II of the Convention establishes the institutions dedicated to the protection and enhancement of human rights. Article 19 establishes the European Court of Human Rights. Various Articles then relate to the appointment of judges and their terms of office. It is worth noting that the judges of the Court serve in their individual capacities (Article 21). The Court is thus impartial and independent of the state parties who are signatories to the Convention. Articles 27–30 state that the Court is organised into Committees, Chambers and a Grand Chamber. The divisions of the Court have slightly different powers in relation to declaring cases inadmissible. After a judgment has been delivered, a party can request that the case be considered by the Grand Chamber. The Grand Chamber will hear the case if it raises an important issue of the interpretation of the Convention.

---

51   See *Ireland* v. *the United Kingdom*, 18 January 1978 and *Guzzardi* v. *Italy*, 6 November 1980, Series A, no. 39, p. 31.
52   *Karner* v. *Austria*, 24 July 2003, para 26.

The powers of the Court can be grouped into three main areas. Article 32 outlines the Court's jurisdiction. Article 32(1) states that it extends to both the interpretation and application of the Convention and its Protocols. The Court also has a general power to determine its own jurisdiction in event of dispute (32(2)). The Convention then describes the two kinds of case that the Court can hear. Article 33 relates to inter-state cases. One state party may refer to the Court any breach of the Convention or its Protocols by another state party. There have only been two judgments in this area by the Court: *Ireland* v. *UK* (1978) and *Cyprus* v. *Turkey* (2001). The scarcity of this kind of case, suggests that the protection of human rights is not primarily achieved through 'hostile' inter-state litigation.

This takes us to a consideration of Article 34 and individual applications. This Article (or at least its forerunner, Article 25) has been described as 'one of the keystones in the machinery for the enforcement of the rights and freedoms set forth in the Convention'.[53] The Court can receive applications from 'any person, non-governmental organisation or group of individuals' who claims that a state party has violated one or more of his/her/their Convention rights. There are also admissibility criteria, which are set out by Article 35. One that is common to Articles 33 and 34 is the need for the applicant to have exhausted 'all domestic remedies'. Furthermore 35(2) states that the Court will not accept anonymous submissions, those that are 'substantially the same' as those it has already considered, or those which are being considered by 'another procedure of international investigation or settlement and contains no relevant new information'. The Court has a wide jurisdiction to declare inadmissible applications that are 'incompatible' with the Convention, are 'manifestly ill-founded' or an abuse of process. The Court also has a wide power to strike out applications (Article 37).

The case law that has developed around Article 34 has addressed the extent to which certain corporate entities have *locus standi*. For instance, in *Danderyds Kommun* v. *Sweden*[54] the Court rejected the idea that a Swedish municipality fell within Article 34, effectively asserting that a public authority could not bring an action under the Convention. The other matter that has been decided upon in the case law is the meaning of the word 'victim'. In *Klass*, the Court stated an important principle in relation to Article 25 (the pre-Protocol 11 version of Article 34):

> Article 25 does not institute for individuals a kind of actio popularis for the interpretation of the Convention; it does not permit individuals to complain against a law in abstracto simply because they feel that it contravenes the Convention. In principle, it does not suffice for an individual applicant to claim that the mere existence of a law violates his rights under the Convention; it is necessary that the law should have been applied to his detriment.[55]

It is clear that Article 25 is somewhat narrow. It does not allow speculative interpretations of the Convention, and can only crystallise into an action for an

---

53   *Klass* v. *Germany*, judgment 6 September 1978.
54   *Danderyds Kommun* v. *Sweden*, application no. 52559/99.
55   Supra n. 57, at para 33.

individual if a law has actually been applied to his or her detriment. One could imagine a much broader operation of the Article that could be used to question potential violations of the Convention, but such a mechanism would lead to a much greater workload for the Court. The Court does point out, however, that a law may 'violate' an individual's rights if they are 'directly affected' by it even without 'any specific measure of implementation'.[56] The point that arose in *Klass* was the extent to which the Court could question secret surveillance measures. The very secrecy of the techniques in question meant that the applicants could not specify the breach that rendered them victims of a violation of their human rights. Interpreting the Convention in a purposive manner, the ECtHR argued that the right to petition the Court was implied in such circumstances. This was because 'the procedural provisions of the Convention' were 'set up to protect the individual' and had to be applied so as to make 'individual applications efficacious'. As unchallengeable secret surveillance would effectively reduce Article 8 to a 'nullity' it was necessary to declare the case admissible. However, the Court stressed that each case had to be considered on its facts, as otherwise a potentially wide exception to Article 25 was created.

This takes us back to Article 34. Another important boundary issue is the extent to which the next of kin of a deceased victim has the right to petition the Court. In *McCann v. UK*[57] the relatives of a deceased member of the IRA were able to bring an action against the UK for breach of Article 2. Later, in *Karner v. Austria*[58] the Court reflected on the principles that related to applications made after the death of the original victim. The Court argued that the Article could not be interpreted in 'a rigid, mechanical and inflexible way'.[59] Allowances had to be made where an heir was either unwilling or unable to continue the deceased's action. These considerations were particularly pressing where the case raised broad 'moral' issues. As the present case concerned the status of homosexuals in Austrian law, it was necessary that it should be heard by the Court.

The admissibility rules have also been interpreted by the Court as they determine threshold criteria that relate to the precise operation of both Articles 33 and 34. In *Isayeva, Yusupova and Bazayeva v. Russia*[60] the Court laid down an important principle for the interpretation of this requirement. They argued that the exhaustion rule was not capable of being 'applied automatically' and that each case had to be considered on its facts. This principle required the Court to consider both the 'formal remedies in the legal system of the Contracting State' and the context of their operation. The critical question was whether, given these concerns, the applicant had done 'everything that could reasonably be expected of him or her to exhaust domestic remedies'.[61] As the 'law enforcement bodies were not functioning properly in Chechnya'[62] the Court

---

56   The Court considered this point in the 'Belgian Linguistic' case and the case of *Kjeldsen, Busk Madsen and Pedersen*, judgment of 23 July 1968, Series A no. 6, and judgment of 7 December 1976, Series A no. 23.
57   *McCann v. UK* (1995) 21 EHRR 97.
58   *Karner v. Austria*, judgment of 24 July 2003; (2004) 38 EHRR 24.
59   Ibid., para 25.
60   *Isayeva, Yusupova and Bazayeva v. Russia*, judgment of 24 February 2005.
61   Ibid., paras 144–5.
62   Ibid., para 151.

did not require the applicants to have formally followed the procedures specified by Russian civil and criminal law.

Once a case has been declared admissible, parties can be asked to submit further evidence. Article 36 provides that in all cases that go before a Chamber or the Grand Chamber, a High Contracting Party has a right to submit written comments and to take part in hearings if one of its nationals is involved in proceedings. NGOs and interest groups can also seek permission to submit written observations. This is an important feature of the Court's democratic mandate. Indeed, it could be argued that the right of non-state parties should be much broader so as to recognise and encourage an international civil society that is not dominated by state powers.

Article 38 provides that once the Court has declared a case admissible, it can itself pursue investigations, for which states must provide 'all the necessary facilities' (38(1)). The Article also specifies that the Court must secure a 'friendly settlement coherent with the Convention'. If a friendly settlement is reached, then Article 39 details that the decision of the Court is limited to a statement of facts. One of the main issues emerging in the case law on friendly settlements is the Court's concern that such settlements are genuine, and show 'respect for human rights' (Article 38(1)(b)).[63] For states, a friendly settlement avoids expensive litigation and the risk of a formal ruling against them; individuals can benefit from speedy resolution of their concerns and enhanced compensation. Depending on the matters at stake, a settlement can also contain an undertaking by a government to desist from activities in breach of the Convention. In *Denmark* v. *Turkey*,[64] for example, the Turkish government undertook to prevent interrogation techniques that were in breach of Article 3.

If the Court finds that there has been a violation of the Convention, and the relevant state party's domestic law does not provide a full set of remedies, the Court has the power to 'afford just satisfaction to the injured party' (Article 41). Article 46 is central to the remedial structure of the Convention. It states that parties undertake to 'abide by the final judgment of the Court'. The execution of judgments is supervised by the Committee of Ministers (Article 46(2)). When the Court has found a breach of the Convention, the Committee invites the relevant state party to inform it as to whether any pecuniary or non-pecuniary damages have been paid, and whether individual measures (i.e. in relation to the applicant him or herself) or general measures (those which relate to a wider group of persons) have been adopted. The Committee of Ministers will keep a case under review until measures have been adopted and/or damages paid. *Loizidou* v. *Turkey*[65] is an example of a respondent state failing (or delaying) implementation of a Court order that had been executed in 1998. The Turkish government eventually paid damages to the applicant in 2003. The Court noted that this was due to the combined efforts of other European states.

This case does suggest one of the peculiar features of international law. For the most part, it is necessary that states accept their obligations voluntarily. A recalcitrant state can be pressured or persuaded, but if the necessary international will to enforce

---

63 For an example of a refusal to accept a friendly settlement, see *Ukrainian Media Group* v. *Ukraine*, judgment 29 March 2005.
64 *Denmark* v. *Turkey*, 5 April 2000.
65 *Loizidou* v. *Turkey* [1995] 20 EHRR 99.

a judgment does not exist, a remedy awarded by an international Court is dramatically limited. We do not have the space to speculate as to why national governments accept international obligations, but perhaps the most compelling argument is that it is in their interests to do so. So long as the advantages of being accepted as a partner by other European states outweigh the disadvantages and inconveniences, it is likely that a state will accept its human rights obligations. If this is a somewhat cynical approach, at least it acknowledges the element of realpolitik that is perhaps a more meaningful influence on policy and state practice than the often rhetorical commitment to human rights. Indeed, the Committee's observation that 'constructive dialogue' rather than 'diplomatic or political pressure'[66] leads to satisfactory solutions in executing Court judgments, suggests that the political will does exist within states to abide by the rulings of the Court. Some have suggested that civil society groups and NGOs should also play a role in the execution of judgments. Such an involvement of non-state parties would assist the Court in building grass roots levels of cooperation and a popular appreciation of the legitimacy of the Court.[67]

The issue of interim measures takes us to an important area of the Court's practice. Interim measures can be used in two distinct ways. They can prohibit a party from taking certain actions; or they can be used to obligate a party to perform certain actions. They are clearly important in human rights cases, as an individual may face abuse or torture should s/he be extradited to another state. Interim measures also obviously raise the issue of the Court's authority. One of the key authorities in this area is *Mamatkulov and Askarov* v. *Turkey*.[68] In this case the applicants were deported from Turkey to Uzbekistan, despite the Court specifically forbidding the Turkish government from so doing. The ECtHR determined that the Turkish government were in breach of Article 34, which creates a duty to refrain from hindering the 'effective exercise' of the Article.

In their appeal to the Grand Chamber, the Turkish government disputed the jurisdiction of the Court to issue interim measures, as it was not expressly created by the Convention. Originally, the Court had indeed empowered itself to make such orders, adopting a practice of the Commission, and issuing Rule 36 in 1974. Clearly the Court does have the power to determine its own procedures, but had it gone too far in assuming the authority to create Rule 36? An early authority, *CruzVaras* v. *Sweden*[69] would suggest that interim orders did not create legal obligations for the parties to whom they were addressed. However, as we saw in the paragraphs above, the Court interprets the Convention in a dynamic manner. The ECtHR argued that the jurisdiction to issue interim measures should be reviewed in the context of the changing practices in international human rights law. The Human Rights Committee of the UN had developed the understanding that failure to comply with interim measures was a breach of the International Covenant of Civil and Political Rights. The Inter-American Court had developed a similar jurisprudence, as had the International Court of Justice.

---

66   Mowbray (2008: 48).
67   Mowbray quoting Leach (2006).
68   *Mamatkulov and Askarov* v. *Turkey*, judgment 4 February 2005.
69   *CruzVaras* v. *Sweden*, 2 March 1991.

In terms of the jurisprudence of the Convention, the Court relied on Article 13 to argue that the idea of an effective remedy meant that it was necessary to prevent actions contrary to the Convention 'whose effects are potentially irreversible'.[70] Ultimately, limiting or denying the jurisdiction would be in breach of both Articles 1 and 34. A positive obligation for a state to abide by interim measures could also be justified by reference to Article 46, which requires a state to 'comply with the final judgment of the Court'.

However, this argument did not compel the assent of all the judges in the Grand Chamber. Those who dissented pointed out that the Convention did not contain the power claimed by the Court. They also argued that the majority's approach abandoned interpretation of the treaty to become judicial law making. Indeed, when Protocol 11 was drafted, recommendations that it should create such a power were not accepted by the contracting states. Where then does the case of *Mamatkulov and Askarov* leave the jurisprudence of the Court? The ECtHR will presumably continue to act upon this authority. Moreover, there is a clear need for such measures, particularly in Articles 2 and 3 cases. To the extent that states themselves accept interim measures, it may be that the practice has become recognised. It will be interesting to see the fate of this most bold assertion of the Court's power.

CONCLUSION

In conclusion to this section, we want to return to the idea of 'constituting' rights and make a single point about the constitutive 'force' of the Convention. The preamble of the Convention refers to the Universal Declaration of 1948. This shows the essential link between these two documents. However, we are primarily concerned with the sentence that describes the 'common heritage of political traditions, ideals, freedoms and the rules of law' that underlies the principles of the Convention.

What is the status of the 'shared' political inheritance between nations to which this sentence appeals? The collapse of democracy before the Second World War suggests that the values of democracy and the rule of law became quickly forgotten in Europe. It is as if the Preamble of the Convention has to be read as constituting the values for which it stands. The Convention serves as a reminder that democracy has to be constantly recreated in the face of extremism, nationalism and racism.

---

70   Ibid., para 124.

9

HUMAN RIGHTS AND THE INTEGRITY OF THE LAW

INTRODUCTION

We use the term 'integrity rights' to describe a grouping of Articles in the European Convention. These Articles serve two main ends. They protect principles that are central to the definition of law and articulate the part that law plays in a democratic political order. Thus, if we look at Article 13 (the right to an effective remedy), Article 7 (no punishment without law) and Protocol 7 (minimum conditions that must apply to criminal justice) we are primarily concerned with law's self-definition. Articles 17 (prohibition on the abuse of rights) and 18 (limitations on the restrictions of rights) take us to the latter concern about law's place in a democratic political culture. It is essential to remember that integrity rights are sites over which rival notions of law and democracy are fought out. This issue is writ large in the first section of this chapter where we examine the very constitution of human rights regimes through a study of the state's power to derogate from and reserve its position on certain human rights obligations. It might seem rather perverse to begin a description of rights regimes with this concern. However, it is to stress the point that rights are arguments over the limits of power. Rights are not absolute and pre-suppose the power of the executive. Executive power is legitimate to the extent it respects the limits placed upon it by human rights. In this sense, integrity rights aim to define the limits of the state use of power. Integrity rights would appear hopelessly deracinated if they were removed from this essential context.

DEROGATIONS AND RESERVATIONS

Our study of integrity rights begins with the issue of derogation. This is crucial as it forces us to think about the very constitution of a human rights regime. At a jurisprudential level, the conventional argument is that human rights are indivisible. In other words, human rights exist as a coherent whole. A document such as the European Convention on Human Rights (ECHR) articulates a complex of rights from which a state cannot pick and choose. It would obviously be contradictory for a state to undertake to uphold, for example, the right of assembly and association, but not the right to freedom of speech. However, in practice, the position is a little different. Although there are some rights from which a state cannot derogate, the Convention itself allows a signatory to either derogate or enter certain reservations to Convention rights. The key issue is the extent to which this is justifiable.

Derogations and reservations are justifiable to the extent to which they are limited and those very limitations place a justification on the state. We will see that this takes us to the very concern with the democratic order and the threats that confront it. We cannot conflate this point with the right to limit or suspend the operation of rights. This issue must largely be dealt with through a study of substantive rights. Our concern here is with the precise operation of integrity rights; and, as far as derogations and reservations are concerns, the power of the state to limit the scope of its human rights obligations.

Thus, derogations and reservations allow a government to effectively opt out of areas of protection that a human rights instrument offers. They can be understood as areas where a government desires to retain either an explicit power to pass certain pieces of legislation, or to reserve a more general policy position that may infringe international rights commitments. There are technical distinctions between the two terms, and it can be difficult to tell them apart, but these issues do not need to detain us. We can observe a fairly robust working definition. Reservations are made at the time a treaty is signed; derogations are made after a treaty is signed and ratified.[1] Reservations and derogations are essential to creating the catalogue of human rights that will enter into force in national law. The jurisprudence of reservation and derogation is thus at the cutting edge of the definition of a human rights regime. There is a very narrow line to tread:

> The possibility of entering reservations may encourage States which consider that they have difficulties in guaranteeing all the rights in the Covenant nonetheless to accept the generality of obligations in that instrument. Reservations may serve a useful function to enable States to adapt specific elements in their laws to the inherent rights of each person as articulated in the Covenant. However, it is desirable in principle that States accept the full range of obligations, because the human rights norms are the legal expression of the essential rights that every person is entitled to as a human being.[2]

Although this passage concerns the International Covenant on Civil and Political Rights, it is an authoritative statement of the core problem with which we are dealing. Reservations allow states to qualify their commitment to international human rights instruments so far as they accept the general tenor of their obligations. Clearly, reservations cannot become so intensive as to destroy the fundamental point of the treaty. Furthermore, in the specific field of human rights, the integrity or totality of rights has to be preserved. This is because there is an 'interplay' between rights to the extent that they back up and support each other. International human rights are thus presented as a framework of obligations that provides the most effective and efficient means for a state to enter into human rights obligations.

---

1   Joint Committee on Human Rights: Inquiry into UK derogations from Convention rights, para 2 at http://www.parliament.uk/commons/selcom/hrpnt13.htm.
2   Para 4, Human Rights Committee, General Comment 24(52), General comment on issues relating to reservations made upon ratification or accession to the Covenant or the Optional Protocols thereto, or in relation to declarations under Article 41 of the Covenant, U.N. Doc. CCPR/C/21/Rev.1/Add.6 (1994) at http://www1.umn.edu/humanrts/gencomm/hrcom24.htm.

Commentators have observed[3] that arguments were made at the drafting stage of the Convention that no reservations would be permitted, as '[s]uch a power would threaten to deprive ... [the Convention] of its practical effects and its moral authority'.[4] Although Article 57 shows that these arguments were not accepted, it does stress that '[r]eservations of a general character will not be permitted', and thus goes some way to preserving the integrity of the Convention. This is writ large in the Temeltasch case.[5] In this case, the Commission asserted that it had a power to review reservations and to determine whether or not particular reservations are in 'accordance' with the Convention. The Commission based its competence to consider these issues on the nature of the Convention itself, specifically the fact that it created 'organs responsible for supervising the enforcement of its provisions by the Contracting Parties'.[6]

The whole point of the Convention was not to allow each nation to pursue its 'national interest', but 'to establish a common public order of the free democracies of Europe with the object of safeguarding their common heritage of political traditions, ideals, freedoms and the rule of law'.[7] To enter into the obligations established by the Treaty is to accept obligations of an 'essentially objective character'. This can be shown by the 'supervisory machinery' that the Convention set up, and is founded on 'a collective guarantee ... of the rights and freedoms set forth in the Convention'.[8] This point was confirmed on and elaborated in *Belios*[9] where the ECtHR affirmed that it, rather than the contracting state, was the correct body to determine the legitimacy of a reservation. However, as commentators have pointed out, the issue of the 'validity'[10] of a reservation would only arise in the event of litigation over an alleged breach of the Convention. This means that, in practice, a degree of uncertainty remains about the reservations entered into by contracting parties. Whether or not this could be remedied by a special procedure is a moot point. It may even suggest that what is constitutive of an international rights regime is a necessary degree of uncertainty over the precise scope of those rights.

Can we find similar issues in the analysis of derogations? Article 15(1) allows a state to derogate from the treaty in 'times of war or other public emergency threatening the life of the nation'. The power of derogation is limited. Article 15(2) specifies that it is not possible to derogate from the right to life (although this would not cover 'deaths resulting from lawful acts of war'), the prohibition on torture (Article 3), the freedom from slavery (Article 4) and the prohibition on retrospective criminal law (Article 7). Protocol 6 also forbids derogation and reservation from the prohibition of the death penalty and the Articles of Protocol 4. This creates a catalogue of minimal rights that include: the right to liberty of movement, the prohibition on the expulsion of nationals and the prohibition of the collective expulsion of aliens. Article 15(1) goes on to specify

---

3   Van Dijk *et al.* (2006: 1102).
4   Ibid., 1102.
5   Temeltasch, Report of 5 May 1982, D and R 31 (1983) p. 120.
6   Ibid.
7   Ibid.
8   Ibid.
9   *Belios* v. *Switzerland*, 29 April 1988.
10 Supra n. 3, at 1104.

that derogations must be limited 'to the extent strictly required by the exigencies of the situation' and must be coherent with general obligations under international law.

The principle that underlies Article 15 is 'the overriding rights of the State to protect its democratic institutions'.[11] Thus the Article is 'more than just a derogation clause'.[12] It has to achieve a difficult task: suspending the operation of certain Articles in extreme moments, but preserving the essential minimum rights detailed above even in the time of emergency or war. Its purpose is thus 'the continuing existence of the democratic rule of law'.[13] The main point raised by the nature of Article 15 though is a peculiarity of human rights law. While reservations relate to the 'power' of the state to determine, albeit in a marginal way, the precise nature of the human rights obligations that it accepts, derogations fulfil a slightly different function. It is the point at which rights have to 'acknowledge' that they can be suspended, provided that the suspension is to protect a wider operation of democracy.

If we compare this power to derogate with the sovereign power to declare a state of emergency to preserve the law, we can glimpse the integrity of rights in the necessary continuation of a set of core values. In this sense, we would have to say that – both at the level of substantive rights, and indeed as far as the theory of integrity rights are concerned – there is an essential and binding core that is definitional of rights. Can we refer to the sovereignty of rights? If this term is useful, we would have to immediately distinguish it from the conventional theory of sovereignty that stresses the omni-competence of a national law-making body with a broad democratic mandate based on a universal franchise. Precisely because human rights have been acknowledged by a sovereign body that has chosen to bind itself to human rights obligations, the sovereignty of rights became a permanent limit on the law-making body, an essential limitation on executive power so long as it continues to remain a signatory to the Convention. This might suggest that a state is legitimate only to the extent that it acknowledges a core set of values that relate to a minimum set of substantive rights, and a structure that preserves the integrity of the law.

Prior to the enactment of the HRA 1998, the United Kingdom had already derogated from Article 5(3) of the Convention to preserve the power of the Secretary of State to extend periods of detention for those suspected of terrorist offences under the Prevention of Terrorism (Temporary Provisions) Act 1984. However, the Terrorism Act 2000 made this derogation unnecessary and it was withdrawn with effect from 1 April 2001. More recently, the UK has derogated from their Article 5 commitments[14] in anticipation of the measures contained in the Anti-Terrorism Crime and Security Act 2001 that permits internment of non-UK nationals without trial.

The Convention also allowed a state to enter a reservation when a law in force is not in conformity with a Convention provision. The UK has a reservation in respect of Article 2 of the First Protocol. The reservations relate to the right to education and the duty of the state to respect the philosophical and religious convictions of parents

---

11   Ibid., 1054, citing Case Law Topics No. 4 Human Rights and their limitations (Strasbourg 1973: 3).
12   Ibid., 1055.
13   Ibid.
14   See Statutory Instrument 2001 No. 3644 Human Rights Act 1998 (Designated Derogation).

in the provision of education and teaching. The reservation accept this right, but only to the extent that it is not incompatible with efficient teaching and avoids excessive expenditure from public funds.

THE RIGHT TO AN EFFECTIVE REMEDY: ARTICLE 13

Article 13 must be read alongside Article 35 (formerly Article 26)[15] as central to the 'co-operative relationship'[16] between national law and European human rights law. The nature of the relationship between national and international law is such that the ECtHR must develop its jurisprudence with a certain degree of sensitivity. The task the ECtHR has set itself is to determine the boundary between the executive's margin of appreciation, and the kind of restriction that would so qualify a right as to make it meaningless. This approach is founded on the principle that it is primarily the responsibility of signatories to the Convention to provide legal remedies for breaches of human rights in their national law. From this perspective, the Commission and the Court are 'subsidiary'[17] bodies and the application to Strasbourg is secondary to a cause of action in a national court.

While this point has undoubtedly featured in the jurisprudence of the ECtHR, other issues have also been pressing. For instance, is Article 13 free standing or does it only apply if another Convention Article has been breached? This question is bound up with other matters. On the broadest of interpretations of the Article, it would amount to an 'obligation to give domestic effect to the Convention'.[18] A narrow interpretation, however, would make the Article almost redundant, as it would apply only when the ECtHR found that there had been a breach of another Article. The Court has attempted to resolve this issue by focusing on 'the nature of the state power' that has come into conflict with the Article. We will also examine the jurisprudence of 'arguability' that has arisen in the Article 13 case law. It may even be the case that the Article is being used as a 'filtering' device to limit the degree to which the Court can intervene in cases where an effective remedy has not been provided.

What then are the limits of Article 13? One of the most celebrated cases here is known as the Greek case.[19] The Commission accepted the argument that as the courts in operation in Greece after the military coup were not independent, there was a breach of Article 13. This case represents one of the more extreme situations in which Article 13 was invoked. The definition of public emergency that the Commission offered suggests that a crisis would have to be serious before a suspension of the Convention was permissible. The Greek case is atypical, because it concerns such a broad breach

---

15 See Protocol 11, which entered into force on 1 November 1998.
16 Harris *et al.* (1995: 443).
17 Ibid.
18 Ibid., 447.
19 The Greek case (12 YB 1, 174 (1969)). 'Such a public emergency may then be seen to have, in particular, the following characteristics: (1) It must be actual or imminent. (2) Its effects must involve the whole nation. (3) The continuance of the organised life of the community must be threatened. (4) The crisis or danger must be exceptional, in that the normal measures or restrictions, permitted by the Convention for the maintenance of public safety, health and order, are plainly inadequate.'

of the Convention. It is not that useful as a guide to the real matters that have emerged in the case law. Once we turn to this body of law, we will see that the fundamental problem is the wide margin of appreciation allowed to the state to determine the nature of remedies when national security matters are at stake.

Klass and Others v. *Federal Republic of Germany*[20] concerned the legitimacy of surveillance techniques. The case concerned a German law that allowed the state to intercept mail and telephone conversations in order to protect the 'free democratic constitutional order' from 'imminent dangers'. This case showed exactly what was at stake in rival interpretations of Article 13. Could it be read as guaranteeing access to the court? This would follow from the fact that an alleged violation of the Article would have to be made before a 'national authority' and would also mean that Article 13 would have to be interpreted as free standing and not dependent on the breach of another Article. On the facts of the case, the applicants alleged that they had suffered a breach of their rights, as the remedies provided were insufficient. An impartial judicial authority had not considered their case. Furthermore, as there was no duty to notify that surveillance was taking place, there was no way in which it could be challenged.

There is something distinctly Kafkaesque about the dilemma in which the applicants found themselves. They may have had certain remedies, but they were unable to petition a court because they did not know whether or not they were under surveillance. However, despite the compelling nature of their claims, it is not difficult to appreciate the arguments that limit the scope of the Article. The reference to a 'national authority' need not necessarily relate to a court, as long as the remedy provided is effective. It is not so much a question of the tribunal that awards the remedy, as its effectiveness given the context of the case.

The ECtHR favoured this narrow interpretation of the Article. They reasoned that the Article could not be read so as to give a right to notification of surveillance. Article 13 had to be coherent with Article 8(2). This prohibits any 'interference' by public authorities except 'as in accordance with the law and is necessary in a democratic society'.[21] To the extent that any surveillance technique falls within this exception, it is not in breach of Article 8. If Article 13 has to be read in this context, there is no requirement that there should be remedies available in court. Moreover, the remedies themselves have to be assessed from the perspective of 8(2). Thus, there is no breach of Article 13 because 'the effectiveness of these remedies is limited and they will in principle apply only in exceptional cases'. While the ECtHR regretted that it had to come to this conclusion, only Judge Farinha (in a partially dissenting judgment) drew attention to the 'risks' inherent in this approach to Article 13. Allowing state surveillance of individuals may be a necessary evil in the defence of democracy, but the checks and balances available in German law effectively failed, leaving too much power in the hands of the executive branch of government. The law allowed the executive to determine that surveillance was necessary, and there was

---

20   *Klass and Others* v. *Federal Republic of Germany Series*, 6 September 1978. 2 EHRR 214.
21   Such restrictions would include limitations on the Article in the interests of national security and the protection of the rights of others. The ECtHR agreed with the government that secret surveillance was necessary for public protection.

no possibility for scrutiny of this decision by an independent judge. Although Judge Farinha did not argue that Article 13 had been breached, he did warn against the breach of the principle of separation of powers that was implicit in the majority judgment.

It would thus appear that Article 13 is not going to be used to question state surveillance practices in any radical manner. The Article has also been argued in cases concerning prison rules and disciplinary regimes. We need to examine the extent to which Article 13 can be used to scrutinise this particular expression of executive power. Article 13 was argued in the context of Article 8 in *Boyle and Rice* v. *United Kingdom*. Boyle and Rice raised issues in relation to the availability of remedies for alleged interference with the correspondence of prisoners. The court held that there had been no breach of either Article 8 or 13.[22] It might appear that *Klass* and *Boyle and Rice* move in different directions. However, we can observe a similar strategy at work in both cases. *Boyle and Rice* needs to be seen in the context of *Silver* v. *UK*.[23] In this earlier case, the court had imposed the test of 'arguability' on an applicant's claim under Article 13. Arguability may have played no role in *Klass*, but in asserting that Article 13 did not give remedies 'in respect of any supposed grievance under the Convention',[24] *Boyle and Rice* is consistent with *Klass*. While a violation of Article 13 is not conditional on the breach of another Convention right, the Article is still required to interface with the Convention. Thus, Article 13 would not 'override' the limits placed on other Convention rights. The pressing question is the nature of the test for arguability.

It suited the British government to urge on the Commission a narrow test. If an argument about breach was 'manifestly ill founded' it would not be possible to make a claim under Article 13. The Commission did not agree with this position and made reference to Article 27(2). This Article contains a variable set of standards that include the test of arguability but also go beyond its terms. The Commission preferred a test that was not too exacting. A case needs only 'to raise a Convention issue which merits further examination' for it to warrant consideration. The standard proposed by the British government was not acceptable, as the conclusion that a claim was 'manifestly ill-founded' would only be possible after taking into account both written and oral argument. The manifestly ill-founded nature of a claim would thus not provide a legitimate threshold condition. It is interesting that the threshold condition test does return to the considerations of *Klass*. Argument about whether or not a substantive Article had been breached would have a degree of bearing on whether or not a claim had passed the threshold.[25] The court backed up its position by asserting that they would not give a definition of 'arguability' as the issue had to be judged on the facts and merits of each case.

If the arguability test restricts the kind of claims that can be heard by the ECtHR, then it is also worth noting that the Court has also held that certain substantive matters

---

22   The ECtHR argued that an effective remedy was available to the applicants, as petition lay to the Secretary of State and there was the possibility of obtaining judicial review.
23   *Silver* v *UK*, 25 March 1983, 5 EHRR 347.
24   *Boyle and Rice*, 27 April 1988, para 53; 10 EHRR 425.
25   Ibid.

fell outside of its competence. In *Boyle and Rice* questions about the legitimacy of the limitation of a prisoner's entitlement to 12 visits a year fell outside the competence of the Court, and was entirely a matter for the relevant national authority. However, in the partly dissenting opinion of Judge Treschsel, a different understanding of the precise scope of Article 13 was articulated. His reasoning concerned the facts of Boyle's case. He indicated that there was at least an arguable case that a trustworthy prisoner (who had been used to a regime in which censorship of letters were not practised) should be exempted from further censorship. This would make Article 13 apply because the prisoner's complaint would raise a question about the compatibility of the prison rules with the Convention and such an issue could not be remedied by a petition to the Secretary of State or by the Scottish courts. On the discrimination point, Judge Treschsel also thought that there was an arguable case. Although it was legitimate for different prisoners to be treated in different ways, it would not be correct to state that there would be no arguable case if a prisoner believed he had been subjected to 'unjustified duress'.[26]

The boundaries of Article 13 can also be traced through a series of cases where the adequacy of the powers of judicial review of UK courts was considered. In *Soering v. UK*[27] the British government countered arguments about a lack of remedies for breach of Article 3, by relying, in part, on the availability of judicial review for the applicant's complaint. In the context of an extradition case, the relevant test applicable by the court would determine whether or not a reasonable Secretary of State would have taken the impugned decision. This would depend on the evidence available that the complainant would suffer inhuman or degrading treatment if extradited. The ECtHR agreed with the government's submission, and did not find it problematic that the 'lack of jurisdiction to award injunctions against the Crown' detracted from the remedy, since 'in practice a fugitive would [not] be surrendered' for extradition before his case had been heard by the Court. The weakness of English law in this area was revealed by *M. v. The Home Office*.[28] This case showed that a minister was willing to act in precisely such a way. Indeed, Soering shows how 'sharp' government practices could continue alongside a formal commitment to the Convention. However, it has to be remembered that Soering was decided before the HRA, when the Convention was not part of domestic law. How has judicial review fared in more recent cases?

In *Chahal v. UK*[29] the applicant argued that judicial review was ineffective in all Article 3 extradition cases. This was because the limitations of the review function of the courts meant that they could not scrutinise the evidence used by the Secretary of State to determine whether or not there were 'substantial grounds' that the person extradited would suffer ill treatment in the country to which he or she was sent. Although the courts could ascertain whether or not the Secretary of State was acting reasonably, this standard of inquiry was far too limited to count as an effective way of providing a remedy. The problem was exacerbated when the state claimed,

---

26 Ibid.
27 *Soering v. UK*, 7 July 1989, 11 EHRR 439.
28 *M. v. The Home Office* [1993] 3 WLR 433.
29 *Chahal v. UK*, 15 November 1996, 23 EHRR 413.

as in *Chahal*, that extradition was for national security reasons. In such cases the reviewing power of the court was even more circumscribed. The British government asserted that the limited powers of the court in these circumstances were entirely coherent with cases such as *Klass* because the remedies provided were 'as effective as they could be' given the national security context. Indeed, in *Vilvarajah*, the Court had held that judicial review was effective in such circumstances where the Home Secretary ruled on a refusal to grant asylum. However, in *Chahal* the ECtHR took a different approach and distinguished the present case from *Vilvarajah*. The fact that there were national security considerations was not material and the principle that a remedy need only be as 'effective as it could be' had to be assessed in the light that the person deported could suffer ill treatment in breach of Article 3. In such a case the 'irreversible nature of the harm that might occur' necessitated 'independent scrutiny' of the extradition decision, and neither the judicial review function of the Court nor the advisory panel that sat in such cases could provide the effective remedy required.

In *Smith and Grady* v. *UK*, national security considerations were also pleaded by the government and also rejected by the court. The case concerned the MoD's policy of preventing homosexuals from serving in the armed forces. The applicants, who had been soldiers with impeccable service records, had been investigated and discharged from their employment. They argued before the ECtHR that they were victims of the breach of Articles 8 and 13. Their point in relation to Article 13 was similar to that examined above in the different context of *Chahal*. A court judicially reviewing decisions to exclude homosexuals from the military could only ask itself whether the 'policy as a whole' was 'so irrational and perverse' that the policy maker had 'taken leave of his senses'.[30] Only the most absurdly made decision would be susceptible to review on this standard. The applicant's problems were compounded by the fact that they bore the burden of proof. Agreeing that there had been a breach of Article 8, the court went on to consider the 'irrationality' test, and whether it provided an effective remedy. The Court concluded that 'the threshold' was 'placed so high that it effectively excluded any consideration by the domestic courts' of the concerns that, under Article 8, would have made the policy justifiable. The reviewing court would have to be able to assess whether or not the blanket ban on homosexuals in the military was proportionate to the requirements of national security, and also the extent to which the policy answered to a pressing social need. In the absence of such powers of review, there was a breach of Article 13.[31]

What sense do we make of Article 13 jurisprudence? We can see that it comes into play in those instances where executive power seeks to exercise itself. This exercise is clearly limited by the law, but nevertheless remains an expression of the state's power. The ECtHR is attempting to hold a line. On one side of the line executive power

---

30 *Smith and Grady* v. *UK*, 27 September 1999, at para 132. 29 EHRR 493.
31 See also *Paul and Audrey Edwards* v. *UK*, 14 March 2002. Breaches of Articles 2 and 13 were found in respect of an inquiry into the death of the applicant's son in prison. The applicants had not been able to participate fully in the inquiry, and were also unable to recover damages for non-pecuniary damages suffered by the deceased. The Court held that the applicants had not had an 'appropriate' means to determine whether or not the authorities had been negligent in failing to protect their son's right to life.

overextends itself in the direction of arbitrary rule; on the other, it is so limited by the law as to be able to protect democratic institutions from abuse. The risk is that in preventing abuse, the state cedes even greater powers to itself. As the dissenting judgment in *Klass* suggests, the surveillance regime was founded on a failure of checks and balances. To the extent that surveillance is necessary, the checks against its abuse must themselves be robust. The ECtHR can thus perhaps be seen as the initiator of dialogue over institutional reform. It must be remembered, though, that the terms of this dialogue are set by the executive. There are areas of state practice that the court cannot examine.

We can make some similar points about Article 13 and judicial review. Certainly the later cases show that the ECtHR appears to be taking a more robust stand in finding breaches of the Article because of the limitations of judicial review. Although concerns with national security run through the case, we have to be aware that they reflect different contexts: *Chahal* concerned the exigencies of the law of extradition and Article 3; *Smith and Grady* drew attention to policies on the sexual orientation of service personnel and Article 8. The state may now have a harder task in justifying national security considerations, but these cases do not in any way suggest that it is not proper for the state to have this argument available. In this sense, Article 13 runs up against its limits. Sovereign power must retain its superiority to the order of rights.

PROHIBITION OF ABUSE OF RIGHTS: ARTICLE 17

Article 17 is very much concerned with the problem of the limit or the exception.[32] It is framed in terms of the 'limitation' or 'destruction' of rights, and can be thought of as structured on the problem of how and why rights should be limited. Commentators tend to point out that it addresses both individuals and the state. If an individual relies on this right against the state, the Article is invoked as a defence against 'totalitarianism' as the alleged breach relates to the state's own violation of human rights. If the state relies on Article 17 against an individual or a group, the Article is being used to prevent the anti-democratic 'subversion' of rights. This 'double regard' of the Article is perhaps best understood as a single coherent idea. The Article is built on the realisation that the state must be allowed to define the boundaries of political discourse, but that this power must be limited to prevent it being used to abuse the very rights the state is meant to be protecting. Thus, the state can limit political activity if it crosses acceptable boundaries, but its own activities must be subject to similar limits.[33]

---

[32] As commentators have pointed out, Article 17 is dissimilar to Article 13 as it is not free standing and relates necessarily to a breach of another right or rights in the Convention.

[33] Article 17 can be used as a kind of filter – thus in *Glimmerveen and Hagenbeek* v. *Norway* (8348/78; 8406/78) the Commission found that preventing a racist political party from participating in municipal elections was justifiable under Article 17. It was held that the applicants could rely neither on Article 10 of the Convention, nor Article 3 of the First Protocol. Alternatively, it is possible to examine a complaint under a different Article, and thus avoid an Article 17 argument. In *X* v. *Austria* (1747/62) the fact that criminal convictions under Austrian law relating to the promotion of National Socialism could be justified under Articles 9 and 10, meant that it was not necessary to justify them under Article 17.

We can consider a couple of indicative cases that show how the Article can be used to define acceptable political behaviour. In *Remer* v. *Germany*[34] the Commission had to consider a prosecution for Holocaust denial under the German Criminal Code. In examining whether there had been a breach of Article 10 the Commission pointed out that the term 'necessary' within the Article 10(2) implies the existence of a 'pressing social need' and, in terms of the Criminal Code, this related to the need to ensure the peaceful coexistence of citizens. This meant that 'Article 17 ... prevents a person from deriving from the Convention a right to engage in activities aimed at the destruction of any of the rights and freedoms set forth in the Convention, inter alia the right to freedom of expression under Article 10'.[35] There is clearly a problem with the court determining the boundaries of acceptable political speech in anything but the most extreme of situations. The court appeared to have acknowledged this point in *Lehideux and Isorni* v. *France*[36] where they considered a prosecution for the crime of 'public defence of war crimes or crimes of collaboration'.[37] The applicants had published an article in a French newspaper, defending the activities of Marshal Petain:[38]

> The Court considers that it is not its task to settle this point, which is part of an ongoing debate among historians about the events in question and their interpretation. As such, it does not belong to the category of clearly established historical facts – such as the Holocaust – whose negation or revision would be removed from the protection of Article 10 by Article 17.

Note that discussion of Marshal Petain's wartime record cannot be equated with Holocaust denial. In *De Becker*[39] the court clarified one of the key principles of Article 17 jurisprudence: the Article is 'limited in scope', and designed only to cover 'persons who threaten the democratic system of the Contracting Parties'. Article 17 would clearly catch Holocaust denial and other forms of racist politics.[40]

When a state uses the Article against an individual, it is necessary for its actions to be 'proportionate' to the seriousness of the threat. The Article cannot therefore be used to deprive people of their Convention rights in their entirety. *Lawless* v. *Ireland*[41] shows the precise terms of this aspect of the Article. The applicant was a

---

34 *Remer* v. *Germany* (25096/94).
35 Ibid.
36 *Lehideux and Isorni* v. *France*, 23 September 1998, 30 EHRR 665.
37 Ibid.
38 The ECtHR held that that prosecution under Article 10 had been disproportionate, and hence it was not necessary to apply Article 17.
39 *De Becker* v. *Belgium* [1958] 59 YB 214.
40 Has the Court remained consistent with this principle? See *Norwood* v. *UK*, 16 November 2004. The applicant displayed a poster expressing anti-Islamic sentiments. There was no breach of Articles 10 or 14, as the display of the poster was covered by Article 17. See also *Garaudy* v. *France*, 24 June 2003. Article 17 applied to a book on Holocaust denial. Therefore there was no breach of Article 10 in prohibiting a book's publication. Also *W.P. and Others* v. *Poland*, 2 September 2004. Article 17 applied so that the applicants could not argue a breach of Articles 11 and 14 in prohibiting the formation of an association called 'The National and Patriotic Association of Polish Victims of Bolshevism and Zionism'.
41 *Lawless* v. *Ireland* [1979–80] 1 EHRR 15.

member of the IRA who had been detained without trial under the Irish Offences Against the State Act. Lawless was arguing that his detention amounted to breaches of Articles 5, 6, 7 and 13. The part of the Irish government's argument that we are interested in relates to Article 17. They asserted that as Lawless had been involved in subversive activities he would not be able to allege breaches of his human rights. The Commission disagreed. The object of the Article 17 was to prevent groups undermining the Convention. This did not mean that members of political or terrorist groups could be deprived of their Convention rights. The ECtHR then went on to distinguish *Lawless* from the case that concerned the banning of the German Communist Party.[42] The ban was legitimate because it prevented the Communist Party from engaging in activities that were designed to subvert democratic government. The facts of *Lawless* were different. Even though the applicant was a member of the IRA, the Irish government could not rely on Article 17 to justify arbitrary arrest and trial. Lawless was not relying on Convention rights to justify his activities, but was addressing the fact that he had been deprived of fundamental human rights relating to his detention.

In the case of *Refah Partisi (the Welfare Party)* v. *Turkey*[43] the Turkish government's attempt to dissolve the Welfare Party came under consideration. The government was alleging that the Welfare Party's political programme was subversive of the secular values on which the state was founded. Members of the Welfare Party were alleged to have made certain statements in favour of sharia law and the wearing of headscarves in public places. The Welfare Party was arguing that any ban on their political activities could not be justified under either Article 11 or Article 17. In relation to the latter, they asserted that they were not a totalitarian party. The Turkish Constitution Court, which heard the case, asserted that secularism was the very foundation of the values of the Turkish state, and was also justified on pluralist principles: 'Persons of different beliefs, desiring to live together, were encouraged to do so by the State's egalitarian attitude towards them'. This implied a right of the state to 'supervise and oversee religious matters'. The Welfare Party's assertion of the supremacy of Sharia law was incompatible with the dominance of secular values. In considering the case through the lens of Article 11(2), the ECtHR argued that it was necessary to review whether the ban on a party was 'necessary in a democratic society'. Answering this question was a prerequisite to considering the Article 17 point.

The ECtHR referred back to the judgment that had been made in the United Communist Party of Turkey case. They had asserted that there was a fundamental link between democracy and the legal order that stems from the Convention and is evidenced by the preamble that makes reference to a 'common heritage' of European democracy. This implied the importance of both political parties and political pluralism. Democracy required the integrity of the process whereby different political programmes could be put before an electorate. It followed that there were 'limits' to the programmes that political parties could put forward. While it was necessary that parties could put

---

42   Application No. 250/57 (1 Yearbook 222).
43   *Refah Partisi (the Welfare Party) and Others* v. *Turkey*, 13 February 2003 [2001] ECHR 495.

forward and recommend for debate issues that were considered 'irksome'[44] there were conditions attached to the way in which a party could promote legal change:

> [F]irstly, the means used to that end must be legal and democratic; secondly, the change proposed must itself be compatible with fundamental democratic principles. It necessarily follows that a political party whose leaders incite to violence or put forward a policy which fails to respect democracy or which is aimed at the destruction of democracy and the flouting of the rights and freedoms recognised in a democracy cannot lay claim to the Convention's protection against penalties imposed on those grounds.[45]

Behind democracy lay a 'compromise' where those enjoying the freedoms of democratic society must agree to certain limits in the name of the 'stability' of the community as a whole.[46] From this perspective, and considering the evidence about the claims that Welfare Party officials had made, the Court considered that there had been no breach of Article 11, and that therefore there was no need to examine whether there had been a breach of Article 17.

We can perhaps think of Article 17 as policing the boundaries of acceptable political discourse. The reflections on the nature of democratic politics in the Welfare Party case are not profound, but the case does suggest that the ECtHR sees its role as the protection and inculcation of democratic values. The negotiations of difference that are required in political debate means that unpopular views have to be tolerated and a broad spectrum of political parties allowed.[47] These most minimum conditions of democratic political culture do not extend to parties sponsoring racism or advocating violent change.

LIMITATIONS ON USE OF RESTRICTIONS ON RIGHTS: ARTICLE 18

Article 18 can be read alongside Article 17. The language of 'limitation' and 'destruction' in Article 17 was clearly too limited to deal with the problem of the restriction of rights.[48] However, although the Convention itself goes to such lengths to limit the

---

44 Ibid., para 97.
45 Ibid.
46 Ibid., para 99.
47 In *United Communist Party of Turkey* v. *Turkey* (1998) 26 EHRR 121. The ECtHR considered a ban by the Turkish Government on the United Communist Party of Turkey ('the TBKP'). The Turkish Constitutional Court had held that the party's commitment to minority rights undermined the unity of the state. The ECtHR held that there had been a violation of Article 11. The Turkish government had argued that because the TBKP were in breach of Article 17, the Article 11 argument did not arise. This argument was supported by reference to the terrorism that was being used against the Turkish state. The ECtHR disagreed with the Turkish government on a matter of fact: the constitution of the TBKP did not commit the party to violence, nor was there any indication that it was not a democratic party. On these facts, there was a breach of Article 11, and Article 17 was not applicable.
48 Supra n. 3, at 1094. Breaches of Article 18 can thus be found in the following areas: the restriction placed in Articles 8–11; Article 2 of the Fourth Protocol, and Article 1 of the Seventh Protocol. Article 18 could also be pleaded in relation to those Articles that exclude people or areas from their application (Article 4(3)), Article 10's exclusion in the second sentence; Article 11(2) and Article 12. Article 18 could also be linked to Articles 15, 16 and 17. This can be seen in *De Becker* v. *Belgium*. De Becker had been accused of collaborating with the Nazis,

state's power to restrict rights, the jurisprudence suggests that Article 18 has been interpreted with a broad margin of appreciation in favour of the state. Arai has argued[49] that Article 18 can be compared to the French public law doctrine of misuse of power (*detournement de pouvoir*). As with the French doctrine, an argument under Article 18 raises a question of the state's motive in placing a restriction on a right; most specifically, it would have to be shown that the motive was not coherent with the restrictions provided by the Convention itself. While this does not amount to showing bad faith, it does place an 'onerous burden of proof' on the person alleging the breach of the Article. In reality, it is very difficult to lead evidence on the 'real motive' of the state, and the applicant would have to rely on difficult arguments about 'inferring' the real motive from the state's action. The case law suggests that it is only in exceptional cases where this argument has succeeded.[50] It is also interesting that in *Bozano*[51] the French Court determined that there had been a misuse of power, while the Commission did not hold that there had been a breach of Article 18.[52]

An approach that suggested that the Commission might take a slightly different approach to the Article was suggested in *Handyside v. UK*.[53] The case concerned the applicant's prosecution under the Obscene Publications Act 1959 for the circulation of a children's book entitled *The Little Red School Book*. Although the case was primarily argued in relation to Article 10, a breach of Article 18 was also pleaded. Handyside lost the case as the book's suppression was justified under 10(2); however, it has been suggested that the Commission at least 'felt a need to evaluate the claim that Article 18 had been violated'.[54] When the Court came to consider the case, they did refer to the applicant's allegations that 'the truth of the matter' was 'an attempt had been made to muzzle a small-scale publisher whose political leanings met with the disapproval of a fragment of public opinion'.[55] While the Commission continued to develop, at least in some cases, this approach to Article 18, the Court has preferred a much narrower test.

Article 18 is not free standing and autonomous. As the Court stressed in *Gusinskiy v. Russia*[56] breach of the Article can only be argued in conjunction with another Article of the Convention. The second important consideration is that the Article can only apply when one of the restrictions of rights determined by the Convention is breached. Thus in *Gusinskiy*, the Court found that there was a breach of 5(1)(c) and Article 18 when the applicant had been pressured to sell his business to a state-owned company while under detention. In *Engel v. Netherlands*[57] the complaints related to disciplinary punishments to which conscript soldiers in the Dutch Army

---

and condemned to death under the Belgian Penal Code, although his sentence was later commuted to a period of imprisonment. The court argued that provisions that were made under Article 15 that related to German occupation of the country were not acceptable if they breached Article 18.

49   Ibid.
50   See *Gusinskiy v. Russia*, 19 May 2004 [2004] ECHR 205.
51   *Bozano v. France*, 18 December 1984.
52   Supra n. 3, at 1100.
53   *Handyside v. UK*, 7 December 1976; 1 EHRR 737.
54   Supra n. 3, at 1099.
55   Supra n. 53, at para 52.
56   Supra n. 50.
57   *Engel v. Netherlands*, judgment 8 June 1976.

had been subjected. The applicants argued that disciplinary proceedings had been taken against them in order to deprive them of Article 6 rights that would have applied to criminal proceedings; they also argued that the disciplinary proceedings were a breach of their right under Article 11 to trade union freedom, and that these breaches amounted to a breach of Article 18. The Court disagreed with both these arguments – also holding that there was no breach of Article 10.

Restricting the scope of Article 18 risks reducing it to little or no purpose.[58] This would show a failure of the ECtHR to develop a jurisprudence that takes the problem of the restriction seriously. The abuse in *Gusinskiy* was so flagrant as to make this case a bad indicator of the more everyday and small-scale restrictions that can be used to cut down the scope of rights. Indeed, the Court were alive to this 'creeping' restriction of rights when they held in *De Becker* v. *Belgium*[59] that the Article prevented the state relying on derogations once the reason for making it had passed. The sense that the Article is very much 'auxiliary' to breach of other Articles also does little to determine a more compelling jurisprudence of the restriction.

Thus far, our discussion has primarily concerned itself with the part that law plays in democratic culture. As argued in the introduction, our interest in integrity rights includes the way in which law defines itself. We now need to examine the Articles of the Convention and the Protocols that allow us to speak of the integral nature of legal processes as defined through human rights.

NO PUNISHMENT WITHOUT LAW: ARTICLE 7

As commentators have stressed, this Article forms a 'primordial part' of the Convention and no derogation is allowed from it even in time of war.[60] The title of the Article shows that it applies to retrospective penal legislation. This is built on two fundamental principles of criminal justice, outlined in 7.1: *nullum crimen sine lege* and *nulla poena sine lege*. These are the principles that a criminal conviction has to be based on the breach of a law that existed at the time of the offence, and that the punishment for the offence cannot be harsher than that specified by the law that was in force at this time. In *Kokkinakis*[61] the ECtHR argued that 7(1) was not restricted to merely the prohibition of retrospective criminal law and developed a third principle: a court should not interpret criminal law to the detriment of the accused. The threshold for this condition is that the criminal law is clear enough for an individual to be certain under what conditions s/he is liable to criminal penalty.

One of the main issues that emerges in the Strasbourg jurisprudence relates to the clarity and accessibility of the law. This is entirely consistent with broader provisions in the theory and practice of human rights, which are set against secret courts and bodies of rules that are not publicly available. Not surprisingly, therefore, the cases draw attention to those areas of national security where a degree of secrecy is

---

58   Harris *et al.* (1995: 515).
59   Supra n. 39.
60   Supra n. 3. at 652.
61   *Kokkinakis* v. *Greece*, 22 June 2000.

arguably necessary even in a democratic society. In *Grigoriades*[62] the ECtHR argued that although the offence of insulting the army was very broadly drawn, it was not in breach of Article 7. Likewise, in *Baskaya and Okcuolu*[63] an offence in Turkish law directed against those who disseminate 'propaganda against the indivisibility of the State' was seen as acceptable because it was necessary for there to be a degree of flexibility in criminal law.

The threshold for Article 7 was also raised in *Ireland* v. *UK*[64] where, in an interstate application, the Republic of Ireland argued that portions of the Northern Ireland Act 1972 fell foul of Article 7 as they created a retrospective offence of not complying with an order of the security forces. However, the Court did not go on to hear the case, as the Attorney General of the UK undertook that the Act would not be applied retrospectively.

The precise operation of Article 7 was tested in *Streltz, Kessler and Krenz and K.-H.W.* v. *Germany*.[65] An important distinction was made in this case between law and practice. The applicants were arguing that the shooting dead of people attempting to cross the border of the GDR was unlawful. According to the law then in force, the actions of the border guards was indeed in breach of Constitutional and other provisions. The case fell outside of Article 7 because the fatal shootings were not therefore a legal penalty.

The doctrine of precedent has also been challenged under Article 7. It would amount to a breach of Article 7 if a judge interpreted the law so as to introduce a new offence with the result that an act or a failure to act which it was not reasonable to foresee as subject to criminal penalty at the time, becomes so at a later date. Although *Shaw* and *Knuller* were not challenged in the ECtHR it would be interesting to speculate as to whether or not these cases would have been in breach of Article 7. While the House of Lords' discovery of a new crime of offences against public morals does amount to retrospective legislation, it might be possible to argue that the offence was reasonably foreseeable. A case that did end up before the ECHR, *X Ltd and Y* v. *UK*[66] concerned the prosecution of *Gay News* for the offence of blasphemy.[67] There was no breach of Article 7 as the court's interpretation of blasphemy amounted to a clarification of the original offence, rather than the creation of a new offence.

In two cases concerning rape in marriage, *S.W.* v. *UK*[68] and *C.R.* v. *UK*[69] the ECtHR asserted that the doctrinal development of the common law was consistent with Article 7 as the judicial developments were 'consistent with the essence of the offence' and reasonably foreseeable. Thus, the abolition of the rule that a man could not be guilty of raping his wife was both foreseeable, and, given the nature of rape, it was not open to an individual to argue that he had been arbitrarily prosecuted.

---

62 *Grigoriades* v. *Greece*, 25 November 1997.
63 *Baskaya and Okcuolu* v. *Turkey*, 8 July 1999.
64 *Ireland* v. *UK* 15 YB76 [1972].
65 *Streltz, Kessler and Krenz and K.-H.W.* v. *Germany*, 22 March 2001.
66 *X and Y* v. *UK* No. 8710/79; 22 DR 77.
67 See *Whitehouse* v. *Lemon* [1979] AC 617.
68 *S.W.* v. *UK*, 22 November 1995.
69 *C.R.* v. *UK*, 22 November 1995.

PROTOCOL 7

In thinking about Protocol 7, our concern is primarily how it allows us to think about the requirements of criminal law from a human rights perspective. The Protocol also tells us something about the European legal order, as defined in opposition to those non-European 'others' who are seeking entry, or have become resident within a European nation.

Our concern will be, first of all, with the distinctions that the Protocol draws between the provisions that relate to criminal law, and those that apply to immigration and asylum law. Arguably, the Convention delineates the criminal justice system as separate and distinct from the systems that deal with asylum and immigration. While this is not unreasonable, unscrupulous governments (for reasons given below) could exploit it. Article 1 provides that an alien in lawful residence can only be expelled by a decision of law. Commentators have stressed that by referring to a 'resident alien' this Article does not apply to those who have just arrived at an airport or border and have not yet been subjected to immigration controls. The 'resident alien' has the right to make a case as to why s/he should not be expelled, a right to representation and the right to have his case reviewed, unless there are compelling reasons of national security to prohibit such a course of action. This can be contrasted with Article 2. This Article contains the right to appeal against conviction or sentence for a criminal offence. This right can be limited in cases of a minor character, and for other technical reasons. The main point is that Article 2 probably does not apply to Article 1. In other words, a deportation order would not be subject to a right of appeal, although, under the terms of Article 1, it might be subject to review. This right could be suspended, and there would then be no way in which Article 2 could be invoked. This argument is interesting from the perspective of the interface of the regimes of immigration law and criminal law. It would appear that the former is more draconian than the latter. It is therefore interesting to note that, at least in the UK, anti-terrorism measures make great use of powers of deportation.

The Protocol goes on to outline other rights that must be minimum conditions of criminal justice systems. Article 3 provides a right to compensation for miscarriages of justice. This must be read alongside Article 5(5), which provides compensation for unlawful detention. The Article contains seven conditions that must apply before compensation is awarded. We are not too concerned with these, as our key interest is why this Article is important. It is central to the regime of the Convention as it provides a way of ensuring that criminal justice is able to monitor and correct itself. It would clearly be a breach of human rights if an individual had been subject to a miscarriage of justice. This is defined as 'some serious failure in the judicial process involving a grave prejudice to the convicted person'.[70] This suggests that miscarriage is to be understood narrowly. The words 'serious' and 'grave' indicate that the Article is concerned with only the most extreme abuses of the criminal justice process. The state is thus under

---

70   Explanatory Report on Protocol 7, para 23.

an obligation to provide a remedy to the aggrieved person(s). The whole schema of the Article presupposes courts independent of the executive.

We can make some similar points about Article 4. The principle behind this Article is expressed in the maxim '*ne bis in idem*'. The principle prohibits trial or punishment for an offence for which a person has already been tried or committed within the same jurisdiction. In other words, an individual could be prosecuted and convicted of the same offence in different jurisdictions. However, the Article does not prevent the reopening of the case if new evidence or facts come to light; or if there is a 'fundamental defect' in the proceedings that impacted on the 'outcome of the case'. Within the Convention, this Article adds to the rights provided by Article 6, which is otherwise arguably silent on double jeopardy.

If we review these Articles in the round, a number of points can be made. There is the clear sense in which they are supplemental to Convention rights. For instance, Article 6 does not appear to mandate a right of appeal that is contained in Article 2; Article 3 provides a more general right than that provided by Article 5(5) and Article 4 also clarifies a matter that does not seem to be implied by Article 6. We would also have to consider the abolition of the death penalty in Article 1 of the Sixth Protocol. This would take us towards a substantive discussion of Articles 2 and 3 of the Convention, which we cannot do here.

The Protocols go some way to clarify the ideal structure of criminal justice. Criminal justice is thus distinct from the body of asylum or immigration law that regulates those who are to become subjects of national law and differentiates between those who are subjects of European human rights, and those who have a more marginal status. To get a better sense of this distinction, we need to turn to the Fourth and Sixth Protocols. According to Article 2, those lawfully within a territory have liberty of movement. This can be read in the context of Article 3, the right of 'nationals' not to be expelled from or forbidden entry to the territory of a state. These rights have to be seen within the much broader context of the rights and civil liberties protected by the Convention that go some way to define citizenship. Non-citizens are not deprived of rights completely. They have fewer rights than citizens. Thus, in terms of the Protocols, Article 4 of the Fourth Protocol provides the prohibition of the 'collective expulsion' of aliens, and we can see how this interfaces with Article 1 of the Seventh Protocol.

CONCLUSION

The distinction that we have made in this chapter between democratic political culture and the way in which the law defines itself is not meant to be hard and fast. Indeed, the two elements of the argument can be brought together to suggest that democratic law does indeed have content: those values and principles that define the basic standards laid down by the Convention and its Protocols. This content is not unproblematic. Indeed, we have described the fundamental distinction the Convention makes between Europe and its others, those who are subject to the rules of asylum and immigration and have lesser rights than European citizens. This boundary creates a zone where Convention rights attempt to define law's proper place in a democratic order where executive power is limited by its obligations to protect human rights. This zone is also therefore bounded by those restrictions and exceptions that define when the state can make use of its sovereign power. In theory this is to protect the normal functioning of human rights, but the Convention acknowledges that the most important concern is precisely the way in which the restriction and the limit, the derogation and the reservation, are both the necessary conditions of, and the most serious threat to, the very possibility of a human rights regime.

10

THE GENERAL JURISPRUDENCE OF HUMAN RIGHTS

INTRODUCTION

This chapter will argue that we can now talk of a general jurisprudence of human rights that exists within the English common law as a body of principles relating to the interpretation and application of the Human Rights Act (HRA) 1998. This body of jurisprudence draws on areas of public law, such as judicial review, but is perhaps most properly thought of as a set of procedures and principles that relate to generic concerns under the Act. This general jurisprudence is related to, but distinct from, the substantive jurisprudence of the Convention. While a great many of the cases we will examine refer to Article 6, we will not read the jurisprudence of the Act narrowly through any single Article. The general procedural jurisprudence that we will attempt to outline can be related back to our argument about integrity rights and the links between law and democracy.

The matters that fall into the general jurisprudence can be described as follows: we will be concerned, first of all, with the general structure of the Act and the mechanisms that it sets up. We will then turn our attention to the linked concerns of the vertical and horizontal effect of the HRA and the vexed question of the definition of public authority. After examining the equally troubled question of the Act's retrospective effect, we will look at the relationship of common law and European human rights law, and the question of whether or not the judges have seized upon the HRA as a catalyst to develop an indigenous human rights law that draws on the traditions of common law as much as the European legal inheritance. We will conclude with some brief observations on the nature of the general jurisprudence of human rights.

THE HUMAN RIGHTS ACT 1998: AN OVERVIEW

As commentators have argued, one of the important areas of argument that has opened up in the jurisprudence of the HRA is the relationship between the court's interpretation of legislation under sections 2 and 3, and the power to issue declarations of incompatibility under section 4.

Section 2(1) of the Act is quite complicated to read, because it brings together at least two major concerns: the interpretative power of the court, and the issue of the Act's retrospective effect. We will deal primarily with the first issue, as a later section will concern itself with retrospectivity. The section specifies that in the interpretation of Convention rights,[1] a court or tribunal must take into account a number of sources of European human rights law[2] if 'in the opinion of the court or tribunal, it is relevant to the proceedings in which that question has arisen'. The court thus has a discretion to determine whether or not the authorities are relevant to the proceedings in question; even if they predate the Act.[3] The Act then goes on to state at 3(1), that as far as the interpretation of legislation is concerned, primary legislation and subordinate or delegated legislation must be read and given effect so that they are compatible with Convention rights, 'so far as it is possible to do so'. Once again, the court has a wide discretion to determine whether or not legislation is Convention compliant. Section 3(2) concerns the extent of this section's operation. It applies, first of all, to primary legislation and subordinate legislation whenever enacted. Bear in mind that incompatibility does not affect the validity or continuing operation of any provision, or the validity or continued operation of incompatible subordinate legislation, if the primary legislation from which it is derived prevents the removal of that incompatibility.[4]

What, then, should happen in the event of a court determining that legislation is incompatible with a Convention right? This takes us to section 4. Section 4(2) states that when a court[5] finds that a provision is incompatible with a Convention right, it may make a declaration of that incompatibility.[6] What effect does a declaration of incompatibility have? We need to look at section 10: 10(1) states that if a provision of legislation has been declared incompatible, and if certain conditions are satisfied with reference to the fact that there will not be an appeal against this incompatibility, then a minister may, under section 10(2), make such an order that the incompatibility will be removed. The Act states that the minister 'may' make an order if there are 'compelling reasons' for so doing. It is not a duty to make an order, because this would effectively

---

1   That is, those under the European Convention on Human Rights – ECHR.
2   These are: (a) judgment, decision, declaration or advisory opinion of the European Court of Human Rights; (b) opinion of the Commission given in a report adopted under Article 31 of the Convention; (c) certain decisions of the Commission in connection with Articles 26 and 27 of the Convention; or (d) decisions of the Committee of Ministers taken under Article 46 of the Convention.
3   Section 2(1) states that the relevant source can be taken into account 'whenever made or given'.
4   Lewis contrasts s.2 of the HRA with 3(1) of the EC Act 1972, which states that UK courts are bound by the decisions of the ECJ, 729. Later, he cites Masterman's rationale for the structure of the HRA, which in turn (at least for the first three points) are taken from statements of Lord Irvine during Parliamentary debate. Domestic courts are not bound to follow the ECtHR because: (a) the Convention is the 'ultimate' source of law but has 'no strict rule of precedent' (731); (b) the Convention states that the UK is bound only by rulings in cases in which it was a party; (c) [from the White Paper] the common law courts must be free to develop Convention law; and (d) as the judgments of the ECtHR are 'declaratory' in nature, it is difficult to follow them as precedent decisions. Lewis cites Clayton's argument (below) that there is a difference between the way in which the ECtHR and common law courts produce their decisions. This makes it all the more necessary to qualify strict adherence to the mirror principle and to develop indigenous interpretations of the Convention.
5   A court is defined as (4(5)): the House of Lords; the Judicial Committee of the Privy Council; the Courts-Martial Appeal Court; in Scotland, the High Court of Justiciary sitting otherwise than as a trial court or the Court of Session; in England and Wales or Northern Ireland, the High Court or the Court of Appeal.
6   Note that, by 4(6), a declaration of incompatibility under this section affects neither the validity, continuing operation, nor the enforcement of the provision in respect of which it is given; and, secondly, the declaration is not binding on the parties to the proceedings in which it is made.

mean that a court could compel a change in the law. The Human Rights Act thus leaves the sovereignty of Parliament in place.[7]

The interpretation of sections 3 and 4 has shown itself to be one of the sites where the scope of the Act has been fought out. As Nicol has observed,[8] those judges 'who wish the HRA to ensure that the Convention rights as interpreted by the European Court of Human Rights become the supreme law of the land' take a broad approach to section 3 that enables the court to strain the literal meaning of an Act to find a Convention-compliant interpretation.[9] Nicol opposes this interpretative faction to those who understand the Act as 'a unique participatory instrument', which must involve the courts and Parliament in a dialogue over the extent of human rights in common law. This tendency prefers narrower interpretations of section 3, with the concomitant reliance on declarations under section 4. Thus, underlying the disagreements over the scope of the Act are different understandings of 'constitutional fundamentals'.[10] Has this argument been resolved in the wake of *Anderson* in favour of the narrow interpretation of section 3? We will examine this claim, and Kavanagh's counter argument[11] in the following section.[12]

In *R. v. A.*,[13] the House of Lords interpreted section 41 of the Criminal Evidence Act 1999 in the light of Article 6. Section 41 prevented evidence being given about the complainant's sexual history without the leave of the court. The instances where the court could allow this kind of evidence were narrowly drawn. Despite the clarity of the wording of the section, the House of Lords interpreted the Act so as to make it compatible with Article 6. In Lord Steyn's judgment, the interpretative powers given to the court under section 3 were broad enough to allow a 'linguistically strained interpretation', even when there was no ambiguity in the Act. Can *Re S* be seen as a reaction to the 'judicial overkill' of *R. v. A.*? The Court of Appeal interpreted the Children Act 1989 in such a way as to make it compatible with Articles 8 and 6. The House of Lords disagreed with this approach, asserting that section 3 did not allow a court to read a statute in such a way as to depart from 'a fundamental feature of the Act':

> [A] meaning which departs substantially from a fundamental feature of an Act of Parliament is likely to have crossed the boundary between interpretation and amendment. This is especially so where the departure has practical repercussions which the

---

7   How often are Declarations of Incompatibility issued? Since 2000, there have been eight declarations relating to various areas of law: mental health, immigration, taxation, offences against the person, sentencing, and embryology. (Statistics based on information supplied to the Human Rights Unit by the Human Rights Act Research Unit, Doughty Street Chambers, London, based on cases reported in Lawtel Human Rights Interactive and Butterworths Human Rights Direct from case transcripts available from 2 October 2000 to 13 December 2001.)
8   Nicol (2004).
9   This approach obviates the need to issue a declaration of incompatibility, and the tension that might result if Parliament does not agree.
10 Ibid., 274.
11 Kavanagh (2004).
12 More detailed discussion of the key cases, *R. v. A.* and *Re S* is contained in the chapter on statutory interpretation.
13 *R. v. A.* [2001] UKHL 25.

court is not equipped to evaluate. In such a case the overall contextual setting may have no scope for rendering the statutory provision Convention compliant by legitimate use of the process of interpretation.[14]

This argument returns to many of the themes that we discussed in earlier chapters. It rests on the distinction between the functions of the executive and the courts. The former are far more able to create policy and assess its impact, as the court is fundamentally passive and limited to responding to the evidence given by parties to a dispute. Judges must therefore restrain the uses that they make of section 3. Lord Nicholls was especially critical of Lord Steyn's position. It was not the case that only express words indicating that Parliament intended that an Act was incompatible with the Convention would limit the court's interpretative duty. There thus appears to be a departure from R. v. A. in Re S – a line of reasoning that was confirmed in Anderson.[15] The argument pressed upon the House of Lords in Anderson was that as the sentencing powers of the Home Secretary in section 29 of the Criminal (Sentences) Act 1997 were incompatible with Article 6, their Lordships should read into this section a requirement for the Home Secretary's power to be limited by the recommendation of the trial judge and the Lord Chief Justice. The House of Lords refused to accept this position, and were unanimous in their agreement that reading section 29 in this way would exceed the interpretative powers of section 3. Lords Bingham, Steyn and Hutton agreed with Lord Nicholls's speech in Re S.

Nicol observes that even Lord Steyn performed a *'volte face'* and appeared to retreat from the arguments made in R. v. A. Precisely because a panel of seven Law Lords decided Anderson, it represents a resolution of the argument about the scope of the court's interpretative powers in the understanding of the position of the court articulated by Lord Nicholls. Later cases, such as Bellinger v. Bellinger[16] are coherent with Anderson. In the former, Lord Steyn referred to Lord Nicholls's speech and, in the latter, a certificate of incompatibility was issued, rather than subject the Matrimonial Causes Act 1973 to a strained reading.

Are we therefore to accept that Re S and Anderson represent the correct statement of the limits of section 3? Kavanagh argues that the significant differences of fact between R. v. A. and Re S mean that Re S cannot be given the status accorded to it by Nicol. R. v. A. concerned judicial interpretation of a specific section of the 1999 Act. In Re S, there were no sections of the Children Act 1989 that could be singled out. The Court of Appeal was thus forced to consider (in Hale LJ's words), not so much what the Act said, but what it did not say.[17] Re S cannot, therefore, be seen as dealing with the same issue as R. v. A. Furthermore, whereas the consequences of the Court of Appeal's decision in Re S would have had significant cost implications for local authorities, R. v. A. concerned an area in which the courts have much greater competence: the regulation of the forensic process. Re S cannot be read

---

14 Re S [2002] UKHL 10, at 41.
15 R. (on the application of Anderson) v. Secretary of State for the Home Department [2002] UKHL 46.
16 Bellinger v. Bellinger [2002] 1 All ER 311.
17 Supra n. 11, at 538.

as a more general statement of a correct judicial attitude to section 3. As Kavanagh puts it:

> Section 3(1) should not be used as a way of radically reforming a whole statute or writing a quasi legislative code granting new powers and setting out new procedures to replace that statute. However, that does not necessarily mean that the decision rules out the type of 'reading in' which was adopted in R. v. A.[18]

If this argument is correct, then cases such as *Anderson* must be seen as specific responses to statutes, rather than as evidence of a coherent judicial attitude adopted to section 3. The refusal of the House of Lords in *Anderson* to read limitations into the power of the Home Secretary under section 29 of the 1997 Act can be explained by reference to the context in which the case was heard. The ECtHR had just issued two rulings against the UK holding that section 29 was in breach of Article 6. As the government was thus 'legally obliged'[19] to change the law, there would have been no point in making a strained interpretation of section 29 and, thus, the better course of action was to issue a certificate of incompatibility. Bellinger shows that the 'case by case' or 'limited' law-making powers of the court were not suitable to interpret the Matrimonial Causes Act in a radical way; it was correct to issue a declaration of incompatibility so that Parliament could assess the policy implications of changes in the law.

What do we make of these two positions? Perhaps the precise scope of section 3 is still open and that (for the most part) the Law Lords are seeking a working relation, rather than a confrontation with Parliament. Klug[20] has specifically taken the notion of dialogue as the key to understanding the operation of the Act:

> Behind the construction of ss.3 and 4 was a carefully thought-out constitutional arrangement that sought to inject principles of parliamentary accountability and transparency into judicial proceedings without removing whole policy areas to judicial determination. In other words it sought to create a new dynamic between the two branches of the State.[21]

Klug argues that Lord Hope's approach in R. v. A. is much closer to the spirit of the Act than that of Lord Steyn. The 'dialogic' relationship envisaged by the Act requires the judges to have the 'courage' to issue declarations, and to engage actively the dialogue with the executive, rather than to see declarations as a last ditch measure. Declarations cannot therefore be seen as a distortion of the judges' relation to Parliament; rather, they are part of a vision of the legislature, the executive and the judiciary 'influencing' each other.

Whether or not this means that *Anderson* correctly states their position is open to question. However, evidence on declarations of incompatibility also suggests that the

---

18   Ibid., 540.
19   Ibid., 542.
20   Klug (2003).
21   Ibid., at 130.

Act is opening up a dialogue between the courts and the executive. The Department of Constitutional Affairs' (DCA) review on the implementation of the HRA specifies that declarations have been made in 15 cases, two of which were under appeal at the time the report was published. In the majority of instances, the government has responded with legislation that has removed the incompatibility by amending primary legislation.[22]

How can we assess the significance of these figures? The DCA report puts them in the context of the HRA's impact on policy and the policy-making process. The fundamental problem is the difficulty of isolating the effect of the Act in the complex series of inputs that feed into policy.[23] The report asserts that overall, on the evidence available, there has been a 'significant' and 'beneficial' influence of the Act on central government.[24] The Act has led to the formalisation of policy-making processes, and has arguably made for changes of behaviour within public authorities, as they become more sensitive to human rights issues. Moreover, litigation under the Act has led to changes in policy and the methods of its implementation. Furthermore, the Act has ensured that the needs of the diverse groups that make up the population of the UK are represented in policy making, promoting 'greater personalisation' and thus 'better public services'. This does indeed suggest that sections 2, 3 and 4 have created mechanisms that have enabled a dialogue to develop between the courts and central and local government. Any substantive assessment of these policy networks would take us beyond the scope of this chapter but we could argue that the HRA has had a structural impact in these areas, and that human rights have become more central to the processes and policies aimed at the delivery of public services. That this was one of the primary aims of the Act takes us towards our next major topic: the definition of public authorities.

PUBLIC AUTHORITIES

What is a public authority?[25]

As has been pointed out, the term 'public authority' was not given a global definition by the Act[26] and it is not an expression defined by the law generally. Given the

---

22 DCA, Review of the Implementation of the Human Rights Act, 20 July 2006. In only one instance was a remedial order issued.
23 Any assessment also depends on the assessor's point of view. For instance, someone assessing whether or not targets for delivery of social services are met is unlikely to be particularly concerned with the role played by the HRA; any consideration of the regulatory framework of the delivery of public services would have to contend with the centrality of the HRA.
24 Supra n. 22, at 22.
25 Section 6(1) of the HRA specifies that it is unlawful for a public authority to act in a way that is incompatible with a Convention right. There is then an important exception to this rule: s.6(1) does not apply to an act of a Public Authority if, as detailed by s.6(2), the authority could not have acted differently because of primary legislation; or in the case of provisions made under primary legislation, which cannot be read in a way which is compatible with the Convention rights, the authority was acting so as to give effect to or enforce those provisions.
26 In s.6(3) a 'public authority' is defined as including a 'court or tribunal' and 'person, certain of whose functions are functions of a public nature'. Note that the definition of a public authority does not include either House of Parliament or a person exercising functions in connection with proceedings in Parliament.

inherent ambiguities of the term, any attempt to grasp its meaning must return to the purpose of the HRA. In a broad sense, the purpose of section 6 is to make 'those bodies for whose acts the state is answerable before the European Court of Human Rights'[27] subject to the rights of the Convention. Thus a public authority must be understood as a 'governmental' body but perhaps this simply introduces another word whose ultimate meaning is unclear. However, it is possible to say which bodies fall within the term. The core meaning of the term would include 'government departments, local authorities, the police and the armed forces'.[28] This would allow us to suggest that a body is governmental to the extent that it possesses 'special powers', is funded by the public, accountable democratically, and constrained to act 'in the public interest'. One consequence of this argument would be that a body that falls within this 'core' definition is not itself a subject of human rights, and thus has no right to action under the Human Rights Act. This is supported by Article 34 of the Convention, which defines those capable of exercising Convention rights as individuals, 'non governmental organizations or groups of individuals'.[29] While this approach provides some certainty to the definition of public authority, there are other complicating factors.

We need to think about the concept of public authority within the context of the modern state, where the tasks of government are organised in different ways. The reality in the UK, particularly since the reforms begun by Margaret Thatcher's regime, is that private bodies now carry out functions that were once within the public sector. Although privatisation is not behind all instances where a private body is given a public function, the commitment of Tony Blair's administration and the present Labour government to market-orientated reforms means that private operators increasingly take over public functions. This begs interesting questions. In the area of transport, for example, there are 'public/private initiatives' that tie in state agencies and private contractors. Are the latter covered by human rights legislation?[30] We could say that the HRA will not apply if the nature of the act is not a 'function of a public nature' but how are we to understand the distinction between public and private? This question is all the more pressing as the Act is silent on the nature of this distinction. A further problem is the nature of 'hybrid public authorities' – or those bodies which exercise both private and public functions. At issue is the 'width' of the definition of 'function of a public nature'; the wider the definition, the more it will cover the kind of acts devolved from government to contractors and private operators. Narrowing the definition will limit the protection offered by the Act. It may allow private operators, enjoying special powers and privileges by virtue of the functions that they carry out to side-step obligations that they would have been held to had they been 'core' governmental authorities.

---

27   'Rights Brought Home', at http://www.archive.official-documents.co.uk/document/hoffice/rights/chap1.htm Para 6.
28   Ibid., para 7.
29   And by 7(7) which effectively gives statutory form to the Article.
30   This point can perhaps be clarified with a reference to *Hansard*: '[D]octors in general practice would be public authorities in relation to their National Health Service functions, but not in relation to their private patients'. (*Hansard* H.L. deb. vol. 583 Col. 811 24 November 8 11.)

We will see that the judges have argued that there is no single test that will allow bodies to be defined as either public, private or, indeed, hybrid. While important factors that tend towards the classification of a body can be specified, this still leaves a certain measure of discretion in the hands of judges. We must thus go on to consider the central issues in relation to the definition of public authority. The first major authority is *Poplar* v. *Donoghue*.[31] Donoghue was disputing the decision of the Poplar Housing Association that she had made herself intentionally homeless, and should thus be deprived of her right to be publicly housed. In part, her arguments relied on a claim that there had been a breach of Article 8. Our concern here, though, is with the definition of a public authority. Obviously, the provisions of the HRA would only apply if Poplar was a public body or performing public functions.

In order to understand the issues in *Poplar*, it is necessary to consider the political and social context of public housing; the 'chronic lack of accommodation for the less well off members of society'[32] and the fact that, particularly in London, demand for social housing 'far outstrips supply'. The determination that Donoghue had made herself intentionally homeless was made by the local authority before it transferred its housing stock to Poplar as a Registered Social Landlord (RSL). Poplar then commenced proceedings against her to evict her from the property. At least from this perspective, it would seem that Poplar had concurred in the decision made by the local authority. Moreover, on the evidence provided by the defendant, Poplar should be considered a public body as it was undoubtedly carrying out a public function and, moreover, the local authority handed over its housing stock while under a 'continuing duty' to provide accommodation.

The court did not agree with this analysis, although it did indeed stress that for section 6, the definition should be given a generous interpretation. This principle is limited to a certain extent by the following argument. The starting point is that simply because a private body takes over a function that a public body would be under a statutory duty to perform, it does not mean that the private body must be considered to be a public authority for the purposes of the Act. Furthermore, if a public body uses a private body to fulfil its duties, then the latter does not become a public body. The policy implications and the purpose that the HRA satisfies suggest that this is not a correct interpretation.[33] Thus, a 'hybrid body' can be both public and private in function:[34] the fundamental question seems to relate to the nature of the act that the body performs. Lord Woolf stressed that this was a matter of 'fact and degree'; a private act becomes public in the extent to which 'a feature or a combination of features ...

---

31   *Poplar* v. *Donoghue* [2001] 33 HLR 73.
32   Ibid., para 33.
33   Lord Woolf (ibid., para 58) argued 'Section 6 should not be applied so that if a private body provides such services, the nature of the functions are inevitably public. If this were to be the position, then when a small hotel provides bed and breakfast accommodation as a temporary measure, at the request of a housing authority that is under a duty to provide that accommodation, the small hotel would be performing public functions and required to comply with the HRA. This is not what the HRA intended. The consequence would be the same where a hospital uses a private company to carry out specialist services, such as analysing blood samples. The position under the HRA is necessarily more complex'.
34   'The fact that through the act of renting by a private body a public authority may be fulfilling its public duty, does not automatically change into a public act what would otherwise be a private act.'

impose a public character or stamp on the act'.[35] On the facts of this case, Poplar was 'so closely assimilated to that of Tower Hamlets that it was performing public and not private functions'.[36] However, this does not necessarily mean that in carrying out other functions, Poplar was a public authority.

We can see a developing jurisprudence in relation to this point if we turn to *Leonard Cheshire*.[37] The Leonard Cheshire Foundation ran a care home for long-stay patients. Acting under powers given to them by the National Assistance Act 1948, local authorities and health authorities placed patients in the care home and provided the Foundation with the funds for their accommodation. In 2000, the trustees who ran the Foundation took a decision to restructure the accommodation offered to residents. In particular, they intended to shut down the largest care home, a property called Le Court, and redevelop a number of smaller properties.

The residents who had been housed in Le Court objected to these plans, and sought to have the trustees' decision judicially reviewed. They argued that the decision was in breach of Article 8. The Foundation was operating as a public authority, even though Le Court had some residents whose funding was provided by local authorities, and others who were privately funded. The residents stressed that, irrespective of the source of patient's funding, the care home provided the same level of service and that this was central in determining the body's status. Relying on *Poplar*, the Court pointed out that while the nature of a body's funding is a factor to take into account, it is not determinative.[38] It was also significant that the National Assistance Act provided the Foundation with no special powers. As it was thus not exercising statutory authority, it was hard to argue that it 'stood in the shoes' of the local authority and its acts were those of a public authority. The Court's conclusion was that the charity was not acting as a public authority.[39]

This jurisprudence was further developed in *Aston Cantlow and Wilmcote with Billesley Parochial Church Council v. Wallbank*.[40] This case concerned an obligation to repair the chancel of a church that was an incident of ownership of the Wallbanks' property. The Wallbanks were arguing that the Parochial Church Council was a public authority. This would allow them to show that the Human Rights Act bound the Council. In enforcing the duty to repair the church, the Council was in fact depriving

---

35   Ibid., para 65, 842.
36   Ibid., para 66, 843.
37   *Leonard Cheshire* [2002] 2 All ER 936.
38   More precisely, the court developed the following test: what can make an act, which would otherwise be private, public, is a feature or a combination of features which impose a public character or stamp on the act. Statutory authority for what is done can at least help to mark the act as being public; so can the extent of control over the function exercised by another body which is a public authority. The more closely the acts that could be of a private nature are enmeshed in the activities of a public body, the more likely they are to be public. However, the fact that the acts are supervised by a public regulatory body does not necessarily indicate that they are of a public nature.
39   However, the Court did point out that the case would have been decided differently had the local authorities attempted to 'divest' themselves of their obligations under Article 8 by 'contracting out' their obligations under the 1948 Act to a private operator. Where a local authority was thus attempting to circumvent s.6, the Court would approach the interpretation of the HRA in such a way as to ensure the relevant human rights are protected. The Court also stressed that, on the present facts, the applicants could reply on their private law rights against the Foundation.
40   *Aston Cantlow and Wilmcote with Billesley Parochial Church Council v. Wallbank* [2004] 1 A.C. 546.

the Wallbanks of their possessions or controlling the use of their property in breach of the general principle of peaceful enjoyment set out in Protocol 1 of the ECHR.

The House of Lords determined that a Parochial Church Council was not a governmental organisation as it had nothing to do with the processes of either central or local government. Furthermore, it was not accountable to the general public for what it did and received no public funding. The statutory powers, which it had been given by the Chancel Repairs Act 1932, were not exercisable against the public generally or any class or group of persons that formed part of it. The appellant was not a core public authority and its status as part of the Church of England did not affect this conclusion.

Lord Nicholls returned to the themes of *Leonard Cheshire* and *Poplar*:

> Clearly there is no single test of universal application. There cannot be, given the diverse nature of governmental functions and the variety of means by which these functions are discharged today. Factors to be taken into account include the extent to which in carrying out the relevant function the body is publicly funded, or is exercising statutory powers, or is taking the place of central government or local authorities, or is providing a public service.[41]

He went on to assert that the Church Council was involved in a private act when it attempted to enforce the liability of the respondents, as this liability was a 'civil debt' and did not relate to 'the responsibilities owed by the public to the state'.

What are we to make of this case? In some senses, the conclusion is rather disappointing. Lord Nicholls himself suggests that the 'ancient liability', the obligation to repair, was 'anachronistic, even capricious'.[42] One could even see the sense in which the imposition of the obligation was a control or interference with property. For the church to demand a considerable figure from individuals, who may have to sell their property to meet the costs, is a draconian power. From this perspective it is hard to agree with their Lordships that it was a mere incident of ownership. It may have been desirable to bring the Church Council within the definition of a public authority because it was able to make use of a power that had such serious consequences on the property rights of individuals. Surely the costs of repair of a public building that is held by the established church with 'special links with central government'[43] should not have to be met by individuals.

We will examine one further authority. In *Regina (Beer (trading as Hammer Trout Farm)) v. Hampshire Farmer's Markets Ltd*[44] the Court of Appeal had to turn from questions about housing charities and church councils to consider another complex set of facts.[45] This case is relevant to our discussion because the law of

---

41 Ibid., para 11.
42 Ibid., para 2.
43 Ibid., para 13.
44 *Regina (Beer (trading as Hammer Trout Farm)) v. Hampshire Farmer's Markets Ltd* [2003] EWCA Civ 1056.
45 The case concerned a farmer's market. This had originally been set up by the Hampshire County Council under powers derived from the Local Government and Housing Act 1989. Anyone who wanted to run a stall on the market had to apply to the council, and Beer had been so accepted. Two years after the scheme had been initiated, the council made a decision to give control of the running of the market to the stallholders themselves. In order to

judicial review is closely linked to the development of Human Rights Act jurisprudence. Judicial review allows the courts to review the acts of decision-making bodies, and determine whether or not they are operating within the powers given to them either by statute or prerogative.[46] If the court finds that a body is acting *ultra vires*, it has the power to quash the decision, and order that it is re-made. Judicial review is thus an important legal mechanism that ensures that executive bodies are acting within the law. There is clearly an important overlap between executive bodies that are susceptible to judicial review, and the definition of a public authority under the Act. The difficulty faced by the court was in determining whether a private company that still had significant links to a local government authority was sufficiently engaged in public administration to be subject to judicial review. One could thus conclude that if it was possible to review Hampshire Farmer's Market's decision, then this kind of body could also be brought within the definition of public authority.

The Court of Appeal held that in a situation such as this, where the empowering statutes did not provide any clear description of the body in question, the determination of whether the body was susceptible to judicial review required a consideration of 'the nature of the power and function' that it exercised. On the facts of the present case, although the market was neither statutory nor charter, the significant issue was that it took place on public land. Furthermore, it had been created by the Council and took over the administrative functions that the council had previously undertaken, and was staffed, in part, by council employees. The court also pointed out that the market was run on a not-for-profit basis in the 'public interest'. Thus the decision to refuse Beer a trading licence could be judicially reviewed, and the market could be considered to be a public authority under 6(3).

Lord Justice Dyson explained that the point of contact between judicial review cases and the 6(3) issue was the problematic definition of a body having a 'public element' that 'can take many forms'. Finding the dividing line between public and private requires an engagement with the authorities on 6(3). In *Poplar*, the significant factors in defining a public act are manifold but, as we saw, *Poplar* remained a private body despite its responsibilities for public housing. Furthermore, the facts in *Beer* make this case very different from those in *Leonard Cheshire Foundation*. In the Leonard Cheshire case, the fact that the Foundation derived some of its funding from a public source was not a determinative factor. In Dyson LJ's opinion, *Aston Cantlow* was coherent with these two earlier authorities. Although the definition of a hybrid authority was of some relevance to *Beer's* case, the correct approach would be to supplement the English authorities with Strasbourg jurisprudence. To the extent that these cases might provide an understanding of the nature of a 'core' authority, they are of great relevance; but they are less helpful in the precise question facing the court: the 'fact

---

facilitate this arrangement, a private company was set up. The company was allowed to use council officers, derived some funding from the council, and drew one of its directors from the council staff. In 2002, Beer was refused a licence to trade and sought judicial review of this decision.

46 Residual common law powers used by the executive for a variety of administrative and political tasks.

sensitive' issue of 'whether in an individual case a hybrid body is exercising a public function'.[47]

How can we understand the court's approach over these four cases? Although the test for establishing that an institution is acting as a public body is broad, it is limited by the argument that a body performing a public activity is not necessarily performing a public function. In other words, a public body can employ a private organisation and the private organisation would not fall within the terms of the definition. The decisions in *Poplar* and *Leonard Cheshire* thus remove certain bodies from the jurisdiction of the Act. From a human rights perspective, this could be criticised as it limits the effectiveness of the Act. This is precisely the point made in the 9th Report of the Joint Committee on Human Rights:[48]

> The tests applied by the courts to determine whether a function is a 'public function' ... have been, in human rights terms, highly problematic ... Effectively, the protection of human rights is dependent not on the type of power being exercised, nor on its capacity to interfere with human rights, but on the relatively arbitrary criterion of the body's administrative links with institutions of State.[49]

The main point is that the test proposed and developed by the courts rests on a notion of the links between the body in question and the state. Given the complexities of the modern state and the fact that a public/private distinction cannot be so easily maintained, might it be suggested that the decisions that we have been considering create too narrow a test for determining whether or not a body is a public body? One of the consequences of these decisions is that due process requirements under the Act will not apply to private bodies. This again raises some difficult issues. There would be no legal compulsion under the Act for a housing association or a charity to employ due process safeguards in determining whether or not someone had a right to housing. Although these bodies are clearly not courts, their decisions they make clearly affect peoples' lives in a serious way. Reflecting on the application of the HRA to care homes, the Joint Committee on Human Rights has criticised the narrow approach taken to the definition of public authority, as 'subjecting private care homes to the Human Rights Act would engender a culture of human rights from which all service users would benefit including those who realistically would not assert rights under the Act'.[50] There are counter-arguments. It would be unreasonable to place too great a burden on decision-making bodies such as housing associations. Besides, as a matter of policy and good practice, such bodies follow guidelines and procedures when they are making decisions. If they do act unreasonably they are in theory open to judicial review if they are bodies established by statute.

---

47   Supra n. 44, at para 28.
48   The Meaning of Public Authority under the Human Rights Act, HL77/HC 410, 28 March 2007.
49   Ibid., Part 2, Conclusion, para 18.
50   See Public Authorities after YL, Johnny Landau, *Public Law* (1997: 630–9), at 639. Landau is commenting on YL *(by her litigation friend the Official Solicitor)* v. *Birmingham CC* [2007] UKHL 27. The report referred to is: 'The Human Rights of Older People in Healthcare', Eighteenth Report of Session 2006–2007, HL 156-I/HC 378-I.

THE RETROSPECTIVE EFFECT OF THE ACT

One of the most problematic questions thrown up by the HRA is the extent to which it has retrospective effect. There are strong arguments against retrospective effect: 'Why should parties that have behaved perfectly properly in the light of the law as it was when they acted find that their legal relations have been profoundly altered ... on account of some subsequent legislative intervention'.[51] It would be perverse to justify a regime of human rights on such a clear breach of a principle of legality, no matter how compelling the claims for 'protection' from abuse of power.[52] However, in Gearty's words, the Act was somewhat 'Delphic'[53] on this crucial issue. What sense could the judges make of the Act? One of the early key authorities is *Wilson v. First County Trust*.[54] In the Court of Appeal, Sir Andrew Morritt wrestled with section 22(4) of the Act. He argued that, first of all, it provides that the provisions in 7(1) that allowed a person to bring proceedings against a public authority acting in breach of the Convention do not apply before 2 October 2000. However, if the 'unlawful act' took place before 2 October 2000, 'it is only where the person who claims to be the victim of that act is party to proceedings brought by or at the instigation of a public authority'[55] that the section applies and the Act has retrospective effect. The Court of Appeal also considered a broader argument, based on an interpretation of 6(1) and 6(3) that would impose a 'dramatic retrospectivity' on the Act; an argument that the House of Lords rejected.

Let us now look at *Lambert* and *Kansal*. *Kansal* suggests that the House of Lords continued to experience certain problems in developing a consistent jurisprudence of retrospective effect. In *Lambert*,[56] the retrospective effect of the HRA was raised in relation to a defence to a criminal prosecution for possession of Class A drugs under the Misuse of Drugs Act 1971.[57] We are concerned with a single point: whether the defendant could rely in his appeal, which took place after the Human Rights Act came into force, on a breach of his rights in a trial which had taken place before the Act had become law. The House of Lords held that as Parliament had not intended that the Act

---

51 Ibid., 165.
52 Parliament can (and has) legislated to change the law retrospectively. See *Burmah Oil* v. *Lord Advocate* [1965] AC 756. The War Damages Act 1965 reversed a House of Lords' decision with 'retroactive effect'.
53 Gearty (2004: 164).
54 *Wilson* v. *First County Trust* [2003] HRLR 33. Mrs Wilson had argued that a loan that she had taken from a pawnbroker and not repaid was unenforceable, because the agreement did not contain all the prescribed terms, contrary to the Consumer Credit Act of 1974. In particular Mrs Wilson was objecting to a fee for preparation of documents that she had been charged and which was not mentioned in the loan agreement. Her argument was that the 1974 Act made the agreement unenforceable. The County Court held that the agreement was enforceable, and Mrs Wilson had appealed to the Court of Appeal, which reversed the County Court's judgment. The Court of Appeal also made a declaration under s.4 of the HRA. The Court of Appeal argued that the 1974 Act was incompatible with the rights guaranteed to the creditor by Article 6(1) of the European Convention on Human Rights ('the Convention'). The Secretary of State, who had been added to the proceedings, appealed, and the House of Lords allowed the appeal.
55 Ibid., para 20.
56 *R.* v *Lambert* [2001] HRLR 55.
57 The defendant argued that there had been a breach of his rights under Article 6, because sections 5(4) and 28 of the 1971 Act placed the burden of proof on the defence, and this was in breach of the right to a fair trial. The Court of Appeal rejected the defendant's arguments, but certified a number of questions for appeal.

should have retrospective effect, the defendant could not reply on the argument about a breach of his rights during his trial.[58]

The key provisions of the Act that were considered in *Lambert* are sections 6 and 7(1)(b). The defendant's argument proceeded on two fronts. The first contention was based on section 6(1) read with section 22 and section 7. Section 6(1) states that '[i]t is unlawful for a public authority to act in a way which is incompatible with a Convention right'. Because 6(3) and (4) define a public authority as a court the provisions of the Act are clearly binding on the courts. Section 7 provides that a person, who 'claims that a public authority has acted' in an unlawful way, may rely on his or her Convention rights to bring proceedings in the appropriate court, provided he or she is a 'victim' of 'the unlawful Act'. Section 22 states that section 7 applies to 'proceedings' that have been brought 'by or at the instigation of a public authority' and, this is the central issue, 'whenever the act in question took place'. Section 7(4) goes on to say that unless a public authority has initiated proceedings, the HRA will not apply. The court was not convinced. As Lord Slynn crisply puts it: 'It seems to me that Parliament was not intending in this case that on an appeal Convention rights could be relied upon in respect of a conviction which took place before the Act came into force'.[59] This position was justified by policy considerations. Parliament thought that it would not be wise to disturb lawful convictions through the retrospective application of human rights.

The second line of argument attempted to link sections 22(4) and 7(1)(b) to the interpretative provisions contained in sections 3(1) and 6(1). This would allow the Act to apply either to the trial judge or the Crown Prosecution Service (CPS). Lord Hope argued that if 6(1) had been law at the time of Lambert's trial, the obligation of 6(3)(a) would have been binding on the trial judge, who would have been compelled by 3(1) to 'give effect' to the 1971 Act in such a way as to make it compatible with Convention rights. However, this argument breaks down because 6(3) must be read alongside 7(1), 7(6) and 22(4), and it would be impossible to assert that a court is a 'public authority by or at the instigation of which proceedings are brought', precisely because the sense of 7(1) is that the public authority is a party to the action, and the court is clearly not. Section 3(1) thus does not apply as the Act itself specifies that the interpretative provision can only be employed 'so far as it is possible to do so'.[60]

Lord Steyn dissented. He argued that the HRA did apply to the present appeal by virtue of 6(1) because to hold otherwise would amount to a breach of the obligations under the Act, as an appellate court would be acting 'incompatibly with a convention right'.[61] Discounting the limit on the scope of 6(1) provided by 6(2), because the 1971 Act could be read compatibly with the Convention, Lord Steyn asserted that there was nothing to limit the general obligation placed on the court by 6(1). Given that 22(4) was so central to the arguments of the majority, Lord Steyn had also to counter the majority's interpretation of this section. Relying on an academic commentary,[62] he argued

---

58   It is worth noting in passing, though, that *Salabiaku* v. *France* (1988) 13 EHRR 37 was cited as authority for interfering with the presumption of innocence.
59   Supra n. 56, at para 9.
60   Ibid., para 109.
61   Ibid., para 30.
62   Clayton and Tomlinson (2000: para 3.75, 142).

that the section is too 'obscure' to have any clear meaning, and cannot be seen to limit the obligations placed on the court under 6(1). He makes a similar argument in relation to section 7. Ultimately, his position rests on the 'plain words' or 'natural meaning'[63] of section 6. Holding otherwise would have the unusual consequence of making certain appeal cases go to the ECHR, rather than allowing the Court of Appeal and the House of Lords to have full competence over the development of an indigenous human rights law.

Kansal is similar in its facts to *Lambert*. Kansal[64] had appealed against his conviction for deception offences and offences under the Insolvency Act. The case was sent to the Criminal Cases Review Commission, who referred it to the Court of Appeal on the grounds that the convictions were unsafe, because the prosecution had relied on answers given under compulsion. The question that the House of Lords had to consider was whether or not a defendant could rely in an appeal on sections of the HRA that had not been in effect at the time of trial. The House of Lords held that Kansal's convictions had been safe at the time they were made and that the HRA should not be given retrospective effect.

The fundamental problem is that it is hard to determine precisely what *Kansal* decided. Lord Slynn argued that *Lambert* was not wrongly decided. If one looks at the disputed sections, 22(4), 7(6) and 7(1)(b), which deal with the issue of retrospection, the Act distinguishes between the language of 22(4) and 7(6), which specifies 'proceedings brought by or at the instigation of a public authority', and an appeal, even though ordinarily 'would be considered as part of legal proceedings'.[65] His fundamental contention was that if Parliament had intended the Act to disturb convictions that were safe at the time of trial, it would have clearly said so in the Act. He also argued that there was no way that *Lambert* can be distinguished on the basis of the distinction between acts of the prosecutor and acts of a judge. Lord Lloyd was critical of the majority in *Lambert*. His major argument is that 7(6) is not clearly enough worded to 'exclude by implication' appeals from the protection offered by the Act. He pointed out that the problem in *Kansal* was that two Law Lords had given supplemental reasons for following *Lambert* and two had argued that the case was wrongly decided. Refusing to 'sit on the fence',[66] Lord Lloyd asserts that *Lambert* was wrongly decided, agreeing with Lord Hope and Lord Steyn. Lord Steyn was against the artificial and strained interpretation of the Act favoured by the majority. He was particularly critical of the interpretation of 22(4).[67]

Lord Hope suggests that Lambert is still correct, for the reasons that he gave in the case. At the same time, though, he amends the central points of his argument. Its fundamental contention was that a court or tribunal cannot be considered as a

---

63   Supra n. 56, at para 30.
64   R. v. *Kansal* [2001] UKHL 62.
65   Ibid., para 8.
66   Ibid., para 17.
67   We now know that 'proceedings brought by or at the instigation of a public authority' in section 22(4) were singled out for special treatment in recognition of the United Kingdom's international obligations under the European Convention for the Protection of Human Rights and Fundamental Freedoms from the date of ratification by the United Kingdom in 1951 or the date of conferment of the right of petition in 1966. This rationale does not support the artificial distinction between criminal trials and appeals.

party to the proceedings. However, Lord Hope now understands that this is a far too narrow interpretation of the Act and such a 'rigid distinction' cannot be maintained, especially in the light of the argument that sections 7–9 lay down a general remedial structure.[68] Despite this point, however, there are still certain judicial acts that can be distinguished on 6(2)(a) of the Act, which determines that if primary legislation so states, a public authority may act inconsistently with the Convention. On the facts of *Lambert*, and given sections 5(3) and 28 of the Act in question, the judge could not have acted differently. This point is not developed but, nevertheless, this argument allows Lord Hope to square his reasoning in the case with that in *Kansal*. As the prosecutor was relying on a piece of primary legislation that was inconsistent with the Convention, he could not have acted differently. The Act did indeed have retrospective effect but the defendant's convictions were safe.

Lord Hutton pointed out that the decision of the Court of Appeal in this case had taken place before the House of Lords had ruled in *Lambert*. It was in the interests of the respondents to make this argument, and to rest on the point that it was the trial judge that had erred in *Lambert*, and the prosecuting authorities in *Kansal*. This position, however, is incompatible with the general statement of the ratio, which is that section 22(4) did not apply to any appeal before 2 October 2000. Furthermore, *Lambert* was not wrongly decided. Lord Hutton insists that there are significant and important differences between the wording in 7(6), which refers 'separately'[69] to 'proceedings brought by or at the instigation of a public authority' and to 'an appeal against the decision of a court or tribunal'. Section 22(4) only then uses one of these phrases 'proceedings brought by or at the instigation of a public authority'. The Act is thus clearly indicating that appeals and proceedings in general should be considered as distinct. This can be backed up with a policy argument. While Parliament intended that 'victims' of human rights violations should be allowed to make use of human rights arguments, this did not extend to upsetting convictions that were 'valid and safe' at the time of trial.[70]

Can we draw any conclusions from *Lambert* and *Kansal*? As Ferguson has argued, 'It is regrettable that the speeches disclose such an array of responses on the important issue of the scope of s.22(4)'.[71] This might suggest that this is not a strong foundation upon which to build consistent principles. From our consideration in Chapter 3 of the perturbations caused in judicial practice by the HRA, it might have been sensible in this case to depart from stability and certainty and to correct error. Critics have also attacked the 'the justice of allowing convictions to remain undisturbed even though they are based on a breach of a Convention which the United Kingdom ratified half a century ago'.[72] In other areas of criminal law, the House of Lords have recognised its errors and attempted to undo them.[73] Although these cases were not cited in *Lambert* and *Kansal*,

---

68   Supra n. 64, at para 79.
69   Ibid., para 102.
70   Ibid., para 103.
71   Ferguson (2002: 14).
72   Ashworth and Barsby (2002: 500).
73   Ashworth and Barsby draw attention to this point, ibid., at 500. See *Moloney* [1985] AC 905 and *Hancock and Shankland* [1986] AC 455, and on impossibility in attempted crime, *Anderton* v. *Ryan* [1985] AC 560 and *Shivpuri* [1987] 1 AC 1.

it might be argued that a coherent jurisprudence of retrospective effect of human rights law in the area of criminal procedure should have taken them into account. Perhaps these cases show that there were more than 'teething problems' in the introduction of the Act.[74]

We cannot look at all the relevant case law but we can examine some important decisions that followed from *Kansal* and *Lambert*. *Wainwright* v. *Home Office*[75] held that acts of courts or tribunals, which took place before 2 October 2000, were not affected by 22(4), provided that the acts were required by primary legislation and were made according to the meaning given to the legislation at that time. So, although the obligation in section 3(1) to interpret legislation as compatible with Convention rights applies to legislation whenever enacted, this obligation cannot be applied to invalidate a decision which was good at the time, if it would involve changing retrospectively the meaning that the court or tribunal had given previously to that legislation. The same view has been taken where the claim relates to acts of public authorities other than courts or tribunals. In *Wainwright* it was held that the HRA could not be relied upon retrospectively to introduce a right of privacy that would make unlawful conduct, which was lawful at the time when it took place. In the Court of Appeal Lord Woolf stated that:

> the claimants [are] seeking to rely on the Convention to change English substantive law … [the 1998 Act] certainly cannot be relied on to change substantive law by introducing a retrospective right to privacy which did not exist at common law.[76]

As the Court of Appeal effectively dealt with this point, the House of Lords did not consider it. Critics have suggested that this avoided difficult questions about 'the scope of Article 8' and its link, if any, with the retrospective effect of the Act.[77] Given the centrality of Campbell (see Chapter 3) to this area of law, *Wainwright* needs to be viewed through the lens of this case. However, as *Campbell* was heard when the HRA was in effect, it would seem that *Wainwright* is a somewhat limited authority.

We will therefore turn our attention to *Re McKerr's Application for Judicial Review*.[78] In this case, the House of Lords had to determine whether or not the failure to conduct an investigation into the killing of an alleged terrorist was in breach of the Human Rights Act. The Court observed that the Act as a whole is not retrospective, and that section 22(4) is an exception to this general rule. Returning to Lord Hope's point in *Wilson*, the Court stressed that this was still problematic: '[A]greements made before the Human Rights Act came into force will often generate obligations requiring performance after 2 October 2000'.

The Court argued that in relation to an unlawful killing, the position is clear. If it occurred before the Act came into force, section 6(1) does not apply.

---

74   Starmer (2003).
75   *Wainwright* v. *Home Office* [2002] QB 1334.
76   Ibid., 1347.
77   Morgan (2004).
78   *Re McKerr's Application for Judicial Review* [2004] 2 All ER 409.

However, the issue before the court was somewhat different. The alleged violation was the failure to conduct a satisfactory inquiry into the death. The death may have occurred before the Act was in force but the investigation would have taken place after the Act became law. The key question was: 'On which side of the retrospectivity line is a post-Act failure to investigate a pre-Act death?' In relation to the interpretation of Article 2 and section 6, this is solved by arguing that the death itself has to occur within the period when the Act is in force:

> Parliament cannot be taken to have intended that the Act should apply differently to the primary obligation (to protect life) and a consequential obligation (to investigate a death).[79]

If one accepts this conclusion, then certain cases may be wrongly decided. To prevent these errors recurring, it is necessary to observe that there is a distinction between Convention rights and rights under the Human Rights Act. Although these rights sit 'side by side', the Court argued that there are differences between them. There are still some Convention rights that are not part of domestic law, because the Convention itself is not part of domestic law. How can we tell the difference between them? The Court went on to argue:

> The extent of these rights, created as they were by the Human Rights Act, depends upon the proper interpretation of that Act. It by no means follows that the continuing existence of a right arising under the Convention in respect of an act occurring before the Human Rights Act came into force will be mirrored by a corresponding right created by the Human Rights Act. Whether it finds reflection in this way in the Human Rights Act depends upon the proper interpretation of the Human Rights Act.[80]

Following *Re McKerr*, it would seem that the key issue is the extent to which a common law right corresponds with a Convention right, prior to the Act becoming law. How might this relate to the issue of retrospective effect? We need to examine *R. (on the application of Richards) v. Secretary of State for the Home Department*.[81] The Court engaged with the following issue: does Article 5(5) of the ECHR give a person a claim for compensation for wrongful detention in the domestic courts of the UK, even though section 6 of the HRA does not apply? The Court decided in the affirmative, partly because of the wording of the Article 5(5) itself: victims 'shall have an *enforceable* right to compensation'. So in this case, a Convention right applied, even though section 6 of the Human Rights Act did not apply. Clearly, if one is considering whether or not the Human Rights Act has retrospective effect, it is necessary to consider each case on its facts. Just because *R. (on the application of Richards)* determined that Article 5(5) had application, this does not mean that all Convention

---

79 Ibid.
80 Ibid.
81 *R. (on the application of Richards) v. Secretary of State for the Home Department* [2004] EWHC 93.

rights were applicable before the Human Rights Act came into force. Indeed, in *Campbell* v. *South Northamptonshire DC*,[82] a case that concerned the interpretation of various social welfare regulations, the court refused to give retrospective effect to Articles 9 and 14. The court also refused to give retrospective effect to Article 5(5) in *R. (on the application of White)* v. *Secretary of State for the Home Department* and distinguished Richards.[83]

To the extent that there are general principles at stake in this area, then they take us to the heart of the rule of law. It would be against the principles of the rule of law to provide retrospective legislation. However, legislation is not retrospective to the extent that the rights in question were already part of the common law. These matters can only be resolved on an Article-by-Article basis and this would take us to matters of substantive law that lie outside this study. It would seem, therefore, that any sensible consideration of this area of the Act must take us to some problematic questions of the relationship between domestic law and European human rights law.

EUROPEAN HUMAN RIGHTS AND THE COMMON LAW

Following Lewis' analysis,[84] we will make reference to the 'mirror' principle that has been influential in articulating the relationship between 'municipal' and Convention rights.[85]

The starting point of our discussion is the idea that the HRA 'incorporates' Convention rights into common law. This would seem a sensible way of thinking about an Act that reproduces the Convention as its substantive human rights provisions. However, while this undoubtedly describes the form of the Act, certain statements in parliamentary debate added significant shades of meaning. If Lord Irving's statements are to be understood, then incorporation is to be interpreted as 'enhancement', suggesting that Convention rights are, in certain senses, more potent than those existing (or indeed not existing) in common law. This suggests that the Act does more than simply incorporate rights. The Act invites the judges to develop an indigenous human rights law.

How might this relate to Lord Nicholls' observation in *Re McKerr*?[86] The first point to stress is that the Act did not simply make the Convention part of domestic law; the Act made it illegal for a public authority to act incompatibly with a Convention right. One consequence of this argument is that the extent of incorporation of the Convention will always be filtered through this application of rights to public authorities. We have examined this concern above but, at this stage, we could speculate that the pressing issue for a common law development of human rights law is the extent to which rights

---

82   *Campbell* v. *South Northamptonshire DC* [2004] EWCA Civ 409.
83   *R. (on the application of White)* v. *Secretary of State for the Home Department* [2006] EWCA Civ 67. In the earlier case, Richards's unlawful detention fell into a period after 2 October 2000. In Wright, the period of detention ran from 1993 to 1999, a period before the Convention was incorporated.
84   Lewis (2007: 720).
85   Lewis citing Laws LJ in *Begum* v. *Tower Hamlets* [2002] EWCA Civ 239.
86   *Re McKerr* [2004] 1 WLR 807, 25, 62–5.

will be given horizontal, as much as vertical application. The second consequence, again as indicated by Lord Nicholls, is that two bodies of rights now exist 'side by side', but with significant differences between them. Convention rights existed before the HRA and, clearly, continue to exist as the contents of an international treaty that are not part of domestic law. The establishment of Convention rights as part of domestic law came into existence when the HRA came into effect on 2 October 2000. The scope of these rights depends on the 'proper interpretation of that Act'. The first issue is one of retrospectivity: just because a right existed prior to 2 October 2000, and which applied to an Act taking place prior to the HRA becoming law, does not mean that it will be 'mirrored' by a right under the Act.[87]

In *R. (on the Application of Ullah)* v. *Secretary of State for the Home Department*[88] the House of Lords considered an appeal from refusals to grant asylum to two individuals who feared religious persecution if they were returned to, respectively, Pakistan and Vietnam. The substance of the refusal of asylum was that the evidence suggested that the 'interference' with the appellant's Article 9 rights fell short of the ill-treatment defined by Article 3. The precise issue on which the House of Lords had to rule was whether any other Articles of the Convention would be engaged by the removal of the applicants from England, even though Article 3 did not apply.

The importance of this case for our analysis is not so much the argument about the technical nature of a refusal of asylum, but what it tells us about the court's understanding of European human rights law. In asserting that Article 2 could be relied upon, the House of Lords affirmed that the courts had a duty to 'keep pace with the Strasbourg jurisprudence as it evolves over time'. On the facts of this case, the jurisprudence of the court establishes that it would be against the humanitarian objectives of the Convention if Article 3 could be relied upon, but Article 2 could not. There were other possibilities under Articles 5, 6 and 8 but the court did not consider it necessary to examine the Convention in its entirety. Furthermore, the House of Lords explained that it had disagreed with the Court of Appeal, because the latter had not taken into account the 'current state' of human rights jurisprudence. The Court of Appeal was criticised for not taking into account *Soering* v. *UK*[89] and the associated cases that stress that the correct approach is to ask whether or not there is a 'real risk' of the violation of the applicant's rights.

Lord Bingham explained that the House was required by 2(1) of the HRA to 'take into account' human rights law and, even though it was not 'strictly binding', the court should try to 'follow' any consistent authorities. In *R. (on the application of Alconbury Developments Ltd)* v. *Secretary of State for the Environment, Transport and the Regions*[90] Lord Slynn explained that it would be wrong not to do so because, in the event of the case going to the ECtHR, that court would make use of its own jurisprudence. In determining the coherent jurisprudence of the ECtHR, it was not necessary to consider every case but to obtain a good sense of key principles. Moreover, as Lord Bingham

---

87   Clayton (2007: 19). These points were developed by Lord Hoffmann in *R.* v. *Lyons* [2003] 1 AC 976.
88   *R. (on the Application of Ullah)* v. *Secretary of State for the Home Department* [2004] UKHL 26.
89   *Soering* v. *UK* (1989) 11 EHRR, 439.
90   In *R. (on the application of Alconbury Developments Ltd)* v. *Secretary of State for the Environment, Transport and the Regions* [2003] AC 295, at para 26.

stressed, the courts should rely on Strasbourg cases, as the ECtHR is the court empowered to give definitive rulings on the meaning of the Convention as an international treaty. Section 6 prevents the court as a public authority from acting incompatibly with the Convention and so any interpretation of Strasbourg cases should not attempt to limit their scope. While national legislatures could supplement Convention rights if they so chose, courts had to be mindful of the need to develop coherently an international jurisprudence, keeping 'pace' with its evolution: 'no more, or no less'.[91]

What are the consequences of this principle? Some authorities have drawn interesting distinctions between Strasbourg case law and that of Commonwealth jurisdictions. In *Brown* v. *Stott*,[92] a case that raised significant points in relation to Article 6, Lord Hope made a qualified reference to the way in which the Canadian courts had approached the issue of self-incrimination in *R.* v *White*[93] and had held it to be 'a principle of fundamental justice under section 7 of the Charter'. However, as Iacobucci J. stated, this did not mean that it was 'absolute'. This approach is similar to that taken by the ECtHR but the Canadian court was not interested in the principles of proportionality and legitimate aim, so the Canadian cases were less useful than the European authorities.[94] Lord Bingham made a similar point in contrasting Article 17 of the Convention with the First Amendment of the United States' Constitution and, noting that the Convention also differed from other 'constitutional systems'. He concluded that the Convention is 'our Bill of Rights'.[95] These concerns continued into *Sheldrake* v. *Director of Public Prosecutions*.[96] Lord Bingham pointed out that in *R.* v. *Lambert*, Lord Steyn and Lord Nicholls in *R.* v. *Johnstone*, had made reference to Commonwealth cases in determining the extent of rights under the Convention. He doubted whether this was entirely correct. Not only was 'caution' necessary in considering different human rights' traditions, but the primary responsibility of the English courts were to give 'full and fair effect to the Strasbourg jurisprudence'.[97]

While the judges have to respect the specificity of the legal instruments with which they are dealing, this rather myopic approach has been criticised as limiting a common law jurisprudence of rights. Clayton, for instance, contrasts the approach of the English courts with that of other nations, in particular France and Germany, and also observes that the South African Constitutional Court has drawn on many different jurisdictions in examining 'universal human rights problems'.[98] Other commentators have come to similar conclusions. Lewis cites Masterman and Klug as arguing that the courts should be able to make use of 'comparative materials'. This area of comparative jurisprudence is precisely one where the common law courts could take the lead, precisely because there is 'little Strasbourg authority' on the use of comparative jurisprudence.[99]

---

91 Ullah, para 21.
92 *Brown* v. *Stott* [2003] 1 AC 681.
93 *R.* v. *White* [1999] 2 SCR 417.
94 Ibid., 724.
95 Ibid., 708.
96 *Sheldrake* v. *Director of Public Prosecutions* [2005] 1 AC 264.
97 Ibid., para 33.
98 Clayton (2007: 19).
99 Lewis (2007: 732).

Lewis has argued that judicial commitment to the mirror principle has severely hampered the creative development of a specifically common law understanding of European human rights. Scrutiny of the White Paper, the extra judicial writing of certain Law Lords and academic commentaries on the potential impact of the HRA, suggest that there was, prior to 1998, a shared understanding that the Act would be a catalyst to a reinvigoration of common law thinking about human rights, and that the Strasbourg jurisprudence would be seen as a 'floor' above which more 'generous' human rights protection could be built. In the wake of *Ullah* and *Alconbury*, this does not seem to be taking place. For instance, in *R. (on the application of Clift)* v. *Secretary of State for the Home Department*,[100] the court refused to extend the protection offered by Article 14, as it was necessary to work within the limits imposed by the ECtHR; similar approaches have been taken to Article 5 in *Secretary of State for the Home Department* v. *JJ*[101] and Article 9 in *R. (on the application of SB)* v. *Denbigh High School*.[102] Lord Bingham was clear in Begum's case that the HRA was not to allow the courts to expand the protection offered by the Convention but to ensure that Convention rights were available in English law.

Have there been any signs that the judges and the Law Lords are willing to take a lead in the development of human rights law? There are instances in which the English courts have moved beyond Strasbourg. In *Campbell* v. *MGM*,[103] the Lords held that Article 8 applied between private parties. Lewis makes reference to a *dicta* in *Huang* v. *Secretary of State for the Home Department*,[104] where Strasbourg jurisprudence was described as 'not strictly binding'. This could be linked with Buxton LJ's argument in *Ghaidan* v. *Godin-Mendoza*. He asserted that it would be possible to depart from a Strasbourg ruling if it was wrong about or misunderstood an aspect of English law. Statements in *Ghaidan* also suggest that it is possible to depart from Strasbourg rulings in 'special circumstances' or, in the language of *Ullah*, where there are 'strong reasons' for so doing. An example of a strong reason or 'special circumstance' was given by Lord Hoffmann in *Alconbury* as one which misunderstood the 'distribution of powers of the British Constitution'.[105]

The mirror principle also appears to be under stress in *Anderson*, where Buxton LJ felt compelled to follow Strasbourg, even though it prevented him from coming to a more appropriate conclusion. The notion that the mirror principle is based on ensuring consistency in the development of European human rights law is also criticised by Lewis. In *M.* v. *Secretary of State for Work and Pensions*[106] the House of Lords had the opportunity to expand the protection offered by Article 14 but refused to take the lead, arguing that any development would have to await a Strasbourg ruling to ensure the uniform interpretation of the Convention. A liberal interpretation of Article 14 could be justified on the basis of a development of municipal rights, which leaves the

---

100   *R. (on the application of Clift)* v. *Secretary of State for the Home Department* [2006] UKHL 54.
101   *Secretary of State for the Home Department* v. *JJ* [2006] EWCA Civ 1141.
102   *R. (on the application of SB)* v. *Denbigh High School* [2006] UKHL 15.
103   *Campbell* v. *MGM* [2004] UKHL 22.
104   *Huang* v. *Secretary of State for the Home Department* [2007] UKHL 11.
105   Supra, n. 99, at 731.
106   *M.* v. *Secretary of State for Work and Pensions* [2006] UKHL 11.

Convention right 'untouched'.[107] The ECtHR has, on other occasions, 'ignored' the English decisions but may follow the lead of the common law courts.

Commentators have been critical of the judicial reluctance to develop an indigenous human rights law. Clayton[108] argues that section 2(1) requires the Court to take into account Strasbourg jurisprudence, but it does not specify what 'weight' is to be given to it, or indeed to follow the cases as if they were precedents. It cannot be seen as a justification for the restrictive approach that the judges have taken.

CONCLUSION

Is it possible to draw together a general jurisprudence of human rights? We have argued in this chapter that there is a body of cases that are authorities on matters of general concern under the Act. Of course, it would be easy to argue that these matters are properly part of public law. To a large extent this is true. However, in arguing for a general jurisprudence of human rights, we want to show how these issues are largely free standing. They define a general jurisprudence concerned with the scope of the Court's interpretative power, the precise boundaries of the Act's application, and the relationship between Convention law and common law. To the extent that we can say anything generally about human rights at common law, we have to take into account these issues and the questions of procedure and policy that they raise.

---

107   Supra, n. 99, at 736.
108   Supra, n. 98, at 19–20.

11

THE JURISPRUDENCE OF ARTICLE 6: DUE PROCESS AND THE COMMON LAW

INTRODUCTION

This chapter looks at a key question: is it possible to define the core fair trial rights, and how does this impact on the common law and its institutions? As well as building up a body of principles that relate to fair trial rights in regular courts, Article 6 also covers the operation of other tribunals, in particular those dealing with military discipline and welfare benefits. The critical question that we have to answer thus applies to both specialist tribunals and courts: do they operate with sufficient fair trial guarantees?

From the perspective of the UK, we are perhaps dealing with one of the particular legacies of the failure to create an adequate notion of due process that was one of the consequences of the politics of the judiciary in the 1940s and 1950s. It is interesting that a great deal of Article 6 litigation against the UK concerns the way in which the courts should regulate the operation of bodies making administrative decisions that impact so heavily on people's lives. However, we should not fall into the error of characterising European human rights jurisprudence as always somehow ahead of the common law in its understanding of due process. Indeed, there are critical voices within European human rights jurisprudence that suggest that it often falls short of articulating the standards that it should.

The chapter will develop as follows. We will first examine the central doctrine of Article 6: the independence and impartiality of the tribunal. We will then turn to the related issue of bias, before turning to consider the doctrine of equality of arms and the requirement for the public pronouncement of judgment. In all these areas, we will outline European principles and show how they have impacted on the common law. We need a complex appreciation of the interfaces between the principles of European human rights law and the doctrines of the common law.

INDEPENDENT AND IMPARTIAL TRIBUNAL

By far the most important guarantee enshrined in Article 6 is that to an independent and impartial tribunal established by law. It is probably also one of the most important guarantees of the whole Convention. In fact, there are two aspects to this guarantee. On the one hand it is an individual human right which ensures that disputes in which the individual is involved are decided by a neutral authority. On the other hand, however, it also has an institutional aspect of constitutional importance: it lays the foundation for what has been labelled ... the third power in a state after the legislative and the executive. While the right to free elections under Article 3 of the First Protocol protects the foundations of democracy, the guarantee to an independent and impartial tribunal lays the foundations necessary for the rule of law.[1]

This passage places Article 6 in the context of the politics of the Convention. It stresses that the Article is central to the very idea of the rule of law, as it guarantees the impartiality of the courts. Indeed, we could even talk about the constitutionalisation of procedure to the extent that the Article provides a foundation for a value that is often enshrined in constitutional documents. This reminds us that procedural law is an essential feature of the politics of democracy. The rule of law requires that the body that adjudicates disputes is not subject to the executive or, at the very least, that the executive and the judiciary respect their mutual spheres of competence. We have seen that this is part of the much broader problem that we have described as the politics of the judiciary and suggested, at least as far as the UK is concerned, that there is a need for dialogue between the courts and Parliament. In this chapter we will attempt to outline the jurisprudence of Article 6, which, as we will see in our analysis of the British cases, is an essential part of the dialogue between the common law courts and the ECtHR.

Perhaps the key theme that underlies Article 6 jurisprudence is the impartiality of the court or tribunal. Should a court be partial, the ECtHR will hold that proceedings are not fair.[2] This reflects the need to affirm the democratic order of the courts against that of 'military' or 'special' courts that retain a right to try civilians, although, as we will see, it also covers the operation of welfare tribunals and professional disciplinary bodies. To cover the range of judicial and quasi-judicial bodies, the jurisprudence of the ECtHR stresses that irrespective of the name given to a body in national law, a court or tribunal must be independent 'in particular of the executive', and 'impartial'. A tribunal must also have in place the procedural guarantees that are provided by the Article.[3] What sense, then, can be made of the particular wording of Article 6; that the tribunal must be 'independent, impartial' and 'established by law'? Are these terms merely amplificatory of the core sense that the court must be independent or do they add distinct substantive requirements?

Arguably, the court sees the requirement that the tribunal is 'established by law' as part of the criteria of impartiality.[4] An impartial body is one established by law and not beholden to a superior body.[5] This does raise issues of definition: to what extent must law regulate every element of the tribunal? Does it leave no room at all for discretion? The consensus appears to be that the 'organisational set up'[6] of the court, including the definition of its jurisdiction and its proceedings, must be determined by law, but there can be some discretion in the hands of the executive, provided that it

---

1 Trechsel (2005: 46).
2 Ibid., 47.
3 *Belios v. Switzerland* [1988] ECHR 4.
4 Trechsel, supra n. 1, citing *Oberschlick v. Austria* 19 EHRR 389.
5 *Zand v. Austria* Application 7360/76.
6 Ibid., para 51.

does not compromise judicial independence. This is perhaps a difficult line to draw. What does seem clear is the sense in which the requirement that a tribunal should be established by law shades into the idea of independence. The case law of the Convention[7] establishes that a tribunal's independence must be judged with reference to the appointment of its members, the 'safeguards' that exist to protect it from pressure to determine a case in a particular manner, and that it actually appears to be independent to the parties concerned.

Thus, independence describes the constitutional position of the court and does not mean that a hierarchical relationship cannot exist between courts, or that a higher court cannot have a supervisory or appellate relationship to a lower court, provided that the impartiality of the tribunal as to the determination of matters of fact and law is ensured. Clearly, impartiality extends to cover the lack of bias of the judge towards either party to the proceedings. On the authority of Findlay,[8] it can be suggested that the court links together impartiality and independence as closely related concepts that are fundamental to the notion of the fair trial. In *Incal*, the court articulated the broader principle at stake in issues of independence and bias: 'What is at stake is the confidence which the courts in a democratic society must inspire in the public and above all ... in the accused'.[9]

Incal v. *Turkey*[10] concerned a trial before the Turkish National Security Court. The applicant had been found guilty of distributing politically inflammatory pamphlets and sentenced to a period of imprisonment. The court was staffed by three judges, one of whom was a member of the Military Legal Service. Arguments concerned the position of the latter. Was the court independent and impartial?[11] The creation and staffing of the court was ultimately justified by Article 143 of the Constitution. National Security Courts were not military courts, but were created to deal with 'offences affecting Turkey's territorial integrity and national unity, its democratic regime and its State security'[12] and to protect the democratic state. The courts relied on military judges because they had experience in dealing with 'illegal armed groups' and 'organised crime'.[13] According to the Turkish government, certain guarantees were provided as to the impartiality of a military judge. Their training is the same as that of civilian judges, and they hold office on similar terms. In particular, 'no public authority may give them instructions concerning their judicial activities or influence them in the performance of their duties'.[14] However, as the ECtHR maintained, because military judges

---

7   *Le Compte and other* v. *Belgium* [1981] ECHR 3, *Incal* v. *Turkey* [1998] ECHR 48.
8   *Findlay* v. *UK*, 27 February 1997.
9   Supra n. 1, at para 56.
10 *Incal* v. *Turkey*.
11 Ibid. Note, at para 65, the inter-relationship of independence and impartiality: 'The Court reiterates that in order to establish whether a tribunal can be considered "independent" for the purposes of Article 6(1), regard must be had, inter alia, to the manner of appointment of its members and their term of office, the existence of safeguards against outside pressures and the question whether it presents an appearance of independence ... As to the condition of "impartiality" within the meaning of that provision, there are two tests to be applied: the first consists in trying to determine the personal conviction of a particular judge in a given case and the second in ascertaining whether the judge offered guarantees sufficient to exclude any legitimate doubt in this respect'.
12 Ibid., para 69.
13 Ibid., para 70.
14 Ibid., para 67.

'still belong to the army', which 'takes its orders from the executive', and because they 'remain subject to military discipline and assessment', there were legitimate doubts over their impartiality. However, before giving judgment, the court indicated that it was not within their competence to determine whether or not it was necessary for the Turkish government to set up special courts 'but to ascertain whether the manner in which one of them functioned infringed the applicant's right to a fair trial'.[15] In so doing, the accused's standpoint is 'important without being decisive' as to whether doubts about the impartiality of the court are 'objectively justified'. The presence of a military judge meant that 'the applicant could legitimately fear' that the court 'might allow itself to be unduly influenced by considerations which had nothing to do with the nature of the case'.[16] This amounted to a breach of Article 6(1).

This takes us to a second point: are administrative tribunals legitimate, as administrative officers rather than judges often staff them? This question is also validly asked of professional bodies with a disciplinary jurisdiction over the profession's members. The question becomes all the more acute with military tribunals that are staffed by military personnel exercising discipline over other serving personnel. In relation to the former point, two key judgments are *Le Compte, Van Leuven and De Meyere* v. *Belgium*[17] and *Albert and Le Compte* v. *Belgium*.[18] Both these cases concerned proceedings by the disciplinary body of the Medical Association (*Ordre des Médecins*) against the applicants. The proceedings had three stages. The case was considered by a Provincial Council, then an Appeals Council, and finally the Court of Cassation. In the *De Meyere* case, the court argued that it was not necessary that each of the tribunals, in particular 'administrative or professional bodies', met with the requirements of Article 6.[19] The *Albert* judgment stressed that even though Article 6 might not apply to professional disciplinary matters:

> [T]he Convention calls at least for one of the two following systems: either the jurisdictional organs themselves comply with the requirements of Article 6 para. 1, or they do not so comply but are subject to subsequent control by a judicial body that has full jurisdiction – that is to say, which has the competence to furnish 'a [judicial] determination ... of the matters in dispute, both for questions of fact and for questions of law' – and does provide the guarantees of Article 6 para. 1.[20]

It is worth remembering, however, that these authorities relate to disciplinary bodies and not to bodies determining 'civil or criminal charges'. They would not be authorities on bodies that were criminal or civil.

How can we think about the British courts from the perspective of Article 6? As we do not have the space to examine all the aspects of Article 6 considered above, we will turn to one particular area: military discipline. A great deal of the cases brought against

---

15   Ibid., para 70.
16   Ibid., para 72.
17   *Le Compte, Van Leuven and De Meyere* v. *Belgium*, 23 June 1981.
18   *Albert and Le Compte* v. *Belgium*, 10 February 1983.
19   Supra n. 17, at paras 50–51.
20   Ibid., para 29.

the UK concern the operation of military tribunals. The key authority is *Findlay* v. *UK*.[21] The appellant, a veteran of the Falklands war, suffered from a post-traumatic stress disorder, which was exacerbated by an accident suffered shortly after his posting to active duty in Northern Ireland. The appellant 'snapped' and held a number of his colleagues at gunpoint, threatening to kill them and himself. He fired two shots, which were not aimed at anyone, then surrendered the pistol and was arrested. Charged with assault, threatening to kill, and with offences against military discipline, Findlay was tried by a court martial. At the time of his trial, the powers and constitution of court martials derived from the Army Act 1955. The case drew attention to the composition of the tribunal, in particular the role of the convening officer, who was responsible for calling the body together, and its procedural correctness. The tribunal was staffed by a president and four other serving officers, all of whom were subordinate in rank to the convening officer. None of them had any legal training. The prosecuting and defending officers were also, at least in theory, subordinate in rank to the convening officer. The court martial was advised on points of law by a judge advocate, who was an assistant judge. As well as advising the tribunal on points of law, the judge advocate (and the president) had to ensure that the defendant did not suffer any disadvantages during his or her trial, and understood the charges and the relevant law.

Findlay pleaded guilty. However, despite convincing medical evidence and the urging of his solicitor that he should be given a lenient punishment, the tribunal ordered a period of imprisonment, a reduction in rank, a dismissal from the army and a reduction in pension entitlement. The applicant then made a number of appeals against his sentence, all of which were rejected by officials who were not legally qualified, although they did receive advice from the Judge Advocate General's office. Neither the nature of this advice, nor the reasons for refusal were revealed to the applicant.

After the failure of an application for judicial review, Findlay applied to the Commission alleging that he had not received a fair trial by an impartial and independent tribunal. The essence of his argument was that the subordinate position of the members of the tribunal to the convening officer, and their lack of legal training, rendered the tribunal incapable of making a fair decision. He also argued that the decisions on the appeal had been made in private and with no rules of procedure. Findlay's arguments also drew attention to the fact that the relevant statute contained no rules on the appointment of the convening officer and reviewing authorities; the tribunal was thus not established by law. The British government did not reply to these allegations, but submitted both to the Commission and the court that the Army Act was being amended in the light of these failures of due process.[22] However, these changes did not apply to the present case, which was dealt with entirely under the old procedures.

---

21   Supra n. 8.
22   In *Morris* the court noted the changes that the British government had made to the system of military justice in the 1996 Act: 'The posts of convening officer and "confirming officer" have been abolished, and the roles previously played by those officers have been separated. The convening officer's responsibilities in relation to the bringing of charges and progress of the prosecution are now split between the higher authority and the prosecuting authority. His duties concerning the convening of the court martial, appointment of its members, arrangement of venue and

Both the ECtHR and the Commission agreed with the applicant's argument. The ECtHR's decision in *Findlay* is consistent with the general jurisprudence on this point, as it asserts the close relationship of the concepts of independence and impartiality. They also stressed that the presence of the Judge Advocate in the court martial, and the availability of advice for the authorities that reviewed the tribunal's decision, were not sufficient enough to dispel the serious doubts about the tribunal's impartiality. Relying on *Pullar* v. *UK*,[23] the court asserted that the tribunal had to be free of both 'personal prejudice' and objectively free of bias.

The court's decision in *Findlay* opened the floodgates. The number of cases received in its wake suggests that there had been major failures in the due process requirements of military justice[24] and that these remained even after reforms of the system.[25] Indeed, *Morris* v. *UK*[26] went even further, casting doubt on the entire structure of the court martial system. The applicant argued that a court martial had to be 'independent of the army as an institution, particularly of senior army command'. The problem was that this was clearly not the case: '[A]t all key stages of the applicant's court martial, including the bringing of charges, the appointment of the members of the court, the reaching of a decision on verdict and sentence, and the review of such verdict and sentence, army institutions were involved'.[27] His argument also showed that there were no statutory guidelines to regulate the appointment of court martial personnel, and the lack of security of tenure of the permanent presidents of the tribunals meant that they were vulnerable to pressure from more senior officers. A related problem was the fact that there could be a difference in rank and seniority between the president and the other members of the court martial, also suggesting that a senior officer might be able to pressure or influence the opinion of a more junior colleague. The 'strong officer corps ethos', which privileged 'discipline' and the need to create examples to deter others, further compromised the independent nature of the court martial.[28]

While not accepting the applicant's point about the role of the Defence Council and the Adjutant General, the court relied on *Incal* v. *Turkey* to find breaches of Article 6 in relation to both the permanent president and the officers who served on the tribunal, and the failure of judicial supervision in relation to appeals from the decision of court martial.

---

summoning of witnesses have been entrusted to the Army Court Service (formerly the Court-Martial Administration Office), whose staff are independent of both the higher and prosecuting authorities. The convening officer's powers to dissolve the court martial have been invested, prior to a hearing, in the Army Court Service and thereafter in the judge advocate, who is now a formal member of the court martial, delivers his summing-up in open court and has a vote on sentence'.
23   *Pullar* v. *UK*, 10 June 1996, at para 30.
24   Cases drew attention not just to these problems in relation to army tribunals, but also to similar bodies presiding over discipline in the RAF (*Cooper* v. *UK Application no. 48843/99*) and the Royal Navy (*G.W.* v. *UK Application no. 34155/96*).
25   See *Hood* v. *UK Application no. 27267/95*; *le Petit (Application no. 35574/97)*; *Thompson* v. *UK (Application no. 36256/97)*; *Miller and Others (Application nos. 45825/99, 45826/99 and 45827/99)*; *Whitfield and Others (Application nos. 46387/99, 48906/99, 57410/00 and 57419/00)*; and *Martin* v. *UK (Application no. 40426/98)*.
26   *Morris* v. *UK*, 26 February 2002.
27   Ibid., para 40.
28   Ibid., para 43.

THE TESTS FOR BIAS

The notion of the independence and impartiality of the tribunal is bound up with the issue of the test for bias. We now need to turn our attention to this essential concern. How does the ECtHR understand bias? Impartiality is compromised by bias. Bias, in this sense, would be one of the fundamental breaches of the right to a fair trial. As the court stated in *Piersack* v. *Belgium*,[29] underlying Article 6 'the confidence which the courts must inspire in the public in a democratic society' underlies Article 6. Given the importance of the concept, the issue that has occupied the courts has been the correct test for bias. In *Piersack* the court pointed out that there are different ways in which bias shows itself. The fundamental distinction is between subjective and objective forms of bias:

> A distinction can be drawn ... between a subjective approach, that is endeavouring to ascertain the personal conviction of a given judge in a given case, and an objective approach, that is determining whether he offered guarantees sufficient to exclude any legitimate doubt in this respect.[30]

At the core of the distinction is the difference between the actual biases of a judge, and the perception of bias that would be justified if there were not ways of showing that the court was operating impartially. However, the ECtHR went on to suggest that it might be difficult to separate the two forms of bias. Citing *Delcourt* v. *Belgium*,[31] the ECtHR argued that if a judge is subjectively biased, then there would be a 'legitimate' reason to doubt the neutrality of the court and, therefore, unless the judge withdrew, there would also be objective bias. On the facts of *Piersack*, the ECtHR had to determine whether the presence of a former public prosecutor, who was now a judge in the same case that he had been prosecuting, breached the test for bias. While it would be 'going to the extreme' to hold that no public prosecutor could ever act as a judge, the facts suggested that there had indeed been bias. The ECtHR's argument, to the extent that it covered the composition of the court and the way in which judges were appointed, also suggests the close connection between the finding of bias and the requirement that a court be independent.

The court followed this approach closely in *De Cubber* v. *Belgium*.[32] The applicant was alleging that he had not received a fair trial from an impartial tribunal, because the presiding judge had acted as an 'investigating judge' in the case against him. *De Cubber* thus goes to the heart of the civilian practice of the investigating magistrate, a role that is not a predominant feature of common law courts. The Belgian government stressed that the investigating judge is 'fully independent' as s/he is not a party to the proceedings[33] and does not perform a prosecutorial role, helping to establish the guilt of the defendant. The investigating judge must 'strike a balance between prosecution and defence' in

---

29   *Piersack* v. *Belgium*, 1 October 1982.
30   Ibid., para 30.
31   *Delcourt* v. *Belgium*, 17 January 1970.
32   *De Cubber* v. *Belgium*, 26 October 1984.
33   Ibid., para 29.

assembling evidence, and presenting to the court an 'objective review' of the progress of the case. The ECtHR disagreed with this argument. Examining the legal definition of the powers of the investigating judge, they found that the office is not strictly separate from that of the prosecutor. In particular, the 'preparatory investigation', which is presided over by the judge is 'inquisitorial', 'secret' and 'not conducted in the presence of both parties'. They concluded:

> One can accordingly understand that an accused might feel some unease should he see on the bench of the court called upon to determine the charge against him the judge who had ordered him to be placed in detention on remand and who had interrogated him on numerous occasions during the preparatory investigation, albeit with questions dictated by a concern to ascertain the truth.[34]

This appeared to amount to a finding of objective bias. There was no reason to doubt the objectivity of the individual judge, but 'his presence on the bench provided grounds for some legitimate misgivings on the applicant's part'. This makes it clear that there is a correspondence between the objective test, and the 'English maxim' that was also cited in the *Delcourt* judgment: 'Justice must not only be done: it must also be seen to be done'.[35]

How has the common law responded to Strasbourg jurisprudence? Before we can properly address this issue, we need to establish the common law approach to bias. As has been explained,[36] English law has three categories of bias: 'actual bias, apparent bias and presumed bias'. The first is evidenced by a prejudice 'against one of the parties', the second category covers the situation where a 'hypothetical fair-minded and informed observer believes that the judge may be biased'.[37] The third situation is a special category that the courts should not be willing to expand, and exists where 'the tribunal has a pecuniary or proprietary interest in the subject matter of the proceedings'. The *Gough* test is an authority on the second form of bias. We will focus exclusively on the second form of bias, as it is the main problem that the case law addresses. It asks the court to consider 'whether, in all the circumstances of the case, there appeared to be a real danger of bias, concerning the member of the tribunal in question so that justice required that the decision should not stand'.[38]

As Lord Goff pointed out in *Gough*, cases of actual bias are 'very rare', and the more pressing issue is 'the degree of possibility of bias'.[39] The law on bias has to negotiate two extremes. If the test were too stringent, it would be too easy to invalidate decisions on the grounds of partiality. An overly lenient test would encourage bad practices. The central idea is that public confidence in the administration of justice requires that the impartiality of the judge be above suspicion. If it is not necessary to prove actual bias, then the fundamental question is how conclusions will be drawn from 'impressions'

---

34 Ibid.
35 *Delcourt* v. *Belgium*, 17 January 1970.
36 Gouldkamp (2008: 32).
37 Ibid.
38 R. v. *Gough* [1993] AC 646, at 647.
39 Ibid., 646.

derived from the circumstances of the case. From the case law, there were two possible ways of thinking about these impressions: one would be from the perspective of the court, the other from that of the reasonable man.[40] However, '[s]ince ... the court investigates the actual circumstances, knowledge of such circumstances as are found by the court must be imputed to the reasonable man', and there should be no real difference between the two perspectives. The related question would be the issue of whether possibility or probability of bias is on the standard of the balance of probabilities. This, in Lord Goff's opinion, would be 'too rigorous'. He concludes:

> I am by no means persuaded that, in its original form, the real likelihood test required that any more rigorous criterion should be applied. Furthermore the test as so stated gives sufficient effect, in cases of apparent bias, to the principle that justice must manifestly be seen to be done, and it is unnecessary, in my opinion, to have recourse to a test based on mere suspicion, or even reasonable suspicion, for that purpose. Finally there is, so far as I can see, no practical distinction between the test as I have stated it, and a test which requires a real danger of bias, as stated in *R v. Spencer* [1987] A.C. 128.[41]

For the moment we must suspend our judgment about whether or not this approach to bias does balance the competing demands that the test must satisfy. The *Gough* test was further elaborated in *Ex parte Pinochet* No. 2.[42] Lord Browne-Wilkinson pointed out that the case was about the 'real danger ... or reasonable apprehension or suspicion' of bias. Returning to the case law, he showed that the test rested on the principles of natural justice: that a man should not be the judge in his own case. However, there are two ways in which this principle could be understood. It may mean that a judge must not try a case in which he or she is a party or has an interest. The very fact that the judge is a party to the action or has an interest would make for his or her automatic disqualification.[43] The second interpretation is broader. It would apply where a judge is not directly party to a dispute and does not have a financial interest but has some concern with the issue at stake, which may make for a suspicion that he is not impartial.

This second interpretation is not, strictly, an application of the principle that a man must not be a judge in his own case at all. It is, more properly, an extension of the general sense of the principle: a judge must not be compromised by any direct or indirect interest in the action.

In *Pinochet*, the judges were aware of Article 6(1) and the differences between the Scottish and English courts on the issue of bias. In the former, a judge had been disqualified on the basis that there was reasonable suspicion about his impartiality.[44] The reasonable suspicion test was obviously different to the real danger test. Was this a problem? Although Lord Hope would speak of the 'uneasy tension' between the tests in *Porter v. Magill*,[45] their Lordships did not seem unduly concerned. They explained that

---

40   Ibid., 667.
41   Ibid.
42   *Ex parte Pinochet* No. 2 [1999] 1 All ER 577.
43   See *Dimes v. Proprietors of the Grand Junction Canal* [1852] 3 H.L. Cas. 759.
44   *Bradford v. McLeod* [1986] SLT 244 and *Doherty v. McGlennan* [1997] SLT 444.
45   *Porter v. Magill* [2002] 2 AC 359.

the tests reflected the differences between two legal traditions. The broad principle was the same; the judge must bring to bear 'an unbiased and impartial mind' and '[h]e must be seen to be impartial'.[46] Although the case of *Locabail*[47] went on to provide some guidance on the issue of 'real danger', the common law remained committed to the *Gough* test and the belief that there was no significant difference between the common and civilian approaches.

Porter v. *Magill*[48] struck a very different note and established that, in the light of Article 6, a new test for bias was necessary. Lord Hope made reference to criticisms of both the real danger and the real likelihood test, as they tended to privilege the view of the court and 'to place inadequate emphasis on the public perception of the irregular incident'.[49] The common law test was out of line with Strasbourg jurisprudence as it lacked the necessary element of objective justification of the fear of bias. Lord Hope went on to look at a passage in *Re Medicaments and Related Classes of Goods*[50] where 'a modest adjustment to the test of *R.* v. *Gough*' was suggested. The new test would involve the court ascertaining 'all the circumstances which have a bearing on the suggestion that the judge was biased', and then asking if 'a fair-minded and informed observer' would come to the conclusion that there was 'a real possibility, or a real danger ... that the tribunal was biased'. Lord Hope stressed that it was necessary to make some adjustments, and 'delete ... the reference to "a real danger" in the test for bias as it "no longer served a useful purpose" '.[51] The fundamental question was 'whether a fair-minded and informed observer having considered the facts would conclude that there was a real possibility that the tribunal was biased'.[52]

What does this mean? This test was further elaborated in *Jones* v. *DAS Legal Expenses Insurance Co. Ltd & Ors*.[53] In this case, the Court of Appeal heard an appeal from an employment tribunal that had presided over a sex discrimination case. The appeal was based on the fact that the chairwoman of the Employment Tribunal was married to a barrister whose chambers took work from DAS, the company that employed the appellant. The appeal was dismissed. In *Jones*, the Court of Appeal returned to a point that had been raised in *Re Medicaments*. The task of the court is to scrutinise all the circumstances that are relevant to the allegation that the judge was biased. In *Re Medicaments*, the court stated that this scrutiny would include taking into account any 'explanation' given by the judge, which, if necessary, would be considered from the perspective of the fair-minded observer. The question for the court is whether 'there was a real danger of bias notwithstanding the explanation advanced'. On the facts of the case, it meant that the test should be applied in the following way: the court is not concerned with precisely what the chairwoman of the tribunal knew. Since, following *Locabail*,[54] the presumption is upon disqualification, the fair-minded

---

46 Supra n. 42, at 595.
47 Locabail v. Bayfield Properties [2000] 1 All ER 65.
48 Porter v. Magill [2002] 2 AC 359.
49 Ibid., at 493.
50 Re Medicaments and Related Classes of Goods [2002] 2 AC 359.
51 Supra n. 48, at 494.
52 Ibid.
53 Jones v. DAS Legal Expenses Insurance Co. Ltd & Ors. [2003] WL 21554681.
54 Supra n. 47.

observer would 'proceed upon a basis that [the chairwoman] knew in general how the system operated and that her husband was to some extent a beneficiary of it even if she did not know all of the detail'. This brings us to a second question: would a fair-minded and informed observer then conclude that there was 'a real possibility that the tribunal was biased'? What qualities must the hypothetical fair-minded and informed observer possess?

Taylor v. *Lawrence*[55] (see also Chapter 13) concerned an appeal before a judge who had made use of the services of the respondent's solicitors the night before he gave judgment. Although the court did not find apparent bias, they offered some reflections on the nature of the test. They stated that judges should be 'circumspect' about 'declaring relationships' where a fair-minded observer would not see it as 'raising a possibility of bias'. Disclosure might itself suggest an 'implication' that the relationship would influence the judge's opinion. In a 'borderline' case the judge should make disclosure and then consider the submissions of either party before making his/her decision about whether or not to withdraw from the case. It had to be stressed that, if disclosure was made, it would have to be full and proper. The court concluded:

> No fair-minded observer would reach the conclusion that a judge would so far forget or disregard the obligations imposed by his judicial oath as to allow himself, consciously or unconsciously, to be influenced by the fact that one of the parties before him was represented by solicitors with whom he was himself dealing on a wholly unrelated matter.[56]

It would seem that the fair-minded observer proceeds on the basis that judges are not biased and that there must be strong evidence to show that there is bias. In other words, the court's interpretation of the test assumes a level of integrity to legal culture in general and to the judiciary in particular. In *Gillies* v. *Secretary of State for Work and Pensions*[57] Lord Hope suggested that the test demands a consideration of the appearance of the facts, rather than raising a question about 'what is in the mind of the particular judge or tribunal member who is under scrutiny'.[58] It would thus seem that any evidence of the judge's intentions would be irrelevant. Does this suggest that the test grants too much to the judges? *Lawal* v. *Northern Spirit Ltd*[59] suggests otherwise. The fair-minded observer can be seen to be critical of the culture with which he or she is familiar and believe in the necessity of high standards for the administration of justice, and 'may not be wholly uncritical of this culture'.[60]

Where does this leave us? The House of Lords has asserted that the test for bias under Article 6 and the common law test are exactly the same. In applying the fair-minded observer test, it is 'unnecessary to delve into the characteristics to be

---

55 *Taylor* v. *Lawrence* [2003] QB 528.
56 Ibid.
57 *Gillies* v. *Secretary of State for Work and Pensions* [2006] UKHL 2, 787.
58 Ibid., 787.
59 *Lawal* v. *Northern Spirit Ltd* [2003] UKHL 35.
60 Ibid.

attributed to the fair-minded and informed observer', and to accept that 'such an observer would adopt a balanced approach'. Importantly, the key reference points return to the common law test: that the observer should be as concerned with the appearance of impartiality as with its actuality. In other words, the impartiality of the decision maker should be assessed to the highest standard, so as not to 'undermine the need for constant vigilance that judges maintain that impartiality'.[61]

EQUALITY OF ARMS

Although Article 6 does not mention 'equality of arms' explicitly, it has come to be seen as an essential component of fair trial rights. However, its definition is a little difficult to pin down. Equality, in this context at least, does not have the sense of a prohibition on discrimination; a meaning that it carries in most human rights law. Trechsel argues that the principle 'implies that each party must be afforded a reasonable opportunity to present his case – including his evidence – under conditions that do not place him at a disadvantage vis-à-vis his opponent'.[62] In the jurisprudence of the court, the concept can also be distinguished from the 'right to adversarial proceedings'. Perhaps the most useful statement of the principle comes from *Kaufman* v. *Belgium*:[63] the defendant in criminal proceedings 'must have a reasonable opportunity of presenting his case under conditions which do not place him at a substantial disadvantage vis-à-vis his opponent'.

The principle of equality of arms also applies to civil as well as criminal cases. In *Dombo Beheer* v. *The Netherlands*,[64] the court made a distinction between the fair trial rights that are relevant in criminal cases and those applicable where civil rights and obligations are at stake. Although contracting states might have a 'greater latitude'[65] in civil cases to determine rules of procedure, there are common concepts shared by both civil and criminal law: most notably that 'the requirement of equality of arms' be understood as making for 'a "fair balance" between the parties'.[66] In relation to litigation between two private parties, this means that each party must have 'a reasonable opportunity to present his case', but national authorities can determine the precise form of the opportunities so afforded. As the majority of the cases concern criminal matters, we will follow this theme.

---

61 What is interesting in our context is the use of the judgment of another court that shares the common law tradition: the Constitutional Court of South Africa, in the case of the *President of the Republic of South Africa & Others* v. *South African Rugby Football Union & Others* [1999] (7) BCLR (CC) 725, 753: 'The reasonableness of the apprehension [for which one must read in our jurisprudence 'the real risk'] must be assessed in the light of the oath of office taken by the judges to administer justice without fear or favour, and their ability to carry out that oath by reason of their training and experience. It must be assumed that they can disabuse their minds of any irrelevant personal beliefs or pre-dispositions ... At the same time, it must never be forgotten that an impartial judge is a fundamental prerequisite for a fair trial'. The court came down on one side of the balance: the tribunal was not biased and the court dismissed the appeal.
62 Supra n. 1, at 96.
63 *Kaufman* v. *Belgium*, 50 DR 98, at 355.
64 *Dombo Beheer* v. *The Netherlands*, 27 October 1993.
65 Ibid., para 32.
66 See also the *Feldbrugge* v. *The Netherlands*, 26 May 1986, at para 44.

The leading cases where the principle of equality of arms has been applied to English law have concerned prosecution disclosure of evidence in the criminal trial. The authorities determine that although there is coherence between the common law and Article 6 on the duty of the prosecution to disclose evidence, in certain instances there are insufficient safeguards to provide equality of arms. However, there is a vocal minority in the ECtHR who see both rights jurisprudence and English law as failing in its duty to ensure equality of arms. As Judge Zupancic argued, unjust limitations on the right of disclosure can 'affect the whole philosophy of criminal procedure'.[67]

In *Edwards*,[68] the applicant had been sentenced to a long period of imprisonment for burglary. He sought to argue that the police had concocted the evidence against him, and that the use of public interest immunity to prevent his counsel having access to the Police Complaints Authority's investigation into the matter rendered his conviction unsafe. After the Court of Appeal rejected his argument, he unsuccessfully petitioned the Home Secretary. Before the ECtHR, he argued that his trial remained flawed because neither the Court of Appeal nor the Home Secretary had seen the report, nor examined police witnesses that, he contended, were vital to his case. The ECtHR affirmed that the common law rules on disclosure of evidence recognised the importance of fairness to the criminal trial and there had, indeed, been 'defects'[69] in Edwards's case. However, the ECtHR went on to say that fairness must ultimately be assessed in the context of the proceedings as a whole.[70] There had been an independent investigation into the conduct of the police, and the Court of Appeal had considered a typescript of the trial and had rejected the applicant's arguments about the credibility of the police witnesses. Moreover, Edwards had been represented by both junior and senior counsel at the appeal hearing. Edwards alleged before the ECtHR that the failure to disclose the independent report rendered his trial unfair but the Court commented that he did not apply to the Court of Appeal for its production.

The dissenting opinion of Judge Pettiti is interesting as it interprets the case through the issue of public interest immunity. He argued that this prevented the disclosure of important evidence at trial, and that the failure of counsel to apply for disclosure before the Court of Appeal was not 'relevant'. He invoked the civilian principle of 'nullity for reasons of public policy'. This doctrine can be employed by the Court itself, and thus relieves counsel of the burden of rectifying procedural faults. The principle is justified by 'the fundamental procedural rule that prohibits the concealment of documents or evidence'. Judge Pettiti's concerns are reiterated in his dissenting judgments in *Fitt* and *Rowe and Davis*.

In *Rowe and Davis*,[71] the applicants had been convicted of a number of charges including murder, assault and robbery. They appealed to the Court of Appeal, arguing that there were 'inconsistencies'[72] in the evidence against them. During the

---

67 *Edwards* v. *UK*, 16 December 1992.
68 Ibid.
69 Ibid., para 36.
70 Ibid., para 34.
71 *Rowe and Davis*, 16 February 2000.
72 Ibid., para 23.

appeal hearing, the prosecution made available to the Court a document that had not been shown to the defence, arguing that it contained sensitive information. Proceeding *ex-parte*, the Court of Appeal held that the document did not have to be disclosed and was protected by public interest immunity. Later, information came to light that the prosecution's case had relied on the evidence of an informer, who had been rewarded for the evidence he provided. The applicants applied to the Criminal Cases Review Commission, who found that the case should be remitted to the Court of Appeal. While the case was waiting to be heard, the ECtHR considered the applicant's argument that they had not had a fair trial. Their argument rested on the understanding that there was no absolute right to disclosure, and that there were legitimate reasons for preventing it; however, 'procedural safeguards' should be in place to ensure the overall fairness of the trial. The ex-parte hearing by the Court of Appeal was not a sufficient safeguard. They argued that there should be a 'special counsel' who would have access to the information and could test the prosecution's case. The government responded that the special counsel system would involve insuperable procedural difficulties and that the present system, in which the trial judge determined whether or not public interest immunity applied, was the best.

The ECtHR followed the principle in *Edwards*, and asserted that it was necessary to consider the proceedings as a whole. They then invoked the equality of arms argument that the prosecution should not enjoy unfair advantages over the defence, linking it to the very idea of the adversarial trial where 'both prosecution and defence must be given the opportunity to have knowledge of and comment on the observations filed and the evidence adduced by the other party'.[73] Article 6(1), and English law in general, were in agreement on the duty of the prosecution to provide 'all material evidence in their possession for or against the accused'. The Court also asserted that this right was not absolute, and it was not for the ECtHR to determine whether any particular refusal of disclosure was legitimate or not, as this fell entirely within the jurisdiction of the national court. However, the problem was that the ex-parte hearing was not a sufficient safeguard to ensure equality of arms between prosecution and defence.

The case of *Fitt*[74] returns to the approach of *Edwards*. It also concerned an ex-parte application from the prosecution to the trial judge. The prosecution argued that evidence from a police informer (C) was protected by public interest immunity and should not be disclosed to the defence. The important point of distinction from *Rowe and Davis* is that the ex-parte hearing in the case took place during the trial itself, rather than in an appeal hearing. This suggests that the ECtHR found a breach of Article 6 in *Rowe and Davis* because the Court of Appeal should have had more robust safeguards in place. This reasoning did not apply to a trial court.

On the evidence presented by the prosecution, Fitt was found guilty of numerous offences, including conspiracy to rob. In his appeal he argued that the evidence of the informer needed to be examined to show that he had been falsely implicated

---

73 See *Brandstetter* v. *Austria*, 28 August 1991, paras 66–7.
74 *Fitt* v. *UK*, 16 February 2000.

in the conspiracy to rob. In particular, he was arguing for disclosure of a series of statements made by C in other cases that would tend to strengthen his case. The Court of Appeal upheld the convictions, and the ECtHR held that the trial had been fair. They stated:

> The Court is satisfied that the defence were kept informed and were permitted to make submissions and participate in the above decision-making process as far as was possible without revealing to them the material which the prosecution sought to keep secret on public interest grounds.[75]

The ECtHR also rejected submissions that there should be a special counsel system to introduce an 'adversarial element' into disclosure hearings. Although there were good reasons for such a system in immigration hearings, there was no argument to extend their operation to criminal trials. The existing law guaranteed equality of arms. For instance, the evidence that was not disclosed in this case never actually formed part of the prosecution's case and was never seen by the jury. This can be distinguished from the kind of non-disclosure issues that lay behind recent major miscarriages of justice, where the 'executive'[76] made use of evidence that the defence never saw. Moreover, the trial judge him or herself provides an important safeguard, as he has a duty to 'monitor ... the fairness or otherwise of withholding the evidence'.[77] Reviewing the relevant case law, the ECtHR held that English law on the matters to be taken into account on disclosure 'fulfils' the 'conditions' laid down by Article 6.

There were a number of powerful dissenting opinions. We will examine those of Judges Palm, Fischbach, Vajić, Thomassen, Tsatsa-Nikolovska and Traja. They held that the principle of equality of arms was breached by the fact that the prosecution had 'access to the judge' during the ex-parte hearing, and were thus able to 'participate in the decision making process' without the presence of the defence. The role of the judge as the neutral umpire could not counterbalance this fundamental in equality in the trial process. This was not to impugn the impartiality and independence of the judge but to assert that in order to make a fair decision, the judge had to hear arguments from both sides. Judge Hedigan relied on the ruling in *Van Mechelen and Others* v. *The Netherlands*.[78] The ECtHR stated: 'Having regard to the place that the right to a fair administration of justice holds in a democratic society, any measures restricting the rights of the defence should be strictly necessary. If a less restrictive measure can suffice then that measure should be applied'.[79] This suggested that the arguments put forward for a special counsel to operate in criminal trials should have been more carefully considered by the British government.

---

75 Ibid.
76 Ibid., para 48.
77 Ibid., para 49.
78 *Van Mechelen and Others* v. *The Netherlands*, 23 April 1997.
79 Supra n. 73, at para 50.

PUBLIC PRONUNCIATION OF JUDGMENT

The requirement that judgment be pronounced publicly is a central element of Article 6. In *Pretto v. Italy*,[80] the Court went some way to articulating the reasons that justified this principle. It protects litigants against the administration of justice in secret with no public scrutiny.[81] The public pronouncement of judgment also makes for public confidence in the courts. Overall, the objective of Article 6 is to make justice 'visible'. Indeed, one definition of a fair trial is that it does not take place in secret. This broader defence of the Article can be linked with the very idea that a publicly pronounced judgment compels the rational defence of the judgment. Secret judgments can be arbitrary because there is no way that they can be scrutinised.

Some cases show that the desire to have judgment pronounced publicly or to have a case heard in open court brings applicants into conflict with a legal culture that stresses the need for secrecy in certain proceedings. The most important cases have tended to concern children. In *B and P v. UK*,[82] the applicant had argued that an application for a residence order should be heard in open court. The judge had refused, as it was a case concerning children, and had conducted the hearings in chambers, warning the applicant that it would be a contempt of court to publicise anything that had taken place during the hearing. The second applicant was asserting that hearings concerning children should be held in open court to ensure the transparency of the decision-making process. The case reached the Court of Appeal.[83] Lord Justice Butler-Sloss argued that under the Children Act 1989 it was necessary to hear cases concerning children in private. Given the 'long established practice' of so doing, it would only be in rare cases where cases are heard in public. The practice of pronouncing judgment in private reflects the interests of the parties involved, although in cases where public interest is at stake, judgment could be given in open court.

When the case came to be heard by the ECtHR, the government restated these arguments: the underlying reason for secrecy in cases concerning children was to protect the children themselves, and to encourage the parties to give 'full and frank' evidence.[84] The judge's discretion to hear cases in public was entirely in keeping with Article 6. The British government argued that the limitations on the right to a public hearing were consistent with Article 6 provided that the restrictions were themselves carefully justified. On the facts of the present case, arguments had been given which asserted that the best interests of the child provided compelling grounds for just such limitations. The applicants argued that the presumption of a private hearing was in breach of Article 6. The correct position would be to assert that all cases, even those concerning children, had to take place in open court. This presumption could then be rebutted, in order to allow a case to be heard privately. Both cases showed that as the interests of the children were not best served by secrecy, the presumption was rebutted. Moreover, the county court

---

80 *Pretto v. Italy*, 8 December 1983.
81 Ibid., 29.
82 *B and P v. UK*, 24 April 2001.
83 *Re P-B (a minor)* [1997] 1 All ER 58.
84 Supra n. 81, at para, 32.

judge had not carried out a 'balancing exercise',[85] which would have made explicit that the interests of the child were not paramount to the need for a public hearing. The second applicant added to these arguments, asserting that a public hearing was particularly important in children's cases because of the operation of 'judicial discretion' and 'the inevitability that judges would decide such cases in accordance with their own personal values and morality'.[86]

The way in which the ECtHR approached this case tells us a great deal about the precise operation of Article 6. The Strasbourg Court reasserted the general principle that the need for a public hearing could be restricted. Most importantly, the Court ruled that there was 'an entire class of case' where there was a compelling argument for closed proceedings. This class would always be subject to the overarching jurisdiction of the Court, but on this issue, 'English procedural law' was entirely consistent with European human rights law. In other words, there was no breach of Article 6.

In relation to the requirement that judgment be pronounced in public, the applicants had relied on *Campbell and Fell* to show that there was no 'implied limitation' to this right. Although a government could determine in national law the precise method to be employed, this discretion did not allow a judgment to be kept 'entirely confidential'.[87] This meant that both the court order and the full judgment itself had to be made public. The court returned to the fundamental principles of the case law. They had held in *Sutter* that Article 6 was satisfied because judgments could be consulted and the position was similar in English law. The ECtHR's interpretation of 'fairness' thus attempts to balance a number of factors, rather than inflexibly assert a predominant requirement for public pronouncement. Indeed, a 'literal' interpretation of Article 6 would privilege 'public scrutiny' over other values, and effectively 'frustrate' the 'primary aim' of the Article.[88]

The dissenting judges argued that the majority had misunderstood the law and practice of the Court. They had held that Article 6 laid down a general rule that civil proceedings should be held in public, and then went on to determine that there was a class of excluded cases that were exceptional to this general rule. Although the majority relied on *Campbell and Fell* to support this statement, the dissenting judges argued that this was not what the case had decided. The court did not simply accept a general principle and then note that it was legitimate to exclude certain cases from it. They examined the case on its facts, and found that it was legitimate to hold the hearing in private. To remain consistent with this approach in the present case, it would be necessary to move to a position much closer to the rejected arguments of the applicants. On an examination of the specific facts of the two cases, it would be necessary to show that the interests of the children took precedence over the requirement of the Article for a public hearing. This would suggest that English law was in breach of the Article:

> We believe that the legal rule in England, to the effect that unless the court directs otherwise hearings of family cases should be in camera, is the reverse of what Article 6 demands, namely, that in civil proceedings such as the present the hearings must be

---

85 Ibid., para 33.
86 Ibid., para 34.
87 Ibid., para 44.
88 Ibid., para 48.

held in public unless the court (and not any general rule of law) decides, exceptionally, in the light of the particular facts, nature or circumstances of the concrete case before it to exclude the press and public from all or part of the trial on any of the grounds specified in Article 6. In actual fact in the present cases, as pointed out above, the courts did not decide to hold private hearings after assessing the relevant facts but proceeded to private hearings because that was the position under the English rules of procedure. This is clearly reflected in the relevant judgments of the domestic courts.[89]

This is not saying that all children's cases should be held in public; rather, that the courts should engage in a balancing exercise in order to arrive at a legitimate argument for holding a particular case in private. The English courts had conducted the argument at a general level, asserting general principles, rather than taking into account specific facts. Ultimately, the majority in the ECtHR had also misunderstood *Sutter* when it asserted that an inflexible and literal reading of the Article meant that the requirement for public hearing could be restricted in the way that the Court believed. *Sutter* merely held that a requirement for an oral delivery of a judgment would be inflexible.

CONCLUSION

How, then, could we characterise this complex relationship between common law and European law? As with our previous chapter, we can perhaps find an ongoing debate both within European law and common law about the way in which due process guarantees are to be realised. To this end, we have examined the interplay between some central aspects of Article 6 jurisprudence and the common law. In some instances we found that the common law had been pushed in the direction of reform after losing in Strasbourg. In other instances, judges have made only slight alterations to common law doctrines. There is also evidence that common law principles remain entirely coherent with those of European human rights law, even though they reflect the differences between legal traditions and their development.

---

89 Ibid.

12

IMAGINING CIVIL JUSTICE

Imagination is more important than knowledge. For while knowledge defines all we currently know and understand, imagination points to all that we might yet consider.

Einstein, as noted by Viereck 1929

This is the Court of Chancery ... which gives to monied might the means abundantly of wearying out the right; which so exhausts finances, patience, courage, hope; so overthrows the brain and breaks the heart; that there is not an honorable man among its practitioners who would not give – who does not often give – the warning, 'Suffer any wrong that can be done you, rather than come here'.

Charles Dickens, *Bleak House* (1853) (Penguin Classics (1971): 51)

INTRODUCTION: FROM *BLEAK HOUSE* TO THE POST-WOOLF LANDSCAPE

Images of justice help determine the acceptability and success of the processes associated with those images. A system of justice appeals to, and gains acceptance by, parties who believe that a specific injustice has occurred, if the ideal behind and the workings of the system are in line with a clear and compelling vision of fairness, procedurally and substantially. While there is always a difference between vision and reality, when the processes and outcomes seem far removed from the core ideals and images of the enterprise, disillusionment and sense of failure is rife.

There is an image of justice oft repeated, reproduced in pictures and sculptures in courtrooms, offices and books: it is of a blindfolded woman, standing straight and tall, with a stretched-out arm that holds a set of scales. In the traditional court-centred understanding of justice, this represents a place of judgment and since the woman is blindfolded, she cannot be swayed by gender, race, wealth, or other influences or advantages that one party might hold. On her scales, the parties to the dispute place their arguments and recounting of the facts, hoping that their side will have more weight. The matter is weighed on these scales in public view, and the balance resolves the matter. The scales themselves are open in their workings and get more precisely balanced after each weighing, after each case. The weight and moment of precise and particular factors are calibrated, and all understand how much factors weigh, this time and for the future. Should a party suspect that the scales were out of balance or the blindfold had been lifted, he may appeal to higher authorities to test the integrity of the process. This process is accessible to all, rich and poor alike.

Figure 12.1

When looking at civil justice our journey begins with Charles Dickens' *Bleak House*. *Bleak House*, the ninth novel of Charles Dickens, was published in instalments from March 1852 through September 1853.[1] *Bleak House* presented a compelling and clear set of images of the abject failure of the British Court of Chancery. Dickens had become

---

1   This is a work that both reflects Dickens' personal life and his desire to fight for a better system (as well as make some money!). Dickens suffered a series of personal difficulties during this time. In 1851 Catherine Dickens, his wife, suffered a nervous collapse. Later Dora Dickens, the youngest daughter of Charles and Catherine, died when she was only eight months old. The father of Charles Dickens also died in 1851. The youngest child of Charles Dickens, Edward, was born in 1852. Dickens had close familiarity with the court system from his time spent as a law clerk. He also had a bad experience with the court in 1844 when he brought a case to Chancery that dealt with

embroiled in matters of Chancery when he was the plaintiff in five Chancery actions to restrain breaches of copyright. Holdsworth[2] tells us that he was victorious but had failed to recover costs and his experience of the system appears to have had a significant impact on him. At that time there were two main types of courts: the Courts of Common Law applied the precedents, principles and rules developed over time by the judges staffing the common law courts; an alternative court, the Court of Chancery, dealt with cases like property disputes and decided on the principles of equity. Equity, often derided as discretion varying with the length of the Lord Chancellor's feet, actually had built up a series of rules and procedures as complex as anything the common law had developed but was even more complicated by the necessity to avoid the set 'forms of action' of the common law procedures and consider each case on its own merits. If this was thought to be an improvement over trying this type of case in the Courts of Common Law, Dickens demonstrated that the Chancery had became as bad, if not worse, as the common law process. The Chancery was ineffective, expensive and technically difficult. The litigants were charged fees at every step of the legal process, fees which went directly to the court officials. The more steps in the justice process, the greater the opportunities to collect fees. The consequence was a bureaucratic nightmare. Sometimes it took years for cases to even come to trial. From that point it could be years before a decision on the case was reached. In the preface of a non-serialised volume of *Bleak House* Dickens writes:

> At the present moment [August, 1853] there is a suit before the court which was commenced nearly twenty years ago, in which from thirty to forty counsel have been known to appear at one time, in which costs have been incurred to the amount of seventy thousand pounds, which is A FRIENDLY SUIT, and which is (I am assured) no nearer to its termination now than when it was begun.

In *Bleak House*, a large group of people, rich and poor (and often made poorer by their involvement in the case), are drawn together by their interest, which is usually financial, in the outcome of the long-running settlement of a disputed inheritance suit. The case is simply known as *Jarndyce* v. *Jarndyce* and Mr Kenge, a lawyer in the story, is astounded when he meets people who have not heard of the case. He says:

> Not heard of Jarndyce – the greatest of Chancery suits known? Not of Jarndyce v. Jarndyce – the – a – in itself a monument of Chancery practice. In which (I would say) every difficulty, every contingency, every masterly fiction, every form of procedure known in that court, is represented over and over again? It is a cause that could not exist, out of this free and great country.

By the end of the novel the case is settled in favour of one of the hopeful litigants but it becomes apparent that there is no money left for any victor in the case because the long delay has eaten all the profits. The only financial winners in *Bleak House*, it seems, are the lawyers and the Court of Chancery.

---

the copyright to *A Christmas Carol*. Dickens won the case; however, his opponents declared bankruptcy. Instead of collecting damages Dickens found himself paying court costs – on a case that he won!
2   Holdsworth (1928a: 80).

Holdsworth[3] makes much of the fact that Dickens' novel opens in physical fog and this fog is indicative of the system at the time. Holdsworth points to four key problems within the system at this time. First, the official machinery of the system was medieval and had been relatively unaltered since that time. Second, the practices of the court had become so technical and so slow and even in uncontested cases the delays were indefensible. Even where new procedures were introduced to attempt to reform the system so the old procedures continued to operate because it was in the officials' interest for them to do so. Finally the court had decided that if it were to act it had to act in entire control of the case. This meant that every time a minute point was raised so the whole procedure had to be undertaken for that point to be resolved. Holdsworth notes that just as Gibbon had commented on the operation of Roman law in much the same way the procedure in the Court of Chancery was 'a mysterious science and a profitable trade'.[4]

Although the two courts were fused in the reforms of the mid-nineteenth century dissatisfaction with civil justice has been widespread and this seems familiar across the common law world. In 1982, US Chief Justice Warren Burger summarised dissatisfaction with litigation: 'Our system is too costly, too painful, too destructive, too inefficient for a truly civilized people'.[5]

The message from Dickens was clear. The system was slow, costly and complicated. Reforms did come when the systems were fused as a result of the Judicature Acts 1872–75, so it was hoped that Dickens' criticisms were no longer unfounded. One hundred and twenty years later and an empirical study, conducted by Professor Hazel Genn, considered what people thought about going to the law.[6] The study did not present a particularly positive portrayal of the civil justice system. One survey respondent said, 'I'd like more access to justice and less access to the courts'.[7] As a quantitative study of the views of 4,125 randomly selected adults, the study offers a valuable insight into how access to justice was often restricted because of the fear of cost and delay associated with use of the courts. The findings of this study confirmed the findings of the National Consumer Council in 1995 who found that the civil justice system was too slow, too complicated and outdated.[8] Given this background the reforms which came in 1997 were apparently timely and necessary if 'access to justice' was ever to become a reality.

The Woolf reforms were implemented by virtue of the Civil Procedure Act 1997 and through the Civil Procedure Rules which followed in 1998. They can be summarised as being concerned with case control, court allocation and tracking and the use of streamlined documentation and procedures.[9] The reforms were meant to simplify the system and speed up the process. This in turn was meant to reduce costs which, although presented as being a marginal concern, were clearly crucial if the reforms were to be seen

---

3   Ibid., 85.
4   Ibid., 87.
5   Burger (1982).
6   Genn (1999).
7   Ibid., 1.
8   See Slapper and Kelly (2006: 293) for details.
9   For a detailed description of these reforms see Slapper and Kelly (2006: 293).

as a marked improvement on the old system. The use of case control has perhaps seen the most significant change in the process as the progress of cases is far more actively managed by the judge in the case whose task it is to ensure that all avenues of dispute resolution are considered before the case arrives at court and can assess more rigorously, and at a much earlier stage, which evidence needs to be presented if the case is to appear in court. The allocation of cases to a newly organised court tracking system means that cases are allocated to the small claims track, the fast track or the multi track.[10] Each track is used to ensure that the cost and complexity of the claim is dealt with in a more carefully defined arena where expert evidence can be utilised more efficiently in accordance with the case. This track allocation is decided upon via a case allocation questionnaire which, when completed by the disputing parties, will be reviewed and a decision[11] taken as to which court the case should be heard in. This limit to access to the High Court for the purpose of minor claims is thought to ensure that access to justice is rather more 'steered' than it ever had been before. This, coupled with a simplification of the language used[12] in the proceedings, was all geared towards making the system more user-friendly in order to meet those earlier criticisms that Genn referred to.

These reforms have now been in place for a decade and some assessment has been made as to their success. The changes to the language used and the track allocation system seem to have been successful in making the system more comprehensible to the parties involved and directing the court's time to the particular issues in each case. The case management changes with their greater reliance on an active judge appear to be less successful in that just as one set of problems disappear (in terms of delay later in proceedings) so another emerges. Richard Burns,[13] a recorder from the county court, has argued that this new front-loading for case management simply moves the delay to earlier in proceedings. He comments that the process has been poorly resourced and appears to place too heavy a burden on the parties to the case at an earlier stage in the resolution of the dispute. The one area where the Woolf reforms appear to have had minimal impact is in the reduction of costs. Evidence[14] suggests that 'Lord Woolf's aspiration that case management would achieve his aims in relation to costs has not been achieved'.[15] In fact the front-loading of cases in some instances appears to have meant that costs have increased rather than decreased as was once hoped for.

THE OVERRIDING OBJECTIVE[16]

Much has been made of the Woolf reforms. The reforms are said to have changed the landscape of the civil justice system to the extent that the system now presents itself

---

10 See Slapper and Kelly (2006: 308).
11 Under Part 26 Civil Procedure Rules.
12 There was a deliberate simplification of terms that took place where arcane terms such as plaintiff were replaced with claimant and formal terms such as particulars of claim were replaced with statement of claim to more clearly indicate what the statement was for.
13 Burns (2000).
14 See discussion in Zander (2007).
15 Peysner and Seneviratne, quoted in Zander (2007: 138).
16 For a useful summary of the application of the overriding objective see Sime (2007).

as being far more in touch with what people require to assist them in resolving their disputes.

The central tenet of these reforms is encapsulated in rule 1.1 of the Civil Procedure Rules, which states: '(1) These rules are a new procedural code with the overriding objective of enabling the court to deal with cases justly'.

This is known as the 'overriding objective' and rather than leaving the term 'just' hanging as a vague and non-specific term, rule 1.1 goes on to explain how a case can be dealt with justly. Given the more active role of judges in the reformed system it is interesting that those who drafted the rules felt the need to explain to judges how to deal with cases 'justly'. After all, this is central to the judicial function. Nevertheless an indicative list is presented to assist the judiciary in their task. To deal with a case justly 'so far as is practicable', it would seem that the judge must:

- ensure that the parties are on an equal footing;
- save expense;
- deal with the case in ways which are proportionate
    - to the amount of money involved,
    - to the importance of the case,
    - to the complexity of the issues, and
    - to the financial position of each party;
- ensure that it is dealt with expeditiously and fairly; and
- allot to it an appropriate share of the court's resources, while taking into account the need to allot resources to other cases.

The list is clear: it tells everyone, including the judge, how cases will be dealt with. But it is also rather mechanical and in some ways it asks more questions than it answers. The reason for this claim is the question of how a judge can ensure that parties are truly on an equal footing. How rapacious must the judge be in attempting to save costs? When dealing with cases proportionately[17] the differences between cases will mean that a starting reference point will be tricky to come by. Will dealing with a case quickly mean the judge runs the risk of not dealing with the case justly? And finally, what share of the courts resources will be 'appropriate'? The list of factors being considered by judges has been considered by the courts[18] but it is not the role of this chapter to go through a host of cases which explain the application of the overriding objective. The cases, like the list, are perfunctory and would fail to enrich the reader's imagining of civil justice.

Instead we intend to imagine what judges should be considering when they are ensuring that a case is dealt with justly. What does 'just' mean for these purposes?

---

17 The concept of proportionality has been central to criminal justice since the writings of Beccaria (1767) and for the sentencing exercise it has been critical since the Criminal Justice Act 1991.
18 If you are particularly interested in seeing how the courts have considered these criteria then see the discussion by Sime (2007: 26–8) and see *Chilton v. Surrey County Council* [1999] LTL 24/6/99; *Cala Homes (South) Ltd v. Chichester District Council* (1999) *The Times*, 15 October 1999; *Maltez v. Lewis* [1999] *The Times*, 4 May 1999; *McPhillemy v. Times Newspapers Ltd* [1999] 3 All ER 775; *Adan v. Securicor Custodial Services Ltd* [2005] PIQR P193; *Re Hoicrest Ltd* [2000] 1 WLR 414; *Re Osea Road Camp Sites Ltd* [2005] 1 WLR 760; *Stephenson (SBJ) Ltd v. Mandy* [1999] *The Times*, 21 July 1999; *Adoko v. Jemal* [1999] *The Times*, 8 July 1999; *King v. Telegraph Group Ltd* [2005] 1 WLR 2282 and *Hertsmere Primary Care Trust v. Administrators of Balasubramanium's Estate* [2005] 3 All ER 274.

To begin with, a judge will need to have a sense of what justice is in order to act justly. So what is justice? Freeman[19] tells us that most contemporary scholarship about justice focuses on the idea of 'distributive justice'. That said the foundations of distributive justice can be traced back to the work of Aristotle who argued that goods should be distributed according to an individual's relative claim. This would necessitate a balancing act where competing claims would need to be resolved. Aristotle suggested that the factors affecting the decision to distribute would be desert, or moral virtue or needs.

Contemporary scholarship does have to resolve the same dilemmas but it is, according to Freeman,[20] the work of John Rawls which offers a modern take on justice and its concerns. In Rawls' *A Theory of Justice*, an argument is made for justice to ensure there is the:

- Maximisation of liberty, subject only to such constraints as are essential for the protection of liberty itself.
- Equality for all, both in the basic liberties of social life and also in distribution of all other forms of social goods, subject only to the exception that inequalities may be permitted if they produce the greatest possible benefit for those least well off in a given scheme of inequality.
- 'Fair equality of opportunity' and the elimination of all inequalities of opportunity based on birth or wealth.

It is not the aim of this chapter to critically evaluate Rawls' claims.[21] Our purpose is to use this modern framework in an attempt to show what a civil justice system ought to be aiming to achieve if it is to confirm its commitment to dealing with cases 'justly'. An examination of key concerns for those using the civil justice system will be considered alongside Rawls' framework so as to demonstrate why civil justice is important and how fertile the system is for the student imagination.

ALTERNATIVE DISPUTE RESOLUTION[22]

One key aspect of civil justice which has grown in importance in the past 40 years is the emergence of alternative methods for dispute resolution. In civil, as in some criminal,[23] cases the use of these alternatives has become central to resolving disputes before recourse to the courts is deemed necessary. So how does this maximise liberty in accordance with the first criterion for Rawls' *A Theory of Justice*? It would appear that by encouraging a wide range of methods for the resolution of disputes, alternative dispute resolution (ADR) ensures that a claimant and defendant are not necessarily straitjacketed into the court process which, for all its reforms, can still prove to be a costly,

---
19 Freeman (2001: 522).
20 Ibid., 522–3.
21 See Freeman for a critical evaluation of Rawls' claims.
22 For a pithy consideration of ADR see Zander (2007).
23 This is especially true in criminal cases involving young people where restorative justice and the use of mediation are central to the attempt to deal with youth offending at an early age. For a lively critique see Fionda (2005).

lengthy and unrewarding experience. Although judges will have a role to play in the case, the view is that with ADR the parties own the process. This again maximises their liberty.

ADR is the broad name for those methods of dispute resolution that do not involve recourse to the court system. These can include mediation, arbitration, conciliation and early neutral evaluation.[24] Mediation can be both formal and informal and it usually involves an experienced person (mediator) who acts as a facilitator to encourage discussion of the parties' concerns and tries to encourage the parties to reach a solution that they are all happy with. Conciliation is slightly different in that the conciliator is authorised to propose a solution for the parties to consider before they reach a conclusion. Neutral evaluation involves an expert considering all of the evidence and reaching a view which, although not binding, is used in an attempt for all parties to see what the effect could be if the case goes to court. It is hoped that both parties will resolve their disputes if they are confronted by this neutral position. Finally, arbitration tends to be used in commercial cases and a professional arbitrator will determine how the case will be resolved. This is a much more formal process than the previous forms of ADR and it is often seen as an expensive but useful alternative.[25]

Back in 1993 a special edition of the *Modern Law Review*[26] was devoted to ADR and a collection of papers were presented which, prior to the Woolf reforms, did consider how ADR was beginning to make its presence felt in the civil justice system. At this stage Cappelletti[27] considered how far the access to justice movement had succeeded throughout the world in promoting ADR as a real alternative to the adversarial process. Glasser[28] confirmed that the principle of orality, so central to the adversarial system, had been in decline within the civil process for some time. Lastly Lord Hoffmann, writing extrajudicially, commented on the civil process in general and confirmed that change had been afoot. Hoffmann's account is interesting in that as a working judge he does raise some concerns about the changes to the civil process. He also calls on research to be undertaken to consider the impact of these changes to the civil process. What is clear from this collection of papers is that ADR had by 1993 been seen as an addition to the process. In 2007, Zander[29] commented that while there has been a significant upsurge in the range of ADR available and the take up by litigants of that ADR, it is not yet directly part of the court system. This is in contrast to the US which has a much more integrated ADR system in place.

Two areas of civil justice which have attempted to embrace ADR, with varying success, have been the construction industry and matrimonial disputes within family law. From 1993 it has been common practice, and the subject of a practice direction,[30] for questions that asked about ADR to be inserted into the pre-trial checklist for both parties to respond to. By 1995 support for ADR came from the Lord Chief Justice

---

24   To understand the advantages and disadvantages of each method see Sime (2007: 65).
25   Ibid.
26   One of the leading law journals in the world.
27   Cappelletti (1993).
28   Glasser (1993).
29   Zander (2007: 141–50).
30   [1994] 1 All ER 34.

and the question was whether solicitors thought ADR would assist in resolving the case. By 1996, judges were prepared, in construction cases, to adjourn the action to see if ADR could, if not already tried, be used to resolve the dispute. At this stage early neutral evaluation may be used as this is likely to be considered positively by both parties. In 1996 the Housing Grants, Construction and Regeneration Act was passed which meant that under s.108 every written construction contract must contain a provision for the right to refer disputes to adjudicators. The procedure is outlined in s.108 and according to Sime the policy is one of 'pay now, argue later'.[31] Parties to the adjudication must provide the adjudicator with evidence of why the dispute has arisen, why the remedy sought is applicable to the party claiming it and all evidence supporting the claim. From this the adjudicator will reach a decision within 28 days. Reasons for the decision must be given and the decision can be court enforced.

Although sometimes proving an expensive option this does appear to be a successful form of ADR. This process, being quite formal, could be seen to be as restrictive as the court which would undermine the maximisation of liberty. That said, its commitment to early intervention does tend to ensure the court is not troubled with these matters which could prove costly. And to refer to adjudicators is a choice not a requirement! This maximises liberty.

Mediation, with its generally informal and flexible approach, was thought to be a useful tool in resolving matrimonial disputes. There was so much confidence in it as a form of ADR that it was announced in 1995 that a new no-fault divorce would be introduced which involved a formal role for mediation. This became law with Part II of the Family Law Act 1996. The thrust of the 1996 Act was to facilitate agreements about the future, to be reached by the parties themselves during a period of 'reflection and consideration', although the courts would retain jurisdiction to approve agreements made and to make orders where mediation had either failed or had been impossible to arrange. By facilitating mediation, parties were not being forced (as this would be counterproductive) but it was strongly recommended. The 'stick' or 'carrot', depending on your view, was that the Legal Aid Board would only approve funding for representation in divorce proceedings if mediation was unsuitable.

Pilot studies for this arrangement were undertaken by the Legal Aid Board. The results were very disappointing but in hindsight not surprising. It should have been apparent that in private matters people do not tend to seek legal redress unless forms of ADR such as mediation are unlikely to work. Mediation requires a willingness to engage in discussion. Often couples have passed the point at which a calm discussion is possible. A good mediator will know that if they list the key issues in the case they should be able to negotiate around the issues not the personalities of the parties involved. But the parties by the stage of mediation appear to have given up hope of reconciliation and are now more interested in ending their marriage and reaching agreement on all ancillary matters.[32]

Given the disappointing findings of these pilot studies it was decided in June 1999 by the then Lord Chancellor, Lord Irvine, that the implementation of Part II of the Family

---

31   Sime (2007: 74–5)
32   A particularly insightful account of the 1996 Act and the rise and fall of Part II is presented by Reece (2003).

Law Act 1996 would be delayed. By 2000 it became clear that Part II and its attempt to insert a formal mediation process into divorce was not going to be implemented. Zander stated that the 'abandonment of the project was plainly a setback for the mediation bandwagon'.[33] It could be explained as a setback if the formal use of mediation in divorce proceedings was a necessary development. However if the non-formal use of mediation, where couples are prepared to engage in a calm discussion about the state of their marriage, can still be accessed then it may have been a blip rather than an end to this form of ADR.

Both the interim and final report from Lord Woolf did demonstrate a commitment to the increased use of ADR. This became an important part of the CPR where under rule 1.4(2)(e) it states that once proceedings have commenced then the court will be under a duty to further the overriding objective of dealing with cases justly by encouraging the parties to use ADR if the court believes this to be appropriate. If time is required for the ADR to take place then under rule 26.4 the parties will be given the opportunity to try to settle the case by ADR. The rules are not meant to be broken! If it appears that one of the parties has adopted an unnecessary approach to ADR then they can be deprived of costs.[34] There is no presumption in favour of ADR as each case has to turn on its facts but the very fact that sanctions can be imposed does show the court treads a fine line between promoting ADR where appropriate and realising that forcing people into mediation, for example, helps no one in the long run as it is unlikely to succeed.

Despite the failure of Part II of the Family Law Act 1996 we have proceeded on the basis that the maximisation of choice in terms of ADR versus court proceedings does in turn maximise liberty as per Rawls' first postulate. It is now important, in offering a balanced picture of the impact of ADR, to consider the realities of its use in the civil justice system. If you imagined that a formal commitment (via the CPR) to generally informal processes would maximise use then you will be disappointed. Professor Zander begins his forensic examination of how ADR is not nearly as popular as Woolf had hoped by suggesting:

> While the "mood music" of the courts is certainly therefore in favour of ADR, it is making slow headway on the ground as a means of resolving civil disputes.[35]

This gloomy picture should be of no surprise as Zander has often taken issue with some of the claims made by Woolf and his supporters in terms of reforming the civil justice process. That said, the figures speak for themselves. He cites the failure of Part II of the Family Law Act 1996 as a clear example of low take-up but he also refers to research undertaken by Professor Hazel Genn[36] in 1996, 2002 and

---

33   Zander (2007: 143).
34   See *Leicester Circuits Ltd* v. *Coates Industries plc* [2003] EWCA Civ 333. For a list of what factors need to be considered for a refusal to be deemed unreasonable see *Halsey* v. *Milton Keynes General NHS Trust* [2004] 1 WLR 3002.
35   Zander (2007: 146).
36   The Central London County Court Pilot Mediation Scheme, LCD Research Series (1998), Court-based ADR initiatives for non-family civil disputes: the Commercial Court and the Court of Appeal (2005) and Mediating Civil Disputes: Evaluating Court Referral and Voluntary Mediation (2007).

2007 to show that take-up of ADR has been modest but there was an increase post-*Dunnett* v. *Railtrack plc*[37] where the courts became more interested in imposing of refusing costs on those who had unreasonably refused to engage in ADR. Genn confirms that if you pressure people into mediation they are less likely to settle as they did not want to mediate in the first place but only agreed for fear of a costs sanction. By 2007 the settlement rate post-mediation was around 42 per cent. Professors Peysner and Seneviratne[38] also conducted research, post-Woolf, in 2003–2004 and confirmed that ADR has not become incorporated into the court process. They identify that lack of both facilities and resources have had an impact on the take-up of ADR.

There is also the question of how ADR fits into the post-Human Rights Act era? To what extent are contemporary rules on ADR consistent with the requirements of Article 6? Is there a possible tension between the 'compulsory or semi-compulsory' nature of ADR and the right of access to the court? This is not, of course, to criticise the emphasis on ADR in the CPR, as ADR provides an alternative to costly and resource intensive litigation. CPR 1.4 (1) and (2) instructs the court to 'encourage' the use of ADR as a means of actively managing cases. These rules interface with CPR Part 26 that allows the court, in circumstances where it considers it appropriate, to stay proceedings and facilitate recourse to mediation. Both parties must consent to ADR.

There does appear to be the inherent problem of 'facilitation' of mediation. Lord Woolf's judgment in *Anufreijeva* v. *Southwark LBC* indicates that '[un]less a party is prepared to use ADR, it could have no access to the courts at all'.[39] This problem has been dealt with by Practice Direction B, which gives a district judge the power to hear the 'objections' to mediation, but also to direct that mediation should proceed. There are similar provisions in the Admiralty and Commercial Court Guide, which allows a judge to 'invite' parties to consider mediation if s/he considers it suitable, and to order an adjournment to 'encourage' the parties to so do. A judge can also issue an ADR order which requires the parties to take 'serious steps' to resolve their dispute through the appointment of a neutral mediator. It seems therefore that the judiciary are keen to emphasise, in accordance with the commitment to Article 6, that a line has to be drawn between encouraging and compelling ADR.

On final analysis the empirical evaluations of Professors Genn, Peysner and Seneviratne, when accompanied by Professor Zander's gloomy but accurate commentary, suggest that ADR may not be nearly as successful as it was once hoped it would be. This is a clear example of where promotion can all too often undermine impact as it is seen that using a 'stick' (cost implications) to cajole individuals into ADR will increase the take-up rate, but means that the settlement rate is lower. The Department of Justice and Treasury may decide that the settlement rate is too low for them to bother to promote ADR any more. This would be a shame as the option to engage in ADR does, on final analysis, maximise liberty because there is a choice to engage or not. The cost sanctions may limit that liberty but not as much as it would if ADR was

---

37   [2002] 1 WLR 2434.
38   The Management of Civil Cases: the Courts and the Post-Woolf Landscape, DCA Research Report 9/2005.
39   [2003] EWCA Civ 1406.

simply not available. Even if settlement rates are low the choice should be there for those parties who want to use it. Glasser suggested that 'among these needs are surely those of developing alternatives to the traditional processes'.[40] These alternatives continue to evolve and in time they may either become more embedded in the civil justice process or they will, like the 1996 Family Law Act reforms, simply wither away. On the one hand ADR maximises liberty. Rawls' only restriction was where constraints were required to protect liberty itself. The end of ADR would do nothing to protect liberty.

DISTRIBUTION OF RESOURCES: MEDICINE AND LAND

Aristotle founded the Western tradition of 'distributive justice' in arguing for money or honour to be equally distributed.[41] This distribution was to be based on merit and the resources available were to be allocated proportionately. Rawls provides a contemporary view for a just distribution in his second postulate, which states:

> Equality for all, both in the basic liberties of social life and also in distribution of all other forms of social goods, subject only to the exception that inequalities may be permitted if they produce the greatest possible benefit for those least well off in a given scheme of inequality.

We will illustrate the importance of a civil justice system to individuals by concentrating on two areas which are currently controversial. So that 'the basic liberties of social life' can be enjoyed equally by the rich and poor we shall consider one example of where there is an attempt for 'social goods' to be distributed equally and another example where the civil justice system would appear to be left wanting. Both examples are witness to how far the court processes are prepared to involve themselves in the resolution of disputes.

ALLOCATION OF MEDICAL RESOURCES: EQUALITY OR LOTTERY?

It is clearly the case that the world's medical resources are distributed unevenly.[42] The developing countries often find themselves running Cinderella services which fail to preserve the lives of their citizens for want of sometimes basic equipment or drugs. This inadequate distribution of resources on the world stage comes at a time when there exist increasingly pandemic levels of infectious diseases.[43] This inequality does suggest that on a global level Rawls' notion of distributing goods equally is not apparent. But what happens nationally?

---

40 Glasser (1993: 324).
41 *The Nicomachean Ethics*, pp. 741–8.
42 See Mason and Laurie (2006: 413).
43 This is certainly the case for HIV and tuberculosis infection.

In the UK the National Health Service[44] was set up in 1948 under the National Health Service Act 1946. The aim of this legislation was to provide the whole population with free and comprehensive health care and to provide access to other social services, which in time would improve the nation's health and reduce the need for intervention. The funding for this service was to come from National Insurance contributions which would be taken at source from an individual's salary and this would ensure that, although not actually free, health care was free at the point of delivery. It was a masterful endeavour. The architect of this plan, Aneurin Bevan, was the first Secretary of State for Health and his vision had seen the development of a system which became the envy of the world. This really was a system which attempted to distribute resources equally, regardless of birth or wealth.

As early as 1951 it became clear that the demand for health care resources was outstripping National Insurance contributions and so to assist in financing the system the introduction of nominal prescription charges took place so that those who could afford to would pay an additional sum for medicines. This continued to work in accordance with distribution on the basis of merit and individuals were not excluded on the grounds of inability to pay. Since 1948 successive governments have continued to prop up the NHS with increased subsidies from the gross national product of the nation and while funding has increased rapidly the perceived quality of service has decreased.

Emily Jackson[45] explains that blame cannot all be laid at the door of the architects of the NHS. She explains that a number of factors have contributed to the present problems with resource allocation in the NHS. Initially the NHS has been a success in that life expectancy is far higher than it was in the 1940s. This means that much of the NHS budget is spent on the elderly and as the elderly sector grows so the demands on limited resources grows. Second, advances in technology have meant that procedures available now are beyond the imagination of those who designed and implemented the NHS. This also means that patient expectations as to what is available and what can be done has increased. This is in line with a growing understanding by the population that the NHS is not a 'free' service for which they should be grateful. It is a (sometimes) free at the point of delivery service which extensive funding continues to prop up. This has meant that demand for the primary services of visiting a general practitioner is often viewed as an entitlement and people insist on visiting their doctor when their ailment may often heal by its own accord. Another problem with dwindling effective distribution of resources is that more than half the resources for the NHS are spent on salaries. Hard-working professional people work for the service and ought to be rewarded adequately but this has, in recent years, continued to place an enormous strain on already strained resources. Finally it is worth remembering that this scarcity of resources is not a national phenomenon. It is a global one. Everyone wants medical assistance to ensure they can live for as long as possible. This expectation is not without its casualties.

---

44 A lively account of the set-up of the NHS and its almost immediate problems can be found in Jackson (2006: 35).
45 Jackson (2006: 36).

Given this expensive exercise in 'balancing the books' it has become clear that difficult decisions need to be made where the resources are inevitably finite. Although it is still the case that the provision of accident and emergency support continues without the cash registers ringing, it has become clear that non-emergency procedures are more difficult to obtain. Medicines that may improve a patient's quality of life may also be difficult to obtain and this is again due to difficult rationing decisions where limited budgets cannot be stretched any more. In this world the possibility of success in any given treatment becomes less and less attractive to those who decide on resource allocation and it is the probable, the safe, which becomes the norm. Since 1980 the housekeeping exercise of ensuring finances are spent wisely in the NHS fell to the district health authorities whose task it is to purchase health care services on behalf of the local population. While it was thought this would ensure that local needs would be prioritised, it has resulted in something of a lottery where a person's postcode can literally decide whether or not they are able to receive medical treatment.[46]

Historically the decision as to whether a particular procedure was undertaken or a particular drug was to be administered was a clinical one. While the local district health authorities will consult with clinicians over a particular procedure, they do now have a responsibility to consider the wider local demands on their budgets. In addition the National Institute for Health and Clinical Excellence (NICE)[47] was established in 1999 with a remit to promote clinical excellence in the health service so as to provide advice and guidance as to what treatments are best for patients on a national scale. It was hoped that NICE would deal with the problem of the emerging postcode lottery for treatment because it would adopt a national view to complement the local view taken by the health authorities. This attempt to redress any perceived inequalities in the distribution of resources was, in reality, difficult to see because as commentators have conceded the decisions of NICE have largely been 'unashamedly moulded to a large extent by their economic effect'.[48]

With the problem of limited resources identified and the local and national attempts to ensure that the distribution of 'social goods' is guaranteed it would appear that civil justice, in its widest sense, is ensured. It is therefore perhaps difficult to see how the civil justice system becomes involved in this process. The answer is that in recent years as difficult decisions have been made and litigants have been disappointed by those decisions reached so they have attempted to use the courts to seek redress. The most fertile avenue for litigation came from the statutory provision in the National Health Service Act 1977[49] which placed a duty on the Secretary of State for Health to produce a comprehensive health service. This duty could be exercised as he or she thinks necessary to meet all reasonable requirements but clearly if a litigant believes the duty has not been exercised to meet their reasonable requirements then litigation can follow.

---

46 For a critical discussion of the different methods of resource allocation which are possible see Newdick (2005).
47 For a wider discussion see Mason and Laurie (2006: 422).
48 Ibid.
49 S.3 as amended in 2006.

The classic case concerned with resource allocation and an indication of whether the courts would be prepared to assist the disappointed litigant came in *Hincks*.[50] In this case, patients in an orthopaedic hospital claimed that they had waited too long for treatment because there was a shortage of facilities. They claimed that the health authority and the Secretary of State were in breach of their statutory duties. At first instance the court decided that as the duty to provide services was accompanied by the words 'to such an extent as he considers necessary' so this discretion could only be successfully challenged if the actions of the Secretary of State frustrated the Act or the policy. On appeal it was held that a failure on behalf of the Secretary of State could only exist if the Minister's[51] action was thoroughly unreasonable. This was a very difficult legal hurdle for the litigants to jump and they once again lost.

When budget holding became a more local issue in 1980[52] it appeared that the lines of accountability could be more clearly drawn and in the *Walker*[53] case the surgery of a baby had been postponed five times due to a lack of skilled nursing staff. This was a non-urgent operation and the court, supported on appeal, stated that the health authority could not be compelled to perform the operation as they had not acted unreasonably. This position was confirmed in a similar case, which this time was urgent,[54] and so the message appeared to be that the civil justice trial process could not be used for litigants to demand performance of a statutory duty unless the decision not to perform was unreasonable. There is of course also a political point to be made here. If the courts had opened the floodgates to permit those suffering delay because of a shortage of resources to either force action or receive redress for failure to act this would have deprived the NHS even further of valuable resources which it can ill-afford to spend.

In the case of *B*,[55] a highly publicised case, funding for what would be an ineffective treatment was refused by the health authority. At first instance the door was left ajar for effective redress when Laws LJ explained that the health authority would have to explain their decision for not providing the necessary resources in this case. He said:

> Where the question is whether the life of a ten year old child might be saved, by more than a slim chance, the responsible authority must in my judgement do more than toll the bell of tight resources. They must explain the priorities that have led them to decline to fund the treatment.[56]

This was overturned on appeal as it was felt unnecessary for health authorities to explain their decision. Bingham LJ in the Court of Appeal said that:

> Difficult and agonising judgements have to be made as to how a limited budget is best allocated to the maximum advantage of the maximum number of patients.[57]

---

50   R. v. *Secretary of State for Social Services, ex p Hincks* [1979] 123 Sol Jo 436.
51   For a discussion of the case see Mason and Laurie (2006: 425).
52   By virtue of the Health Services Act 1980.
53   R. v. *Central Birmingham Health Authority, ex p Walker* [1987] 3 BMLR 32 CA.
54   R. v. *Central Birmingham Health Authority, ex p Collier* [1987] 6 January.
55   R. v. *Cambridge Area Health Authority ex p B (A Minor)* [1995] 25 BMLR 5.
56   R. v. *Cambridge Area Health Authority ex p B (A Minor)* [1995] 25 BMLR 5, p. 17.
57   R. v. *Cambridge Area Health Authority ex p B (A Minor)* [1995] 1 WLR 898.

Recent cases have bucked this trend in that it would seem that the courts will now require health authorities to honour their promises even if the pressure on the existing resources is great. In R. v. *North West Lancashire Health Authority, ex parte A and Others*[58] the applicants suffered from gender identity dysphoria and it had long been thought that they should have had gender reassignment surgery. Although clinical need was apparent their cases were lowered in priority due to pressures on the authority's budget. The applicants wanted to seek treatment outside of the authority's area and they were refused. This refusal was quashed by the court and the Court of Appeal upheld this decision. In R. v. *North and East Devon Health Authority ex parte Coughlan*[59] a promise made that residents of a residential home which was prohibitively expensive to run, was upheld by the court and the Court of Appeal spoke of the parties having a legitimate expectation to stay in this home for the rest of their lives. These cases demonstrate the courts' increasing willingness to adjudicate effectively and sympathetically to the extent that the blanket raising of resources as a defence to a decision not to treat will likely be insufficient in future. This is certainly the view of Newdick.[60] King has recently argued[61] that the Human Rights Act 1998 has ensured that questions of resource allocation are no longer no-go areas for the courts. He says:

> A new fault line has emerged under the Human Rights Act 1998. The non-justiciability doctrine no longer applies. The notion of a judicial 'no-go area' of resource allocation has effectively been put to rest where human rights are at issue.[62]

The distribution of the 'social good' of medicine in the UK is largely based on utilitarian principles where the community as a whole must be considered. This is in accordance with Rawls' postulate. The civil justice trial process is now being used to ensure that those disappointed by these rationing decisions can use the courts to hold those who have their hands on the purse strings and make these decisions accountable.[63]

USE OF LAND BY MINORITIES: THE GYPSY'S LOT

While the availability of medicine is critical to a nation's health, so the availability of land is also crucial if only to ensure that people have somewhere to live. When examining resource allocation we were particularly concerned about equality of access for all. We now turn our attention to how the civil justice process has been used to attempt to secure occupational land rights for one of our minority groups: the gypsy.

---

58 [2000] 1 WLR 977.
59 [2001] QB 213.
60 Newdick (2005).
61 King (2007: 197).
62 King (2007: 224).
63 For a recent high profile case involving resource allocation, see NICE and the availability of the drug herceptin which is proven, if administered early enough, to stall the development of breast cancer. Initially NICE decided this stalling was not cost-effective because the drug was very expensive and it was thought the impact was temporary. After a large publicity campaign involving a hostile media the decision of NICE was reversed.

According to Barnett[64] gypsies were first recorded in the sixteenth century.[65] She goes on to explain that the legal system's response to them has been one of 'expulsion, repression, discrimination and uneasy tolerance'.[66] Barnett importantly acknowledges the difficulty associated with accommodating minorities within any given domain. For the past 50 years the gypsy has caused problems for the legislature and the courts not just in terms of deciding who is a gypsy but also how and when their occupation of land will be legal.

The Highways Act 1959 offered no definition of 'gypsy'. It merely decided they would be guilty of an offence if they encamped on a highway. The Caravan Sites Act 1968 decided that 'gypsies' would be broad in definition as it is 'clear that "gypsies" do not constitute a cohesive and separate group within our society'.[67] The courts decided that 'gypsy' should be construed as meaning 'any person having a nomadic way of life'.[68] This wide definition saw the courts struggle when considering whether a sign saying 'no travellers' outside a public house was in contravention of the Race Relations Act 1976.[69] Although the court recognised that it was difficult to identify gypsies as a cohesive whole they did take the view that they were still a racial group who deserved protection under the 1976 Act.

The wide definition of 'gypsy' proved to be a blessing and a curse because under s.16 Caravan Sites Act 1968 local authorities had to make site provision for *all* nomadic peoples. This would have included 'new age travellers' under the Race Relations Act 1976 but it did not apply to the Caravan Sites Act 1968 because the latter legislation did not consider race but the currently adopted way of life as central to its decision making. A series of cases[70] saw the courts wrestle with local authority decisions to take possession of land which had been inhabited by gypsies. Barnett argues that these decisions generally show that attempts to distinguish between 'real' gypsies and others who appear to have been, on occasion, living a nomadic lifestyle ensured restrictive practises could be exercised and the statutory duty to provide accommodation was limited in its impact. The restrictions it appears did not end there. S.6 Caravan Sites Act 1968 imposed a duty for the local authority to provide adequate accommodation 'so far as may be necessary'. This 'get out' clause along with other statutory provisions[71] was supposed to effectively balance the needs of the gypsies and the concerns of the community. The legislation was meant to ensure that 'no gypsy residing in or resorting to the area is without a suitable place to go',[72] but in reality there was a significant shortfall in lawful sites provided for gypsies.

---

64   Barnett (1995: 133).
65   In 1530 an Act was passed which prevented gypsies from entering the realm.
66   Barnett (1995: 133).
67   Ibid., 142.
68   *Mills* v. *Cooper* [1989] 2 WLR 17.
69   *The Commission for Racial Equality* v. *Dutton* [1989] 2 WLR 17.
70   *Greenwich London Borough Council* v. *Powell* [1959] 1 AC 995; *Horsham District Council* v. *Secretary of State for the Environment* (1989) *The Guardian*, October 31; *R.* v. *Shropshire County Council ex p Bungay* [1990] 23 HLR 195; *R.* v. *South Hams District Council ex p Gibb and others* [1993] EGCS 179.
71   S.6(2) and s.12 Caravan Sites Act 1968.
72   Department of the Environment Consultation Paper.

The duty prescribed under the Caravan Sites Act 1968 was subsequently repealed by the Criminal Justice and Public Order Act 1994. Part V strengthens the provisions of the Public Order Act 1986 to enable a police officer to move on trespassers to land where they have been asked to leave. This is usually in response to violent or threatening behaviour on the part of the gypsy or if there are six or more vehicles on the land. If the gypsies fail to abide by this provision then this can result in the vehicles being seized. The 1994 Act is committed to finding permanent housing for gypsies. This is, according to Barnett, 'anathema'[73] to travelling gypsies. The language used by the government is punitive. Circular 1/94 confirms that gypsies wanting a nomadic existence should be permitted one but this should only ever be within the confines of the law. This means that at the present time gypsies are to be encouraged to purchase their own land for their sites so that the local authorities do not have to provide sites for them. The problem here is that just as occupation of the land can be controversial so obtaining the land with the correct planning provision can also be very difficult.

The difficulty of obtaining planning permission was raised in *South Bucks* v. *Porter*, *Wrexham CBC* v. *Berry* and *Chichester DC* v. *Keet and Searle*[74] where it was noted:

> In the case of Gypsies, the problem [i]s compounded by the features peculiar to them: their characteristic [nomadic] lifestyle debarred them from access to conventional sources of housing provision. Their attempts to obtain planning permission almost always met with failure: statistics quoted by the European Court ... [found that] 90% of applications made by Gypsies had been refused whereas 80% of all applications had been granted. But for many years the capacity of sites authorized for Gypsies had fallen far short of that needed.

The tide does appear to be turning. In *South Bucks* v. *Porter*, *Wrexham CBC* v. *Berry* and *Chichester DC* v. *Keet and Searle*[75] it became apparent that the court were prepared to consider an applicant's Article 8 rights under the European Convention on Human Rights when it comes to the granting of planning permission.[76] Historically Lord Scarman had said that 'the courts should be reluctant to accommodate individual rights in a manner that compromised effective enforcement of planning policy'.[77] This post-*Porter* did not initially appear to be the path being taken by the courts.[78] By the time the Court of Appeal ruled on *Smith* v. *Buckland*[79] in 2007 it would appear that to respect gypsy human rights, domestic law does now provide, when they reside on local authority sites, procedural safeguards against conviction.

'The history of Gypsies is one characterized by intolerance.'[80] It would appear that this intolerance has also involved reluctance by the community to allow this minority

---

73   Barnett (1995: 161).
74   [2003] 2 WLR 1547.
75   [2003] 2 WLR 1547.
76   For a discussion of the case and its potential impact see Loveland (2002: 906).
77   Loveland (2002: 922).
78   See *Leeds City Council (Respondents)* v. *Price and others* (FC) [2006] UKHL 10 where Article 8 rights were not upheld as the right of local authorities to evict was upheld.
79   EWCA Civ. 1318.
80   Barnett (1994: 464).

group to live the nomadic life they crave. When statute attempted to prescribe a duty on local authorities to find sites for the gypsy caravans this legislation was littered with exceptions. Gypsies then became victims of the community's mistrust of 'new-age travellers' when the Criminal Justice and Public Order Act 1994 was passed. The result was that the community decided that instead of providing sites for gypsies the local authority would expect the gypsy to purchase their own land for their own sites. This seemed equitable enough but it then emerged that when gypsies applied for the requisite planning permission to turn the land they had purchased into a site they were on most occasions refused. Human rights jurisprudence may save the gypsy in the long run but at the moment case law suggests that success for the gypsy, when either seeking legal redress or subject to legal sanction, is patchy. The distribution of this social good; that is, land, would appear to be sporadic for this minority and while Rawls always insisted 'that inequalities may be permitted if they produce the greatest possible benefit for those least well off in a given scheme of inequality' the gypsy lot appears to be a precarious one. They are clearly subject to inequalities when one considers the success rate of those planning applications and they are often the least well-off individuals in society.

ACCESS TO JUSTICE: ACCESS TO LEGAL REPRESENTATION

It has been argued elsewhere in this book that a central right of an individual who is trying to secure access to justice is that they should have access to legal representation. In criminal cases statute ensures[81] that an individual has the right to legal advice following arrest. The civil justice system is rather less generous in its funding of litigation. There are practical reasons for this. The effect of losing a civil case is not, generally, as catastrophic as losing a criminal case where the latter could involve the loss of liberty. There is a wide range of methods of funding litigation which will be explored later.[82] For now it is important to return to the final postulate of Rawls where he states there should be:

> "Fair equality of opportunity" and the elimination of all inequalities of opportunity based on birth or wealth.

Here for our purposes we shall be considering access to legal representation both for the commencement and defence of civil actions as an example of where the law should be providing 'fair equality of opportunity'. Clearly if you have sufficient resources then such actions will not be prohibited but it is also clear that there are hostages to the limitations that have been placed on the funding of litigation.

First, it is clear that solicitors are under a professional duty to ensure that their clients are clear as to the options available to them. Under the Solicitors' Costs Information and Client Care Code 1999 solicitors are to discuss with their clients how the funding of their case is to be managed. The traditional method of payment is termed

---
81 S.58 Police and Criminal Evidence Act 1984.
82 Sime (2007: 36–49)

a retainer and it involves the client paying an agreed hourly rate with the solicitor. There is also legal expenses insurance which some clients have access to. This is usually the case with home and motor insurance policies. There also exists after-the-event insurance where a premium is paid in an attempt to cover the possibility of paying the successful party's costs. Such premiums can be very expensive given the risk involved. If a solicitor wishes to take on a case where the client cannot afford the costs then the solicitor may choose only to recover costs if the claim is successful. Historically such agreements were thought to be illegal and unenforceable because they 'savour of champerty and maintenance'.[83] This is still the case and actions which come from those litigants who cannot afford these costs will normally be recommended for a conditional fee agreement (CFA). The CFA can be used where a solicitor agrees that a client will be liable for the costs if the action is successful. Here the usual costs and a success fee will be payable. This success fee cannot be more than 100 per cent of the solicitor's usual fees. Finally, limited funding may be available for civil cases from the Legal Services Commission (LSC). The criteria for allocation can be strict although if a case is particularly deserving it may receive full public funding. There are some actions which are excluded from assistance though. These include boundary disputes, the making of wills, conveyancing and, controversially, defamation and malicious falsehood.[84]

The result is that in the civil justice system an interesting dichotomy emerges. Given the restrictions in entitlement only those with modest means can secure financial assistance from the LSC. If a litigant is of significant means then they will be able to afford the litigation. That must mean there is a group in the middle who are neither entitled nor blessed with sufficient funds. The result for them is a distinct non-access to justice. That said, Zander[85] points out that there is an interesting anomaly here. We spend much of our time being critical of the current limits to the funding of legal aid in the UK and yet an international comparison[86] suggests that we have the highest per capita expenditure on legal aid of any country in the world. This is for both criminal and civil litigation but perhaps, as with medical resources, there will never be enough!

Up until now we have been talking generally about those who wish to bring an action against someone. This is not to say the aforementioned methods of funding do not apply to individuals defending a case but the issue of financing a defence in a civil case is perhaps more critical in the civil justice process. If the civil justice system does not fund your defence to a claim against you then you could, if unsuccessful, find yourself financially ruined. The most celebrated case where this happened in the recent history of civil justice was in the now infamous 'McLibel' case.

Whilst the 'McLibel' case is considered later in this book its importance here is in the current restriction on funding for defending an action brought against someone. The facts of the 'McLibel' case are well known[87] but the key point was that in an aggressive

---

83   Sime (2007: 41). 'Maintenance' refers to supporting litigation without just cause and 'champerty' is an advanced form of this on the basis the solicitor seeks to obtain a share in the proceeds of the suit.
84   Controversial because following *Steel* v. *UK* [2005] it was held that a denial of public funding for a libel case was in breach of the European Convention on Human Rights.
85   Zander (2007: 629).
86   Flood and White (2006).
87   See Nicholson (2000).

leafleting exercise Helen Steel and Dave Morris, among others, broadly attacked the McDonald's Corporation for their working practices as well as holding them largely responsible for the growth in consumerism, corporatism and materialism. Their leaflet entitled 'McCancer, McDisease and McGreed' was distributed widely. While the protest by Steel and Morris may not have been wise it was certainly effective. It must have been as McDonald's reacted very strongly to the leaflet by infiltrating the group who were disseminating it and finally a libel action was brought against Steel and Morris. The trial took place in June 1994 and became the longest trial in British history, lasting for 313 days. The significance here was that because the case against Steel and Morris was for libel it was excluded from public funding. This was the case in 1994 due to the Legal Aid Act 1988 and it would also be true today under the Access to Justice Act 1998.[88] This was a true battle between 'David and Goliath' as Steel and Morris had nothing to defend themselves with whereas McDonald's secured high levels of expensive legal representation. The result was never really in doubt given the inflammatory nature of the comments made by Steel and Morris. However, interestingly the claims made by them that McDonald's food was unhealthy by virtue of its fat and salt content were received with sympathy by the Court of Appeal. The result was that, according to Vick and Campbell:[89]

> Most observers concluded at the time of the High Court's verdict that McDonald's had won the battle but lost the war, suffering a tremendous public relations backlash in the United Kingdom, the United States and elsewhere.

Not only were Steel and Morris not able to fund a defence because public funding is not available for defamation proceedings, but the law of defamation was to all intents and purposes curtailing their right to trial under Article 6 and freedom of expression under Article 10 of the European Convention on Human Rights. Having been denied an appeal to the House of Lords, Steel and Morris decided to take their case to Strasbourg in an attempt to assert their Convention rights.

At Strasbourg the applicants were successful. The Court found that the denial of legal aid violated their rights under Article 6(1) as it contributed to an unacceptable inequality between Steel and Morris and McDonald's.[90] We have claimed elsewhere in this book that there is a general commitment to 'equality of arms' so this should not be of any great surprise. The Court recognised that there was no absolute right to legal aid but each case should be assessed and it seems the Court were not in favour of the blanket ban on public funding for defamation cases given the 'David and Goliath' spectre that followed. This seems a sensible criticism of the present rules, especially if individuals are having to defend themselves in cases where the stakes are so high. Scolnicov has argued that as a result of the decision of the European Court of Human Rights the law 'should be rectified ... by change in the provision of legal aid'.[91] It seems that Rawls'

---

88   Although they could obtain special authorisation from the Lord Chancellor.
89   Vick and Campbell (2001: 218).
90   The Court also accepted Steel and Morris' Article 10 claim. They felt that free speech here was akin to that given to journalists and they had made a valuable contribution to the debate.
91   Scolnicov (2005: 311, 314).

final postulate with its emphasis on equality of opportunity is, in the context of legal aid for civil justice, left wanting, for a fairer, more just distribution of resources reform is required.

CONCLUSION

To imagine civil justice is to imagine a system which provides the opportunity for disputing parties to resolve their disagreements in an effective and expeditious way while remembering that a good decision is a just decision. An examination of the system in light of the Woolf reforms has at best shown that the present process is better than before[92] but not nearly as effective as it could be. At this stage we can ask whether Dickens would have been any happier assessing the process than he was some 170 years ago? Holdsworth[93] tells us: 'What Dickens is concerned with is the machinery by which the law was enforced, the men who enforced it, the conditions in which these men lived, and the actual effects of the rules of law, substantive and adjective, upon the men and women of his day. Hence we get in his books that account of the human side of the rules of law and their working.' When we then consider some of the current issues in civil justice, when judged against Rawls' criteria and Dickens' vision we can see that uncertainty and injustice do remain for some who seek recourse to a system designated for just dispute resolution.

---

92 Although Zander (2007: 140) argues that on balance the disadvantages outweigh the advantages. This view does not appear to be that of most.
93 Holdsworth (1928a: 7).

13

THE PRINCIPLES OF CIVIL PROCEDURE

INTRODUCTION

This chapter concerns the fundamental principles that underlie civil procedure.[1] In the most general sense, these principles are known by their Latin tags: *nemo judex in causa sua* and *audi alteram partem*. However, an in-depth study of civil procedure shows that we need to engage with a more specific body of principles that relate to the perennial conflicts animating procedural case law if we want to understand the nature of the subject. So, in this chapter, we will first examine the tensions that exist between disclosure and privilege, and the related requirement for legal proceedings to be held in public. We will then turn our attention to self-incrimination before examining the notion of finality in litigation, and how it can come into conflict with the right to appeal. Returning to the structuring principles of natural justice, we will consider the duty to give reasons for a decision. In the final section we will discuss the relationship between alternative dispute resolution (ADR) and fair trial rights. We will see that civil procedure requires ongoing judicial interpretation and adaptation. The law has to respond to disputes that raise challenging questions about the precise balance of the competing interests.

THE NATURE OF CIVIL PROCEDURAL LAW

As we have seen in the previous chapter, the Civil Procedure Rules (CPR) are central to the operation of the civil courts. Although these rules are important, it is worth bearing in mind that civil procedure is also shaped by the general law, in particular the law of evidence, and human rights. In this chapter we will also appreciate the importance of equity and the jurisdiction that the courts have to regulate their own procedure. Returning to Chapter 12, our starting point is the CPR's definition of the values that inform civil justice.[2]

The CPR describes itself as a 'new procedural code with the overriding objective of dealing with cases justly'.[3] It then goes on to define 'justly'. Justice includes: 'ensuring

---
1   We can follow the distinction made by Andrews between 'leading principles' and constitutional, to the extent that they provide 'fundamental procedural guarantees' to civil procedure. See Andrews (2003: 49).
2   The CPR, which came into effect in April 1999, replaced two distinct bodies of rules that regulated the operation of the courts. The Rules of Supreme Court covered the High Court and the Court of Appeal and the County Court Rules covered The County Court. Consequently there is a 'unified' (Andrews, 2003: 4) body of rules that relate to the High Court, the County Court and the Court of Appeal. The House of Lords sits somewhat outside of this body of rules, and is regulated by its own 'practice rules' (ibid.).
3   The Overriding Objectives, CPR Part 1.

that the parties are on an equal footing'; 'saving expense'; dealing with cases which are proportionate to what is at stake in the litigation; making sure that cases are dealt with 'expeditiously and fairly'; and taking into account the general allocation of resources in the civil justice system. When we turn to an analysis of the leading authorities on procedural law, we will see that, even though some of them predate the CPR, they share this overarching concern with the fairness of proceedings.[4] However, before we develop this argument, it is worth bearing in mind that this interplay is not without its tensions, and requires choices to be made between conflicting principles. Thus, an important aspect of the quest for the principles of civil justice is an understanding that judges are required to act creatively in the development of procedural law. Indeed, the values that underlie these principles are not inert, but take the shape that they do through a process of judicial articulation, which is also necessarily a balancing and shaping of the competing priorities of procedural law. This, in turn, raises issues about the CPR and human rights. Work remains to be done on the human rights context in which the CPR was drafted. Such issues are best debated in detail, and this chapter does not intend to discuss in any coherent way the human rights elements of the Woolf reforms. Our focus remains on the inherent conflicts between competing principles that articulate different aspects of the concept.

DISCLOSURE, PRIVILEGE AND THE PUBLICITY OF LEGAL PROCEEDINGS

The civil justice system has to balance the competing values of disclosure and privilege, two principles that are 'equally important to the administration of justice'.[5] As far as the former is concerned, litigation is best served if both parties make a full and frank account of the relevant documents that they have under their control and allow their inspection. However, there are also legitimate arguments for limiting the degree to which a party in litigation should have to reveal sensitive information to his or her opponent. The case law shows the courts attempting to resolve or at least manage this tension. We will examine a key case: *Waugh v. British Railways Board*.[6]

Lord Simon's judgment is interesting as it discusses the constitution of the competing principles. Underpinning disclosure was the principle stressing the availability of all 'relevant evidence' to the court. On the other hand, the principle supporting privilege tended to reflect the adversarial culture of litigation, and made for a far more minimal approach to the disclosure of documents. Lord Wilberforce explained the context in which the principles had developed. He argued that one justification for disclosure related to the 'exigencies' of litigation itself. A litigant is allowed to prepare his case, and not to disclose to the other side certain important details before they are made public in open court.[7] As the parties themselves drove litigation, legal procedure merely provided

---
4 The general judicial approach has been to move away from the pre-CPR case law, but not to reject principles that remain congruent with the objectives of the CPR (ibid.: 9–10).
5 Lord Simon in *Waugh v. British Railway Board* [1979] 3 WLR 521, at 526.
6 *Waugh v. British Railway Board* [1979] 3 WLR 150.
7 Lord Wilberforce, at ibid., 531.

the form of litigation. Its 'contents' were properly the concerns of the parties. This has the virtue of removing the judge from the cut and thrust of forensic argument, and leaves him/her to concentrate on a neutral adjudication of the dispute. It is important to realise that this is rooted in the broader culture of the common law, the fundamental principle that 'a litigant must bring forward his own evidence to support his case, and cannot call on his adversary to make or aid it'.[8]

However, the interests of litigation do not necessarily trump other competing reasons for making information and facts publicly available. For instance, public safety should not be compromised by claims that information is protected because it was given to a lawyer in confidence. Disclosure represents the practice of the Court of Chancery, and the mitigation of common law principles by equity. The 'conscience of the court' would be 'affronted' if one party should win 'merely through the silent non-cooperation of the defendant'.[9] If we consider this conflict of values from this historical perspective, then, we can invoke the spirit of 'compromise' and accommodation that allows equity and common law to work hand in hand, balancing the competing interests of disclosure and privilege. This is because neither principle is 'absolute' and 'both are subject to numerous exception'. How should these arguments be related to the facts in *Waugh*?

The litigation in this case was initiated by Mrs Waugh. She alleged that the defendants were liable in negligence for the accident that had killed her husband. She was seeking disclosure of a report that had been prepared for the British Railways Board. The Board argued that the report contained private advice by their solicitor and was thus protected by legal professional privilege. The House of Lords held in favour of Mrs Waugh, arguing that the 'due administration of justice' required that the report be made available as it contained witness statements that were important evidence as to the cause of the accident. How was this conclusion justified? The court stated that legal privilege would only 'override' disclosure if the legal advice that the document contained was the 'dominant purpose' for which the report had been written. As the document prepared for the Board contained both important evidence and legal advice, it could not be argued that the latter was the dominant function of the document.

The concept of dominant purpose is problematic as it is somewhat ambiguous. Even if one posits that the court's 'dominant purpose' was to 'find out what happened', how is it possible to determine precisely what this principle meant? Dominant purpose is capable of bearing a number of meanings. For instance, the Board were arguing that there was no single dominant purpose; how would one choose, for instance, between determining whether the dominant purpose was one of preventing litigation or furthering safety at work? Lord Edmund Davies thought that these concerns could be avoided if dominant purpose was defined as substantial purpose. It would then be possible to articulate the substantial reason for the preparation of the report. If this definition of the word was acceptable, Lord Edmund Davies argued that the test would still have to be fair between the parties, and easy to apply to the facts of any given case.

---

8   Ibid., 536.
9   See Y.B. 9 Ed. IV, Trin. 9. Cited in Waugh at 536.

Lord Wilberforce's reasoning supported this approach. He pointed out that English case law contained a generous test for privilege. A document would not have to be disclosed if 'one of its purposes (even though subsidiary)' was to seek advice from a lawyer about litigation. In order to create a more balanced test, Lord Wilberforce turned to the Australian case *Grant v. Downs*.[10] In this case, the court considered a series of reports that had been prepared for a number of reasons; one of which had been the purpose of soliciting legal advice. The judgment of the court stressed that professional privilege could only attach itself to documents 'brought into existence for the sole purpose of submission to legal advisers for advice or use in legal proceedings'.[11] This articulation of the principle corresponds with the Court of Appeal's reasoning in the present case, albeit that they preferred the language of dominant reason. On the balance of the facts and arguments in this case, it was thought necessary to order disclosure as the report was 'certainly the best evidence as to the cause of the accident'.[12]

Concerns with disclosure and privilege can also be considered as part of a broader issue: to what extent should legal proceedings be public?[13] In Lord Bingham's words, this area shows the 'tension between efficient justice and open justice'. This takes us to the process known as discovery.[14] Discovery is an interference with the private affairs of an individual: an invasion of 'the right of privacy'. This interference is justifiable only to the extent that the court needs access to all relevant information when resolving a dispute. Discovery is thus limited, and documents that have been subject to discovery cannot be used for purposes outside of litigation. Thus, a person who is a 'recipient' of documents is under an 'implied undertaking' not to reveal information to others. A breach of the implied undertaking amounts to a contempt of court.

The key issue is the extent to which a person who is in receipt of information from documents subject to discovery is still bound, despite the fact that the documents have been read in open court. In *Harman v. Home Office*,[15] the House of Lords held that a person was so bound, and revelation of information would be a contempt of court. The minority in this case argued that this position was in breach of Article 10 of the ECHR. Lord Scarman referred to *Scott v. Scott*[16] and invoked the principle of the public administration of justice:

> there is also another important public interest involved in justice done openly, namely, that the evidence and argument should be publicly known, so that society may judge for itself the quality of justice administered in its name, and whether the law requires modification. When public policy in the administration of justice is considered, public knowledge of the evidence and arguments of the parties is certainly as important as

---

10   *Grant v. Downs* [1976] 135 CLR 674.
11   Supra n. 6, at 533.
12   Ibid., 531–2.
13   These comments are based on Sir Nicolas Browne-Wilkinson's judgment in *Derby v. Weldon* (No. 2) (unreported, 19 October 1988).
14   Since the CPR, now known as Disclosure. In the Interim Report, Lord Woolf defined discovery as the 'obligation on a party to disclose documents which are damaging to his own case'. Supra n. 3, at Chapter 21, Para 1.
15   *Harman v. Home Office* [1983] 1 AC 280.
16   *Scott v. Scott* [1913] AC 417.

expedition: and, if the price of expedition is to be the silent reading by the judge before or at trial of relevant documents, it is arguable that expedition will not always be consistent with justice being seen to be done.[17]

Although we have encountered similar arguments in our consideration of Article 6, this argument does not make explicit reference to human rights. It is largely one of principle; the fundamental value of civil process has to be that of the openness of the courts, and the possibility of public scrutiny of legal processes. Indeed, the European Commission ruled on *Harman*, and the case was 'settled' when the British government promised that they would reform the law of contempt.[18]

Lord Scarman's powerful dissent stresses the openness of justice, but how should this principle be applied when the practice of the court changed? After *Harman*, procedural rules were amended, so that it was no longer the case that documents were read aloud in the court. Documents were to be made available to the judge to read through and to comprehend. The proceedings in court could then proceed more quickly as counsel could make references to material that the judge already understood, rather than having to lead the judge through all the documents, and thus waste court time.[19]

The requirement for streamlined and transparent procedure thus seems to come back into tension with the need to limit the uses of information made available through discovery. The key authority in this area is *SmithKline Beecham Biologicals SA* v. *Connaught Laboratories Inc.*[20] During the course of litigation over a vaccine for whooping cough, the defendants had disclosed a number of technical documents to the plaintiffs. An order had been made under the rule of the Supreme Court, and this referred to documents being read to or referred to in open court. The issue thus related to trade secrets to which the judge or counsel might make reference during proceedings. The question that the Court of Appeal had to address was a variation on the *Harman* point: was the party 'to whom disclosure had been made' no longer bound by the 'ordinary duty' to use the documents only in the course of litigation?

So, how are the rights of the parties to protect confidential information, and the public interest in the open administration of justice to be balanced in the light of this new practice?[21] Lord Bingham held that even though both parties had marked their documents as confidential, they did not contain sensitive information. Indeed, if the case had come to a full hearing, the court would not have sat *in camera*. In patent actions such as this one, an *in-camera* sitting would only be held if a party applied

---

17 Supra n. 15, at 317.
18 So that publication of information that had been made public through a reading in court would not be an offence. This led to Order 25, rule 14A. The law now requires one of the parties to the action to show that there are 'special reasons' not to allow information to be made publicly available.
19 The rationale was: 'The result is that a case may be heard in such a way that even an intelligent and well-informed member of the public, present throughout every hearing in open court, would be unable to obtain a full understanding of the documentary evidence and the arguments on which the case was to be decided' (511–12).
20 *SmithKline Beecham Biologicals SA* v. *Connaught Laboratories Inc.*, CHPCI 1998/1432/3.
21 *Derby* v. *Weldon* (No. 2) shows that Order 24 rule 14A applies even though it has not been read out in open court. However, Connaught were seeking to argue that this authority did not apply, as this case was a 'fully contested' hearing and that different rules had to apply to protect the secrecy of the information that they had provided. In particular they referred to a confidentiality agreement between themselves and *SmithKline*. However, the court was not convinced by this argument.

for such a hearing and if it was considered necessary. It is a question of balance. Lord Bingham argued that Connaught Laboratories had a legitimate interest in controlling access to trade secrets. However, there was a compelling reason not to protect this information. A patent protects a particular scientific or technical discovery, but it does so by 'restricting competition'. If a court is dealing with patented material, then this restriction on competition is legitimate, and discovery should not be ordered. However, in the present case there was a public interest in the development of a vaccine for whooping cough, and it would be wrong if the record of the court's reasons for making its decision did not include reference to sensitive, though not patented, material.

To what extent did Lord Woolf's reforms of civil justice qualify these principles? In the Interim Report[22] Lord Woolf explained that the primary problem with discovery was that it made litigation unnecessarily expensive. Especially in commercial litigation, discovery of documents was a 'huge task', and its cost was not entirely justified by its results, which tended to lead to the general lengthening of trials. However, it was not a question of simply doing away with discovery, as it did play an important role in making information available to the court. Lord Woolf's solution was thus to accept:

> the desirability of retaining discovery, because of its contribution to the just resolution of disputes. However, the benefits of a system of discovery will only outweigh the disadvantages if substantially greater control over the scale of discovery is exercised than at present.[23]

In the Final Report[24] Lord Woolf recommended that discovery should now be called disclosure, and that it should be limited to 'relevant documents of whose existence a party is aware'.[25] Although this test was not without its problems, the guiding concern was to achieve a procedure which balanced the duty to disclose with workable limits on what should be disclosed. Thus CPR 31, which applies to all cases except those on the small claims track,[26] is framed in terms of the 'right to inspect'[27] a disclosed document. The CPR creates the concept of 'standard disclosure',[28] which applies both to documents on which a party seeks to rely,[29] as well as those which are detrimental to his/her case.[30] This is balanced against a party's right to argue that disclosure would be 'disproportionate to the issues in the case'.[31] Disclosure can also be withheld on the grounds that it would damage the public interest.[32] Furthermore, a party to whom

---

22 Access to Justice, Interim Report, 1995, at http://www.dca.gov.uk/civil/interim/woolf.htm.
23 Ibid., para 18.
24 Access to Justice, Final Report, 1996, at http://www.dca.gov.uk/civil/final/intro.htm.
25 Ibid., chapter 9, para 7.
26 Supra n. 3, at 31.1.
27 Ibid., 31.1.
28 Ibid., 31.6.
29 Ibid., 31.6.a.
30 Ibid., 31.6.b.i. This includes those documents that 'adversely affect another party's case (ii); or support another party's case' (iii).
31 Ibid., 31.1.2.
32 Ibid., 31.19.1.

disclosure has been made may make use of the document only 'for the purpose of the proceedings in which it is disclosed'.[33]

Although Lord Woolf was concerned primarily with the cost of litigation, we can see that the new rules attempt to balance the values that we have been studying; although Andrews criticises the 'open texture' of the rules, which perhaps do not provide sufficient means of foreclosing the issues over which lawyers 'bicker' and thus drive up the costs of litigation, this perhaps suggests that the fundamental structure of the old law remains, especially if one allows that this might be a bickering over matters of principle.

SmithKline was decided under the old Rules of the Supreme Court (RSC) Order 14, but Order 14 was 'readopted' or 'codified' in 31.22[34] and thus still serves as a good example of how the courts attempt to balance conflicting values. While litigation privilege was criticised by Scott VC in *Secretary of State for Trade and Industry* v. *Baker*,[35] his views have in turn attracted much criticism and it is perhaps unlikely that either the House of Lords or legislation will abolish this head of privilege. Our tentative conclusion then, is that the law of civil procedure, even after the CPR and other recent developments, continues to navigate the tensions produced by the clash between the values of disclosure and privilege.

SELF-INCRIMINATION

The law against self-incrimination can be defined as 'the right not to answer questions or produce material which might have the effect of incriminating oneself or one's spouse'. These principles mean that an individual can refuse to either answer questions or disclose documents if these actions would lead to criminal proceedings. The key authority is *R.* v. *Director of Serious Fraud Office, ex parte Smith*[36] where Lord Mustill argued that the fundamental concern of the right to silence was protection of 'abuse of power' by those investigating crime. What are the boundaries of this principle, and how can any limitations on the privilege be justified? Does it amount to '[a] general immunity, possessed by all persons and bodies, from being compelled on pain of punishment to answer questions the answers to which may incriminate them'? The essential problem is that the privilege can be claimed to 'thwart' the claims of justice. There is certainly a sense that the judges themselves think that the privilege should be tightly defined:

> the privilege against self-incrimination exercisable in civil proceedings is an archaic and unjustifiable survival from the past when the court directs the production of relevant documents and requires the defendant to specify his dealings with the plaintiff's property or money.[37]

Is the privilege simply a historical remainder? The history of the common law indeed shows that the courts have reacted to 'abuses of judicial interrogation'. In the 1600s,

---
33   Ibid., 31.22.1.
34   Supra n. 1 at 611.
35   *Secretary of State for Trade and Industry* v. *Baker* [1998] Ch. 356, at 371.
36   *Reg.* v. *Director of Serious Fraud Office, ex parte Smith* [1993] AC 1.
37   Ibid., 31.

the Prerogative Courts of the King had the power to extract confessions, and, even once these abuses of process had been removed, magistrates had certain interrogatory powers. If one turns to the criminal trial, then the right not to self-incriminate is justified by the poor evidential value of confessions, unless they can be shown to have been made in a voluntary fashion.

Our key authority is *AT&T Istel Ltd. v. Tully*.[38] The case concerned a complicated commercial transaction. The facts with which we are concerned relate to a contract that had been obtained by the plaintiff company under circumstances that were redolent of fraud and breach of trust. It was alleged that the defendant had 'swindled' the Wessex Health Authority through false accounting and double invoicing for work. The plaintiffs began their own investigations into the Wessex contracts, and sought discovery of numerous accounting documents.

In civil proceedings, both plaintiffs and defendants are normally able to obtain disclosure of all documents that are relevant to the case. The plaintiff company had obtained orders compelling the defendant company to disclose various documents that related to the allegedly fraudulent transaction. However, the orders specified that the information obtained was not to be used in criminal prosecutions. On an application by the defendants, the court set aside the order as it amounted to self-incrimination. When the plaintiffs appealed against this decision, the CPS were asked whether they wanted to intervene in proceedings. Although the CPS declined the offer, they asserted that they would make use of evidence against the defendants that they obtained independently of the court order. The Court of Appeal dismissed the appeal, and the plaintiffs took the case to the House of Lords. The House of Lords held that although the defendant's privilege against self-incrimination still stood, it could not be used in such a way as to deprive the plaintiff of his/her rights.

Underlying the right not to disclose incriminatory information is the general principle that one's own affairs are private. However, this would not apply in this case as the allegations concerned the defendant's handling of money that belonged to others. In other words, the privacy principle is clearly limited by the requirement that crimes are detected and punished. If these general principles show themselves to be somewhat distant from this civil requirement, then any clarification of the correct approach will depend on an analysis of the statutes that regulate this and related areas of law. In the criminal field, the Theft Act 1968 limits the privilege against self-incrimination, provided that such evidence is not produced through pressure being placed on the suspect. The order with which the court was concerned had nothing to do with criminal charges, but was analogous to the extent that the plaintiffs were attempting to trace embezzled funds. Further limitations of the privilege can be found in section 72 of the Supreme Court Act 1981, where, in an action for breach of intellectual property rights, a person cannot plead that disclosure of documents would lead to prosecution. There are similar provisions under section 434 of the Companies Act 1985. The common law privilege against self-incrimination has thus been 'abrogated' or 'modi[fied]', and although the present case does not fall under any of the relevant sections of the statutes discussed above, it does raise issues

---

38   *AT&T Istel Ltd v. Tully* [1993] AC 45.

that are sufficiently analogous to be covered by the general principles articulated in these Acts.[39] The defendant could possibly plead that he was not compelled to abide with the court order as it would lead to a criminal prosecution, but he should not be allowed to rely on the privilege to frustrate the plaintiff's investigations of his financial dealings.

In order to assess development in this area of law, we need to consider the impact of human rights on procedural principles. The cases of *Saunders* v. *UK*, which will be discussed in Chapter 15, led to legislative reform that impacted on the law relating to material obtained under compulsion. Important post-*Saunders* decisions are *R.* v. *Hertfordshire County Council, ex parte Green Environmental Industries Ltd*[40] and *Brown* v. *Stott*.[41] How do these cases elaborate the jurisprudence that we have been considering?

Ex parte Green Environmental Industries Ltd began with a prosecution for the illegal storage of clinical waste under section 71(2) of the Environmental Protection Act 1990. Hertfordshire County Council had served a notice on the appellants, requesting information about the storage and handling of waste, and refusing to give undertakings that the information so obtained would not be used in any later prosecution. The appellants had sought judicial review of the Council's decision in the Divisional Court, which rejected the application. Their appeal was turned down by the Court of Appeal and the House of Lords. The House of Lords took a broad approach to the Act, and argued that its purpose would be frustrated if people were allowed to rely on the privilege against self-incrimination and refuse to provide information. Moreover, this was coherent with Strasbourg jurisprudence. This principle was qualified by the discretion of the trial judge to exclude unfairly prejudicial evidence.

In his judgment Lord Hoffmann referred back to Lord Templeman's speech in the *AT&T* case. He argued that the privilege against self-incrimination was meant to 'preserve the fairness of the trial' by prohibiting confessions that had 'doubtful probative value'.[42] However, he stressed the point that this principle is open to statutory exception, and that even the 'most general immunity from being made to answer questions' is qualified by numerous 'duties to provide information'.[43] Lord Hoffmann was therefore able to create a principled defence of the notion that the 1990 Act has to be understood in the context where self-incrimination is limited by the need to 'protect public health'.[44] Furthermore, both EU law and the law of human rights were relevant. Lord Hoffmann thus moves his focus to Article 6(1), the concept of a 'fair and public hearing' and the presumption of innocence in Article 6(2).[45] Article 6(1) did not apply because an 'extrajudicial inquiry' was not, under Strasbourg jurisprudence, an 'adjudication';

---

39   Ibid., 67.
40   *R.* v. *Hertfordshire County Council, ex parte Green Environmental Industries Ltd. and Another* [2000] 2 WLR 373.
41   *Brown* v. *Stott* [2001] 2 WLR 681.
42   Supra n. 39, at 419.
43   Ibid.
44   Ibid., 420.
45   Saunders was not relevant in this case because no evidence had been obtained by investigation under the 71(2) notice.

thus to the extent that the inquiry fell outside the notion of a 'judicial process' it was not covered by the Article.

In *Official Receiver* v. *Stern*[46] the official receiver had brought proceedings against the directors of a wound-up company. The directors had been interviewed under section 235 of the Insolvency Act 1986, and the official receiver was seeking to use their replies to disqualify them from acting as directors in the future. The judge had determined that there had been a breach of neither EU law nor human rights law, and the Court of Appeal confirmed that the use of 'compelled evidence' in the context of the liquidation of a company did not breach Article 6(1). The court approached this case in a way that was similar to *ex parte Green Environmental Industries*. It was determined that the purpose of the statute was to gain information to allow the liquidation of a company, not to 'acquire incriminating material'. There were a number of factors that had to be taken into account in assessing whether or not there had been a fair trial. It had to be borne in mind that these were civil rather than criminal proceedings, and that although there was a certain 'stigma' associated with disqualification, the public interest in administration had also to be taken into account. Within proceedings for disqualification, the decision as to whether or not evidence was prejudicial was best left to the trial judge. This involved distinguishing *Saunders* from the present case. Even though evidence had been obtained under compulsion, it could be used in 'non-criminal' proceedings.[47]

Although the Privy Council case *Brown* v. *Stott*[48] concerned a criminal prosecution, we can usefully consider it in this section. The defendant had pleaded not guilty to theft and a road traffic offence of driving under the influence of alcohol. The prosecution were seeking to make use of evidence that she had been compelled to provide. The defendant was arguing that precisely because she had been compelled to provide the evidence, it amounted to a breach of her fair trial rights under Article 6(1). Confirming her conviction, the Privy Council held that although the right to a fair trial was 'absolute', the privilege against self-incrimination was not. Distinguishing the case from *Saunders*, the court argued that there was a significant difference between the hours of interviews to which Saunders had been subjected and the procedure under the Road Traffic Act 1988. Any qualifications on the right not to self-incriminate oneself had to take into account the 'legitimate aim' which such limitations served, and had to be proportionate to that goal. The 'serious social problems' and the 'high incidence of death' that resulted from drunken driving meant that there was a 'public interest' in road traffic legislation. As far as the Act in question was concerned, the defendant was compelled to answer 'one simple question'. The fact that the penalty for refusing to answer the question was 'moderate and non-custodial' meant that there was not a disproportionate coercion placed on the defendant. The Privy Council argued that the trial judge had the discretion to exclude evidence obtained through 'improper coercion'.[49]

These three cases show that the privilege not to incriminate oneself is open to many qualifications. They also show that these qualifications are not contrary to the focus on both EU law and human rights law on Article 6. While *ex parte Green Environmental*

---

46   *Official Receiver* v. *Stern* [2001] BCC 121.
47   Ibid., 122.
48   Supra n. 40.
49   Ibid., 682.

Industries avoids the application of the article by asserting that investigations under the 1990 Act were extrajudicial, Stern makes a central distinction between evidence obtained in criminal proceedings, and that obtained in the context of the winding up of companies. *Brown* v. *Stott* is coherent with this limitation of the reach of Article 6. It would be wrong to argue that this run of cases shows that these recent developments have somehow forgotten the common law's commitment to the privilege, as we have seen that the common law contains similar qualifications. The more accurate question would be the extent to which the law now achieves an effective balance between the protection of the defendant's liberties, and the public interest. Whether or not one agrees that these cases have struck that balance, it would be hard to assert that there is an absolute human right not to incriminate oneself.

FINALITY IN LITIGATION

What are the limits to which a case can be appealed or reopened? The rule that once a court has pronounced judgment, the case should not be reopened does not derive from statute, but from the 'fundamental principle' that litigation must have an end.[50] A central authority is *Ladd* v. *Marshall*.[51] Underlying *Ladd* v. *Marshall* is a foundational common law rule that stresses the finality of litigation.[52] This means that the decision of the court is binding on the parties and 'definitive'. Related to this is the rule that parties must put before the court all the relevant information, and cannot seek to reopen a case at a later stage.

The Ampthill Peerage Case[53] contains an important elaboration of this procedural principle. Lord Wilberforce stressed that all mature legal systems contain an 'essential' set of principles that place limits on the right of the individual to 'reopen disputes'. In English law, this principle can be found in the Legitimacy Declaration Act 1858 and is related to other rules such as the operation of limitation periods. However, underlying these rules is an understanding of the necessarily limited nature of legal proceedings. Legal processes cannot seek to include and consider every single piece of evidence that relates to a dispute, and must do the best that they can with the information available at the time. Lord Wilberforce admits that this can lead to a tension between 'justice and truth', and while the law attempts to make these two values coincide, it has to be acknowledged that the truth may not fit into the parameters with which the law has to operate. It may be that 'the certainty of justice prevails over the possibility of truth'. Justice, then, requires finality, but finality that is itself subject to 'safeguards'. Indeed, this provides a rationale for appeals, which in rare cases are even permissible outside of the set time limits. Safeguards would also allow the exceptional challenge to a judgment on the grounds of fraud, and also the extension of limitation periods.

The creation of the Court of Appeal by the Supreme Court of Judicature Act 1873 was itself an acknowledgement of these principles and a qualification to the principle

---

50   *Ladd* v. *Marshall* [1954] 1 WLR, at 538.
51   535.
52   Ibid.
53   *The Ampthill Peerage Case* [1977] AC 547.

that the judgment of a court was final. Indeed, the Court of Chancery had a practice that allowed the impeachment of a judgment 'obtained by fraud', and the Act of 1873 can be seen as a further articulation of this equitable principle. Would fresh evidence also allow a case to be reopened? This point was considered in *Re Barrell Enterprises*.[54] In theory, the jurisdiction of the Court of Appeal to reopen an appeal because of fraud was not removed by the 1873 Act. However, the Court was impressed by the argument that there had never been a single successful instance where a case was reopened because fresh evidence was discovered. Is the conclusion, therefore, that the Court cannot reopen cases? As the Court of Appeal was created by statute, the definitive answer to this question would lie in an analysis of the relevant Acts. An analysis of (among others) the Supreme Court Act 1981; its predecessor, the Supreme Court of Judicature Act 1873; and the Administration of Justice Act 1934, which empowered the Court of Appeal to hear appeals from the County Court, showed that the Court could not reopen an appeal case, and that the correct course of action would be to appeal to the House of Lords.[55]

However, this principle does need to be qualified. There are authorities, such as *Flower* v. *Lloyd*[56] that do suggest that in very specific and limited circumstances, the Court could reopen a case if a fraud had been 'practiced upon it'. Although this authority cannot be seen as standing unequivocally as a statement of principle, there are other more recent judgments that can be read as suggesting that in 'exceptional circumstances' cases can be reopened. Lord Woolf usefully relates this jurisdiction to the functions of the Court of Appeal. The Court has the dual function of ensuring justice between parties, and 'public confidence in the administration of justice' by both correcting 'wrong decisions' and 'developing the law'.[57] Moreover, these functions correctly belong to the Court of Appeal, rather than the House of Lords, because the latter, due to the weight of its own work, cannot take appellate responsibility over all issues. There is an argument that appeals such as the one in the present case are more properly dealt with by a court less senior to the House of Lords.

These issues run through *Taylor* v. *Lawrence*.[58] The case concerned a property dispute over the positioning of a boundary wall. The claimants had begun an action for trespass against the defendants, alleging that the latter had built the wall on their land. At the trial, where the defendants acted for themselves, the judge revealed that the solicitor for the claimants had drafted his will. Neither party objected to this fact. However, when judgment was given for the claimants, the defendants alleged that the judgment was compromised because of the 'appearance of bias' on behalf of the judge. After the appeal against the judgment had been dismissed, the defendants found out that the judge had not paid for the services of the solicitor, and had made amendments to his will on the night preceding the judgment in the case. Despite having the opportunity to do so, the judge never revealed this fact to the Court. The defendants applied to have the

---

54 *Re Barrell Enterprises* [1973] 1 WLR 19.
55 The House of Lords determined in *R.* v. *Bow Street Metropolitan Stipendiary Magistrate, Ex p Pinochet Ugarte* No. 2 [2000] 1 AC 119 that it could reopen an appeal where the appearance of bias compromised its judgment.
56 *Flower* v. *Lloyd* [1877] 6 Ch D 297.
57 *Taylor and Another* v. *Lawrence* [2003] QB 528.
58 Ibid.

appeal reopened. While the Court of Appeal agreed that the appeal should be reopened, they dismissed the application.

Lord Woolf argued that the case raised two issues of fundamental importance: the jurisdiction of the Court of Appeal in relation to the reopening of appeals, and the possible bias of the judge. The fundamental principle was that the Court of Appeal would not hear new evidence in an appeal, if that evidence was not available at trial.[59] The plaintiffs were arguing that application of this rule would prevent the defendants from submitting an argument about the judge's possible bias, as the evidence on which they relied was not available at the original hearing. Given the broader points raised by this case, the application of this rule had to be suspended.

Counsel for the applicants was trying to urge the Court to acknowledge that it did indeed have a jurisdiction that was somewhat wider than might at first be believed.

Arguments, in part, relied on *Wood v. Gahlings*.[60] In this case the Court had ordered a retrial because of a fraud perpetrated not in the Court of First Instance, but on the Court of Appeal itself. Counsel was arguing that this was part of a much broader principle, that as the Court of Appeal could 'reopen a decision where it has been obtained by fraud', it could also do so 'in other exceptional cases'[61] in order to 'regulate the implementation and enforcement of its own orders'. Counsel relied on a series of cases concerning children to further this argument, and on the bold idea that the Court of Appeal 'had a jurisdiction similar to that exercised by the House of Lords' in the Pinochet case. This would, of course, bring the present case within the category of exceptional instances, as it would apply to allegations that a judgment was biased.

The court did not completely accept this argument, as there are important differences between the Court of Appeal and the House of Lords. However, it did prompt Lord Woolf to clarify the principle that should determine the outcome of the present appeal. This returns to the principle articulated above:

> As an appellate court [the Court of Appeal] has the implicit powers to do that which is necessary to achieve the dual objectives of an appellate court.[62]

This means that it has a power to 'control its own procedure so as to prevent it being used to achieve injustice'.[63] All the authorities, and the statutes must be interpreted in the light of this power. However, this does indeed lead to a 'a tension between a court having a residual jurisdiction of the type to which we are here referring and the need to have finality in litigation'.[64] The only sensible response to this tension is to ensure that cases are only reopened when it is absolutely necessary to do so, and that therefore the threshold must be exacting: 'It should be clearly established that a significant injustice has probably occurred and that there is no alternative effective remedy'.[65] Bias may

---

59   Supra n. 49.
60   *Wood v. Gahlings* (*The Times*, 29 November 1996; Court of Appeal (Civil Division) Transcript No. 1525 of 1996).
61   Supra n. 56, 542.
62   Supra n. 57, 546.
63   Ibid.
64   Ibid.
65   Ibid.

fall into this category, provided it is a significant breach of the rules of natural justice. However, on the facts of this case, and for reasons that will become clearer when we consider the issue of judicial bias, the fair-minded observer would not conclude that there was a danger of bias in this case.

How do these principles relate to the 'changed landscape' of civil procedure after Woolf? We cannot consider the broader issues that come out of the defence of an appellate system in civil justice within the confines of this chapter. Suffice to say that Woolf is congruent with the general recommendations of the Evershed Committee that stressed the importance of appeals in correcting error, and the opinion of the Committee of Ministers of the EU that an appeals system is necessary in civil law.[66] It goes without saying, however, that as appeals are expensive and use up the resources of the civil justice system, some restrictions are necessary. Andrews stresses that the whole drive of the CPR is to sustain a framework where appeals are kept to a minimum through a requirement for permission.[67] As Article 6 stresses access to Courts of First Instance, and does not provide a right to appeal, this is entirely coherent with the human rights framework. To the extent that an appeals process is made available, it must comply with due process. Thus, any limitations must serve a proportionate end.[68] Any assessment of *Ladd* v. *Marshall* and *Taylor* v. *Lawrence* must take place against this general backdrop.

How have the restrictions on producing new evidence on appeal in *Ladd* v. *Marshall* fared? The CPR provide that an appeal court will not receive oral evidence or evidence which was not placed before the lower court unless it orders otherwise.[69] This largely reflects the approach of *Ladd* v. *Marshall*, but the approach of the courts is best described by Lord Phillips in *Hamilton* v. *Al Fayed*,[70] where he made reference to the 'overriding objectives', rather than the 'straitjacket of previous authority' as the guide for allowing fresh evidence. He stressed however, that pre-CPR authorities would remain 'powerful persuasive' authorities as they are indicative of the need to 'strike a fair balance' between finality in litigation and the achievement of 'the right result'. These authorities are also coherent with the 'overriding objectives' of the CPR. *Taylor* v. *Lawrence* also accords high regard to *Ladd* v. *Marshall*, and cites the case as evidence of a 'fundamental principle of our common law' – the finality of litigation.[71] Lord Phillips' words are thus measured – while the courts regard the CPR as a new horizon for civil justice, they will look back to those cases whose principles are consistent with the 'overriding objectives'. As maximising the opportunities for appeal is not an objective of the system, it is not surprising that chances to introduce fresh evidence are similarly restricted.

---

66   Supra n. 1, 900.
67   The general structure of the new rules are provided by CPR 52.11(3). This provides that an appeal will be allowed when the decision of a lower court is 'wrong' or 'unjust because of a serious procedural or other irregularity in the proceedings in the lower court'. CPR 52.3.6. states that permission to appeal will be granted when there is 'a real prospect of success' or 'some other compelling reason'.
68   Ibid., 901–2.
69   Supra n. 3, at 52.11.2. There is also a power to draw 'inferences of fact' that are 'justified by the evidence'; see CPR 52.11(4).
70   *Hamilton* v. *Al Fayed* (unreported, 21 December 2000), cited Andrews, supra n. 1 at 905.
71   Ibid., 909.

THE PRINCIPLE OF DUE NOTICE

As Andrews points out, the 'core' value that due notice protects is the 'need for a legal system to show respect for a person's individuality'. This means that it is the 'antithesis of justice' if a case is decided either in the absence of the defendant, or without allowing 'reasonable opportunity'[72] for the defendant to make his or her own case. However, the courts have to reconcile this fundamental principle with other exigencies of the forensic process and broader demands placed on the court. If we consider this matter from the perspective of 'without notice' injunctions to freeze assets of alleged fraudsters,[73] then it does seem justifiable that in certain circumstances, orders should be made that do not put the person who will be subject on notice. These issues are writ large in Anton Piller orders.

An Anton Piller order is made to prevent evidence being destroyed, and would clearly be useful in a situation where a defendant might take such actions prior to litigation. Applications are made without the other party being present. Scott J outlined the application procedure in *Columbia Picture Industries Inc. and Others* v. *Robinson and Others*.[74] It is 'implicit' in the nature of the injunction that they are applied for in secret. Practice differs between Queen's Bench Division and Chancery. In the former, the application is heard in chambers; in the latter, the court sits in camera. The award of an Anton Piller injunction thus does not depend on notice. They tend to be accompanied by Mareva injunctions that freeze the bank account of the respondent and thus prevent them making financial transactions. Scott J dramatically outlined the effects of such injunctions on a respondent's private and public life. The seizure of documents and stock in trade could effectively mean the end of the respondent's business. Equally 'traumatic' is the right of the applicant to:

> search and rummage through the personal belongings of any occupant of [a private address] and to remove the material they consider to be covered by the terms of the order.[75]

As the effects of these injunctions are so severe, a party is under a strict duty to the court to present all the relevant material, and to ensure that they are not served in an oppressive manner. Anton Piller orders derive from the case *Anton Piller KG* v. *Manufacturing Processes Ltd*.[76] The best way of introducing ourselves to the issues at stake in an Anton Piller order are to consider the words of Lord Denning MR:

> Let me say at once that no court in this land has any power to issue a search warrant to enter a man's house so as to see if there are papers or documents there which are of an incriminating nature, whether libels or infringements of copyright or anything else of the kind. No constable or bailiff can knock at the door and demand entry so as to inspect

---

72 Ibid., 85.
73 See s.37(3) Supreme Court Act 1981 and s.7 Civil Procedure Act 1997.
74 *Columbia Picture Industries Inc. and Others* v. *Robinson and Others* [1986] 3 WLR 542.
75 Ibid., 73.
76 *Anton Piller KG* v. *Manufacturing Processes Ltd* [1976] Ch. 55.

papers or documents. The householder can shut the door in his face and say 'Get out'. That was established in the leading case of Entick v. Carrington (1765) 2 Wils.K.B. 275. None of us would wish to whittle down that principle in the slightest. But the order sought in this case is not a search warrant. It does not authorise the plaintiffs' solicitors or anyone else to enter the defendants' premises against their will ... The plaintiffs must get the defendants' permission. But it does do this: it brings pressure on the defendants to give permission. It does more. It actually orders them to give permission – with, I suppose, the result that if they do not give permission they are guilty of contempt of court.[77]

There are a number of points to bear in mind. An Anton Piller order is not an indiscriminate search warrant. As the key authority *Entick* v. *Carrington* shows, no court can make a general order for the search of premises to find incriminating material. An Anton Piller order is a way in which a defendant is compelled to give their permission, at the risk of being in contempt of court. It is fundamentally a civil rather than a criminal measure. Suffice to say that the circumstances in which an order can be made are tightly controlled. Lord Denning outlined these 'extreme' cases. The applicant would have to show that 'there is a grave danger that vital evidence will be destroyed, that papers will be burnt or lost or hidden, or taken beyond the jurisdiction'. Ormrod LJ elaborated the conditions: there has to be 'an extremely strong prima facie case'. The applicant then has to show that the damage they are likely to suffer is 'very serious'; the applicant must also show that there is 'clear evidence' that 'incriminating documents' or material are in the defendant's possession, and that there is a 'real possibility' that they might be destroyed.[78] As Shaw LJ stressed, precisely because the Anton Piller injunction stands outside the 'normal processes of the law', the court has to ensure they are only awarded when absolutely necessary.

For both the Anton Piller and the Mareva injunction, the essential safeguard is the 'liberty' that the respondent has to apply to the court for the order(s) to be discharged. While this is an effective safeguard in relation to Mareva injunctions, it tends to be less so in the case of Anton Piller injunctions, as once it is served, it is already too late, as the applicant may already have taken possession of documents and materials. The respondent cannot object to search and seizure on the grounds that s/he intends to apply to go to court to object to the order. The order should also contain the undertaking to compensate the respondent for any loss suffered, as assessed by the court. A third safeguard is the duty placed on the applicant to disclose all the relevant evidence to the court. The inherent problem with this safeguard is that the legal advisers to the applicant will act in his or her best interest. The solicitor overseeing the application, and the service of the order, is thus not in the neutral position of the court.

When the Anton Piller injunction was first awarded, it was intended that it would be used sparingly. However, by 1986, the injunction was commonly used, especially in cases involving audio and video piracy. Should the courts look again at such a draconian order? Scott J argued that the case raised a 'fundamental principle' of 'civil jurisprudence'. This rested on the maxim *audi alteram partem*, and meant that, if a citizen is to be deprived of their property, there is a need for a hearing. How can this be

---
[77] Ibid., 60.
[78] Ibid., 61.

squared with the fact that the regular award of court orders 'depriv[es] citizens of their property and clos[es] down their businesses ... on applications of which they know nothing'?[79] The safeguards mentioned above do not go all the way to satisfying these objections; objections which could only be served by allowing the respondent a chance to address the court. These issues were raised in *Pamplin* v. *Express Newspapers Ltd*.[80] The case concerned a taxing issue (the way in which the court assess the costs that the losing party will pay to the winner). The plaintiffs challenged some of the charges that had been raised by the defendants. They applied for a review of the charges, arguing that they should have been given the chance to see the documents that the defendants had lodged with the court. The court held that these documents were confidential, and refused the application for the review. The plaintiffs asked for this decision to be reviewed by a judge, but the decision of the taxing master was upheld. How could this decision be justified?

Justice Hobhouse presented the case as a 'conflict between two legal principles'. The 'principle of natural justice' requires that when a court or a tribunal is making an order that will bind another party, that each party should have a right to be heard. In relation to evidence, the same principle demands that parties should be able to examine evidence placed before the court, and to submit 'counter material'[81]; in other words, '[o]ne party may not make secret communications to the court'. This principle comes into conflict with the right to legal privilege, which, as we know, enables full and frank discussions between individuals and their legal representatives. However, this principle is waived when a document is given in evidence. The plaintiffs had pleaded that it would be a breach of natural justice for the documents to be kept from them, and the defendants objected that the documents were covered by privilege.

Applying these principles to the matter in hand require a determination of the precise status of taxation within the civil justice system. As Justice Hobhouse points out, the proceedings are 'hybrid', and can be 'administrative or supervisory' rather than adversarial like litigation. A dispute on a taxation matter, though, comes closer to the adversarial than the supervisory. The taxing master must hear the parties, and must make decisions on both fact and law.[82] However, although taxation proceedings can take an adversarial form, taxation is excluded from the rules that cover normal litigation. RSC Order 62 thus represents a 'self-contained code'; it does not contain, for instance, rules on discovery and inspection that govern litigation. Despite its distinct nature, however, 'the rules of natural justice apply to taxation proceedings', and the pressing issue is how the legitimate interests of the parties are balanced.

Justice Hobhouse has to privilege one principle over another:

> The answer is that, ultimately, the principle that each party must have the right to see any relevant material which his opponent is placing before the tribunal, and which that tribunal is taking into account in arriving at its decision, must prevail.[83]

---

79   Ibid., 74.
80   *Pamplin* v. *Express Newspapers Ltd* [1985] 1 WLR 689.
81   Ibid., 691.
82   Ibid., 695.
83   Ibid.

This means that a party must elect whether to submit a document in evidence to the court and thus waive his or her privilege, or to not make use of the document in evidence. Normally, as most taxation hearings are uncontentious, the issue will not arise. The plaintiff was arguing that litigation rules should apply to taxation matters. Justice Hobhouse thought that this would 'place a serious obstacle in the way of the efficient and fair conduct of taxations', and that it made for the correct balance of the parties' interests for taxation matters to be covered by Order 62.

How do Lord Woolf's reforms of civil justice relate to the judicial development of Mareva and Anton Piller orders? The interim report made it clear that both orders were 'invaluable'[84] so long as the behaviour of both parties adhered to 'the standard of conduct' required by the court.[85] The present practice direction also makes clear the standard of conduct required, and presupposes the judicial attempts to balance the competing interests that are at stake in interim injunctions. It is worth noting that the orders have been renamed, and are now known as freezing orders and search orders.[86] The practice direction goes on to state that an application for an order must be supported by evidence that specifies the 'facts on which the applicant relies for the claim being made against the respondent'.[87] Applications can still be made without notice, and 'except in cases where secrecy is essential, the applicant should take steps to notify the respondent informally of the application'.[88] Protection is provided for the respondent as the court may order that the applicant provides an undertaking to pay damages if the court deems it necessary; in the case of a freezing order the applicant's solicitor as well as the applicant may have to give undertakings for damages.[89] The practice direction goes on to specify that the solicitor serving a search order must be experienced in their 'operation';[90] there must be an 'independent and supervisory solicitor' who is not an employee of the applicants. There are also detailed rules provided for their service[91] and the custody of seized materials.[92]

The general framework of the practice directions suggests that Lord Woolf has not significantly altered the form of the orders. Has human rights law had a significant impact? The key case is *Chappell* v. *UK*[93] where an Anton Piller order was challenged under Article 8. The court held unanimously that there had been no breach. Their judgment is interesting as it shows how procedure is 'translated' into the language of human rights. Thus, the court argued that although there had been an 'interference' with the applicant's 'private life' and his 'home', it was 'legitimate' as it protected 'the rights of others'. We are, of course, familiar with this argument. There is no such thing as an absolute right. More properly, the issue is how is the legitimacy of the interference

---

84   Supra n. 22 at chapter 19, para 11.
85   Lord Woolf cites (chapter 19, para 11) the Practice Direction by the Lord Chief Justice, the President of the Family Division and the Vice-Chancellor, 28 July 1994.
86   Supra n. 3 at 25.1.1.
87   Ibid., 25.3.3.
88   Ibid., 25.4.3. (3).
89   Ibid., 25.6.2.
90   Ibid., 25.7.2.
91   Ibid., 25.7.4.
92   Ibid., 25.7.5.
93   *Chappell* v. *UK* [1990] 12 EHRR 1.

determined? Following the terms of Article 8, the court held that there was a legal basis for the order, and that safeguards existed, such as the undertakings given by the applicants and the availability of remedies if the order was misused.

Chappell led to a re-examination of the safeguards on injunctions,[94] and these were incorporated in the new practice direction. In particular, the CPR stresses the role of the supervisory solicitor, and the opportunities for the respondent to set aside a search order. The role of human rights in this area of procedure thus appears to be that of fine-tuning the principles developed incrementally by judges; in this sense, it would be apt to cite the Scottish case *HM Advocate* v. *Montgomery*,[95] the principles of European human rights law 'soak through and permeate' domestic law.[96] Matters articulated in civil law or common law are largely coherent with international standards.

THE DUTY TO GIVE REASONS

The requirement that a court should give reasons for its decision brings us to one of the most intriguing areas where common law rules of civil procedure and Article 6 come together. There are three main authorities on the duty to give reasons.[97] We will examine *Flannery and Another* v. *Halifax Estate Agencies Ltd. (trading as Colleys Professional Services)*[98] first of all. The case concerned an appeal against a judge's decision that he preferred the defendant's expert evidence to the plaintiff. The judge had not given any reasons for this preference. The Court of Appeal allowed the plaintiff's appeal, holding that the failure to give reasons breached the principle that the court had to show fairness to both parties. The court began its judgment by affirming the common law duty to give reasons.[99] However, this duty is not absolute or unqualified. It does not 'usually' apply in the magistrate's court, or in orders for costs.[100] Moreover, it would not be correct to specify a single rule in relation to the different aspects of the forensic process. For instance, if a judge is considering oral evidence, then it is acceptable to assert that one witness was simply more credible than another. However, with expert evidence, a judge should probably always give reasons why one expert's evidence is more credible than another. Bingham LJ in *Eckersley* v. *Binnie*[101] argued that '[i]n resolving conflicts of expert evidence' a judge had to issue a 'coherent reasoned rebuttal' of evidence that had been presented, but was not convincing.

---

94   See *Practice Direction (Mareva Injunctions and Anton Piller Orders)*, 28 July 1994.
95   *HM Advocate* v. *Montgomery* [2000] JC 111 at p. 117A–B.
96   Cited by Charteris (2000: 275).
97   Andrews points out that the CPR only require small claims court judges to give reasons – CPR 27.8(6). Supra n. 1 at 97.
98   *Flannery and Another* v. *Halifax Estate Agencies Ltd (trading as Colleys Professional Services)* [2000] 1 WLR 377.
99   See *R.* v. *Knightsbridge Crown Court, Ex parte International Sporting Club (London) Ltd* [1982] QB 304; *R.* v. *Harrow Crown Court, Ex parte Dave* [1994] 1 WLR 98. In *Eagil Trust Co Ltd* v *Pigott-Brown* [1985] 3 All ER 119, 122 Griffiths LJ argued that the judge does not have to deal with every argument made by counsel.
100 Supra n. 98, at 381.
101 *Eckersley* v. *Binnie* [1988] 18 ConLR 1, 77–8.

The Court of Appeal attempted to clarify these principles by articulating a set of general comments. The duty to give reasons is part of due process, and its 'rationale'[102] has two elements. Fairness requires that the party that has lost the case knows the reason why; this is to ensure that the Court has not 'misdirected itself', and to ascertain whether or not an appeal is possible. Indeed, failure to give reasons may itself constitute grounds of appeal. It could be suggested that fairness is related to 'transparency'.[103] The second principle might be described as a forensic discipline: it encourages good practice as judgments must be soundly reasoned. As mentioned above, this duty must be sensitive to context. The key issue is the 'subject matter' of the case. Once evidence moves beyond the oral and, in particular, once it is disputed expert evidence, the duty to give a coherent reasoned judgment is triggered.

Flannery was revisited in *English* v. *Emery Reimbold & Strick Ltd*.[104] Since the case had been decided, the Human Rights Act had made Article 6 part of English law. Article 6, as we have seen, does not contain the duty to give reasons. However, as was pointed out in *North Range Shipping*, 'the right to a fair hearing generally carries with it an obligation to give reasons'.[105] Thus, since 1998, the courts have changed their practice. In particular, magistrate's courts now have to give reasons for the decisions that they have made. So, it was necessary to recast the language of *Flannery* in relation to Article 6. The Court of Appeal held that decisions affecting the 'substantive' rights of parties should be reasoned, while other decisions, such as those on 'interlocutory case management' did not require a reasoned justification. How can this distinction between substantive and procedural rights be justified?

After reviewing the Strasbourg case law, Lord Philips argued that Article 6 relates not to the merits, but to the procedure of a case. For a judgment to be compliant with Article 6, it would have to show that the 'essential issues' raised by the case have both been considered by the court and 'resolved'.[106] In other words, fairness does not require that all elements of a decision are explained, for instance, 'interlocutory decisions in the course of case management'. However, costs orders after the CPR do require some justification. This reflects the fact that, in the new culture of civil litigation, costs do not simply 'follow the event', but reflect the conduct of the parties. In relation to evidence, the Strasbourg jurisprudence does not require a judge to give reasons for preferring one piece of evidence to another. Indeed, common law reasoning, in comparison with that of civilian jurisdictions, tends to give much greater detail.

In Lord Philips opinion, the common law has always generally acknowledged that a judgment should be reasoned,[107] although this general acknowledgement has not been expressed as a human right. His discussion of the relevant authorities largely amplifies the common law understanding of this topic as articulated by *Flannery*. However, he adds some interesting reflections. The common law's commitment to a binding system of precedent cannot in itself explain why there is an acknowledgement of the duty to

---

102 Ibid., 381.
103 Ibid., 382.
104 *English* v. *Emery Reimbold & Strick Ltd* [2002] EWCA Civ 605.
105 Ibid., 1403.
106 Ibid., 2416.
107 Ibid., 2417.

give reasons, as the fundamental nature of the judgment is that it binds the parties to the case, not that it 'delineate[s]' or 'develop[s]' the law.[108] Lord Philips also places the duty to give reasons in the context of the appellate system. Given that appeals require permission, it is necessary that a judge set out the grounds on which he or she has made his or her decision. This provides a further measure for the level of detail required. It is not necessary for the judge to deal with every argument given, and refute it on a point by point basis: what is crucial is to show 'the issues the resolution of which were vital to the judge's conclusion and the manner in which [they have been] resolved'.[109]

A third important decision is *North Range Shipping Ltd* v. *Seatrans Shipping Corporation*.[110] This case, also decided after the Human Rights Act, concerned an appeal from the decision of a High Court judge to refuse to give more than the briefest of reasons to explain why he refused to consider an appeal from an arbitration decision. The Court of Appeal affirmed the judge's reasoning, arguing that he had been correct under the relevant statute, and that it was only in rare cases that it would consider appeals against 'adequacy of reasons'. Appeals in this area had become something of a 'cottage industry'. It was therefore correct to restrict the circumstances under which they could be made. This necessity also reflects a commercial environment, where arguments about a possible appeal conceal a 'reluctance' to abide by a court's order. Whether or not these observations are convincing, the weight of applications for appeal on grounds of a failure to give reasons, might suggest that in the light of Article 6 common law practices are not as focused as they might be.

Tuckey LJ's opinion stressed that judges in commercial courts – who are the gate-keepers for appeals from arbitration decisions – have enjoyed the privilege of not having to give as thoroughly reasoned judgments as those in other common law courts.[111] Practices tended to differ, but the 'common approach' appeared to be simply to refer to the statutory grounds on which the appeal had been refused.[112]

The question of whether or not this practice was compliant with Article 6 reflects the peculiar context of arbitration appeals. The practice had been laid down in 1985, with the case *The Antaios*.[113] Lord Diplock had indicated that as the judge was not determining a question of law, but dealing solely with whether or not an appeal should be allowed, he 'should do no more than say whether the application was granted or refused'.[114] As far as Article 6 applies to arbitration, the parties to 'consensual arbitration' waive their rights, 'in the interest of privacy and finality'. However, as this case concerns the appeals process, it does not raise the issue of Article 6's applicability to arbitration hearings.

---

108   Lord Philips citing Mahoney JA in *Soulemezis* v. *Dudley (Holdings) Pty Ltd* [1987] 10 NSWLR 247, 273, at ibid., 2417.
109   Ibid., 2417.
110   *North Range Shipping Ltd* v. *Seatrans Shipping Corpn*. [2002] EWCA Civ 405.
111   See Bingham LJ, 'Reasons and Reasons for Reasons: Differences Between a Court Judgment and an Arbitration Award' (1988) 4 Arb Int 141.
112   Supra n. 110, at 2400.
113   *The Antaios* [1985] AC 191.
114   Ibid., 199.

What guidance can be obtained from the Strasbourg case law? In *X* v. *Federal Republic of Germany*,[115] the Commission argued that where a domestic court is considering an appeal, it is acceptable simply to make reference to the statutory framework. This appears to be backed up by another Commission case: *Webb* v. *United Kingdom*.[116] *Webb* concerned the failure of the Privy Council to give reasons for dismissing an application for appeal against conviction. The commission stated that an appellate court had to be considered within its context, and the 'very limited reasoning'[117] may be acceptable when refusing leave to appeal.

It would thus appear that arbitration appeals are not covered by the requirement to give reasons. This does not 'subvert[s] the arbitral process' as the judge may adopt the reasoning of the arbitrators themselves; this would also appear to be coherent with Article 6 and its application to appellate procedures.

CONCLUSION

This chapter has engaged with the principles of civil procedure. We have not attempted to outline civil procedure in its entirety, and have kept our focus on the fundamental issues that underlie the areas that we have chosen to consider. Civil procedural law can be understood as animated by certain tensions that relate to the competing requirements of due process within this area. For instance, we have seen that the judges have tried to find a balance between privilege and the disclosure of documents, finality and justice, efficiency and human rights. These very tensions suggest that the role of the judge in the development of procedural law is central. Even though the CPR are important, the rules still need to be interpreted and developed through general principles of law. These general principles also relate to human rights, and perhaps most specifically Article 6.

---

115   *X* v. *Federal Republic of Germany* (1981) 25 DR 240.
116   *Webb* v. *United Kingdom* [1997] 24 EHRR CD 73.
117   Ibid., 74.

14

IMAGINING CRIMINAL JUSTICE

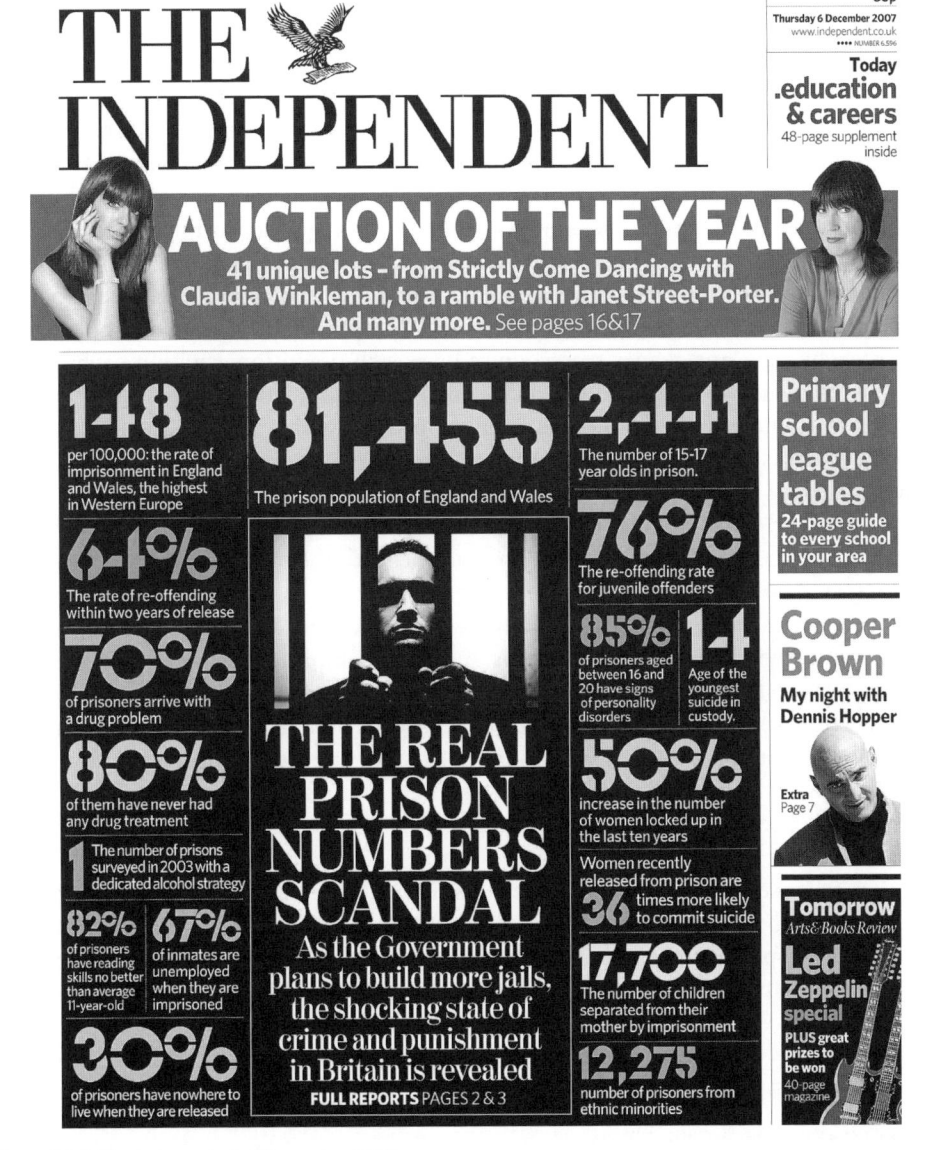

Figure 14.1 The Independent, 6 December 2007.

> The criminal sanction is at once prime guarantor and prime threatener of human freedom. Used providently and humanely it is guarantor; used indiscriminately and coercively it is threatener. The tensions that inhere in the criminal sanction can never be wholly resolved in favour of guaranty and against threat. But we can begin to try.
> Herbert Packer, *The Criminal Sanction* (1968), p. 366

INTRODUCTION: A FORTUNE WITH HOSTAGES?

Traditional accounts of criminal justice tend to assume that there exists a system with a collection of seamless processes which begins with intervention by the police and ends in the punishment of the offender. Such accounts are useful to demonstrate how the institutions of the criminal justice system work but their assumption that the process operates in an objective fashion with one common aim and a seamless 'system' is unfounded. Since Herbert Packer's famous account[1] of how the criminal justice process of any country can be evaluated by considering whether its processes are committed to crime control or due process far more attempts have been made to try and understand the underlying values within any criminal justice system. In England and Wales more recent academic commentary has concerned itself with the inherent conflicts and dilemmas that are faced by those who practice within the criminal justice process.[2] These practitioners face competing values every day in their work and an appreciation of this encourages any reader to recognise how each practitioner within each institution has its own 'working credos'.[3] With such variations within each institution it is difficult to see how there can be one seamless process with a single aim. The criminal justice system is best understood therefore as a series of processes with many of its practitioners working with different values. This could suggest chaos, but in fact it is at worst organised chaos because the machinery of the institution tends to drive through a particular course and practitioners often work beneath the radar to preserve their own working credos.

Once we understand that the system is not objective, it is not uniform, we can begin to imagine what criminal justice is and how it impacts upon an individual. The majority of us lead law-abiding lives and so will not encounter the criminal justice system. However it is also important to remember that those who do encounter it should be subject to practices which are defensible and bear critical scrutiny. Some who encounter the process will be guilty but there will also be those who are innocent and yet have been a victim of a miscarriage of justice. These miscarriages may be due to discriminatory police practices, it may be due to incompetent scientific evidence or the over-reliance of the court on expert testimony. In imagining criminal justice we need to remember that where mistakes are made by those who have power within the process so this power, when abused, can have critical consequences. These people are often hostages to the fortune of the process.

---

1   Packer (1968).
2   See in particular Rutherford (1993).
3   A term used by Rutherford.

But our story is not simply one of mistakes. It is also a story of the battle for power. It involves a consideration of the arguments that continue to rage within any evaluation of the criminal justice process. The battle between the judiciary and the executive/legislature over the sentencing of a convicted person, and also over the effects of an expansionist policy towards the use of prison, continue to haunt the processes we think about. In these battles we would expect to be supportive of the executive/legislature, for their task is to represent us in our liberal democracy. However, sometimes they too become blinkered in their search for fortune (in the form of re-election and the consolidation of political power) that they forget that there will be hostages to their decision making. Helena Kennedy warns us of how even the most benevolent of governments with significant influence over the legislature[4] can often forget how powerful they have become and the responsibility which accompanies that power. She says:

> Once people 'are the state' or have their hands on the levers of the state they have amnesia about the meaning of power and its potential to corrupt. They forget the basic lessons that safeguards and legal protections are there for the possible bad times which could confront us, when a government may be less hospitable, or when social pressures make law our only lifeline. They forget that good intentions are not enough, that scepticism about untrammelled power is essential. No state should be assumed benign, even the one you are governing.[5]

The state is therefore not benign. The criminal justice process with its institutions who advance their commitment to 'justice' are not benign either. The process may be littered with good intentions but whilst those intentions manifest themselves into practices which marginalise or vilify the few then our imagining of criminal justice soon becomes the darkest of visions.

POLICING: LOCAL BATTLES AND NATIONAL WARS

We begin our tour through the criminal justice process by considering the current extent of police powers and some of the controversies which have emerged during the exercising of those powers. Policing in England and Wales has long been considered to have been by consent.[6] This means that those who are policed tacitly consent to allow the police to have powers which enable the police to preserve public order, ensure citizen safety and to protect citizen property where appropriate. This has been the traditional view of policing since reforms to policing were carried out during the nineteenth century. Any evaluation of policing in the twenty-first century can see that although there continues to be widespread support for the police there has, over the last

---

4 Given the fact that our government is almost exclusively selected from the legislature the term 'executive/legislature' is used to demonstrate how powerful the executive in the UK is.
5 Kennedy (2004: 41–2).
6 For a fuller discussion of policing by consent and its efforts at attainment see Joyce (2006).

30 years, been a decline in policing by consent. This is in part due to the fragmentation of local communities where those being policed have felt for some years that the powers possessed by the police have become too intrusive and are being used in a discriminatory way to target particular groups within that local community. While these local battles continue to rage we have also seen developments on the world stage which has led to increased police powers which have been implemented in an attempt to respond to the perceived increased threat of terrorism.[7] These powers have also proved controversial in their use by police. The result being a general recognition that heightened policing may be a necessity but a far keener eye is now placed on how the police exercise these powers, both locally and nationally, to ensure they are used carefully.

Local battles

Policing has always been a local business. Historically, policing was organised and controlled by the local community. This arrangement, with 43 police forces in England and Wales, has continued and so there is not currently a national police force. That said, in recent years there have been legislative reforms which have resulted in greater centralisation[8] and indeed the Home Office suggests that they 'fund the police and have overall responsibility as overseer and coordinator'.[9] This localised arrangement means that each police force is permitted, within limits, to target its resources at particular priorities within that local community.[10] Local justice has always been preferred as a means of targeting local problems. There would be little point directing valuable resources towards preventing a particular type of crime which is a concern for one police force but not for another. This division has been particularly noted when considering the priorities for policing in rural as opposed to urban areas. One 'local' problem[11] for the London Metropolitan Police Service since the publication of the MacPherson Report[12] has been how to deal with the criticism by that report that the service is 'institutionally racist'. There have been a whole host of initiatives[13] to attempt to combat this charge. However, on a local level there remains a crucial test of how racist,[14] or not, the police are. This is in their day-to-day exercising of their stop and search powers.

---

7   Although terrorist threats have been local to the UK since the 1970s due to the Troubles in Northern Ireland the extent of these threats have been heightened since 9/11 and the death of 3,017 people.
8   For an excellent discussion of the structure of the police and issues currently facing them see Uglow (2002: 35).
9   See http://www.homeoffice.gov.uk/police/about/?version=3 for an overview.
10   Although Uglow (2002) questions how far this is really possible given that the 'Home Office increasingly lays down a general strategy, which all forces are expected to follow' (2002: 54), suggesting the Home Office tacitly direct affairs!
11   Racial discrimination is a concern for all police but is more critical for those areas where there are large populations of people from ethnic minority groups.
12   Report of the Inquiry into the Matters Arising from the Death of Stephen Lawrence (Home Office, London, 1999).
13   The Home Office website cites an increase in defining racist incidents, more community and race relations training for police officers and the mobilisation of the Independent Police Complaints Commission to independently review police actions. There has also been an attempt to increase the recruitment of ethnic minority police officers. See http://www.homeoffice.gov.uk/police/about/?version=3 for more details.
14   And this refers to a police officer being racist in their decision making rather than an institution whose processes discriminate against those from an ethnic minority background.

Historically, with the exception of Londoners,[15] there was no police power to stop and search. Any police officer stopping and attempting to search a citizen could be sued for assault. This changed in 1984 when s.1 of the Police and Criminal Evidence Act (PACE) permitted police, on reasonable suspicion, to stop and search any person or vehicle that the police believed were carrying stolen goods or other prohibited items. This search was limited to a search of bags or pockets. This new power was seen as a crucial development for the police as they had argued they could not prevent or detect crime if they were unable to detect people carrying stolen goods and prevent people who were in possession of items which may be criminal[16] or facilitate a future crime.[17] All stop and searches have to be recorded and each police force publishes statistics on those searches in their annual reports. The controversy surrounding the exercising of these powers was considered in MacPherson and does remain an indicative measure of the working practices of police officers.

To stop and search an individual there must be 'reasonable suspicion' on the part of the police officer. It is the formation of this suspicion, based around societal stereotypes and discriminatory beliefs, which causes the most concern. As Sanders and Young have stated, 'Police working rules do not impact equally upon all sections of society'.[18] It has become apparent that black people in deprived socio-economic conditions are no more likely to commit crimes than their white counterparts[19] and yet they figure disproportionately in the stop-and-search figures. The same is true for those who are unemployed and low paid.[20] Back in 1970, prior to the supposed rigours of PACE, Lord Devlin stated that:

> suspicion arises at or near the starting point of an investigation of which obtaining of prima facie proof is the end ... Prima facie proof consists of all admissible evidence. Suspicion can take into account matters that could not be put in evidence at all.[21]

This view tended to grant police officers *carte blanche* to stop who they wanted even though they had no statutory power to do so.[22] Things did not appear to improve after PACE. Sanders and Young explain that in 2003/2004 a black person was 6.4 times and an Asian person 1.9 times more likely to be subject to a stop and search by a police officer than a white person.[23] They explain that this could be due to both direct and indirect discrimination. The direct discrimination is where the stop and search is founded by police prejudice and reliance on negative stereotypes (all black

---

15   S.66 Metropolitan Police Act 1839.
16   Possession of drugs which s.23 Misuse of Drugs Act 1971 did permit stop and search on the basis of reasonable suspicion.
17   Possession of a dangerous weapon.
18   Sanders and Young (2007: 153).
19   Ibid., 155.
20   We are concentrating on the issue of race here in light of the MacPherson Report.
21   *Shaaban Bin Hussein* v. *Chong Fook Kam* [1970] AC 942 at 948–9.
22   With the exception of Londoners. We have already stated there was no statutory power to stop and search and yet police officers often did in a particularly arbitrary way. An assault claim could follow against an officer but few individuals would know this and in accordance with 'policing by consent' would submit to a search if asked.
23   Sanders and Young (2007: 81).

people are drug users and all Asians, especially Muslims, are terrorists). Indirect discrimination occurs where the exercising of police powers is based on criteria which inadvertently results in unjustified disparities. It could also be due to black people actually exhibiting behaviour which is objectively more suspicious.[24] We should not assume that the reasons are easy to locate within the police officer on the street exercising reasonable suspicion. It could be a combination of all three. The problem is that even if black people are exhibiting behaviour which is objectively more suspicious, which makes the stop and search 'legitimate', their over-representation in the figures does suggest that direct and/or indirect discrimination is also apparent and this does need to be addressed.

To understand how the exercising of stop-and-search powers is racially discriminatory we need to understand what the motivation is of those who exercise these powers. Quinton *et al*.[25] conducted an extensive survey of those who stop and search and noted that one police officer said, 'You see someone and you just know he's not right'. Decisions are often based on instinct and experience which, by its nature, can be negatively grounded in racial prejudice. This research confirmed that those who experienced stop and search often found the experience aggressive and intimidating. It also stated that 'the legal requirement of reasonable suspicion is probably not fulfilled for some searches'.[26] This research confirms the 'suspicions' long held over the use of stop and search and it seems apposite that 'the aggravation, distrust and resentment currently caused was seen to outweigh any perceived positive outcomes'.[27]

Quinton *et al*.'s research was conducted directly after the MacPherson Report was published in an attempt to offer some guidelines on good practice for the use of stop-and-search powers. It now remains to ask if things have improved. Foster *et al*.[28] conducted research which attempted to assess the impact of the MacPherson Report on the London Metropolitan Police Service. They indicate that some improvements are apparent[29] but now police are very anxious about stopping and searching for fear of being accused of being racist. This does suggest that police have become more aware of how their behaviour can be construed as being racist. It is also understandable that police officers may find themselves working in a more defensive way. We should, however, have no problem with this. Police make decisions to stop and search and these decisions should be defensible. Police officers may well be anxious about exercising those powers but it is an anxiety which should inform and assist in their decision to stop and search. It is not a decision that should be taken lightly. Foster *et al*. do offer a caveat to the many positives they identify by suggesting that 'forces – perhaps understandably – have tended to focus on those changes that were most obviously identifiable and achievable'.[30] Changes in attitude, especially in the canteen and on the streets, may prove rather more difficult to alter over such a short period of time.

24   Sanders and Young (2007: 81) describe this as 'legitimate disparities'.
25   Quinton *et al*. (2000a).
26   Quinton *et al*. (2000b).
27   Quinton *et al*. (2000b).
28   Foster *et al*. (2005).
29   Racist language in the workplace appears to have been eliminated although those black and ethnic minority officers interviewed tended to suggest this was something of a cosmetic change.
30   Ibid., viii.

On final analysis, Bowling and Phillips[31] remain sceptical. They conclude that as of 2007 black people in England and Wales were now six times more likely to be stopped and searched based on their numbers in the general population. They argue that unlawful racial discrimination continues to operate and this can be supported in two ways. First, they argue that this does have an unfavourable impact on those people of African-Caribbean origin because it continues to undermine any trust and confidence that these communities may have ever held for the police. Second, they point to evidence which continues to show damning examples of police prejudice towards ethnic minorities. One cited example is a film in 2003 which used covert recordings to show extreme racism was alive and well in a National Police Training Centre. Officers were shown demonstrating extreme racial hatred and even admiration for those who murdered Stephen Lawrence.[32] The film also showed a serving police officer boasting about his use of discretion in stopping and searching people from ethnic minority backgrounds. Their final rallying cry is for 'the police power to detain a person on the street for the purpose of a search should be restricted to situations where a constable has a genuine and reasonable belief that wrongdoing is afoot, rather than the merest of suspicions'.[33] A sound sentiment but we are left imagining how 'genuine and reasonable belief' will be construed by a serving officer who appears to be confronted with, if not thoroughly adhering to, the stereotypical views of police officers about those from ethnic minority backgrounds.

National wars

The 'war on terror' is now a common feature of crime prevention and detection in this country. Police appear to tour the streets in far greater numbers than they did prior to 9/11 and 7/7[34] and we as citizens are all encouraged to be far more vigilant as we go about our everyday lives. Such a response is understandable. But it is also responsible for instilling a growing sense of paranoia between citizens. Imagine the following: a young Asian man in his twenties gets onto a busy bus or a busy underground carriage in London with a large rucksack on his back. He is wearing traditional Muslim dress. Some people will not notice him, but others may flinch, even momentarily, and worry that the man is in fact a suicide bomber. That worry is borne out of experience for some people and media-filled fear for others. Such paranoia is understandable if not legitimate. To combat this fear we expect our government and our police force to keep us safe. The methods for ensuring that safety may appear draconian but we often think they are necessary given the current climate. The 'war on terror' is the defence for policing which would otherwise appear indefensible. The reality is that for these policing methods to be truly defensible there is no greater time for them to be defended than in times of fear for national security. As John Wadham has commented, 'Draconian

---

31 Bowling and Phillips (2007).
32 A teenager who was killed in 1993 in south-east London for simply being black. His murder prompted the MacPherson Review.
33 Bowling and Phillips (2007: 961).
34 7/7 refers to the terrorist attacks which took place in 2005 in London. Fifty-six people died and over 700 were injured. It was the largest and deadliest terrorist attack on London in history.

anti-terrorist laws ... have a far greater impact on human rights than they ever will on crime'.[35]

Since the 'war on terror' began after 9/11, the law enforcement agencies have been granted ever more extensive powers to attempt to counter terrorism. The head of the Anti-Terrorist Branch of the Metropolitan Police said 'public safety demands earlier intervention'.[36] Earlier intervention required greater stop and search powers than were already in existence. Moeckli[37] charts the increase in police powers. The Terrorism Act 2000 had already created a power for police officers to carry out blanket stop and searches. The Anti-Terrorism Crime and Security Act 2001 introduced new powers for the Treasury to freeze terrorist funds and control orders on terrorist suspects can be imposed under the Terrorism Act 2005. The Terrorism Act 2006 gives police the power to detain terrorist suspects for up to 28 days and at the time of writing the government are pushing, once again, for this to be increased to 42 days. Our interest here is once again to consider how far these powers have impacted upon individual liberty. Just as the stop-and-search powers under PACE could be seen to be disproportionately aimed at black citizens so the terrorist powers have been disproportionately applied to Asian citizens. Moeckli suggests that after 9/11 the searches of Asian persons rose by 302 per cent. Black and Asian people were more likely to be stopped under the provisions of the Terrorism Act 2000 than white people.

There is apparently an inevitability to this rise. Hazel Blears, Home Office Minister at the time, stated that it 'inevitably means that some of our counter-terrorist powers will be disproportionately experienced by people in the Muslim community'.[38] The Chief Constable of the British Transport Police was even blunter when he said 'We should not waste time searching old white ladies. It is going to be disproportionate. It is going to be young men, not exclusively, but it may be disproportionate when it comes to ethnic groups'.[39] Moeckli suggests that this strategy is tantamount to ethnic profiling and when exploring the judgments in the *Gillan*[40] case he explores how this form of profiling can be compatible with the European Convention on Human Rights, which under Article 14 prohibits discrimination. Lord Scott in *Gillan* comments that the stop-and-search powers under the Terrorism Act 2000 may 'require some degree of stereotyping in the selection of the persons to be stopped and searched and arguably therefore, some degree of discrimination' he felt this would be validated by existing legislation which permits discrimination on the grounds of race[41] if this is for the purpose of safeguarding national security. This in itself is, to Moeckli, difficult to defend. Targeting terrorists is the purpose of the Terrorism Act 2000, not persons of Asian appearance who may, just may, be involved in terrorist activity. This is difficult to defend in the context of Article 14 which can be mobilised when the Article 8 right to privacy has been infringed.

---

35   *The Guardian*, 14 November 1999.
36   House of Commons Home Affairs Committee, *Fourth Report of Session 2005–6: Terrorism Detention Powers* HC 910-I, 54.
37   Moeckli (2007).
38   Hazel Blears quoted in House of Commons Home Affairs Committee, *Sixth Report of Session 2004–5: Terrorism and Community Relations*, HC 165-I, 46.
39   Dodd (2005).
40   *R (Gillan) v. Commissioner of Police for the Metropolis* [2006] 2 AC 307.
41   See Race Relations (Amendment) Act 2000.

Moeckli[42] is also more concerned on a practical level with the use of Asian appearance as a factor which defends this discriminate form of stop and search. He points out that only half of those who are Asian are Muslim and so the criteria are too broad. Many who are stopped will not be Muslim and the overwhelming majority of those who are Muslim have nothing to do with terrorism. These broad criteria serve once again to alienate the ethnic minority communities and give police the power to interfere with people's lives. The justification is that these people are of a particular ethnic origin and the current threat means that this interference is inevitable. Inevitable for some though, not inevitable for all.

Terrorist attacks are tragic. They often involve an indiscriminate taking of civilian life and represent a breakdown in the democratic process which is there to ensure that dissatisfied citizens can voice their concerns about national and international developments which affect them either directly or indirectly. Increased powers of policing may be necessary to contain the threat of terror and to ensure national security is maintained. However, these powers should not be used at any cost. One tragic reminder of the need to defend decisions taken in times of heightened security is the death of Jean Charles de Menezes. Jean Charles, 27, was a Brazilian National who had been living in London since 2002. On 22 July 2005 he was shot dead by Metropolitan Police armed officers. The armed officers shot him eight times. Following his death it transpired that the police had been following de Menezes believing that he fitted the description of a terrorist suspect who had been foiled the previous day in the attempt to blow up a London Underground train. Mystery surrounds the identity of the armed officers who shot him. This was a tragic case of mistaken identity.[43] Alarming too was the response of the police to the incident. Initially it was claimed that de Menezes had been wearing bulky clothes in the height of summer; he had jumped over the ticket barrier, which added to the officers' suspicions; and had not responded when challenged before he was shot. The Independent Police Complaints Commission later confirmed that none of this was true. It would appear that these details were fabricated by eye-witnesses and the police in an attempt to provide some 'justification' for the incident. Public reaction appeared mixed.[44] Some appeared to recognise that the police had made a split-second decision and it was tragic. It appeared to some that it was collateral damage in the 'war on terror'. Three weeks earlier, 52 people had died, excluding 4 suicide bombers, in the 7/7 attacks and it was understandable that the police should be vigilant and tragedies happen. Others were far more critical, believing this to be a further example of police brutality. What does appear evident is that the exercising of police powers needs to be based on more accurate intelligence if such incidents are to be avoided. De Menezes was Brazilian and mistaken for a naturalised British citizen who was originally from Ethiopia. One man was South American, the other of African descent. Ethnic profiling in this instance had tragic consequences. As Moeckli speculates, 'One wonders whether the shooting of Jean Charles de Menezes ... was

---

42   Moeckli (2007: 667).
43   Although it is not suggested that it would have been fine for Hussain Osman, the suspected terrorist who the officers mistook de Menezes to be, to have been shot dead, unless he demonstrated an immediate threat to public safety.
44   BBC News, 'Is police anti-terror policy justified?', 26 July 2005.

not a tragic consequence of the over reliance on stereotypical characteristics such as ethnic appearance in antiterrorism operations'.[45] The lesson is clear. When police powers are increased for the protection of citizens from terrorist attack they need to be employed even more carefully to ensure that citizens do not become as vulnerable to the police as they do to the terrorist attack. Lucia Zedner explains it best when she concluded:

> The London bombings were a stark reminder both of the threat posed by terrorist acts to fundamental rights and the importance of security measures in protecting them. Yet, when the pursuit of security is permitted to proceed at such a speed and with such sway as to trample basic liberties, it runs counter to the very purpose of securing liberty. One of the ironies of pursuing security is that whilst claiming to protect liberty from one source – terrorism, it diminishes the protection of liberty from another – the state.[46]

COURTROOM: SCIENCE AS TRUTH, EXPERTS AS TRUTH TELLERS

One area within the criminal justice system which has increased dramatically is the reliance on science in the courtroom. While the English legal system has a long history of consulting expert advice on scientific matters, the growing developments in forensic science have meant that reliance on science is greater than ever before. This should be welcomed. As Roberts confirms:

> The increasing use of science in the modern criminal process should be welcomed as an overwhelmingly positive development. Forensic science is good for justice in the same way that all modern science improves on the knowledge and technology of the past. Aeroplanes are more effective conveyances than hot-air balloons, key hole surgery is preferable to treatment with leeches, and rape is easier to prove with DNA evidence than without it.[47]

It is the growth of reliance on DNA evidence which is to be particularly welcomed. Historically the criminal trial used witness testimony and statements by the accused along with documents and real evidence to attempt to establish truth. Alongside lawyer submissions and judicial directions this was thought to make for a court system which, although adversarial, did ensure that the truth was established. The celebrated miscarriages of justice cases[48] from the 1970s have all demonstrated the limitations of these methods. DNA is more foolproof, but DNA evidence is not to be relied on without caution. Uglow[49] considers an example where a sample taken from a scene of a burglary led to a suspect who lived 200 miles away, suffered from Parkinson's disease,

---

45 Moeckli (2007: 667).
46 Zedner (2005).
47 Roberts (2002).
48 See the Guildford Four, Birmingham Six and Maguire Seven.
49 Uglow (2002: 168).

who could not drive and could barely dress himself. His blood sample had been taken during a previous arrest and the police refused to accept his alibi when he protested his innocence. A retest established that there had been a mistake but it demonstrated that once DNA evidence is found, its mythical qualities of absolute truth tends to dissuade even the most compelling counter-evidence. These mistakes are likely to be increased where the growth of the DNA database continues. This database was set up in 1995 and by 2006 it had over four million different people's DNA stored on it. The database records the DNA of all those who are arrested. Given that this is when they are arrested rather than charged, the use of DNA in this way is controversial, not least because of its potential invasion of privacy and given the concerns about over-reliance on it as a type of evidence. It is more foolproof than witness testimony but reliance on it should not be at the expense of all other evidence which can, on balance, be compelling.

The increased use of scientific evidence is generally supported. Back in 1993, following the unmasking of the infamous miscarriages of justice cases it became apparent that techniques of interrogation by the police were flawed and Mike McConville proclaimed that we should have 'more detection, less interrogation'.[50] Given our discussion of the potential and actual abuse of police powers earlier in this chapter this may be a desirable development. However, it should not be utilised without caution. Scientific evidence has to be presented in the courtroom within the context of the adversarial system and Walker has commented that 'the evidential value of expert testimony has been overestimated in a number of instances only for it later to emerge that the tests being used were inherently unreliable, that the scientists conducting them were inefficient or both'.[51] In the case of the Maguire Seven the prosecution case was heavily based around the fact that the defendants had knowingly handled nitroglycerine for an unlawful purpose. The charge required a positive trace on the body or clothing of the defendants and innocent contamination had to be discounted. The scientific evidence presented at trial was used to construct a narrative of bomb preparation. In fact, Stockdale asserts that later tests showed the 'brittle nature of legal extrapolation from scientific fact'[52] and there were a number of explanations as to how these traces of nitroglycerine could have found their way onto the defendants' bodies. By the time a successful appeal was granted all but one of the defendants had served their prison sentences. One of the defendants, Giuseppe Conlan, father of Gerard Conlan who was one of the Guildford Four, died in prison in 1980. He would never know that his name had been cleared. The Maguire Seven case reminds us that it is not just the accumulation of scientific evidence that is important but also its presentation in the courtroom. To demand more scientific evidence as though it is a panacea to all the problems associated with other forms of evidence is to look 'for a chimera – forms of evidence which can be presented in court unsullied by fallible human processes'.[53]

As well as the type of evidence presented and the over-reliance on evidence which happens to be scientific, the reliance on and deification of the 'expert' has also led to calls

---

50 McConville (1993).
51 Walker (1999: 53–4).
52 Stockdale (1999: 133).
53 Ibid., 150.

for increasing caution surrounding the use of expert testimony. Concerns surrounding the jury attempting to understand scientific evidence are not new. Stephen[54] back in 1860 said:

> Few spectacles, it might be said, can be more absurd and incongruous than that of a jury composed of twelve persons who, without any previous scientific knowledge or training are suddenly called upon to adjudicate in controversies in which the most eminent scientific men flatly contradict each other's assertions.

What has become clear in the last decade is that there has been greater reliance on expert evidence usually because of increased sophistication in the collection of scientific data. This in turn has led to a more extensive use of the expert who often presents their findings as the truth, unable to recognise alternative explanations. The three cases here concern the phenomenon of sudden infant death syndrome (SIDS). This is where death occurs and following an autopsy the apparent cause is still unknown. This immediately presents us with a problem. We do not know why the child has died so we speculate. And although we refute 'suspicious circumstances' we need to find out why. We turn to an expert to assist and through this informed, specialist, all-knowing expert, we believe what we are told. Why would we doubt the expert?

Our story begins with the case of Sally Clark. She was convicted of murdering two of her babies in November 1999. The murders took place within 14 months of each other. At her trial the expert paediatrician, Professor Sir Roy Meadow, said that the chance of two babies dying as a result of SIDS[55] was 1 in 73 million. He had famously stated that 'one sudden infant death in a family is a tragedy, two is suspicious and three is murder unless proven otherwise'. This became known as Meadow's law.[56] During her appeal against conviction in 2001 the Court of Appeal recognised that Meadow had reached his calculation incorrectly but the appeal was still disallowed. Soon after Clark's failed appeal, Angela Cannings[57] was convicted of a double murder when she had lost three babies to SIDS although she was only convicted of murdering two of her three children. This time, the Meadow's statistic appeared to hover over the trial like the ghost at the feast. Given the media coverage, it was unlikely the jury had not learned of Meadow's erroneous calculation.[58] At this trial, he refuted the suggestion that the prevalence of death to Angela Cannings' children could be attributed to a medical condition, when he said:

> Well, is it possible it is a condition that is not yet understood by doctors or described by them? And that must always be a possibility, but nevertheless as a doctor of children I am saying these features are those of smothering.[59]

---

54 Stephen (1860).
55 Colloquially known as a 'cot death'.
56 See Taylor (2003).
57 For a lively discussion of the case see Ward (2004).
58 See Nobles and Schiff (2004) for a discussion of the Sally Clark case and the media's presentation of that case.
59 As quoted in *R. v. Cannings* [2004] 1 All ER 725.

The Court of Appeal noted in Cannings' appeal that:

> Experts in many fields will acknowledge the possibility that later research may undermine the accepted wisdom of today. 'Never say never' is a phrase which we have heard in many different contexts from expert witnesses.[60]

It would seem however that this was a concession that Meadow was reluctant to acknowledge.

Soon after this case the second appeal of Sally Clark was heard and this time it was decided that Meadow's statistics were manifestly wrong and grossly misleading. Clark was freed having spent over three years in prison. Just before the successful appeal of Angela Cannings in 2003 another woman, Trupti Patel, was charged with killing three of her babies. This time there was no conviction as Patel's grandmother appeared as a witness and explained that five of her twelve children had died within six weeks of birth. There was a genetic defect that could account for the deaths. As could be commonly concluded, multiple deaths made a genetic link just as likely as a case of serial murder.

As an expert Professor Sir Roy Meadow had been raised up by the trial system. Deified as an expert who had explained how the death of Sally Clark's children could not have been anything but murder. However, following these cases he was investigated and in December 2005 he was found guilty of serious professional misconduct by the General Medical Council (GMC). Meadow appealed to the High Court in 2006 and was successful. The GMC then appealed to the Court of Appeal who upheld Meadow's appeal. He had been cleared of serious professional misconduct but would never act as an expert again. It would appear that Meadow had been too focused on confirming his own suspicions without considering the alternative explanations for the SIDS. This was understandable in that he had long launched a crusade against those who wilfully injured their children. He was an early campaigner in the medical recognition of Munchausen syndrome by proxy and it seems he became so focused on the prosecution and conviction of those he thought were guilty that he forgot that he was an expert opinion, not the only expert opinion. He had also miscalculated his statistics and this meant there could be an alternative explanation. He was likened to a Witchfinder General by Jenkins[61] who suggested that during Meadow's court appearances:

> The courts of justice are the same as tried the Salem witches. They summon juries to pass public judgment on these wretched women, calling in aid a witch-finder general, the hawkish Professor Sir Roy Meadow … Sir Roy is said to possess the courtroom presence of Judge Danforth in Arthur Miller's Salem witches play, *The Crucible*. He can whip any jury into finding these women guilty.

The criminal justice system had asked a medical expert to offer an explanation as to how the deaths of these children had occurred. Professor Sir Roy Meadow offered such an explanation but it was negligently formed by someone who had forgotten to

---

60 See *R. v. Cannings* [2004] 1 All ER 725.
61 Jenkins (2003).

recognise the limits of his own opinion. He had offered a view but it appeared he delivered a verdict. Delivering a verdict in the adversarial trial is the task of the jury, not the expert, and Meadow ultimately paid the price for his folly. There is a tragic end to our story though. In March 2007 Sally Clark was found dead at her home, four years following her release from prison. Her death reminds us of the very real costs often borne by victims of miscarriages of justice and her case serves as a reminder of why 'expert' testimony too has its flaws.[62]

SENTENCING: ART OR SCIENCE?

Once an offender has been convicted they will be sentenced. There has long been a power struggle between the judiciary and the executive over who controls sentencing. Believing it to be an art, the judiciary have argued that sentencing, to be just, has to be very carefully navigated to consider not only the offence committed but the offender themselves. As one judge explained:

> At the end of the day, the exercise of discretion in sentencing must remain in human hands. You cannot programme a computer to register the 'feel' of a case, or the impact that a defendant makes upon the sentencer.[63]

The executive, on the other hand, have argued for there to be far more consistency in application and this has meant the pursuit of statutory penalties for offences which limit the extent of judicial discretion. This has really been a battle for control over punishment because increasingly successive governments adopt an agenda of taking crime seriously and part of this agenda is the attempt to exert pressure on the judiciary to mete out harsher punishments. This is not to suggest that the judiciary have never administered harsh punishments but they have generally demonstrated a reluctance to lose their own discretion in favour of satisfying the executive's political aspirations of the day. This battle has seen a number of key twists and turns which we shall now explore.

Thomas[64] explains that in early English criminal law sentencing was a straightforward matter. If a person committed a felony[65] then they would receive the death penalty. If a person committed a misdemeanour[66] they would be subject to an unlimited fine or an unlimited prison sentence. The law was harsh and unforgiving. Over a period of time the judiciary developed procedures which mitigated the harshness of the law. One such procedure was known as the 'benefit of clergy'. If a defendant was convicted of a felony they were sentenced to death. One way of avoiding this was if the defendant was a priest. Being a priest meant the defendant could be dealt with by the ecclesiastical court. There existed no formal records as to who was or was not a priest and so the

---

62   See Taylor and Wood (1999: 247).
63   Cooke (1987: 58).
64   Thomas (2002: 473).
65   This would now be an indictable offence.
66   This would now be a summary offence.

only measure was the defendant's literacy. A defendant would be asked in court to read extracts from the Bible to demonstrate their membership of the clergy. Although most defendants could not read many would learn extracts from the Bible verbatim and recite them when prompted in the courtroom. This would result in the felon's release. This early circumvention of the common law demonstrated a common dilemma for judges and one they still face today. What right do they have to circumvent the existing law? Their answer: it is in the interests of justice to do so.

The 'benefit of clergy' dwindled in importance during the eighteenth century and it was then that the power for judges in sentencing was at its apogee. They could transport the offender if friends of the offender could secure a royal pardon. The pivotal point for the judge was where they either decided to sentence the offender to death or they granted a temporary reprieve for the offender to seek the royal pardon. The operation of this discretion was totally arbitrary and did according to Thomas result in 'a lottery of justice'.[67] While the exercising of power in an arbitrary way is always frowned upon, the key principle of establishing judicial discretion in the sentencing process is a key feature in the argument by the judiciary that sentencing is an art not a science.

By the nineteenth century sentencing was still very much in the hands of the judiciary but statutes were passed, prompted by the executive, to further restrict judicial discretion. Fixed penalties were enforced so that it was clear that if you were guilty of murder then the death penalty followed. Given that the death penalty[68] had been reduced in scope so that it only remained for the most serious of offences this meant there could be no further justification for the judiciary to depart from the existing legislative provisions. By the end of the nineteenth century consistency in sentencing was again seen as elusive and so by 1907 the Court of Criminal Appeal was established. This court was charged with ensuring that there was parity in sentencing. If a defendant believed their sentence was excessive then they could appeal to this appellate court that would have a sense of how similar cases were being dealt with across the country. It was also hoped that the spectre of appeal would encourage the judiciary to be more consistent in their decisions on sentencing. Just as the executive had attempted to curb excessive disparity in the awarding of sentences by the creation of the Court of Criminal Appeal, so the executive had also widened sentencing powers to include probation, which after 1907 was an alternative to custody.

By the time the Court of Criminal Appeal was renamed the Court of Appeal (Criminal Division) in 1964 it had become clear that the plea for consistency had not been overly successful. Few defendants appealed against sentencing and there was a lack of systematic reporting and analysis of sentencing decisions. This was altered after 1964 thanks to the work of Lord Chief Justice Parker and the arrival of the Judicial Studies Board[69] but by 1991 there was still a feeling that the executive wanted to use sentencing as a tool by which they could demonstrate their commitment to tougher sentencing. In fact their statutory enshrinement of 'just deserts' in the Criminal Justice Act 1991 demonstrated a commitment to proportionality which the judiciary

---

67   Ibid.
68   Ibid., 474.
69   A training forum for judges to keep abreast of new developments.

had arguably always worked towards anyway. Ordinal and cardinal proportionality[70] had always been used to ensure that similar cases received similar sentences taking into account any mitigation or aggravating factors. The 1991 Act also introduced the custody threshold under s.2(2)(a) where it was made clear to the judiciary when they should be sentencing a defendant to custody. This was largely ignored by the judiciary. Believing the custody threshold was a matter for 'recognising elephants' they did not believe a statutory provision could explain when custody should be used. The judges, with their experience, felt they knew when custody was appropriate. By the late 1990s the Court of Appeal had come to all but ignore the 1991 Act.

By 1996 there was a real concern that the executive had prompted the legislature to legislate far beyond what was reasonable and the judges felt their 'art' of sentencing was being reduced to a science as the executive began to legislate for mandatory sentencing.[71] Mandatory sentencing clips the judicial wings in that it prescribes what sentences must be awarded for what offences. The Crime (Sentences) Act 1997 saw offenders who were convicted for a second time of a violent or sex offence receiving an automatic life sentence. Similarly, an offender convicted of domestic burglary with two previous convictions for similar offences would receive a mandatory sentence of three years. This was popularly known as the 'three strikes and you are out' rule. These reforms had taken place during a period of penal populism where the Conservative administration, desperate to show they were responding to perceived increases in crime, had decided that sentences needed to be harsher. Lord Chief Justice Taylor was publicly very critical of these reforms feeling they were ill-considered and symptomatic of an executive interference which should be ceased immediately. Lord Donaldson was equally concerned that interference with the judicial power to sentence posed a threat to the individual citizen who was excessively punished because politicians had decided that an example needed to be set. Finally Lord Hailsham, a former Lord Chancellor, had argued that the legislation imposed upon the independence of the judiciary.[72] There was, however, a critical loophole in the 1997 legislation. The provisions for the second life sentence stated that the automatic life sentence should be imposed 'unless there were genuinely exceptional circumstances' which the court would have to justify. In 2000 the Court of Appeal effectively quashed this rule by arguing that as long as the defendant posed no substantial risk to the public the life sentence did not need to be passed. Again consistency and 'honesty in sentencing'[73] had been used to defend the passing of the Crime (Sentences) Act 1997 but the judiciary had seen an out with the 'exceptional circumstances' section and seized upon it to limit the impact of the legislation.

Further attempts have been made to promote consistency in sentencing. The Labour government has been as keen as the Conservative government had been to add to the

---

70   Ordinal proportionality is where offences are considered among themselves so a rape is considered against another rape. Cardinal proportionality is where different offences are considered against each other so, for example, a burglary is compared with a rape.
71   A very public battle emerged between the then Lord Chief Justice, Lord Taylor, and the Home Secretary, Michael Howard. See Ashworth (2005) for more details.
72   This controversy is discussed further by Joyce (2006: 254).
73   The mantra used by Michael Howard during the passing of the Crime (Sentences) Act 1997 to defend mandatory sentences.

list of mandatory punishments for offences committed.[74] They have, however, adopted a more conciliatory approach by establishing the Sentencing Advisory Panel in 1998 whose task it has been to stimulate sentencing guidelines. Given that the membership includes senior judges it would appear a sense of cooperation is being fostered between all those involved and influencing the sentencing function. The Criminal Justice Act 2003 also established the Sentencing Guidelines Council whose job it is to provide sentencers with comprehensive and practical guidance. Again membership is mixed but this time it is chaired by the Lord Chief Justice. It seems that in this long battle to keep sentencing an art rather than reducing it to a science a fine balance has been reached. The executive will now continue to allow the judiciary, with all their experience, to carry out the sentencing function as though it were an art but will insist on some consistency which in turn will ensure it is marginally scientific in its approach. This balance is however subject to change. An executive seeking to gain greater political support may decide to increase the powers and remit of the Sentencing Guidelines Council while introducing further mandatory sentences for offences which they decide need to be dealt with in a more punitive way. It is a clever judiciary that continues to find ways of retaining their power base just as they had done when they introduced the benefit of clergy some centuries before.[75]

As a coda to this discussion of the judiciary and sentencing it is interesting to note a recent development which recognises why judges and not the executive should control sentencing. The example here is the historic power of the Home Secretary to fix and review the tariff of a prisoner serving a life sentence. The Court of Appeal has long issued guideline judgments which set out the proper approach to be adopted by a judge in dealing with offences within a particular category. They are not meant to be prescriptive but they usually indicate a tariff or range in which judges, according to the severity of the offence, will impose a sentence. Things have always been slightly different for those convicted of murder. This offence carries a mandatory sentence of life imprisonment. Since 1948 the Home Secretary has had the power to decide when a life prisoner can be released from prison. Under s.29 Crime (Sentences) Act 1997 the Home Secretary was able to decide on the date of release for the lifer on licence and they were also able to set the tariff which saw them decide how long a lifer should remain in prison. As this power was a judicial one the separation of powers had once again long been compromised.

By 2004 this position had become untenable. A series of cases before the courts, since the Human Rights Act 1998 had come into force, had been critical of the Home Secretary's power and the decision in the *Anderson* case,[76] and finally withdrew the power. A panel of seven Law Lords decided that the court rather than the Home Secretary should decide on the tariff for a lifer convicted of murder.

---

74 See Crime and Disorder Act 1998 and Youth Justice and Criminal Evidence Act 1999.
75 Of course it could be argued that the judiciary have no right to circumvent the will of the people via their elected representatives. Andrew Ashworth argues that more consistency in sentencing is required and the judiciary should be required to be consistent. The author agrees but clearly legislative sledgehammers should not be used to trounce judicial discretion. Better judicial discretion is maintained and navigated through a path towards some relative consistency. The judiciary need to believe they are controlling sentencing as they believe this is their function within the constitution.
76 *R. v. Secretary of State for the Home Department ex p Anderson* [2002] UKHL 46.

The Home Secretary's sentencing role was seen to be in direct conflict with the Article 6 right to a fair trial as per the European Convention on Human Rights. The right to a fair trial demands an independent and impartial tribunal. The Home Secretary was not independent or impartial. The reaction by the executive was one of anger and the then Home Secretary, David Blunkett, insisted he would circumvent the rule with legislation. The result was s.269 Criminal Justice Act 2003 which requires the court to have regard to certain principles when setting a tariff for a convicted murderer. Once again however there is a loophole in the legislation in the form of the term 'normally' which allows the court to consider all factors and continue to be creative in their exercising of their function.

This change in the law cannot be underestimated. First, the reiteration by the judiciary of the constitutional role of the judge in sentencing is important at a time when questions are being asked as to the legitimacy of that role. Lord Steyn views the separation of power to be critical here and has argued that:

> [N]owhere outside Britain, even in democracies with the weakest forms of separation of powers, is the independence of the judiciary potentially compromised in the eyes of citizens by relegating the status of the highest court to the position of subordinate part of the legislature. And nowhere outside Britain is the independence of the judiciary potentially compromised in the eyes of the citizen by permitting a serving politician to sit as a judge at any level.[77]

In addition, a very famous case in English legal history demonstrates the potential injustice that can befall a defendant under that power which was once held by the Home Secretary. Myra Hindley was convicted of killing four children with her partner Ian Brady in 1966. At trial the judge imposed a life sentence, as was mandatory, along with a tariff of 25 years. This meant she was due for parole in 1990. By 1985 the then Home Secretary, Leon Brittan, decided under his political power to extend the tariff so that she would in fact serve 30 years before being eligible for parole. By 1990, following revelations of further involvement in other murders, the then Home Secretary, David Waddington, imposed a whole life tariff on Hindley insisting she would never leave prison. Hindley was not notified of this decision until 1994 when the prison service were told they were obliged to inform all prisoners of when they could expect to be considered for parole. Between 1997 and 2000 Hindley appealed against the whole life tariff a total of three times, each time arguing that she was a reformed prisoner who no longer posed a risk to the public. All three appeals were rejected. Hindley died in prison in November 2002. Two weeks later the House of Lords confirmed in the *Anderson*[78] decision that the Home Secretary should no longer decide on the tariff for convicted murderers. Hindley's crimes were clearly abhorrent but the decisions by successive Home Secretaries to alter her tariff and prevent her consideration for release were political and not based on sound legal principle. It is not clear whether Hindley would have ever been released from prison even if the power to set tariffs had been with

---

77   Lord Steyn (2002: 382, 383).
78   *R. v. Secretary of State for the Home Department ex p Anderson* [2002] UKHL 46.

a judge rather than a politician. Although not a sympathetic figure, Hindley did prove, ironically, to be a victim of the partiality of the criminal justice process in this regard.

OVERCROWDED PRISONS: A CRISIS OF NUMBERS AND CONDITIONS

Convicted offenders sometimes receive custodial sentences. They are then sent to prison to serve those sentences. According to Cavadino and Dignan[79] there exists a penal crisis. This crisis is concerned with a number of issues which impact upon the legitimacy of the process and more importantly the lives of prisoners. There currently exists a managerial crisis, a crisis of security, a crisis of control and authority, a crisis of accountability and a crisis of legitimacy. The impact of these crises should not be underestimated but it is the crisis of numbers which impacts upon prison conditions which is most worrying at this time. At the time of writing there are 82,655 prisoners in custody.[80] The last decade has consistently seen records broken as to the number of prisoners in custody and if an expansionist policy was the current government's aim then the numbers would point to success. This unprecedented increase does however have its casualties. Cavadino and Dignan explain that as many of the current prison cells were designed for single occupancy, at least 22 per cent of the prison population are being held in overcrowded conditions.[81]

Overcrowded prisons feed the crisis of conditions. This crisis is three-fold[82] in that it involves the physical accommodation that prisoners have to live in, the repressive regimes they are often subject to[83] and the breakdown with family ties that often occurs as a result of local prisons being full and inmates being transported around the country to places difficult for visitors to travel to. This final consequence is said to feed offender bitterness and hostility while in prison which then contributes to their recidivism upon release.[84] We will contain our discussion to the physical accommodation and its related conditions as this has the most direct impact upon the prisoner's life and reminds us of a political battle that was once won by the executive but which proved the judiciary to see into the future and the developments that would occur. The Howard League for Penal Reform has commented on how two or more prisoners are often housed in cells designed for one and they are using unscreened toilets which 'fail to provide them with the most basic of human rights'.[85] These 'inhuman and degrading conditions'[86] are not

---

79 Cavadino and Dignan (2007).
80 Her Majesty's Prison Service population figures as of 30 May 2008. Can be accessed at http://www.hmprisonservice.gov.uk/assets/documents/10003A8330052008_web_report.doc.
81 Cavadino and Dignan (2007: 214). This figure is likely to be much higher four years on.
82 This classification is confirmed by Cavadino and Dignan (2007: 215).
83 For example it was reported in 2006 that the Lord Chief Justice announced that overcrowding was proving 'fatal' for prisoner treatment. In fact he said that drug addicts were often committing offences in order to access treatment in prison. See http://www.politics.co.uk/issue-of-the-day/public-services/prisons/prison-overcrowding/prison-overcrowding-$441353$441353.htm.
84 Cavadino and Dignan (2007: 215).
85 Howard League for Penal Reform, Campaign to End Prison Overcrowding, 2006, accessed at http://www.howardleague.org/index.php?id=overcrowding.
86 As confirmed by the European Committee for the Prevention of Torture (1991).

new but the current prison crisis of numbers and overcrowding is likely to exacerbate rather than reduce these squalid conditions. The practice of prisoners 'slopping out' their overnight waste did come to an end in 2006 but this was some 15 years after the Woolf Report cried out for a cap on prison numbers and a review of prison conditions.

The Woolf Report was in response to the Strangeways and other prison riots in 1990. The enquiry that followed was chaired by the then Lord Justice Woolf. His terms of reference were to 'inquire into the events which began on April 1st 1990 and the action taken to bring it to a conclusion, having regard also to the serious disturbances which occurred shortly thereafter in other prison establishments'.[87] Interestingly sentencing practice was not included in these terms of reference for fear that Woolf would comment on the expansionist policy that the government of the day was beginning to adopt following a dip during the 1980s. The key point to Woolf's approach was, he believed, that there was no single cause to a riot. This meant that there was no simple solution or action which will prevent this from happening again. There were a total of 12 recommendations. Most significant for the discussion here was that, in light of prison conditions and the executive thirst for recourse to the prison, a new prison rule should be implemented which would prevent an establishment holding more prisoners than is provided for in its normal certified level of accommodation. This recommendation was never adopted in the package of reforms which followed the publication of the report. Woolf also wanted the executive power of release to be used if prisons became overcrowded.[88]

By 2007 Cavadino and Dignan comment that Woolf's call for a new prison rule to limit overcrowding appears 'fanciful'.[89] And yet a member of the judiciary had asked for an executive power, to continue to fill up prisons beyond their natural capacity, to be curtailed. Lord Woolf had been wrong about one thing though. He had declared that prison overcrowding was a thing of the past and yet prisons are now overcrowded beyond anything he could have imagined. Answers to the current problem could be 'increasing prison capacities or crisis driven changes in sentencing'.[90] The problem with these solutions is they tend to be short term and isolated. Losel offers a more profound course of change when he suggests that a reduction in the prison overcrowding crisis may come if we improve offender rehabilitation which will reduce recidivism. He also advocates a reduction in short-term incarceration and a greater commitment by government to developmental prevention and early intervention.[91]

Back in 1987 Vivien Stern described our prisons as 'bricks of shame'.[92] Woolf commented in 1991 that justice itself is compromised if prisoners are held in overcrowded conditions that are 'inhumane and degrading, or are otherwise wholly inappropriate'.[93] Seventeen years on and the prison numbers have escalated beyond

---

87   Woolf and Tumim (1991).
88   Ibid., para 1.189.
89   This classification is confirmed by Cavadino and Dignan (2007: 215).
90   Losel (2007: 513).
91   Losel (2007: 514–17).
92   Book title.
93   Woolf and Tumim (1991: para 10.19).

what could have ever been imagined. Crowded cells see prisoners sitting on toilets as a means of sitting down whilst eating their meals.[94] This time has seen improvements in prison conditions but there are still improvements to be made and these tend to be compromised when overcrowding is at such a peak. The prison service, in collusion with the government, suggests they have a useable operational capacity of 83,487. This would suggest at the time of writing that there are still 832 places going spare! Cavadino and Dignan are however suspicious of the method of calculating these figures suggesting they 'mask the true extent of the problem'.[95] The Prison Reform Trust has suggested[96] that one very serious effect of this prison overcrowding is that the incidence of self-harm increases. This cannot be defensible. The experience of prison for the prisoner is directly affected by this commitment to an expansionist policy which at the present time cannot keep up with its own enlargement.

CONCLUSION: DREAMS AND NIGHTMARES

Sanders and Young believe that the time has come to 'set the primary goal of the criminal justice system as the promotion of freedom of all citizens and social groups alike' (Sanders and Young, 2007, p. 673). This dream is a noble one. To promote freedom within a process that often prizes crime control over due process and routinely discriminates against vulnerable groups within society may be desirable but is it realistically attainable? At the beginning Packer said we should try. We should try to attain the unattainable for if we stop trying we will fall even further short of finding guaranty and eliminating threat. This chapter has considered some of the winners and the losers in our current criminal justice processes. The winners appear to be the state and its vast machinery charged with delivering justice in a way that satisfies many. It should satisfy all, but on final analysis it is a process that is left wanting. The losers are those who have suffered nightmares at the hands of a process which in both its structures and its practices has left critics believing that it is a process in need of repair. We only need the process to be fair when we encounter it. On this evidence the many will hope they don't encounter for fear of being treated like the few.

---

94 See http://www.prisonreformtrust.org.uk/subsection.asp?id=333.
95 Cavadino and Dignan (2007: 213).
96 See http://www.prisonreformtrust.org.uk/subsection.asp?id=333.

15

THE PRINCIPLES OF CRIMINAL PROCEDURE

INTRODUCTION

Building on our analysis of civil procedure in the previous chapter, we will now turn to consider criminal procedure. Although there is something of an overlap between the two areas, no single model can cover both areas of procedure. This is due to the different functions that civil and criminal procedures serve. The distinctive nature of the latter is due to the fact that it is the state and its agencies that both police and prosecute crime. The values of criminal process return us to this fundamental issue. At a general level, we could say that criminal procedure shows a tension between the values of due process and crime control. While this model of criminal justice has a relevance to our consideration of arrest, for example, we will see that the notion of crime control is simply too remote from criminal procedure to be a generally useful term. This suggests that we are far more concerned with arguments about the form of due process itself, and the tensions that characterise the forensic process. To what extent can the court articulate a balance between values and principles that operate in favour of defendants, and those that suit the prosecution? We will refer to these as defence- and prosecution-orientated values. How can we develop our analysis of these issues?

Although there is a rhetorical commitment to due process values, commentators have often pointed out that English criminal process operates in favour of the prosecution. While this is perhaps generally true, we will see that there is an ongoing commitment to defence-orientated values in the common law and, in recent years, an interesting relationship between the common law and European human rights has developed. Human rights law carries within it the same tensions that we have described above. However, human rights cases do suggest new ways of thinking about the clash of values in the criminal procedural law, and the broader operation of the courts in a democratic society committed to the rule of law.

As it would be impossible in a book of this length to cover criminal procedure in its entirety, we will focus on a number of issues that are illustrative of broader tensions. Our first concern will be with arrest, as this is the point at which an individual enters the criminal process. Some of the most important issues relate to the policing of terrorism, and the extent to which both the criminal law and criminal process respond to this threat to the democratic state. We will then consider issues that are cross-cutting. This will take us to a consideration of the presumption of innocence and the privilege against self-incrimination. We will deal with the consequences of the refusal to answer police questions at the pre-trial stage, before turning to silence during the trial and the human rights context. The final section of the chapter will deal with the jury and the issue of bias, as this shows the tensions and correspondences that exist between a common law institution and the principles of human rights law.

POWERS OF ARREST AND HUMAN RIGHTS

The common law has always understood that arrest serves a valid function in the apprehension of criminals or those suspected of being criminals. However, it is a power that can be easily abused. The common law has therefore attempted to safeguard individual liberty, or 'the sense of freedom from arbitrary detention'. Indeed, the protection of 'personal freedom' is fundamental to the libertarian conscience of the common law that Lord Bingham described as 'dating back to chapter 39 of Magna Carta 1215'.[1] Liberty is given specific form in the writ of habeas corpus, the right to damages for false imprisonment and the narrow interpretation of any exceptions to the 'most basic guarantee of individual freedom'.[2] While it is true to say that the common law provides remedies for unlawful arrest, we need to look critically at the constitution of arrest in both common law, and the Police and Criminal Evidence Act (PACE) 1984. The critical issue is: does the common law achieve a balance between crime control and due process? We will examine this question by considering the 'threshold' for a valid arrest. This is a fundamental concern, as the test itself must ensure that powers of arrest are not easy to abuse, while acknowledging the practical issues that face a police officer making an arrest.

As Lord Devlin pointed out in *Shaaban bin Hussien* v. *Chong Fook Kam*,[3] the threshold condition or the 'test of reasonable suspicion ... has existed in the common law for many years'. In *Dumbell* v. *Roberts*,[4] Scott J explained that reasonable grounds for 'suspicion of guilt' are a 'safeguard' designed for the 'protection of the public'. However, as he also pointed out, the 'requirement is very limited' and falls far short of the evidence required for conviction. Moreover, suspicion can be based on matters that are not 'admissible evidence'.[5] The problem is precisely this 'malleability'[6] of the standard required for arrest. One would have thought that if the common law were so committed to the protection of civil liberties, it would have required a far more exacting threshold. In order to investigate these issues, we need to look in more detail at the contemporary law defining arrest.

Powers of arrest without warrant are now primarily defined by statute. However, as has been pointed out, PACE preserves[7] the 'ancient' power of the citizen's arrest, and this informs the way in which arrest powers are described by the Act.[8] The most

---

1   *A.* v. *Home Secretary* [2004] UKHL 56; [2005] HRLR 1.
2   *Austin* v. *Metropolitan Police Commissioner* [2005] HRLR 20, para 37.
3   *Shaaban bin Hussien* v. *Chong Fook Kam* [1970] AC 942, at 948.
4   *Dumbell* v. *Roberts* [1944] 1 All ER 326, at 329.
5   Supra n. 3, at 949.
6   Feldman (2002: 332).
7   PACE at 24(4) and (5).
8   Robertson (1993: 10).

important section is 24(4). An individual can make an arrest if there are reasonable grounds for suspecting that an arrestable offence is in the process of being committed or when an arrestable offence has been committed. The powers of arrest given to police officers are more extensive. A police officer can arrest on reasonable grounds of suspicion that an arrestable offence has been committed. In other words, an officer is effectively protected from a civil action if he makes an arrest and an offence has not been committed.[9] A constable also has a preventative power of arrest[10] that is not available to a private citizen.[11]

PACE preserves the fundamental common law safeguard on arrest: the threshold of reasonable suspicion. But how do the courts understand this key term? The requirement of 'reasonable suspicion' is based on the information available to the arresting officer at the time that s/he makes the arrest.[12] The court has determined that this issue must be assessed at the time of arrest and not from the perspective of hindsight.[13] It is also necessary to acknowledge that an arrest may be based on a 'spur of the moment' decision.[14] So, critical questions relate to what the officer knew or had in mind when he or she made the arrest. But how are we to understand the concept of reasonable suspicion? One of the central authorities is *Castorina* v. *Chief Constable of Surrey*.[15] The trial judge defined 'reasonable cause'[16] as an 'honest belief founded upon reasonable suspicion leading an ordinary cautious man to the conclusion that the person arrested was guilty of the offence'. This argument was based on the authority of *Dumbell* v. *Roberts* that applied to arrests the principle that 'everyone is innocent until proven guilty'. The Court of Appeal disagreed, asserting that the proposed test was too severe and should be objective. The trial judge's reference to 'honest belief' was misleading, as it raised questions of subjective belief.

Thus, it would appear that reasonable cause does not mean that an ordinary cautious man would conclude that the person was guilty of the offence; it would be enough to suspect that he was guilty. *Castorina* was further elaborated in *Holgate-Mohammed* v. *Duke*.[17] The House of Lords determined that 'where a police officer reasonably suspects an individual of having committed an arrestable offence, he may arrest that person with a view to questioning her at the police station'.[18] This decision can only be judicially reviewed if the constable acted improperly by taking something irrelevant into account.

Commentators have pointed out that this case law errs too far on the side of crime control. The law also allows the space for the investigation of crime to be based

---

9   PACE 24(6).
10 PACE 24(7).
11 The only exception is the power to make an arrest when an imminent breach of the peace is anticipated. A citizen (as well as a constable) may then make a preventative arrest.
12 See *Redmond-Bate* v. *DPP* [1999] Crim LR, 998. This principle is elaborated by a later case: *Clarke* v. *DPP* [14 November 1997, unreported]. It must be made clear to the court what the officer had in mind when he or she made the arrest. See Bailey *et al.* (2001: 281).
13 *Redmond-Bate* v. *DPP* 163 J.P. 789 DC.
14 *G.* v. *Chief Superintendent of Police, Stroud* 86 Cr.App. R.92 DC.
15 *Castorina* v. *Chief Constable of Surrey* [1988] 138 NLJ 180, CA.
16 Under 2(4) of the Criminal Law Act 1967, now 24(6) PACE.
17 *Holgate-Mohammed* v. *Duke* [1984] 1 All ER 1054.
18 Ibid.

on 'hunches'. An arrest is made to provide reasons for either confirming or denying a police officer's 'feeling' that an individual has committed an offence. The courts have shown themselves unwilling to question those decisions that arresting officers have made. Moreover, section 25 of PACE created arrest powers for non-arrestable offences. The fact that the courts have been careful to construe this power narrowly indicates that there may be due process constraints over these additional police powers. However, it would be wrong to suggest that the courts have always taken this approach to arrest powers.

While in some cases the courts are attempting to control power of arrest, in others they have been less interventionist. For instance, the police make extensive use of common law breach of the peace powers – both to make arrests and to take steps short of arrest. In *Chief Constable of Cleveland Police* v. *McGrogan*,[19] powers of arrest for breach of the peace were construed narrowly but in *Austin*,[20] the court was less willing to examine the use of breach of peace powers.[21] As these powers are useful in policing public order situations, it is likely that the court does not want to interfere unduly with operational decisions, although it will censure more extreme abuses.

We can observe a similar pattern in relation to the court's consideration of the safeguards on the power of arrest. At common law, it was necessary for the person making the arrest to make it clear to the person under arrest by either physical means or through clear oral communication that s/he had been arrested.[22] PACE supplements the common law with further requirements. An arrest under PACE has to meet with the formalities contained in section 28(1). Section 28 states that the arrest is not lawful until the person arrested is told of the reason for arrest, and this must be done as soon as is practicable after the arrest. Moreover, the person arrested must be informed of the ground of the arrest under section 28(3). In section 28(3) an arrest is not lawful unless the arrestee is informed of the ground for arrest: *Christie* v. *Leachinsky*[23] gives the reason:

> a person is *prima facie* entitled to personal freedom [and] should know why for the time being his personal freedom is being interfered with ... No one, I think, would approve of a situation in which when the person arrested asked for the reason, the policeman replied 'that has nothing to do with you: come along with me ...' And there are practical considerations ... if the charge ... is then and there made known to him, he has the opportunity of giving an explanation of any misunderstanding or of calling attention to the other persons for whom he may have been mistaken,

---

19 *Chief Constable of Cleveland Police* v. *McGrogan* [2002] 1 FLR 707, CA (Civ. Div.).
20 *Austin* v. *Metropolitan Police Commissioner* [2005] HRLR 20, para 37.
21 A related issue is the extent to which the courts are willing to question the arrest power of private security guards. Given the privatisation of policing, this matter should be given more attention than it presently receives.
22 In terms of the common law definition of arrest, the element of compulsion is also essential. The arresting officer must, therefore, indicate that the suspect is under arrest either physically or orally. The problem in relation to indicating arrest by oral means alone is that it may not indicate the required compulsion. See *Alderson* v. *Booth* [1969] 2QB 216. Note: the requirements under s.28 are strictly separate from this necessity to indicate that the detainee is under compulsion.
23 *Christie* v. *Leachinsky* [1947] AC 573.

with the result that further inquiries may save him from the consequences of false accusation.[24]

This statement suggests that the courts take the requirements of section 28 with great seriousness. The words spoken on arrest are important as they specify the reason for the arrest and thus give the detained person the factual basis for any legal challenge. If there were no requirement to give reasons or the courts allowed a valid arrest to be constituted by vague and imprecise reasons, the law would not effectively prevent the arbitrary use of power. Viscount Simonds' words in *Wilson v. Chief Constable of Lancashire Constabulary*[25] are an instructive guide to the court's attitude. An arresting officer is not entitled to 'keep to himself' the grounds of arrest or give an untrue ground. Indeed, failure to inform the detained person of the correct grounds for arrest constituted false imprisonment. However, at the same time, the requirement to give reasons for arrest cannot hinder the practical task of making an arrest. The words used by the arresting officer need not be technically correct[26] – it is a matter of 'substance ... and turns on the elementary proposition that ... a person is ... entitled to his freedom and is only required to submit to restraints on his freedom if he knows in substance the reason why it is claimed that this restraint should be imposed'.[27]

ARTICLE 5

To what extent is the common law consistent with European human rights? Article 5 is an essential element of human rights, as it is concerned with limiting the power of the state, and preserving the liberty of the individual. In *Kurt v. Turkey*,[28] the ECtHR stressed that:

> the fundamental importance of the guarantees contained in Article 5 for securing the right of individuals in a democracy to be free from arbitrary detention at the hands of

---

24 Ibid.
25 *Wilson v. Chief Constable of Lancashire Constabulary*, Daily Telegraph, 5 December 2000, CA (Civ Div), pp. 587–8.
26 In *Lewis v. The Chief Constable* [1991] 1 All ER 206, CA, the plaintiffs were told of the fact of the arrest but the police delayed telling them the grounds. The court stated that an arrest arose as a question of fact from the deprivation of a person's liberty: as it was a continuing act, what had started as an unlawful arrest could *become* a lawful arrest; in other words an arrest becomes lawful once a ground is given. *DPP v. Hawkins* [1988] 1 WLR 1166 is authority for the fact that if it is not practicable for reasons to be given at the time of the arrest, the arrest is lawful and remains so until such time as reasons should be given. The arrest does not need to be confirmed by words such as 'I arrest you'; a statement of the fact of the arrest is sufficient. Zander (1995: 74–5) suggests that the *Abbassey* [1990] 1 All ER 193 has the key statement of the law here. There was no need for the technical or precise language to be used, provided the person knew that they had been arrested. This was a question of fact to be answered by the jury. However, the reason given must be the correct reason. 'If an incorrect reason is given the arrest is unlawful' – see *DPP v. Edwards* [1993 DC]; see also *Mullady v. DPP* [1997 DC].
27 Ibid.
28 *Kurt v. Turkey* (1998) 27 EHRR 373, para 122.

the authorities [and to the need to interpret narrowly any exception to] a most basic guarantee of individual freedom.[29]

This statement of general principle appears broadly consistent with the values articulated by the common law courts. But, as always, the devil is in the detail. It is necessary to take a close look at Article 5. Article 5(1) states the fundamental guarantee: deprivation of liberty can only take place in the circumstances stated in the Article, and only 'in accordance with a procedure prescribed by law'. The remainder of 5(1) covers these circumstances. They range from the requirement that detention should be 'after conviction by a competent court' through to arrest for non-compliance with a court order, to detention of various classes of persons. This basic summary gives some sense of the range of the Article. As we need to focus on what it tells us about arrest, we are not concerned with the challenges to mandatory life sentences, the confinement of the mentally ill or the concept of the 'supervision of minors' that emerge in Article 5 jurisprudence. Although this approach does limit our understanding of the Article, it does allow us to focus on the paradigmatic instance of the suspension of a person's liberty.

So far as this first paragraph of the Article is concerned, our focus is on 5(1)(c), which states that detention is lawful to the extent that it is based on 'reasonable suspicion' and 'effected for the purpose of bringing [an individual] ... before the competent legal authority'. How is reasonable suspicion defined?

The ECtHR has held that 'the "reasonableness" of the suspicion on which an arrest must be based forms an essential part of the safeguard against arbitrary arrest and detention'. Article 5(1)(c) requires that some facts exist which 'would satisfy an objective observer that the person concerned may have committed the offence', although the Court pointed out that reasonableness depends on the facts of the case.[30] A fair proportion of the cases brought against the UK in relation to this point concern anti-terrorism legislation in Northern Ireland. Anti-terrorism legislation tends to allow arrest to take place on the basis of information that, for reasons of security, can be withheld from the person arrested or even from the court. The jurisprudence of the Convention attempts to balance a tension between competing values. It recognises that non-disclosure is justifiable but that the concept of reasonableness should not be exploited by the state and its agencies. Thus, the state is under a duty under Convention law to reveal at least some information that justifies detention.[31]

What is the nature of this information? The test is not too stringent. Information used to justify an arrest does not have to be of the quality to justify charges against the detainee. It can be linked to an arrest, the purpose of which is to question the detainee about the suspicion that might have arisen that made the arrest necessary in the first place.[32] In *O'Hara*,[33] for instance, the applicant was arrested on suspicion of murder. He was held and questioned for over six days – but remained silent. The ECtHR did not

---
29 Ibid.
30 *Fox, Campbell and Hartley* v. *the United Kingdom*, judgment of 30 August 1990, Series A no. 182, p. 16, §32).
31 Ibid., 16–18.
32 *Brogan and Others* v. *the United Kingdom*, judgment of 29 November 1988, Series A no. 145-B, p. 29, §53, and *Murray* v. *the United Kingdom*, judgment of 28 October 1994, Series A no. 300-A, p. 27, §55.
33 *O'Hara* v. *the United Kingdom*, judgment of 16 October 2001.

find a breach of Article 5(1)(c), partly because the applicant had not raised this issue in the domestic courts. On the facts, it was thus legitimate to rely on the evidence of informers to justify the detention. *Brogan*[34] is largely consistent with this position. It was possible to rely on evidence that could not be produced in court and, to the extent that it was not possible to show that the investigations were motivated by bad faith, the detention of those suspected of terrorist offences was justifiable.

We will look in detail at *Murray* v. *UK*[35] to determine what is at stake in these terrorism cases. Murray had been arrested under section 14 of the Northern Ireland (Emergency Provisions) Act 1978 on suspicion of being involved with the procurement of arms for a terrorist organisation, the Irish Republican Army (IRA). Before the ECtHR, Murray argued that the arresting officer did not have the 'requisite suspicion' to justify the arrest. The ECtHR began its judgment by referring to the political context of the case, noting that 'due account will be taken of the special nature of terrorist crime, the threat it poses to democratic society and the exigencies of dealing with it'.[36] The question for the ECtHR was whether this was sufficient, given that Article 5(1) laid down a standard of 'reasonable suspicion'.

In *Fox*, the ECtHR had held that reasonable suspicion 'presupposed' facts that would 'satisfy an objective observer that the person concerned may have committed the offence'.[37] Importantly though, reasonableness required that all relevant circumstances be taken into account. This, of course, meant that the specific concern with the investigation of terrorist offences had to be taken seriously. The 'risk of loss of life and human suffering' requires that the authorities 'act with utmost urgency'. It may be necessary to act on information from sensitive or secret sources. This may be 'reliable' but cannot be made known to the suspect for fear of compromising the sources. Therefore the standard that justifies 'reasonable suspicion' cannot be the same as that used in 'conventional crime', but this does not mean that 'reasonableness' can be 'stretched' to the point that the 'safeguards' put in place by Article 5 are negated.[38] By the same token, the Article cannot be interpreted to 'put disproportionate difficulties in the way of the police authorities of the Contracting States in taking effective measures to counter organised terrorism'. This element of appreciation means that the ECtHR will not require the compromise of secret sources of information in anti-terrorism cases. However, a government must 'furnish at least some facts or information capable of satisfying the Court that the arrested person was reasonably suspected of having committed the alleged offence'. This requirement becomes all the more serious when the relevant law sets the threshold of 'honest suspicion', which is not as exacting a standard as 'reasonable suspicion'.[39]

Following *Brogan*,[40] the threshold of suspicion falls below that required to bring charges. The length of detention also had to be taken into account. On the facts of the

---

34 *Brogan* v. *UK*, supra n. 32.
35 *Murray* v. *UK*, supra n. 32.
36 Ibid., para 47.
37 Supra n. 30.
38 Supra n. 35, para 51.
39 Ibid.
40 *Brogan*, supra n. 34.

instant case, it had been limited to the maximum period allowed by the Act, which was four hours. The ECtHR's balancing act required them to acknowledge the need to combat terrorism but not to restrict the protection offered by Article 5. The following paragraph is worth citing in full:

> As to the present case, the terrorist campaign in Northern Ireland, the carnage it has caused over the years and the active engagement of the Provisional IRA in that campaign are established beyond doubt. The Court also accepts that the power of arrest granted to the Army by section 14 of the 1978 Act represented a bona fide attempt by a democratically elected parliament to deal with terrorist crime under the rule of law.[41]

From this position, the ECtHR can approach the government's argument much more positively than the Commission and attach a much greater level of credibility to the evidence against Murray. Applying *Fox*, though, the government still had to show that there were some facts to justify honest suspicion. The ECtHR considered that the fact that Murray had associated with her brothers in the United States, that they were prosecuted for attempting to procure arms, and that the evidence showed that they were liaising with someone 'trustworthy' in Northern Ireland, was sufficient to pass the minimum standard.

We now turn from our consideration of the legitimate grounds of detention to the second paragraph of the Article that specifies the safeguards that should operate. These have been described as 'elementary' and an 'integral' part of Article 5. They state that a person who has been arrested should know that this is the case.[42] The Article requires that 'any person arrested must be told, in simple, non-technical language that he can understand, the essential legal and factual grounds for his arrest'. The ECtHR has also held that while it is necessary that the detained person must be promptly[43] told that s/he is under arrest, the arresting officer need not tell the detainee everything. Indeed, there appears to be something of a sliding scale. If a person is arrested on the basis that s/he has committed a crime, it is not necessary to specify the precise crime or charge nor even to use a particular form of language.[44] Extradition proceedings require a lower threshold still,[45] although the court has insisted on the requirements of promptness.[46]

The fundamental reason for this safeguard is to allow the detained person to 'challenge' the lawfulness of his/her arrest. This links together paragraphs (2) and (4) of Article 5. An equally important requirement is that the person is told 'promptly'. There is a great deal of case law on this element of the Article, and we can only review the fundamental reason for this particular requirement. The court's explanation of

---

41   Ibid.
42   Supra n. 30, para 40.
43   Promptness must be assessed on the facts of the case: see *Bordovskiy* v. *Russia*, no. 49491/99, 8 February 2005.
44   *X* v. *Germany*, no. 8098/77, Commission decision of 13 December 1978, DR 16, p. 111.
45   *K.* v. *Belgium*, no. 10819/84, Commission decision of 5 July 1984, DR 38, p. 230.
46   See *Saadi* v. *UK Judgment*, 11 July 2006.

the promptness requirement links it to protection against the 'arbitrary' powers of the state.[47] The court has further elaborated this point:

> Judicial control of interferences by the executive ... is implied by the rule of law [this is] one of the fundamental principles of a democratic society ... [and] is expressly referred to in the Preamble to the Convention[.][48]

Section 5(3) is seen to flow directly from the fundamental values of the Convention. The ECtHR's approach acknowledges the fine line that exists between legitimate policing and the use of power unchecked by law. This means that the ECtHR has been keen to interpret the word 'prompt' in a very narrow way, as it means a person has been kept from appearance before a judge or a court through an executive act that has not been justified before an independent body. Even in anti-terrorism cases, the ECtHR has insisted on the need to bring a detainee before a court.

If we link 5(3) with 5(4), we can understand more precisely the schema of the Article. Article 5(4) specifies that a detained person must have the opportunity to challenge the 'lawfulness of his detention'. This, in turn, requires further guarantees:

> Certain procedural and substantive guarantees ensure that judicial control: the judge (or other officer) before whom the accused is 'brought promptly' must be seen to be independent of the executive and of the parties to the proceedings; that judge, having heard the accused himself, must examine all the facts arguing for and against the existence of a genuine requirement of public interest justifying, with due regard to the presumption of innocence, a departure from the rule of respect for the accused's liberty, and that judge must have the power to order an accused's release.[49]

It would be far too limited to think in terms of the writ of habeas corpus to address these issues from the perspective of the common law.[50] Indeed, the ECtHR has suggested that in certain circumstances, the writ is itself too limited.[51]

---

47   The *Bozano* judgment of 18 December 1986, p. 23, para 54.
48   Ibid.
49   S.B.C. v. *the United Kingdom*, judgment of 19 June 2001.
50   From the perspective of the common law, this gives us the terms in which to judge the operation of habeas corpus. Habeas corpus has been described as 'the fundamental instrument for safeguarding individual freedom against arbitrary and lawless state action', *Harris* v. *Nelson*, 394 US 286, 290–92 (1969). Although it is perhaps less important in English law today, it retains a hold on the legal imagination. It is the means by which the court can make a determination of the legality of a person's detention. As well as questioning the technical reasons for an arrest and detention, habeas corpus can also be used to enquire into the abuse of power. See *R.* v. *Governor of Brixton Prison, ex parte Sarno* [1916] 2 King's Bench Reports 742 and *R.* v. *Brixton Prison (Governor), ex parte Soblen* [1962] 3 All England Law Reports 641.
51   *X* v. *United Kingdom*, judgment of 5 November 1981, para 57: 'Although X had access to a court which ruled that his detention was "lawful" in terms of English law, this cannot of itself be decisive as to whether there was a sufficient review of "lawfulness" for the purposes of Article 5, para. 4'. However, at para 58, the court commented: '58. Notwithstanding the limited nature of the review ... the remedy of habeas corpus can on occasions constitute an effective check against arbitrariness in this sphere. It may be regarded as adequate, for the purposes of Article 5 para 4 , for emergency measures for the detention of persons on the ground of unsoundness of mind. The authority empowered to order emergency detention of this kind must, in the nature of things, enjoy a wide discretion, and this inevitably means that the role of the courts will be reduced'.

What should we make of the terrorism context of these cases? Although the nature of terrorist offences means they must be policed in a different way to non-terrorist criminal activity, has the ECtHR taken into account the rights of the suspects in any meaningful way? Arguably, in some cases, and *Murray* would be a good example, there are factors that suggest the Court has ceded too much to executive power.

Taking into account Murray's health, the fact that she had four young children and no previous criminal record, meant that there should be 'higher level of suspicion', a 'stricter standard' put in place. Moreover, the interrogation was characterised by 'vague questions' and Murray could not therefore have come to the conclusion that she had been 'informed of the reasons for her arrest'.[52] According to the interpretation of the Article in *Fox*, the basic safeguard of Article 5(2) was that 'any person arrested must be told, in simple, non-technical language that he can understand, the essential legal and factual grounds for his arrest, so as to be able, if he sees fit, to apply to a court to challenge its lawfulness in accordance with paragraph 4'. The facts in the instant case suggest that this 'basic standard' had been breached.[53] We will need to return to these considerations when we examine the basic safeguards that exist at common law to protect the detained or accused person: the presumption of innocence and the privilege against self-incrimination.

THE PRESUMPTION OF INNOCENCE

What is the presumption of innocence? One might imagine that there is a simple answer to this question, given the importance of the presumption to criminal procedure, and the ideology of the common law in general. Before we can elucidate the clash of values that animates the case law on the presumption of innocence, we need to isolate its precise nature. Following Roberts and Zuckerman's analysis, this principle could be presented as: 'the right of the innocent not to suffer criminal conviction and punishment'.[54] This clearly states a due process value. Building this argument means understanding that, at least at common law, the presumption of innocence makes most sense as a body of 'rules of evidence' relating to 'the burden and standard of proof'.[55] This point is clearly made in the celebrated speech of Viscount Sankey in *Woolmington* v. *DPP*:[56]

> Throughout the web of the English Criminal Law one golden thread is always to be seen, that it is the duty of the prosecution to prove the prisoner's guilt ... subject to what I have already said as to the defence of insanity and subject also to any statutory exception. If, at the end of and on the whole of the case, there is a reasonable doubt, created by the evidence given by either the prosecution or the prisoner ... the prosecution has not made out the case and the prisoner is entitled to an acquittal. No matter what the charge or where the trial, the principle that the prosecution must prove the guilt of

---
52   Supra n. 32, *Murray*, para 6.
53   Ibid., para 7.
54   Supra n. 36, at 329.
55   Ibid., 327.
56   *Woolmington* v. *DPP* [1985] AC 462.

the prisoner is part of the common law of England and no attempt to whittle it down can be entertained.[57]

Viscount Sankey's speech shows that the prosecution carry the duty of proving the guilt of the accused. The standard of the credibility of the prosecution evidence must show that the accused is likely to be guilty beyond reasonable doubt. This principle was elaborated in *Mancini v. DPP*:[58]

> Woolmington's case is concerned with explaining and reinforcing the rule that the prosecution must prove the charge it makes beyond reasonable doubt, and, consequently, that if, on the material before the jury, there is a reasonable doubt, the prisoner should have the benefit of it. The rule is of general application in all charges under the criminal law.

If the prosecution cannot prove their case beyond reasonable doubt then the accused should not be found guilty. Although the House of Lords affirmed this principle in *R. v. Hunt*,[59] they also returned to a second central argument in *Woolmington*: the exceptions to the rule. Although the burden rests with the prosecution 'throughout the trial', there may be certain issues that the defence has to prove. We will return to this point presently, for there is an important prior issue. As Roberts and Zuckerman point out, the crucial issue is the status of the presumption itself. Viscount Sankey's speech suggests that the presumption must be a rigorous one and requires the prosecution to prove not simply that the accused had the 'opportunity' to commit the crime, but that the evidence shows that the person in the dock did act in such a way as to satisfy both the mental and the physical elements of the crime. It is worth remembering that we are concerned here with a common law court that does not act inquisitorially. In other words, the parties present the evidence and the court acts as a neutral umpire. The standard of proof is effectively the threshold that the prosecution must pass in order for a jury to be very sure that the defendant is guilty of committing a crime.

There have been profound problems of definition in explaining precisely what is meant by beyond reasonable doubt. In *Bater v. Bater*,[60] Lord Denning differentiated between the civil and the criminal standard of proof, but suggested that different definitions of the standard of proof may be no more than a 'matter of words',[61] and that there might not be an 'absolute standard', of either criminal or civil cases,[62] as the standard of proof 'depends on the subject matter'.[63] Thus a civil court considering fraud would require a higher level of probability than when considering negligence. Lord Denning went on to provide an explanation for the differences between civil and criminal courts. He posited that it rests on 'our high regard for the liberty of the individual, a doubt may be regarded as reasonable in the criminal courts, which would not

---

57 Ibid., 481–2.
58 *Mancini v. DPP* [1942] AC 1, 369.
59 *R. v. Hunt* [1987] AC 352.
60 *Bater v. Bater* [1951] P. 35.
61 Ibid., 36.
62 Ibid., 37.
63 Ibid.

be so in the civil courts'.[64] Lord Scarman's judgment in *Khawaja v. Secretary of State for the Home Department* resonates with this case.[65] Khawaja was a judicial review case but the substance of Lord Scarman's argument suggests that the risk of loss of liberty of an individual justifies a higher burden of proof. This position is perhaps most thoroughly elaborated by Lord Bingham in *McIntosh v. Lord Advocate*:[66]

> There is a paradox at the heart of all criminal procedure, in that the more serious the crime and the greater the public interest in securing convictions of the guilty, the more important do constitutional protections of the accused become. The starting point of any balancing inquiry where constitutional rights are concerned must be that the public interest in ensuring that innocent people are not convicted and subjected to ignominy and heavy sentences, massively outweighs the public interest in ensuring that a particular criminal is brought to book ... Hence the presumption of innocence, which serves not only to protect a particular individual on trial, but to maintain public confidence in the enduring integrity and security of the legal system.[67]

Lord Bingham considers the presumption as a 'paradox' within criminal justice. The contradiction appears to be that the rules of criminal procedure both seek to convict the guilty and provide safeguards that make it very difficult to do so. When faced with conflicting values, the courts can only try to reach a compromise. But should there be a predominant value? Arguably, it is that the innocent should not be convicted. Thus, the presumption of innocence is not only to do with the protection of liberty, as Lord Scarman and Lord Denning suggest, but can also be related to the maintenance of public confidence in the criminal justice system as a whole.

THE PRESUMPTION OF INNOCENCE AND ARTICLE 6

The jurisprudence of Article 6 is more or less consistent with the common law.[68] The issue that has tended to arise in human rights law is the extent to which it is justifiable that the accused should bear the burden of proof. One of the leading cases is *Salabiaku v. France*.[69]

Salabiaku had been convicted of offences relating to smuggling goods. He had collected a trunk from Roissy Airport, which he believed had been sent to him by a relative in Zaire. When officials opened the trunk, it was found to contain cannabis seeds. Salabiaku claimed that he had picked up the trunk by mistake. His case before the French court focused on the 'almost irrebuttable' presumption of his guilt. Under the Customs Code, this presumption was based on the mere fact of

---

64 Ibid., 38.
65 *Khawaja v. Secretary of State for the Home Department* [1983] 2 WLR 321.
66 *McIntosh v. Lord Advocate* [2001] 3 WLR 107.
67 Ibid., 570.
68 Section 6(2) applies only to criminal charges and would thus have no application to the investigation of crime, see *X v. Germany* (1962) 5 YB 192.
69 *Salabiaku v. France* (Application no. 10519/83).

possession of the trunk. Salabiaku argued that this amounted to a breach of Article 6(2) and 6(1).

The court argued that the problem was not with the presumption of guilt, as all legal systems make presumptions of both fact and law. From the perspective of Article 6, the real issue was the extent to which the presumptions were consistent with the Convention. Certainly, a presumption of guilt could amount to a breach of due process, as it would effectively deprive the court of its 'genuine power of assessment', and make a nonsense of the presumption of innocence.[70] The critical question thus becomes: does the presumption of guilt go beyond 'reasonable limits' to such an extent that it limits the 'rights of the defence'? Under the relevant legislation, the 'possession of smuggled goods' is a finding of fact. However, this finding of fact does not immediately show the guilt of the accused. The court pointed out that the defence of extenuating circumstances was available to Salabiaku. Shifting the burden of proof to the defence is not in itself a breach of the Article, provided that this operates within 'reasonable limits' and acknowledges the fundamental issues in the case and the 'rights of the defence'. *Hoang v. France*[71] further elaborates this position. Article 6 is not breached so long as the primary burden for proving guilt rests with the prosecution.

So, it is not the case that human rights law simply elaborates due process values. There is a tension between due process and crime control values in the reasoning of the ECtHR. We can appreciate that the common law is not in breach of Article 6 to the extent that it requires the defence to bear the burden of proof in certain instances. An important case here is *R. v. Lambert*.[72] The appellant had been charged under the Misuse of Drugs Act 1971 with possession of a controlled substance. He argued that although he was in possession of a bag containing the prohibited drugs, he neither knew nor had reason to suspect that drugs were in the bag. Furthermore, he argued that his defence should not have been based on the balance of probabilities, as this amounted to a breach of the presumption of innocence under Article 6(2). The House of Lords held that the Misuse of Drugs Act could be interpreted in such a way as to make it compatible with Article 6. The court agreed that it would be incompatible with human rights jurisprudence if an accused was required to prove or disprove, to the standard of the balance of probabilities, part of an offence or defence. However, an 'evidentiary presumption from which a trier of fact may (as opposed to must) draw an inference of guilt' was acceptable. This does not mean that the burden shifts to the defence. It does mean that the 'reverse onus is satisfied' if the defence uses evidence which raises an issue which the prosecution must then prove to the 'contrary beyond reasonable doubt'.[73] As it was possible to read the 1971 Act in this way, it was not necessary to consider a breach of Article 6.[74]

Clearly, these three cases are merely indicative of a much wider body of principles. Our main point is that, leaving aside the myriad complexities that are attendant on

---

70 Para 28.
71 *Hoang v. France* [1992] 16 EHRR 53.
72 *R. v. Lambert* [2001] 2 AC 545.
73 Ibid., 573.
74 See *R. v. DPP, ex parte Kebilene* [2000] 2 AC 326.

coordinating two different legal cultures, there is a broad congruence between the common law and human rights jurisprudence.

THE PRIVILEGE AGAINST SELF-INCRIMINATION

The privilege against self-incrimination 'confers a freedom to refuse to answer questions when the reply might incriminate the person to whom the question is addressed'.[75] This privilege is limited to 'suspects and the accused'.[76] Lord Mustill in *ex parte Smith*[77] pointed out that the so-called right to remain silent is in fact a cluster of 'immunities', which, despite their different histories and provenance, have been brought together under a single heading. These rights have been limited and redefined by statute. If we take these considerations together, it makes the 'right to silence' appear somewhat high-sounding: a rhetorical claim rather than a legal reality. We must ascertain whether or not the courts have achieved justice between the prosecution and the defence in their elaboration of due process in this area. We will begin our analysis by briefly examining the key common law authorities.

Lord Mustill's analysis divides the right to silence into six categories.[78] If we take the categories as a whole, we can see that they generally reflect the common law's civil libertarian underpinnings, to the extent that the right to silence respects a person's privacy.[79] However, it is worth bearing in mind Lord Mustill's warning. As the immunities appear to protect 'citizens' from 'abuse of powers from those investigating crimes' it might be safe to 'assume that they are all different ways of expressing the same principle'. This would be wrong as they are 'embedded' in different legal contexts.[80] This suggests that although they enshrine defence-orientated values in criminal procedure, the common law has always been equally concerned with their limitation, and has never seen the privilege against self-incrimination as its single fundamental and underlying justification.[81]

---

75 Roberts and Zuckerman (1994: 392).
76 Ibid., 393.
77 R. v. *Director of Serious Fraud Office, ex parte Smith* [1993] AC 1 30-2.
78 The first category covers a 'general immunity' to refuse to answer questions; the second category is more precise in that it covers a general immunity to refuse to answer incriminatory questions. The third and fourth categories reflect the immunity from compulsion to answer police questions, and the immunity during the trial from the compulsion to give evidence. The fifth immunity covers the refusal to answer police questions that relate to the offence to which they have been charged, and the sixth relates to the immunity from adverse comment during the trial on either failure to answer pre-trial questions, or failure to give evidence.
79 This is particularly true of the general immunities, although their practical importance has been decreased by various statutes that place a citizen under a duty to provide information in situations such as tax liability. In the language of human rights, these liberties could be coordinated with Articles 8 and 10.
80 Lord Mustill goes on to argue: 'In these circumstances I think it clear, given the diversity of immunities and of the policies underlying them, that it is not enough to ask simply whether Parliament can have intended to abolish a long-standing right of silence. Rather, an essential starting point must be to identify what variety of this right is being invoked, and what are the reasons for believing that the right in question ought at all costs to be maintained'.
81 So what different principles are at stake here? The first two principles reflect the view that 'one person should so far as possible be entitled to tell another person to mind his own business'. While this may have some links to legal notions of privacy, and hence to due process, this immunity is subject to numerous statutory interventions, and so cannot be seen as an overarching due process value. A second principle, in some ways distinct from the

For instance, consider Lord Mustill's examination of what appears to be the central principle underlying the immunities: the 'instinct that it is contrary to fair play to put the accused in a position where he is exposed to punishment whatever he does'. The right of the accused to remain silent would thus be based on the idea that it would not be fair to allow him to 'condemn himself out of his own mouth' or to punish him for refusing to answer questions. This appears to be a firm commitment to defence values: 'the desire to minimise the risk that an accused will be convicted on the strength of an untrue extra-judicial confession, to which the law gives effect by refusing to admit confessions in evidence except upon proof that they are "voluntary" '. However, this defence-orientated value has to be put in the general context of criminal procedure.[82] The accused's legitimate refusal to provide incriminating information comes into tension with the public interest in the conviction of the guilty. The fundamental question is whether the courts have managed to balance defence and prosecution values. Assessing this balance means that we have to take into account the fact that the great majority of those interrogated do 'crack' and do not remain silent.[83] We will return presently to the issue of confession evidence, but for the moment we will remain with the consequences of an accused's silence.

The common law has primarily grappled with two related issues: to what extent is pre-trial silence an admission of guilt; and to what extent is it acceptable for the accused's silence to be commented on during their trial?[84] There was an appreciation during the nineteenth century that it would be wrong, given the inherent ambiguity of a defendant's silence, to link refusal to answer questions with guilt. The courts should thus approach an accused's silence cautiously. However, there were also authorities indicating that refusal to provide specific forms of evidence could be commented upon in court and adverse inferences drawn. In *R. v. Chandler*,[85] Lawton LJ reviewed the law and explained that although the accused had a privilege against self-incrimination, it did not imply that 'the failure to answer an accusation or question when an answer could reasonably be expected' could not 'provide some evidence in support of an accusation'. In other words, the silence of the accused during interrogation was never necessarily sacrosanct and could, in certain circumstances, be used by the prosecution in court.

As far as silence during the trial is concerned, the Criminal Evidence Act of 1898 provided that the 'failure' of 'any person charged with an offence to give evidence' could

---

first, also underlies the immunities that relate to pre- and post-trial proceedings. Lord Mustill roots these in the 'long history of reaction against abuses of judicial interrogation'. Going back to the seventeenth century, the King's prerogative courts had the power to extract confessions and, although these courts were swept away by the civil war, magistrates had a power to interrogate the accused, which only came to an end in the 1840s. While this again sounds promising as a presentation of the common law's historical commitment to defence values, one cannot use this history to understand the different immunities. For instance, since the Criminal Evidence Act 1898, the accused giving evidence in court could be questioned by prosecuting counsel as well as the judge.

82   It is specific to the accused; other witnesses can be compelled to give evidence. There is an exception that applies to giving evidence in court that might incriminate the witness but, in general, the duty to give evidence is compulsory. The accused's privilege also covers pre-trial processes; the police may be able to interrogate a suspect but the suspect is not compelled to answer.

83   As Roberts and Zuckerman argue (supra n. 75, at 396): '[c]ontrary to the popular TV scenario of the scheming professional criminal taking advantage of the right to silence ... in real life perhaps as little as five per cent of suspects remain completely silent or give "no comment" answers to police questioning'.

84   Ibid., 473.

85   *R. v. Chandler* [1976].

not be made 'the subject of any comment by the prosecution'.[86] This section concerns a person charged with an offence, and so it was necessary to develop case law on the status of the silence of an accused prior to charge. The first thing to note is that although the 1898 Act prevented the prosecution from making comments on the accused's silence, it did not prevent the judge from so doing. There was some confusion about the precise form of the comments that the judge could make. In *R. v. Rhodes*[87] Lord Russell argued that the matter fell within the judge's discretion, and that it was certainly acceptable that the judge could pass comment on the accused's 'absence from the witness box'. Two later cases,[88] *R. v. Corrie and Wilson* and *R. v. Bernard*, showed that the judge could direct the jury to draw adverse inferences from the accused's silence when 'the facts pointed so strongly to guilt as to call for an explanation'. Later cases[89] established the important safeguard that the judge's discretion to comment was subject to appeal. *R. v. Bathurst*[90] established the form of words that would lead to the model direction to the jury. The judge must explain that the accused 'is not bound to give evidence, [and] can sit back and see if the prosecution have proved their case'.[91] The jury must not assume that '[the accused] is guilty because he has not gone into the witness box'.[92]

Subsequent cases failed to clarify certain pressing points about the precise nature of the judge's comments. In *Martinez Tobon*,[93] Lord Taylor CJ suggested that it was hard to see where the distinction lay between 'permissible and impermissible comment'.[94] He reasserted that the starting point were the directions in *R. v. Bathurst*. These stressed that the defendant did not have to testify, and the jury were not permitted to assume guilt from his or her silence. The judge could then go on to comment on facts given in evidence by the defence, which contradict prosecution evidence and which the defendant must have known about. The law in this area of criminal evidence has been changed by section 34 of the Criminal Justice and Public Order Act 1994.

Section 34 is controversial. It states that when an accused gives evidence in his defence, which, at the time that the offence was charged or when s/he was questioned under caution, s/he 'failed to mention'. The court or the jury may then draw such inferences as 'appear proper'. The section also covers the situation where the accused 'could reasonably have been expected to mention information when s/he was 'questioned, charged or informed'. In this situation the court or the jury would also be allowed to draw such inferences as appeared appropriate. Section 35(2) and (3) provide something of a safeguard. The accused had to be put on notice that if s/he chooses not to give evidence, then the court or the jury can draw inferences about a refusal 'without good cause ... to answer any questions'. Section 38(3) goes further: a person cannot be convicted 'solely on an inference' drawn from his or her silence.

---

86   Supra n. 83 at 438.
87   *R. v. Rhodes* [1899] 1 QB 77.
88   *R. v. Corrie and Wilson* (1904) 20 TLR 365 and *R. v. Bernard* [1908] 1 Cr. App. R. 218.
89   *Waugh v. the King* [1950] AC 203 but cf. *R. v. Fisher* [1964] Crim LR 150.
90   *R. v. Bathurst* [1968] 2 QB 99.
91   Ibid., 107.
92   Ibid.
93   *Martinez Tobon* [1994] 1 WLR 388.
94   Ibid., 397.

The case law relating to this section suggests that the courts have been very careful to stress the narrow meaning of an accused's silence.[95] The judge has to remind the jury that on arrest and at the start of any police interview, the defendant had to be cautioned, and warned about the consequences of refusing to answer questions. In his summing up, the judge must then tell the jury that the accused's defence had relied upon evidence that was not mentioned during police interview. The judge must go on to explain the precise terms of the prosecution case. The judge must then explain that it was for the jury to decide what inferences could be reasonably drawn, stressing that failure to mention information cannot itself establish the accused's guilt. The jury must always bear in mind that the defence may have produced evidence that explains the accused's silence or failure to answer questions and, only if this fails to offer an 'innocent explanation', should inferences be drawn against the accused. In *Argent*, the court stressed that whether or not the accused had received legal advice was an important factor to be taken into account by the jury.

Within the scope of this chapter it is difficult to offer any final assessment of the status of the privilege against self-incrimination. While the 1994 Act certainly seems to work in favour of the prosecution rather than the defence, it would be premature to conclude that the cases we have examined all privilege prosecution values. We can see that the common law has never simply committed itself to protecting the 'right' of the accused not to give evidence, and to refuse to reply to police questions. There have been numerous statutory interventions, and the immunities against self-incrimination have been consistently restricted or limited. At the same time, the common law has not abandoned a certain commitment to defence-orientated values. For instance, the concern with the precise words that the judge can use to comment on silence, and the right of appeal if the direction is prejudicial to the defence, suggest that the law is concerned with holding a line between the prosecution and the defence.

SELF-INCRIMINATION AND HUMAN RIGHTS

To understand the law of ECHR on self-incrimination, we need to appreciate that the jurisprudence links together the immunity against self-incrimination with a related issue: the status of evidence unfairly obtained under compulsion. This kind of evidence would also include confession evidence, which tends to incriminate the accused, and is rendered unreliable because it was obtained by 'oppression'. The relevant provisions of domestic law are contained in the Police and Criminal Evidence Act 1984. In the following section, we will see that while the common law is broadly consistent with international standards of procedural law, we can trace the similar tensions around the status of immunities against self-incrimination as we noted in the section above.

---

95 See R. v. *Argent* ([1997] Criminal Appeal Reports 27, para 35). See also R. v. *Roble* [1997] Criminal Law Reports, 449 which stressed the importance of making it known to the jury that the defendant had remained silent on the basis of legal advice. Importantly, R. v. *Doldur* (judgment of 23 November 1999, *The Times*, 7 December 1999) confirmed that inferences can only be drawn by the jury once the prosecution have established a strong prima facie case.

A reading of Article 6 reveals that it does not lay down any rules to deal with incriminating evidence. This might suggest the rather startling conclusion that such rules are not part of European human rights jurisprudence. *Saunders v. the United Kingdom*[96] put forward the argument that 'the right not to be compelled to contribute incriminating evidence' was 'implicit' in Article 6[97] and should be 'linked' to the 'presumption of innocence' which was 'expressly guaranteed' by Article 6(2).

Saunders had been convicted on numerous charges including false accounting and theft. He argued that the use of the Department of Trade and Industry (DTI) inspector's interviews in the trial had made the proceedings unfair. The ECtHR agreed with *Saunders* in principle. Although Article 6 did not contain an explicit mention of either the right to silence or the privilege against self-incrimination, both principles are recognised 'international standards' of a fair trial. The 'right' not to self-incrimination is thus 'closely linked to the presumption of innocence contained' in Article 6(2).[98] The court held that there had indeed been a breach of the right not to incriminate oneself. They did not accept the British government's arguments that the complex nature of crimes of fraud justified 'such a marked departure ... from one of the basic requirements of fair procedure'.[99]

John Murray v. the United Kingdom raises a similar point to *Saunders*, but in a different context: the investigation of terrorist offences. Murray had refused to answer any questions either at the time of his arrest or during the 21-hour period of his questioning. It was only towards the end of this period that he was allowed access to a solicitor, although the solicitor was not present during the final hours of the interrogation. Before the ECtHR, Murray relied on the case law of the Convention to argue that the right to remain silent had to be understood as the refusal to answer police questions and to refuse to testify at trial. Fair trial guarantees would also be breached if adverse inferences could be drawn from either silence in questioning or at trial. These are 'absolute rights which an accused is entitled to enjoy without restriction'.[100] To allow limitations on these rights would 'subvert ... the presumption of innocence and alter the fundamental structure of the trial, where the prosecution have the burden of showing the defendant's guilt'. These arguments were supported by information drawn from Amnesty International, Liberty and Article 14(3)(g) of the United Nations International Covenant on Civil and Political Rights.[101]

---

96   *Saunders v. United Kingdom*, 17 December 1996.
97   This was recognised by the court in *Funke v. France* (25 February 1993, Series A no. 256-A, p. 22, para 44) and *John Murray v. the United Kingdom* (8 February 1996, Reports of Judgments and Decisions 1996-I, p. 49).
98   *Murray*, para 68. The court went on to assert that the right to remain silent 'does not extend' to the use of evidence obtained under compulsion that 'has an existence independent of the will of the suspect'. The key examples are 'breath, blood ... urine' and 'DNA samples'. The instant case does not, however, raise concerns with this kind of evidence: the sole question relates to the evidence obtained under DTI interview (para 69).
99   Supra n. 96, Para 74.
100 Supra n. 97, Para 41.
101 This explicitly provides that an accused shall 'not be compelled to testify against himself or to confess guilt'. The international context of this principle was also demonstrated by reference to Rule 42 (A) of the Rules of Procedure and Evidence of the International Criminal Tribunal for the Former Yugoslavia which also stresses the right of the accused to remain silent. The wording of the Draft Statute for an International Criminal Court further elaborates: the right to silence is not to be limited by 'silence being a consideration in the determination of guilt or innocence'. Cited at para 42. The British government were not particularly impressed by

The ECtHR refused to give 'an abstract analysis of the scope' of the 'immunities' and refused to comment on the issue of 'improper compulsion'.[102] Instead, they argued that Murray's case required consideration of whether or not the immunities are 'absolute' to the extent that the accused's silence cannot be 'used against him in court' or whether (more precisely) the warning that his silence may be used against him amounts to 'improper compulsion'.[103] There can be no question of solely basing a conviction on silence; but, likewise, the accused should not be able to hide behind his or her silence to frustrate the court.[104] This would suggest that the ECtHR sees the right to silence as limited, and open to qualification. The defendant's silence can therefore have implications at trial. Was there compulsion of the applicant?

The court noted that Murray's silence did not in itself amount to an offence or to contempt of court.[105] If, following the government's case, this silence is not in itself an inference of guilt, then it would be hard to link this to the other cases on compulsion. In *Funke*, charges had been brought in order to compel the defendant to provide evidence of offences that he was suspected of committing. This clearly amounted to a breach of Article 6. However, the case was distinguishable from the facts of *Murray*.

What do we make of these cases? In asserting that the immunity against self-incrimination was linked to the presumption of innocence, and that both were implied by Article 6, *Saunders* stressed the centrality of these due process guarantees to European human rights law. The case did not hold that they were absent from the common law; rather, it made a narrower point about reliance on a certain kind of evidence during fraud trials. In this sense, *Saunders* brings the common law into line with international standards and prevents a national government creating different standards of evidence for different criminal offences. *Murray* also confirms that the common law remains consistent with international standards as far as the status of silence is concerned. The ECtHR argued that:

> Whether the drawing of adverse inferences from an accused's silence infringes Article 6 is a matter to be determined in the light of all the circumstances of the case, having particular regard to the situations where inferences may be drawn, the weight attached to them by the national courts in their assessment of the evidence and the degree of compulsion inherent in the situation.[106]

The use of silence in court must be assessed in the context of the case and the checks and balances that exist in a national legal system. While this might seem much too broad to be a useful clarification of an international standard, it does allow a degree of flexibility to the precise way in which a national court draws inferences on silence. It would not be a breach of international standards to warn an accused that their silence

---

these arguments. They asserted that the sources used by the applicants 'did not demonstrate any internationally accepted prohibition on the drawing of common-sense inferences from the silence of an accused whether at trial or pre-trial.
102   Ibid., para 46.
103   Ibid.
104   Ibid.
105   Ibid.
106   Ibid., para 47.

might be used against him or her at trial. The ECtHR's position is probably justifiable as a balancing of defence- and prosecution-orientated values but, before we draw a final conclusion, we should consider one final authority: *Condron* v. *UK*.[107]

Condron is an authority on section 34 of the Criminal Justice and Public Order Act 1994. The applicant was alleging that the judge's decision to leave to the jury the question of whether they should draw adverse inferences from the accused's silence had breached Article 6(1). While accepting (on the basis of the John Murray judgment) that the right to silence was not absolute, the applicants contended that the necessary safeguards were not in place. In particular, the trial judge had not taken into account the applicant's solicitor's 'honest belief' that the applicants were not fit to be interviewed and were 'vulnerable and confused'.[108] Despite this fact, the judge advised the jury that they could draw negative inferences from their silence in the interview. The judge had not reminded the jury that the applicants' silence may have been due to the fact that they had been so advised, and were suffering from the symptoms of drug withdrawal. Nor had the trial judge reminded the jury that the prosecution had to establish a strong prima facie case.

The ECtHR took issue with the judge's advice to the jury. Although he had reminded them of the solicitor's advice, his direction was in such terms as to leave the jury to draw inference 'notwithstanding' that the explanation appeared reasonable:

> In the Court's opinion, as a matter of fairness, the jury should have been directed that it could only draw an adverse inference if satisfied that the applicants' silence at the police interview could only sensibly be attributed to their having no answer or none that would stand up to cross-examination.[109]

In other words, the direction should have been much more precise. The ECtHR found that this was a serious fault, given the fact that the judge's directions to the jury were an important safeguard in the absence of the jury's explanation for its decision. Despite agreeing with the British government that other safeguards were in place, the ECtHR argued that the nature of the judge's directions were such as to compromise the fairness of the trial. The Strasbourg court held unanimously that there had been a breach of 6(1).

Condron suggests that the checks and balances in the common law only operate in an acceptable way from a human rights perspective if the judge's direction to the jury is precise. The other safeguards in criminal procedure will not offset a mistaken direction. For instance, the ECtHR noted the British government's arguments that the applicants had been issued with a clearly worded caution, and had indicated that they understood the consequences of remaining silent. Moreover, they had had the advice of a solicitor and the usual safeguards of a criminal trial. It is also interesting that the ECtHR made an important distinction between the Court of Appeal's ruling that the accused's 'convictions' were safe, and the issue of whether or not there had been a fair trial.

---

107 *Condron* v. *UK*, 2 May 2000.
108 *Condron*, para 44.
109 Ibid., para 61.

Even if convictions appear sound, it could thus be the case that there were issues in the trial that made its procedure unfair. This suggests a more demanding standard than that of the safety of conviction. It is perhaps proper that criminal procedure should be held to this higher threshold, as it poses the power of the state and its resources against the individual. Condron suggests that for the jury to be an acceptable institution within a criminal trial, it needs to be carefully advised by the judge, and if this safeguard fails, then it is likely that the trial itself is compromised.[110]

BIAS, HUMAN RIGHTS AND THE JURY

In this final section, we argue that both the ECtHR and the English courts have failed to reconstruct the role of the jury in a way that effectively balances due process and the requirement for finality in the criminal trial. The essential issues in this area of criminal procedure are focused by Lord Steyn's speech in *R. v. Mirza*.[111] Lord Steyn stressed the context of the problem: the accused is entitled to trial before an 'impartial tribunal'[112] and, should there be allegations that the tribunal showed bias, then there must be a robust way of examining this allegation. How does this 'fundamental'[113] fair trial guarantee sit alongside the common law rule that prevents any examination of the jury's deliberations? What are the risks of this approach? It would appear that the law places the 'efficiency of the jury system' above the possibilities of 'miscarriages of justice'.[114] More specifically, we will see that the law is consistently downplaying the 'corrosive'[115] effect of racism within the jury.

The common law and human rights jurisprudence have not taken this problem of racism seriously enough. It is, of course, easy to argue that a person who has been found guilty of an offence will want to reopen his/her case. However, this does not get to the real issue: the problem of biased jury decisions. To understand this issue, we need to examine the leading cases. In *Gregory v. UK*[116] evidence emerged of jury bias. After the jury had retired to consider its verdict a note was passed to the judge

---

110   For a case that falls on the other side of this line, see *Brown v. Stott* [2001] HRLR 9. Brown had been under compulsion under s.172(2)(a) of the Road Traffic Act 1988 to admit that she had been the driver of her car. Could this information be used in a separate prosecution under 5(1)(a) of the same Act? Brown argued that using the evidence of her admission would be in breach of the privilege against self-incrimination. The Appeal Court in Scotland accepted this argument, and the Crown appealed to the Privy Council. The basis of their argument was that the privilege was not absolute, and that the relevant sections of the 1988 Act provided a 'legitimate and proportionate interference'. The Privy Council held that although the 'overall fairness of a criminal trial' could not be 'compromised', the 'constituent rights' could be, provided the limitations were 'legitimate and proportionate'. The court had to achieve a balance between the general interest of the community and the personal rights of the individual. In so deciding, they distinguished *Saunders*. On the facts, the large number of fatalities in road traffic accidents indicted that s.172 was 'legitimate'. It was proportionate because it did not license long and oppressive questioning, and the penalty for refusing to answer was 'moderate and non-custodial'.
111   *R. v. Mirza* [2004] HRLR 11.
112   Ibid., para 5.
113   Ibid.
114   Ibid.
115   Ibid., para 151 (Lord Rodger)
116   *Gregory v. UK*, 25 February 1997.

which read: 'Jury showing racial overtones. One member to be excused'.[117] The judge went on to show the note to both the prosecution and the defence, and warned the jury that they had to ignore any prejudice and try the case on its facts. The jury found the defendant guilty by a verdict of 10 to 2. The applicant argued before the ECtHR that he had not received a fair trial and his rights under Article 6 and Article 14 had been breached.

What should the judge have done? The relevant test for bias at the time of the trial was *R. v. Gough*.[118] Once the judge became aware of bias on the part of the jurors he should have considered whether there was a possibility of actual bias. He should have asked whether individual jurors could be shown to be biased or, failing that, was it possible to find a 'real danger of bias affecting the mind of the relevant juror or jurors'. This is the so-called objective test. Gregory argued that although the note itself was not evidence of actual bias, the judge should still have discharged the jury or, at the very least, put the question to the jury as to whether they were able to continue trying the case, and able to put bias out of their minds.

The ECtHR did not agree with him. They began from the principle that it was of 'fundamental importance' that the criminal courts maintain the confidence of the public, and to this end it was necessary to ensure that they were 'impartial' decision-makers.[119] This returns, in part, to the *Pellar* case,[120] which linked the lack of partiality to the fundamental Article 6 guarantee of a trial before an independent and impartial tribunal. In *Gregory*, the court held that the rule that maintained the secrecy of jury deliberations was 'crucial and legitimate'[121] to the operation of common law courts, as it guaranteed 'open and frank deliberations among the jurors'.[122] They then distinguished Gregory's case from another important authority, *Remli v. France*.[123] In *Remli*, the judge had not taken any action when a member of the jury had been overheard saying that he was a racist. The ambiguous nature of the note that the judge received in *Gregory* meant that the judge's actions were reasonable.

The dissent of Judge Voegel is interesting, as it suggests one way in which the law could respond to racism in the jury. He pointed out that as the jury is 'the ultimate arbiter of the facts of a case'[124] it is of paramount importance that jurors are made aware of the problem of bias especially as no warning or training is given, and their personal experiences may be a poor substitute for a more structured approach. He argued that, in these circumstances, a speech from a judge would not 'dispel racial prejudice'[125] and the only real remedy would have been to discharge part of the jury or to conduct a more thorough investigation into the note itself. This was not possible because of the rule on jury secrecy.

---

117 Ibid., para 9.
118 *R. v. Gough*
119 Supra n. 116, (1993) A.C. 646, at para 49.
120 *Pellar v. UK* (1996) 22 EHRR 391, at para 32.
121 Supra n. 116, at para 44.
122 Ibid.
123 *Remli v. France* 22 EHRR 253.
124 Supra n. 116, para 18.
125 Ibid., para 40.

We could thus suggest that the law is more properly stated by the dissenting judgment in *Gregory*. Does this suggest that, as Gregory's case was distinguished in *Sander* v. *UK*,[126] this latter case is a more desirable statement of the law? Sander had been convicted of conspiracy to defraud but his trial was adjourned because the judge received a complaint from one of the jurors that two other members of the jury had been making racist comments. The judge then received a letter from one of the jurors apologising and a letter from the jury as a whole denying racial prejudice. Rather than discharging the jury, the judge chose to redirect them. The applicant argued that this was a fundamental error that deprived him of a fair trial. As there was a real danger of bias, the jury should have been discharged.

The ECtHR argued that there had been a breach of Article 6. Following *Piersack* v. *Belgium*,[127] the court held that the impartiality of the decision-maker must be presumed until there is evidence to the contrary and, on these facts, there was evidence that the jury was racially biased. The judge was not sure that there was not actual bias in the jury, and should have made further investigations. On these facts, the applicant had not received a fair trial. What seems central to the reasoning of the court is that the judge 'had both been informed of a serious allegation and received an indirect admission that racist remarks had been made'.[128] In such a situation, the judge should have discharged the jury. It would appear that the distinction between *Gregory* and *Sander* is one of differences of fact. Indeed, we cannot expect a clear statement of the need to reform the jury from the ECtHR because, given the role and function of the court, it would not take the lead on the issue in such a way. The matter is nuanced. The secrecy rule is not clearly in breach of Article 6. If jury reform is necessary, then it would be up to the English courts to articulate the way forward. In our reading of *R.* v. *Mirza*[129] we show that this matter has been firmly taken off the agenda.

In *Mirza*, the House of Lords affirmed the centrality of the secrecy rule to the workings of the jury, even if this meant that the partiality of the jury could not be examined:

> The general common law rule was that the court would not investigate, or receive evidence about, anything said in the course of the jury's deliberations while they were considering their verdict in their retiring room. Attempts to soften the rule to serve the interests of those who claimed that they were unfairly convicted should be resisted in the general public interest, if jurors were to continue to perform their vital function of safeguarding the liberty of every individual.[130]

Why, then, is there such a commitment to jury secrecy? What role does it play in the criminal trial? There is a useful consideration of the underlying rationale of the rule in the Canadian of case of *R.* v. *Pan*[131] Secrecy allows jurors to consider the aspects of

---

126   *Sander* v. *United Kingdom*, 9 May 2000.
127   *Piersack* v. *Belgium*, 1 October 1982, Series A no. 53, para 30.
128   Supra n. 117, at para 39.
129   Ibid.
130   Ibid., H5.
131   *R.* v. *Pan* [2001] 2 SCR 344.

the case 'without fear of exposure to public ridicule, contempt or hatred'.[132] The virtue of secrecy is that it also allows the jurors a degree of protection from 'harassment' and 'reprisals', an important consideration in the criminal trial.[133] Furthermore, as the case might concern an 'unpopular accused' or someone 'charged with a particularly repulsive crime', this requirement protects the integrity of the decision-making process.[134] Most importantly, though, this has to be taken on faith. Arbour J simply asserts that it is 'sound' and does not need any further justification. The second rationale stresses the 'finality' of the jury's verdict. This is perhaps less convincing in a legal system that allows appeals and reviews of decisions, and should not perhaps 'trump' other due process values.[135]

In *Mirza*, Lord Slynn described the other safeguards that protected both the composition and the integrity of the jury. The principle of random selection means that it is composed of a cross-section of the population who are acting on oath. As far as the operation of the jury in the court is concerned, the fact that the judge gives directions allows irregularities to be dealt with effectively, as does the possibility of an appeal. Indeed, the cases of bias and 'improper behaviour'[136] show the system is sensitive to these matters and that they do come to light. Of course, there are exceptions to the secrecy rule. These exceptions relate to those instances when the jury is allegedly affected by 'extraneous influences'[137] (although this was not an issue in the present case). Another problem was also considered: if it was alleged that 'the jury as a whole declined to deliberate at all, but decided the case by other means such as drawing lots or by the toss of a coin'[138] then the court would intervene, as such behaviour would 'amount to a complete repudiation by the jury of their only function which, as the juror's oath put it, was to give a true verdict according to the evidence'.[139] The exceptions do not compel the conclusion that there is any profound need to reform jury practices, and that any problems cannot be dealt with by the existing law.

Lord Hobhouse pointed out that since section 17 of the Juries Act 1974 (which requires majority, rather than unanimous verdicts) there will always be situations where the views of one or two jurors have not been followed. While this may be a 'fertile scenario for a dissident juror',[140] the system itself contains sufficient checks to guarantee the legitimacy of the result. Besides, without definite evidence of 'actual bias', the bias of an individual cannot affect the decision. Furthermore, the trial judge supervises the trial and can give jurors directions and guidance; prejudicial evidence can be excluded. Most importantly, the jury trial represents a particularly common law approach to human rights;[141] 'a bastion of the criminal justice system against domination of the state and a safeguard of the liberty of its citizens'. While this does indeed stress the foundational

---

132 Supra n. 117, at para 114.
133 Ibid.
134 Ibid.
135 Ibid.
136 Ibid., para 50.
137 Ibid., para 102.
138 Ibid., H 55.
139 Ibid., para 123.
140 Ibid., para 135.
141 Ibid., para 144.

values of due process, it is interesting that Lord Hobhouse distinguishes the jury system in the US, with its 'very thorough and public procedure of jury vetting which precedes the empanelling of the jury' and allows 'an investigation of their prejudices' from that of the UK.[142] He appears to be arguing that the US approach is not necessary; if the confidentiality rule was rejected there would be 'no stopping point in the other changes which would consequentially have to be made short of introducing a full-blown pre-trial procedure of jury vetting in order to maintain an acceptable minimum level of finality and public confidence in the jury verdict'.

Perhaps we can leave the last word to Lord Slynn:

> it is difficult to see how it would promote public confidence in the criminal justice system for the public to be informed that our appellate courts observe a self denying rule never to admit evidence of the deliberations of a jury even if such evidence strongly suggests that the jury was not impartial. In cases where there is cogent evidence demonstrating a real risk that the jury was not impartial and that the general confidence in jury verdicts was in the particular case ill reposed, what possible public interest can there be in maintaining a dubious conviction?[143]

Lord Hobhouse's approach suggests that there is a failure to appreciate the nature of racism. As it is a social problem and an issue of people's prejudices, arguments about the jury as a defence against the state miss the point. Likewise, arguments stressing the liberty of the individual do not necessarily deal with racism. A defendant who alleges jury bias is not making an argument about liberty, but about distorted perceptions that make objective judgments impossible.

CONCLUSION

This chapter has discussed the tensions that exist between defence- and prosecution-orientated principles in criminal procedure. Rather than cover criminal procedure in its entirety, we have focused on certain pre-trial and criminal evidence issues. We have shown that while the principles in these areas can be analysed in terms of human rights, there is also the sense in which they are immanent to the common law. Their status and development owe more to the 'logic' of the common law than to the European Convention. The case law of the ECtHR shows that although there have been instances in which common law fell short of international standards of due process, it is broadly coherent with Articles 5 and 6. However, there are also critical voices, most notably that of Lord Slynn in *Mirza*. It would be far too complacent to think that there are no problems with common law institutions, particularly in the light of the institutional racism that remains a persistent problem in criminal justice.

---

142 Ibid.
143 Ibid., para 16.

16

THE POLITICS OF REPRESENTATION: LEGAL AID, HUMAN RIGHTS AND ACCESS TO JUSTICE

INTRODUCTION

This chapter will consider legal aid reform within the broader context of access to justice and human rights. It is necessary to think through the connections between these terms, because legal aid reform should not simply be seen as an exercise in economics. Although legal aid policy is driven by the need to control costs and achieve value for money, there are also ways in which it is influenced by concepts of access to justice, and arguments drawn from both European human rights law, and those elements of EU law that are congruent. While legal aid provision remains thoroughly within the hands of the nation state, any sensible assessment must also take into account the influence of these bodies of law.

There is a detailed history of the term 'access to justice'. We will define it as 'equality of access to law and legal services'.[1] In order to analyse the term, we will make use of the analytical distinction between formal and economic access. It is worth remembering that the range of the term extends far beyond its use in the government White Paper, *Modernising Justice*, or Lord Woolf's report into civil justice. Indeed, the concept of access to justice has to be seen as contested and open to political debate. This is why we will be examining ideas of access that come from sources that are often distinct from, and even in opposition to, the ideology of the present government's reforms.

Why should it be necessary to make these points? At stake is a vision of law, and how it should operate. As Le Sueur points out:

> Radical legal and political theorists question what, if any, value can be attached to the formal equality conferred on people by the courtroom – it is the real thing which should matter, they say. Pretending to be equal only helps disguise where real power lies; a fair hearing in court of a repossession action cannot alter the fact that in our society landlords and building societies are powerful institutions, and tenants and borrowers are not.[2]

The position developed in this chapter is that access to justice must be understood as more than a pretence. It thus relates to the arguments that we made in Chapter 12.

---

1 Jacob (1987: 277) cited in Andrews (2003: 221).
2 Le Sueur (2000).

Access to justice is a doctrine that affirms that the courts should allow citizens to protect their rights against powerful bodies. Democratic politics requires that the courts operate against the powerful. If necessary, the state should provide the means for this holding to account to take place. While this may be a political vision out of step with government policy, it provides a principled means of developing a 'thick' notion of access to justice as an element of democratic politics.

A SHORT HISTORY OF LEGAL AID

> Legal aid is ... an expensive, open ended, social service, whose demand led budgetary needs are hard to forecast and create a steady drain on government funds. To policy makers, legal aid may seem a second order need ... certainly secondary to the right of minimum existence which underlies social assistance; or the highly prized 'right' to health care which heads the popular list of human rights in the UK; less productive than services such as education or housing.[3]

This paragraph describes the fundamental dilemma of legal aid, at least from the perspective of government. Since 1945, legal aid policy has been driven by the need to control the costs of a potentially open-ended service, and to ensure that other areas of the welfare state receive their fair share of government funds. Indeed, compared to the need to fund welfare services such as housing, health and education, legal aid appears somewhat secondary. However, the politics of the post-war period are marked by a broad consensus that the welfare state is to be supported by central government. The crucial question is how this support is to be provided. The financing of public services has become a matter of fierce debate. Are these to be provided by general taxation or by privatised, profit-driven organisations? The period of Conservative administration from 1979 to 1994, and of Labour government from 1994 to the time of writing shows that a market model for the provision of social services commands government policy. While bitter arguments have taken place over the appropriateness of the delivery of public services through either private or market mechanisms, it would probably be fair to say that, while the state continues to provide some financial resources, there is continued government commitment to private delivery of welfare services.

However, lest it seem that the only issue in this area is that of privatisation, we need to review some other key concerns. Arguments as to why legal aid proved to be prohibitively expensive are necessarily contentious. Indeed, there would be some who argue that, given the political will, funds could be centrally provided for the adequate funding of welfare and legal aid, and that too much has been 'surrendered' to market-orientated reforms. While these arguments can be convincing, there are other factors that we need to take into account. The model of legal provision in the UK has been that of lawyers in private practice.[4] Arguably this is, in itself, an expensive way of employing

---
3 Carol Harlow, 'Access to justice as a human right', in Alston (1999: 189).
4 There is a variation on this argument that would link the costs of legal aid to the adversarial system, which places the onus on the parties to prepare the case, rather than the judge. This, it is suggested, drives up the cost of legal aid. Blankenburg notes this argument, but also indicates that it is not the sole factor in the costs of litigation. See Blankenburg (1995).

lawyers, and had there been more extensive experiments with law centres and salaried legal services, a solution to the rising costs of legal aid might have been discovered earlier on. The hold of the model of private employment perhaps owes something to institutional inertia, and something to the lobbying power of the Law Society and the Bar Council, who have been able to use their influence to preserve this pattern of legal employment. A second and perhaps equally important factor to take into account is the way in which lawyer's bills are calculated 'after the event'. Some have suggested that this has created inappropriate financial incentives, and has never encouraged lawyers to control the costs of their cases.

Social and economic factors also have to be taken into account, in particular because law, and indeed litigation, tend to be responsive to broader social and economic patterns. Goriely[5] has argued that legal aid was primarily driven by the rising divorce rate after the Second World War.[6] While it would be difficult to speculate as to why this took place, it did produce a great demand for legal services. Likewise, the periods of economic depression, and the associated patterns of social breakdown that they created, impacted on the need for different kinds of litigation. It may also be the case that lawyers do not manage their own time well.[7] However, we also need to take into account the broader politics of legal aid. While legal aid has never perhaps had the same popular support as the National Health Service, there has always been an element of both popular and governmental support for legal aid. The ongoing commitment to criminal legal aid in particular represents an acknowledgement that it would be problematic to have no provision for those facing the threat of criminal sanction.

There are, of course, different ways of providing criminal legal aid, and more or less minimal and maximal models of provision. However, criminal legal aid remains an important element of a criminal justice system that retains a commitment to due process values. These arguments might be more difficult to make in relation to civil legal aid, but the point is that the complete abolition of legal aid has never been seriously on the political agenda. Critics would point out that the present legal aid system has led to such restrictions in legal aid provision, that there is a de facto 'abolition' as legally aided lawyers cannot be found to do certain kinds of work.[8] While this may be an unintended consequence of government policy, only a conspiracy theorist would argue that the real intent is to destroy the legal aid system.

---

5   Goriely (1994).
6   Ibid.
7   Modernising Justice (1998) (CM 4155, 1998, para 1.4: '[I]n many instances, the assumptions and working practices of the legal profession, taken as a whole, are outdated and inefficient. The taxpayer often meets the cost of that inefficiency. So the Government's proposals present a challenge to the profession: to adapt to a modern and rapidly-changing society, in order to provide a better service, and better justice, for the public'.
8   LAG asserts that 'in practice, certain people may have no option at all as to who advises and represents them – and indeed may be very lucky to find anyone at all who is willing to take their case' (LAG: The Future of Publicly Funded Legal Services, 2004: 16). These findings are supported by the NAO report 2002–3: the number of solicitor firms providing specialist services has dropped, but this is, to some extent, offset by a rise of service providers in the not-for-profit sector, which now accounts for around 8 per cent of the 'total supplier base'. Since the introduction of new contracting arrangements, there has been a decline in the number of solicitor firms providing legal aid services from 4,866 in January 2000 to 4,427 by July 2002. However, the number of not-for-profit firms providing services has risen from 344 to 402 over the same period. (National Audit Office Press Release, 22 March 2004 http//www.nao.org.uk).

We can also introduce another point at this stage. The Labour governments from 1994 to the time of writing have shown a commitment to social reform. While, as we will see, this can be linked to human rights, it is also free standing. Access to justice is part of a broader commitment to equality of opportunity, and these ideas do inform present government thinking, whether or not they are successfully achieved. Legal aid reform is thus not entirely motivated by cost and efficiency, although these requirements do provide the dominant values. The real debate would be over the extent to which social reform, and hence the reform of legal aid, is compatible with the reliance on market mechanisms. There is no easy answer to this question, but it is worth pointing out that the last 12 years of British politics have been presided over by a party that (at least once) described itself as socialist.

CONCEPTS OF ACCESS TO JUSTICE

Access to justice can be analysed as having formal and economic aspects. Formal access is defined as 'the various checks and controls which ensure that cases are technically sound, or within the court's jurisdiction ... these restrictions ... are formal [as] they are independent of the litigant's financial capacity to meet the costs of litigation'.[9] Economic access is perhaps more difficult to define. Definitions tend to stress the requirement that the legal system is efficient or effective. In this chapter, economic access will be defined by the dominant government discourse on the reform of legal aid; a discourse not simply about funding, but also about the appropriateness of the bodies that have dispute-resolving functions.[10] These terms are useful in identifying aspects of the problem, but the distinction between formal and economic aspects is not as hard and fast as it may seem. Indeed, the concept of access to justice requires that the formal and the economic be brought together. Let us consider the government's definition of access to justice:

> 'Access to justice' means that, when people do need help, there are effective solutions that are proportionate to the issues at stake. In some circumstances, this will involve going to court; but in others, that will not be necessary. Someone charged with a criminal offence should have access to proper legal advice and representation, when the interests of justice require it. But in civil matters, for most people, most of the time, going to court is, and should be, the last resort. It is in no-one's interest to create a litigious society. People must make responsible choices about whether a case is worth pursuing; whether to proceed by negotiation, court action, or in some other way; and how far to take a relatively minor issue.[11]

The argument begins with a statement about proportionality. This brings together arguments about economy and formal legal mechanisms. Access to justice means making the right choice about the proportionate relationship of means and ends. An effective

---
9 See Andrews (2003: 216).
10 There is, of course, more to economic access than the funding of legal aid. It would also cover the funding of the courts themselves, and thus the broader reforms in civil and criminal justice.
11 Supra n. 7, at 1.10.

legal system is one where the way in which the means of dispute resolution bears a relationship to both the remedy awarded. To take a rather simplistic example: it would be inefficient to require the High Court to deal with disputes over parking tickets. In civil law, efficiency as a concept of access requires[12] that people do not use the courts. This is peculiar for a number of reasons, but we will return to this argument below.[13] We need to deal with a more embracing concern. How is the broader philosophy of access defended in the White Paper?

In *Modernising Justice*, access to justice is placed within a context of legal reform that returns to 'first principles'.[14] The legal system allows people to enforce their rights and to 'protect' society from crime.[15] The legal system is thus one of the key foundations for 'peaceful social and economic activity'.[16] This function of law is specifically linked to the efficiency of the system. A peaceful and cooperative society requires an efficient legal system 'because [people] know that rights and obligations can ultimately be enforced; this in turn means that relatively few people should actually need to use the courts'.[17] This is an interesting statement, but it is not backed up with any evidence. Indeed, it seems to be based on a rather strange way of indicating the efficiency of a system: the small numbers of people actually making use of it. One might think that the efficiency of the legal system would be better measured by some indication of the time it took to resolve the disputes that were submitted to the courts. How could it be possible to measure the number of people who were not using the courts?

This returns us to the argument that we studied above. It is worth noting that access is seen as essentially a failure of the system to respond to the needs of the middle classes. The civil law is not efficient because costs limit the use of the courts to a small portion of society who can afford to litigate, and even then, litigation costs are 'unpredictable'. The very poor may qualify for legal aid, but the vast majority, composed of neither the very rich nor the very poor, feel 'unable to turn to the law for assistance and remedies'. The conclusion is that the 'remedies sought ... are often disproportionate to the issue at stake'.[18] While this may undoubtedly have been one of the problems of the legal system, it is interesting that it takes such a privileged position in the argument. It clearly links to an agenda that pushes alternative dispute resolution (ADR) as a way of resolving disputes that does not require the use of court resources, but it also links to the more basic argument that any resolution to the problems of the system is not going to be based on making more money available:

> The affordability of legal services is also important for the Government, which funds legal aid and the courts. It is in the interest of both taxpayers and those who use publicly-funded services that these services should be the highest possible quality at the best possible price.[19]

---

12   See supra n. 9, at 206. Andrews describes this as 'Orwellian double think'.
13   There is no evidence to suggest a link between the availability of legal aid and the volume of litigation.
14   Supra n. 7, at 1.6.
15   This privileges one of the values of criminal justice; we cannot let this distract us here.
16   Supra n. 7, at 1.4.
17   Ibid.
18   Ibid., 1.7.
19   Ibid., 1.8.

It could perhaps be safely stated that access to justice, as a plank of the policy of the Labour government is primarily an economic concept. This is apparent from the concern with giving the 'taxpayer' the best possible service. Any 'significant increase in access to justice'[20] is thus entirely subordinate to this primary goal. How is this potential contradiction between 'quality' and 'price' to be resolved?

It is necessary to rethink the centrality of law, courts and lawyers for dispute resolution. As far as the provision of legal services is concerned policy will be driven by providing a 'range of different services'.[21] Rather than rush to a lawyer, people will be encouraged to seek advice from a 'voluntary agency',[22] and then to make use of different mechanisms. Mediation or negotiated settlements would thus replace the need to make use of legal representation in court. By being 'less formal and adversarial' they can 'allow disputes to be resolved more quickly and cheaply'. We can thus appreciate that a formal requirement, that a dispute be resolved through ADR, connects with an economic argument that this is the best use of legal resources.

Access to justice thus goes further than a redesign of the courts. It means root and branch reform of the legal profession itself. These reforms are also driven by a very specific agenda. Efficiency is to be provided by 'market mechanisms':

> The Government therefore intends to remove unjustified restrictive practices, and encourage greater competition ... We will fundamentally reform the legal aid scheme: contracts will define quality standards, encourage greater efficiency, and require lawyers to compete for work. This will mean better value for the taxpayers' money, and a better service for people who use the scheme.[23]

Reshaping the legal profession began with the Courts and Legal Services Act 1990. This statute ended the solicitors' monopoly on conveyancing and the bars on representation in the higher courts. These 'restrictive practices' limited healthy competition and competition is 'good' because it drives down prices. However, this is not simply leaving regulation of the profession to the market. The most competitive way of doing legal work would be to cover the greatest volume of work at maximum profit. The market therefore has to be shaped by quality stipulations. This is part of a coherent policy vision:

> The justice system is top heavy – it is dominated by lawyers, courts, and outdated legal practices and jargon. The Government will refocus legal aid spending on social welfare cases, and expand the role of voluntary advice agencies, so helping to correct this imbalance.[24]

Behind the rhetoric of this claim lurks one of the fundamental problems of this approach to formal/economic access. If the primary driver is cost, then there is the risk that the 'voluntary sector' will be relied upon to deliver services that would be

---

20 Ibid., 1.9.
21 Ibid., 1.16.
22 Ibid., 1.19.
23 Ibid.
24 Ibid., 1.18.

more appropriately provided by lawyers. Thus, the commitment to 'refocus legal aid spending on social welfare cases' may conceal the desire to remove this sort of case from the courts, and from the state's obligation to provide legal services, rather than merely supporting volunteers.

Any human rights considerations are more or less driven by the prevailing argument about cost. Thus, the justification for the Human Rights Act is as follows:

> It does not serve access to justice if someone has to go to a higher tier of court – likely to be less accessible and more expensive – than is necessary to deal properly with his or her case.[25]

If the HRA represents a 'radical extension of the jurisdiction of the courts in the UK'[26] it is because people no longer have to endure the costs of taking a case to Strasbourg. Once again, we can appreciate that formal and economic factors come together in defining both the need to domesticate the Convention and to redefine the jurisdiction of the courts vis-à-vis the ECtHR. Can human rights be restricted to this concept of efficiency? It is undoubtedly a benefit that litigants can now rely on Convention rights in UK courts, but it would be hard to understand the impact of the HRA merely through this optic. The HRA has invigorated democratic politics to the extent that it is redefining the relationship between the executive and the judiciary around concepts of rights and their application to social and economic life. When we look at the right to representation, we will see that there is a far more problematic relationship between notions of representation, the rule of law and access to the courts than the thinking of the government in *Modernising Justice* might allow.

ACCESS TO JUSTICE AND THE CARTER REVIEW

The best way of understanding the present impact of these broader political patterns on legal aid provision is to examine the recent Carter Review. The Carter Review opens with some broad statements of the problem, and the principles that will be used to resolve it:

> the steady increase in spending on legal aid in recent years is unsustainable. The overall budget has increased by £500 million since 1997 alone to £2 billion last year, and the steep rise in criminal legal aid is putting severe pressure on what is available to fund civil and family legal aid.[27]

These concerns can be traced back, at least in recent years, to the Middleton Review of 1997 which showed that the problem was an increase in legal aid expenditure without any concomitant improvement of efficiency. Prior to Middleton, there had been ad hoc attempts to achieve reform. The legal aid budget had been 'capped' and standard

---

25 Ibid., 1.21.
26 Ibid., 1.22.
27 'Legal Aid: a Market-based Approach to Reform', Lord Carter's Review of Legal Aid Procurement, July 2006, available at http://www.legalaidprocurementreview.gov.uk/publications.htm.

fees introduced. In the area of civil legal aid, the Courts and Legal Services Act 1990 introduced conditional fee arrangement in an attempt to displace the costs of funding of legal aid onto the insurance industry and litigants themselves.

Middleton's recommendations also moved in the direction of centralisation. The review's key proposal was the need for a central body to fund and coordinate the delivery of legal aid. This body would replace the Legal Aid Board, which played an essentially passive role. If the central body itself purchased the services of lawyers, then, so the argument ran, there would be the benefit of economics of scale, and also a greater degree of control over the work that was being funded. Moreover, because the central body controlled funding, an element of competition could be introduced into the system, which would mean that lawyers would have to compete with each other to provide the best value for money. These ideas fed into the Access to Justice Act 1999.

The Access to Justice Act 1999 created the Legal Services Commission (LSC) which was charged with establishing, maintaining and developing a Community Legal Service and a Criminal Defence Service (CDS). Funding decisions by the LSC were to be based on two main principles: planning and contracting. While the former would allow a sensitive allocation of resources, the latter would enable the imposition of quality standards and the achievement of value for money. The CDS scheme replaced the old criminal legal aid system. It now covers representation in court and advice and assistance for suspects being questioned by the police. The CDS was also founded on the principle of contracting, and the creation of a system of salaried defenders who would work alongside lawyers in private practice.

The Carter Review draws attention to the need to continue reforming legal aid:

> It is clear to us that the fairest and most sensible way forward is to move towards a market-based approach which rewards efficient firms providing a quality service at the best value to the taxpayer. We recognise however that to secure a thriving and sustainable supply base, change needs to be implemented in a phased way over a three-year period.[28]

Carter's fundamental proposal is to move away from the present way in which fees are assessed and paid at hourly rates, to a system based on competitive tendering for block contracts of work. Competition would effectively determine the rates that the LSC would pay.[29] Note in the passage above the objectives that the review sets out: how best to ensure access to justice and how to deliver greater value for money. The tension between these two ideas is resolved by a very clear statement of the over-riding objective: to 'secur[e] ... value for money without compromising quality and access to legal advice'.[30] The review argued that costs increased because of 'systemic weaknesses in the way legal aid services are procured and therefore inefficiencies in the way those services are delivered'.[31] In other words, legal aid policy attempts to square efficiency and access to justice within a model of the delivery of public services largely determined

---

28 Ibid., chapter 4, para 5.
29 Select Committee on Constitutional Affairs, Third Report, para 10 at http://www.publications.parliament.uk/pa/cm200607/cmselect/cmconst/223/22304.htm#a2.
30 Supra n. 27, at para 35.
31 Ibid., para 6.

by the politics of the free market. After Carter, funding legal services will no longer be based on payments for hourly rates, but on the basis of 'best value tendering' – best value being understood as a relationship of 'quality, capacity and price'.[32]

ASSESSING LEGAL AID REFORM

Can we assess the balance between the access to justice agenda, and the drive for efficiency in the wake of the Carter Report? The key criticisms were made by the chairman of the Parliamentary Select Committee on Constitutional Affairs. Commenting on the finding of the Committee, he framed his argument in terms of access to justice:

> It is important that experienced professionals are prepared to stay in the field providing Legal Aid services for the most vulnerable members of society, such as individuals with mental health problems or children.[33]

What has been the impact of the market-driven reforms? Recently published research suggests that the reforms have had a largely negative impact on legal aid suppliers.[34] The overall impression is of an increasingly shrinking number of solicitors' firms who are willing to take on legal aid work.[35] In some areas, there are simply no firms willing to take on legal aid work at all.[36] In the area of family law, there is evidence that fewer contracts are being awarded and fewer cases are being begun. Solicitors' firms have begun giving up family law work because of the administrative burden of applying for contracts, poor rates of remuneration and problems both retaining and recruiting sufficiently qualified staff.[37] Similar patterns have been observed in mental health work. There are now 25 per cent fewer firms offering advice and representation in this area, while those requiring their services have grown by 10 per cent since 2000. Evidence from reports presented to the LSC suggest that criminal legal aid firms operate 'on the edge of their profitability'. There is concern that this retreat from legal aid work may become more pronounced when Carter's recommendations are implemented.[38]

---

32 Ibid.
33 Alan Beith MP: http://www.accesstojusticealliance.org.uk/PN22LegalAidReformonpublication.doc.
34 However, one of the major problems in this area is the lack of data. The Parliamentary Select Committee were critical of the way in which the LSC performed its 'statistical research' into costs (supra n. 19, at para 127) and the lack of significant data about legal aid suppliers (supra n. 29, at para 128).
35 Supra n. 29, at para 39. There were 4,854 firms with civil contracts in 2001, 3,632 by March 2006. This is a decline of about 25 per cent. There has been a 10 per cent decline in the number of firms holding criminal legal aid certificates from 2001–2006.
36 The Select Committee quote the Director of the Advice Services Alliance, Richard Jenner. He stated that 'provision in social welfare law (including housing, debt, welfare benefits and community care) [are] patchy in different areas of the country and in some areas even "fairly poor"'.
37 Supra n. 29. Two senior legal aid solicitors informed the Select Committee they had to 'turn away between 20% and 75% of family cases ... and 40–50% of those approaching the firm for advice in social welfare law'.
38 This would also find some support with the earlier concerns of the National Audit Office report on the Community Legal Service and the Introduction of Contracting (Report by the Comptroller and Auditor General, HC 89 2002–2003): 'Since the introduction of new contracting arrangements, there has been a decline in the number of solicitor firms providing legal aid services from 4,866 in January 2000 to 4,427 by July 2002. However, the number of not-for-profit firms providing services has risen from 344 to 402 over the same period. The reduction in the

Legal aid reforms have not solved the problem of legal fees. Research from the University of Manchester suggests that when criminal legal aid fixed fees were introduced in Scotland in 1999, legal aid firms increased the number of cases that they took, but decreased the number of interviews with prosecution witnesses for each client. The research predicted that there would be a similar impact on criminal legal aid work in England.[39] Although, as pointed out above, there are attempts to oversee and control the quality of work done by legal aid practitioners, there are doubts over whether the system of 'peer review' would identify the problems identified in Scotland, and the 'reliance' on 'case volume' as a 'precondition for adequate remuneration for legal aid work'[40] exacerbates the inbuilt encouragement to achieve volume, rather than quality of work.[41]

This can be linked to a broader set of criticisms about the general failure to make use of standards that are relevant to access to justice. The LSC uses contracts to determine and police standard requirements. This represents a move on from the franchise model, which was still based on the Law Society as the guarantor of standards. The LSC makes reference to the Legal Aid Franchise Quality Standard (LAFQAS). However, LAFQAS are limited because they cannot be used to assess whether the correct advice was given or the correct legal strategy pursued. This can be evidenced by the fact that certain immigration firms were awarded contracts, but showed themselves incapable of doing the work to the correct standards. It is thought that there are similar problems with the audit procedures in assessing criminal contracts.[42] Ways of assessing quality need to be completely revised. The fundamental problem is that the LSC should not be in the position where it assesses quality and awards contracts, as there is too great a potential for the development of conflicts of interest between these two roles. The risk is also that quality standards will ultimately be determined by those who control budgets. This means that the predominant criteria will always refer to efficient resource management, rather than the best interests of those who rely on legal aid to seek remedies.[43]

The 1999 reforms have certainly led to a growth in the voluntary, or not-for-profit sector (NfP).[44] The Community Legal Services Partnerships (CLSPs), begun

---

supplier base is partly a deliberate move away from reliance on a large number of generalist support firms towards a smaller number of specialist quality-assured providers. However, the reduction also reflects concern among some firms about the level of remuneration offered on civil legal aid work. The Commission has identified gaps in provision in some parts of the country, particularly in rural areas, and in some areas of law, for example family law, but has had some success in attracting suppliers to immigration work'. Executive summary at http://www.nao.org.uk/pn/02-03/020389.htm.

39   Ibid., quoting Professor Frank Skinner.
40   Ibid., para 68.
41   Ibid., para 106 contains a stark warning about the parlous state of criminal legal aid: 'In the light of the current economic fragility of the criminal legal aid supplier base, these planned reductions in income for criminal defence practitioners may prove to be unsustainable. It remains unclear whether criminal legal aid lawyers have the capacity to absorb such rate cuts by changing their working practices or through business restructuring, especially in the short time of the transitional period'.
42   Bridges (2000).
43   Karen Mackay.
44   LSC Annual Report 2005/6, p. 28: 32 per cent of Legal Help expenditure and 68 per cent of expenditure in social welfare law. Contracts for immigration advice and social welfare work stand at £95 million. At http://www.legalservices.gov.uk/docs/about_us_main/56543TSOLegalServicesRpt_WEB.pdf.

in April 2000, are aimed at allowing grassroots input into planning the provision of legal services. CLSPs bring together local authorities, charities, local lawyers and advice groups and are meant to identify legal needs at the local level, and communicate this to the Regional Legal Services Committees. CLSPs interface with the Regional Legal Services Committees. These committees are charged with determining 'bid zones', which reflect regional requirements for legal services. However, the Commission and its activities are themselves expensive; it is estimated that the planning initiatives cost £2.8 million.[45]

The reforms have made for significant changes in the provision of legal aid. In the areas of 'debt and welfare benefits' NfPs now hold 60 per cent of civil legal aid contracts.[46] The Carter Review was critical of the way in which NfPs were paid under existing arrangements, as they did encourage 'effective working' and proposed certain technical changes to systems of remuneration.[47] There are concerns that the new payments system will not cover the costs that NfPs have to bear, particularly as they deal with a high percentage of clients with 'disability, medical, health or psychological problems'.[48] The Director of the Advice Services Alliance expressed his concern that NfPs were effectively being under-funded and being treated as a cheap way of doing work that would be more effectively done by specialist solicitors.[49]

Criticisms could also be made of the government's belief that legal aid reforms have created a 'seamless referral network'[50] where different assistance agencies and lawyers' firms provide a coordinated field of advice and representation. While we should not reject the notion of a 'mixed economy' of legal provision, there are certain unresolved problems. If choice is one of the policy objectives of legal aid reforms, then it is a matter of concern that provision of services in certain areas has actually decreased. Legal Action Group (LAG) asserts that 'in practice, certain people may have no option at all as to who advises and represents them – and indeed may be very lucky to find anyone at all who is willing to take their case'.[51]

Government reforms can also be criticised as creating undemocratic and non-transparent bodies. It is important to bear these points in mind, as our broad concern is with the democratic culture of legal aid. Consider the LSC. As there is little scrutiny by an outside body, it is not satisfactory that it should retain control of such a large legal aid budget. In particular, there is a risk of conflict of interest between the role of the LSC in awarding contracts, fixing contract prices and monitoring those contracts. There is a need for a body to oversee the LSC. The principle that should inform the operation of the LSC is 'independence from local and central government'.[52] These criticisms can

---

45   LSC annual report, quoted by Goriely (2001). There are other innovations: legal aid firms should make use of government proposals to set up 'community interest companies' (CICs). CICs 'will be a new type of company, designed for social enterprises that want to use their profits and assets for the public good' (LAG: The Future of Publicly Funded Legal Services [London: LAG] 2003, p. 16/17). This would also allow more flexibility to agencies who have traditionally been reliant on grants to fund their operations.
46   Supra, n. 8. The Future of Publicly Funded Legal Services, at 95.
47   Ibid.
48   Ibid., para 97.
49   Ibid., para 99.
50   Ibid., p. 17.
51   Ibid., p. 16.
52   LAG argues that there should be an overseeing 'a body at arm's length from the Commission' (ibid., p. 3/4).

also apply to the giving of advice by government departments. Once again there is a potential conflict of interest if providers of services are also providing help and advice in relation to those services. Advice should be provided by an independent and impartial third party.

THE ECHR AND THE RIGHT TO REPRESENTATION

> Everyone charged with a criminal offence has the following minimum rights: … (c) to defend himself in person or through legal assistance of his own choosing or, if he has not the sufficient means to pay for legal assistance, to be given it free when the interests of justice so require.

It might seem somewhat strange to argue that Article 6 does not actually guarantee a right of access to the courts. However, if one carefully reads the first sentence, then it is clear that these words are never used. Moreover, it would be entirely possible to interpret the argument as applying to civil rights and obligations, or criminal charges that are already 'sub judice', or already under consideration by the court. These issues were considered in *Golder* v. *UK*,[53] which is a central authority on the 'reach' of the right to representation in Article 6.

The British government sought to impress upon the ECtHR a narrow interpretation of Article 6, in order to limit its effectiveness. The ECtHR resisted this interpretation, and linked a broad interpretation of the Article to the concept of the rule of law. Argument focused on the preamble to the Convention. The rule of law is linked to 'the common heritage of political traditions' of the European nations, and the need to preserve the rights 'stated in the Universal Declaration'. The British government were arguing that the wording of the preamble suggested that the Convention does not actually refer to the rule of law as one of the purposes of the treaty, but merely a 'feature of the common spiritual heritage of the member States'; it should thus be seen as somewhat 'rhetorical' and not be used to interpret ambiguities in the Treaty itself. Both the Commission and the ECtHR rejected this approach, seeing the rule of law as central to the elucidation of 6(1). As they succinctly pointed out: 'in civil matters one can scarcely conceive of the rule of law without there being a possibility of having access to the courts'.[54] Article 6, then, can be understood as stating a right of access to the courts:

> Taking all the preceding considerations together, it follows that the right of access constitutes an element which is inherent in the right stated by Article 6 para. 1. This is not an extensive interpretation forcing new obligations on the Contracting States: it is based on the very terms of the first sentence of Article 6 para. 1 read in its context and having regard to the object and purpose of the Convention and to general principles of law.[55]

---

53 *Golder* v. *UK*, 21 February 1975.
54 Ibid., para 34.
55 Ibid., para 36.

The ECtHR's approach in this paragraph is interesting. They explain that they are not creating new law. An admission that the ECtHR was so doing would weaken both the Convention and the degree to which sovereign governments would accept their human rights obligations. The right of access to the courts that underlies Article 6 is 'implicit' given the wording of the Article and its context within a Treaty dedicated to preserving the rule of law. The ECtHR went on to locate the right of access within the broader concept of a fair trial right:

> In this way the Article embodies the 'right to a court', of which the right of access, that is the right to institute proceedings before courts in civil matters, constitutes one aspect only. To this are added the guarantees laid down by Article 6 para. 1 as regards both the organisation and composition of the court, and the conduct of the proceedings. In sum, the whole makes up the right to a fair hearing.[56]

The right of access is understood as the right to 'institute' proceedings. This rejects the British government's argument that the right only applied to proceedings that had been instigated. But this is only an aspect of due process. As we have seen, due process has to be understood as relating, in both criminal and civil justice, to the composition of the court itself. Access to justice must thus be seen as an element of a much broader jurisprudence. This is not to say, however, that the right of access to the courts cannot be limited. The ECtHR drew an analogy with a ruling on the right to education contained in Article 2 of the 1952 Protocol. The right to education can be limited with respect to available resources, and access to the court must be considered in the same way. However, the important caveat is that the right must not be so limited as to 'injure the substance of the right'.[57] As far as the facts of the present case were concerned, Golder's petition to the Home Secretary for access to a solicitor should not have been refused. Golder intended to initiate legal proceedings against a prison officer, who he accused of libelling him in relation to a matter of prison discipline. The Home Secretary's own determination that Golder's case was not likely to succeed was not a valid limitation on his access to the court.

Golder can be read alongside *Airey v. Ireland*.[58] Mrs Airey was arguing that because legal aid was not available for separation proceedings, the state was effectively denying her access to court in breach of Article 6. The Court asserted that as separation proceedings concerned civil rights and obligations, Article 6 did apply. Furthermore, as judicial separation was only available in the High Court, it involved difficult issues of procedural law making it unlikely that a person could represent themselves; besides, a litigant in person would have 'an emotional involvement that is scarcely compatible with the degree of objectivity required by advocacy in court'.[59]

The Irish government attempted to refute the applicant's arguments by distinguishing the case from *Golder*. In *Golder*, a breach of Article 6 was found because of the obstacles that the Home Secretary placed in the way of the applicant's access to court.

---

56   Ibid.
57   Ibid., para 38.
58   *Airey v. Ireland*, 9 October 1979.
59   Ibid., 24.

In the instant case, Airey's inability to initiate proceedings were not a product of an act of the government, but of her own lack of financial resources for which the government could not be held responsible. The ECtHR rejected this argument in forthright terms:

> Although this difference between the facts of the two cases is certainly correct, the Court does not agree with the conclusion which the Government draw therefrom. In the first place, hindrance in fact can contravene the Convention just like a legal impediment ... Furthermore, fulfilment of a duty under the Convention on occasion necessitates some positive action on the part of the State; in such circumstances, the State cannot simply remain passive.[60]

The Irish government saw this as asserting that the Convention required a state to provide 'free legal aid', a position that the Court similarly rejected, noting that 6(3)(c provided only a qualified right. However, just because the essentially 'civil' and 'political' rights that are contained in the Convention become effectively 'social' and 'economic' rights, as they include commitments for state spending, does not mean that rights such as Article 6 must be interpreted narrowly. The court also stressed that Airey's situation could not be generalised and that any award of legal aid should not be seen as opening the floodgates, and requiring all determinations of civil rights and obligations to require free legal representation. The court found that there was a breach of 6(1).

What is the impact of this case law on the UK? We can return to the consideration of *Steel and Morris* v. *United Kingdom*.[61] The applicant's arguments focused on the denial of legal aid. The impact of this on the case is vividly illustrated by the ECtHR:

> At the time of the proceedings in question, McDonald's economic power outstripped that of many small countries (they enjoyed worldwide sales amounting to approximately 30 billion United States dollars in 1995), whereas the first applicant was a part-time bar worker earning a maximum of GBP 65 a week and the second applicant was an unwaged single parent. The inequality of arms could not have been greater.[62]

Against the financial might of McDonald's who employed one of the 'largest firms in England'[63] specialising in libel, the pro bono work of largely inexperienced barristers and solicitors would count for very little. Indeed, during the trial, the applicants bore the burden of proof in relation to the allegations that they had made. Without counsel to argue points of law, they also had to cross-examine witnesses and lacked means of paying for associated costs of photocopying and expenses for witnesses. The ECtHR sums up their problems well:

> 'All they could hope to do was keep going: on several occasions during the trial they had to seek adjournments because of physical exhaustion'.[64]

---

60   Ibid., 25.
61   *Steel and Morris* v. *United Kingdom*, 15 February 2005.
62   Ibid., para 50.
63   Ibid.
64   Ibid., para 51.

The ECtHR framed the Article 6 argument as follows. Central to the notion of the fair trial is the idea that the plaintiff or defendant should be able to present his or her case 'effectively', and that this required 'equality of arms' – in other words, that there should not be, as there was in this case, an unequal access to legal resources and representation. The legal aid scheme provided just such an equality of arms. However, whether or not legal aid was required had to be determined on the facts of each case. Important determining factors were the complexity of the issues raised, and the extent to which the applicant was able to represent him or herself.[65] This was not to say, of course, that there is an absolute right to legal aid. Any restrictions on this right, however, had to be both legitimate and proportionate. Acceptable factors included chances of success and the financial means of the person applying for legal aid. This meant that it was not necessary that 'complete equality of arms' be maintained, but what was important was that both parties to the action had a 'reasonable opportunity' to present his or her case in such conditions that one party was not at a 'substantial disadvantage' in relation to the other.[66]

On the facts of the present case, the ECtHR determined that legal assistance would have been necessary to ensure a fair trial. This was because the defendants were defending their right to freedom of expression in an action that raised many complex points of law. Moreover, the financial consequences for the applicants in losing the case were significant. Although the applicants had proved themselves to be articulate, and did receive pro bono work from lawyers, this was not sufficient to ensure a fair trial. In other words, 'the disparity between the levels of legal assistance enjoyed by the applicants and McDonald's had been so great that it must have given rise to unfairness'.[67] There was thus a breach of Article 6.

CODA: EUROPEAN COMMUNITY LAW AND THE RIGHT OF ACCESS TO THE COURT

As Harlow points out in the early years of its creation, the EU 'adopted a limited view of access to justice' as the matter was seen as falling within the competence of

---

65   See *P, C and S v. United Kingdom* [2002] 35 EHRR 31 was a case that raised an Article 6 point in relation to removal of children from the parental home. P had been convicted of offences against her son in 1995, and was found to be suffering from Munchausen's syndrome. In 1996, the relevant authorities began care proceedings against P in relation to her second child, S. The judge ordered that the child should be removed from her care. P had represented herself during the care proceedings. The applicant alleged (inter alia) to the ECHR that her rights under Article 6 had been breached, and the court accepted her arguments. The court argued that the key principle underlying the Article was fairness. Even though an individual might be able to conduct him or herself in court without representation, the question may still be asked as to whether the procedure was fair. A key issue was the seriousness of the issues at stake. Within the context of this test, it was not necessary to show that there had actually been prejudice from the failure of legal representation – such a test would be too stringent, and would deprive litigants of Article 6 protection. This decision reflects the facts of the case. At the beginning of the care proceedings, S was represented by a team of lawyers. However, they asked to be removed from the case, as S was asking them to conduct the case in an 'unreasonable manner'. The judge considered that S was capable of conducting the case in their absence, and was also acting on expert evidence that it was necessary to resolve the care issue before S's first birthday. Against these facts, the ECHR argued that both the emotive issues involved, the voluminous documentation in the case and S's own distress at the proceedings required representation in order to make the trial fair.
66   Supra n. 59, at para 62.
67   Ibid.

nation states. However, the peculiar nature of EU rights meant that there was an implicit understanding of the centrality of access to the courts as a means of creating a European legal order through 'actions brought by private parties in the courts of the Member states'.[68] As the European Court of Justice (ECJ) stated:

> By contrast with ordinary international treaties, the EEC treaty has created its own legal system which, on the entry into force of the Treaty, becomes an integral part of the legal system of the member states and which their courts are bound to apply ... the member states have limited their sovereign rights, albeit within a limited field, and have thus created a body of law which binds both their nationals and themselves.[69]

This over-arching statement of the nature of the European legal order can thus be read as an elaboration of a particular doctrine of access to the court, and hence access to justice. The EEC Treaty is distinct from other international treaties as it creates rights that become part of domestic legal systems, and which domestic courts are bound to apply. In the UK, the EC Act 1972 acknowledges this political and legal reality. The limitation of a nation's sovereign rights is thus also the concept that underpins the individual's access to European rights. In more technical terms, this is linked to the doctrine of direct effect. At its simplest, this means that a Treaty Article can be relied upon by an individual against a national government before a national court:

> The European Economic Community constitutes a new legal order of international law for the benefit of which the states have limited their sovereign rights, albeit within limited fields, and the subjects of which comprise not only the member states but also their nationals.
>
> Independently of the legislation of member states, community law not only imposes obligations on individuals but is also intended to confer upon them rights which become part of their legal heritage. These rights arise not only where they are expressly granted by the treaty but also by reason of obligations which the treaty imposes in a clearly defined way upon individuals as well as upon the member states and upon the institutions of the community.[70]

Van Gend en Loos extends the reach of European law in domestic legal systems, thus broadening the range of rights that an individual has access to as part of his/her 'legal heritage'. These rights arise 'independently of the legislation of member states',[71] – in this sense effectively sidelining a national government. Clearly, the crucial question for us is two-fold: how does this interface with notions of legal aid; and to what extent do European rights invigorate a democratic polity where the powerful can be held to account?

Since 1999 and Treaty of Amsterdam, the EU has taken a far more active and interventionist role in legal aid, and policy is now focused on achieving minimum standards

---

68   Supra, n. 3, at 191.
69   *Costa* v. *ENEL* [1964] ECR 585.
70   *Van Gend en Loos* v. *Nederlandse Administratie der Belastingen*, case 26-62 (5 February 1963).
71   Ibid.

across the Union to allow the funding of cross-border cases. The Green Paper stressed that this was not simply a matter that appealed to corporate litigators, but concerned the daily affairs of normal citizens. Cross-border litigation could thus concern a holiday injury, purchase of goods that turn out to be faulty, or custody disputes. Given the diversity of legal cultures within the EU, a global definition of legal aid is necessary. The Commission argues that it includes certain minimum elements that cover pre-litigation advice, free or low-cost advice or representation, possible exemption from court and other help with expenses linked with litigation.[72] The fundamental issue with cross-border litigation is that legal aid is almost exclusively linked to litigation within national courts and has not adapted itself to the culture where a litigant resident in one country may commence proceedings in the courts of another country. It is probably the case that models of legal aid are national, and do not, as yet, include the further costs of international litigation. Moreover, returning to the fundamental idea of European law, such a system should be in place to actualise the very idea of universal rights.

Thus, it is now necessary to think of civil legal aid from a European perspective. This means that provision of legal aid must be analysed through the underpinnings of the common market. Member states tend only to grant legal aid to disputes in their own territory, and link the availability of legal aid to 'nationalist or residence requirements'.[73] This would appear to be inconsistent with the principles developed by the ECJ stemming from Article 12E of the 1957 Treaty which prohibits discrimination on the grounds of nationality. Relying on this principle, the ECJ has stressed that 'any beneficiary of a Community law right (including a cross-border recipient of services or purchaser of goods) is entitled to equal treatment with nationals of the host country as regards both formal entitlement to bring actions and also the practical conditions in which such actions can be brought'. This development of the law of legal aid is interesting as it fills a void left by the ambiguities of Article 6.

The whole issue of thresholds for eligibility would have to be re-examined. As we have seen, legal aid operates through criteria relating to both financial need and, among other matters, the extent to which the case may be successful. The Commission argue that financial eligibility would have to take into account 'difference of income levels'[74] between different nations. Otherwise, litigants in poorer countries would be discouraged from commencing actions in nations where the cost of living, and hence the cost of legal services, was much higher than they could afford. The Commission also drew attention to the subjective element in decisions to award or withhold legal aid funding: it will be necessary to achieve much greater transparency.[75]

In November 2003, a directive was issued[76] and steps taken to harmonise English law with the new requirements. Rather than concern ourselves too much with the technical aspects of this process, we will turn to consider our second main point. To what

---

72   Green Paper on Legal Aid in Civil Matters, p. 2, at http://europa.eu/eur-lex/en/com/gpr/2000/com2000_0051 en01.pdf.
73   Ibid., para 9.
74   Ibid., para 15.
75   Ibid., para 16.
76   2002/8/EC. The Community Legal Service Amendment (No. 2) Order 2004 conferred powers on Legal Services Commission to fund cross-border actions.

extent can cross-border litigation be linked to the ability of normal citizens to use the courts to hold the powerful to account? Harlow points out that this is, in part, a question of standing in European law. One of the main problems is that the state, 'normally the defendant in human rights proceedings',[77] has more enhanced standing than individuals or non-governmental organisations (NGOs). The latter have to show that they are 'directly affected' by the litigation in order to intervene in proceedings. The case law of the court also shows some confusion as to the precise test to be applied to individuals and groups. There is also a restrictive understanding of when a 'public interest action' can take place. This is related to the ECJ's reluctance to develop principles relating to NGOs, who have to bring themselves within narrowly framed rules before they can initiate an action.

Although there are other significant factors in play, one of the consequences of this restrictive approach to standing, despite the availability of legal aid for cross-border litigation, is that the 'docket of the ECJ is ... largely dominated by corporate and commercial entities'.[78] Arguably, this reflects the Commission's own policy on access to justice which is 'sufficiently ensured if economic interests are at stake'.[79] The logic of this position is that litigation will be funded by commerical actors who have an interest in sustaining the 'framework for prosperous business'.[80] This clearly ignores that access to justice may also be concerned with those who are affected by the economic decision of corporate and commercial entities, and seek to use the courts to defend their rights; it also ignores areas of litigation, such as welfare, immigration or asylum which are not driven by commerical interests.

But perhaps the ECJ has to operate with a limited notion of access to justice. It is not a court of human rights. *S.P.U.C.* v. *Grogan*[81] is indicative. The ECJ did not argue that case by reference to freedom of expression, although arguably this was precisely what was at stake. There is a further concern that providing broader rules on standing would merely encourage 'corporate and commercial litigation', by virtue of the 'advantages corporate actors already possess in the Brussels lobbying system'.[82] Cautious reforms of the standing rules to allow NGOs an enhanced position would be achievable, but Harlow warns against a sudden surge of 'test cases' in the ECJ.

CONCLUSION

The politics of representations concerns itself with the ideologies and funding of legal aid and access to justice. We have analysed how recent legal aid reforms can be assessed, and the extent to which legal aid can be coordinated with ideas of human rights. The last section of the chapter argued that we need to see legal aid as operating within

---

77 Ibid., 193.
78 Ibid., 195.
79 Ibid.
80 Supra, n. 3, at 195. Harlow is citing a Communication from the Commission: Implementing Community Environmental Law (1996) COM (96) 500, at para 36.
81 *S.P.U.C.* v. *Grogan*, case C 159/90.
82 Supra n. 3, at 197.

a European context. Running through all these themes is an engagement with a doctrine of access to justice that asserts that the courts should be open to all and should not be a preserve of the rich and powerful. Democratic culture requires an efficient system of courts and a means for people to make use of legal services. Whether or not 'the market' can provide these public goods remains a pressing question.

CONCLUSION

If there was a single way of summing up the key thesis of this book, it might be as follows: the common law is characterised by due process. Due process is important but it must be located within a culture of human rights. Human rights allow us to make arguments about the legitimacy of the state and legal processes. However, human rights do not replace politics. For us a democratic political order is defined by social pluralism and a desire to engage in the ongoing and progressive reform of institutions. Rather than revisit and recap exhaustively on these themes, we want to offer a couple of general final points.

The first part of the book was focused on the post-colonial and on law's part in the construction of plural communities. We were very much concerned with the forms of life that the law either destroys or makes possible. We see the common law as bound up with a vast repository of narratives that are accounts of the law's proper role in the social and political world. This avoids nineteenth century arguments that linked the common law with the development of a 'spirit' of a 'people'. Surely, in our times, this is a corrupt and exhausted language. There is no such thing as a people; there are no coherent cultural identities. We are all bastards; the products of hybrid cultures; vast patterns of migration and dislocation that have displaced and scattered different people speaking different languages throughout different cultures of the world (which were never coherent in the first place). If the common law speaks to us today, it must talk polyglot.

The second part of the book moved on to consideration of various 'technical' concerns. In these sections our concern with human rights was, in part, an engagement with a language of analysis. Human rights provide a way of thinking about the common law. Whether or not this language becomes adopted as a general way of understanding the common law is open to question. We hope that we have also been alive to the way in which principles have developed at common law in an immanent manner. The principles of natural justice are a good example of common law ideas that are not expressed in terms of human rights, but can be seen in terms of due process and Article 6. To repeat a point made earlier on: this use of the language of rights allows us to place common law ideas in an international context. This is an essential element of an argument that has sought to examine the legitimacy of law. Even if the common law in the future separates itself from international traditions of rights, the question of the legitimacy of common law institutions remains.

The final part of the book was focused upon matters of procedure. We wanted to engage our institutional imaginations. Procedural law is so frequently presented as dull or simply the province of the practitioner. To remain authentic to our theme, we considered it necessary to present procedure as an articulation of principles that (in part) return us to ideas of due process. However, the civil and criminal procedural systems are immensely complicated. The language of due process is not, in itself, sufficient. Thus an important element of our engagement was to be aware that civil and criminal procedure is animated by tensions. These reflect competing agendas about their function and the ways in which the system attempts to negotiate their inner tensions.

We have saved the most difficult point until the very last moment. How does this book fit into legal pedagogy?

To the extent that the common law has been studied as part of an LLB syllabus, it has been done so through a subject called either 'legal method' or 'English legal system'. As Kavanagh has pointed out, this tends to be the Cinderella subject of legal education – or at least Cinderella before the kiss. Its concern is with the drudgery of legal reasoning, with what remains behind the scenes, or at least somehow prior to the proper study of law. The subject is seen as either an irrelevance or a trial for both those who have to teach it and those who are forced to study it. In part, this is a valid response to courses (and indeed books) that are lacking in structure, imagination and any sense of the contemporary dynamics of the common law.

The subject thus needs to be reinvented. We hope that this book might re-orientate 'legal system' or 'legal method' and give the subject the coherence and foundations that it is otherwise lacking. We believe the subject has a relationship to both public law and jurisprudence. Indeed, it should be presented in just such terms. Thus, rather than being cast adrift from the syllabus, 'legal system' can be informed by ideas drawn from those subjects that most directly engage in broader questions about the nature of law, its animating concerns and its possible futures.

London 2008

BIBLIOGRAPHY

Allan, T.R.S. (2003) 'Constitutional dialogue and the justification of judicial review', *Oxford Journal of Legal Studies* 23: 563–84.
Allison, J.W.F. (2007) *The English Historical Constitution – Continuity, Change and European Effects* (Cambridge: Cambridge University Press).
Alston, P. (1999) *The European Union and Human Rights* (Oxford: Oxford University Press).
Anderson, B. (1991) *Imagined Communities: Reflections on the Origin and Spread of Nationalism* (London: Verso).
Anderson, D. (2005) 'Burying the bones of the past', *History Today* 55(2): 2–3.
Anderson, D. (2005) *Histories of the Hanged* (London: Weidenfeld & Nicolson).
Anderson, D., Bennett, H. and Branch, D. (2006) 'A very British massacre', *History Today* 56(8): 20–2.
Andrews, N. (2003) *English Civil Procedure: Fundamentals of the New Civil Justice System* (Oxford: Oxford University Press).
Aristotle (1925) *The Nicomachean Ethics* (Oxford: Oxford University Press).
Armitage, A. (1995) *Comparing the Policy of Aboriginal Assimilation: Australia, Canada and New Zealand* (Vancouver: UBC Press).
Arnull, A. et al. (2002) *Accountability and Legitimacy in the European Union* (Oxford: Oxford University Press).
Ashworth, A. (2005) *Sentencing and Criminal Justice* (Cambridge: Cambridge University Press).
Ashworth, A.J. and Barsby, C. (2002) 'Human rights – post conviction change in the law', *Criminal Law Review*, 498–501.
Auden, W.H. (1976) *Collected Poems* (London: Random House).
Bailey, S.H. Harris, D.J. and Ormerod, D.C. (2001) *Civil Liberties* (Butterworths: London).
Baker, J.H. (1993) 'Statutory interpretation and parliamentary intervention', *Cambridge Law Journal* 52: 353.
Baker, J.H. (2002) *An Introduction to English Legal History*, 4th edn (London: Butterworth Lexis Nexis).
Bales, K. (1999) *Disposable People: New Slavery in the Global Economy* (Berkeley: University of California Press).
Balibar, E. and Wallerstein, I. (1991) *Race, Nation, Class: Ambiguous Identities* (London: Verso).
Ball, H. (1999) *Prosecuting War Crimes and Genocide: The Twentieth-Century Experience* (Kansas: University Press of Kansas).
Banton, M. (1991) 'The race relations problematic', *British Journal of Sociology*, 42: 115–30.
Barber B.R. (2003) *Fear's Empire: War, Terrorism, and Democracy* (New York: W.W. Norton & Co.).
Barnett, H. (1994) 'A privileged position? Gypsies, land and planning law', *The Conveyancer* (Nov/Dec): 454–64.
Barnett, H. (1995) 'The end of the road for gypsies', *Anglo American Law Review* 24(2): 133–67.
Baucom, I. (2005) *Specters of the Atlantic – Finance Capital, Slavery, and the Philosophy of History* (Durham and London: Duke University Press).
Becker, C.L. (1942) *The Declaration of Independence: A Study in the History of Political Ideals* (New York: Random House).

Bentham, J. (1928) *A Comment on the Commentaries*, Everett, C.W. (ed.) (Oxford: Clarendon Press).
Blackstone, W. (1765) *Commentaries on the Laws of England*, vol. I [original edition 1765, used 9th edition as prepared by Wayne Morrison] (London: Cavendish Publishing).
Blankenburg, E. (1995) 'Access to justice and alternatives to courts', *Civil Justice Quarterly* 14(Jul): 176–89.
Bowling, B. and Phillips, C. (2007) 'Disproportionate and discriminatory: reviewing the evidence on police stop and search', *Modern Law Review* 70(6): 936–61.
Bracton (*c.* 1235) *De Legibus et Consuetudinibus Angliae* [On the laws and customs of England], fols 1b and 2.
Bridges, L. (2000) *Quality in Criminal Defences Services*, LSC.
Burger, W. (1982) 'Isn't there a better way? Annual Report on the State of the Judiciary, Remarks at the Mid-Year Meeting of the American Bar Association', *American Bar Association Journal* 68: 274, 275.
Burns, R. (2000) 'A view from the ranks', *New Law Journal* 150: 1829–30.
Camenish, P.F. (1983) *Grounding Professional Ethics in a Pluralist Society*, (New York: New Haven Publications).
Cappelletti, M. (1993) 'Alternative dispute resolution processes within the framework of the World Wide Access to Justice Movement', *Modern Law Review* 56(3): 282–96.
Cardozo, B. (1921) *The Nature of the Judicial Process* (New Haven: Yale University Press).
Cassell (1902) *Cassells's History of England. Vol. I* (London: Cassell and Company).
Cavadino, M. and Dignan, J. (2007) *The Penal System* (London: Sage).
Chrimes, S.B. (1965) *English Constitutional History*, 3rd edn (Oxford: Oxford University Press).
Churchill, W. (1997) *A Little Matter of Genocide: Holocaust and Denial in the Americas, 1492 to the Present* (San Francisco: City Lights Books).
Clayton, R. (2007) 'The Human Rights Act six years on: Where are we now?', *European Human Rights Law Review* (3): 11–16.
Clayton, R. and Tomlinson, H. (2000) *The Law of Human Rights* (Oxford: Oxford University Press).
Clayton, R. and Tomlinson, H. (2001) *Fair Trial Rights* (Oxford: Oxford University Press).
Cohn, M. (2007) 'Judicial activism in the House of Lords', *Public Law* 1: 95–115.
Cooke, R.K. (1987) 'The practical problems of the sentencer', in D. Pennington and S. Lloyd-Bostock (eds) *The Psychology of Sentencing* (Oxford: Centre for Socio-Legal Studies).
Cownie, F. and Bradney, A. (1996) *English Legal System in Context* (London: Butterworths).
Craig, D. (2007) *EU Administrative Law* (Oxford: Oxford University Press).
Cross, R. and Harris, J.W. (1991) *Precedent in English Law* (Oxford: Clarendon).
De Burca (1996) 'The quest for legitimacy in the European Union', *Modern Law Review* 359: 368–71.
De Certeau, M. (2006) *The Practice of Everyday Life* (Berkeley: University of California Press).
Dodd, V. (2005) 'Asian men targeted in stop and search', *The Guardian*, 17 August.
Douzinas, C. and Gearey, A. (2005) *Critical Jurisprudence* (Oxford: Hart Press).
Dworkin, R. (1986) *Law's Empire* (Cambridge, MA: Harvard University Press).
Dyrberg, P. (2002) 'Accountability and legitimacy: what is the contribution of transparency', in A. Arnull and D. Wincott (eds) *Accountability and Legitimacy in the European Union* (Oxford: Oxford University Press).
Ekins, R. (2003) 'A critique of radical approaches to rights consistent statutory interpretation', *European Human Rights Law Review* 6: 641–50.
Ellis, E. (ed.) (1999) *The Principle of Proportionality in the Laws of Europe* (Oxford: Hart).
Elkins, C. (2005) *Imperial Reckoning: The Untold Story of Britain's Gulag in Kenya.* (NY: Henry Holt).

Everson, E. (with Eisner, J.) (2007) *The Making of a European Constitution* (London: Routledge-Cavendish).
Fanon, F. (1963) *The Wretched of the Earth* (New York: Grove Press).
Fanon, F. (1986) *Black Skin, White Masks* (trans. C. Lam Markmann) (London: Pluto).
Feldman, D. (1999) 'Proportionality and the Human Rights Act 1998', in E. Ellis (ed.) *The Principle of Proportionality in the Laws of Europe* (Oxford: Hart Publishing). pp. 117–44.
Feldman, D. (2002) *Civil Liberties and Human Rights in England and Wales* (Oxford: Oxford University Press).
Fenwick, H., Masterman, R. and Phillipson, G. et al. (2007) *Judicial Reasoning under the UK Human Rights Act* (Cambridge: Cambridge University Press).
Ferguson, P.W. (2002) 'Human rights and their retrospective effect', *Scots Law Times* 2: 11–17.
Finberg, A.J. (1961) *The Life of J.M.W. Turner, R.A.*, 2nd edn (Oxford: Clarendon Press) 474.
Fionda, J. (2005) *Devils and Angels* (Oxford: Hart).
Fitzpatrick, P. (1987) 'Racism and the innocence of law', in P. Fitzpatrick and A. Hunt (eds) *Critical Legal Studies* (London: Blackwell). pp. 119–32.
Fitzpatrick, P. (1992) *The Mythology of Modern Law* (London: Routledge).
Fitzpatrick, P. (2001) *Modernism and the Grounds of Law* (Cambridge: Cambridge University Press).
Flood, J. and White, A. (2006) 'What's wrong with legal aid? Lessons from outside the UK', *Civil Justice Quarterly* 25: 80–98.
Foster, J., Newburn, T. and Souhami, A. (2005) 'Assessing the impact of the Stephen Lawrence Inquiry', *Home Office Research Study* 294 (London: Home Office).
Frankena, W.K. (1973) *Ethics*, 2nd edn (Englewood Cliffs: Prentice-Hall).
Freeman, M.D.A. (2001) *Lloyd's Introduction to Jurisprudence* (London: Sweet and Maxwell).
Fryer, P. (1984) *Staying Power* (London: Pluto Press).
Fryer, P. (1993) *Aspects of British Black History* (London: Index Books).
Galligan, D. (1996) *Due Process and Fair Procedure* (Oxford: Clarendon Press).
Gearty, C. (2004) *Principles of Human Rights Adjudication* (Oxford: Oxford University Press).
Genn, H. (1999) *Paths to Justice* (Oxford: Hart).
Gilroy, P. (1987a) 'The myth of black criminality', in P. Scraton (ed.) *Law, Order and the Authoritarian State* (Milton Keynes: WUL).
Gilroy, P. (1987b) *There Ain't No Black in the Union Jack: The Cultural Politics of Race and Nation* (London: Routledge).
Glasser, C. (1993) 'Civil procedure and the lawyers – the adversary system and the decline of the orality principle', *Modern Law Review* 56(3): 307–24.
Goodrich, P. (1986) *Reading the Law* (London: Basil Blackwell).
Goodrich, P. (1990) *Languages of Law* (London: Weidenfeld and Nicolson).
Goriely, T. (1994) 'Rushcliffe fifty years on: the changing role of civil legal aid within the welfare state', *Journal of Law and Society* 21(4): 545–66.
Gouldkamp, J. (2008) 'Facing up to actual bias', *Civil Justice Quarterly* 27(1): 32–9.
Griffith, J.A.G. (1977) *The Politics of the Judiciary* (London: Fontana).
Guillaum, C. (1995) *Racism, Sexism, Power and Ideology* (London: Routledge).
Hale, H. (1971) *The History of the Common Law.* (Chicago: University of Chicago Press).
Hale, B. (2001) 'Equality and the judiciary', *Public Law* (Autumn) 489–504.
Harpers Magazine (2003) 'We were calling to death', *Harpers Magazine* (February): 14–15.
Harris, B. (2002) 'Ongoing search', *Law Quarterly Review* 118(Jul): 408–27.
Harris, B.V. (2002) 'Final appellate courts overruling their own "wrong" precedents: the ongoing search for principle', *Law Quarterly Review* 118(Jul): 408–27.
Harris D.J., O'Boyle, M. and Warbrick, C. (1995) *Law of the European Convention on Human Rights* (London: Butterworths).

Harris, D.J., O'Boyle, M. and Warbrick, C. (2005) *The Law of the European Convention on Human Rights* (London: Butterworths).
Hepple, B. (1992) 'Have twenty five years of race relations Acts in Britain been a failure?' in B. Hepple and E.M. Szyszczak (eds) *Discrimination: The Limits of the Law* (London: Mansell).
Hesiod (1983) 'Works and days' in *Hesiod: Theogony, Works and Days, Shield II* (trans. A.N. Athanassakis) (Baltimore: Johns Hopkins University Press).
Hilbink, L. (2007) *Judges beyond Politics in Democracy and Dictatorship: Lessons from Chile* (Cambridge: Cambridge University Press).
Hobbes, T. (1991 [1651]) Richard Tuck (ed.) *Leviathan* (Cambridge: Cambridge University Press).
Hobbes, T. *Dialogue Between a Philosopher and a Student of the Common Laws of England*.
Hochschild, A. (2005) *Bury the Chains – The British Struggle to Abolish Slavery* (London: Pan Macmillan).
Hoffman, D. and Rowe, J. (2003) *Human Rights in the UK* (Harlow: Pearson Longman).
Holdsworth, W. (1928a) *Charles Dickens as a Legal Historian* (New Haven: Yale University Press).
Holdsworth, W.S. (1928b) *Some Lessons from Our Legal History* (New York: Macmillan).
Holmes, O.W. (1881) [1923 reprint] *The Common Law* (Boston: Little Brown).
Holmes C. (1998) *John Bull's Other Island* (London: Macmillan).
House of Commons Home Affairs Committee. *Fourth Report of Session 2005–6: Terrorism Detention Powers* HC 910-I, 54.
House of Commons Home Affairs Committee. *Sixth Report of Session 2004–5: Terrorism and Community Relations* HC 165-I, 46.
Huntington, S.P. (1996) *The Clash of Civilizations and the Remaking of World Order* (London: The Free Press).
Jackson, E. (2006) *Medical Law* (Oxford: Oxford University Press).
Jacob, J. (1987) *The Fabric of English Civil Justice* (London: Stevens and Sons).
Jacob, J. (2007) *Civil Justice in the Age of Human Rights* (Aldershot: Ashgate).
Jamieson, K.H. (1992) *Dirty Politics: Deception, Distraction and Democracy* (Oxford: Oxford University Press).
Janis, M.W., Bradley, A.W. and Kay, R.S. (2007) *European Human Rights Law* (Oxford: Oxford University Press).
Jenkins, S. (2003) 'Trupti Patel and the rotten courts of Salem', *The Times*, 13 June 2003.
Jordan, J. (1995) 'In the land of white supremacy', *The Progressive*, 18 June: 21.
Joseph, P. (2007) *Constitutional and Administrative Law in New Zealand*, 3rd edn (Wellington: Thomson Brookers).
Joyce, P. (2006) *Criminal Justice: An Introduction to Crime and the Criminal Justice System* (Devon: Willan).
Judt, T. (2005) *Post War: A History of Europe Since 1945* (New York: Penguin Press).
Juss, S.S. (1993) *Immigration, Nationality and Citizenship* (London: Mansell).
Kavanagh, A. (2004) 'Statutory interpretation and human rights after Anderson: A more contextual approach', *Public Law* (Autumn) 537–45.
Kennedy, H. (2004) *Legal Conundrums in our Brave New World* (London: Sweet and Maxwell).
King, J. (2007) 'The justiciability of resource allocation', *Modern Law Review* 70(2): 197–224.
King, M. (2003) *The Penguin History of New Zealand* (Auckland: Penguin Books).
Klug, F. (2003) 'Judicial deference under the Human Rights Act', *European Human Rights Law Review* 2: 125–33.
Kriegel, B. (1995) *The State and the Rule of Law* (trans. M.A. LePain) (New Jersey: Princeton University Press).
The Lawrence Inquiry, (1999) Cm 4662-I. (London: HMSO).

Le Sueur, A. (2000) 'Access to justice and human rights in the UK', *European Human Rights Law Review* 5: 457–75.
Leach, P. (2006) 'The effectiveness of the Committee of Ministers in supervising the enforcement of judgments of the European Court of Human Rights', *Public Law* 443–56.
Lenaerts, K. (2004) 'In the union we trust: trust enhancing principles of community law', *Common Market Law Review* 41: 317–43.
Lester, A. (2000) 'Politics of the Race Relations Act 1976', in M. Anwar, P. Roach and R. Sondhi (eds) *From Legislation to Integration; Race Relations in Britain* (London: Macmillan).
Lewis, J. (2007) 'The European ceiling on human rights', *Public Law*: 720–47.
Lord Denning (1979) *The Discipline of the Law* (London: Butterworths).
Lord Hailsham (1978) *The Dilemma of Democracy* (London: Collins).
Lord Irvine (1999) 'Activism and restraint: human rights and the interpretative process', *European Human Rights Law Review* 4: 350–402.
Lord Steyn (2002) 'The case for a Supreme Court', *Law Quarterly Review* 118: 382.
Lord Steyn (2004) 'Dynamic interpretation amidst an orgy of statute', *European Human Rights Law Review* 3: 245–57.
Lord Steyn (2005) 'Democracy, The rule of law and the role of judges', *European Human Rights Law Review* 3: 243–53.
Losel, F. (2007) 'Counterblast: the prison overcrowding crisis and some constructive perspectives for crime policy', *Howard Journal of Criminal Justice* 46(5): 512–19.
Loveland, I. (2002) 'Injunctions, planning enforcement and human rights', *Modern Law Review* 65(6): 906–18.
Luban, D. (1994) *Legal Modernism* (Michigan: University of Michigan Press).
Lustgarten, L. (1980) *Legal Control of Discrimination* (London: Macmillan).
MacInnes, C. (1934) *England and Slavery* (London: Arrowsmith).
Macpherson, W. (1999) *The Stephen Lawrence Inquiry* (London: Home Office).
Mamdani, M. (1996) *Citizen and Subject* (Princeton: Princeton University Press).
Mason, J.K. and Laurie, G.T. (2006) *Mason and McCall Smith's Law and Medical Ethics* (Oxford: Oxford University Press).
Mathew, P., Hunter, R. and Charlesworth, H. (1995) *Thinking About Law – Perspectives on the History, Philosophy and Sociology of Law* (Sydney: Allen & Unwin).
Maughan, C. and Webb, J. (2005) *Lawyering Skills and the Legal Process* (Cambridge: Cambridge University Press).
McConville, M. (1993) 'Wanted: more detection, less interrogation', *The Times*, 2 March 1993.
McCrudden, C., Smith, D.J. and Brown, C. (1991) *Racial Justice at Work* (London: Policy Studies Institute).
McHugh, P.G. (2001) 'A History of Crown Sovereignty in New Zealand', in *Histories Power and Loss: Uses of the Past – a New Zealand Commentary*, A. Sharp and P. McHugh, eds, (Wellington: Bridget Williams Books).
Mead, P. (1991) 'The obligation to apply European law', *European Law Review* 16(6): 490–501.
Miles, R. (1989) *Racism* (London: Routledge).
Miles, R. and Phizacklea A. (1987) *White Man's Country* (London: Pluto Press).
Moeckli, D (2007) 'Stop and search under the Terrorism Act 2000: A comment on *R (Gillan) v. Commissioner of Police for the Metropolis*', *Modern Law Review* 70(4): 654.
Morgan, J. (2004) 'Privacy torts: out with the old, out with the new', *Law Quarterly Review* 120(Jul): 393–8.
Morrison, T. (1992) *Playing in the Dark: Whiteness and the Literary Imagination* (London: Routledge).
Morrison, W (2005) 'Rethinking Penal Narratives in Global Context', in Pratt, J. Brown, D. Brown, M. Holdsworth, S. and Morrison, W, eds, *The New Punitiveness* (Devon: Willan).

Morrison, W. (2006) *Criminology, Civilisation and the New World Order* (London: Routledge-Cavendish).
Mowbray, A. (2007) *Cases and Materials on the European Convention on Human Rights* (Oxford: Oxford University Press).
Newdick, C. (2005) *Who Should We Treat?* (Oxford: Oxford University Press).
Nicholson, M.A. (2000) 'McLibel: A case study in English Defamation Law', *Wisconsin International Law Journal* 18: 1–114.
Nicol, D. (2004) 'Statutory interpretation and human rights after Anderson', *Public Law*.
Nicol, D. (2006) 'Law and politics after the Human Rights Act', *Public Law*, 722–51.
Nobles, R. and Schiff, D. (2004) 'A story of miscarriage: law in the media', *Journal of Law and Society* 31(2): 221–44.
Packer H. (1968) *The Limits of the Criminal Sanction* (Stanford: Stanford University Press).
Pannick, D. (1989) *Judges* (Oxford: Oxford University Press).
Partington, M. (2003) *Introduction to the English Legal System*, 2nd edn (Oxford: Oxford University Press).
Paul, K. (1997) *Whitewashing Britain; Race and Citizenship in the Postwar Era* (Ithaca: Cornell University Press).
Peysner and Seneviratne (2005) *The Management of Civil Cases: the Courts and the Post-Woolf Landscape*. DCA Research Report 9/2005.
Phillips, C. and Bowling, B. (2002) 'Racism, ethnicity, crime and criminal justice' in M. Maguire, R. Morgan and R. Reiner (eds) *The Oxford Handbook of Criminology* (Oxford: Oxford University Press), 579–619.
Phillipson, G. (2007) in Fenwick *et al.* (ed.) *Horizontal Effect after Campbell in Judicial Reasoning under the UK Human Rights Act* (Cambridge: Cambridge University Press).
Pollock, F. and Maitland, F.W. (1898) *History of English Law*, 2nd edn, vol. I (Cambridge: Cambridge University Press).
Potter, H. (1943) *An Historical Introduction to English Law*, 2nd edn (London: Sweet & Maxwell Ltd).
Quinton, P., Bland, N. and Miller, J. (2000a) 'Police stops, decision-making and practice', *Police Research Series Paper 130* (London: Home Office).
Quinton, P., Bland, N. and Miller, J. (2000b) 'Police Stops and Searches: Lessons from a programme of research', *Briefing Note* (London: Home Office).
Reece, H. (2003) *Divorcing Responsibly* (Oxford: Hart).
Reynolds, H. (1971) *An Indelible Stain? The Question of Genocide in Australia's History* (Camberwell: Penguin Viking).
Reynolds, H. (1987) *The Law of the Land* (Camberwell: Penguin Books Australia).
Roberts, P. (2002) 'Science, experts and criminal justice', in M. McConville and G. Wilson (eds) *The Handbook of Criminal Justice* (Oxford: Oxford University Press).
Roberts, P. and Zuckerman, A. (1994) *Criminal Evidence* (Oxford: Oxford University Press).
Robertson, G. (1993) *Freedom, the Individual and the Law* (London: Penguin).
Rubinstein, W.D. (2004) *Genocide: A History* (London: Pearson, Longman).
Rutherford, A. (1993) *Criminal Justice and the Pursuit of Decency* (Oxford: Oxford University Press).
Sanders, A. and Young, R. (2007) *Criminal Justice* (Oxford: Oxford University Press).
Scolnicov, A. (2005) 'Supersized speech – McLibel comes to Strasbourg', *Cambridge Law Journal*: 311–14.
Sedley, S. (1995) 'Human rights: a twenty first century agenda', *Public Law* (3): 386–440.
Sedley, S. (2001) 'The common law and the political constitution', *Law Quarterly Review* 117(Jan): 68–70.
Seuffert, N. (2006) *Jurisprudence of National Identity: Kaleidoscopes of Imperialism and Globalisation from Aotearoa New Zealand* (Aldershot: Ashgate Publishing).

Sharp, G. (1773) Granville Sharp's diary. Gloucestershire Archives, 19 April 1773, Ref D3549 13/4/2 book G.
Sharp, G. (1786) Granville Sharp's letter to the Archbishop of Canterbury. Gloucestershire Archives, 1 August 1786, Ref: D3549 13/1/C3.
Sharp, G. (1820) *Prince Hoare, Memoirs of Granville Sharp*. London.
Shyllon, F.O. (1974) *Black Slaves in Britain* (Oxford: Oxford University Press).
Sibley, D. (1995) *Geographies of Exclusion: Society and Difference in the West* (London: Routledge).
Sime, S. (2007) *A Practical Approach to Civil Procedure* (Oxford: Oxford University Press).
Simpson, A.W.B. (1973) 'The common law and legal theory' in *Oxford Essays in Jurisprudence* (Oxford: Clarendon Press).
Simpson, A.W.B. (1984) *Cannibalism and the Common Law* (Chicago: University of Chicago Press).
Simpson, A.W.B. (2001) *Human Rights and the End of Empire* (Oxford: Oxford University Press).
Sivandan, A. (1982) *A Different Hunger* (London: Pluto Press).
Slapper, G. and Kelly, D. (2006) *English Legal System* (Oxford: Routledge-Cavendish).
Solomos, J. (1993) *Race and Racism in Britain* (London: Macmillan).
Stannard, D.E. (1992) *American Holocaust: The Conquest of the New World* (Oxford: Oxford University Press).
Starmer, K. (2003) 'Two years of the Human Rights Act', *European Human Rights Law Review* 1: 14–23.
Stephen, J.F. (1860) 'On trial by jury: and the evidence of experts', *Two Papers Read before the Juridical Society* 236.
Stevens, R. (2002) *The English Judges: Their Role in the Changing Constitution* (Oxford: Hart).
Stockdale, R. (1999) 'Forensic evidence', in C. Walker and K. Starmer (eds) *Miscarriages of Justice* (Oxford: Blackwell).
Summers, S. (2007) *Fair Trials* (Oxford: Hart).
Taguieff, P.-A. (1988) *La Force du Prejuge, Essai Sur Le Racisme et Ses Doubles* (Paris: Editions la Decouverte).
Tate, W. (2003) 'Pre-Wi Parata: early native title cases in New Zealand', *Waikato Law Review* 6.
Taylor, M. (2003) 'Cot death expert to face investigation', *The Guardian*, December 19, 2003.
Taylor, N. and Wood, J. (1999) 'Victims of miscarriages of justice', in C. Walker and K. Starmer (eds) *Miscarriages of Justice* (Oxford: Blackwell).
Thomas, D.A. (2002) 'The sentencing process', in M. McConville and G. Wilson (eds) *The Oxford Handbook of Criminal Justice* (Oxford: Oxford University Press).
Tomkins, A. (2002) 'In defence of the political constitution', *Oxford Journal of Legal Studies*: 22(1), 157–75.
Tomkins, A. (2005) *Our Republican Constitution* (Oxford: Hart).
Trechsel, S. (2005) *Human Rights in Criminal Proceedings* (Oxford: Oxford University Press).
Tuitt, P. (2004) *Race, Law, Resistance* (London: Glasshouse Press).
Twining, W. (1992) *How to Do Things with Rules* (London: Weidenfeld and Nicolson).
Uglow, S. (2002) *Criminal Justice* (London: Sweet and Maxwell).
Usher, J.A. (1998) *General Principles of EC Law* (London: Longman).
Van Caenegem, R.C. (1986) *Judges, Legislators & Professors: Chapters in European Legal History* (Cambridge: Cambridge University Press).
Van Cleve (2006) Sommersetts Case and its Antecedents', *Law and History Review*, 24(3).
Van Dijk, Van Hoof, G. (eds) (2006) *Theory and Practice of the European Convention on Human Rights* (Antwerp: Intersentia).
Vick, D.W. and Campbell, K. (2001) 'Public protests, private lawsuits, and the market: the investor response to the McLibel case', *Journal of Law and Society* 28(2): 204–41.

Wadham, J. (2003) *The Human Rights Act 1998* (Oxford: Blackstone Press).
Walker, C. (1999) 'Miscarriages of justice in principle and practice', in C. Walker and K. Starmer (eds) *Miscarriages of Justice* (Oxford: Blackwell).
Wallerstein, I. and Balibar, E. (1991) *Race, Nation, Class* (London: Verso).
Walvin, J. (1992) *Black Ivory – A History of British Slavery* (London: Fontana Press).
Ward, A. (1999) *An Unsettled History: Treaty Claims in New Zealand Today* (Wellington: Bridget Williams Books).
Ward, T. (2004) 'Experts, juries and witch-hunts: from Fitzjames Stephen to Angela Cannings', *Journal of Law and Society* 31(3): 369–86.
Watson, A. (1985) *The Evolution of Law* (Baltimore: Johns Hopkins University Press).
Williams, G. (1973) *Learning the Law*, 9th edn (London: Stevens).
Williams, P. (1997) 'The Genealogy of Race: Towards a Theory of Grace', Reith Lectures, BBC, London.
Wilson, B. (1988) 'The making of a constitution: approaches to judicial interpretation', *Public Law* (3): 370–84.
Woolf, H. and Tumim, S. (1991) *Prison Disturbances April 1990*, Cm 1456 (London: HMSO).
Young, K.E. and Connelly, N. (1981) *Policy and practice in the multi-racial city* (Report) (London: Policy Studies Institute).
Zander, M. (1995) *The Police and Criminal Evidence Act 1984* (London: Sweet and Maxwell).
Zander, M. (2007) *Cases and Materials on the English Legal System* (Cambridge: Cambridge University Press).
Zedner, L. (2005) 'Securing liberty in the face of terror: reflections from criminal justice', *Journal of Law and Society* 32(4): 507–33.
Zimmerer, J. (2004) 'Colonialism and the Holocaust: Towards an archaeology of genocide', in A. Dirk Moses (ed.) *Genocide and Settler Society*. (New York: Berghan Books).

INDEX

A v. Secretary of State (no. 2) [2005] 140–1
A and others v. *Secretary of State for the Home Department* [2005] 139
abolition of slavery *see* slavery
Aborigines *see* Australian Aborigines; Maoris
access to justice 132, 199–200, 379, 382–5, 390–1, 393–6; *see also* legal aid; legal representation; standing
Access to Justice Act [1999] 386
accountability *see* democratic accountability
administrative tribunals 128, 274
adversarial proceedings 44–5
Airedale NHS v. *Bland* [1993] 92
Airey v. *Ireland* [1979] 391–2
Al-Jubail v. *Council of the European Communities* 200
aliens *see* immigration; resident aliens
alternative dispute resolution 295–300, 383–4
Ampthill Peerage Case 321
Anderson case 251, 252–3, 269, 351–2
Anderton v. *Ryan* [1985] 82–3
anti-discrimination law 178–81
Anton Piller orders 325–7, 328–9
Aotearoa *see* New Zealand
appeals 263, 321–2, 323–4, 330, 331–2; *see also* Court of Appeal; House of Lords
arguability: test of 235
arrest and detention: grounds for 358–61; regulations 355–8, 363; safeguards 361–3; of terrorists 132, 340, 359–61, 363
Aston Cantlow ... PCC v. *Wallbank* [2004] 256–7, 258
asylum *see* immigration
AT&T Istel Ltd. v. *Tully* [1993] 318, 319
Atlanta AG v. *Commission* [1999] 194–5
audi alteram partem 199–200, 326–7
Australia: UK origin of law 19, 167
Australian Aborigines 161, 165–8
authority *see* precedent

B case 303
B and P v. *UK* [2001] 286–7

Bater v. *Bater* [1951] 364–5
Beer case 257–9
Begum case 147–50, 269
Bellinger v. *Bellinger* [2002] 251, 252
Bentham, Jeremy 8–9, 72
bias 277–82, 322–4, 374–78; *see also* impartiality
binding precedent 74, 79–80
Birmingham Declaration 196
blackness: and whiteness 158–9
Blackstone, William: *Commentaries* 40–1, 161
Bland case 92
Bleak House (Dickens) 290–2
bodily integrity *see* torture
Boyle and Rice v. *UK* [1988] 235, 236
breach of the peace: and arrest powers 357
Bristol Aeroplane Co. case 85, 86–7
British nationality: definition of 177–8
Brixton Disorder: Scarman report 181
Brogan v. *UK* [1988] 359, 360–1
Brown v. *Stott* [2001] 319, 320, 321, 374
burden of proof *see* presumption of innocence

C. v. *DPP* [1995] 91–2
Campbell v. *MGM* [2004] 94–5, 269
Canning, Angela 344–5
Caravan Sites Act [1968] 305–6
care orders: and judicial interpretation 117–18
Carter Review 387, 386–7, 389
Carvel and Guardian Newspapers v. *Council* [1995] 196–7
case control: in civil justice 292–3
case law 29, 48–50, 72, 79; *see also* judicial law making; precedent
Castorina v. *Chief Constable of Surrey* [1988] 356
censorship *see* privacy
Chahal v. *UK* [1996] 236–7, 238
Chandler case 368
Chappell v. *UK* [1990] 328–9

Charter of Fundamental Rights [2000] 185–9, 198
children's cases 91–2, 286–8
Chile: role of judiciary 137
Christie v. *Leachinsky* [1947] 357–8
citizen's arrest 355–6
civil justice: alternative dispute resolution 295–300, 383–4; in *Bleak House* 290–2; juries in 44; and legal aid 308–9, 381, 386, 391–2, 395; overriding objective 293–5, 311–12; public perceptions 292; reforms 46, 292–3, 298, 316, 328–9; *see also* distributive justice
civil procedural law: characteristics 311–12; and disclosure and privilege 312–17, 327–8; due notice principle 325–9; duty to give reasons 329–32; and finality of litigation 80, 321–4; and self-incrimination 317–21
Civil Procedure Act and Rules [1997/8] 46, 292–3, 294, 298, 324, 327–8
civil society: rights in 221
Clark, Sally 344–6
Clegg case 90–1
Code of Conduct (European Commission and Council) 196, 197
Collingwood, Luke (slave trader) 60–2, 65
colonial consciousness 165
colonial law: UK origins 19–24
colonialism: and genocide 161–2, 166; and immigration 175–6; and indigenous land rights 159–60, 161, 163–8, 169, 171–2; legal principles 161; and race 175; and repression 169–74; and spread of common law 157–8, 162, 165
Commentaries on the Laws of England 40–1, 161
commercial law: development 38
common law: characteristics 28, 39, 40–1, 48–9, 78–9; and ECHR 266–70; origins 24–8, 29–32; spread through colonialism 157–8, 162, 165; *see also* case law; civil justice; *Commentaries*; criminal justice; positive law
Common Law Procedure Act [1854] 42–4
Commonwealth Immigration Acts 176, 177
community interest companies 389
Community Legal Services Partnerships 388–9
conditional fee agreements 308
Condron v. *UK* [2000] 373–4
confession evidence 368

confidentiality laws: and judicial decision making 94–5
conjoined twins: legal case on separation 69–70
Connor v. *UK* [2004] 98
Constitutional Reform Act [2005] 143–5
construction industry: dispute resolution in 296, 297
corruption *see* bias; electoral corruption
Coughlan case 304
Council of Europe: and the ECHR 212
Council of the European Union: role 206
Court of Appeal 84–8, 321–2, 323, 347–8
Court of Chancery 290–2
Court of First Instance 206, 208
court tracking system: in civil justice 293
courts: and administrative tribunals 128; as adversarial proceedings 44–5; hierarchies 74, 76, 77, 79, 80, 84–8, 97–100, 273; Medieval development 26–8; *see also* juries; legal procedures; Queen's Bench; tribunals
courts martial *see* military tribunals
crime control: and arrest 356–7
Crime (Sentences) Act [1997] 93, 348, 349
Criminal Defence Service 386
Criminal Evidence Act [1898] 368–9
criminal justice 220, 243, 244, 245–6; *see also* arrest and detention; evidence; police; presumption of innocence; self-incrimination
Criminal Justice Act [1991] 347–9
Criminal Justice and Public Order Act [1994] 306, 307, 369, 373
cross-border litigation: and legal aid 394–6
customary law: recognition of 163–6

D v. *East Berkshire Community NHS Trust* [2004] 99
Davis v. *Johnson* [1974] 85–6, 87–8
De Cubber v. *Belgium* [1984] 277–8
De Menezes, Jean Charles 341–2
declaratory theory of case law 28, 72, 79
democratic accountability: of the judiciary 141–2
deportation: of resident aliens 245
derogations: from the ECHR 138, 229–33, 243
detention *see* arrest and detention; prisons
Dickens, Charles: *Bleak House* 290–2
disclosure of evidence 44–5, 196–7, 202, 283–5, 312–17, 327–8, 359; *see also* self-incrimination

discrimination 180, 222, 337–9, 340–2; *see also* bias; institutional racism; Race Relations Acts; religious discrimination; sexual discrimination; stop and search powers
dispute resolution *see* alternative dispute resolution; civil justice
distributive justice 295, 300–10
diversity: in the judiciary 146; *see also* plural society
divorce *see* matrimonial issues
DNA evidence 342–3
document disclosure *see* disclosure
doli incapax 91–2
Dombo Beheer v. *The Netherlands* [1993] 282
Domesday Book 27
double jeopardy 246
Douglas v. *Hello* [2001] 94, 95
Dudley and Stephens case 57–60, 69
due notice: principle of 325–9
due process 2, 11–12, 187, 220; *see also* access to justice; fair trial; procedural law; standing; transparency
Duke v. *GEC Reliance* [1988] 109–110
Dumbell v. *Roberts* [1944] 355, 356
duress: and murder 83–4

ECHR *see* European Convention on Human Rights
economic rights: in ECHR 221
Edwards v. *UK* [1992] 283
effective remedy: right to 233–8
electoral corruption 39–43
English v. *Emery Reimbold & Strick Ltd* [2002] 330–1
Equal Pay Act [1970] 110–11
equality of arms 282–5, 309, 392–3; *see also* legal aid
Equiano, Olaudah 62
ethics: of the judiciary 137; *see also* human rights; morality
ethnicity *see* Australian Aborigines; blackness; discrimination; Maoris
EURATOM 205, 208
European Coal and Steel Community 204–5, 208
European Commission 196, 197, 200–3, 205–6
European Commission on Human Rights 212, 213

European Convention on Human Rights: on arrest and detention 359, 361; Article 6 text 14–15; on asylum and immigration 245; background 6–7, 210–13; and the common law 266–70; on criminal justice systems 220, 245–6; derogations/reservations from 138, 229–33, 243; in English law 214–16, 249–50, 265–7; on extra-legal punishment 220, 243–4; on independent tribunals 271–6; institutions 223–8; on legal aid 390; on presumption of innocence 365–7; protocols 222; on rights limitations 238–43; rights summary 217–22, 231; on rule of law 390; on self-incrimination 370–1
European Council: access to documents 196–7
European Court of Human Rights: creation 212, 213; evidence and investigations 226; execution of judgments 226–7; interim measures 227–8; judgments on arrest 358–63; judgments on bias 375–6; judgments on burden of proof 366–7; judgments on extradition 237; judgments on fair trial 273–4, 276, 277–8, 283–5, 286–8, 328–9; judgments on freedom of expression 239, 242; judgments on legal aid 309, 390–3; judgments on political activity 240–1; judgments on privacy 216, 225, 234–6, 238; judgments on retrospective application of laws 243–4; judgments on self-incrimination 371–4; judgments on sexual discrimination 237; powers 224; and precedents 98–9, 249, 267–70; role 223; standing in 224–6, 235–6
European Court of Justice 206, 209, 394, 396
European Economic Community 205
European law: and access to justice 393–6; challenge in national courts 191–2; due process in 187; in English law 214–15; judicial interpretation 108–112, 215–16; and judicial law making 130; overview 206–7; and sovereignty 31, 34–7, 394; standing in 395–6; transparency in 196–202
European Parliament: role 206
European Union 6, 186, 204–6
evidence 32–3, 226, 342–8, 364–5, 368; *see also* Anton Piller orders; disclosure; presumption of innocence; self-incrimination
executive: role in sentencing 348, 347–51

executive power 10, 237–8; *see also* judiciary, independence of
expert witnesses 343–6
extra-legal punishment: and the ECHR 220, 243–4
extradition: and judicial review 236–7

fair-minded observer: in bias tests 280–2
fair trial: in the Charter of Fundamental Rights 188–9; ECtHR judgments 273–4, 276, 277–8, 283–5, 286–8, 328–9; and the European Commission 202; and independent tribunals 271–6; judicial interpretations 113–17; principles 14–15; and public pronouncement of judgment 286–8; *see also* appeals; bias; equality of arms; self-incrimination; sentencing; transparency
Family Law Act [1996] 297–8
Fanon, Franz 158–9
Findlay v. *UK* [1997] 273, 275–6
Fiskano v. *EC Commission* [1995] 199–200
Fitt v. *UK* [2000] 284–5
Fitzleet Estates v. *Cherry* [1977] 96–7
Flannery v. *Halifax Estate Agencies* [2000] 329–30
forensic science *see* scientific evidence
Fox, Campbell and Hartley v. *UK* [1990] 359, 360, 361
freedom of assembly and association: rights to 220–1
freedom of expression 133–6, 220, 239, 242
friendly settlements: in the ECtHR 226
funding: for the NHS 301

Garland v. *British Rail Engineering Ltd* [1982] 109
genocide 161–2, 166, 184
Ghaidan v. *Godin-Mendoza* [2004] 118–19, 120, 269
Gillan case 340
globalised legal order 153–5
'Glorious Revolution': effects 42
Golder v. *UK* 390–1
good administration: right to 187–8
Gough test of bias 278–80, 375
Grant v. *South Western Trains* [1998] 112
Greek case 233–4
Green Environmental Industries case 319–21
Gregory v. *UK* [1997] 374–6
Griffith, J.A.G.: *Politics of the Judiciary* 124–6, 146–7

Gusinskiy v. *Russia* [2004] 242, 243
gypsies: access to land 304–7

habeas corpus 32, 50, 53, 355, 362
Halsbury, 1st Earl 126–7
Hampshire Farmer's Market case 257–9
Handyside v. *UK* [1976] 242
Hansard: use in judicial interpretation 105–6
Harman v. *Home Office* [1983] 314–15
Harrow LBC v. *Qazi* 98
Havana Railways case 84–5
Heintz van Landewyck SARL v. *Commission* [1980] 202, 203
Henry II: legal reforms 26
Hey Bros 160–1
Hincks case 303
Hindley, Myra 352–3
Hobbes, Thomas 34–7, 169
Hogarth, William: on electoral corruption 42–3
Hola massacre (Kenya) 173–4
Home Secretary: and sentencing tariffs 349–51
homicide *see* murder
House of Lords Appellant Committee 79–80, 84–8
Howe case 83–4, 91
human rights: legitimisation of 12–14; limits to 238–43; and role of judiciary 130–2, 133–6, 137, 138–41; typology 217; *see also* Charter of Fundamental Rights; discrimination; due process; European Convention on Human Rights; European Court of Human Rights; slavery
Human Rights Act [1998]: and the ECHR 265–7; effects 96–100, 253; and judicial interpretation 112–19, 249–53; and judicial law making 92–6, 120, 269–70; and public authorities 253–9, 261, 262–3, 266; retrospective effect 260–6; White Paper 112, 130
hybrid public authorities 254, 255, 258–9

IFAW v. *Commission* [2004] 197–8
immigration 175–8, 245, 267–8; *see also* Race Relations Acts
Immigration Acts [1971, 1976] 177
impartiality of tribunals 271–6; *see also* bias
Incal v. *Turkey* [1998] 273–4, 276
independence: of tribunals 271–6
indigenous people *see* Australian Aborigines; genocide; Maoris

indirect discrimination 180, 337–8
innocence 82–3, 363–7
institutional legitimacy 77–8, 81, 102–5, 130–2
institutional racism 180–3, 336, 338
insurance: for slave deaths 61, 62, 63, 64–5
integrity rights: definition 2, 7–8, 229; and derogations 229–33, 243; in the ECHR 220; and effective remedy 233–8
interpretation *see* judicial interpretation
investigating judges: risk of bias 277–8
Isayeva, Yusupova & Bazayeva v. Russia [2005] 225–6

Jackson case 133
Jégo-Quéré v. Commission [2002] 193–4
Jodie (conjoined twin) 69–70
John (King of England): and Magna Carta 29–32
John Murray v. UK [1996] 371–2
Jones v. DAS Legal Expenses Insurance [2003] 280–1
judge-made law *see* case law; judicial law making; precedent
judgment: public pronouncement of 286–8
judicial appointments 126–8, 141–6
judicial interpretation: of European law 108–112, 215–16; on fair trial 113–17; and the HRA 112–19, 249–53; and institutional legitimacy 102–5; *Pepper v. Hart* 105–8, 115, 130; and precedent 73, 76–7; presuppositions 104–5; principles 103, 106–8, 117, 118–21; and proportionality 113, 114, 116, 117, 119–20, 135–6; purposive 104, 106–8, 110–12, 114–15
judicial law making 77–8, 79–84, 88–92, 92–6, 120, 130, 269–70; *see also* case law; policy making; precedent
judicial power: definition 10–11
judicial reasoning 28, 329–32
judicial review 190, 236–7, 238, 257–9
judiciary: democratic accountability 141–2; ethics 137; globalisation of 153–5; and human rights 130–2, 133–6, 137, 138–41; independence of 72, 134–5, 143–4, 271–6, 346; and Parliament 130–1, 132–5; in a plural society 146–50; reform proposals 128–9; role 37–9, 46, 125–33, 136–7; sentencing powers 346–8; *see also* courts; investigating judges
juries 34, 44, 374–78

justice: images of 289; and legal certainty 89; miscarriage of 245–6, 343; principles 294–5, 311–12; *see also* access to justice; civil justice; criminal justice; law

Kansal case 96, 97, 262, 263–4
Kaufman v. Belgium 282
Kay v. London Borough of Lambeth [2006] 97, 100
Kearley case 91
Kenya *see* Mau Mau
Kenyatta, Jomo 171, 172, 173
Kikuyu: oppression of 172–3
Klass v. Germany [1978] 224, 225, 234–5, 238
Kurt v. Turkey [1998] 358–9

labour relations *see* trade unions
Ladd v. Marshall [1954] 321, 324
Lambert case 96, 97, 120, 260–4, 268, 366
land access: distributive justice in 304–7
Land Freedom Army *see* Mau Mau
land law: Norman Conquest 27–8
land rights: indigenous 159–60, 161, 163–8, 169, 171–2
law: concepts 37, 39, 51, 55; discourse of 68; integrity of *see* integrity rights; language of 45–6; and morality 57–60; perceptions of 175; *see also* commercial law; common law; courts; customary law; justice; land law; private law; rule of law; Sharia law
Law Lords: appointment of 126–8
Lawless v. Ireland [1979–80] 239–40
Lawrence Inquiry 181–3, 336, 338
Leeds City Council v. Price [2006] 97, 98–9, 100
legal aid: access by middle classes 385; in civil cases 308–9, 381, 386, 391–2, 395; costs 380–2, 384–5; and cross-border litigation 394–6; ECtHR judgments 309, 390–3; and market mechanisms 380–1, 382, 384, 386–7; quality control 388; reforms 385–90; statistics 385, 387–8, 389
Legal Aid Franchise Quality Standards 388
legal education 19–24, 39, 49, 77, 78, 79, 399
legal positivism *see* positive law
legal procedures 8–10; *see also* evidence; procedural law; sentencing
legal representation: access to 307–310; *see also* legal aid
Legal Services Commission 386, 388, 389–90

legal system: globalised 153–5; Henry II's reforms 26; and legal aid costs 382–4; reform proposals 128–9, 381, 383–5
Lehideux and Isorni v. *France* [1998] 239
Leonard Cheshire case 256, 258, 259
Leviathan (Hobbes) 34–7, 169
libel cases: legal aid for 308–9
life and liberty: right to 219, 231; *see also* slavery
litigation: finality in 80, 321–4; *see also* appeals; precedent
Litster v. *Forth Dry Dock* [1989] 111
locus standi see standing
London Tramways v. *London City Council* [1898] 79–80, 87, 127
Lord Chancellor: and judicial appointments 142–5
Lynch case 83, 91

Maastricht Treaty 198, 208
Mabo case 165–8
MacPherson Report 181–3, 336, 338
Magna Carta 29–32, 355
Maguire Seven 343
Malone v. *Metropolitan Police Commissioner* No. 2 [1979] 215–16
Mancini v. *DPP* [1942] 364
mandatory sentences 93, 348–9
Mandla v. *Lee* 180
Mansfield, 1st Earl 38, 50, 53, 54, 56, 63–4, 71
Maoris 158–60, 163–5, 166
Mareva injunctions 325, 326, 328–9
market mechanisms: and legal aid 380–1, 382, 384, 386–7
Mary (conjoined twin) 69–70
matrimonial issues: dispute resolution in 296, 297–8
Mau Mau rising 168–73
McIntosh v. *Lord Advocate* [2001] 365
McKerr case 264–5, 266–7
'McLibel' case 308–9, 392–3
McLoughlin Appellant v. *O'Brian* [1983] 88–9
Meadows, Roy 344, 345–6
mediation 296, 297, 299
medical resources: distributive justice in 300–4
Medicaments case 280
middle classes: access to legal aid 383
Middleton Review 385–6
Miliangos v. *George Frank* [1975] 81–2, 85

military tribunals 273–6
minority groups *see* Australian Aborigines; gypsies; Maoris; plural society
Mirza case 374, 376, 377
miscarriage of justice 245–6, 343
Modernising Justice (White Paper) 381, 383–5
morality: and law 57–60; *see also* ethics; human rights
Morris v. *UK* 275–6
murder: and duress 83–4; and necessity 57–60, 68–70; sentencing tariffs 349–51; of slaves 60–5; *see also* genocide
Murray v. *UK* [1994] 359, 361, 363

National Health Service *see* medical resources
national sovereignty *see* sovereignty
Native Land Court (New Zealand) 163, 164–5
necessity: in law 57–60, 63, 64–5, 68–70
Netherlands v. *Council* [1996] 197
neutral evaluation 296, 297
New Zealand: legal education 19–24; *see also* Maoris
NICE 302, 304
non-governmental organisations *see* voluntary sector
Norman Conquest 25–8
North Range Shipping v. *Seatrans Shipping Corporation* [2002] 330, 331
not-for-profits *see* voluntary sector

oaths: and issues of proof 32–3
objective innocence 82–3
Offen case 93
openness *see* transparency
Orkem v. *EC Commission* [1989] 200
overriding objective of civil justice 293–5, 311–12

P, C and S v. *UK* [2002] 393
PACE 337, 355–6, 357, 358
Pamplin v. *Express Newspapers Ltd* [1985] 327
Parliament 4, 130–1, 132–5; *see also* European Parliament; executive
participation: in legal procedures 9–10; *see also* access to justice
Patel, Trupti 345
Pepper v. *Hart* 105–8, 115, 130
Pickstone v. *Freemans* [1988] 110–11
Piersack v. *Belgium* [1982] 277
Pinochet case 279

planning permission: and gypsy access to land 306
Plaumann v. *Commission* [1963] 190–1, 193
plural society 146–50, 222–3, 398; *see also* discrimination; gypsies; immigration
police: institutional racism in 181–3, 336, 338
Police & Criminal Evidence Act [1984] 337, 355–6, 357, 358
policing: and arrests 355–8; by consent 335–6; local 336–9; national 339–42; stop and search powers 336–9, 340
policy making: in legal decisions 88–9, 91, 92, 113, 120
political life: right to 220–1, 240–1
Politics of the Judiciary (Griffith) 124–6, 146–7
Poplar v. *Donoghue* [2001] 255–6, 258, 259
Porter v. *Magill* [2002] 279–80
positive law 34–7, 54–6, 79, 137
power: dangers of 335; forms of 10–12; *see also* executive power; judicial power; separation of powers
Practice Statement [1966] 80–1, 82–3, 87, 96–7, 98
precedent: concept 74–5; and court hierarchies 74, 76, 77, 79, 80, 84–8, 97–100; and the ECtHR 98–9, 249, 267–70; effect of HRA 96–100; identification of 72–5; and interpretation 73, 76–7; as judicial practice 75–9; legal education on 77; principles 71–2, 79–84; social function 80; *see also* case law; judicial law making
Prendergast, James 162–4
presumption of innocence 363–7
Pretto v. *Italy* [1983] 286
prisons: overcrowding 351–3; *see also* sentencing
privacy 93–6, 216, 221, 225, 234–6, 238
private law: application of HRA 93–6
privatisation *see* market mechanisms
privilege: and disclosure of evidence 312–17, 327–8
procedural law 28; *see also* arrest and detention; civil procedural law; due process; evidence; police; presumption of innocence; self-incrimination
ProLife Alliance case 133–6
proof: standard of 364–5; *see also* evidence
property rights 52–6, 63, 97–8, 118–19; *see also* land rights

proportionality: of access to justice 382–3; in civil justice 294; and judicial interpretation 113, 114, 116, 117, 119–20, 135–6; in sentencing 347–8; of terrorism regulations 139, 239–40
public authorities: and the HRA 253–9, 261, 262–3, 266
public hearings 286–8, 314–15, 326–7
public interest immunity: and disclosure of evidence 283–4
public pronouncement of judgment 286–8
punishment *see* extra-legal punishment; prisons; sentencing
purposive interpretation 104, 106–8, 110–12, 114–15

Qazi case 98
Queen's Bench 42–5

R. v. A [2001] 93, 113–17, 120, 250, 251–2
R. v. *North West Lancashire Health Authority, ex parte A and Others* [2000] 304
R. v.: *see also* names of parties to cases, e.g. *Ullah* case
Race Relations Acts 178–81
Race Relations Board 178, 179
racism *see* bias; colonialism; discrimination; institutional racism; Race Relations Acts; stop and search powers
rationing *see* medical resources
Rawls, John: *A Theory of Justice* 295, 300, 307
Re S [2002] 117–18, 250–2
reasonable suspicion: and arrest 355, 356, 359–61
reasons *see* judicial reasoning
recidivism: and prison overcrowding 351
Refah Partisi v. *Turkey* [2003] 240–1
Regina v. *R.* [1991] 89–90, 91
religious discrimination: cases 147–50, 180
Remer v. *Germany* [1994] 239
Rent Act [1977] 118–19
reoffending *see* recidivism
reopening cases: principles 321–4; *see also* appeals; double jeopardy
reservations from ECHR 231, 232–3; *see also* derogations
resident aliens: deportation of 245
Revolution of 1688: effects 42
Richards case 265–6

rights *see* human rights; integrity rights; land rights; property rights
Rights Brought Home (White Paper) 112, 130
Roma *see* gypsies
Rookes v. *Barnard* [1964] 85, 129
Rowe and Davis v. *UK* [2000] 283–4
rule of law 13–14, 31, 35, 42, 72, 134–5, 272, 390–1
Rwandan genocide 184

S. v. *H.M. Advocate* [1989] 90
Salabiaku v. *France* 365–6
Sander v. *UK* [2000] 376
Saunders v. *UK* [2000] 319, 320, 371, 372
school uniform: cases 147–50, 180
Schorsch Meier v. *Henin* [1975] 84–5
scientific evidence 342–6
secrecy: of jury proceedings 375–7
'secret soundings' 142, 144
self-incrimination 200, 317–21, 367–74; *see also* disclosure
sentencing 93, 346–51; *see also* prisons
Sentencing Advisory Panel 349
Sentencing Guidelines Council 349
separation of powers 42, 134, 144, 350
Sex Discrimination Act [1975] 109–110, 111–12
sexual discrimination: ECtHR judgments 237
Sharia law 150–1
Sharp, Granville: and slavery 47, 50, 51, 52–3, 63, 64
Shivpuri case 82–3, 84
silence: right of 367–70, 371–3
single market: development of 208
Slave ship (Turner) 65–8
slavery: abolition movement 63, 64, 67; legal proceedings 47, 50–7, 62, 63, 64–5; prohibited in ECHR 221, 231; *Zong* slave ship 60–5, 66, 67–8
Smith and Grady v. *UK* [1999] 237, 238
SmithKline Beecham Biologicals v. *Connaught Laboratories* [1998] 315–16, 317
social goods *see* land; medical resources
social rights: in ECHR 221
Soering v. *UK* [1989] 236, 267
Somerset case [1772] 50–1, 53–7
sovereignty 4, 31, 34–7, 169, 394
Spath Holme case 107–8
special counsel system: in disclosure hearings 284, 285

standing 189, 190–5, 224–6, 235–6, 395–6; *see also* access to justice
stare decisis 73, 74
state power *see* executive power; judicial power; separation of powers
statistics: misuse of 344–6
statutory interpretation *see* judicial interpretation
Steel and Morris v. *UK* [2005] 308–9, 392–3
Stephen Lawrence Inquiry 181–3, 336, 338
Stern case 320, 321
stop and search powers 336–9, 340
Streltz [et al.] v. *Germany* [2001] 244
Strong, Jonathan (slave) 47, 50, 52
subsidiarity 205, 208, 209
substantial purpose: and disclosure of evidence 313–14
surveillance *see* privacy
Sytravel case 201

taxation proceedings: regulations 327–8
Taylor v. *Lawrence* [2003] 281, 322–4
terrorism 138–41, 168–73, 232, 239–40, 339–42
terrorists: arrest and detention 132, 340, 359–61, 363
A Theory of Justice (Rawls) 295, 300, 307
'three strikes' sentencing rule 348
torture 138, 140–1, 219, 231
trade unions 127, 129, 220
Transocean Marine Paint Association v. *Commission* [1974] 199
transparency 196–202, 329–32; *see also* disclosure
Travellers *see* gypsies
Treaty of Amsterdam [1997] 205, 208–9
Treaty on European Union 198, 208
Treaty of Lisbon [2007] 209
Treaty of Nice [2001] 205, 209
Treaty of Rome [1957] 185–6, 205, 207
Treaty of Waitangi 159–60, 163, 164, 166
trespass regulations 306
trial by ordeal 32–3
tribunals 128, 271–6; *see also* courts
Turner, J.M.W.: *Slave ship* 65–8
twins *see* conjoined twins

Ullah case 267–8
Unión de Pequeños Agricultores v. *Council of the European Union* 191–2, 193–4
Universal Declaration of Human Rights 12, 211

Van Duyn v. *Home Office* [1975] 207
Van Mechelen and Others v. *The Netherlands* [1997] 285
Vassa, Gustavus 62
Venables and Thompson v. *Newsgroup Newspapers* [2001] 93–4
voluntary sector 386–7, 390–1, 396

Wainright v. *Home Office* [2002] 264
Walker case 303
'war on terror' 339–42
Waugh v. *British Railway Board* [1979] 312–14
Wednesbury test 135
Welfare Party *see* Refah Partisi
welfare state: legal regulation of 127–8
whiteness: and blackness 158–9
Wi Parata v. *Bishop of Wellington* [1871] 163–4, 165, 166
William the Conqueror 25–6, 41

Williams, Rowan: on Sharia law 150–1
Wilson v. *Chief Constable of Lancashire Constabulary* [2000] 358
Wilson v. *First County Trust* [2003] 112–13, 260
Woolf reforms of civil justice 46, 292–3, 298, 316, 328–9; *see also* Civil Procedure Act and Rules
Woolf Report (on prisons) 352–3
World Development Movement case 130

X v. *UK* [1981] 362

Yorke-Talbot ruling on slavery 52, 53, 56
Young v. *Bristol Aeroplane Co.* [1944] 85, 86–7
Youth Justice and Criminal Evidence Act [1999] 93, 113–17, 250

Zong slave ship 60–5, 66, 67–8